Edited and designed by

Time Out Magazine Limited
Universal House
251 Tottenham Court Road
London W1P OAB
Tel: 0171 813 3000
Fax: 0171 813 6001
E-mail: net@timeout.co.uk
http://www.timeout.co.uk

Editorial

Managing Editor Peter Fiennes
Editor Julie Emery
Copy Editor Dave Rimmer
Researchers Eveline Hagenbeek, Sue Cowell
Indexer Dorothy Frame

Design

Art Director Warren Beeby
Art Editor John Oakey
Designers Paul Tansley, Mandy Martin
Ad Make-up David Pepper
Picture Editor Catherine Hardcastle

Advertising

Group Advertisement Director Lesley Gill
Sales Director Mark Phillips
Advertisement Manager (Amsterdam) David Pepper
Advertisement Sales (Amsterdam) Maxim van Wijk

Administration

Publisher Tony Elliott
Managing Director Mike Hardwick
Financial Director Kevin Ellis
Marketing Director Gillian Auld
Production Manager Mark Lamond

Features were written and researched by:

Introduction Andrew Thompson. **Essential Information** Eveline Hagenbeek. **Getting Around** Eveline Hagenbeek; **Ticket to Ride** Andrew Thompson. **Accommodation** Rina Vergano. **Sightseeing** Aleida Strowger; **Jewish Amsterdam** Sally Swingewood, Andrew Thompson. **Architecture** Rodney Bolt. **Amsterdam by Season** Willem de Blaauw; **Queen for a Day** Andrew Thompson. **Early History** Sophie Marshall; **XXX Marks the Spot** Sophie Marshall; Blaauw. **War & Reformation** Sophie Marshall. **The Golden Age** Sophie Marshall. **Decline & Fall** Sophie Marshall. **Between the Occupations** Sophie Marshall. **World War II** Kees Neefjes. **Post-war** Mark Fuller; **Provocations** Steve Korver **Amsterdam Today** Jules Marshall. **Amsterdam by Area** Pip Farquharson, Steve Korver, Andrew Moskos. **Canals** Steve Korver. **Restaurants** Julie Emery, Steve Korver, Rina Vergano; **Indonesian for Beginners** Maxim van Wijk. **Cafés & Bars** Julie Emery, Andrew Thompson; **Oompah pah party** Andrew Thompson. **Coffeeshops** Andrew Thompson. **Shopping** Johanna Stoyva. **Services** Eveline Hagenbeek. **Galleries** Sally Swingewood. **Museums** Aleida Strowger; **Lair of the CoBrA** Steve Korver. **Media** Jules Marshall. **Clubs** David Pepper. **Dance** Lisa Sove. **Film** Aleida Strowger. **Music: Classical & Opera** Andrew May. **Music: Rock, Folk & Jazz** Jo Bartlett; **Amsterdam in Song** Andrew Thompson. **Sport & Fitness** Andrew Thompson. **Theatre** Lisa Sove. **Early Hours** Johanna Stoyva, Andrew Thompson. **Business** Sue Cowell. **Children** Rina Vergano. **Gay & Lesbian** Willem de Blaauw, Pip Farquharson. **Students** Eveline Hagenbeek. **Women** Pip Farquharson. **Beyond Amsterdam** Angela Jameson, Eveline Hagenbeek. **Excursions in Holland** Pip Farquharson, Anne Campbell Lord. **The Randstad** Willem de Blaauw, Pip Farquharson, Angela Jameson. **The Provinces** Ailsa Camm, Eveline Hagenbeek**. Survival** Eveline Hagenbeek.

Maps by Mapworld
Photography by Nick Feeney except for: pages 21, 67, 73 **Hulton Getty**; 185 **Deen van Meer**; 244, 249 **Netherlands Board of Tourism**; 252 **Rotterdam VVV**.
Pictures on pages 187, 189 were supplied by the featured establishments.

Amsterdam Guide

Penguin Books

PENGUIN BOOKS

Published by the Penguin Group
Penguin Books Ltd., 27 Wright's Lane, London W8 5TZ, England
Penguin Books USA Inc., 375 Hudson Street, New York, New York 10014, USA
Penguin Books Australia Ltd., Ringwood, Victoria, Australia
Penguin Books Canada Ltd., 10 Alcorn Avenue, Toronto, Ontario, Canada M4V 3B2
Penguin Books (NZ) Ltd., 183–190 Wairau Road, Auckland 10, New Zealand

Penguin Books Ltd., Registered offices: Harmondsworth, Middlesex, England

First published 1991
Second edition 1993
Third edition 1995
Fourth edition 1996
10 9 8 7 6 5 4 3 2 1

Colour reprographics by Precise Litho, 34–35 Great Sutton Street, London EC1V
Mono reprographics, printed and bound by William Clowes Ltd, Beccles, Suffolk NR34 9QE

Contents

About the Guide

This is the fourth edition of the *Time Out Amsterdam Guide*, one in series of city guides that includes London, Paris, New York, San Francisco, Berlin, Budapest, Prague, Brussels, Barcelona, Madrid and Rome. The latest edition has been thoroughly revised, updated and, where necessary, rewritten by people who live and work in the Dutch capital. It covers all the major sights and attractions, but also directs you to hundreds of the city's more obscure and eccentric venues. Since 1993, *Time Out Amsterdam* – now available online at *http//:www.timeout.nl* – has been covering everything that's new in the Dutch capital. We tell you both what's worth seeing, and what's worth crossing the road to avoid.

The *Time Out Amsterdam Guide* is updated every two years and we've sweated and slaved to make it as useful as possible. Addresses, telephone numbers, transport details, opening times, admission prices and credit card details are all included in our listings. And, as far as possible, we've given details of facilities, services and events. Cross-referencing is extensive, and where a building, musuem or venue appears in bold in chapters such as History or By Area, this means it is listed elsewhere and will be found in the index.

CHECKED AND CORRECT

All the information in the guide was checked and correct at time of writing: but please bear in mind that owners and managers can change their arrangements at any time. We urge you to phone, before you set out, to check opening times, the dates of exhibitions, admission prices and other important details. In Amsterdam, most people speak English as well as Dutch. We have tried to include information on access for the disabled, but it's always wise to phone and check needs can be met.

PRICES

The prices listed throughout the guide should be used as guidelines. Fluctuating exchange rates and inflation can cause prices, in shops and restaurants especially, to change rapidly. If prices and services somewhere vary greatly from those we've quoted, ask if there's a good reason. If not, go elsewhere. Then, please let us know. We try to give the best and most up-to-date advice, so we always want to hear if you've been overcharged or badly treated.

CREDIT CARDS

Throughout the guide the following abbreviations have been used for credit cards: AmEx: American Express; DC: Diners Club; JCB: Japanese credit cards; MC: Mastercard/Access; V: Visa.

LET US KNOW

It should be stressed that the information we give is impartial. No organisation or enterprise has been included in this guide because its owner or manager has advertised in our publications. Impartiality is one reason our guides are so successful and well respected. We hope you enjoy the *Time Out Amsterdam Guide* and that it helps you make the most of your stay. But if you disagree with any of our reviews, let us know; your comments on places you have visited are always welcome. There's a reader's reply card inserted into this book.

There's an on-line version of this guide, as well as weekly events listings for Amsterdam and other international cities, at:
http//:www.timeout.co.uk.

Introduction

Like the naughty kid who sits at the back of the classroom, Amsterdam has a reputation to live up (or down) to. Usually perceived internationally as the black sheep of Europe, mainly because of its government's policy of tolerating soft drugs, Amsterdam is in fact the European capital closest in character to London. It is for the main part populated by north European caucasians who are not so remarkably different from their British counterparts, excepting the fact that they all seem to be a lot taller. And although they don't call a spade a spade, they do call a station a station and a rollmop a rollmop; there are in fact a great many similarities between the world's most popular language and a tongue which most people take great delight in proclaiming unintelligible.

And yet, Amsterdam is one of the world's strangest cities, with myriad sights and sounds that assault the senses of all visitors and make the place uniquely alien to all visitors, including most Dutch people. If there was ever some theory asserting that capital cities were microcosms of their respective nations then Amsterdam rips it up; it's a city state in all but name and as completely removed from the rest of Holland as can be imagined. It is as if it was put there as some sort of complex psychological practical joke on the rest of Europe: the young seem to get it whilst the old become ever more perplexed.

Perhaps most of all, Amsterdam is a city of anomalies – how does a place popularly conceived as the manifestation of the pleasuredome come to be populated entirely by people hell bent on making money? Everyone seems to be sitting at a terraced café saying 'we'll do it tomorrow' when the reality is that they did it yesterday and have just banked the money. Even stranger is the phenomenon of a city that collectively seem to eat chips, drink beer and smoke but who never appear unduly obese or die from heart disease or cancer.

It is equally perverse that this supposed den of iniquity is one of the most astoundingly beautiful cities in existence, steeped in a cultural history so deep that it is difficult to provide explanations as to how modern-day Amsterdam could have become so incongrously Americanised. There has been an almost complete submission to the Big Mac/MTV culture with neon billboards nestling between classical gables.

But then again, Amsterdam is a city of clichés and contradictions; where some visitors choose to spend their time so stoned that they can't remember anything about the city by the time they've got home, and where others will spend every minute of their trip rushing around museums and galleries and taking photographs of seventeenth-century architecture. Those who have most fun seem to do both. *Andrew Thompson*

Essential
Information

Banks and insurance, time zones and tipping, weather and queuing, visas and vocabulary – a brief on the basics.

Find **Thomas Cook** on Dam Square. See pages 6-7.

Amsterdam is a surprisingly user-friendly city: its compact size and excellent public transport system make it easy to get around in, and Amsterdammers' ease with the English language means that there are few communication problems. But there are still some essentials that you'll need to know to get by: the following list is designed to help get your visit off to a good start. More detailed advice on staying healthy and dealing with emergencies can be found in *chapter* **Survival**. The abbreviations used within this guide are explained on *page vi* **About the Guide**.

Visas

A valid passport is all that is required for a stay of up to three months in the Netherlands, if you are an EC national or from the USA, Canada or New Zealand.

If you are unsure of visa requirements or need a visa, contact your nearest Dutch embassy or con-

sulate at least three months before your departure. For stays of longer than three months EC citizens need a residence permit, which will only be available upon production of an employment contract, colour passport photographs and certificate of registration with the local council. It is also important to remember that when moving from one locality to another you are required to sign off from the locality you're leaving before registering with the new locality in which you will be residing. Residence permits are available from the Aliens' Police (**Bureau Vreemdelingenpolitie**, *listed below*). For information on work and residence permits *see chapter* **Business**.

Bureau Vreemdelingenpolitie (Aliens' Police)

Bijlmerdreef 90 (general enquiries 559 6300). Metro Bijlmer. **Open** 8.45am-5pm Mon-Fri.
The Vreemdelingenpolitie deal with up to 300 applications for visas every day in Amsterdam alone (and these are the ones applying to live here legally) so expect a long wait. For

those with the correct visa, a residence permit for three months can usually be obtained on the day of application, free of charge. To extend this permit, you need to return to the Vreemdelingenpolitie with proof of employment or sufficient legal funding; EC residents are charged *f*50, non-EC residents *f*1000 at this stage of registration. Appointments are not required but queues start at around 7am and you can expect a wait of up to two hours. Once you are through the queue it takes a few minutes for the interviewer to process your application and grant you a visa. You will need to take ID, proof of an address in the Netherlands, and a contract of employment or proof of sufficient funds for a longer stay. Regulations concerning identification require that everyone carries some form of identification in the following circumstances: when opening accounts at banks or other financial institutions; when looking for work; when applying for benefits; when found on public transport without a valid ticket and when going to a professional football match (ID will only be asked for if there are signs of potential disturbance).

Customs

EC nationals over the age of 17 may import limitless goods into the Netherlands for their personal use. It is important to note that other EC countries may still have limits on the quantity of goods they permit on entry.

• For citizens of non-EC countries, the old limits still apply:

• 200 cigarettes or 50 cigars or 250g (8.82oz) tobacco

• 1 litre (1.76 pints) of spirits (over 22 per cent alcohol) or 2 litres of fortified wine (under 22 per cent alcohol) or 2 litres of non-sparkling wine

• 50g (1.76oz) of perfume

• 500g (1.1lb) coffee

• 100g (3.52oz) tea

• Other goods to the value of *f*380

• The import of meat, meat products, fruit, plants, flowers and protected animals is forbidden.

Insurance

EC countries have reciprocal medical treatment arrangements with the Netherlands. British citizens will need form E111, which can be obtained by filling in the application form in leaflet SA30, available in all Department of Social Security (DSS) offices and the Post Office. Make sure you read the small print on the back of form E111 so that you know how to obtain medical or dental treatment at a reduced charge, since the chances are you'll have to explain this to the Dutch doctor or dentist who treats you. If you should need treatment, photocopy your insurance form and leave that with the doctor or dentist who treats you.

Citizens of other EC countries should make sure they have obtained one of the forms E110, E111 or E112. Citizens of the following non-EC countries can also receive medical treatment at reduced rates by producing the appropriate form: Morocco form MN111; states of former Yugoslavia YN111; Tunisia TUN/N111; Turkey TUR/N111.

A fistful of guilders.

Citizens from all other countries should take out private medical insurance before their visit. Dutch medical treatment costs about half what it would in the USA, which is still more than enough to make travelling without insurance unwise.

As always when travelling abroad, visitors should take out insurance on personal belongings before leaving for Amsterdam. Such insurance is usually included in package holidays, but be sure to check.

Money

The unit of Dutch currency is the guilder (or occasionally, florin), variously abbreviated as *f*, fl or Hfl. Throughout this guide the abbreviation '*f*' is used. The guilder is divided into 100 cents, rather more obviously abbreviated to c. Coins in use are 5c, 10c, 25c, *f*1, *f*2,50 and *f*5. The 5c coin is copper, 10c, 25c, *f*1 and *f*2,50 coins are silver coloured and the *f*5 coin is gold coloured (it closely resembles the £1 coin). The 5c coin is also known as a *stuiver*, the 10c coin as a *dubbeltje*, 25c as a *kwartje* and the *f*2,50 coin is called *a rijksdaalder*. Notes come in *f*10, *f*25, *f*50, *f*100, *f*250 and *f*1,000 denominations. The *f*10 note is blue, *f*25 pink, *f*50 yellow, *f*100 brown and *f*250 purple. Raised symbols give the denominations for blind people.

Since the Dutch no longer have 1c or 2c coins, prices are rounded up or down to the nearest 5c, so *f*1,53 will be charged as *f*1,55 and *f*1,52 will be charged at *f*1,50.

Amsterdammers prefer to use cash for most transactions, although the larger hotels, shops and most restaurants will accept one or more of the major credit cards (American Express, Diners Club, Eurocard, Mastercard, Visa) and many will take Eurocheques with guarantee cards, and travellers' cheques with ID such as a passport.

Banks

Banks and bureaux de change offer similar rates of exchange although banks tend to charge less commission. Most banks are open from 9am to 4pm Monday to Friday. As yet no banks open on Saturdays but exchange facilities are available at the bureaux de change listed below. Dutch banks buy and sell foreign currency and exchange travellers' cheques and Eurocheques, but few give cash advances against credit cards. For this you'll need to go to a bureau de change (*see below*).

For a full list of banks in Amsterdam *see chapter* **Business** or consult the *Amsterdam Yellow Pages* (*Gouden Gids*), under 'Banken'. *Gouden Gids* can be found in post offices, hotels and phone centres (*see chapter* **Survival**).

Bureaux de Change

Bureaux de change can be found throughout the city centre, especially on Leidseplein, Damrak and Rokin. Those listed below give reasonable rates, although they charge more commission than banks. Avoid using hotel and tourist bureau exchange facilities (*see below* **Tourist Information**) as these are generally more expensive.

American Express
Damrak 66 (504 8777). Tram 4, 9, 14, 16, 24, 25.
Open 9am-5pm Mon-Fri; 9am-noon Sat.
This office has a 24-hour cash machine for card holders and an automatic travellers' cheque refund service. Mail can also be sent poste restante if you are a cardholder; the service is

Vocabulary

The vast majority of Amsterdammers speak English quite well and are happy to show off their linguistic talents. However, some knowledge of the absolute basics of the language will be useful – and polite – particularly if you intend to venture out of the city. As in any foreign country, the attempt to speak in the native tongue is well received. Pronunciations given are the nearest approximation we could find.

Pronunciation

ch – like 'ch' in 'loch'
ee – like 'ay' in 'hay'
g – similar to 'ch' (*above*) (this has to be heard to be imitated)
ie – like 'ea' in 'lean'
j – like 'y' in 'yes', except when preceded by i in which case it should be pronounced as a y (*see below*).
oe – like 'o' in 'who'
oo – like 'o' in no
ou, au – like 'ow' in 'cow'
ui – similar to above (has to be heard to be imitated)
tie – like 'tsy' in 'itsy bitsy'
tje – like 'ch' in 'church'
v – like 'f' in 'for'
w – like 'w' in 'which', with a hint of the 'v' in 'vet' thrown in
y / ij – (written as either) a cross between 'i' in 'hide' and 'ay' in 'way'.

Useful Phrases

hello – hallo (hullo) or dag (darch)
goodbye – tot ziens (tot zeens)
yes – ja (yah)
no – nee (nay)
please – alstublieft (als-too-bleeft). Also commonly used to replace the phrase 'there you are' when exchanging items such as money with others.
thank you – dank u (dank-oo)
excuse me – pardon (par-don)

I'm sorry, I don't speak Dutch – Het spijt me, ik spreek geen Nederlands (et spate meh, ik spraykhane nayderlants)
I don't understand – Ik begrijp het niet (ik begripe t neet)
What does (...) mean? – Wat betekent (...)? (Vot bitaykent (...)
Do you speak English? – Spreekt u Engels? (spraykt oo engels)
sir – meneer (munnear)
madam – mevrouw (muffrou). NB: the progressive Amsterdammers rarely address anyone as 'Miss'
waiter – ober
open – open
closed – gesloten
I want... – ik wil graag...
how much is...? wat kost...?
could I have a receipt? – mag ik een bonnetje alstublieft?
how do I get to...? – hoe kom ik in...?
how far is it to...? – hoe ver is het naar...?
left – links
right – rechts
straight ahead – rechtdoor
far – ver
near – dichtbij
street – straat
canal – gracht
square – plein
good – goed
bad – slecht
big – groot
small – klein

Numbers

0 – nul; 1 – een; 2 – twee; 3 – drie; 4 – vier; 5 – vijf; 6 – zes; 7 – zeven; 8 – acht; 9 – negen; 10 – tien; 11 – elf; 12 – twaalf; 13 – dertien; 14 – veertien; 15 – vijftien; 16 – zestien; 17 – zeventien; 18 – achttien; 19 – negentien; 20 – twintig; 21 – eenentwintig; 22 – tweeëntwintig; 30 – dertig; 31 – eenendertig; 32 – tweeëndertig; 40 – veertig; 50 – vijftig; 60 – zestig; 70 – zeventig; 80 – tachtig; 90 – negentig; 100 – honderd; 101 – honderd een; 110 – honderd tien; 200 – tweehonderd; 201 – tweehonderd een; 1,000 – duizend

Information retrieval at the VVV.

free. Letters should be addressed, with your name, to Client Mail Service, American Express, Damrak 66, 1012 LM Amsterdam. When collecting mail you need to show ID and your AmEx card.

Change Express
Damrak 86 (624 6681/624 6682). Tram 4, 9, 14, 16, 24, 25. **Open** 8am-11.30pm daily.
Branch *Leidsestraat 106 (622 1425).* **Open** 8am-midnight daily.

GWK
Centraal Station (627 2731). Tram 1, 2, 4, 5, 9, 13, 16, 17, 24, 25. **Open** 24 hours daily.
Branches: Amsterdam Schiphol Airport (in the railway station) (653 5121). **Open** 24 hours daily; **Leidseplein** 123 (622 1415). **Open** 8am-midnight daily. At the Leidseplein branch you can also exchange coins.

Thomas Cook
Dam 23-25 (625 0922). Tram 4, 9, 14, 16, 24, 25. **Open** 9am-6pm Mon-Sat; 9am-6pm Sun.
Branches: *Damrak 1-5 (620 3236).* **Open** 8am-8pm Mon-Sat; 8.30am-8pm Sun; *Leidseplein 31A (626 7000).* **Open** 8.30am-6pm Mon-Sat; 10am-4pm Sun.
There is no charge when cashing Thomas Cook travellers' cheques here.

Tourist Information

The national tourist information organisation is the VVV (pronounced 'Vay Vay Vay'). Although it is a private organisation, many of the individual offices are subsidised by local councils.

There are three offices in Amsterdam and about 450 throughout the rest of the Netherlands, all offering services similar to those listed below. In the larger branches all the staff speak English,

German and French, and English is spoken by almost all the staff in the smaller offices.

Many phone centres (*see chapter* **Survival**) run a booking service for theatres, car hire, hotels and excursions.

AUB Uitburo
Leidseplein 26 (621 1211). Tram 1, 2, 5, 6, 7, 10, 11. **Open** 9am-9pm Mon-Sat; 9am-9pm Thur.
AUB Uitburo provides information and advance tickets for theatre, concerts and other cultural events. It is possible to make a reservation over the phone if you have a credit card. The reservation fee is *f*2, or *f*5, including postage and packing. You can also get the Cultureel Jongeren Passport (CJP) here (*f*20), which is valid for a year and entitles people under 26 to discounts on museum entrance and cultural events nationally. An essential stopping-off point for everyone interested in exploring the city's culture, it has chatty and helpful staff, plus a comfortable café area where visitors can leaf through listings guides and brochures at leisure. Centrally located, it's a good place to arrange to meet friends.

Dutch Tourist Information Office
Damrak 35 (638 2800). Tram 4, 9, 14, 16, 24, 25. **Open** 8am-10pm Mon-Sat; 9am-10pm Sun.
Recently opened, this single Dutch office concentrates on a booking service for theatres, car hire, hotels and excursions, rather than the all-round information provision of the VVV. Nevertheless it provides an alternative when the VVV offices are full, especially in high summer.

VVV
Stationsplein 10 (06 340 34066). Tram 1, 2, 4, 5, 9, 11, 13, 16, 17, 24, 25. **Open** 9am-5pm daily.
This is the main office of the VVV. Both here and at the branch listed below English-speaking staff can change money and provide information on transport, entertainment and exhibitions as well as day-trip ideas for the whole of the Netherlands. The VVV can also arrange theatre and hotel

bookings for a fee of ƒ5, and excursions and car hire for free. There is a comprehensive range of brochures for sale detailing walks and cycling tours as well as cassette tours, maps and, for ƒ3,50, the useful (if dull) fortnightly English-language listings magazine *What's On*. The VVV runs a general information line on the number listed above which features an English-language service. Bear in mind that it will cost about 75c per minute (as do all 06 numbers), which is rather trying if you are in a public telephone box.

Branches: Leidseplein 1. **Open** 8am-9pm daily. *Centraal Station (inside station).* **Open** 8am-9pm daily.

Maps

Many of the brochures and leaflets that you will find scattered around in hotels and bars will have some kind of sketchy map. But if you require more detail, the Falk Pocket Book Map (ƒ10) and the Falk fold-out map (ƒ7) are useful and accurate, and have a full street index on the back. Cheaper and smaller, but perfectly adequate, is Falk's small fold-out plan (ƒ5,50). Steer clear of the complicated Falk 'patent-folded' map unless you're keen on origami. If you prefer to use a map book, ask for a *stratengids* (street map); the Cito Plan spiral bound map book is recommended. All these can be bought from newsagents and bookshops (*see chapters* **Shopping** *and* **Survival**).

What's On

Dutch-language free papers and leaflets with general entertainment information can be picked up in Amsterdam's theatres, cafés, bars and libraries. Most of the information is easy to follow even without an understanding of Dutch.

Time

Amsterdam, like the rest of continental Europe, is one hour ahead of Greenwich Mean Time (GMT). It used not to be so, but the clocks on CET (Central European Time) now go back and forward on the same spring and autumn dates as GMT.

Climate

Amsterdam's climate is very changeable and often wet and windy. January and February are the coldest months, with icy winds whipping around the narrow streets and down the canals. It can be very humid in the summer, when mosquitoes thrive on the canals and in campsites. The average daytime temperatures are: January 4.6°C (40.3°F); February 5.4°C (41.7°F); March 8.4°C (47.1°F); April 11.9°C (53.4°F); May 16.4°C (61.5°F); June 19.2°C (66.6°F); July 20.6°C (69.1 °F); August 20.9°C (69.6°F); September 18.2°C (64.8°F.); October 14.2 °C (57.6°F); November 8.9 °C (48° F); December 5.8° C (42.4°F). If you can speak Dutch there is a 24-hour recorded information weather line on 068003.

Public Holidays

Called Nationale Feestdagen in Dutch, they are: New Year's Day; Good Friday; Easter Sunday and Monday; 30 April (Koninginnedag, the former Queen Juliana's Birthday, *see chapter* **Amsterdam By Season**); Ascension Day; Whit (Pentecost) Sunday and Monday; Christmas Day and the day after Christmas.

Opening Times

The opening times of all businesses are currently under review and there may be changes to the law in 1996. For all our listings in this guide we give full opening times, but in general shops are open from 1pm to 6pm on Monday; 9am to 6pm on Tuesdays, Wednesdays and Fridays; 9am to 9pm on Thursdays; and 9am to 5pm on Saturdays. Smaller, specialist shops tend to open at varying times; if in doubt phone first. For shops that are open late *see chapter* **Shopping**.

The city's bars open at various times during the day and close around 1am Monday to Thursday and at 2am on Fridays and Saturdays, reverting to 1am on Sundays. Restaurants are generally open for business in the evening from 5pm until 11pm (though some close as early as 9pm), and for seven days a week, although some close on Sunday and Monday.

Tipping

Although by law a service charge is included in hotel, taxi, bar, café and restaurant bills most Amsterdammers generally also round up the change to the nearest five guilders for large bills and to the nearest guilder for smaller ones, leaving the extra in small change rather than putting it on a credit card. In taxis the most common tip is around ten per cent for short journeys. Because of the compulsory service charge, never feel obliged to leave a tip; use your discretion and do so only when the service warrants it. Taxi drivers we spoke to say the best tippers are American and British, and the worst, apparently, are the Dutch themselves.

Queuing

A ticketing system is widely used here which cuts out the need for the traditional queue. From supermarket delicatessen counters and information bureaux to doctors' surgeries, you tear off a numbered ticket from a small machine and then wait until your number is either called or appears on an electronic screen. This allows you to seek somewhere comfortable to wait; you can even wander off for a while, but beware, if you miss your turn it will take some persuasive arguments if you are to be served, and you will usually end up having to take another ticket.

Getting Around

Trams and boats and planes and a perplexing profusion of pushbikes – Amsterdam is easy to negotiate, as long as you don't mind some of the Continent's most curmudgeonly cab drivers.

Getting around Amsterdam is fairly easy. The city has an efficient and reasonably priced tram and bus system. In this compact-sized town it's also possible to cycle or walk to most places of interest. Cycling is the preferred method of transport for many Amsterdammers and, true to the cliché, the streets are busy with bike traffic all day and most of the evening. There are also pleasure boats, commercial barges and water taxis on the canals.

If you're thinking of bringing a car to Amsterdam for a short stay – don't. Trams, bikes and buses jostle alarmingly at the larger junctions and jams are common on the narrow one-way systems around the canals. Parking places are elusive and expensive. On the other hand, public transport provision for those with disabilities is dire and, although there are lifts at all Metro stations, the staff can't always help people in wheelchairs. So if you can't do without a car *see chapter* **Survival** for information on car hire,

parking and what to do in case of breakdown. For details of orientation and where to get maps *see chapter* **Essential Information**.

To and From the Airport

Schiphol Airport Rail Service

Schiphol Airport/Centraal Station (information 06 9292). **Times** Trains daily at 15 minute intervals 4am-midnight; then hourly from 12.44am. **Tickets** *single* ƒ6; ƒ2,50 under-12s with adult; free under-4s; *return* ƒ10,25; ƒ2,50 under-12s with adult; free under-4s.
The journey to Centraal Station takes about 20 minutes.

KLM Hotel Bus Service

Main exit Schiphol Airport (649 1393/5651). **Times** buses at 30-minute intervals 6.30am-3pm, then on the hour until 10pm daily. **Tickets** *single* ƒ17,50; *return* ƒ30. This service is available to anyone; you don't need to have travelled on the airline or be staying at one of the hotel stops. The route starts at Schiphol, then goes to the Golden Tulip Barbizon (Leidseplein), Pulitzer (Westermarkt-Keizers-

Amsterdam's three-line **Metro** *is mostly used by commuters.*

gracht), Krasnapolsky (Dam Square), Holiday Inn and Renaissance (Nieuwzijds Voorburgwal), Barbizon Palace (Zeedijk) and back to Schiphol again.

Taxis

There are always plenty of taxis outside the main exit. It's pricey, however: at the time of writing about ƒ60 from the airport into central Amsterdam, and even more at night. For details of car hire firms operating from Schiphol Airport *see chapter* **Survival**. For more details about Amsterdam's taxi service, *see below* **Taxis**.

Airline Information

For general airport enquiries ring Schiphol Airport on **06 35034050**. Major airlines can be reached at the following addresses. Staff answering the telephone will almost certainly speak English.

British Airways

Neptunusstraat 31, Hoofddorp (Booking: 02503 50066, Schiphol information desk: 601 5413). **Open** 8.30am-6pm Mon-Fri. **Credit** AmEx, DC, MC, V.
It is also possible to book tickets on the British Airways Schiphol information number, or in person at the desk. Open 6am-9pm Mon-Fri; 6am-8pm Sat; 7am-9pm Sun.

British Midland

Ticket desk Schiphol Airport (604 1459/reservations 662 2211). **Open** 6am-5.30pm Mon-Fri; 6am-7pm Sat; 8am-9pm Sun. **Credit** AmEx, DC, MC, V.

KLM

Gabriel Metsustraat 226 (474 7747 24-hour information and reservations). Tram 2, 5, 16. **Open** 8.30am-5.30pm Mon-Fri; 10am-2pm Sat. **Credit** AmEx, DC, MC, V.

TWA

Singel 540 (627 4646). Tram 4, 9, 14, 16, 24, 25. **Open** 9am-12.30pm, 1.30-5pm, Mon-Fri. **Credit** AmEx, DC, MC, V.

AIR UK

W Sacrestraat, building 72, Schiphol-East (601 0633). **Open** 24 hours daily. **Credit** AmEx, DC, MC, V.

Transavia Airlines

Westelijke Randweg 3, Schiphol (604 6518). **Open** 9am-5.30pm Mon-Fri; 9.30am-4pm Sat. **Credit** AmEx, DC, MC, V.

Public Transport

For information, tickets, maps and an English-language brochure explaining the city's ticket system visit the Municipal Transport Authority (*below*). But if all you need is information on Amsterdam's ticketing system *see below* **Tickets**.

GVB (Amsterdam Municipal Transport Authority)

Stationsplein 15 (069292 6am- midnight daily). Tram 1, 2, 4, 5, 9, 11, 13, 16, 17, 24, 25. **Open** 7am-10.30pm Mon-Fri; 8am-10.30pm Sat.
The GVB runs Amsterdam's Metro, bus and tram services. **Branches**: GVB Head Office, Prins Hendrikkade 108; Amstel Railway Station, Julianaplein.

Metro

The Metro system in Amsterdam uses the same ticketing system as trams and buses (*see below* **Tickets**), but mainly serves suburbs to the south and east. There are three lines, all terminating at Centraal Station. Trains run from 6am Mon-Fri (6.30am Sat, 7.30am Sun) to about 12.15am daily.

Trams and Buses

As a visitor to Amsterdam you will find buses and trams a particularly good way to get around the city centre. Tram services run from 6am Monday to Friday, 6.30am on Saturday and 7.30am on Sunday, with a special night bus service taking over after midnight. Night buses are numbered from 71 to 77, with numbers 73 to 76 running through the city centre. Night bus stops are indicated by a black square at the stop with the bus number printed on it. Buses run between 1am and 5.30am Monday to Friday and until 6.30am on Saturday and Sunday.

Yellow signs at tram and bus stops indicate the name of the stop and further destinations. There are usually maps of the entire network in the shelters and diagrams of routes on board the trams and buses. Amsterdam's bus and tram drivers are generally courteous and will happily supply directions if asked. Like other Amsterdammers, most are sufficiently fluent to do this in English.

The yellow and decorated varieties of tram are as synonymous with Amsterdam as the red double-decker bus is with London. The vehicles make for fast and efficient travel, but other road-users be warned that they will stop only when absolutely necessary. Cyclists should listen out for the tram's warning bell and motorists should avoid blocking tramlines – cars are only allowed to venture on to them if they're turning right. It doesn't pay to argue with a tram. Cyclists should also be careful to cross tramlines at an angle that avoids the front wheel getting stuck – easily done and usually the cause of an undignified tumble. To get on or off a tram, wait until it has halted at a stop and press the yellow button by the doors, which will then open. On some trams you can buy a ticket from the driver at the front; on others from either a machine in the middle, or a conductor who stands at the back.

Tickets

Strip tickets (strippenkaarten): In Amsterdam a strip ticket system operates on trams, buses and the Metro, which is initially confusing but ultimately good value for money. Prices range from ƒ3 for a strip with two units to ƒ11 for 15 units

Cyclists should be careful to cross tramlines at an angle that avoids the front wheel getting stuck.

and ƒ32,25 for 45 units. Foreign pensioners and unemployed unfortunately aren't entitled to any reductions on ticket prices but children under four travel free and older children pay reduced fares for two-day tickets (*see below*). Ticket prices increase every year. Tickets can be bought at GVB (Public Transport) offices (*see above*), post offices (*see chapter* **Survival**), train stations and many tobacconists. The tickets must be stamped on board a tram or bus and on entering a Metro station. The city is divided into five zones: Noord (north), West, Centrum, Oost (east) and Zuid (south); most of central Amsterdam falls, not surprisingly, within zone Centrum. Strip tickets are also valid on trains that stop at Amsterdam train stations, with the exception of Schiphol.

For travel in a single zone, two units must be stamped, while three are stamped for two zones, four for three zones and so on. In trams you can stamp your own tickets in the yellow box-like contraption near the doors. Just fold it so the unit you need to stamp is at the end. On buses, drivers stamp the tickets and on the Metro there are stamping machines at the entrance to stations. An unlimited number of people can travel on one card, but the appropriate number of units must be stamped for each person. The stamps are valid for one hour, during which time you can transfer to other buses and trams without having to stamp your card again. If your journey takes more than an hour you have to stamp more units, but no single tram journey in central Amsterdam is likely to take that long. There is no set expiry date on *strippenkaarten*.

Day tickets (dagkaarten): A cheaper option for unlimited travel in Amsterdam, a day ticket costs ƒ12, two days cost ƒ16 and three days ƒ19,75, with each additional day costing an extra ƒ3,75. Only Dutch pensioners and the unwaged are eligible for cheaper travel, but for a child (aged four to 11) a two-day ticket costs ƒ8 and three days ƒ10, with each additional day costing a further ƒ2. Child day tickets are valid on night buses. A day ticket is valid on trams, buses and Metro on the day it is stamped until the last bus or tram runs. You need to buy a new ticket for night buses. Only the one-day ticket and the less economical hourly ticket (ƒ3) can be bought from drivers on trams and buses.

Season tickets (sterabonnement): These can be bought from GVB offices, tobacconists and post offices, and are valid for a week, a month or a year. A weekly pass for the central zone (Centrum) costs ƒ16, a monthly one ƒ54 and a yearly one ƒ540. Teenagers between the ages of 12 and 18 can buy season tickets for approximately a third of the price. Children between the ages of four and 11 can get all the passes at half price. You will need a passport photo to get a season ticket.

Beware of travelling on a bus or tram without a ticket. Uniformed inspectors make regular checks

Amsterdam's taxis: notorious for rudeness.

and those without a valid ticket – or an exceptionally good excuse – will be asked for ID and fined ƒ60 on the spot. Playing the ignorant foreigner rarely works.

Taxis

Amsterdam's taxi drivers were once notorious for their rudeness. These days, part of the qualification to be a taxi driver is a compulsory course in politeness. Most of them are still pretty stroppy, even so. Always check that the meter initally shows no more than the minimum charge and ask the driver for an estimate of how much the journey will cost before setting out. Even short journeys are expensive; after paying an initial ƒ5,60, it works out at ƒ2,80 per kilometre between 6am and midnight and rises to ƒ3,25 per kilometre thereafter. Note that on the narrow streets around the main canals, you may get stuck behind an unloading lorry and end up paying a fortune for the privilege.

If you feel you have been ripped off, ask for a receipt, which you are legally entitled to see before handing over any money. If the charge is extortionate, refer it to the central taxi office (677 7777) or the police. We stress that such rip-offs are relatively rare – taxi drivers have too much to lose if they are caught.

You are not meant to hail a taxi in the street (though occasionally one may stop) as there are ranks dotted around the city. Places you are likely to find a taxi waiting in a rank include Centraal Station; the bus station at the junction of Kinkerstraat and Marnixstraat; Rembrandtplein and Leidseplein. You generally can't book a cab in advance, but if you call Amsterdam's 24-hour central taxi control on 677 7777 a taxi will arrive almost immediately. The line is often busy on Friday and Saturday nights, but there's a telephone queuing system.

Wheelchairs will only fit in taxis if folded. If you're using a wheelchair, phone the car transport service for wheelchair users on 613 4134. The office is generally open between 9am and 6pm, Monday to

Friday, but the office hours are casual and you might well find someone there outside these times, even on the weekend. You need to book your journey one or two days in advance and it costs around ƒ2,80 per kilometre.

Water Taxis

It would be somewhat extravagant to use this service as a regular taxi – most Amsterdammers use water taxis only for special occasions. However, it is possible to hire a taxi – with guides, food and drink provided by the company at extra charge – and use it for your own personal canal tour or water-borne party. The boats are mostly modern and well maintained, with both covered and on-deck seating.

For details of canal tours *see chapter* **Sightseeing**.

Water Taxi Centrale

Stationsplein 8 (622 2181). Tram 1, 2, 4, 5, 9, 11, 13, 16, 17, 24, 25. **Open** 8am-midnight daily. **Cost** 8-person boat ƒ90 for first half-hour, then ƒ2 per minute; 16-person boats ƒ180 for first half-hour, then ƒ60 per 15 minutes; 35-person boat ƒ210 for first half-hour, then ƒ75 per 15 minutes. **Credit** AmEx, DC, MC, V (accepted only prior to boarding).

Advance booking is advisable as the service is usually busy, particularly in high season. Water taxis can be hailed as they're sailing along a canal – but it's unlikely they'll be free.

Canal Buses

Canal Bus

Weteringschans 24 (623 9886). Tram 6, 10. **Open** 10am-7pm daily. **Cost** day ticket ƒ19,50; ƒ15 under-12s; two-day ticket ƒ26; ƒ26 under-12s.

The 52-seater canal buses are the latest addition to Amsterdam's water transport system. They offer a regular service through the canals from the Rijksmuseum to Centraal Station, stopping at Leidseplein, Leidsestraat/Keizersgracht and Westerkerk/Anne Frankhuis. The service operates every day between 10am and 8pm at 30-minute intervals.

Cycling

Cycling is widely considered the most convenient means of getting from A to B in Amsterdam: there are bike lanes on most roads, marked out by white lines and bike symbols. Some drivers insist on using bike lanes as parking spaces, but most motorists are used to the abundance of cyclists and collisions are rare. Remember that cycling two abreast is illegal, as is going without reflector bands on both front and back wheels.

Never leave your bike unlocked, as there's a thriving trade in stolen bikes. Police are currently trying to clamp down on this, partly because of bike theft's association with junkies trying to raise a fast buck. Be sure to use a sturdy lock or even

Ticket to ride

It's an all too familiar scene. You're in the middle of a magical Dutch public transport adventure; you've sampled the peculiar delights of a double-decker train, maybe even a bus with the bendy bit in the middle and finally, you're on the tram. This is the way to travel, clanking along in a manner that would have your dad lost in misty nostalgia. And then suddenly, upon reaching a tram stop, all the little kids (and some of the grown-ups) bolt like rabbits out of the tram which is suddenly filled with a swarm of blue uniformed ticket inspectors. The *Kontrol*. They want to see your ticket and er, well... you haven't got one. Spot fine: ƒ60. And it isn't even your fault, you bluster, you wanted to get a ticket but as far as you could see there weren't any.

Once upon a time, upon proclaiming that you had no money on you, the ticket inspectors, then endowed with a pathetically touching faith in human nature, would produce a small book and pen. You would supply your name and address back home, they would send you the fine, and you would pay up because otherwise they'd follow up with a court summons. And so Dick

Head of 999 Letsbe Avenue would pass into the annals of Dutch legal procedure as a confirmed fare dodger and you would go about your holiday scot free.

Alas, those times are no more. The *Kontrol* have become cynical and tough. If you have no valid ID when caught without a ticket, then it's off to the police station – you're nicked. What the relevant authorities don't seem to realise is that the whole procedure surrounding the buying of tickets for the tram is as clear as mud. It all hinges around the *strippenkaart* (*see above* **Tickets**). Validating the *strippenkaart* should be simple: shove it in one of the little yellow boxes on the tram whereupon the box goes 'ding' and the the ticket is stamped. Or it isn't, because it's pot luck as to whether said yellow box is working or not. If not then the driver will stamp it for you, but that means battling up to the front and the one thing that Amsterdam trams were definitely not made for is battling up to the front. Hé Hé (pronounced Her Her) is a Dutch expression of exasperation. Learn it.

More bikes than you can shake a spoke at.

better, two sturdy locks; some thieves are equipped with powerful cutters which will make short work of thin chains. If someone in the street offers you a bike for sale (*'fiets te koop'*), don't be tempted: it's almost certainly stolen. There's no shortage of firms where a good bike can be hired for about ƒ10 a day. Below we list four reputable companies; others can be found in the *Amsterdam Yellow Pages* (*Gouden Gids*) under 'Fietsen en Bromfietsen Verhuur' (Bikes and Motorbikes Rental).

Bike City
Bloemgracht 70 (626 3721). Tram 17, 13. **Open** 9am-6pm daily in summer; varies in winter. **Cost** ƒ10 per day plus ƒ50 deposit and passport, or credit card imprint. **Credit** AmEx, DC, EC, MC, V.

The Bulldog
Oudezijds Voorburgwal 220 (624 8248). Tram 4, 9, 14, 16, 24, 25. **Open** Apr-Sept 9am-6pm daily. **Cost** ƒ10 per day plus ƒ200 deposit and passport.

Rent-A-Bike
Pieter Jacobszoondwarsstraat 7-13 (625 5029). Tram 4, 9, 14, 16, 24, 25. **Open** 9am-6pm daily. **Cost** ƒ10 per day plus ƒ50 deposit and passport/ID card, or credit card imprint. **Credit** AmEx, DC, MC, V.
Rent-A-Bike offers a ƒ1 per day discount to anyone mentioning that they heard of them through *Time Out*.

Take-A-Bike
Centraal Station, Stationsplein 6 (624 8391). Tram 1, 2, 4, 5, 9, 11, 13, 16, 17, 24, 25. **Open** 6am-10pm Mon-Fri; 7am-10pm Sat; 8am-10pm Sun. **Cost** ƒ8 per day (8am-10pm) or ƒ32 per week plus ƒ200 deposit.
Here you can both hire (until 10pm) and store (up to midnight) a bike.

Trains

From Centraal Station, one of the biggest railway terminals in Europe, you can get direct trains to most major cities across the continent. The ornate neo-Renaissance station, designed by PJH Cuypers, is one of Amsterdam's most imposing structures and gives a bustling first impression of the city. All conceivable needs of the newly-arrived visitor are catered for here, from shower facilities and restaurants inside the station to hotel, travel and entertainment booking services on Stationsplein outside. As most of the city's bus and tram services begin and end here it is also an ideal starting point for trips around the city. A year-round procession of flower-sellers, street entertainers and useless hippy buskers singing 'All You Need Is Love' in front of the main entrance adds to its character, though beware of pickpockets, street hustlers and rip-offs.

But be warned, you must obtain a reservation for international trains and the reservations office gets very crowded during the summer season. Tickets can be reserved over the phone (620 2266) but you must do this seven days in advance. For more information on rail travel, *see chapter* **Beyond Amsterdam**.

Centraal Station Information Desk
Stationsplein 13 (information 069292). Tram 1, 2, 4, 5, 9, 11, 13, 16, 17, 24, 25. **Open** information desk 6.30am-10pm daily; reservations office 6.30am-10pm daily. **Credit** MC, V.

Accommodation

A five-star suite with hot tub, a room with canal view or a bed in a budget dorm? Amsterdam can accommodate you.

It's hardly surprising that in a city as densely populated and as popular with tourists as Amsterdam, accommodation – whether it's a long-term flat or a hotel room for the night – is not always easy to come by. The main rule is, reserve well in advance: two to three weeks is advisable, and even earlier in peak periods and during public holidays.

The good news is that hotel standards are generally high, with clean functional rooms and facilities, so although prices are on the steep side, you get your money's worth. You are unlikely to encounter the seedy grottiness endemic to many a Parisian hotel, nor are you likely to run into the Dutch counterpart of Basil Fawlty. Amsterdam's hoteliers are generally an honest bunch.

Canal houses which have been converted into hotels have a pleasant, typically Dutch atmosphere but few have lifts and their staircases are invariably steep and narrow. Since these are the most popular among first-time visitors it is best to check details thoroughly and book well in advance. Many of the moderately priced hotels we list are family-run and have a friendly, relaxed atmosphere. Of the de luxe and expensive hotels listed, several give discounts at weekends, so it's worth checking by phone for bargains.

Amsterdam's importance as a business centre is reflected in the increasing number of business hotels, especially around the RAI (*see chapter* **Business**) and Schiphol Airport. All provide comprehensive business facilities, including fax, telephones, conference and meeting rooms, at extra cost.

Only the more expensive hotels have their own car parks (indicated under individual hotel descriptions below, where present). Some have paid valet parking or offer reduced price parking coupons. Finding your own parking space is a problem: since the introduction of paid parking in central Amsterdam, spaces are scarce and expensive. Illegally parked cars are clamped or towed away (*see chapter* **Survival**), and cars with foreign plates are extra liable for break-ins. So it's smart to leave your wheels at home.

The hotels we have selected are classified into price groups on the basis of the cost of a double room with WC and shower or bath en suite for one night in the high season: **Deluxe** (over ƒ500); **Expensive** (ƒ300-ƒ500); **Moderate** (between ƒ160-ƒ300); **Budget** (under ƒ160). The room prices listed run from a basic room off-peak to the hotel's best room in the high season.

For listings of other hotels and university halls of residence, *see chapters* **Gay & Lesbian**, **Students** *and* **Women's Amsterdam**.

Unless otherwise stated, breakfast is included in the room price.

RESERVATIONS

There are several ways of making reservations. Booking a travel and hotel package direct with your local travel agent is a reliable option and can work out cheaper. If you book yourself, advance bookings need to be made in peak periods as demand is high. Most hotels will require a deposit; if the establishment does not accept credit cards, this will have to be sent by post. Alternatively you can make use of the free Dutch hoteliers' reservation service (*see below*), which handles bookings for the whole of

Untold luxury at the **Amstel**. *Page 17.*

THE HEART OF AMSTERDAM

De Lairessestraat 11
1071 NR Amsterdam
Tel: 020 675 0051
Fax: 020 675 3934
Ask for Time Out Rates
(Short and Long Term)

*All postmodern conveniences at the **Hotel Winston**. Page 27.*

the Netherlands. For those already in the country, the VVV tourist information offices at Centraal Station and Schiphol Airport (*see chapter* **Essential Information**) also offer a national hotel booking service. In Amsterdam, this costs ƒ5 per person (plus a deposit of ƒ5 per person which is later deducted from your hotel bill). Enquiries are only taken in person. The VVV also produces a comprehensive guide to hotels in the city, available from their offices at ƒ4,50.

Nationaal Reserverings Centrum

PO Box 404, 2260 AK Leidschendam (070 320 2500/fax 070 320 2611). **Open** 8am-8pm Mon-Fri; 8am-2pm Sat.
Many of the hotels recommended by the VVV can be booked through this bureau free of charge. The VVV can provide a brochure of the hotels the centre deals with and, if you decide to book through them, they will send confirmation of your reservation by post.

Deluxe: over ƒ500

American Hotel

Leidsekade 97 (624 5322/fax 625 3236). Tram 1, 2, 5, 6, 7, 10, 11. **Rates** *single* ƒ295-ƒ425; *double* ƒ425-ƒ600; *extra bed* ƒ75. **Credit** AmEx, CB, DC, JCB, MC, TC, V.
A listed art deco building just off Leidseplein, the American Hotel was designed by Willem Kromhout in 1902 and extensively modernised in the 1980s. The stunning ground-floor Café Americain is the hotel's centrepiece and is busy throughout the year. The rest of the building has been renovated in a more modern style with constant echoes of art deco in colour, lighting, textile patterns and furniture design. The rooms are large, airy and luxuriously appointed, some with a picturesque canal view, others overlooking the bustle of Leidseplein. Double glazing throughout, however, means all the rooms are quiet. The illuminated, red 'American Hotel' sign

on the roof offers a good night-time landmark for the newly-arrived – and easily lost – visitor. Breakfast costs an extra ƒ30.
Hotel services *Bar. Café. Conference rooms. Dry cleaning. Fitness centre. Gift shop. Lifts. Terrace. Valet.* **Room services** *Babysitting. Minibar. Room service (24-hour). Telephone. TV and in-house movies.*

Amstel Intercontinental Amsterdam

Professor Tulpplein 1 (622 6060/fax 622 5808). Tram 6, 7, 10. **Rates** *single* ƒ720-ƒ800; *double* ƒ775-ƒ850; *suites from* ƒ1000. **Credit** AmEx, DC, JCB, MC, TC, V.
After a ƒ70 million renovation in 1992, the five-star Amstel is the most luxurious and expensive hotel in the whole of the Netherlands. Running since 1867, part of its lasting appeal is its beautiful and quiet location on the River Amstel. The service is calm and discreet, ideal for those seeking star treatment – celebrity spotters take note. The communal areas are exceptionally sumptuous. Breakfast costs ƒ38,50.
Hotel services *Bar. Banqueting halls. Brasserie. Business centre. Conference rooms. Fitness centre with sauna. Lifts. Limousines. Motor yacht. Parking (and valet service). Restaurant. Reuters news wire. Secretarial services. Shops. Swimming pool. Terrace. Wheelchair access with assistance.* **Room services** *Air-conditioning. Fax. Minibar. Room service (24-hour). Stereo CD player. Telephone. TV and in-house movies. Video.*

Amsterdam Hilton

Apollolaan 138-140 (678 0780/fax 662 6688). Tram 5, 24. **Rates** *single* ƒ415-ƒ485; *double* ƒ445-ƒ515; under-12s free if sleeping in same room as parents; *extra bed* ƒ85. **Credit** AmEx, DC, MC, JCB, TC, V.
This enormous, rather anonymous building houses 271 rooms which overlook either the Amstel or the Apollolaan. The decor throughout is unexciting, but the comprehensive hotel facilities and services give few other causes for complaint. Beatlemaniacs can book the suite where John Lennon and Yoko Ono staged their 'Bed-In'. Breakfast not included.
Hotel services *Banquet facilities for up to 650. Bar. Boat hire. Business facilities. Café. Conference rooms. Dry*

Hotel Belga

Hotel Belga is a comfortable one star family hotel. The hotel was designed by Rembrandt's frame-maker. It is situated in the old centre of Amsterdam, so walking in the neighbourhood (for example along the canals) is like living 300 years ago. Most rooms have a shower and a toilet and all rooms have cable colour TV and telephone with wake up system. You can pay cash or by credit card. The rates include breakfast.

For reservations: Hotel Belga
Hartenstraat 8, 1016 CB Amsterdam
Tel: 00 31 20 624 9080 Fax: 00 31 20 623 6862

Hotel Café Utopia

Budget bed and breakfast.
In this small "smokers' friendly" hotel in the heart of the centre. You will find a relaxed atmosphere in our well stocked bar.Utopia is the ideal place for the budget traveller. Being only a few minutes walk from every interesting place to see in Amsterdam. Like the bars, coffeeshops, red light area and shopping centre. We have single rooms, double rooms and rooms for groups.

For reservations: Hotel Utopia
Nieuwezijds Voorburgwal 132,1012 SH Amsterdam
Tel: 00 31 20 626 1295 Fax: 00 31 20 622 7060

Hotel Peters

Small and quite family hotel with eight rooms. The rooms are nicely decorated and have TV, fridge, shower and toilet.
Breakfast is served in the room. The hotel is located round the corner from the Concertgebouw, the van Gogh museum, Leidseplein and congress centre RAI. We have single, double, triple and group rooms.

For reservations: Hotel Peters
Nicolaas Maesstraat 72, 1071 RC Amsterdam
Tel: 00 31 20 673 3454 Fax: 00 31 20 623 6862

The opulent art deco **American.** *Page 17.*

cleaning. Hairdresser. KLM bus service. Laundry. Lifts. Parking. Restaurants. Shops. Terrace. Water taxi service. Wheelchair access with assistance. **Room services** *Minibar. Room service (24-hour). Stereo. Telephone. TV and in-house movies.*

The Grand
Oudezijds Voorburgwal 197 (555 3111/fax 555 3222). Tram 4, 9, 14, 16, 24, 25. **Rates** *single* ƒ545; *double* ƒ645. **Credit** AmEx, DC, MC, TC, V.
This five-star hotel is in the old part of the city in what used to be Amsterdam's City Hall. It opened in 1992 and has 182 rooms and suites that have been designed to reflect the building's history. The restaurant Café Roux is inspired by the world famous chef Albert Roux; dishes served are extremely good at surprisingly moderate prices.
Hotel services *Bar. Banqueting room. Conference rooms. Health spa. Parking (valet). Restaurant. Sauna and steam room. Swimming pool.* **Room services** *Minibar. Room service (24-hour).Telephone. TV and in-house movies.*

Grand Hotel Krasnapolsky
Dam 9 (554 9111/fax 622 8607). Tram 1, 2, 5, 13, 14, 16, 17, 24, 25. **Rates** *single* ƒ350-ƒ500; *double* ƒ405-ƒ575; *extra bed* ƒ85; *under-12s in parents' room at half price; under-2s free.* **Credit** AmEx, DC, MC, TC, V.
An enormous building on Dam Square opposite the Royal Palace, this externally impressive five-star hotel dating from 1866 has over 429 rooms of differing sizes. Inside, the impression is functional rather than grand. The hotel offers particularly good business facilities, including 14 convention rooms accommodating 1,500 people. The Winter Garden restaurant in the centre of the hotel offers a daily lunch buffet. There is also a Japanese Teppan Yaki restaurant.
Hotel services *Bar. Beauty parlour. Brasserie. Conference rooms. KLM bus service. Lifts. Parking.*

Shopping arcade. Restaurants. Wheelchair access. **Room services** *Air-conditioning. Minibar. Radio. Telephone. TV and in-house movies.*

Hotel de L'Europe
Nieuwe Doelenstraat 2-8 (623 4836/fax 624 2962). Tram 4, 9, 14, 16, 24, 25. **Rates** *single* ƒ475-ƒ515; *double* ƒ575-ƒ650. **Credit** AmEx, DC, MC, TC, V.
Built in 1895 and with extensive renovations carried out in 1995, this centrally located five-star hotel retains a period charm and elegance. The rooms are large and tastefully furnished and there's an attractive ground-floor terrace overlooking the River Amstel and the Munttoren (Mint tower). Many of the rooms have balconies overlooking the river. Haute cuisine can be enjoyed in the Excelsior restaurant: *see chapter* **Restaurants.** Breakfast is an additional ƒ22,50.
Hotel services *Bar. Business facilities. Café. Fitness centre. Lifts. Limousine service. Massage parlour. Parking. Private boat landing. Restaurants. Sauna. Swimming pool. Terrace.* **Room services** *Air-conditioning. Minibar. Room service (24-hour). Telephone. TV and in-house movies.*

Okura Hotel Amsterdam
Ferdinand Bolstraat 333 (678 7111/fax 671 2344). Tram 12, 25. **Rates** *single* ƒ375-ƒ475; *double* ƒ420-ƒ520. **Credit** AmEx, DC, JCB, MC, TC, V.
The luxurious Hotel Okura is one of the leading five-star hotels in the Netherlands. It is just five minutes' walk from RAI Congresgebouw and the World Trade Centre and has ten multifunctional banquet rooms that can be used for conferences and meetings. The largest room can seat up to 650 people. There are two Japanese restaurants as well as the French Le Ciel Bleu on the the 23rd floor, with its fantastic view over the city. Breakfast costs an extra ƒ37,50.
Hotel services *Bar. Café. Conference/banqueting rooms. Health centre. Lifts. Parking. Restaurants. Secretarial services. Shopping arcade.* **Room services** *Air-conditioning. Minibar. Room service (24-hour). Telephone. TV and in-house movies.*

Hotel Pulitzer
Prinsengracht 315-331 (523 5235/fax 627 6753). Tram 13, 14, 17. **Rates** *single* ƒ395-ƒ470; *double* ƒ455-ƒ540. **Credit** AmEx, DC, JCB, MC, TC, V.
Arguably the best of Amsterdam's five-star hotels, the Pulitzer comprises 24 seventeenth-century canal houses between Prinsengracht – the hotel's entrance – and Keizersgracht. The architecture may be charming but it does mean that there's a labyrinth of angular corridors and steep stairs. It's ideal, however, if you're seeking a characterful and intimate atmosphere. All the 231 rooms are different and many have a view of the canals, but the most pleasant overlook the gardens in the hotel's inner courtyard. Breakfast costs an extra ƒ33.
Hotel services *Airline reservations. Art gallery. Bar. Café. Conference rooms. Currency exchange. Dry cleaning. Garden. Gift shop. KLM bus service. Laundry. Lifts. Restaurant. Valet parking (ƒ42,50).* **Room services** *Minibar. Room service (24-hour). Safe. Telephone. TV and in-house movies.*

Victoria Park Plaza
Damrak 1-5 (623 4255/fax 625 2997). Tram 4, 9, 14, 16, 20, 24, 25. **Rates** *single* ƒ325-ƒ355; *double* ƒ395-ƒ425. **Credit** AmEx, DC, MC, TC, V.
The four-star hotel has been refurbished in a conventional yet tasteful style and proves popular as an elegant business hotel just opposite Centraal Station. The Victoria Gallery is light, airy and has dozens of plants, characteristics common to all the communal areas. Breakfast costs an extra ƒ27,50.
Hotel services *Bar. Beauty salon. Business facilities. Conference rooms. Fitness centre. Hairdresser. Parking nearby. Swimming pool. Restaurant. Terrace.* **Room services** *Minibar. Telephone. TV.*

Expensive: ƒ300-ƒ500

Hotel Dikker & Thijs Fenice
Prinsengracht 444 (626 7721/fax 625 8986). Tram 1, 2, 5, 11. **Rates** *single ƒ250-ƒ280; double ƒ315-ƒ415.* **Credit** AmEx, DC, EC, MC, TC, V.
A small intimate hotel with 25 rooms, newly decorated throughout in plush classic style, located on the corner of the Prinsengracht canal and Leidsegracht canals, right in the centre. Good French/Italian food in the restaurant.
Hotel services *Bar. Small conference room. Laundry. Lift. Parking nearby. Restaurant. Secretarial services.* **Room services** *Babysitting. Room service. Telephone. TV.*

Estherea
Singel 303-309 (624 5146/fax 623 9001). Tram 1, 2, 5, 11. **Rates** *single ƒ185-265; double ƒ210-ƒ365; triple ƒ390-ƒ415; quad ƒ440- ƒ475.* **Credit** AmEx, DC, JCB, MC, TC, V.
The Estherea is made up of eight seventeenth-century canal houses which have been converted into a comfortable, family-run four-star hotel. All of the 75 bedrooms have recntly been renovated, and some overlook the canal. Some rooms are very small, but even those are uncluttered as furnishings are comfortable and neat.
Hotel services *Bar. Lift. Lounge. Wheelchair access with assistance.* **Room services** *Room service (7am-11pm).Safe. Telephone. TV.*

Holiday Inn Crowne Plaza
Nieuwezijds Voorburgwal 5 (620 0500/fax 620 1173). Tram 1, 2, 5, 11, 13, 17. **Rates** *single ƒ420-ƒ470; double ƒ395-ƒ400.* **Credit** AmEx, DC, JCB, MC, TC, V.
This overtly luxurious five-star hotel is within a stone's throw of Dam Square, on the corner of Nieuwezijds Voorburgwal and Nieuwendijk. The rooms are spacious, quiet and decorated in unobtrusive good taste (there is a choice of queen-size, king-size and twin rooms). That said, once inside you could be in any Holiday Inn in the world. Breakfast costs an extra ƒ33.
Hotel services *Bar. Brasserie. Business facilities. Conference rooms. Fitness centre. KLM bus service. Parking. Restaurant. Sauna. Solarium. Swimming pool. Wheelchair access (limited).* **Room services** *Air-conditioning. Minibar. Room service (24-hour). Telephone. TV and in-house movies.*

Jan Luyken Hotel
Jan Luykenstraat 58 (573 0730/fax 676 3841). Tram 2, 3, 5, 12. **Rates** *single ƒ250-ƒ275; double ƒ290-ƒ350;* **Credit** AmEx, DC, MC, V.
In a peaceful location, close to the Concertgebouw, this is one of the city's few four-star hotels that is not part of a chain. The 63 bedrooms have been recently redecorated and are well furnished. The Jan Luyken Residence opposite the hotel has facilities for conferences.
Hotel services *Bar. Business centre. Conference rooms. Exchange facilities. Lifts. Lounge. Parking. Wheelchair access.* **Room services** *Minibar. Room service (7am-midnight). Telephone. TV.*

Marriott Hotel
Stadhouderskade 21 (607 5555/fax 607 5511). Tram 1, 2, 5, 6, 7, 10, 11. **Rates** *single ƒ440; double ƒ490,* discounts at weekends, under-18s free in parents' room. **Credit** AmEx, DC, MC, TC, V.
A modern, large and efficient five-star hotel adjacent to Vondelpark and within easy reach of Leidseplein and the museums. The hotel has recently redecorated rooms and a health club with a sauna, as well as business facilities. There is a bright and pleasant café area overlooking the busy Stadhouderskade. Breakfast costs an extra ƒ32,50.

Hotel Babylon

Every major city has its rock 'n' roll hotels and naturally Amsterdam is no exception. The **Amstel** was the scene of much hysteria in April 1996 when heart-throbs Take That stayed there on the day of their farewell appearance on Dutch TV. The **American** is the hotel that most visiting pop stars grace with their presence, and has been the scene of many a debauched post-gig shindig. The city's most famous hotel happening however, was John Lennon and Yoko Ono's prolonged stay in bed at the **Hilton** in March 1969. For seven days the couple stayed in bed as 'a protest against war and violence in the world'. Like, radical, man.

Hotel services *Bar. Café. Hairdresser. Health club. Laundry. Lifts. Parking. Restaurant. Sauna. Secretarial services. Shop. Valet. Wheelchair access.* **Room services** *Air-conditioning. Minibar. Room service (24-hour). Telephone. TV and in-house movies.*

Park Hotel
Stadhouderskade 25 (671 1222/fax 664 9455). Tram 1, 2, 5. **Rates** *single ƒ270; double ƒ375; triple ƒ450; extra bed ƒ90.* **Credit** AmEx, DC, MC, TC, V.
In the bustling heart of the city, a few minutes from the Rijksmuseum and the Van Gogh Museum. The hotel is on a busy road, but double glazing makes for relative quiet in all front-facing rooms. Seventh floor rooms have spectacular views across Amsterdam. Staff are well-trained and multilingual. Breakfast included.
Hotel services *Bar. Business facilities. Conference room. Hairdresser. Lift. Parking. Restaurant. Secretarial services. Shops.* **Room services** *Coffee and tea-maker. Hair-dryer. Room service (24-hour).Telephone. TV. Trouser press.*

Schiller Karena
Rembrandtplein 26-36 (623 1660/fax 624 0098). Tram 4, 9, 14. **Rates** *single ƒ245-ƒ270; double ƒ315-ƒ340.* **Credit** AmEx, DC, MC, V.
Refurbished in 1993, the building housing this four-star hotel dates from the late nineteenth century, when the painter Schiller threw down his brush in favour of architecture. To commemorate its creator, the hotel features his paintings

Filosoof: worth thinking about. *Page 25.*

throughout and these, along with the art deco furnishings, lamps and wood panelling, give the building its unique personality.
Hotel services *Business facilities. Café. Laundry. Lifts. Restaurant.* **Room services** *Telephone. TV.*

Moderate: ƒ160-ƒ300

Acro
Jan Luykenstraat 44 (662 0526/fax 675 0811). Tram 2, 5. **Rates** *single ƒ105-ƒ150; double ƒ140-ƒ195.* **Credit** AmEx, DC, MC, V.
Good, modern hotel, stylishly refurbished, and handy for the museums. There is a comfortable bar and self-service restaurant. Breakfast is included.
Hotel services *Bar. Restaurant.* **Room services** *TV. Telephone.*

Agora
Singel 462 (627 2200/fax 627 2202). Tram 1, 2, 5, 11. **Rates** *single ƒ115-ƒ170; double ƒ135-ƒ200.* **Credit** AmEx, DC, MC, V.
Built in 1735 and renovated in 1989, the Agora is a small, comfortable hotel situated on the Singel canal, close to the flower market. There are masses of plants in the pretty communal areas and a large family room at the top of the house with angled ceilings and exposed beams. Most of the 15 bedrooms have private facilities and some overlook the canal.
Room services *Room service. Telephone. TV.*

Ambassade Hotel
Herengracht 341 (626 2333/fax 624 5321). Tram 1, 2, 5, 11. **Rates** *single ƒ240; double ƒ295.* **Credit** AmEx, DC, MC, V.
A good value three-star hotel on the Herengracht, home of

embassies and consulates, comprising nine seventeenth- and eighteenth-century merchant houses. All the rooms are individually furnished in a variety of refined styles but, as is typical in canal houses, the stairs are narrow and steep and not all houses are accessible by lift. The ground-floor lounge and breakfast room have huge ceiling-to-floor windows, affording a fine canal view. Antique furnishings help the building retain much of its former graciousness.
Hotel services *Laundry and dry-cleaning service. Lift.* **Room services** *Room service (24-hour). Safe. Telephone. TV.*

Amsterdam Wiechmann
Prinsengracht 328-332 (626 3321/fax 626 8962). Tram 1, 2, 5, 11. **Rates** *single ƒ135-ƒ150; double ƒ195-ƒ225; triple ƒ250.*
The friendly hoteliers take great pains to ensure their establishment is scrupulously clean and comfortably furnished. Pleasantly situated and with a canal view, the hotel is close to the Anne Frankhuis. The breakfast room and lounge have been completely refurbished.
Hotel services *Lounge. Bar.* **Room services** *Telephone. TV.*

Bridge Hotel
Amstel 107-111 (623 7068/fax 624 1565). Tram 3, 6, 7, 10. **Rates** *single ƒ100-ƒ130; double ƒ150-ƒ175; triple ƒ230.* **Credit** AmEx, DC, MC, V.
Overlooking the famous 'Skinny Bridge' on the Amstel river, The Bridge hotel is within walking distance of the Waterlooplein flea market and the nightlife on Rembrandtplein. The hotel has been recently renovated throughout by the new owners. There are de luxe and standard rooms all with en suite facilities and stripped pine furniture.
Hotel services *TV lounge. Parking coupons.* **Room services** *Telephone.*

Canal House Hotel
Keizersgracht 148 (622 5182/fax 624 1317). Tram 13, 14, 17. **Rates** *single ƒ210-ƒ265; double ƒ225-ƒ265.* **Credit** AmEx, DC, MC, TC, V.
The American owner has lovingly restored this seventeenth-century canal house (actually a two-house conversion) close to the Jordaan in a quiet residential area. Antiques adorn every nook and cranny and there are exposed beams, patchwork quilts and an attractive garden. The hotel's charm is reflected in a long waiting list for weekends in high season.
Hotel services *Bar. Garden. Lift.* **Room services** *Hair-dryer. Telephone.*

Concert Inn
De Lairessestraat 11 (675 0051). Tram 16. **Rates** *single ƒ140; double ƒ185-ƒ205; extra bed ƒ65.* **Credit** AmEx, DC, MC, V.
The rooms vary in size and though some are a little cramped for the price, all are spotlessly clean, have private bathrooms and are plainly furnished. There is a pleasant breakfast room with garden. The hotelier is friendly and welcoming.
Hotel services *Lift. Wheelchair access with assistance.* **Room services** *Hair-dryer. Telephone. TV.*

Eden Hotel
Amstel 144 (626 6243/fax 623 3267). Tram 4, 9, 14. **Rates** *single ƒ135-ƒ180; double ƒ175-ƒ240.* **Credit** AmEx, DC, MC, V.
Backing on to the busy Rembrandtplein and overlooking the Amstel River, the newly renovated Eden is made up of several canal houses dating back to the seventeenth century. In April 1997, the new brasserie opens, offering the possibility of full board. All rooms have en suite facilities and there's a romantic bridal suite for honeymooners.
Hotel services *Hair-dryer. Lifts. Wheelchair access. Laundry. Exchange.* **Room services** *Babysitting. Telephone. TV and video.*

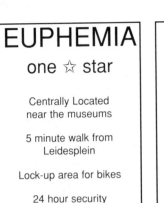
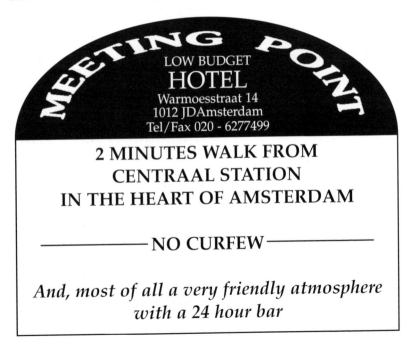

Clock up some Zzzzzzzzs at the **Arena**. *Page 26.*

Hotel de Filosoof

*Anna van den Vondelstraat 6 (683 3013/fax 685 3750).
Tram 1, 6, 11/bus 171, 172.* **Rates** *single ƒ125-155;
double ƒ145-ƒ185; triple ƒ165-240; quad ƒ225-295.*
Credit AmEx, MC, V.
You don't have to be a philosophy enthusiast to stay in this
small hotel, but it helps. Even the decor has a philosophical
theme, with each room in the style of a well-known thinker.
The Plato room, for example, is decorated in black and white,
with paintings mounted on *trompe l'œil* pedestals. All rooms
with en suite facilities.
Hotel services *Bar.* **Room services** *TV. Telephone.*

Hotel de Munck

Achtergracht 3 (623 6283/fax 620 6647). Tram 4.
Rates *single ƒ85-ƒ115; double ƒ125-ƒ165; triple ƒ165-
ƒ210; quad ƒ220-ƒ280.* **Credit** AmEx, DC, MC, V.
Recently refurbished, all 14 rooms are modern and tasteful.
In a peaceful area, close to the centre, the building dates from
1727, when it was a captain's residence. Could be a bargain
in the low season, as the owner gives a ten per cent discount
from January 3 to March 15, and if business is quiet, you may
get a luxury room for the price of a standard.
Hotel services *Bar. Garden.* **Room services** *Minibar.
Radio. Telephone. TV.*

Owl Hotel

*Roemer Visscherstraat 1 (618 9484/fax 618 9441).
Tram 1, 3, 6, 11, 12.* **Rates** *single ƒ115-ƒ140; double
ƒ150-ƒ190; triple ƒ190-ƒ220.* **Credit** AmEx, DC, MC, V.
A friendly family hotel with a garden, backing on to the
Vondelpark, and handy for the museums. All rooms with
shower and WC en suite.
Hotel services *Bar. Lift. Garden.* **Room services**
Hair-dryer. TV and radio. Telephone.

Hotel Prinsen

*Vondelstraat 36-38 (616 2323/fax 616 6112) Tram 1, 3,
6, 11, 12.* **Rates** *single ƒ 135-ƒ155; double ƒ175-ƒ195; triple
ƒ195-ƒ250; quad ƒ245-ƒ300;* **Credit** AmEx, DC, MC, V.

A recently renovated hotel in a quiet, leafy residential street
near to Vondelpark, the Leidseplein and the museums. All
rooms have en suite facilities, new carpets and curtains and
continental quilts. There is a pretty, secluded garden at
the back.
Hotel services *Bar. Lift. Garden.* **Room services** *Coffee
and tea maker. Cot (ƒ15). Hair-dryer. TV. Telephone.*

Hotel Prinsenhof

Prinsengracht 810 (623 1772/fax 638 3368). Tram 4.
Rates *single ƒ80-ƒ85; double ƒ125-ƒ175; triple ƒ175-
ƒ210; quad ƒ210-ƒ290.* **Credit** AmEx, DC, MC, V.
The Prinsenhof is simply and tastefully decorated throughout.
Two of the ten rooms have private bathrooms. A charming,
friendly and reasonably priced hotel, close to the River Amstel.
Room services *Clock radio. Telephone.*

Seven Bridges

Reguliersgracht 31 (623 1329). Tram 16, 24, 25. **Rates**
single ƒ100-180; double ƒ130-ƒ220. **Credit** AmEx, MC, V.
A lovely hotel at the viewpoint of the seven bridges (*see chapter* **Canals**). The 11 rooms are tastefully furnished with new

A tasteful time at the **Seven Bridges**.

carpets and curtains throughout. As there is no dining area, breakfast is served in the room.
Room services *TV.*

Hotel Terdam
Tesselschadestraat 23 (683 1811). Tram 1, 2, 3, 5, 6, 11, 12. **Rates** *single f180; double f260.* **Credit** AmEx, DC, JCB, MC. TC, V.
Very popular with tour operators, this three-star hotel is in a quiet, pretty street close to Leidseplein. There is a pleasant art deco bar and lounge and the staff are well-informed and helpful.
Hotel services *Bar. Exchange facilities. Lift. Lounge.* **Room services** *Telephone. TV.*

Toren
Keizersgracht 164 (622 6352/fax 626 9705). Tram 13, 17. **Rates** *single f80-f245; double f120-f265; triple f210-f230; quad f230-f250.* **Credit** AmEx, DC, MC, V.
A seventeenth-century canal house, close to the beautiful Jordaan area. A gentle atmosphere is created by the tall ceilings, elegant decor and antiques. All rooms have en suite facilities.
Hotel services *Bar. Dining-room.* **Room services** *Hair-dryer. Room service. Safe. Telephone. TV.*

Budget: under f160

De Admiraal
Herengracht 563 (626 2150). Tram 4. **Rates** *single f80-f130; double f105-f155.* **Credit** MC.
A friendly and homely hotel close to the Rembrandtplein. Room six has four beds and a stunning view of the Reguliersgracht and Herengracht. Hearty Dutch breakfasts are not to be missed at f7,50.
Room services *Colour TV. Safe.*

Arena
's-Gravesandestraat 51 (694 7444/663 2649). Tram 3, 6, 9, 10, 14/Metro Weesperplein. **Rates** *double f90-f110; triple f130-f140; six bed apartments f230-f260; large dormitories f22,50 per person; small dormitories (4- 8 beds) f34-f39 per person, linen rental for dorms f5.* **Key deposit** *f40.*
A unique, recently renovated centre in an old listed convent close to Oosterpark, and three stops on the metro from central Amsterdam. The Arena is open all year round and has become one of the main centres of youth culture in the city. Features include an excellent international live music programme, tourist and cultural information centre, a stylish restaurant and bar, a huge garden and car park (f5). The dormitories (free lockers) are closed between 11am and 3pm for cleaning, but there is no night-time curfew. The newly decorated, simple rooms at the top of the building all have shower and WC, and are great value for money. One of the best budget options in town. (*See also chapter* **Music: Rock, Folk & Jazz**).
Hotel services *Bar. Bike rental. Live music. Lobby garden. Pool table. Restaurant. Tourist info. Video room. Wheelchair access.*

Bob's Youth Hostel
Nieuwezijds Voorburgwal 92 (623 0063/fax 675 6446). Tram 1, 2, 5, 11, 13, 17. **Rates** *4-18-bed dormitories f22 per person.*
Big (160 beds), brash and commercial, the hostel's low prices and central location mean it is extremely popular with international backpackers all through the year. Those with a preference for quiet may not enjoy the noise and surrounding decadence. Most dorms are mixed, but there are four women-only dorms sleeping four to 16. The bar (snacks available) is open from 8am to 2am daily.

There's a 3am curfew, and breakfast and sheets are included in the price.
Hotel services *Bar. Lockers f25 deposit. Showers in all rooms.*

La Bohème
Marnixstraat 415 (624 2828/fax 627 2897). Tram 1, 6, 7, 10. **Rates** *single f55-f60; double f100-f105.*
This small hotel was taken over by a young enthusiastic team in 1994, under the slogan 'two-star facilities for a one-star price'. It's in the heart of the city, a stone's throw from Leidseplein. All rooms have shower and WC.
Hotel services *Bar. Lounge. Internet. Fax.* **Room services** *TV. Telephone.*

Euphemia Hotel
Fokke Simonszstraat 1-9 (tel/fax 622 9045/e-mail euphjm@pi.net). Tram 16, 24, 25. **Reception open** 8am-11pm daily. **Rates** *single f40-f100; double f75-f150; triple f27,50-f50 per person; quad f22,50-f40 per person; breakfast f7,50.* **Credit** AmEx, DC, EC, MC, V.
A comfortable, friendly hotel near to the museums that offers cheap, clean accommodation. The rooms for four, complete with lockable storage facilities, are rather cramped, but the double rooms are quiet, pleasant and all have televisions. The owner has also created a separate TV/video and breakfast room that's open to all hotel guests.
Web address: http//www.channels.nl..80/euphemia.html.

Hans Brinker Budget
Kerkstraat 136-138 (622 0687/fax 638 2060). Tram 1, 2, 5, 11, 16, 24, 25. **Rates** *single f75-f89; double f115-f143; dormitory f39,50-f42.* **Credit** AmEx, DC, MC, V.
A very popular and lively hotel, awash with international backpackers in high season. Facilities are basic but the building is well-maintained and clean. Its location is a definite bonus, being just a short distance from the Leidseplein night-life.
Hotel services *Café. Lifts. Wheelchair access with help.*

De Harmonie
Prinsengracht 816 (625 0174/fax 6220174). Tram 4. **Rates** *single f70-f80; double f110-f140; triple f150-f165.* **Credit** AmEx, DC, MC, V.
Nicely situated, close to the Rembrandtplein and River Amstel, De Harmonie has been recently redecorated and now has several rooms with en suite facilities. The friendly Irish manager will point you towards Amsterdam's best Irish bars. Good value for money.

Hotel Washington
Frans van Mierisstraat 10 (679 7453/fax 673 4435). Tram 3, 12, 16, 24. **Rates** *single f80-f115; double f115-f195; 3 bed apartment (min one week) f195 per night.* **Credit** AmEx, DC, MC, V.
In a quiet street near the Museumplein, this small, clean and intimate hotel is popular with classical music-lovers and visiting musicians playing at the nearby Concertgebouw.
Room services *Telephone. TV.*

Hotel Wilhelmina
Koninginneweg 167-169 (662 5467/fax 679 2296). Tram 2, 16. **Rates** *single f55-125; double f115-155; extra bed f35.* **Credit** AmEx, MC, V, DC, TC.
In Amsterdam's most fashionable area, ideally placed for business visitors and tourists. Offering a high level of comfort at low level prices, the hotel is also in the midst of elegant shops and plush residences. In a free parking zone.
Room services *Shower. Toilet. TV and radio.*

Parkzicht
Roemer Visscherstraat 33 (618 1954/fax 618 0897). Tram 1, 2, 3, 5, 6, 11, 12. **Rates** *single f60-f90; double f120-f150.* **Credit** AmEx, MC, V.
A simple, quiet hotel, close to the museums. Most of the

rooms have en suite shower and toilet. The chunky wooden furniture is a little worn, but this and the dark wooden panelling make for an authentic Dutch feel.
Room services *Telephone. TV in most rooms.*

PC Hooft
PC Hooftstraat 63 (662 7107/fax 675 8961). Tram 2, 3, 5, 12. **Rates** *single ƒ55-ƒ75; double ƒ90-ƒ105.* **Credit** MC, V.
A small, one-star hotel with 16 rooms, the PC Hooft is very basic but clean and cheerful. It's close to the museums on a busy road which is home to some of Amsterdam's most elegant shops. Vondelpark is a short walk away.
Hotel services *Café.*

Van Ostade
Van Ostadestraat 123 (679 3452/fax 671 5213). Tram 12, 25. **Rates** *single ƒ70; double ƒ90-ƒ135;*
In the Pijp, this small friendly 'bike-hotel' rents bikes from only ƒ7,50 per day. Maps and ideas about tours are also available. The rooms are basic, but scrupulously clean, and parking for cars is available for ƒ25 per night. Breakfast is included.

Hotel Royal Kabul
Oudezijds Voorburgwal 3 (638 1461/fax 638 1046). Tram 1, 2, 4, 5, 9, 13, 17, 16, 24, 25/Metro Centraal Station **Reception open** 24hrs daily.
Slightly smarter sister of the Young Budget Hotel Kabul (*see below* **Hostels**) with more double and triple rooms with shower and WC available. The facilities and room prices are otherwise the same.

Winston Hotel
*Warmoestraat 123-129 (623 1380/fax 639 2308/e-mail winston.@xs4all.nl) Tram 4, 9, 16, 24, 25.***Rates** *single ƒ65-ƒ80; double ƒ80-ƒ135; triple ƒ120-ƒ185; 8 person dorm ƒ200-ƒ300.* Credit AmEx, DC, MC, V.
On Amsterdam's oldest street you'll find the city's most innovative hotel. The Winston, which opened in a flurry of publicity in January 96, is an on-line, multi-media arts centre offering 67 rooms either with en suite facilities or shared bathrooms. Each room is individually designed and decorated by an artist, and sponsored by a brand name. There are live performances of music and poetry in the Winston Kingdom bar (*see also chapter* **Music: Rock, Folk & Jazz**), and the food served in the restaurant is great value: breakfast ƒ7, lunch ƒ10, dinner ƒ15 or full board for just ƒ35. Let's hope it lives up to expectations and doesn't disappear up its own web site.
Room services *Internet. Powerbook. TV. Video conferencing.*

Hostels

The Dutch Youth Hostels Association (NJHC) has two hostels in Amsterdam (*listed below*). You have to be a member of the International Youth Hostel Federation (IYHF), but you can enroll on arrival; membership costs ƒ30 for non-natives (no concessions available), but Federation membership can be slightly cheaper if you join in your own country. For information on NJHC hostels throughout the Netherlands, contact the NJHC, Professor Tulpplein 4, 1018GX Amsterdam (551 3155); the office is open for enquiries from 9am to 5pm, Monday to Friday.

NJHC Hostels
Vondelpark *Zandpad 5 (683 1744/fax 616 6591). Tram 1, 2, 5, 6, 7, 10, 11.* **Stadsdoelen** *Kloveniersburgwal 97 (24 6832/fax 639 1035). Tram 4, 9, 14, 16, 24, 25.* **Both open** 7am-2am daily.

Multinational staff provide a cheery welcome at both sites, of which the Vondelpark is larger and far more pleasantly situated; the Stadsdoelen is in a seedy area on the edge of the Red-Light District. Rates at Zandpad are ƒ26 per night for 6-22 bed dormitories. Accommodation is also available in smaller rooms. Single ƒ66-ƒ71, double ƒ77-ƒ87, 3-4 beds ƒ134-ƒ144 and 5-6 beds ƒ156-ƒ168. The rooms are locked between 10.45am and 2.30pm each day. Accommodation at Kloveniersburgwal is in dormitories for 20 people, charged at ƒ24 per night. These prices are for IYHF and NJHC members – non-members pay an additional ƒ5 per night at both sites. Both hostels charge a seasonal supplement of ƒ2 on dormitory prices for July and August. Linen hire costs ƒ6,25. Facilities at both sites include communal rooms, non-smoking areas, kitchen, lockers and a bar. At Zandpad there is a lift. The curfew at both sites is 2am. Groups are advised to book at least two months in advance.

Adam and Eva
Sarphatistraat 105 (624 6206/fax 638 7200). Tram 6, 7, 10/Metro Weesperplein. **Rates** *ƒ19,50-ƒ21,50 per person; sheets ƒ6.*
A sensible option for those on a tight budget seeking no-frills accommodation. There are 90 beds in mixed and single-sex dorms accommodating between six and 20 each; there is no night-time curfew. The bar is open every day from 4pm to 2am. It's a ten-minute walk from Rembrandtplein. Breakfast is included in the price.
Hotel services *Bar. Restaurant. Garden. TV.*

The Flying Pig Hostels
The Flying Pig Downtown *Nieuwendijk 100 (420 6822/fax 624 9516). Tram 1, 2, 5, 11, 13, 17/Metro Centraal Station.* **The Flying Pig Vondelpark** *Vossiusstraat 46-47 (400 4187/fax 400 4105). Tram 2, 3, 5, 12.* **Reception open** both 24hrs daily. Reservations for more than four persons via head office (421 0583).
Rates *double ƒ100; quad ƒ31-ƒ33,50 per person; 6 person room ƒ29-ƒ30 per person; 8 person room ƒ27-ƒ28 per person; dormitory ƒ23,50.* **Credit** AmEx, EC, DC, MC, V.
The Flying Pig has two hostels in Amsterdam, one on the edge of the Vondelpark and one right by Centraal Station. Both are clean, laid-back and run by an enthusiastic crew who are seasoned travellers themselves and therefore understand the needs of backpackers. Both hostels offer free use of a fully equipped kitchen and good tourist information facilities, and almost all rooms have showers and WCs. There is no curfew. Situated next to the Downtown hostel is the Twin Pigs Café, with cheap snacks and meals and live music seven nights a week. This is the best deal in central Amsterdam for the young backpacker. *See also chapter* **Music: Rock, Folk & Jazz**.
Hotel services *Bar. Kitchen facilities. No commission exchange. Free lockers and luggage storage. Tourist information. Web address: http://www.hostelwatch.com/hostels/-flyingpig.html.*

International Budget Hotel
Leidsegracht 76 (624 2784). Tram 1, 2, 5. **Reception open** 9am-11pm daily. **Rates** *double ƒ75-ƒ150; quad ƒ22.50-ƒ40 per person.* **Credit** AmEx, DC, EC, MC, V.
A youth hostel in the heart of Amsterdam, overlooking a tree-lined canal. All rooms have showers and WCs, there are free maps, lockers, and linen, plus music and movies in the communal video lounge. It's good value for money and ideal for backpackers, with its relaxed policy on smoking on the premises.

Meeting Point
Warmoestraat 14 (tel/fax 627 7499). Tram 4, 9, 16, 24, 25/Metro Centraal Station. **Open** 24hrs daily. **Rates** *10-15 bed dorms ƒ25-ƒ35 per person; 4-5 bed dorms ƒ35-ƒ45 per person (including linen); breakfast ƒ5.*
Very close to Centraal Station, this hostel boasts a 24-hour

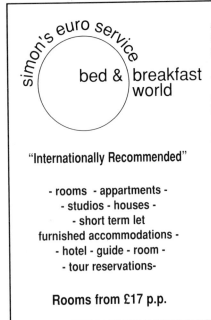

bar. This of course means that there is also no curfew. The pool table and the convenient, slightly sleazy surroundings make this a very free and easy place.
Hotel services Bar. Hot showers. Safe deposit boxes.

Young Budget Hotel Kabul

Warmoesstraat 38-42 (623 7158/fax 620 0869). Tram 4, 9, 14, 16, 24, 25. **Rates** *single ƒ67-ƒ72;* *double ƒ82-ƒ105; triple ƒ120-ƒ137; 4-16 bed dorms ƒ26-ƒ40 per person.*
In three seventeenth century buildings on the edge of the Red-Light District, the Kabul's rooms and dormitories are basic and rather cramped, but all have lockers, sheets and breakfast included in the price. There is no curfew and the bar regularly plays host to live musicians through to the early hours. The restaurant has meals at budget prices and the bar has a daily happy hour from 11pm to midnight. (*See also* **Hotel Royal Kabul** *under* **Budget** *above.*)
Hotel services *Two bars. Pool tables. Hotel open 24 hours. Lockers. Restaurant.*

Barge

Amstel Botel

Oosterdokskade 2-4 (626 4247/fax 639 1952). Tram 1, 2, 5, 9, 13, 17, 24, 25. **Reception open** 24 hours daily. **Rates** *single ƒ119-ƒ129; double ƒ136-ƒ148; triple ƒ180-ƒ190.* **Credit** AmEx, DC, EC, MC, V.
This is Amsterdam's only floating hotel, docked close to Centraal Station on the River IJ. If you like the cross-Channel ferry, then you'll love the Botel, as it's simply a large boat moored to the edge of the train tracks. The view over the river is pleasant, but if you're unfortunate enough to book a room on the land-side, you'll have to endure the stench of stagnant water and a view of rubbish-filled river.
Hotel services *Bar. Breakfast room. Parking.* **Room services** *Shower. Toilet. Telephone. TV, in-house movies.*

Private accommodation/B&B

There are very few bed and breakfasts in Amsterdam but there are places where you can stay in private accommodation, with a similar service. It does not need to be a risky business providing you are sensible and inspect the room first. However, despite the B&B name tag, breakfast may not always be included and you may be expected to tidy your room yourself.

Holiday Link

PO Box 70.160, 9704 AD Groningen (050 313 4545/fax 050 313 3177). **Open** 9.30 am-4pm Mon-Fri.
This Groningen-based organisation recommends bed and breakfast accommodation throughout the Netherlands. It also publishes an annual guide 'Bed and breakfast in Holland and budget accommodation' available in major bookshops and from national VVV offices (ƒ7,50). This handy little book contains around 200 addresses offering reliable B&B accommodation, ranging from around ƒ30-ƒ50 per person per night. The book can be ordered by post or with the order form displayed on their web site.
Web address: http://ovv.xxlink.nl/lovv

Marcel van Woerkom

Leidsestraat 87 (622 9834/fax same). Tram 1, 2, 5. **Rates** *ƒ55-ƒ65 per person.*
Designer and graphic artist Marcel van Woerkom has four double rooms all with private bathrooms in his house on Leidsestraat just round the corner from bustling Leidseplein. Marcel has lovingly restored his home over 25 years and filled it with contemporary designer furniture as well as

retaining many original features (folder with colour photos of the house available on request). Marcel offers immaculate rooms for two, three or four people sharing. He is also pleased to offer his guests all kinds of insider tourist tips and information. The popularity of Marcel's is largely due to the fact that many visitors return and in turn recommend this B&B to their friends, as Marcel's collection of delighted thank-you letters attests. If you like a home-from-home feel to your holiday accommodation, this is the place for you.

Campsites

There are a number of camping grounds in and around Amsterdam; we list four, all recommended by the VVV. Two are just a 15-minute bus ride north from the centre, two are further out and more rural. Remember that though the climate is changeable, you can always hire a cabin if it rains. During the summer, the weather is reliably mild. Vliegenbos and Zeeburg are classified as youth campsites, while the other two are more family-orientated campsites with separate areas for camping.

Gaasper Camping Amsterdam

Loosdrechtdreef 7 (696 7326/fax 696 9369). Metro Gaasperplas/Bus 59, 60, 158. **Reception open** *June-Aug* 8am-10pm daily; *Sept-May* 9am-9pm daily. **Rates** (all per night) per person ƒ6; under-12s ƒ3,50; car ƒ5,50; camper ƒ10; caravan ƒ8; tent ƒ6-ƒ8; electrical connection ƒ4,50; hot showers ƒ1,50; dog ƒ3,75.
This campsite is in the south-east of greater Amsterdam, easily accessible by either Metro or bus. It's on the edge of the Gaasperplas park, which has a lake with a watersports centre. Ground facilities include shop, café, bar and restaurant.

Het Amsterdamse Bos

Kleine Noorddijk 1, 1432 CC Aalsmeer (641 6868/fax 640 2378). Bus 171. **Reception open** *Apr-Oct* only 8am-10pm daily. **Rates** (all per night) per person ƒ8,25; 4-12s ƒ4,25; under-4s free; car ƒ4,25; tent ƒ5,25; electricity for caravans/campers ƒ3,50.
The site is several miles from Amsterdam, a long and dreary cycle ride. However, half-hourly bus services for the 30-minute trip into town stop 300m from the grounds, which are on the southern edge of the beautiful Amsterdamse Bos, a large park with facilities for horse-riding and watersports. Wooden cabins sleeping up to four people can be hired for ƒ60 per night. These are equipped with stoves and mattresses, but you will need to provide your own cooking utensils and sleeping bags. Site facilities include phones, a shop, a bar and a restaurant, lockers, and bike hire in July and August.

Vliegenbos

Meeuwenlaan 138 (636 8855/fax 632 2723). Bus 32/Night bus 72. **Reception open** *April-June* 9am-9pm daily; *July-Aug* 9am-10pm daily. **Rates** (all per night) over-30s ƒ10,75 per person; 15-30s ƒ9,25; 3-14s ƒ7,75; under-3s free; car including driver ƒ13,50; motorbike ƒ12,50; camper including two people ƒ24,50, with electricity ƒ28,20; all prices include showers, tent pitch and tourist tax.
The grounds are close to the River IJ to the north of Amsterdam, a ten-minute bus journey from Centraal Station. Facilities include a bar, a restaurant, a safe at reception, and a small shop with exchange service. Cabins sleeping up to four people cost ƒ63 per night.

Zeeburg

Zuiderzeeweg 29 (694 4430/fax 694 6238). Bus 37. **Reception open** *April-May* 9am-1pm daily; *June-Aug* 8am-11pm daily. **Rates** (all per night) ƒ6,50 per person;

5-12s ƒ2,50; under-5s free; tents ƒ3,50; motorbikes ƒ3,50; cars ƒ6; camper ƒ10,50; electricity ƒ4; hot showers ƒ1,50. Facilities at these grounds, just north of the River IJ, include a bar, a small restaurant, lockers, a shop and bike hire. Cabins sleeping four people cost ƒ80 per night and cabins for two cost ƒ40 per night including bedding.

Flat hunting

Flat-seekers in Amsterdam require two vital commodities: tenacity and luck. Competition for apartments is fierce, and landlords in the private housing sector have little trouble in filling empty properties, whatever their size and location.

Don't count on a cheap flatshare, which is rare here in comparison to London or Paris. The Dutch seem rather shy of sharing their living space and many of the available properties are simply too small to accommodate more than one person. However, it is common for the Dutch to let their flats during holidays or periods spent working abroad.

The property agencies (listed below under **Apartment Rentals**) – others can be found in the *Gouden Gids* (*Yellow Pages*) – may be worth contacting but be prepared for a hefty commission if they find you a flat. You can also try looking in the daily newspapers *De Telegraaf* and *De Volkskrant* under the *Te Huur* (To Let) sections, particularly on Wednesdays, Fridays and Saturdays, when there are more ads. Otherwise try the *Via Via*, published every Thursday. If you spot something, act swiftly: most desirable properties are usually snapped up within a few hours. Also, don't be surprised if the landlord instantly dismisses your enquiry if you can't speak Dutch.

The noticeboard in the main public library (*see chapter* **Survival**), plus many supermarkets and tobacconists, display cards advertising available lets. If you're having no luck it may even be worth placing a few cards or ads saying you are looking for a place. You can also place an ad free of charge in the *Via Via* (626 6166).

Many people simply find a place through word of mouth, so be sure to let your friends, workmates, associates, anybody and everybody, know that you are looking.

When you find a flat, the landlord will probably charge you a *borgsom*, a refundable deposit ranging from a week's to a month's rent. The previous occupants may also attempt to charge an *overname* (key money) to cover the costs of any furniture they leave. Though often unavoidable, such charges are often inflated and can only be recouped by similarly charging the next tenant when you leave.

Apartment Rentals

Amsterdam Apartments

Krommewaal 33 (626 5930/fax 622 9544). **Open** 9am-5pm Mon-Sat.
Amsterdam Apartments have details of privately owned, furnished, self-contained flats in central areas of town. Rates

start from ƒ700 per week for a one-person studio or one-bedroom flat. The minimum let is one week, maximum two months.

Apartment Services AS

Maasstraat 96 (672 3013/672 1840/fax 676 4679). Tram 4, 12, 25. **Open** 9.30am-5pm Mon-Fri.
This reliable, friendly agency deals with a wide variety of mainly furnished accommodation, from simple short-let flats whose owners are away, to apartments and whole houses. Rentals start at around ƒ1,000 per month, and a minimum let of three months is usual, although they sometimes let properties for one or two months as well. There is a registration fee of ƒ30 and the bureau takes one month's rent as commission.

Intercity Room Service

Van Ostadestraat 348 (675 0064). Tram 3, 4. **Open** 10am-5pm Mon-Fri.
The place to try if you're in Amsterdam and require something – anything – very quickly. This agency specialises in flatshares, and occasionally offers entire apartments. Flatshares in the centre of town cost from ƒ60 per day, self-contained flats from ƒ1,200 per month. The minimum stay is one day, maximum is indefinite. The agency charges two weeks' rent as commission.

Riverside Apartments

Amstel 138 (627 9797/fax 627 9858). Tram 4, 9, 14. **Open** 9am-5pm Mon-Sat; by appointment other times. **Credit** AmEx, DC, MC, V.
These privately-owned, luxuriously furnished flats in central Amsterdam cost ƒ4,750 per month for two people. Studios cost ƒ2,500 per month for one or two people and ƒ5,500 for three to four. Services include telephone, fax, laundry, cleaner and linen. The apartments are available for a minimum of one week.

Housing associations

In order to obtain a much sought-after controlled rent flat (under ƒ1007,50 per month), the new guidelines are as follows: when you have obtained your *verblijfvergunning* (resident's permit) from the *Vreemdelingenpolitie* (Aliens' Police) (*see chapter* **Essential Information**), and have registered at *Bevolkingsregister* (Population Register), the next step is to register with one of the three housing association clusters – **Woonwerk** (524 4566), **Archipel** (511 8911) and **Spectrum** (618 0909) – who together control two-thirds of the available accommodation in this sector.

Registration costs ƒ35, which includes a year's subscription to the housing bulletin. You will then be put on a waiting list. Housing lists are extremely long, so don't be surprised if you end up kicking your heels from three to five years before anything happens. For a detailed brochure in English outlining procedures call the head office of the Stedelijke Woningdienst Amsterdam (596 9111), or call the accommodation information line (680 6806).

Bevolkingsregister

Herengracht 531-537 (551 9911). Tram 4, 9, 14. **Open** 8.30am-3pm Mon-Fri.
This is the main office of the Bevolkingsregister (Population Register), which deals with the registration of both Dutch and foreign people moving into the city.

Amsterdam by Season

Flower parades, silent processions, marathon runs and absolutely any excuse for a party – there's action in Amsterdam all year round.

The canals are used as skating rinks whenever they freeze over.

The Netherlands' heritage is steeped in Calvinist morals, allowing for the survival of only a few ancient traditions. However, when the Dutch, and especially Amsterdammers, start to celebrate, nothing is going to stop them. This is best experienced on *Oudejaarsavond* (New Year's Eve) and *Konninginedag* (Queen's Day), the year's two best excuses for city-wide partying. These only get topped when Ajax wins an important match and thousands of supporters gather in and around Leidseplein and Rembrantplein to celebrate.

The Royal Family tends to keep a low profile – your best chance of seeing Queen Beatrix is at the opening of parliament (**Autumn**) or on Remembrance Day (**Spring**). Other seasonal events in Amsterdam and the rest of the country are listed in entertainment chapters such as **Dance**, **Film**, **Music** and **Theatre**. The AUB

and VVV (*see chapter* **Essential Information**) have up-to-date information on all events in the city and the latter publishes a calendar in its *What's On* magazine (*f*3,50). For a list of public holidays, *see chapter* **Essential Information**.

Spring

Bicycles and windmills. These two signature sights get fêted every spring. The second Saturday in May is National Windmill Day: about 650 of the country's 950 windmills turn their sails and are open to the public, including Amsterdam's four working mills (*see chapter* **Sightseeing**). Windmills open to the public carry a blue banner (details from the Vereniging De Hollandse Molen on 623 8703). National Cycling Day also takes place on the second Saturday in May; roads are even more full of cyclists than usual. About 200 routes are worked out for the occasion (details from the AVN on 071 560 5972).

In such a watery country, it's no surprise that there's an annual boat show, HISWA. In 1997 the show, always held in Amsterdam's RAI (*see chapter* **Business**) takes place on 1-9 March. The Meervaart (Osdorpplein 205, 610 7498) hosts a blues festival which is gradually growing in status (phone for dates).

Every Sunday from March until October or November (depending on the weather), two open-air art and crafts markets are held on Spui (tram 1, 2, 4, 5, 9, 11, 14, 16, 24, 25) and on Thorbeckeplein (tram 4, 9, 14 to Rembrandtplein). Opening hours of both markets are 10am-5pm. These are pleasant places to browse, but although they're called art markets, don't expect to find the new Jeff Koons. Most of the jewellery, paintings, vases and bargain ornaments are rather mediocre. Buskers playing and touting CDs or tapes on Thorbeckeplein top the bill perfectly.

Stille Omgang (Silent Procession)

Dates 15-16 March 1997. **Contact** Gezelschap van de Stille Omgang, Zandvoortseweg 59, 2111 GS Aerdenhout (023 245415). Phone after 7pm.
Every year on the Sunday closest to 15 March, local Catholics commemorate the Miracle of Amsterdam with a silent night-time procession through the city. The Miracle took place in 1345; the story goes that a dying man vomited up the bread given in communion as part of the last rites. It was thrown on the fire and was found undamaged among the ashes the following morning. The sick man is said to have subsequently recovered (*see chapter* **Early History**). The Procession follows the road that pilgrims have used for centuries, called, for that reason, Heiligeweg – Holy Way. The silent procession through the bustling Red-Light District is a remarkable sight.

National Museum Weekend

Dates 12, 13 April 1997.
During National Museum Weekend many state-run museums offer reduced or free admission and mount special exhibitions and activities such as treasure hunts. Opening hours are often extended, but even so most museums are predictably busy. Call the Vereniging Museum Jaarkaart (667 0111) for further information.

Koninginnedag (Queen's Day)

All over Amsterdam. **Date** 30 April.
This is the party to end all parties, Europe's biggest birthday party. Queen's Day starts on the eve of the 29th and finally fizzles out the following night. *See* **Queen for a day**.

Herdenkingsdag & Bevrijdingsdag (Remembrance Day & Liberation Day)

Remembrance Day *National Monument, Dam. Tram 1, 2, 4, 5, 9, 11, 13, 14, 16, 17, 24, 25.* **Date** 4 May.
Liberation Day *Vondelpark. Tram 1, 2, 3, 5, 6, 12. Leidseplein. Tram 1, 2, 5, 6, 7, 10, 11.* **Date** 5 May.
On 4 May, those who died during World War II are remembered in a ceremony at the National Monument on the Dam. The service starts at 7.30pm; the Queen lays a wreath at 8pm; there follows a two-minute silence before the Chief of the Armed Forces and other dignitaries lay wreaths. Although homosexuals who died during World War II are now remembered in the ceremony as well, the Dutch gay organisation COC organises their own remembrance service at the Homomonument (*see chapter* **Gay & Lesbian**). Liberation

is celebrated on the following day with various activities throughout the city. Vondelpark, Museumplein, Leidseplein and Rokin are the best places to be, with performances by local and national bands, speeches and information stands organised by political and ideological groups and a free market where you can sell all the unwanted things you bought on Queen's Day – if you've recovered from the hangover.

Oosterparkfestival

Oosterpark. Tram 3, 6, 9, 14. **Date** first week in May.
The Oosterpark in the east of Amsterdam hosts this annual free festival. The idea of the two- or three-day event is to bring together the people of different nationalities who live in this eclectic neighbourhood. It links with Remembrance Day (May 4th) since many local Jews were deported during World War II. With today's increase of racism, the organisers make a special effort to broaden peoples' minds regarding other cultures and customs. Festivities include performances by singers and groups of various nationalities, food stalls serving authentic foreign dishes and sports matches for the youngsters.

Open Garden Days

A unique opportunity to see the often beautiful and rather ostentatious gardens of some of the houses on Amsterdam canals. For more than ten years now, this annual selection of private gardens, many designed by landscape gardeners, is open to the public for a few days around 15 May when these oases are at their best. For as little as ƒ15 you not only get ideas for your own garden, but can also glimpse how the rich on Herengracht, Keizersgracht and Leidsegracht actually live. Check the local press for details of this low-key event.

Drum Rhythm Festival

The annual Drum Rhythm Festival generally takes place in mid-May. This commercial festival offers a mix of 'rhythm and roots' with often well-known bands and artists performing in the Westergasfabriek on four different stages. *See chapter* **Music: Rock, Folk & Jazz**.

Open Ateliers

An interesting and fun biennial event (the next one is in 1998). For three days at the end of May, around 50 Jordaan artists open their studios to the public. From the designated starting point, map and catalogue in hand, you can wander in and out of artists' studios and scrutinise their living/working quarters in envy (or pity). Keep an eye open for posters announcing the event or contact the organisation: Open Ateliers Jordaan (*638 1885; 10am-noon Fri*), *Eerste Laurierdwarsstraat 6, 1016 PX Amsterdam.*

Summer

With the arrival of the sun, Amsterdam's events move outdoors. Four book markets spring up in summer; two along the Amstel (mid-June, mid-August) and two on Dam (mid-July, mid-September). Antique and bric-à-brac lovers should head for the Nieuwmarkt where, between May and October, a small antiques market is held every Sunday (10am-5pm).

In June there are six rowing contests in Amsterdamse Bos and four later in the year (*see chapter* **Sightseeing** or call the Koninklijke Nederlandse Roeibond 646 2740 for details). A bit out of town but worth the trip are the motor races at Zandvoort (*see chapter* **Sport**) which get into full swing in June. A lesser-known and more ancient pursuit is ring tilting, in which costumed horsemen try to catch rings on their spears. There are ring tilting events in July in Friesland and Zeeland; the best is at Middelburg (*see chapter* **The Provinces: Zeeland**). More civilised is the Holland Festival with performances by well-known dance companies in The Hague (1, 5, 6 June 1997) and Amsterdam (2, 3 and 8, 9 June 1997). Local music talent can be watched and heard at the Arena (*see chapter* **Music: Rock, Folk & Jazz**) during the Amsterdam Pop Prijs festival in June, organised by Stichting GRAP.

KunstRAI (RAI Arts Fair)

RAI Congresgebouw, Europaplein (549 1212). Tram 4, 25/NS railway from Schiphol Airport to RAI Station. **Open** *office and enquiries* 9am-5pm Mon-Fri. **Dates** between mid May and early June.
This annual exhibition of contemporary art includes everything from ceramics and jewellery to paintings and sculpture. About a hundred Dutch and international galleries take part (*see chapter* **Art Galleries**).

Echo Grachtenloop (Canal Run)

Information Echo Newspaper, Basisweg 30 (585 9222). **Date** 9 June 1997.
Around 5,000 people take part in this five-, 10- and 18km (three-, six- and 11-mile) run along the city's canals (Prinsengracht and Vijzelgracht) on the second Sunday in June every year. You can register on the spot at the Stadsschouwburg on Leidseplein (*see chapter* **Theatre**), where the run starts and finishes. Start times run from 11am. Leidseplein is a good place to watch but gets crowded; for a more relaxed viewpoint, stand on the banks of Prinsengracht.

Paardendagen

Spaarndammerstraat. Bus 22, 28.
Generally held over a June weekend, on the Saturday there are various parades, including special breeds of horses; on Sunday there are short trotting races. On both days there are performances by local singers, a fair and a small market. Although far from being Amsterdam's answer to Ascot, this free annual event, which originally started out as a neighbourhood festival, has become more and more popular over the last few years, and now attracts spectators from all over Amsterdam.

Prinsengracht Classical Concert

Information *Stichting Cristofori, Prinsengracht 579 (626 8485/8495).* **Date** one evening during last week in August.
Musicians play a classical concert from a boat in front of the Pulitzer Hotel (*Prinsengracht 315-331*). The hotel organises the event with the piano manufacturers Cristofori. Get there early for a good view. It's free, but liable to be cancelled if it rains (*see chapter* **Music: Classical & Opera**).

Uitmarkt

Dam. Tram 4, 9, 14, 16, 24, 25. **Dates** 29-31 August 1997.
A wonderful tradition, the Uitmarkt previews the Netherlands' coming cultural season with a huge fair on and around Dam, giving information on amateur and professional theatre, opera, dance and music of all sorts. There are also performances on outdoor stages and in the city's various theatres. Everything is free and, not surprisingly, it gets very crowded all day and into the evening (*see chapter* **Theatre**).

Autumn

The Jordaan Festival takes places every year in September (*see chapter* **Amsterdam By Area**) with performances from local talents keeping alive the spirit of Jordaan artists like Johnny Jordaan and Tante Leen. If you're not an animal-rights activist you can experience the thrill of a show-jumping competition at the RAI (Europaplein) in

Up in Smoke

Remember the old firework code? Pets indoors, biscuit tins, only with a grown-up, and so on? Not even a rumour in Amsterdam. Far from caring about drab old safety regulations, here pyrotechnical mayhem is absolutely *de rigeur* at year's end as the whole city sees in the New Year by going absolutely crazy.

For one night, the city goes completely off its cake in a fashion which slightly resembles Queen's Day here but has no English equivalent. Every street has a party raging. December 31, from dusk onwards, resembles a war zone. There are deafening 20-minute firecrackers and a host of other fireworks that the manufacturers wouldn't even jokingly try to get a license for in more cautious countries. Dutch bangers are nearer the size of the English gastronomic equivalent and their fireworks make even the most energetic of British Roman Candles seem like a poor excuse for a barbecue flare. And then

there are all manner of devices which, once lit, will lie dormant for anything between one and 30 seconds before randomly shooting off in any direction. Including into the nearest face.

Because inevitably, for all the overt jollity and healthy libertarian disregard for fuddy-duddy guidelines, the number of casualties caused by fireworks is appallingly high; over 800 in Amsterdam alone on New Year 1996, including two fatalities. Even worse is the fact that 40 per cent of those injured were simply spectators. And these figures are trumpeted as a 27 per cent reduction in the casualty rate.

The problem is, no one here really cares. If you visit Amsterdam for New Year you are guaranteed a fantastic time; this city parties like no other on God's earth. But you should also be prepared for the fact that no matter how much you might remonstrate, people are going to throw fireworks at you – and find it hilarious.

October. Out of Amsterdam, a revered annual antiques and art fair (absolutely nothing modern) takes place in Delft (*see chapter* **The Randstad**) in mid-October. One of the Netherlands' few state occasions is the opening of parliament in The Hague on the third Tuesday in September. The Queen drives to the Binnenhof, the parliament building, in a gilded coach, accompanied by soldiers in ceremonial uniform. If you're in The Hague, the best place to go is the Binnenhof; if you're not, you can watch it all on television.

Bloemen Corso (Flower Parade)

Route *leaves from Aalsmeer at 9.30am; Olympic Stadium, Stadionplein at 1pm (Tram 16); Overtoom (Tram 1, 6); Leidseplein (Tram 1, 2, 5, 6, 7, 10, 11); Leidsestraat (Tram 1, 2, 5, 11); Spui (Tram 1, 2, 5, 11); Spuistraat (Tram 1, 2, 5, 11); Dam (Tram 1, 2, 4, 5, 9, 11, 13, 14, 16, 17, 24, 25) around 4pm; Rembrandtplein (Tram 4, 9, 14); Vijzelstraat (Tram 16, 24, 25); Weteringschans (Tram 6, 7, 10).* **Date** early September.

For over 40 years a spectacular parade of floats bearing all kinds of flowers (except tulips, which are out of season) has made its way from Aalsmeer (the home of Holland's flower industry – *see chapter* **Excursions in Holland**) to Amsterdam on the first Saturday of September. Crowds line the pavements for a glimpse of the beautiful and fragrant displays. At 4pm the parade reaches the Dam, usually packed, where there is a civic reception, after which it returns for an illuminated cavalcade through Aalsmeer (9-10pm).

National Monument Day

Monumentenzorg, Keizersgracht 123 (626 3947). **Date** September. **Admission** free.

On the second Saturday in September the National Monument Society arranges for as many as possible of the Netherlands' listed buildings to be open to the public. In Amsterdam, this means you can see inside around 30 of the city's finest canal houses, as well as windmills and pumping stations. In 1996 it celebrates its tenth anniversary, with an extra open day on the following Sunday. Write or phone for details as the buildings open to the public change every year.

Kunstroute De Pijp

An exhibition of local work, displayed in the windows of shops, cafés and offices in this area which is becoming more and more the 'Quartier Latin' of Amsterdam. The Kunstroute is usually held during the first two weeks in September. A combined route map and catalogue can be obtained from the VVV (*see chapter* **Essential Information**).

Winter

The conversion of Leidseplein into an ice rink signals the advent of winter – usually in mid-October, depending on the weather. For the Dutch, St Nicholas' Day (5 December) is as important as Christmas. In the evening gifts are exchanged, sometimes seasonal sweets like *speculaas* (cinnamon gingerbread) and chocolate initials, accompanied by poems hinting at the nature of the gift and the character of the recipient. The Dutch festivities are very family orientated and the city closes down early. New Year's Eve is also celebrated in a big way, mainly in the streets (*see below*). Hordes of tourists descend on the city, so all reasonably priced hotels are booked up well in advance. There are festive New Year concerts at Nieuwekerk and Westerkerk (*see chapter* **Sightseeing**), usually accompanied by mulled wine. On Scheveningen beach (*see chapter* **The Randstad: The Hague**) there's a New Year's Day dive. On February 25 every year there's a ceremony at the Dokworker statue in Amsterdam to commemorate the protest strike of 1941; *see chapter* **History: World War II**.

Sinterklaas

Route Barbizon Palace Hotel, Prins Hendrikkade (Tram 1, 2, 4, 5, 9, 11, 13, 16, 17, 24, 25); Damrak (Tram 4, 9, 14, 16, 24, 25); Dam (Tram 1, 2, 4, 5, 9, 13, 14, 16, 17, 24, 25); Raadhuisstraat (Tram 13, 14, 17); Rozengracht (Tram 13, 14, 17); Marnixstraat (Tram 7, 10); Leidseplein (Tram 1, 2, 5, 6, 7, 10, 11). **Dates** mid-Nov, 5 Dec.

In mid-November, Sinterklaas – the Dutch equivalent of Santa Claus – marks the beginning of the Christmas season when he steps ashore from a steamboat at Amsterdam's Centraal Station before parading through the city on his traditional white horse while his helpers – Zwarte Pieten (Black Peters) – distribute sweets. He is given the keys to the city by the Mayor on the Dam, but it's best to watch the early stages of the procession from Utrechtsestraat and Rembrandtplein). On 5 December small presents and specially-written poems are exchanged, but unfortunately for Dutch parents, the indigenous culture has been so diluted that they now have to fork out for two lots of presents. Mainly because of American influence, the bugger now comes back on 25 December, albeit without his little friend, but still bearing gifts. Don't worry too much. The average income of a Dutch family means they can afford it.

Oudejaarsavond (New Year's Eve)

All over Amsterdam. **Dates** 31 Dec, 1 Jan.

Along with Koninginnedag (*see above* **Spring**), New Year's Eve is Amsterdam's best celebration. There's revelry throughout the city but the best spots are Nieuwmarkt and Dam, both of which get seriously crowded. The Dutch celebrate by having a special evening with coffee, spirits and *oliebollen* (a deep fried delicacy, not dissimilar to a doughnut, but lacking in either holes or jam in the middle) with family until midnight; many bars don't open until then. *See* **Up In Smoke**.

Carnaval

Information Stichting Carnaval Mokum (623 2568). **Route** *Prins Hendrikkade (Tram 1, 2, 4, 5, 9, 11, 13, 16, 17, 24, 25); Damrak (Tram 4, 9, 14, 16, 24, 25); Dam (Tram 1, 2, 4, 5, 9, 13, 14, 16, 17, 24, 25); Rembrandtplein (Tram 4, 9, 14); Vijzelstraat (Tram 16, 24, 25); Weteringcircuit (Tram 6, 7, 10, 16, 24, 25); Stadhouderskade (Tram 6, 7, 10); Leidseplein (Tram 1, 2, 5, 6, 7, 10, 11).* **Date** February.

Carnaval was originally a southern tradition celebrating the coming of spring, but not wanting to miss out on an opportunity to party, Amsterdammers have adopted it over the last decade. It must be said, however, that the festivities in the capital are nowhere near as much fun as the three-day jamborees in the provinces of Noord Brabant and Limburg (*see chapter* **The Provinces**). Also, Southerners look a little askance at the attempts of Northerners to join in. The main activity is drinking, with the emphasis on pub crawling, to the accompaniment of Dutch oom-pah-pah songs (including entertainingly bizarre brass-band versions of the biggest Dutch hit ever, 2 Unlimited's 'No Limits'). Everybody, irrespective of age, wears fancy dress. To try and feel part of Carnaval without creating a daft outfit is a serious *faux pas*.

Queen for a Day

Even the most ardent republican would find it hard to object to the Dutch royal family. They are of course, unspeakably dull, and Queen Beatrix did herself no favours with her subjects by getting hitched to a German in 1966, but they keep it all very low profile. They don't take the piss out of the taxpayer and rarely lay themselves out to get flayed by the media (the Windsors fulfil the capacity of media fall guys here too). What Queen Bea does do, and the nation loves her for it, is give her birthday over to *en masse* public frolickings. The whole shebang, which goes under the name of Queen's Day, is actually her mum Juliana's birthday, April 30. With typical Dutch common sense Beatrix deemed her own birthday, January 31, a tad too chilly for nationwide merry-making.

Thus Queen's Day has been April 30 since the end of World War II and will only shift by three days when heir Willem-Alexander accedes, as his birthday is on April 27. The actual festivities kick off the night before and from around 6pm, Amsterdam swings into full party mode as only Amsterdam can – the place goes berserk. The streets are so jammed with people that from 8pm public transport, including taxis, is suspended and even cycling is impossible; if the crowds don't get you then streets full of broken glass will because, with most bars and cafés staying open all night, an awful lot of drinking gets done.

There is no agenda – apart from getting drunk – but with all restrictions suspended, there are an almost unlimited number of parties and when these pall, there are more parties. They range from live music in bars to full-blown club nights which spill outdoors, providing a constant barrage of noise to compete with a bewildering variety of culinary aromas that further confuse the already alcohol-befuddled senses. There are also all sorts of informal (and mostly free) performances, from singing to custard pie slinging, throughout the city centre (focal points are Leidseplein, Spui and Dam). More sophisticated entertainment is provided by many bars, which erect outdoor stages for all sorts of bands from jazz to pop (try along Egelantiersstraat and Spui) and traditional Dutch folk (in the Jordaan). The whole phenomenon winds itself up to a perfectly surreal pitch in Reguliersdwaarsstraat where Queen's Day is given an altogether more contemporary interpretation (*see chapter* **Gay and Lesbian**).

The other main feature of Queen's Day is the proliferation of street selling: children and grown-ups arrange their junk on home-made stalls, or simply tip it all out on the pavements in front of their homes in the city centre, turning Amsterdam into a huge open-air bazaar. There really are no rules; and anyone can sell anything they choose, be it small children flogging off unwanted Barbie dolls and Disney comics, or sharp market traders making a killing through the fleecing of unwitting drunkards.

It is truly amazing how the most useless tat can suddenly become an essential purchase when enough alcohol is consumed, so be warned. Pink budgie cages and miniature shopping trollies may seem the last word in accessories but in the hard morning light they will be revealed for the pure junk they are. If nothing else consider it a graphic metaphor for how much shit you talk when inebriated.

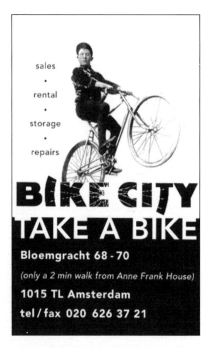

Sightseeing

**Towers, canals, windmills, diamond workshops, secret gardens –
Amsterdam's attractions can be toured by foot, by boat, or even by
helicopter.**

Amsterdam is a surprisingly user-friendly city. As
capitals go it's pretty small: the official population
is 722, 350. The city centre is compact and easy to
get around, as you can walk almost everywhere.
The Red-Light District can be both intimidating
and exciting, but you only need to walk for two
minutes beyond its boundaries to reach some of
the most serene and picturesque sites on offer anywhere in the world. Both aspects are postcard
clichés, but it is constantly surprising that such
paradoxical facets can exist in harmony in such
close proximity.

The city's cinemas, clubs and theatres provide
a whole scala of amusement, but some good entertainment can be found on the streets. Tourist spots
such as **Leidseplein** and **Dam** (*see below* **Focal
Points**) attract every kind of street performer, day
and night, throughout the year; but buskers seem
to play in every park and lurk on every street corner. Most of them are absolute rubbish, although
every now and then you might catch Amsterdam's
premier buskers, the Robin Nolan Quartet. George
Harrison liked them so much he flew them over to
England to play at his birthday party.

At night many of the canalside buildings and
most of the bridges are illuminated, a beautiful sight
and a good opportunity for making pictures. The
city is still wide awake at two in the morning and
the liveliness doesn't just evolve around the clubs
and bars. The streets are relatively safe to walk at
night, as long as you use your common sense .

This chapter refers briefly to major sights (as well
as some of the less familiar ones); most of the places
listed appear elsewhere in the guide in greater detail:
consult the index at the back of the book.

Focal Points

Like most cities, Amsterdam has several well-
known areas where tourists tend to congregate.
These have an international flavour – bright lights,
billboards, buskers and pavement cafés – so don't
expect to find the 'real' Amsterdam. For more on
these areas of the city, *see chapter* **Amsterdam
by Area**.

Dam

Tram 1, 2, 4, 5, 9, 11, 13, 14, 16, 17, 24, 25.
Dam has been the heart of the city since the first dam was
built here across the Amstel in 1270. Although it provides

Many canal bridges are illuminated at night.

an easy meeting point for nearly every tourist, this square
is now one of the least atmospheric parts of the city.
Nevertheless, there are a number of important landmarks on
and around it. The west side is flanked by the **Koninklijk
Paleis (Royal Palace)** (*see below* **Heritage**) and the
Nieuwe Kerk (*see below* **Churches and Viewpoints**); in
the middle of the eastern side is the **Nationaal Monument**.
This 22-metre-high obelisk is dedicated to the Dutch ser-
vicemen who died in World War II. Designed by JJP Oud,
with sculptures by John Raedecker, it incorporates 12 urns:
11 filled with earth collected from the then 11 Dutch
provinces, the 12th with soil from war cemeteries in
Indonesia, which was a Dutch colony until 1949. The monument, however, is in danger of falling apart and at time of
writing there was much disagreement in the city about the
best way to repair it.

Leidseplein

Tram 1, 2, 5, 6, 7, 10, 11.
The area around Leidseplein probably has more cinemas, theatres, nightclubs and restaurants than any other part of the
city. It is also one of the most touristy areas. The square is dom-

inated by the **Stadsschouwburg** (municipal theatre) as well as numerous cafés which take over the pavements during the summer. You can also take a drink on the elegant (but pricey) terrace of the **American Hotel**, a prominent feature on the square's south side and a good place to watch all the street performers. During the summer, fire-eaters, jugglers, acrobats, singers and small-time con-artists fill the square (watch out for pickpockets). The development of the Leidseplein over recent years has meant that there are now fast food restaurants on every corner and many locals feel the essential Dutch flavour of the district has been destroyed for a fast buck. Just off the square, in the Leidsebos, is the Adamant, a white pyramid-shaped sculpture given to Amsterdam by the city's diamond industry in 1986 to commemorate 400 years of the trade. Designed by Joost van Santen at a cost of ƒ75,000, it uses light to create a rainbow hologram.

Red-Light District
Tram 4, 9, 14, 16, 24, 25.
The lure of Amsterdam's Red-Light District, known colloquially as *de walletjes* because it's the area within the old city walls, proves irresistible to most visitors. Sex for money is on offer in and around one of Amsterdam's oldest streets, Warmoesstraat. Obviously the area attracts more than its fair share of crime, but if you stay away from the Nieuwmarkt end of Zeedijk, the Red-Light District is safe enough. Note, however, that cameras are not welcomed by local 'entrepreneurs' and snapshotters are likely to be pounced upon. Prostitutes are mainly concentrated along Oudezijds Voorburgwal, Oudezijds Achterburgwal and the small interconnecting alleyways. They take up their shop window positions at about 10am and are still there well into the small hours. While this area draws the bulk of the tourists, there are smaller red-light districts in two other parts of town.

Rembrandtplein
Tram 4, 9, 14.
Gloriously tacky, Rembrandtplein is full of sunbathers by day and funseekers by night. The square is home to a variety of places, from the faded fake elegance of traditional striptease parlours to seedy peep-show joints and nondescript cafés and restaurants. Nevertheless, there are a few exceptions to this exuberant display of trash (such as the art deco **Café Schiller** and the **Tuschinski Cinema**). Just round the corner on the Amstel is a stretch of gay cafés (*see chapter* **Gay Amsterdam**).

Waterlooplein
Tram 9, 14/Metro Waterlooplein.
This fast-developing district is dominated by the ultra-modern **Stadhuis-Muziektheater** (*see below* **Cultural Centres**). This opened in 1985 amid great controversy; the area, once the centre of Jewish life in the city, had become a squatter's paradise in the 1970s. The squats were demolished to make way for the theatre, nicknamed the Stopera. The **Waterlooplein Market** and **Rembrandthuis** (*see chapter* **Museums**) are also here.

Heritage

Anne Frankhuis (Anne Frank House)
Prinsengracht 263 (556 7100). Tram 13, 14, 17. **Open** *Sept-May* 9am-5pm Mon-Sat; 10am-5pm Sun, public holidays; *June-Aug* 9am-7pm Mon-Sat; 10am-7pm Sun, public holidays. **Admission** ƒ8; ƒ4,50 10-17s, CJP card holders; free under-10s; group discount (min 10 people).
One of the most visited attractions in town – the seventeenth-century canalside house where the young Jewish girl Anne Frank spent over two years in hiding during World War II, from June 1942 to August 1944. It is not a cosy recreation of a family home: the Nazis destroyed the furniture and the interior has been left bare, although you can still see the diary and the bookcase which concealed the entrance to the annexe

A favourite with sunbathers: **Vondelpark**.

where the family hid, sustained by friends. The Anne Frank Foundation was founded in 1957 to maintain the house and to fight fascism and racism. Regular exhibitions are held, but visit very early to avoid the crowds. *See also chapters* **World War II** *and* **Museums**.

Begijnhof
Spui. Tram 1, 2, 5, 11. **Open** 9am-11pm daily.
Admission free.
A quiet backwater hidden behind a doorway just off Amsterdam's noisy main shopping area, the Begijnhof is a group of houses built around a secluded courtyard and garden. It was established in the fourteenth century to provide modest homes for the Beguines, a religious sisterhood of unmarried women of good families who, although not nuns, lived together in a close community and often took vows of chastity. They did a lot of charitable work, especially in education and nursing. The last sister died in 1971. Most of the neat little houses were modernised in the seventeenth and eighteenth centuries. In the centre of the courtyard stands the English Reformed Church (Engelsekerk), built in about 1400 and given in 1607 to English-speaking Presbyterians living in the city. It is now a principal place of worship for Amsterdam's English community (*see chapters* **Music: Classical & Opera** *and* **Survival**). The pulpit panels were designed by Mondriaan. You can also see a Catholic church, secretly converted from two houses in 1665, following the banning of the Roman Catholic faith after the Reformation. The wooden house at number 34 is dated 1477 and is the oldest house standing in the city. Number 35 is a café and information centre. This is the best known of the city's numerous *hofjes*; for details of others, *see below* **Hofjes**.

Beurs van Berlage
Damrak 277 (626 5257/fax 620 4701). Tram 4, 9, 14, 16, 24, 25. **Open** *office and enquiries* 9am-5pm Mon-Fri.

Designed in 1896 by Hendrik Petrus Berlage as the city's stock exchange, the Beurs represents an important break with nineteenth-century architecture and prepared the way for the modern lines of the Amsterdam School (*see chapter* **Architecture**). No longer used as a stock exchange, the building has been sensitively converted into a conference and exhibition centre (*see chapter* **Business**) with two concert halls, a café and a restaurant. Tours can be arranged by Archivise, *see below* **Tours**.

Koninklijk Paleis (Royal Palace)

Dam (624 8698 ext 217). Tram 1, 2, 4, 5, 9, 13, 14, 16, 17, 24, 25. **Open** *June-Sept 12.30-5pm daily.*
Admission *f5; f3 CJP card holders, students, over-65s; f1,50 under-13s; free under-5s; f50 groups up to 10 persons; f35 10-25 persons.*
The Royal Palace was designed by Jacob van Campen in the seventeenth century along classical lines and was originally intended to be the city hall. The exterior is not particularly impressive for a building of its stature and betrays its municipal origins. Inside it's a different story, with chimney pieces painted by artists such as Ferdinand Bol and Govert Flinck, both pupils of Rembrandt. The city hall was transformed into a royal palace in 1808 after Napoleon made his brother, Louis, King of the Netherlands (*see chapter* **Decline & Fall**). A fine collection of furniture from this period can be seen on a guided tour of the building. The Palace became state property in 1936 and is still used occasionally by the royal family.
Guided tours June-Sept, 2pm Wed (f5; f3 students, over-65s; f1,50 under-12s). Group tours (min 10 people) can also be arranged Oct-May, phone for details.

Munttoren (Mint Tower)

Muntplein. Tram 4, 9, 14, 16, 24, 25.
On Singel between the floating flower market (*see below* **Markets**) and the start of Kalverstraat (the pedestrianised shopping street), this medieval tower was the western corner of the Regulierspoort, a gate in the city wall in the 1480s. In 1620 a spire was added by Hendrik de Keyser, the foremost architect of the period. It's called the 'mint tower'

because the city authorities used it to mint coins for a short period in 1672 when Amsterdam was cut off from its money supply during a war with England, Munster and France. There's a shop on the ground floor selling fine Dutch porcelain, but the rest of the tower is closed to visitors. The Munttoren is prettiest at night, when it's floodlit; although daytime visitors may be able to hear its carillon, which often plays for 15 minutes at noon.

Schreierstoren (Weeping Tower)

Prins Hendrikkade. Tram 1, 2, 4, 5, 9, 13, 16, 17, 24, 25/Metro Centraal Station.
The most interesting relic of what's left of Amsterdam's medieval city wall is the Weeping Tower. Legend relates that the wives of sailors leaving on trade expeditions stood here and waved tearful farewells to their men. Built in 1487, it was successfully restored in 1966. In 1927, a bronze memorial plaque was added by the Greenwich Village Historical Society of New York: its English text states that it was from this point on 4 April 1609 that Henry Hudson departed in search of shorter trade routes to the Far East. He ended up colonising a small island in the mouth of a river in North America. The river was later named after him and the colony was called New Amsterdam; only to have its name changed by the English to New York. In 1956 some stones from the Schreierstoren were taken to Chicago and placed into the wall of the *Chicago Tribune* building alongside similar chunks from famous buildings around the world, including Athens' Parthenon, Paris' Notre Dame cathedral and the Great Wall of China. Visitors are not allowed inside the Schreierstoren.

De Waag (Weigh House)

Nieuwmarkt. Tram 9, 14/Metro Nieuwmarkt.
The Waag, previously called St Antoniespoort, stands in the centre of the Nieuwmarkt and dates from 1488, when it was built as a gatehouse for the city defences. It's an odd, squat building with turrets protruding from unlikely places. Over the years it has housed various institutions: in 1617 the ground floor was a public weigh house while the first floor held the trade guilds of smiths, bricklayers, painters and sur-

*The **Koninklijk Paleis** betraying its municipal origins. Page 40.*

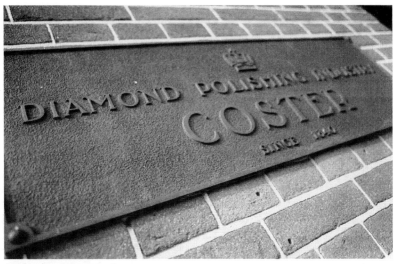

Diamond workshops are forever.

geons. The surgeons' annual anatomy lectures were the inspiration of Rembrandt's 1656 painting, *The Anatomy Lecture of Dr Jan Deyman*, which hung here from 1691 until it was damaged by fire in 1723. It now hangs in the Rijksmuseum (*see below* **Cultural Centres** *and chapter* **Museums**). Since 1819, the building has been put to a variety of uses: it was the Jewish Historical Museum from 1932 to 1986, but after ambitious plans to convert it into a cultural centre and a children's book centre/museum fell through, it fell into disuse. It is currently under restoration; for the latest news contact the **VVV**.

Attractions

Artis Zoo

Plantage Kerklaan 40 (623 1836). Tram 7, 9, 14. **Open** 9am-5pm;buildings close at 4.30 pm. Admission *f*20; *f*13 under-12s. Group discount (*f*2,50 per person, min 20 persons)

Amsterdam Zoo was established in 1838, making it the oldest zoo in the Netherlands. It's home to over 6,000 animals. Though popular, it is never too crowded to prevent enjoyment of the beautifully laid out gardens and broad range of exhibits. The liberal use of perspex allows generally unrestricted views, and the aquarium, one of the zoo's best features, boasts over 2,000 fish and a wide variety of species. Don't miss the seals being fed at 11.30am and 3.45pm; or the penguins at 3.30pm. Also recommended are the reptile house, the luxuriant tropical greenhouse, the young animals' section, the children's farm (*see chapter* **Children & Parents**) and the spectacular planetarium (with Dutch commentary, but an English-language summary is available). Unfortunately, a few of the enclosures, particularly for the big cats, rhinos and hippos, are criminally small. The guidebook is in Dutch. *Café and restaurant. Guided tours by prior arrangement (free). Schools' educational programme. Shop. Wheelchair access and toilets for the disabled.*

Diamond workshops

Amsterdam's association with diamonds dates back to the sixteenth century. The largest diamond ever found, the

Cullinan, and the world-famous Koh-I-Noor, part of the British Crown Jewels, were cut by Amsterdam workers. The smallest 'brilliant cut' diamond (a brilliant cut has 57 facets) was also cut here, a tiny sliver of sparkle – just 0.0012-carat (it can be seen in **Van Moppes & Zoon**). There are numerous diamond-polishing factories and shops in Amsterdam. The five bigger firms listed below are members of the Diamond Foundation and welcome visitors (you are under no obligation to buy). All of the tours are similar, and can last from around 20 minutes to an hour.

The guides provide a brief history of the diamond industry and Amsterdam's strategic importance in it. You'll probably be shown a worker polishing or setting a diamond, but the real thrill (only offered to those in large groups) is when the guide nonchalantly pours diamonds from a black velvet bag onto a table for your inspection. **Gassan Diamond House**, built in 1879 as a diamond factory, offers one of the more enjoyable tours. There's not much to choose between the others, but be prepared for an unenthusiastic commentary and a very brisk walk around to the sales room if you're not part of a group. Tours can be given in any European language.

Amsterdam Diamond Centre *Rokin 1-5 (624 5787). Tram 4, 9, 14, 16, 24, 25.* **Open** 9.30am-5.30pm Mon-Fri; 10.30am-5.30pm, 7-8.30pm Sun, Thur.

Coster Diamonds *Paulus Potterstraat 2-6 (676 2222). Tram 2, 3, 5, 12.* **Open** 9am-5pm daily.
Both these establishments run tours throughout the day on request, free with soft drink at end of tour.

Gassan Diamond House *Nieuwe Uilenburgerstraat 173-175 (622 5333). Tram 9, 14/Metro Nieuwmarkt.* **Open** 9am-5pm daily. **Tours** throughout the day on request, free with soft drink at end of tour.

Stoeltie Diamonds *Wagenstraat 13-17 (623 7601). Tram 4, 9, 14.* **Open** 8.30am-5pm daily. **Tours** throughout the day on request, free with soft drink at end of tour.

Van Moppes & Zoon Diamond *Albert Cuypstraat 2-6 (676 1242). Tram 16, 24, 25.* **Open** 8.30am-5pm daily. **Tours** throughout the day on request, free but here with no soft drink.

Heineken Brewery

Stadhouderskade 78 (523 9239/ Recorded information 523 9666). Tram 6, 7, 10, 16, 24, 25. **Tours** 9.30am and 11am Mon-Fri.

Beer production at the old Heineken Brewery was stopped at the beginning of 1988 amid some outcry – after all, Heineken is virtually the Dutch national drink. But the company remained public-spirited and now runs tours round this famous old brewery (phone for details). The fee is ƒ2, which goes to charity, and snacks and beer are served at the end. No bookings are taken and participants must be over 18 years old.

Madame Tussauds Scenerama

Peek & Cloppenburg, Dam 20 (622 9239). Tram 4, 9, 14, 16, 20, 24, 25. **Open** 10am-5.30pm daily; *July, Aug* 9.30am-7.30pm daily. **Admission** ƒ17,50; ƒ15 under-15s, over-65s, ƒ57,50 family ticket A (2 adults, 2 children), ƒ63,50 family ticket B (2 adults, 3 children).

Tussauds' only branch outside the UK, the show is housed in the top two floors of the Peek & Cloppenburg department store at the Dam. An express lift whisks visitors from ground level to be greeted by Claes Janszoon, Amsterdam Man, a five metre figure clothed in windmills, buccaneers, tulips and all the clichés. Visitors walk through a series of elaborate, climatically controlled scenes, many using impressive audio-animatronic technology and special effects. On the first floor the emphasis is on the Golden Age of commerce and empire. Merchants and peasants, artists and kings are all depicted. On the second floor there are models of the Dutch royal family and local celebrities; international political leaders such as Nelson Mandela, George Bush and Mikhail Gorbachev; record and film stars, including Michael Jackson, Tina Turner and Madonna; and famous people from the twentieth century, notably Einstein and Charlie Chaplin.

Cultural Centres

Amsterdams Historisch Museum

Kalverstraat 92 (523 1822). Tram 1, 2, 4, 5, 9, 14, 16, 24, 25. **Open** 10am-5pm Mon-Fri; 11am-5pm Sat, Sun. **Admission** ƒ8; ƒ4 under-17s.

The city's elegant historical museum is a wonderful cluster of buildings and courtyards, located on the site of St Lucy's Convent (built in 1414). The museum used to house an orphanage and is one of the most underrated attractions of the city centre. Exhibits are well displayed but not interactive. *See also chapter* **Museums**.

Concertgebouw

Concertgebouwplein 2-6 (ticket reservations 671 8345 10am-5pm daily/recorded information in Dutch 675 4411). Tram 3, 5, 12, 16. **Open** *box office* 10am-7pm Mon-Sat; 45 mins before performance for ticket sales and collection. **Tickets** ƒ30-ƒ175; reductions for CJP card holders. **Performances** 8.15pm. **Credit** AmEx, DC, MC.

Amsterdam's venerable Concertgebouw, known as one of the world's three most acoustically perfect concert halls (the others are in Boston and Vienna), was actually outside the city limits when it opened in April 1888. For the event, the 422 horse-drawn carriages bearing the city's élite to the first concert were lined up from Museumplein to the Amstel River. A century later, the hall celebrated its centenary with a face-lift that involved replacing the 100-year-old wooden pilings with concrete ones, and the addition of a controversial glass side wing – the performers never missed a beat. Currently about 500 performances a year are given for some half million visitors.

Rijksmuseum

Stadhouderskade 42 (06 88981212). Tram 2, 5, 6, 7, 10/Bus 63, 170. **Open** 10am-5pm daily, public holidays. **Admission** ƒ12,50; ƒ5 under-18s, CJP card holders;

ƒ7,50 over-65s; free with Museum Card; group discounts (min 20 people).

The Dutch national museum is an imposing sight on the otherwise boring Stadhouderskade. It's one of The Netherlands' most prestigious museums and houses the largest collection of Dutch paintings in existence, including works by the seventeenth-century greats Rembrandt, Vermeer and Frans Hals. Many visitors go to the Rijksmuseum just to see Rembrandt's *Night Watch* and the Vermeers, but with approximately seven million works of art you could easily spend several days here. It is advisable to decide beforehand which parts of the museum you want to visit. *See also chapters* **Architecture** *and* **Museums**.

Stadhuis-Muziektheater

Waterlooplein 22 (625 5455). Tram 9, 14/Metro Waterlooplein. **Open** *box office* 10am-8pm Mon-Sat; 11.30am-8pm Sun. **Tickets** *opera* ƒ17,50-ƒ100; *ballet* ƒ20-ƒ45; reductions for CJP card holders, over-65s. **Performances** *opera* 8pm; *ballet* 8.15pm. **Credit** AmEx, DC, MC.

Dominating the Waterlooplein, the modern Music Hall/City Hall complex is home of the **Netherlands Opera** and **Dutch National Ballet**. Designed by Wilhelm Holtzbauer and Cees Dam and opened in 1985, it occupies 30,000 square metres and cost ƒ300 million to construct. The project has had a troubled history ever since it was first mooted in the 1920s, although it was not until 1954 that the City Council selected Waterlooplein as the site and 1979 before the decision was made to combine the civic headquarters with an opera house. The decision was a controversial one – as was the design itself. Indeed, one of Holland's top composers called the proposed building 'a monument of deceit, mediocrity and lack of taste – a European scandal'. Amsterdammers showed their discontent by organising demonstrations and continued to protest during construction (*see chapter*

Seeing red: the famous **Red-Light District**.

Architecture). Finally, in 1982, a riot caused a million guilders' worth of damage to construction equipment. The building is now universally known as the Stopera. In the passage between the City Hall and the Muziektheater there is a display of geological information, the Amsterdam Ordnance Project. This includes a device showing the NAP (normal Amsterdam water level) and a cross-section of the Netherlands showing its geological structure.

Stedelijk Museum

Paulus Potterstraat 13 (573 2911/Dutch recorded information 573 2737). Tram 2, 3, 5, 12, 16. **Open** 11am-5pm daily; 11am-4pm public holidays. **Admission** *f*8; *f*4 under-17s, CJP card holders, over-65s; free with Museum Card, under-7s.

The most lively of the trio of mighty institutions – the others are the Rijksmuseum (*see above*) and the van Gogh Museum (*see below*) – that dominate Museumplein. A refreshingly light and airy building, it holds art from 1850 to the modern day and includes paintings, sculpture, graphic art, photographs, video arts, industrial design and posters. Highlights include paintings by Picasso, Monet, Cézanne, Kirchner, Matisse and Chagall. The main exhibition is in the summer with the rest of the year being given over to special exhibitions. *See also chapter* **Museums**.

van Gogh Museum

Paulus Potterstraat 7 (570 5200). Tram 2, 3, 5, 12, 16. **Open** 10am-5pm Mon-Sat; 1-5pm Sun, public holidays. **Admission** *f*12,50; *f*5 under-18s; free with Museum Card; *f*7,50 over -65s; group discounts (min 20 people).

The van Gogh Museum opened in 1973 to provide a permanent home for over 700 letters, 200 paintings and 500 drawings by Van Gogh, including *Sunflowers* and several self-portraits. Also on display are works by contemporaries such as Gauguin and Toulouse-Lautrec. Some of the early paintings on display are less than inspiring, but it's interesting to see van Gogh's progression from dull, earthy colours to the gaudy, bright colours that he is known for. In 1990 the Dutch flung themselves into celebrating the centenary of van Gogh's death with great vigour and everything from van Gogh wine to van Gogh potatoes were sold, while a whole van Gogh village appeared on Museumplein. There are also temporary exhibitions from time to time. *See also chapters* **Architecture** *and* **Museums**.

Churches and Viewpoints

Nieuwe Kerk

Dam (Nieuwe Kerk foundation 626 8168/recorded information 638 6990). Tram 1, 2, 4, 5, 9, 13, 14, 16, 17, 24, 25. **Open** 10am-5pm daily. **Admission** free.

While the Oude Kerk (*see below*) was built in the fourteenth century, the Nieuwe Kerk dates from about 1408. It is not known how much damage was caused by the fires of 1421 and 1452, or how much rebuilding took place, but most of the pillars and walls were erected after that period (*see chapter* **Architecture**). Iconoclasm in 1566 left the church intact, although statues and altars were removed in the Reformation (*see chapter* **War & Reformation**). In 1645 the church was completely gutted by the Great Fire; the ornately carved oak pulpit and great organ (the latter designed by Jacob van Campen) are thought to have been constructed shortly after this. Of interest is the tomb of naval hero Admiral de Ruyter who died in 1676. Behind his black marble tomb is a white marble relief depicting the sea battle in which he died. Poets Pieter Cornelisz Hooft and Joost van den Vondel are also buried here. The Nieuwe Kerk is no longer used as a place of worship, but for exhibitions, organ recitals and state occasions, such as the crowning of sovereigns, including Queen Beatrix in 1980.

Oude Kerk

Oudekerksplein 1 (625 8284). Tram 4, 9, 16, 24, 25, 26. **Open** 11am-5pm Mon-Sat; 1-5pm Sun. **Admission** *f*5; *f*3,50 CJP card holders, over-65s, groups. Tours by appointment.

Originally built in 1306 as a wooden chapel and constantly renovated and extended between 1330 and 1571, this is Amsterdam's oldest and most interesting church (*see chapter* **Architecture**). All furnishings were removed by iconoclasts during the Reformation, but the church retains a wooden roof painted in the fifteenth century with figurative images, a Gothic and Renaissance façade above the northern portal, and stained glass windows, parts of which date from the sixteenth and seventeenth centuries. The church is also noted for its carillon and large organ built in 1724 and restored in 1738, which is still in use (*see chapter* **Music: Classical & Opera**). Rembrandt's wife Saskia, who died in 1642, is buried under the small organ. Some restoration work was being carried out at time of writing.

Westerkerk

Prinsengracht 281 (624 7766). Tram 13, 14, 17. **Open** *church* 10am-4pm Mon-Sat; *tower June-Sept* 10am-4pm Wed-Sat. **Admission** *tower f*3.

The neo-classical Westerkerk was built in 1631 by Hendrik de Keyser and its 85m tower, topped with a somewhat gaudy gold, blue and red crown, dominates the city skyline. The story goes that in 1489, Maximillian, the Holy Roman emperor, granted the city the right to include this crown on the city arms. It's worth climbing to the top of the tower (186 steps to the sixth floor) for the superb view of the city – and while you recover from the exertion, ponder the fate of one of Amsterdam's most famous sons, Rembrandt van Rijn: it is thought that the painter is buried somewhere in the graveyard here, although no-one knows exactly. Rembrandt died a pauper, and though his burial on 8 October 1669 was recorded in the church register, the actual spot was not spec-

Don't tyre yourself out on a canal bike.

*The **Nieuwe Kerk**, parts of which date back to 1408.*

ified. There's a good chance that he shares a grave with his son, Titus, who died a year earlier. Inside the church is a monument to the painter. *See also chapter* **Architecture**.

Parks and Gardens

Although there are 28 parks in Amsterdam, the city really only has a few green spaces worth visiting: **Amsterdamse Bos**, **Beatrixpark**, **Flevopark**, **Hortus Botanicus** (Botanical Gardens), **Vondelpark** and **Amstelpark**. Some residential neighbourhoods are fortunate enough to have their own (smaller) areas of green, which are transformed into sheets of colour by beautiful displays of tulips and crocuses; **Sarphatipark** in the Pijp and **Oosterpark** in the east are prime examples. The world and his wife go to the Vondelpark to sunbathe. For gardens outside Amsterdam, *see chapter* **Excursions in Holland**. Admission to all the parks listed below is free except for the Hortus Botanicus.

Amstelpark
Bus 8, 48, 49, 60, 158, 173. **Open** dawn-dusk daily.
Created for Floriade 1972, a garden festival held in a different location every ten years, this major park offers recreation and respite in the suburb of Buitenveldert (near the RAI business centre). A formal rose garden and rhododendron walk are among the seasonal floral spectacles. Art shows at the Glass House (Glazenhuis), pony rides, a children's farm, and tours aboard a miniature train are available. The Rosarium Restaurant serves expensive meals; its outdoor café is somewhat less pricey.

Amsterdamse Bos
Bus 170, 171, 172. **Open** 24 hours daily.
Created in the 1930s, partly as a job creation scheme to ease what was a chronic unemployment problem, the 2,000-acre (800 hectare) *Bos* (wood) is a favourite retreat for Amsterdam

families, especially at weekends. The man-made *Bosbaan* (canal) is used for boating and swimming, with canoe and pedalo rental available. Other attractions include a **horticultural museum**, play areas, jogging routes, a buffalo and bison reserve, a watersports centre, horse-riding stables and a picnic area. The non-subsidised goat farm sells various cheeses, milks and ice cream and you can also feed the goats. In the outdoor pancake restaurant, the peacocks have a habit of flapping noisily from table to table and low-flying aircraft roar by overhead.
Bicycles for hire (Mar-Oct) at main entrance.

Beatrixpark
Tram 5. **Open** dawn-dusk daily.
A little off the beaten tourist track, though on the doorstep of the RAI business centre in the elegant south of the city, this is one of Amsterdam's loveliest parks. Beatrixpark was extended and renovated in 1994. It's always very peaceful and is a good place to repair if you want to avoid the crowds on a hot summer's day. Worth visiting is the Victorian walled garden. There is also a pond complete with ducks, geese, black swans and herons. Amenities include a large children's wading pool and well-equipped play area. There are concerts in July and August.

Flevopark
Tram 14. **Open** *pool* 10am-5pm, 7-9pm (on days warmer than 25°), daily. **Admission** *f* 4,25.
Supremely peaceful and much bigger than it looks on the map, Flevopark has both extensive wooded areas and wide open spaces. Its size means that there are always places to sit in peace and quiet and added bonuses are the two open-air swimming pools which, although highly populated in the summer, the extra sunbather always seems to find space to lie on the surrounding grass.

Hortus Botanicus
Plantage Middenlaan 2A (625 8411). Tram 7, 9, 14. **Open** *Oct-March* 9am-4pm Sat, Sun, public holidays; *April-Sept* 9am-5pm Mon-Fri; 11am-5pm Sat, Sun, public holidays. **Admission** *f* 7,50; *f* 4,50 under-15s; free under-5s. Guided tours by appointment.

The University of Amsterdam has had its own medicinal plant garden since 1638, and it has been at this location since 1682, making the Hortus Botanicus one of the oldest gardens in the Netherlands as well as one of the most beautiful. Best of all are the greenhouses, planted with tropical and subtropical vegetation: one is filled with carnivorous plants, while the palm house (which includes a 400-year-old cycad, reputed to be the oldest potted plant in the world) also has several large tanks of tropical fish. A magnificent greenhouse was opened in 1993, the aim of which is to give the visitor a more genuine impression of flora around the world. You can also seek out van Gogh's favourite plants with the help of a special leaflet. Information and suggested route guides are available in English. Amsterdam also boasts another botanical garden, run by the Free University (*see chapter* **Museums**).

Vondelpark

Tram 1, 2, 3, 5, 6, 7, 10, 12. **Open** dawn-dusk daily.
Named after the city's most famous poet, Joost van den Vondel (1587-1679), this is the most central of Amsterdam's major park. It was designed in the 'English style' by Zocher, with the emphasis on natural landscaping. The original 10 acres were opened in 1865. It has several ponds and lakes (no boating, though), several cafés

(the most pleasant being the Filmmuseum's Café Vertigo, which backs on to the park, *see chapter* **Bars & Cafés**), and assorted children's play areas. The park is exceptionally lively on Sundays when any open space tends to be taken up by ramshackle impromptu football and volleyball matches. Theatre productions, film screenings and pop concerts are also held here.

Canals

A stroll along any of Amsterdam's 160 canals is always pleasant, but the four concentric city-centre canals – Singel, Herengracht, Keizersgracht and Prinsengracht – and the tiny streets that connect them, are the most interesting to wander round. Some smaller, connecting canals worth seeking out for their charm include Leliegracht, Egelantiersgracht, Bloemgracht, Spiegelgracht and Brouwersgracht.

Seeing Amsterdam from the water is an unforgettable experience. There are plenty of tours (*see*

Jewish Amsterdam

Amsterdam suffered terribly at the hands of the occupying forces, as monuments dotted around the city will testify. But it is the appalling legacy of the Holocaust that is most visible, not simply because of Anne Frank but also through the preservation of the **Jodenhoek**, the traditional Jewish area of the city which was isolated by the Germans in order to contain the Jewish population; it now provides a graphic reminder of a horrific period.

The Jodenhoek (Jewish corner) is in the east of the city centre and the walk covers a large section of this area, starting at the Waterlooplein and ending at the Hollandse Schouwburg on Plantage Middenlaan.

The Waterlooplein, then as now a thriving marketplace, was at the heart of the Jewish neighbourhood and together with Plantage Middenlaan provided the focal point for much of everyday life. With the onset of the occupation it remained a focal point, but for more sinister reasons. Much of the rounding up of the Jewish community took place here, to the extent that even non-Jewish people became afraid to go to the Waterlooplein because of the random nature of arrests. There is now a monument to the occupation behind the Stopera building on the corner of Amstel and Zwanenburgwal.

From the Waterlooplein, cross over the street to JD Meijerplein where the **Joods Historisch Museum** is located. The museum, housed in a series of linked former synagogues, contains a wealth of information about the surrounding area as well as Jewish culture and history in general. On the JD Meijerplein stands the **Dockworker statue**, sculpted by Mari Andriessen, commemorating one of the most notorious moments of the occupation. In early 1941, in response to the killing of a Dutch Nazi by the resistance, the Germans rounded up over 400 Jews, the first mass round-up. There was widespread protest to this action by Amsterdammers which culminated in a general strike led by the dockers and which was brutally suppressed after two days. Although there was much collaboration with the Nazis and many Amsterdammers had no real love of Jewish people there was genuine horror and outrage at the actions of the Germans; slogans began to appear on walls

stating 'Get your dirty hands off *our* dirty Jews'. As a warning against future anti-semitism, a ceremony is held at the statue each year on 25 February.

Across from JD Meijerplein is the **Portuguese Synagogue** (above), more than anything a symbol of the practical annihilation of the Jewish community; Amsterdam had a huge Jewish population but by the cessation of hostilities there was no more than a handful of families left alive.

Walking down Plantage Parklaan towards Plantage Middenlaan, the Wertheim Park, to the left, is today a peaceful monument. Named after nineteenth-century Jewish banker and philanthropist AC Wertheim, the park is now home to a glass monument declaring *Nooit meer Auschwitz* (Auschwitz never again). Its official opening in 1993 saw a sea of flowers of remembrance laid on the stone platform in front of it by local residents.

The **Desmet** cinema served as the Rika Hoppertheater before and during the war. During the occupation the premises were off limits to non-Jews. Crossing the road, on the left is Plantage Kerklaan, site of a notorious arson attack on number 36, which was then the office for population registration. On 27 March 1943, a resistance group headed by Gerrit van der Veen torched the building in an attempt to destroy records of Jewish residents. Sadly, the identity cards were so closely packed that the flames could not take a hold on them. Twelve participants in the attack were arrested and shot; van der Veen survived but was later shot after leading another resistance action. Today, a text written by van der Veen remains on the powerful, violent sculpture (Plantage Middenlaan, by Plantage Westermanlaan) which commemorates the bravery of resistance fighters.

With your back to the sculpture you face the Artis Zoo, one time hiding place of 150-300 young Jewish men trying to avoid deportation to Germany. Also on this side of the road is a brightly coloured building which, then as now, serves as a kindergarten. Along with the **Hollandse Schouwburg**, opposite, the crèche was a pivotal site during deportations. The Hollandse Schouwburg was originally an operetta theatre, founded in 1892. In 1941 the name was changed to the Joodsche Schouwburg and, as *below* **Tours**), but if you prefer to drift at will, hire a pedal boat or, if money is no object, a water taxi. And don't forget to navigate on the right-hand side of the waterways. *See also chapter* **Canals**.

Canal Bike
Weteringschans 21 (626 5574). **Open** 10am-6pm Tue-Sun. **Moorings** *Leidsekade at Leidseplein, between Marriott and American Hotels; Stadhouderskade, opposite Rijksmuseum; Prinsengracht, by Westerkerk; Keizersgracht, on the corner of Leidsestraat.* **Hire costs** *4-person pedalo f12,50 per hour for the first two people.* The third and fourth person each pay *f*8 per hour. **Deposit** *f50-f250.* **Credit** £TC.
Canal Bike has four-seater pedalos for hire.

Roell
Mauritskade 1, by the Amstel (692 9124). Tram 6, 7, 10. **Open** *Apr-Sept* 11am-9pm Wed, 8am-9pm Thur-Sun; *Oct-Feb* 11am-6pm Wed, 8am-6pm Thur, Fri, Sat. For groups it's possible to call outside opening times as Roell is quite flexible. **Hire costs** *2-person pedalo f20 per hour; 4-person pedalo f30 per hour; 4-person motor boat f70 for*

1½ hours, *f85 for two hours; partyboat f400 for 1½ hours in summer, f300 for 1½ hours in winter.* **Deposit** *pedalo f50; 4-person motor boat f150.*
Roell is a general watersport centre which has four-seater pedal and motor boats for hire.

Water Taxi Centrale
Stationsplein 8 (622 2181). Tram 1, 2, 4, 5, 9, 11, 13, 16, 17, 24, 25. **Open** 8am-12am daily. **Cost** *8-person boat f90 for first half-hour, then f2 per minute; 16-person boats f180 for first half-hour, then f60 per 15 minutes; 35-person boat f210 for first hour, then f300 per hour.* **Credit** (accepted only prior to boarding) AmEx, DC, MC, V.
You can't hail a taxi from this company – you have to book by phone. The boats can take up to 30 passengers and charge a tariff based on the duration of your trip (*f2 per minute*).

Bridges
With so many canals, it's logical that Amsterdam should also have a fair number of bridges – in fact there are over 1,400 of them. There's a point on Reguliersgracht, at the junction with

with the Rika Hoppertheater, only Jewish performers and audiences were permitted to attend.

In 1942 the theatre underwent its most sinister transformation, into a holding base for those to be sent to the camps. The Germans had formed the Jewish Council, a so-called interest group for Dutch Jews, whose members were forced to prepare the deportations of their own people. One member was Etty Hillesum, whose published diary, *Etty: A Diary*, recounts her voluntary decision to go to Westerbork (she ended up at Auschwitz), explaining the apparent submissiveness of so many Dutch Jews as a refusal to play the role of victim in an unequal fight. Jews who didn't show up voluntarily for 'work' in Germany were dragged out of their houses or hiding places and

brought to this building, which had been a Jewish theatre since 1941. In the theatre there was a Resistance group led by Walter Süskind, who helped Jews escape deportation, and there's a plaque here to his memory.

Without food, drink or even fresh air some 60,000 people passed through between June 1942 and July 1943 before being herded on to trains headed for Westerbork. Today a list of the 6,700 families who never returned stands as a moving testament to the building's horrific past. The crèche was used to hold the children to be deported. Through the help of both Jewish and non-Jewish resistance workers around 1,100 children were smuggled from the crèche to safety in adoptive homes both in and out of Holland.

Keizersgracht, where you can see seven parallel bridges, floodlit by night. One of Amsterdam's most unusual bridges is the Magerebrug (Skinny Bridge), which was originally built in the seventeenth century. The story goes that two sisters who lived either side of the Amstel were bored by having to walk all the way round to visit each other, so the bridge was built for them. Uniquely, it's made from wood and has to be repaired every 20 years. It links Kerkstraat and Nieuwekerkstraat and is opened by hand whenever a boat needs to pass. the Blauwbrug, which links Amstelstraat with Waterlooplein. It was inspired by the elaborate Pont Alexandre III in Paris.

Windmills

Amsterdam is not the best place to see windmills – go to nearby **Zaanse Schans** to see some more impressive examples in action. If you are keen, there are six in the city, but you can only look at them from the outside. All the mills are capable of working, or at the very least turning their sails, and do so on **National Windmill Day**. With the exception of D'Admiraal, which was built in 1792 to grind chalk and is now empty, all are private homes or shops. The best example is De Rieker, on the banks of the Amstel, which can be reached by walking through Amstel Park. Built in 1636 to drain the Rieker polder, it's beautifully preserved and is now a private home. This was a favourite

spot of Rembrandt's and there is a small statue of him close by.

There are two mills on the Haarlemmerweg: 1200 Roe (circa 1632) – a roe is an old-fashioned unit used to calculate the distance from the city centre – and the corn mill De Bloem (1768). The other mills are De Gooyer (1725) on Funenkade in the east of the city, which was another corn mill and is now home to a brewery and bar; and 1100 Roe, an old water mill in a western suburb.

Amsterdam's windmills

D'Admiraal *Noordhollandschkanaaldijk, near Jan Thoméepad. Bus 26, 36, 37, 39.*
De Bloem *Haarlemmerweg, near Nieuwpoortkade. Bus 18.*
De Rieker *Amsteldijk, near De Borcht. Bus 148.*
1200 Roe *Haarlemmerweg, near Willem Molengraaffstraat. Bus 85.*
De Gooyer *Funenkade. Tram 6, 10/bus 22, 28.*
1100 Roe *Herman Bonpad, Sportpark Ookmeer. Bus 19, 23.*

Tours

For advice on how to get around town under your own steam, *see above* **Canals** *and chapter* **Getting Around**.

Walking

Amsterdam is compact enough to be a great city for walking around, but it isn't the world's best for stilettos, pushchairs or wheelchairs because of its uneven streets and tramlines. The tourist organisation **VVV** has a series of English-language brochures outlin-

Hello sailor!

Hofjes

It is a little publicised fact that tucked behind certain Amsterdam doors are courtyards rich in greenery and calm. These almshouses or hofjes date from the seventeenth and eighteenth centuries, when many were built by wealthy tradesmen to house the poor, elderly or needy. The Begijnhof (*see above* **Heritage**) is the classic example, but those prepared to stray from the standard tourist routes will gain a behind-the-scenes glimpse at more intimate (and inhabited) sites. Hofje-spotting requires patience, the boldness to push open apparently closed doors and the discretion to avoid disturbing the residents or outstaying your welcome.

The highest concentration of small *hofjes* is around the Jordaan (*see chapter* **Amsterdam by Area**), although many of the best examples are in Haarlem (*see chapter* **The Randstad: Haarlem**). People live and work in them; they are not signposted as sights and it is up to their residents to choose whether or not to leave doors open for public access – meaning that they are open irregularly. Visit in small groups (three's a

crowd) and bear in mind that although residents don't usually mind you having a look, you are in fact standing in their garden.

Hofjes are often liberally decorated with the gablestones that were used to identify homes until house numbers were introduced and with commemorative plaques in memory of the charitable donors. Our listings cover a selection of Jordaan *hofjes*. Not all of the doors will open when you push them, but they are close together and if you can't get in, the area itself is still an attractive and interesting part of Amsterdam for wandering around.

All *hofjes* listed below are in the Jordaan. *Tram 10, 13, 14, 17.*

Bon's Hofje
Prinsengracht 171.
Newer, noisier and slightly less bijou than some of the more carefully preserved *hofjes*; but it's often open. Keep the door closed because of Jasper the cat.

Claes Claesz Hofje
Eerste Egelantiersdwarsstraat, gate opposite No 4.
Actually two *hofjes* (dating from the early seventeenth century) which were combined in 1945 and have an impressive wooden tower. It's now inhabited by music students and is often open to the public.

Hofje Venetia
Elandsstraat 106-138.
This large *hofje* was originally built by a trader in Venetian goods in 1650. Partly restored in 1957 and with further renovation work completed in 1994, it has an especially beautiful garden.

Sint Andrieshofje
Egelantiersgracht 107-145.
Built in 1617 with the inheritance of cattle farmer Ivo Gerritszoon, this is one of the oldest *hofjes* in Amsterdam and it has been very well restored. The engraving in the courtyard means 'peace be with you'.

Suyckerhofje
Lindengracht 147-165.
This hofje was built in 1670 by Peter Jansz Suyckerhof for forsaken Protestant women. The beautifully overgrown garden was restored in 1989.

---

ing easy-to-follow walks, including ones in the city centre and the Jordaan and themed walks around Rembrandt, van Gogh, Maritime, architecture, and Jewish Amsterdam. The following operate guided tours; English is spoken on all of them.

Archivisie
PO Box 14603, 1001 LC Amsterdam (625 8908/fax 6206 791).
Archivisie organises tailor-made architectural tours, and runs regular theme tours. Phone for appointment and details of charges, which vary greatly.

Mee in Mokum
Hartenstraat 18 (625 1390). Tram 13, 14, 17. **Tours** (last 2-3 hours) 11am Tue-Fri, Sun. **Cost** *f* 4; free under-12s. Groups with a minimum of seven persons can call for appointment outside opening times.
Long-time residents of Amsterdam, all over 55, give highly personal and individual tours of the old part of the city and the Jordaan. They're more of an informal walk than a professional guided tour, but are highly informative and enjoyable. The tour guides are all volunteers and each guide has his own route and his own story to tell about the city (in English as well as Dutch). Tours leave from the Amsterdam Historisch Museum. Advance booking is necessary.

Boats

The best way to see Amsterdam is undoubtedly from the water. Don't be put off by the hordes of coach parties lining up to get on board one of the various tour boats. There are plenty of tour operators, most of them with embarkation points along Rokin and opposite Centraal Station; we list the main ones below.

All the tours cover the same canals, give the same information and carry the same bunch of gawping tourists: the only real choice is whether to take a boat with a live guide or one where you just listen to a pre-recorded voice announcing the points of interest as you pass them.

Some of them also offer night-time cruises, when many of the buildings and most of the bridges are illuminated. Some of the trips include a stop at 'a real Amsterdam pub' and all evening tours offer cheese and wine, although the quality usually leaves plenty to be desired.

Tours generally follow the same routes from different directions. They meander up and down the Herengracht, through the Amstel and chug around the Ij behind Centraal Station, giving plenty of opportunities for nosey peeks into some of Amsterdam's 3,000 houseboats. On sunny days it's pleasant to sit in the open air at the back of the boats but this can defeat the object of the tour as the noise of the engine will override the voice of the guide. Mind you, this can also be no bad thing.

The Best of Holland

Damrak 34. Depart from Rederij Lovers landing stage opposite Centraal Station (623 1539). Tram 4, 9, 16, 24, 25. **Open** *Apr-Oct* 9am-10pm daily; *Nov-Mar* 9am-5.30 daily.**Cruises** approx every 30 mins, 9am-6pm daily; *night cruise* (reservation required) 9pm daily, Wed, Sat in Winter. **Duration** *day cruises* 1 hour; *night cruise* 2 hours. **Tickets** *day cruises: 1-hour* ƒ12; ƒ8 under-13s; *candlelight cruise* ƒ42,50; ƒ17,50 under-13s. **Credit** MC, V.

Holland International

Prins Hendrikkade 33A.Depart opposite Centraal Station (622 7788). Tram 1, 2, 4, 5, 9, 11, 13, 16, 17, 24, 25. **Cruises in Summer** approx every 30 mins, 9am-10 pm daily; *brunch cruise* (reservation required) 11am Wed, Sat, Sun *candlelight cruise* (wine, cheese, stop-off at bar; reservation required) 9.30pm and 11.30pm daily; *dinner cruise* (4-course dinner, reservation required) 8pm Tue, Thur-Sat; *afternoon tea cruise* 3pm Sun. Cruises in Winter approx every 30 mins 10am-6pm daily; *brunch cruise* 11am Sun; *candlelight cruise* 8pm daily; *dinner cruise* 7pm Tue, Fri; *afternoon tea cruise* 3pm Sun. **Duration** *day cruises* about 1 hour; *luncheon cruise* 3 hours; *candlelight cruise* 2 hours; *dinner cruise* 3 hours. **Tickets** *day cruises* ƒ12,50; ƒ7,50 under-13s; *brunch cruise* ƒ55; ƒ50 under-13s; *candlelight cruise* ƒ45; ƒ25 under-13s; *dinner cruise* ƒ145; ƒ115 under-13s; *afternoon tea cruise* ƒ45; ƒ40 under-13s. **Credit** AmEx, MC, V.

One of the most commercial companies, which attracts coach parties by the score.

Lindbergh

Damrak 26 (622 2766). Tram 4, 9, 16, 24, 25. **Cruises** *March-Oct* approx every 15 mins, 10am-6pm daily; *Nov-Apr* approx every 30 minutes, 9am-4pm daily; dinner cruise 7.30pm (Nov-Apr 7.30pm daily); *candlelight cruise* (wine, cheese) 9pm daily (*Nov-Apr* 9.30pm Wed, Sat). **Duration** *day cruises* 1 hour; *dinner cruises* 2½ hours; *candlelight cruises* 2 hours. **Tickets** *day cruises* ƒ12,50; ƒ8 4-13s; *dinner cruises* ƒ99; ƒ49,50 4-13s; *candle light cruises* ƒ42,50; ƒ21,25 4-13s (*Nov-Apr* ƒ39; ƒ19,50). **Credit** MC, V.

Lovers

Prins Hendrikkade (opposite 25-27) by Centraal Station (622 2181). Tram 1, 2, 4, 5, 9, 11, 13, 16, 17, 24, 25. **Cruises** approx every 30 minutes, 9am-6pm daily; *dinner cruise* (reservation required) 7.30pm; *candlelight cruise* (reservation required) 9.30pm. **Duration** *day cruise* 1 hour; *dinner cruise* 2½ hours; *candlelight cruise* 2 hours. **Tickets** *day cruises* ƒ12.50; ƒ8 under-13s; *dinner cruise* ƒ99; ƒ48 under-13s; *candlelight cruise* ƒ42,50; ƒ21,25 under-13s. **Credit** AmEx, DC, MC, V.

As the name suggests, Lovers offers a range of tours for all the honeymooners and romantically inclined couples who drift into Amsterdam. Instead of a guide they have talking video monitors and a driver who mutely points to the sights as you drift by.

Rondvaarten

Kooy BV Rokin (opposite 125) at the corner of Spui (623 3810). Tram 4, 9, 16, 24, 25. **Cruises** *Mar-mid Oct* every 30 minutes 9am-10pm; *mid Oct-Feb* every 30 minutes 10am-5pm. **Duration** 1 hour. **Tickets** ƒ12; ƒ8 under-14s.

Rondvaarten's boats are slightly more upmarket than some of those sitting outside Centraal Station, seem to attract fewer coach parties and their guides speak an impressive four languages, repeating each piece of information in Dutch, English. German and French. The company also offers candlelight wine and cheese tours from April to mid October at 9.30pm. The tours last two hours and cost ƒ35.

Cycling

Cycling may be the best way to get around Amsterdam, but be careful of resident cyclists and car drivers who delight in cutting up tourist cyclists. Most people who cycle around Amsterdam have nerves of steel, so cycling is not recommended for those of a nervous disposition. Rental of a bicycle for the duration of the tour is included in the prices below. For bicycle hire shops, *see chapter* **Getting Around**.

Yellow Bike

Nieuwezijds Voorburgwal 66 (620 6940). Tram 1, 2, 5, 11, 13, 17. **Open** *Apr-Nov* 9am-5pm daily.

Glide past Amsterdam's main sights with Yellow Bike's **City Tour**; it takes three hours, departs at 9.30am and 1pm every day from Nieuwezijds Kolk 29 and costs ƒ30. The **Waterland Tour** takes you further afield and lasts about 6½ hours; the trip includes a visit to a cheese factory and a clockmaker and a return or outward bus journey. Tours depart at 9am daily from the Beurs van Berlage or at noon from Centraal Station, and cost ƒ30 (excluding lunch).

Helicopter

KLM Helicopter Tours

(649 2041). **Open** 9am-5pm Mon-Fri.

If you're keen to get an aerial view of Amsterdam and its surroundings, you can charter a helicopter through KLM. Mind you, it'll cost ƒ4,500 (10 passengers) or ƒ5,500 per hour (25 passengers). The helicopters take a maximum of 25 people.

Architecture

From wooden huts on muddy mounds through the Dutch Renaissance and gables galore to billowing modernist brickwork, Amsterdam's architecture charms with detail rather than ostentation.

'The colours are strong and sad, the forms symmetric, the façades kept new,' wrote Eugene Fromentin, the nineteenth-century art critic, of Amsterdam, 'We feel that it belongs to a people eager to take possession of the conquered mud...'. Amsterdam is a merchants' town, built on a bog. Protestant restraint and the treacherously soft soil put strictures on most attempts at monumental display. Warehouses, domestic architecture, the stock exchange and city hall, not palaces, make up the architectural highpoints.

Amsterdam's architectural epochs have closely followed the pulse of the city's prosperity. The dainty gables and decorative façades of wealthy seventeenth- and eighteenth-century merchants' houses still line the canals. A splurge of public spending in the 1880s gave the city two of its most notable landmarks – Centraal Station and the Rijksmuseum. Social housing projects in the early twentieth century stimulated the innovative work of the Amsterdam School. Amsterdam's late-1980s resurgence as a financial centre and transport hub led both to an economic upturn and to thickets of bravura modern architecture sprouting on the city outskirts.

Prime viewing-time for Amsterdam architecture is late on a summer's afternoon, as the sun gently picks out the varying colours and patterns of the brickwork. Then, as twilight comes, the canal houses – most of them more window than wall – light up like strings of lanterns, and you get a glimpse of the beautifully preserved, rather opulent interiors that lie behind the façades.

MUDDY BEGINNINGS

Amsterdam is built on reclaimed marshland. Below the topsoil is a thick, soft layer of clay and peat. About 12 metres down is a hard band of sand, deposited 10,000 years ago during the Little Ice Age. Below that, after about five metres of fine sand, there is another firm layer, this one left by melting glacial ice after the Great Ice Age. Another 25 metres down, through shell-filled clay and past the bones of mammoths, is a third hard layer, deposited by glaciers over 180,000 years ago.

The first Amsterdammers built their homes on muddy mounds, making the foundations from tightly packed peat. Later, they dug trenches, filled them with fascines (thin, upright alder trunks) and built on those. But still the fruits of their labours sank slowly into the swamp. By the seventeenth century, builders were using longer underground posts and were rewarded with more stable structures, but it wasn't until around 1700 that piles were driven deep enough to hit the first hard sand layer.

The method of constructing foundations that then developed has remained essentially the same ever since – though nowadays piles may reach the second sand level, and some even make the full 50-metre journey to the third hard layer. A double row of piles is sunk along the line of a proposed wall (since World War II, concrete has been used instead of wood), then a crossbeam is laid across each pair of posts, planks are fastened longitudinally on to the beams, and the wall is built on top.

From time to time piles break or rot. Amsterdam is full of buildings that teeter precariously over the street, tilt lopsidedly, or prop each other up in higgledy-piggledy rows.

STICKS AND STONES

Early constructions were timber-framed, built mainly from oak with roofs of rushes or straw. Wooden houses were relatively light, and so less likely to sink into the mire, but after two devastating fires (in 1421 and 1425) the authorities began stipulating that outer walls be built of brick – though wooden front gables were still permitted. The first brick gables were shaped in direct imitation of their spout-shaped wooden predecessors.

Amsterdammers took to brick with relish. Some grander seventeenth-century buildings were built of sandstone, plastered façades made an appearance a hundred years later, and reinforced concrete made its inevitable inroad this century. But Amsterdam is still essentially a city of brick – red brick from Leiden, yellow from Utrecht, grey from Gouda, all laid in curious formations and arranged in complicated patterns. Local architects' attachment to – and flair with – brick reached a zenith in the fantastical, billowing façades designed by the Amsterdam School early this century.

EARLY DAYS

Only two wooden buildings remain in central Amsterdam: one (built in 1460) in the quiet square of the Begijnhof, and the other on the Zeedijk. **Het Aepgen** (Zeedijk 1) was built around 1550 as a lodging house (it got its name from the monkeys that impecunious sailors used to leave behind in payment). Although the ground floor dates from the nineteenth century, the upper floors provide a clear example of how, in medieval times, each successive wooden storey protruded a little beyond the previous one, allowing rainwater to drip on to the street rather than run back into the body of the building. Early brick gables had to be built at an angle over the street for the same reason – so some of Amsterdam's apparent wonkiness is intentional. (These leaning façades also prevent loads bumping against the wall as they are hauled up using the hooked hoist beams that protrude from the top of nearly every building in town.)

Amsterdam's oldest building is the **Oude Kerk** (Old Church, Oude Kerksplein 23), which was begun in 1300 – though only the base of the tower actually dates from then. Over the next three hundred years the church developed a barnacle crust of additional buildings, mostly in Renaissance, some in a localised Gothic style. Nearly all of them retain their original medieval roofs – making the church unique in the Netherlands. The only full Gothic building in town (in the style of towering French and German churches) is the **Nieuwe Kerk** (Dam/Nieuwezijds Voorburgwal) – still called the 'New Church' even though building began at the end of the fourteenth century.

When gunpowder was invented in the fifteenth century, Amsterdammers realised that the wooden palisade that surrounded their settlement would offer scant defence against invaders, and so they set about building a new city wall. Watchtowers and gates left over from this wall make up a significant proportion of remaining pre-seventeenth-century architecture, though most have been considerably altered over the years. The **Schreierstoren** (Prins Hendrikkade 94-5; built 1480) has kept its original shape, with the addition of doors, windows and a pixie-hat roof. The base of the **Munttoren** (Muntplein) originally formed part of the Regulierspoort, a city gate built in 1490. Another city gate, the **St Antoniespoort** (Nieuwmarkt 4; built 1488) was converted into a public weighhouse ('Waag') in 1617, then further refashioned to become a Guild House.

DUTCH RENAISSANCE

A favourite sixteenth-century amendment to these somewhat stolid defence towers was the addition of a sprightly steeple. Hendrick de Keyser (1565-1621) delighted in designing these spires, and it is largely his work that gives Amsterdam's present skyline a faintly oriental appearance. He added a lantern-shaped tower with an openwork orb to the Munttoren, and a spire that resembled the Oude Kerk steeple to the **Montelbaanstoren** (Oude

Schans 2; a sea-defence tower that had been built outside the city wall). His **Zuiderkerk** (Zandstraat 17; built 1603) sports a richly decorative spire, said to have been much admired by Christopher Wren.

De Keyser's appointment as city mason and sculptor in 1595 had given him free reign, and his buildings represent the pinnacle of the Dutch Renaissance style. Since the beginning of the century, Dutch architects had been gleaning inspiration from translations of Italian pattern books, adding lavish ornament to the classical system of proportion they found there. Brick façades were decorated with stone strapwork (scrolls and curls derived from picture frames and leather work). Walls were built with alternating layers of red brick and white sandstone, a style that came to be called 'bacon coursing'. The old spout-shaped gables were replaced with cascading step-gables, often embellished with vases, escutcheons and masks.

The façade of the **Vergulde Dolphijn** (Singel 140-142), designed by De Keyser in 1600 for Captain Banningh Cocq (the commander of Rembrandt's Nightwatch) is a lively combination of red brick and sandstone, while the **Gecroonde Raep** (Oudezijds Voorburgwal 57) has a neat step gable with riotous decoration featuring busts, escutcheons, shells, scrolls and volutes. The magnificent **Huis Bartolotti** (Herengracht 170-172; De Keyser, 1617) is the finest example of the style.

This decorative step-gabled style was to last well into the seventeenth century. But, gradually, a stricter use of classical elements came into play – the façade of the Bartolotti house already features rows of Ionic pilasters. The Italian pattern books that had inspired the Dutch Renaissance were full of the less-ornamented designs of Greek and Roman antiquity.

This appealed to the young architects who succeeded De Keyser, and who were to develop a more restrained, Classicist style. Many, such as Jacob van Campen (1595-1657), went on study tours of Italy, and returned fired with enthusiasm for symmetric designs, simple proportions and austerity of Roman architecture. The buildings that they constructed during the Golden Age are among the finest that Amsterdam has to offer.

THE GOLDEN AGE

The seventeenth century was a boom time for builders as well as for business. Amsterdam's population more than quadrupled during the first half of the century. Grand new canals were constructed, and wealthy merchants lined them with mansions and warehouses. Jacob van Campen and fellow architects Philips Vingboons (1607-78) and his brother Justus (1620-98) found ample expression for their ideas in a flood of new commissions.

Stately façades constructed entirely of sandstone began to appear, but brick remained the most popular building material. **The Witte Huis**

*Housing project in the **Dagerad** with the billowing brickwork of the Amsterdam School.*

(Herengracht 168; Philips Vingboons, 1638) has a white sandstone façade with virtually no decoration; the regular rhythm of the windows is the governing principle of the design. The house **Vingboons** built in 1648 at Oude Turfmarkt 145, has a brick façade adorned with three tiers of classical pilasters (Tuscan, Ionic and Doric) and with the festoons that were also characteristic of the style. The crowning achievement of the period was Amsterdam's boast to the world of its mercantile supremacy and civic might – the **Stadhuis** (city hall) on the Dam, designed by Jacob van Campen in 1648 and now a Royal Palace.

There was one fundamental point of conflict between classical architecture and the requirements of northern European building. Wet northern climes required steep roofs; yet low Roman pediments and flat cornices looked odd with a steep, pointed roof rising behind them.

The architects solved the problem by adapting the Renaissance gable, with its multiple steps, into a tall, central gable with just two steps. These simpler elevated neck-gables had a more suitable classical line. Later, neck-gables were built with no step at all, just a tall central oblong. The right-angles formed at the base of neck-gables (and again at the step of elevated neck-gables) were often filled in with decorative sandstone carvings, called claw-pieces.

Dolphins, sea monsters and other marvels of the world being explored by the Dutch East India company ships became themes for claw-piece design. At **Oudezijds Voorburgwal 187** exotic men with feather head-dresses recline on bales of tobacco. Later, the space occupied by the claw-piece was filled in with brick, rather than by sandstone carving, to form the aptly named bell-gable. These were often trimmed with sandstone decoration.

On exceptionally wide houses it was possible to construct a roof parallel to the street rather than end-on, making a more attractive backdrop for a classical straight cornice. The giant **Trippenhuis** (Kloveniersburgwal 29), built by Justus Vingboons in 1662, has such a design, with a classical pediment, a frieze of cherubs and arabesques, and eight enormous Corinthian pilasters. It was only in the nineteenth century, when zinc cladding became more affordable, that flat and really low-pitched roofs became feasible.

THE EIGHTEENTH CENTURY

Working towards the end of the seventeenth century, Adriaan Dortsman (1625-82) had been a strong proponent of the straight cornice. His exceptionally stark designs – such as for the **Van Loon** house at Keizersgracht 672-674 – ushered in a style that came to be known as Restrained Dutch Classicism. It was a timely entrance. Ornament was costly, and by the beginning of the eighteenth century the economic boom was over. The great merchant families were still prosperous, but little new building went on. Rather, they gave their old mansions a facelift, or revamped the interiors. Thus a number of seventeenth-century houses got new sandstone façades (or plastered brick ones, which were cheaper).

The house of star architect **PJH Cuypers.**

French taste was all the rage. As the century wore on, ornamentation regained popularity. Gables were festooned with scrolls and acanthus leaves (Louis XIV), embellished with asymmetrical rococo fripperies (Louis XV), or strung with disciplined lines of garlands (Louis XVI). The baroque grandeur of the house at **Keizersgracht 444-446** hardly seems Dutch at all.

Straight cornices appeared even on narrow buildings, and became extraordinarily ornate – a distinct advantage as this hid the steep roof that lay behind. Decorative balustrades added to the deception. The lavish cornice at **Oudezijds Voorburgwal 215-217** is a prime example.

THE NINETEENTH CENTURY

Fortunes slumped even lower after 1800. During the first part of the century more buildings were demolished than built. When things picked up after 1860, architects raided past eras for inspiration. Neo-classical, neo-Gothic and neo-Renaissance features were sometimes lumped together in the same building in a mix-and-match Eclectic style.

The **Krijtberg church** (Singel 446; 1881) has a soaring neo-Gothic façade and a high, vaulted basilica; the interior of the **Hollandse Manege** (Vondelstraat 140; AL van Gendt, 1881) combines the Classicism of the Spanish Riding School in Vienna with a state-of-the-art iron-and-glass roof;

the **Concertgebouw** (Van Baerlestraat 98; AL van Gendt, 1888) borrows heavily from the late Renaissance; and the **City Archive** (Amsteldijk 67; 1892) is Hendrick de Keyser revisited. **The Adventkerk** (Keizersgracht 676) manages a classical rusticated base, Romanesque arches, Lombardian moulding and fake seventeenth-century lanterns.

Star architect of the period was PJH Cuypers (1827-1921), who landed the commissions for the **Rijksmuseum** (Stadhouderskade 41; 1877-1885) and **Centraal Station** (Stationsplein; 1882-1889). Both are in traditional red brick, adorned with a wealth of Renaissance-style decoration in sandstone and gold leaf. Here Cuypers turns away from eclecticism and organises each building according to a single coherent principle. This idea became the basis for modern Dutch architecture.

MODERN TIMES

Brick and wood – good, honest, indigenous materials – appealed to HP Berlage (1856-1934), as did the possibilities offered by industrial developments in the use of steel and glass. A rationalist, he took Cuypers' ideas a step further in his belief that a building should openly express its basic structure, with just a modest amount of ornament in a strictly supportive role. His **Beurs** (Beursplein; 1898-1903) – all clean lines and functional shapes, with the mildest patterning in the brickwork – was startling at the time, and earned him the reputation of being the father of modern Dutch architecture.

Apart from the odd shopfront and some well-designed café interiors, the Art Nouveau and Art Deco movements had little direct impact on Amsterdam, though there were a few eccentric flourishes at the time, such as the **Tuschinski Cinema** (Reguliersbreestraat 26; HL de Jong, 1918-21), a delightful piece of high-camp fantasy. Instead, Amsterdam architects developed a style of their own, an idiosyncratic mixture of Art Nouveau and Old Dutch using their favourite materials: wood and brick.

This movement, which became known as the Amsterdam School, reacted against Berlage's sobriety, producing whimsical buildings with waving, almost sculptural brickwork. Built over a reinforced concrete frame, the brick outer walls go through a series of pleats, bulges, folds and curls that earned the movement's work the nickname *schortjesarchitectuur* (apron architecture). Windows may be trapezoid or parabolic; doors are carved in strong, angular shapes; brickwork is decorative and often polychromatic; brick and stone sculptures abound.

The driving force behind the Amsterdam School came from young architects Michel de Klerk (1884-

Gables galore – a seventeenth-century stepped version cosies up to its postmodern cousin.

KSNM Eiland – *new architecture in the redeveloping eastern docklands.*

1923) and Piet Kramer (1881-1961). Commissions for social housing projects from two Housing Associations, one for **Dageraad** (around PL Takstraat; 1921-23) and another for **Eigen Haard** (in the Spaarndammerbuurt; 1913-1920) allowed them to treat entire blocks as single units, and the adventurous clients gave them complete freedom to express their ideas.

In the early 1920s a new movement emerged that was the complete antithesis of the Amsterdam School. Developing on, rather than reacting against, Berlage's ideas, the Functionalists believed that new building materials such as concrete and steel should not be concealed, but that the basic structure of a building should be there for all to see. Function was supreme; ornament was anathema. Their hard-edged, concrete-and-glass boxes have much in common with the work of Frank Lloyd Wright in the USA, Le Corbusier in France and the Bauhaus in Germany.

Early Functionalist work, such as the **Round Blue Teahouse** (Vondelpark; 1937) and the **Cineac Cinema** (Reguliersbreestraat 31; 1934), has a clean-cut elegance, and the Functionalist garden suburb of **Betondorp** (literally 'Concrete Town'; 1921-26) is far more attractive than the name might suggest. But after World War II, Functionalist ideology became an excuse for dreary, derivative, pre-fabricated eyesores. The urgent need for housing, and town-planning theories that favoured residential satellite suburbs, led to the appearance of soulless, high-rise horrors on the edge of town, much the same as in the rest of Europe.

A change of heart during the 1970s refocussed attention on making the city centre a pleasant jumble of residences, shops and offices. At the same time a quirkier, more imaginative trend began to show itself in building design. The **ING Bank** (Bijlmerplein 888; 1987), built in brick and according to anthroposophical principles, has hardly a right-angle in sight. A use of bright colour, and a return to a human-sized scale, is splendidly evident in the **Moederhuis** (Plantage Middenlaan 33; Aldo van Eyck, 1981). New façades – daringly modern, yet built to scale – began to appear between the old houses along the canals.

The 1980s also saw, amid much controversy, the construction of the **Stopera**, a combined city hall (stadhuis) and opera house on Waterlooplein. The eyecatching brick and marble coliseum of the Muziektheater is decidedly more successful than the dull oblongs that make up the city hall.

Housing projects of the 1980s and 1990s have provided Amsterdam with some of its most imaginative modern architecture. The conversion of a nineteenth-century army barracks, the **Oranje Nassau Kazerne** (Sarphatistraat/Mauritskade) into studios and flats, with the addition of a row of rather zanily designed apartment blocks, is one of the more successful ones. Building at present underway on the **KNSM Eiland** and other islands in the derelict eastern docklands combines an intelligent conversion of existing structures with some highly inventive new architecture. The hard lessons of the 1950s and 1960s have clearly been learned.

History

Key Events

Middle Ages

1204 Gijsbrecht van Amstel builds a castle in the coastal settlement that is to become Amsterdam.
1270 The River Amstel is dammed at Dam Square.
1275 Count Floris V grants Aemstelle Dam a toll privilege charter – the first historical record of Amsterdam.
1300 Amsterdam granted city rights by Bishop of Utrecht.
1306 Work begins on the Oude Kerk.
1313 The Bishop of Utrecht grants Aemstelledamme full municipal rights and leaves it to William III of Holland.
1342 City walls (burgwallen) are built.
1345 The 'Miracle of Amsterdam'. From this date Amsterdam attracts large number of pilgrims.

1400-1535

1421 Saint Elizabeth's Day Flood; Amsterdam's first great fire.
1452 Fire destroys most of Amsterdam's wooden houses. Building with slate and stone obligatory from this date.
1489 Maximilian grants Amsterdam the right to add the imperial crown to its coat of arms.
1534 Anabaptists seize the City Hall. They are captured and a period of anti Protestant repression begins.

Under Spanish Rule

1562 Amsterdam has 5,728 houses, 30,000 inhabitants.
1565 A winter crop failure causes famine among Calvinist workers; William the Silent organises a Protestant revolt against Spanish rule.
1566 The Beeldenstorm (Iconoclastic Fury) is unleashed. Protestant worship authorised in public for the first time.
1568 Eighty Year War with Spain begins.
1572 William of Orange (1533-84) joins beggars revolt.
1577 Prince of Orange annexes Amsterdam.
1578 Catholic burgomasters and officials are replaced with Protestants in a coup known as 'The Alteration'.
1579 The Union of Utrecht is signed, allowing freedom of religious belief but not freedom of worship.
1585 Antwerp falls to Spain; mass exodus to the north.

1600-1700

1602 Inauguration of Verenigde Oost Indische Compagnie.
1606 Rembrandt van Rijn is born.
1609 Amsterdam Exchange Bank established.
1611 Zuiderkerk is completed.
1613 Construction of the western stretches of Herengracht, Keizersgracht and Prinsengracht begins.
1621 West Indische Compagnie (WIC) is inaugurated. Amsterdam's population is 105,000.
1623 WIC colonises Manhattan Island. Peter Stuyvesant founds New Amsterdam two years later.
1634 Tulipmania!
1638 Athenaeum Illustre opens. Westerkerk is completed.
1642 Rembrandt finishes 'The Night Watch'.
1648 The Treaty of Münster, ending war with Spain. Jacob van Campen starts to build the City Hall on Dam. Daniel Stalpert finishes it in 1654.
1654 England starts first war against United Provinces.

1665 England is at war with the United Provinces again.
1667 England and the Netherlands sign Peace of Breda.
1663 The plague takes its toll: 23,000 people die.
1672 England and the Netherlands are at war; Louis XIV of France invades the Netherlands.
1674 West Indies Company is dismantled. Amsterdam has a population of 200,000.
1675 The Portuguese Synagogue is completed.
1685 French protestants take refuge in Amsterdam after the revocation of the Edict of Nantes.
1689 William of Orange, Stadholder of the Netherlands, becomes King William III of England.
1696 Undertakers riot against wedding and funeral tax.

1700-1815

1780 Fourth war with England, Dutch fleet destroyed.
1787 Frederick William II, king of Prussia, occupies Amsterdam in support of his brother-in-law.
1795 French Revolutionary armies are welcomed into Amsterdam by the Patriots. The Batavian Republic is set up and administered from Amsterdam.
1806 Napoleon's brother is made King of the Netherlands.
1811 King Louis is removed from the Dutch throne.
1813 Unification of the Netherlands. Amsterdam is no longer a self-governing city.
1815 Amsterdam becomes capital of Holland.

1824-1940

1824 North Holland Canal completed.
1848 The city's ramparts are pulled down.
1876 Noordzee Kanaal links Amsterdam with North Sea.
1877 Gemeentelijk Universiteit (later UvA) set up, followed in 1880 by the Vrije Universiteit Amsterdam.
1880s Oil is discovered on the east coast of Sumatra; foundation of the Royal Dutch Company (Shell Oil).
1883 Amsterdam holds the World Exhibition.
1887 The Rijksmuseum is finished.
1889 Centraal Station opens.
1922 Women are granted the vote.
1928 The Olympic Games are held in Amsterdam.
1934 Amsterdam has a population of 800,000.

WWII to Present Day

1940 May 15, German troops invade Amsterdam.
1941 February strike against the deportation of Jews.
1944-1945 The Hunger Winter; over 2,000 people die.
1945 May 8, Canadian soldiers free Amsterdam.
1947 Anne Frank's diary is published.
1966 Provo (Provocation) movement. Marriage ceremony of Princess Beatrix and Prince Claus ends in riots.
1968 IJ tunnel opens.
1973 Amsterdam's football team, Ajax, win the European Cup for the third successive year.
1975 Cannabis is decriminalised.
1978 First Metrolijn (underground) opens.
1980 Riots on Queen Beatrix's Coronation Day (30 April) in Nieuwe Kerk. This day becomes National Squatters' Day.
1986 Stopera is built amid much controversy.
1992 Boeing 747 crashes into block of flats in Bijlmermeer.

Early History

A mere marsh until medieval times, Amsterdam was born when the Amstel was dammed and built its prosperity on beer.

Although the Romans occupied other parts of Holland, they didn't reach the north. Waterlogged swampland was apparently not the stuff empires were built on, so the legions headed for firmer footholds elsewhere in northern Europe. Archaeologists have found no evidence of settlement at Amsterdam before 1000AD, although there are prehistoric remains further east in **Drenthe**.

Amsterdam's site was partially under water for most of history and the River Amstel had no fixed course until enterprising farmers from around Utrecht began the laborious task of building dykes during the early eleventh century. Once the peasants had done the work, the nobility took over.

During the thirteenth century, the most important place in the newly reclaimed area was Oudekerk aan de Amstel. In 1204, the Lord of Amstel built a castle near this tiny hamlet on what is now the outskirts of Amsterdam. Once the Amstel was dammed (in about 1270), a village grew up on the site of Dam Square, acquiring the name *Aemstelledamme*. The

*The **Oude Kerk**.*

Lord of Amstel at this time was Gijsbrecht, a pugnacious man continually in trouble with his liege lord, the Bishop of Utrecht, and with his nearest neighbour, Count Floris V of Holland.

Tension increased in this power struggle when Floris bestowed toll rights – and thus some independence – on the young town in 1275. Events culminated in Floris' murder by Gijsbrecht at Muiden (where Floris' castle, **Muiderslot** can still be seen). Gijsbrecht's estates were confiscated by the Bishop of Utrecht and given to the Counts of Holland, and Amsterdam has remained part of the province of North Holland ever since.

FOR WHOM THE BEER TOLLS

The saying goes that Amsterdam's prosperity was launched in a beer barrel. This is based on the commercial boost which came courtesy of a later Count of Holland, Floris VI, who in 1323 made the city one of only two toll points in the province for the import of brews. This was no trivial matter at a time when most people drank beer instead of water (drinking the local water was practically suicidal). Hamburg had the largest brewing capacity in northern Europe and within 50 years a third of that city's production was flowing through Amsterdam. Because of its position between the Atlantic and Hanseatic ports, Amsterdam increased its trade in an assortment of essential goods. The city's ships became a common sight in European harbours.

STICKS AND STONES

Although a major trading centre, Amsterdam remained little more than a village until well into the fifteenth century. In 1425, it consisted of a few blocks of houses with kitchen gardens and two churches, compactly arranged along the final 1,000-metre stretch of the River Amstel and bordered by the present Geldersekade, Kloveniersburgwal and Singel. The buildings, like the **Houtenhuis**, were virtually all wooden, so fire was a constant threat. In the great fire of May 1452, three-quarters of Amsterdam was razed.

Few buildings predate 1452, and those built later had to be faced with stone and roofed with tiles or slates. A certain amount of urban expansion began around this time. Foreign commerce led to shipbuilding development. Numerous craftsmen in related trades set up shop outside the city walls (the only remains of which are **Schreierstoren** and St Antoniespoort) in what is now the **Nieuwmarkt** quarter.

A CLOISTERED LIFE

In early medieval society, the Catholic Church permeated every aspect of life throughout Europe, and Amsterdam was no exception. Contemporary chronicles show that the city became an independent parish sometime before 1334. Documents dating from this period are the first to refer to the **Oude Kerk**; the **Nieuwe Kerk** was built at the start of the fifteenth century.

Cloisters proliferated as the city grew and became more prosperous; no fewer than 18 were dotted around the tiny urban enclave. The only remaining example is the **Begijnhof**. One reason for this concentration of cloisters could be the 'miracle' of 1345 (*see below* **XXX marks the spot** *and chapter* **Amsterdam by Season**). The Heiligeweg (Sacred Way) was the road within the city which lead to the chapel on Rokin, close to where the miracle took place. Its length (roughly 70 metres) is an indication of just how small Amsterdam then was.

The cloisters were also the main source of social welfare, providing hospital treatment and orphanages. Nothing remains of these complexes, as the Protestant élite which took over the city after the Reformation obliterated every single trace of popery.

XXX marks the spot

Amsterdam's XXX-rated coat of arms.

When in Amsterdam, it's impossible to avoid the city's coat of arms: it's plastered everywhere, especially in the tourist areas, covering canal boats, tacky T-shirts, mugs and pencils. But consult any Amsterdammer about the meaning behind the three crosses, the lions, or the motto "Heldhaftig, Vastberaden, Barmhartig" and you'll be lucky to receive a coherent answer.

Amsterdam's coat of arms comprises a red shield with a thick black stripe running down the centre, embossed with three white crosses. There are a couple of explanations for its origins. In one, the pennant with three crosses is ascribed to the crusaders, *Heren van Persijn* (Lords of Persia), predecessors of the *Heren van Aemstel*; the crosses probably appeared in their pennant. Another version is that the central black strip represents the river Amstel and that

the three white crosses depict the three disasters (the two terrible fires of 1421 and 1452, the St Elizabeth's Day flood of 1421) that shook the city early in its history.

The first lion in Amsterdam's emblematic history appeared on a town seal in 1416, although this lion as we know them now only appeared after the sixteenth century, and no one seems to know how they got there.

Historians are at least agreed on how Amsterdam won the crown at the top of its town arms. In 1345 a dying man was given the last sacrament and later vomited up the host. The vomit was thrown into a fire but the host emerged from the ashes undamaged. The man recovered. From that time on, Amsterdam attracted a large number of pilgrims, one of whom was the Austrian King (later Emperor), Maximillian. After recovering from an illness in 1489, he bestowed Amsterdam with the right to add the crown on top of its town arms.

The words "Heldhaftig, Vastberaden, Barmhartig" (heroic, determined, merciful) were added in 1948 by Queen Wilhelmina, in recognition of Amsterdam's suffering during World War II.

More recently, the three crosses were copied onto Amsterdam's many anti-parking bollards (known as *Amsterdammertjes*). Though hated by drivers, the design of the *Amsterdammertje* became so popular that many Amsterdammers (especially those leaving the city) stole the bollards for their back gardens. Café owners now use them for plant decorations (or even as table tops) to liven up their street terraces and one smart manufacturer has started producing chocolate miniatures.

War & Reformation

Amid revolts and religious struggles, Amsterdam begins to emerge as one of the world's great trading powers.

None of the wealth and glory of Amsterdam's Golden Age would have been possible without the turbulent events that preceded it. During the sixteenth century, Amsterdam's population increased five-fold, from about 10,000 (a low level even by medieval standards) to 50,000 by 1600. Its first major urban expansion took place to accommodate the growth, yet people flocked to the booming city only to find poverty, disease and squalor in the hastily erected working-class quarters. But Amsterdam's merchants weren't complaining. During this century the city started to emerge as one of the world's major trading powers.

Amsterdam may have been almost autonomous as a chartered city, but on paper it was still subject to absentee rulers. Through the intricate and exclusive marriage bureau known as the European aristocracy, the Low Countries (the Netherlands and Belgium) had passed into the hands of the Catholic Austro-Spanish House of Habsburg. The Habsburgs were the mightiest monarchs in Europe and Amsterdam was a comparative backwater among their European possessions, but events in the sixteenth century soon gave the city a new prominence.

REVOLT & REPRESSION

Amsterdam's burgeoning trade led to the import of all kinds of radical religious ideas which were flourishing throughout northern Europe at the time, encouraged by Martin Luther's audacious condemnation of the all-powerful Catholic Church in 1517. The German princelings sided with Luther, but the Habsburgs gathered all the resources of their enormous empire and set about putting the protesters back in the Catholic Church.

Although Luther's beliefs failed to catch on with Amsterdammers, many people were drawn to the austere and sober creeds of first the Anabaptists and later Calvin. Advocating a revolutionary Christian equality, the Anabaptists insisted on adult baptism. Calvinist doctrine was intertwined with principles of sober, upright citizenship.

When the Anabaptists first arrived from Germany in about 1530, the Catholic city fathers tolerated the new movement. But when they seized the Town Hall in 1534 during an attempt to establish a 'New Jerusalem' on the River Amstel, the authorities clamped down. The leaders were arrested and executed, signalling a period of religious repression unparalleled in the city's history. Protesters of every persuasion had to keep a low profile – heretics were burned at the stake on the Dam.

Calvinist preachers came to the city from Geneva (where the movement started), or via France (the Principality of Orange, in the south of France, had links with Holland and was one of the few pockets of Protestantism outside Switzerland and parts of Germany). Their arrival caused a transformation in Amsterdam. In 1566, religious discontent erupted into what became known as the Iconoclastic Fury, the most severe such outbreak in European history. In the space of two months, a spontaneous uprising led to the sacking of many churches and monasteries. The Iconoclastic Fury had two major effects: one was that a church in Amsterdam, the **Zuiderkerk**, was allocated to the Calvinists; the other was Philip II of Spain's decision to send an army to suppress the heresy.

UNITY AGAINST SPAIN

The Eighty Years' War (1568-1648) between the Habsburgs and the Dutch is often seen as a struggle for religious freedom, but there was more to it than that. The Dutch were looking for political autonomy from an absentee king who represented little more than a continual drain on their coffers. By the last quarter of the sixteenth century, Philip II of Spain was fighting wars against England (to which he sent his Armada) and France; in the East against the Ottoman Turks, and in the New World for control of his colonies. The last thing he needed was a revolt in the Low Countries.

During the revolt, Amsterdam toed the Catholic line, ostensibly supporting Philip II until it became clear that he was losing. Only in 1578 did the city patricians side with the rebels, who were led by William of Orange. A year later the Protestant states of the Low Countries united in opposition to Philip when the first modern-day European Republic was born at the Union of Utrecht. The

Republic of Seven United Provinces was made up of Friesland, Gelderland, Groningen, Overijssel, Utrecht, Zeeland and, most importantly, Holland. Although lauded as the start of the modern Netherlands, it wasn't the unitary state that William of Orange had wanted, but a loose federation with an impotent States General assembly.

Each province appointed a *stadhouder* (viceroy), who commanded the Republic's armed forces and had the right to appoint some of the cities' regents or governors. The *stadhouder* of each province sent delegates to the assembly, which was held at the **Binnenhof** in The Hague. The treaty enshrined freedom of conscience and religion – except for Catholics (until the end of the Republic in 1795).

THE NEW ELITE

From its earliest beginnings, Amsterdam had been governed by four burgomasters and a city council representing citizens' interests. By 1500 city government had become an incestuous business. The city council's 36 members were appointed for life and themselves 'elected' the burgomasters from among their own ranks. Selective intermarriage meant that the city was, in effect, governed by a handful of families. When Amsterdam joined the rebels in 1578, the only real change in civic administration was that the formerly Catholic élite was replaced by a Calvinist faction comprising equally wealthy families.

However, social welfare was transformed. Formerly the concern of the Catholic Church, it was now incorporated into city government. The Regents, as the Calvinist élite became known, took over the convents and monasteries, establishing charitable organisations including orphanages and homes for the elderly. But the Regents' hardwork ethic and abstemious way of life would not tolerate any kind of excess. Crime, drunkenness and immorality were all condemned and these offences were punishable by a spell in a house of correction.

Law and order in the city was maintained by the civic guard or militia who, fortunately for artists like Rembrandt, had a penchant for having their portraits painted.

BENEFICIAL BLOCKADES

During the two centuries before the Eighty Years War, Amsterdam had developed a powerful maritime force, expanding its fleet and broadening its trading horizons to include Russia, Scandinavia and the Baltic States. Even so, Amsterdam remained overshadowed by Antwerp until 1589, when it fell to the Spanish.

The Habsburg Spanish, rather than engaging in pitched battles, adopted siege tactics, primarily in what is now Belgium. Thus Amsterdam was unaffected by the hostilities and benefited from the crippling blockades suffered by rival commercial ports. Thousands of refugees fled north, including Antwerp's most prosperous Protestant and Jewish merchants. These refugees brought with them the skills, the gold and, most famously, the diamond industry that would set Amsterdam on course to becoming the greatest trading city in the world.

The **Begijnhof** *is the only original cloister that can be seen today.*

The Golden Age

Over several decades of relative peace, Amsterdam's commerce and culture flourished as never before.

European history seems to be littered with Golden Ages, but in Amsterdam's case the first six decades of the seventeenth century truly deserve the title. The small city on the Amstel came to dominate world trade and establish important colonies, resulting in a population explosion at home and a frenzy of urban expansion. The elegant girdle of canals excavated around the city centre is one of the greatest engineering feats of that century. Extraordinarily, this all happened while the country was at war with Spain, the century's ailing superpower. And equally startling for the period, this growth was presided over not by kings but by businessmen.

The East India Company doesn't have much of a ring to it, but the name of the mighty Verenigde Oost Indische Compagnie (VOC) definitely loses something in translation. This was the world's first ever transnational company. The VOC was created by a States General charter in 1602. Its initial purpose was to finance the wildly expensive and hellishly dangerous voyages to the East. Drawn by the potential fortunes to be made out of trade in spices and silk, the shrewd Dutch saw the sense in sending out merchant fleets, but they also knew that one disaster could leave an individual investor penniless. As a result, the main cities set up trading 'chambers' which evaluated the feasibility (and profitability) of ventures, then equipped ships and sent them eastwards. The power of the VOC was far-reaching: it had the capacity to found colonies, establish its own army, declare war and sign treaties. The VOC's history is well charted in the **Scheepvaart Museum** on Kattenburgerplein.

STRAITS OF LEMAIRE

The story of Isaac Lemaire, whose name was to become immortalised in atlases, is a good illustration of just how powerful the VOC became. Lemaire fled to Amsterdam from Antwerp in 1589 and became a founder member of the VOC, initially investing ƒ90,000 – about £30 million in today's terms. Later, accused of embezzlement, he was forced to leave the company and industriously cast around for ways to set up on his own. But the Republic had given the VOC a monopoly on trade with the East via the Cape of Good Hope and at that time there was no alternative route.

However, Portuguese seamen claimed the Cape route was not the only passage to the East. They believed the fabulous spice islands of Java, the Moluccas and Malaya could also be reached by sailing to the tip of South America where a strait would lead into the Pacific. In 1615, Lemaire financed a voyage, led by one of his sons, which discovered the strait that still bears his name. His son perished on the voyage home and Isaac died of a broken heart.

While the VOC concentrated on the spice trade, a new company received its charter from the Dutch Republic in 1621. The Dutch West India Company (*West-Indische Compagnie, WIC*) although not as successful as its sister, did dominate trade with Spanish and Portuguese territories in Africa and America. In 1623 the WIC was also first to colonise Manhattan Island. The settlement was laid out on a grid system similar to Amsterdam's and adopted the Dutch city's name. New Amsterdam flourished and areas were named after other enterprising towns with a stake in the colony: Haarlem (Harlem) and Breukelen (Brooklyn). Staten Island was so called in honour of the States General, the 'national' council of the Republic.

After the Duke of York's invasion in 1664, the peace treaty between England and the Netherlands determined New Amsterdam would change its name to New York and come under British control. The Dutch got Surinam as consolation prize.

STRAIGHT TO THE BANK

Extensive though commerce with the Indies became, it never surpassed Amsterdam's European business. The city became the major European centre for distribution and trade. Grain from Russia, Poland and Prussia, salt and wine from France, cloth from Leiden and tiles from Delft all passed through the port. Whales were hunted by Amsterdam's fleets, generating a flourishing soap trade, and sugar and spices from Dutch colonies were distributed to ports throughout Scandinavia and the north of Europe. This activity was financed by the Bank of Amsterdam, a bank set up in the cellars of the City Hall by Amsterdam's municipal council as early as 1609. It was a unique initiative and was considered the money vault of Europe, its notes being readily exchangeable throughout the trading world – the seventeenth-century equivalent of an AmEx Gold Card.

ORANGE PIPPED

The political structure of the young Dutch Republic was complex. When the Treaty of Utrecht was signed in 1579, no suitable monarch or head of state was found, so the existing system was adapted to new needs. The seven provinces were represented by a 'national' council known as the States General. In addition, the provinces appointed a *stadhouder* (*see chapter* **War & Reformation**).

The most popular and obvious choice for *stadhouder* after the treaty was William of Orange, the wealthy Dutch nobleman who had led the rebellion against Philip II of Spain. William was succeeded by his son, Maurits of Nassau, who was as militarily successful against the Spanish as his father had been, securing the Twelve Years' Truce (1609-1621). Although each province could, in theory, elect a different *stadhouder*, in practice they usually chose the same person. It became something of a tradition to elect an Orange as *stadhouder* and by 1641 this family had become sufficiently powerful for William II to marry a British princess, Mary Stuart. It was their son William III who, backed by Amsterdam money, set sail in 1688 to accept the throne of England in the so-called Glorious Revolution.

But the Oranges weren't popular with everyone. The provinces' representatives at the States General were known as regents, and Holland's (and therefore Amsterdam's) regent was in a powerful enough position to challenge the authority and decisions of the *stadhouder*. In 1650 this power was exercised. The crisis was precipitated by Holland's decision to disband its militia after the end of the Eighty Years' War with Spain. The *stadhouder*, William II of Orange, wanted the militia maintained (and paid for) by Holland. In response to the disbandment, he got a kinsman, William Frederick, to launch a surprise attack on Amsterdam. Although there was no resistance to the attack, William II died three months later. The leaders of the States of Holland then called a Great Assembly of the provinces, which decided (apart from Friesland and Groningen, which remained loyal to William Frederick) that there should be no *stadhouders*. Johan de Witt, Holland's powerful regent, swore no prince of Orange would ever become *stadhouder* again. This became law in the Act of Seclusion of 1653.

THE NEW ORDER

The powers that be in Amsterdam, the Heren XLVIII (a sheriff, four mayors, a 36-member council and seven jurists) kept a firm grip on all that went on both within and without the city walls. Although this system was self-perpetuating, these people were merchants rather than aristocrats, and anyone who made enough money could, in theory, become a member. The mayors and the council usually came from a handful of prominent families, the most powerful being the Witsen, Bicker,

Six and Trip families – who are also commemorated on Amsterdam street names. Their wives, nieces and daughters made up boards of governesses at the multitude of charitable institutions scattered throughout the city.

The less elevated folk, the craftsmen, artisans and shopkeepers, were equally active in maintaining their position. A system of guilds had developed in earlier centuries, linked to the Catholic Church, but under the new order guilds were independent organisations run by their members. The original Amsterdammers were known as *poorters*, deriving from the Dutch for gate (they originally lived within the gated walls of the city). As the city rapidly expanded, the *poorters* began to see their livelihoods threatened by an influx of newcomers who were prepared to work for lower wages.

Things came to a head when the shipwrights began to lose their trade to less expensive competitors in the nearby Zaan region. The shipwrights' lobby was so strong that the city regents decreed that Amsterdam ships had to be repaired in Amsterdam yards. This kind of protectionism extended to almost all industrial sectors in the city and effectively meant that most crafts became closed shops. Only *poorters* or those who had married *poorters'* daughters were allowed to join a guild, thereby protecting Amsterdammers' livelihoods.

ELEGANCE & EXPANSION

In 1600 Amsterdam's population was no more than 50,000 but in the space of about 50 years that figure quadrupled. The city was obliged to expand. The most elegant of the major canals circling the city centre was Herengracht (lords' canal); begun in 1613, this was where many of the Heren XLVIII had their homes. So that there would be no misunderstanding about who was the most important, Herengracht was followed further out by Keizersgracht (emperors' canal) and Prinsengracht (princes' canal). Immigrants were housed rather more modestly in the Jordaan quarter.

The **Amstelkring Museum** has preserved Amsterdam's only surviving attic church in its entirety. (The only other remaining clandestine church is the **Begijnhof**.) During the seventeenth century, Roman Catholic worship was banned in the city and this chapel, 'Our Lord in the Attic', was one of several used for secret services. The rest of the house is preserved in its seventeenth-century state, giving an insight into the domestic life of the period. **Museum Van Loon** is housed in a beautifully restored and rather grand seventeenth-century home. The Van Loon family was then one of the most powerful in Amsterdam – Willem Van Loon helped found the VOC in 1602. Among the collection of period pieces there is an enormous number of family portraits, all excellent examples of contemporary portraiture.

Despite the city's wealth, and the reputation of its people as masters of transport, famine hit Amsterdam with dreary regularity in the seventeenth century. Guilds had benevolent funds set aside for their members in times of need, but social welfare was primarily in the hands of the ruling merchant class. Amsterdam's élite was noted for its philanthropy, but only *poorters* were eligible for assistance and they had to fall into a specific category, described as 'deserving poor'.

Those seen as undeserving were sent to a house of correction. Initially, the philosophy behind these places had been rather idealistic, run on the premise that hard work would ultimately produce reformed, useful citizens. But this soon changed and the institutions became little more than prisons.

PAINTERS & PIONEERS

Amsterdam's seventeenth-century Golden Age encompassed both commercial life and the arts. Rembrandt and hundreds of long-forgotten artists made a good living during the period. Those artists united in the Guild of St Luke are estimated to have produced an extraordinary 20 million paintings. Art historians have good reason to believe that almost every family had at least three or four paintings in their home. Though Rembrandt died in poverty, he had a remarkably comfortable life – when he managed to keep his temper and not offend his rich patrons. The house where he lived in Jodenbreestraat still exists as the **Rembrandthuis Museum** and it's no garret.

Unlike other European countries, the Netherlands wasn't liberally scattered with ancient universities. In fact, Amsterdam didn't have one at all. The first move towards establishing a centre of higher education came in 1632 when the Athenaeum Illustre was opened. It was attended by (male) members of the élite who studied Latin, Greek, law and the natural sciences. But two of the era's scientific pioneers, physicist Christiaan Huygens and Anthonie van Leeuwenhoek, who pioneered microbiology, didn't go to a university at all. They did their work in improvised laboratories at home. Amsterdam's guild of surgeons, as Rembrandt and other artists have recorded, held public demonstrations of anatomy, using the bodies of executed criminals for dissection practice.

Headquarters of the **East India Company**, *the world's first multinational.*

Decline & Fall

After the intoxicating Golden Age came the inevitable hangover.

Although Amsterdam remained one of the wealthiest cities in Europe until the early nineteenth century, after 1660 its dominant trading position was lost to England and France. Wars and invasions would gradually milk the country dry.

The United Provinces spent a couple of centuries bickering about trade and politics with Britain and the other main powers. Wars were frequent. Major sea conflicts included battles against the Swedes and no fewer than four Anglo-Dutch wars, from which the Dutch came off slightly worse. It wasn't that the Dutch didn't win any wars; more that the small country ran out of men and money. Amsterdam became the most vociferous opponent to the Orange family's attempt to acquire kingdoms – although it strongly supported William III when this Orange crossed the sea to become King of England in 1688. The city fathers believed a Dutchman on their rival's throne could only be an advantage. For a while that proved true, but William was soon knocking on the Amsterdammers' doors for more money to fight even more wars – this time against France.

MARITIME MONUMENTS

The admirals who led the wars against Britain are Dutch heroes, and the **Nieuwe Kerk** has monuments to admirals Van Kinsbergen (1735-1819), Bentinck (1745-1831) and, most celebrated of all, Michiel de Ruyter (1607-1676). The most famous incident, though not prominent in British history books, was during the Second English War (1664-1667) when de Ruyter sailed up the Thames to Chatham, stormed the dockyards and burnt the Royal Charles, the British flagship, as it lay at anchor. The Royal Charles' coat of arms was stolen, and is now displayed in the Rijksmuseum.

Despite diminished maritime prowess, Amsterdam retained the highest standard of living in Europe until well into the eighteenth century. The Plantage district was the period's principal city development. Tradesmen and artisans flourished and their role in society can still be gauged by the intricate shapes and carvings on gablestones.

THE FINAL BLOW

The Dutch Republic began to lag behind the major European powers in the eighteenth century. The Agricultural and Industrial Revolutions didn't get off the ground in the Netherlands. Amsterdam was nudged out of the shipbuilding market by England, and its lucrative textile industry was lost to other provinces, but the city managed to exploit its position as the financial centre of the world – until the final and most devastating Anglo-Dutch War (1780-1784). The British hammered the Dutch merchant and naval fleets, crippling the profitable trade with their far-eastern colonies.

The closest the Dutch came to the republican movements of France and the United States was with the Patriots. During the 1780s the Patriots managed to shake off the influence of the *stadhouders* in many smaller towns, but in 1787 they were foiled in Amsterdam by the intervention of the Prince of Orange and his brother-in-law, Frederick William II, King of Prussia. Hundreds of Patriots fled to exile in France, where their welcome convinced them Napoleon's intentions towards the Dutch Republic were benign. In 1795 they returned, backed by a French army of 'advisers'. With massive support from Amsterdam, they celebrated the new Batavian Republic.

It sounded too good to be true, and it was. According to one contemporary: 'The French moved over the land like locusts'. Over f100 million (about a f1 billion today) was extracted from the Dutch. The French also sent a standing army, all 25,000 of whom had to be fed, equipped and billeted by its Dutch 'hosts'. Republican ideals seemed increasingly hollow when Napoleon installed one of his brothers as King of the Netherlands and the symbol of Amsterdam's mercantile ascendancy and civic pride, the City Hall of the Dam, was requisitioned as Louis Bonaparte's royal palace. Even Louis was disturbed by the increasing impoverishment of a nation that had been Europe's most prosperous. After Louis had allowed Dutch smugglers to break Napoleon's blockade of Britain, he was forced to abdicate in 1810 and the Low Countries were absorbed into the French Empire.

Government by the French wasn't an unmitigated disaster for the Dutch. The foundations of the modern Dutch state were laid in the Napoleonic period, a civil code was introduced and education improved. Trade with Britain ceased, however, and the growing price of Napoleon's wars prompted the Dutch to join the revolt against France. After Napoleon's defeat in 1815, Amsterdam became the capital of a constitutional monarchy, incorporating what is now Belgium. William VI of Orange was crowned King William I in 1815. But although the Oranges still reign in the northern provinces to this day, the United Kingdom of the Netherlands, as it then existed, was to last only until 1831.

Between the Occupations

Amsterdam expands, modernises, unionises and occasionally thrives during an invasion-free century.

When the French were finally defeated and left Dutch soil in 1813, Amsterdam emerged as the capital of the new kingdom of the Netherlands – but very little else. The city wasn't even the seat of government. With its coffers almost totally depleted and its colonies occupied by the British, Amsterdam would have to fight hard for recovery.

This was made more difficult by two huge obstacles. First, Dutch colonial assets had been reduced to present-day Indonesia (then known as the Dutch East Indies), Surinam and the odd island in the Caribbean. Secondly, the Dutch were slow to join the Industrial Revolution. The Netherlands has few natural resources to exploit and Dutch business preferred to keep its hands clean by relying on the power of sail. Moreover, Amsterdam's opening to the sea, the Zuider Zee, was too shallow to accommodate the new, larger, steam-ships.

In an attempt to link the city to the North Sea port of Den Helder, the circuitous Great North Holland Canal was dug in 1824. But because it had so many bridges and locks, it was slow and expensive, both to construct and to use. Rotterdam gradually took over the capital's position as the most progressive industrial centre.

ECONOMIC ADVANCES

Prosperity returned to Amsterdam after the 1860s. The city readjusted its economy to meet modern demands, and its trading position was greatly improved by the building of two canals. The opening of the Suez Canal in 1869 speeded up the passage to the Orient, producing a giant increase in commerce. But what the city needed most was easy access to the major shipping lanes of Northern Europe. The North Sea Canal enabled Amsterdam to take advantage of German industrial trade and to become the Netherlands' greatest ship-building port again – at least temporarily.

Industrial machinery was introduced late to Amsterdam. However, by the late nineteenth century, the city had begun to modernise production of the luxury goods it would become famous for – chocolates, cigars, beers and cut diamonds.

Although there had been a local railway track between Haarlem and Amsterdam since 1839, the city finally got a major rail link and a new landmark in 1889. **Centraal Station** was designed by PJH Cuypers in 1876, an influential architect known mainly for his neo-Gothic churches. The terminal was initially intended to be in the Pijp, and when it was decided that the track should run along the Zuider Zee, shutting the city off from its seafront, much objection ensued. There was also controversy when the **Rijksmuseum** was sited at what was then the fringe of the city, and about the selection of Cuypers as its architect. The result was, like Centraal Station, uniquely eclectic and led to the museum being ridiculed as a 'cathedral of the arts' – a not entirely inappropriate label, given the contemporary boom in culture.

In 1877, the Carré Theatre opened, followed a year later by the **Concertgebouw**, then in 1894 by the **Stadsschouwburg**, in 1895 by the **Stedelijk Museum** and, in 1926, the Tropen Institute (now the **Tropenmuseum**). The city's international standing improved to the point that in 1928 it hosted the Olympic Games.

REAPING THE BENEFITS

Social welfare in Amsterdam, long dependent on charity and the goodwill of the élite, was transformed in the nineteenth century. But until prosperity returned in the last third of the century, the living conditions of the working population continued to be appalling. Amsterdam's solution before 1850 was to follow central government policy and round up the destitute, sending them off to do hard agricultural labour. Yet throughout this period, Amsterdam spent a relatively large amount of money on relief of the poor.

In the second half of the century, however, the idea grew that assistance only made the poor lazy, and relief was cut back. But towards the end of the 1800s, the newly formed trade unions set up some forms of relief of the poor for their members. Socialist ideas began to permeate, and the way was paved for the development of one of the best social security systems in the world.

THE DIAMOND AGE

The story of diamonds in Amsterdam is also the history of social change in the city (to visit working factories, *see chapter* **Sightseeing**). The first records of diamond-working in Amsterdam go as far back as 1586. Fabulous stones such as the Koh-i-Noor (Mountain of Light), one of the British crown jewels, was cut by an Amsterdammer. But as the industry was entirely dependent upon the discovery of rare stones, it was in a continual state of flux. In the early 1870s, diamond cutters could light cigars with ƒ10 notes (the average weekly wage for the rest of the workforce was then ƒ8). A decade later, the city would prohibit working diamond workers from begging naked in the streets. The working classes, meanwhile, had become more politicised, so the ideas behind the old guild system took on a new resonance. Funds were established to protect diamond workers during slumps, and this led to the formation of the first Dutch trade union.

In the early days of the union movement, socialists and the upper classes co-existed relatively harmoniously, but by the 1880s things were changing. The movement found an articulate leader in Ferdinand Domela Nieuwenhuis, who also set up a political party, the Social Democratic Union. The SDU faded into obscurity after a split in 1894, but a splinter group, the Social Democratic Labour Party (SDAP), later won the first ever socialist city-council seat for the diamond workers' union chief, Henri Polak in 1901. The SDAP went on to introduce the welfare state after World War II.

Educational reform was perhaps the greatest step forward made in the late nineteenth century. A network of free primary schools was set up to teach the working classes the rudiments of reading, writing and arithmetic.

NEW DEVELOPMENTS

Amsterdam's population had stagnated at around a quarter of a million for two centuries after the Golden Age, but between 1850 and 1900 it more than doubled. The increased labour force was desperately needed to meet the demands of a revitalised economy, but the major problem was how to house the new workers. Today, the old inner city quarters are desirable addresses, but they used to be the homes of Amsterdam's poor. The picturesque Jordaan, where riots broke out with increasing regularity in the 1930s, was occupied primarily by the lowest-paid workers. Canals were used as cesspits and the mortality rate was high. Oddly, the Jordaan was the first area in the city to have Tarmac streets. The decision wasn't philanthropic; it came after Queen Wilhelmina had been pelted by Jordaan cobblestones.

Around the old centre, new neighbourhoods were constructed. The new housing developments – the Pijp, Dapper and Staatslieden quarters – weren't luxurious by any means, and most were cheaply built by speculators, but at least they had simple lavatory facilities (though no bathrooms). Wealthier city-dwellers found elegance and space in homes built around Vondelpark and in the south of the city.

WAR & DEPRESSION

The city didn't fare badly in the first two decades of this century, but Dutch neutrality during World War I brought problems. While the élite lined their pockets selling arms, the poor were confronted with continual food shortages. In 1917, with food riots erupting, especially in the Jordaan, the city had to open soup kitchens and introduce rationing.

The army was called in to suppress another outbreak of civil unrest in the Jordaan in 1934. This time the cause was unemployment, endemic throughout the industrialised world after the Wall Street Crash of 1929. Historians estimate that in 1936 19 per cent of the workforce was unemployed.

Unfortunately, the humiliation of means testing for unemployment benefit meant that many families suffered in hungry silence. Many Dutch workers even moved to Germany where National Socialism was creating new jobs. At home, Amsterdam initiated extensive public works under the 1934 General Extension Plan, whereby the city's southern outskirts were developed for public housing. The city was just emerging from the Depression by the time the Nazis invaded in May 1940.

Ferdinand Domela Nieuwenhuis.

World War II

War and Nazism brings persecution, pestilence, hunger and the Holocaust.

Amsterdam endured World War II without being flattened by bombs, but its buildings, infrastructure and inhabitants were reduced to a terrible state by Nazi occupation. The Holocaust also left an indelible scar on a city whose population in 1940 was ten per cent Jewish. Photographs and relics of the World War II collection can be seen at the **Amsterdams Historisch Museum**.

Early in the morning of 10 May 1940, German bombers mounted a surprise attack on Dutch airfields and military barracks in order to destroy the Dutch Air Force. The government and people had hoped that the Netherlands could remain neutral, as they had in World War I, so the armed forces were unprepared for war. Yet the Dutch aimed to hold off the Germans until the British and French could come to their assistance. This hope was in vain. Queen Wilhelmina and the government fled to London to form a government in exile, leaving Supreme Commander Winkelman in charge of state authority.

Rotterdam was destroyed by bombing and when the Germans threatened other cities with the same treatment, Winkelman capitulated on 14 May 1940. The Dutch colonies of Indonesia and New Guinea were invaded by the Japanese in January 1942. After their capitulation on 8 March, Dutch colonials were imprisoned in Japanese concentration camps and the Indonesian nationalists Sukarno and Hatta proclaimed an independent republic.

NATIONAL SOCIALISM

Hitler appointed Arthur Seyss-Inquart, an Austrian Nazi, as Rijkskommissaris (State Commissioner) of the Netherlands. His policy was to tie the Dutch economy to the German one and to Nazify Dutch society. The National Socialist Movement (NSB) was the largest and most important fascist political party in the Netherlands, although in the 1939 elections it won less than five per cent of the votes. Naturally, it was the only Dutch party not prohibited during the occupation. Its doctrine greatly resembled German Nazism, but the NSB wanted to maintain Dutch autonomy under the direction of Germany.

During the first years of the war, the Nazis allowed most people to live relatively undisturbed. But rationing made the Dutch vulnerable to the black market, while cinemas and theatres eventually closed because of curfews, censorship and dis-

Dutch kids fail to resist the Nazi advance.

rupted transport. This soft approach failed to Nazify the locals, so the Germans adopted more aggressive measures. Dutch men were forced to work in German industry and economic exploitation assumed appalling forms. In April 1943 all Dutch soldiers – who'd been captured during the invasion and then released in the summer of 1940 – were ordered to give themselves up as prisoners of war. In an atmosphere of deep shock and outrage, strikes broke out during April and May throughout the country, only to be suppressed bloodily.

PATTERNS OF COLLABORATION

To begin with, ordinary people, as well as the political and economic élite, had no real reason to make a choice between collaboration and resistance. But, as Nazi policies became more virulent, opposition swelled and a growing minority of people were confronted with the difficult choice of whether to obey German measures or to resist.

There were several patterns of collaboration. Some people joined the NSB, others intimidated Jews, were involved in economic collaboration or betrayed people in hiding or members of the Resistance; a small number even signed up for German military service. In Amsterdam several social institutions gave information about Jews to the Germans. The most shocking institutional collaboration was by the police, who dragged Jews out of their houses for deportation. The Dutch Railways

also assisted the Nazis by transporting Jews to their deaths and received money for doing so. After the war between 120,000 and 150,000 people were arrested for collaborating. Mitigating circumstances – as in the case of NSB members who helped the Resistance – made judgements very complicated and eventually 60,000 people were brought to justice.

GOING UNDERGROUND

The Resistance comprised chiefly Calvinists and Communists. The latter gained public support, although the Calvinist élite ensured that there was no Communist takeover after liberation. Anti-Nazi activities took several forms. Illegal newspapers, unlike the censored press, kept the population properly informed and urged resistance. Originals can be seen in the **Verzetsmuseum** and copies were reprinted for sale across the Netherlands in 1993-4. The monument on Apolloaan is of three men about to be executed as a reprisal for killing a German espionage agent.

There were many kinds of underground groups, which spied for the Allies, fought an armed struggle against the Germans through assassination and sabotage, or falsified identity cards and food vouchers. A national organisation took care of people who wanted to hide and helped the railway strikers, Dutch soldiers and illegal workers being sought by the Germans. Other groups helped Jews into hiding. By 1945, more than 300,000 people had gone underground in the Netherlands.

HUNGER WINTER

In 1944 the Netherlands was plunged into the 'Hunger Winter'. Supplies of coal ceased after the liberation of the south and a railway strike, called by the Dutch government in exile to hasten German defeat, was disastrous for the supply of food. In retaliation for the strike, the Germans damaged Schiphol Airport and the harbours of Rotterdam and Amsterdam, and appropriated everything they could. Walking became the only means of transport, domestic refuse was no longer collected, sewers overflowed and the population, suffering malnutrition and cold, was vulnerable to disease.

To survive, people stole fuel. More than 20,000 trees were cut down and 4,600 buildings were demolished. Floors, staircases, joists and rafters were plundered, causing the collapse of many houses, particularly those left by deported Jews. Supplies were scarce and many people couldn't even afford to buy their rationing allowance, let alone the expensive produce on the black market. By the end of winter, 20,000 people had died of starvation and disease and much of the city was damaged.

The **Resistance Monument** *on Apollolaan stands as a tribute to all who died.*

FREEDOM NOW

The Allies liberated the south of the Netherlands on 5 September 1944, Dolle Dinsdag (Mad Tuesday). Complete liberation came after the Hunger Winter on 5 May 1945, when it became apparent that the Netherlands was the worst hit country in Western Europe. In spite of the chaos, destruction, hunger and the loss of so many lives, there were effusive celebrations. But in Amsterdam tragedy struck on 7 May, when German soldiers opened fire on a crowd gathered on Dam Square to welcome their Canadian liberators, killing 22 people.

THE HOLOCAUST

'I see how the world is slowly becoming a desert, I hear more and more clearly the approaching thunder that will kill us,' wrote **Anne Frank** in her diary on 15 July 1944. As well as to Jews, Anne's words applied to the gypsies, homosexuals, the mentally handicapped and political opponents, who were all severely persecuted during the war. Antisemitism in Holland had not been as virulent as in Germany, France or Austria. Yet most – but not all – of the Dutch closed their eyes to the persecution and there's still a feeling of national guilt as a result.

There were three stages to the Holocaust. First came measures to enforce the isolation of the Jews: the ritual slaughter of animals was prohibited, Jewish government employees were dismissed, Jews were banned from public places such as restaurants, cinemas and libraries and, eventually, all Jews were made to wear a yellow Star of David. Some non-Jewish Dutch courageously wore the badge as a demonstration of solidarity. Concentration was the second stage. From the beginning of 1942 all Dutch Jews were obliged to move to three areas in Amsterdam, which were isolated by signs, drawbridges and barbed wire.

The final stage was deportation. Between July 1942 and September 1943, most of the 140,000 Dutch Jews were deported, via Kamp Westerbork. Public outrage at the first deportations provoked the most dramatic protest against the anti-semitic terror, the impressive February Strike.

The Nazis had also wanted to eliminate Dutch gypsies. More than 200,000 European gypsies, about 200 of them Dutch, were exterminated in concentration camps. Homosexuals were also threatened with extermination, but their persecution was less systematic. Public morality acts prohibited homosexual behaviour and gay pressure groups ceased their activities. Men arrested for other activities were punished more severely if they were discovered to be gay.

In Dutch educational history books, the extermination of gypsies and homosexuals is still often omitted, but Amsterdam has the world's first memorial to persecuted gays, the **Homomonument**, which incorporates pink triangles in its design, turning the Nazi badge of persecution into a symbol of pride.

Post-war

Both prosperity and provocations mark the revival of the Netherlands.

The Netherlands was deeply scarred by the German occupation, losing about ten per cent of all its housing, 30 per cent of its industry and 40 per cent of its total production capacity. The transport system had been immobilised and some of the country's dykes had been blown up, leaving large areas flooded. Although Amsterdam had escaped the bombing raids which devastated Rotterdam, it had borne the brunt of the deportations, and only 5,000 out of a pre-war total Jewish population of 80,000 remained.

Despite intense poverty and drastic shortages of food, fuel and building materials, the Dutch tackled the massive task of post-war recovery and restoration with the spirit of the Resistance. There was a strong sense of optimism and unity, which was sustained until the end of the 1940s. In 1948, people threw street parties, firstly to celebrate the inauguration of Queen Juliana and later the four gold medals won by Amsterdam athlete Fanny Blankers-Koen at the London Olympics.

Some Dutch flirted briefly with Communism directly after the war, but in 1948 a compromise was struck between the Catholic party, KVP, and the newly created Labour party, PvdA. The two governed in successive coalitions until 1958. Led by Prime Minister Willem Drees, the government resuscitated pre-war social programmes and laid the basis for the country's lavish welfare state. The Dutch reverted to the virtues of a conservative, provincial society: decency, hard work and thrift.

The country's first priority after the war was economic recovery. The Amsterdam city council concentrated on reviving the two motors of its economy: Schiphol Airport and the port of Amsterdam, which was boosted by the opening of the Amsterdam-Rhine Canal in 1952. Joining Belgium and Luxembourg in the Benelux brought the country trade benefits and the Netherlands was the first to repay its Marshall Plan loans. The authorities dusted off pre-war development plans and embarked on rapid urban expansion. To the west, garden cities were created, such as Slotervaart, Geuzenveld and Osdorp. The architecture was sober, the setting spacious. But as people moved out to the new suburbs, businesses moved into the centre, worsening congestion on the already cramped roads, which had to deal with an explosive growth in traffic. Road casualties soared.

COLONIAL CONNECTIONS

After the war, the Dutch colonies of Indonesia and New Guinea were liberated from the Japanese and pushed for independence. With Indonesia accounting for 20 per cent of their pre-war economy, the Dutch launched military interventions on 20 July 1947 and 18 December 1948. These could not prevent the transfer of sovereignty to Indonesia on 27 December 1949. The dispute with New Guinea dragged on until 1962 and did much to damage the Netherlands' international reputation. Colonial immigrants to the Netherlands, including the later arrival of Surinamese, and of Turkish and Moroccan 'guest workers', now comprise 16 per cent of the population. Although poorer jobs and housing have usually been their lot, racial tension has been relatively low until recently, with the rise of neo-fascism in the shape of the CD party.

The economy revived in the 1950s, the welfare state was in place, but there was still civil unrest. Strikes flared at the port and council workers defied a ban on industrial action. In 1951, protesters clashed with police outside the Concertgebouw, angered by the appointment of a pro-Nazi as conductor. In 1956, demonstrators besieged the Felix Meritis Building, the base of the Dutch communist party from 1946 until the late 1970s, hurling stones in outrage at the Soviet invasion of Hungary.

In the late 1940s and 1950s, Amsterdammers returned to pre-war pursuits: fashion and celebrity interviews filled the newspapers and cultural events mushroomed. In 1947, the city launched the prestigious **Holland Festival**. The élite held an annual event called the 'Boekenbal', where writers met royalty and other dignitaries. New avant-garde artistic movements emerged, notably the **CoBrA** art group, whose 1949 exhibition at the Stedelijk Museum caused an uproar. The *vijftigers*, a group of experimental poets led by Lucebert, shocked the literary establishment. Many of these writers and artists gathered in brown cafés (*see chapter* **Cafés & Bars**) around Leidseplein.

WELFARE OR WELL-BEING?

The 1960s were one of the most colourful decades in Amsterdam's history. There were genuine official attempts to improve society and make it more prosperous. The IJ Tunnel eased communications to North Amsterdam and the national economy took off. There were high hopes for vast rehousing developments, such as the **Bijlmermeer** and there was influential new architecture by Aldo van Eyck and Herman Herzberger.

Yet the generous hand of the welfare state was being bitten. 'Welfare is not well-being', was a popular slogan. Discontent began on a variety of issues: the nuclear threat; rampant urban expansion and industrialisation; the consumer society and authority in general. Amsterdam saw the creation of popular movements similar to those in other West European cities, but with a zaniness all of its own. Because protest and dissent have always been a vital part of the Netherlands' democratic process, and the Dutch have a habit of keeping things in proportion, many popular demonstrations took a playful form.

PROVO PRANKS

The discontent gained focus in 1964, when pranks around 't Lieverdje statue, highlighting political or social problems, became the springboard for a new radical subculture, the Provos (*see* **Provocations**). Founded by Roel van Duyn, a philosophy student, the Provos only numbered about two dozen, but had a much wider appeal.

On 10 March 1966, protests about Princess Beatrix's wedding to Claus von Amsberg turned into a riot. Amsterdam's police chief was forced to resign, followed a year later by the city's mayor. As opinion turned against the council's large-scale planning, the Provos won 2.5 per cent of the municipal vote and a seat on the council in 1966. However, their manifesto – the so-called White Plans – tended towards the Utopian and by May 1967 the Provos had outgrown themselves and disbanded.

Van Duyn next led the Kabouters, named after a helpful gnome in Dutch folklore. They set up an alternative 'Orange Free State', with its own 'ministers' and policies, and had considerable success in the early 1970s, adopting some of the more realistic White Plans and winning five seats in Amsterdam. The movement disintegrated in 1981 amid quarrels about ideology.

The Provo actions somewhat overshadowed the beginnings of the Dutch feminist, gay and pacifist movements; for these, *see chapters* **Gay Amsterdam**, **Women's Amsterdam** *and* **Students**. However, the Provos forced little change on the traditional, conservative power-base.

HIPPY HEAVEN

Meanwhile, foreign hippies flocked to the city, attracted by its tolerant attitude to soft drugs. Although the possession of up to 30g (1oz) of hash wasn't decriminalised until 1978, the authorities turned a blind eye to its use, preferring to prosecute dealers, who increasingly pushed hard drugs. Amsterdam subsequently suffered a heroin (and AIDS) epidemic and has since developed a well-defined drugs policy (*see chapter* **Survival**).

The focal points of hippy culture were the **Melkweg** and **Paradiso**, both of which emitted such a pungent aroma of marijuana that it could be smelt hundreds of metres away in Leidseplein. In March 1969 John Lennon and Yoko Ono gave the city's subculture some global publicity through their 'sleep-in' for peace in the **Amsterdam Hilton**.

Towards the end of the decade, with the Dam and Vondelpark becoming unruly camp sites, public tolerance of the hippies waned. In the 1970s Amsterdam's popular culture shifted towards a tougher expression of disaffected urban youth. Yet Vondelpark, the Melkweg and the Dam remain a Mecca for both ageing and new age hippies, even into the 1990s.

HOUSING HORRORS

Perhaps the most significant catalyst for discontent in the 1970s – which exploded into full-scale civil conflict by the 1980s – was housing. Amsterdam's compact size and historic city centre had always been a nightmare for city planners. There was a dire housing shortage and many inner city homes were in need of drastic renovation. The population increased during the 1960s, reaching its peak (nearly 870,000) by 1964. The numbers were swelled by immigrants from the Netherlands' last major colony, Surinam. Many of these were dumped in the forbidding Bijlmermeer high-rise housing project (*see also chapters* **Architecture** *and* **By Area**) which quickly degenerated into a ghetto. It was here that an aeroplane crashed in October 1992. The number of fatalities was never ascertained because many victims were illegal residents and not registered.

The Metro link to the Bijlmermeer is itself a landmark to some of the most violent protests in Amsterdam's recent history. Passionate opposition erupted against the proposed clearance in February 1975 of a particularly sensitive site – the Jewish quarter of the Nieuwmarkt. Civil unrest culminated on 'Blue Monday', 24 March 1975, when heavy-handed police tactics once again sparked off violent clashes with residents and over 1,000 supporters. Police fired teargas into the homes of those who had refused to move out and battered down doors with armoured cars. Despite further clashes a few weeks later, the plans went ahead and the Metro was opened in 1980, though only one of the four lines planned for the city was completed.

City planners were shocked by the fervent opposition to their schemes for large, airy suburbs and the wholesale demolition of old neighbourhoods. It was simply not what people wanted; they cherished the narrow streets, the small squares and cosy corner cafés. The shortage of residential space in the city centre made it a target for property speculators. The public felt that the council was selling out to big

Provocations

Between 1965 and 1967, Amsterdam's Provos were the archetypal bonkers 1960s politics-as-theatre grouping. Their style not only influenced later anti-war demonstrations in America, but also set the tone for the Dutch capital's continuing love of all politics that lean liberal, and all theatre that is absurd and spectacular.

The movement was sparked by the meeting of two minds: that of 'anti-smoke magician' Robert Japser Grootveld, and that of anarchist Roel van Duyn. Grootveld was already known as an inspired freak after his one-man campaign against consumer society in general and smoking in particular. He gleefully picked up on tobacco addiction as a symbol for the enslavement of the consumer, and went about decorating billboard cigarette ads with a large 'K' for cancer. This got him 60 days in jail. He was soon back at it, hyping Amsterdam as the 'magical centre of the universe' and himself as some wacky voodoo high priest of the 'K-temple', a hang-out off the Leidseplein.

The K-temple became the happening place on a Saturday night. Grootveld would rave out some inspired anti-smoke sermon (himself often smoking to take on the burden of humanity's sins), accompanied by a communal chorus of 'ugge-ugge-ugge' – the chant of a smoker's hack. Other regulars included Johnny the Selfkicker, a bellowing poet who would go into a trance and throw himself from scarily high places, and the 'semi-doctor' Bart Hughes, who testified on the benefits of trepanation – the act of drilling a hole in one's head, said to open the third eye and induce a pleasantly permanent high. The end came on one such night with the temple catching fire under mysterious circumstances. A body-painted Grootveld danced on the roof while it burnt. For that he got a suspended sentence, and promptly went more public by moving his show outdoors to the Spui by the Lieverdje statue. It was the summer of 1965.

A figure of a boy in goofy knee socks that had been donated by a multinational tobacco company, the 'Little Darling' statue was deemed an auspicious spot to exorcise the demons of consumer addiction. The Saturday night theatrics continued, and the crowds swelled making the happenings yet more happening. But it took the responsible young anarchist, van Duyn to focus all the chaos into an agenda.

Roel van Duyn shared with the original artier types both a sense of humour and a media savvy, but after years of experience in the Ban The Bomb movement brought with him a more serious political agenda. He began distributing newsletters under the name of Provo, which were obviously meant to provoke (hence the name). Orchestrated mind-games had police busting houses for the possession of what turned out to be hay. The cops started confiscating issues of Provo and being a little looser with truncheons and arrests on Saturday nights. When the newly-dubbed Provos donated a white bicycle to the city for the use of all who happened to need it, with the hopes that many more would follow (a project attempted years later by the city council), the police reacted by impounding said bicycle.

There were other 'White Plans'. The 'White House Plan' promoted squatting and made free white paint available for redecorations. The 'White Corpse Plan' suggested that the asphalt be chiselled away from under each cyclist snuffed by a car and replaced with white cement as an eternal reminder. The 'White Constable Plan' envisioned cops in white who distributed lights for joints, chickens to the hungry and oranges to the thirsty.

Oranges, neatly enough, have the same representative colour as the Dutch Royal Family who were also in the limelight at the time. Daughter and present Queen, Beatrix, was to be married expensively in Amsterdam to ex-Nazi Claus von Amsberg. It was a touchy subject and paranoia ran rife. The Provos implemented a strategy of ridicule. Actions were rumoured for the wedding day: LSD in the water supply, LSD in the horsefeed, lion shit on the streets to craze the horses, laughing gas in the church...

Millions worldwide saw it on television. With a huge puff from a simple smoke-bomb, the Royal Carriage emerged like a dream from the clouded screen. It was live drama, a fairy tale wedding from hell – especially when the police started beating heads. The Provos won another media war and the Mayor and Chief of Police were sacked. Some of the more serious of the Provos even ended up getting elected into the city government, but that spelt the beginning of the end.

Finally the politico side, with van Duyn carrying the banner, formed the Kabouters to annoy the State from within the system, while the artier types just went on being arty on their own. Grootveld is currently hoping to bring floating styrofoam islands of greenery to the definitely ungreen waterways of Amsterdam. If you start seeing some colour, you will know who's responsible.

Hippies turned Dam Square into an unruly camp site.

business and complained that the city centre was becoming unaffordable for ordinary people. Eventually, in 1978 the council decided to improve housing through small-scale development, renovating houses street by street. But with an estimated 90,000 people (13 per cent of the city's population) still on Amsterdam's housing list in 1980, there was growing public concern about the shortages.

THE SQUAT MOVEMENT

Speculators who left property empty caused justifiable, acute resentment, which was soon mobilised into direct action – vacant buildings were occupied illegally by squatters. The squatting movement took off through two significant events in 1980. In March, police turned against the squatters for the first time and used tanks in evictions from a former office building in Vondelstraat; the ensuing battle attracted hundreds of demonstrators and flung the city into chaos. The building was quickly resquatted and the movement was further strengthened by the riots on Coronation Day a month later. Defeat and the expense of eviction forced the council to rethink its tactics.

In 1982, while the squatting movement reached its peak with an estimated 10,000 members in Amsterdam, clashes with police escalated. The eviction of Lucky Luyk, a lavish villa in the museum area of the city, was the most violent and expensive. Riots went on for three days and, after a tram went up in flames, the mayor was forced to declare a state of emergency. A year later, Amsterdam had a new mayor, Ed van Thijn, who took tough action to eradicate the squatters. One of the last of the city's important squats, Wyers, fell amid tear-gas in February 1984 and was pulled down to make way for a Holiday Inn. The squatters were no longer a force to be reckoned with, although their ideas of small-scale regeneration have since been absorbed into official planning.

BACK TO BASICS

Born and bred in Amsterdam, Ed Van Thijn embodied a new strand in Dutch politics. Although a socialist, he took tough action against 'unsavoury elements' – hard drug traders, petty criminals, squatters – and upgraded facilities to attract new businesses and tourists. A new national political era also emerged, with the election in 1982 of Rotterdam millionaire Ruud Lubbers as leader of the then centre-right coalition government of Christian Democrats and right-wing Liberals (VVD). He saw to it that the welfare system and government subsidies were trimmed to ease the country's large budget deficit, and aimed to revitalise the economy with more business-like policies (*see chapter* **Business**). In February 1984 Van Thijn resigned to become Home Affairs Minister.

The price of Amsterdam's new affluence (among most groups, except the poorest) has been a swing towards commercialism. Van Thijn has found it hard to live down a clumsy remark he made about turning Amsterdam into a 'pleasure park'. Yet the evidence of his intentions can be seen in the new casino, luxury apartments and shopping complex at the Leidseplein and the massive redevelopment of its docklands (*see chapters* **Amsterdam by Area** *and* **Amsterdam Today**). Van Thijn also pushed through plans to build the Stadhuis-Muziektheater (City Hall-Opera House) complex, dubbed 'Stopera!' by the campaign waged against it (*see chapter* **Sightseeing**).

But the hordes of squatters were largely supplanted by well-groomed yuppies. Flashy cafés, galleries and nouvelle cuisine restaurants replaced the alternative scene and a mood of calm settled on the city. Still, a classic example of Dutch free expression was provoked by the city's mid-1980s campaign to host the 1992 Olympics. Amsterdam became the first city ever to send an (ultimately successful) official anti-Olympics delegation.

Amsterdam Today

**As the city authorities try to soften Amsterdam's image abroad,
what are the consequences for those that live, work and play here?**

The biggest question today is whether Amsterdam is the urban-developmental haven it is cracked up to be, or whether a decade of courting international business and pandering to Dutch banks and property developers has jeopardised its unique atmosphere.

This swing to the right began in the early 1980s, when, with much of the city centre apparently lost to drug dealers or tatty shops and bars, and regularly disrupted by battles between squatters and police, the city collectively agreed to clean the place up, attract a 'better' visitor and reposition itself in the increasingly international competition for investment.

The private-public partnership devised to solve these problems has largely been successful. Once peppered with lurking junkies, areas such as Zeedijk and Nieuwmarkt have been gentrified; the city has a swanky new casino and several new shopping malls while the inner city squats have mostly been emptied or legalised. A rolling infrastructure improvement programme has seen many of Amsterdam's streets repaved and utilities re-laid. That this has been achieved at the same time as the sex, drugs and rock'n'roll cliché of Amsterdam's attractions has remained intact is a testament to the durability of the city's mythology. Although the Dutch tourist board sticks with the gently marketable 'tulips, windmills and clogs' image, it can't be too much of a secret that many tourists are attracted to Amsterdam by its liberal traditions.

SEX & DRUGS & ROCK & ROLL

Sex remains a two billion guilder-plus domestic business, split roughly 50-50 between pornography and prostitution. The average Dutchman contributed ƒ260 to the sex industry in 1994, according to a study by Erasmus University (compared with ƒ12,50 per woman). Significant recent developments in the Amsterdam sex trade have included the building of two *tippelzones* – legal kerb-crawling areas – complete with cafés for the girls, police patrols, council-provided litter bins for condoms and bizarre rows of 'cattle stalls' for the 'transactions'. One in the deserted eastern docks was pretty uncontroversial but a later *tippelzone*

built in the new suburb of Sloterdijk encountered strong local opposition. The council, determined to grapple with the problem of heroin-addicted prostitutes patrolling behind Centraal Station, has stood firm. In 1995, the Prostitution Information Centre on Ouderkerksplein organised a brief trial of male window prostitutes, for female clients. No significant help has, however, been extended to the often underage and usually foreign boys involved in homosexual street prostitution, and problems of exploitation, particularly of Eastern European and Far Eastern women, remain to be solved. But with the relative legal protection and public acknowledgement the profession enjoys, at least there's a chance of doing so.

Technological innovations in the pornography trade included live sex shows in the Red Light District being distributed on the Internet (*see chapter* **Media**). Amsterdam's online reputation may well find itself the victim of shrill US-led protests in the near future, and it will be interesting to see how the authorities react.

As for drugs, in April 1995 the new socialist mayor, Schelto Patijn, announced a crackdown on coffeeshops, promising to close around half Amsterdam's 400 dope dens and tighten up the application of rules to the remainder. Whether this was a calculated piece of bluster designed to placate Holland's Schengen 'Euro-superstate' partners, we can't say, but the threat has yet to materialise. While raids and closures do occur, they don't amount as yet to a crackdown. Even the most committed Amsterdam tokers agree there are too many poor quality dives and there's been no real protest.

However, even ardent critics of coffeeshops dislike having President Chirac trying to dictate drug policies. When Atomic Jacques cancelled a trip to Holland early in 1996 – explicitly because of his disapproval of the country's drugs laws – the Dutch simply pointed to their vastly superior HIV and drug addiction figures compared with France's and told him to shove his visit.

In a curious court case, Conscious Dreams (http://neturl.nl/codreams/), a shop selling legal psychotropic plant products including dried magic mushrooms, was busted and got off by re-classifying itself as a greengrocers (and therefore allowed to sell fresh 'shrooms, which they do to this day). The city retains a small but knowledgeable and well-sourced underground researching the more arcane aspects of the psychedelic experience, including an active ayuhuasca (a holy Amazon drink) church.

The Amsterdam establishment's policy of tolerance and compromise (or failing that, the crack ME riot police) has seen off both the Green intellectual threat and the the challenge posed by the anarchist-squatter movement. Amsterdam's future now lies firmly in its relationship to the flows of increasingly mobile global capital. The city may once, briefly, have appeared to belong to the people, but today it is firmly in the pocket of the grey financial acronyms of banks ABN-AMRO, ING and KPN.

VIRTUAL AMSTERDAM

As Amsterdam wealth has gone virtual, so its population has begun to follow. 1994 saw the establishment of the city's newest *wijk*, or neighbourhood, The Digital City. A remarkable example of the relaxed partnership between different factions that is possible in Amsterdam, the DDS, as it's known, was built by former anarcho-hackers and financed by the city council. With its own mayor, and increasingly complex and graphical capabilities, the DDS offers a mix of access to councillors and city information, one-on-one chat, an increasing range of commercial services, electronic art and Web Home Pages. It has become the model for a Benelux-wide network of digital cities and has attracted interest – and tens of thousands of visitors – from around the globe (*see chapter* **Media** for details).

In addition, a small but talented base of theorists and practitioners, taking advantage of the California cyber-elite's fondness for Amsterdam as watering hole, has given the city some groundbreaking conferences over the years. The Dutch Design Institute has been established here for three years and organises the Doors of Perception conference each November; the Society for Old and New Media has sprung up, housed in the newly refurbished, historical Waag building in Nieuwmarkt; cultural institutions such as the Paradiso and the Balie have hosted significant cyber-events such as the Next Five Minutes and the Galactic Hacker Party, while the RAI convention centre regularly attracts a large mainstream audience to digital events.

The upshot of all this activity is that although physical protest may no longer be a feature of the Amsterdam scene, resistance to the model of the future being presented by the multinational institutions and governments – a problem-free Electronic New World Order – is relatively well-developed in Amsterdam. The questions of privacy, freedom of speech, security, electronic cash and access to tools within the increasingly important digital domain – questions whose answers are currently being forced upon American citizens but which remain open in Europe –- are being actively explored by several Amsterdam-based institutions.

MILLENNIAL WORRIES

Back in the Amsterdam of flesh and blood reality, problems loom on the horizon, and as darkly as in any other European city. The developmental issues mentioned earlier are merely the surface eruptions of wider questions at the end of the century: where are we going to put all the garbage, find the low-cost housing and create jobs? How big should the city become, and who should be allowed to live here? How will we travel to and through it?

Some of these questions have been answered better than others. The thorny issue of foreigners, who currently make up around 30 per cent of the city's population, is still only just being asked.

Professor Christopher Mullard, father of anti-racist education in Britain, took on the first European chair in ethnic studies and education at the University of Amsterdam in 1984. He pioneered research revealing 'institutionalised' racism in Dutch economic, social and cultural life, and accusations against him by university authorities led to a libel action settled out of court.

The reaction of Holland's efficient bureaucracy to fears of being 'swamped' by refugees from Eastern Europe and the southern Mediterranean has been to computerise everything that moves, either in or out of the country, issue everyone with ID cards following a once-and-for-all amnesty of illegal aliens, criminalise employers of black labour and sign the Schengen Agreement with its mainland European neighbours to cooperate along similar lines, and share computer information.

One result of relevance to tourists should be the reminder that 123 Leeds United fans with tickets to last season's football match against Eindhoven were arrested and spent the night in jail – for not having their passports on them. Several were later arrested entering other European countries when their records had been passed on to other police forces. It is worth bearing in mind before trying to test the boundaries of Amsterdam's famously cool police. Dealings with the Amsterdam cops as a victim or innocent tourist is generally a pleasant experience – which is just as well since nine per cent of all tourists and a record-breaking 13 per cent of British tourists are the victim of a crime while in Holland, most of which happen in Amsterdam.

Beneath the surface, the police are currently registering an all time low in public satisfaction. The so-called IRT Affair, still unravelling in Dutch courts, has uncovered wide-scale and systematic corruption, including the sale of confiscated drugs back to the criminal world. Complaints against the police, principally for discriminatory arrest, were up more than 40 per cent in 1994.

The blame for some of these bugs in the Amsterdam system can be laid at the feet of the treasured national principle of *verzuiling* (compartmentalisation) – what many foreigners would consider an overriding concern for the ordered separation of people, objects and ideas into meticulously segregated – and thus inflexible – categories.

PLANS & PLANNERS

Some blame must also lie with the change in city planning principles over the last decade. The human-centred architecture that made the city so user-friendly for the last four centuries has now been abandoned. The new suburbs of Sloterdijk and Hoofdorp, for example, look like blown-up architect's models; mediocre car-orientated office blocks separated by vast, windy and intimidating open spaces. Recent housing projects have bifurcated between waterside yuppie flats and unimaginative, functional boxes.

The logic of the planners was impeccable: Amsterdam's well-educated workforce, proficient language skills and relatively Anglo-Saxon business attitudes meant it could compete with Paris, Berlin or London as a location for European headquarters of global firms. The city would capitalise on traditional trading and distribution skills, extending them to the new virtual world of telecommunications.

The infrastructural consequences of all this have started to produce protest. A projected new North-South Metro line is deeply unpopular and uncertain to go ahead, as is the extension of the four current runways at Schiphol Airport and the addition of a fifth. Passions are already high; the recent air crash into the flats in the Bijlmer, an Amsterdam suburb, showed the city the price it had to pay for having such a conveniently-located international airport. Just how big does it have to be, and for whom? Dutch Friends of the Earth (*Milieudefensie*) have bought crucial land around Schiphol and sold it off in small lots to delay construction, but if the extensions get the absolute go-ahead, these can be compulsorily bought.

Elsewhere, long-standing plans by a Danish architect to re-develop the museums neighbourhood could also get underway in 1996. The plan includes removal of more than 200 trees from the Museumplein, extending the Stedelijk and van Gogh museums, and building an underground hypermarket, bus station and car park for 1000 cars. It remains to be seen how effective protests by the genteel local population will be.

Also in the city centre, there was a recent loss of nerve over radical plans to develop the entire Amsterdam docklands waterfront by Rotterdam-based architecture superstar Rem Koolhaas. The partnership between the council and the banks fell

One of the city's squatted buildings.

apart when the latter decided the plans did not realise sufficient return on investment (in other words they wanted more luxury flats and office space than the city did), and to date, only a piecemeal development on the KNSM Island has been completed.

Amsterdam's shilly-shallying about its future is probably symptomatic of a realisation that ignoring the needs of the local population in favour of courting fickle corporate wealth does not necessarily lead to the best city to live in.

Amsterdam by Area

Amsterdam
by Area

Amsterdam may be diminutive, but its different districts are divertingly diverse.

Few visitors to Amsterdam venture beyond the *grachtengordel* (girdle of canals) that defines the city centre, except to stroll south to the area around Museumplein, where the major museums are concentrated. As you might expect with an historic city, the further from the centre you travel, the newer the areas are. Within the centre are the medieval buildings, the old port, the earliest and prettiest canals and the seventeenth-century merchants' houses. Slightly further out are quarters built to house the various waves of incoming workers.

After World War II, new self-contained 'garden neighbourhoods' were built further out, including those to the west at Osdorp and Slotermeer. More recent building projects have been completed nearer the centre: in the east, around the old port area (*see below* **The Waterfront**), new homes have been built to replace old housing and warehouses

are being converted. Amsterdam Noord, across the River IJ behind Centraal Station, has always been considered to be out on a limb, but it has been opened up, traffic permitting, by the IJ tunnel. Apart from the impressive Flora Park, there is very little to see in Amsterdam Noord and the best part of a trip there will probably be the ferry journey for pedestrians and cyclists which leaves from behind Centraal Station.

The Red-Light District

This area, found roughly in a triangle formed by Centraal Station, the Nieuwmarkt and the Dam, is where Amsterdam garners most of its international reputation. The world's desperate and horny imagine breasts eagerly pancaked against red neon-framed windows, canals awash with bodily

Everything you always wanted to know about sex – the **Prostitutes Information Centre.**

fluids. The postcards present a sort of small, cutesy Vegas. The cheesy joke shop has here become the sex shop, with electric palm buzzers and nose glasses being replaced by multi-orificed inflatables and huge dildos. Most of the history – of which there is plenty; this is the oldest part of Amsterdam – has been greasily veneered with that oldest of trades: marketing. Sex is secondary to window shopping. People do buy (it's a ƒ1 billion per year trade) but mostly they wander in groups, stopping here and there to gawp. The choice is ample with 5,000 professionals, 2,000 of whom are available on any given day. Most of these window girls are self-employed and even though prostitution is technically illegal, the women are taxed and have a union, De Rode Draad, that has represented them since 1984. They are indeed, mostly women. Despite attempts to launch male and transsexual prostitution, men have so far found it difficult to get their dicks into this particular door of opportunity.

As at more traditional markets like the Albert Cuyp, where cheese merchants line up alongside cheese merchants and fishmongers group with fishmongers, women of similar specialisations also tend to clump together. Sultry Latins gather on the Molensteeg and the beginning of Oudezijds Achterburgwal, African mamas on the Oudekerkplein, ambigiously sexed Thais on Stoofstraat, and the vaguely model-ish but definitely anorexic on Trompettersteeg, Amsterdam's smallest street. But there is much else to absorb in this most iconoclastic of neighbourhoods. Prostitutes, clerics, schoolkids, junkies, carpenters and cops all interact with a strange brand of social cosiness. The tourists are mere voyeurs. It's all fun and harmless enough, as long as you remember that window girls do not like having their pictures taken and that drug dealers react to eye contact like a dog to a bone.

Zeedijk

Facing away from Centraal Staion, on the left is the St Olaf Chapel (locally known as the Cheese Church because it was the cheese exchange for many years). To the right of it one can enter Zeedijk, a street with a rich and tattered history. Before this dyke was built around 1300, Amsterdam was a fishing village with barely enough bog to stand on. But by the fifteenth and sixteenth centuries, with the East India Company raking in the imperialist dollars, Zeedijk was where sailors could come to catch up on their boozing, brawling and bonking. Just off the street towards the harbour down Oudezijds Kolk, one can spot the **Scheiierstoren** – the 'Wailing Tower'. Wives would cry there, perhaps with relief, when husbands set off on a voyage, and then cry again if the ship returned with the bad news that the husband was lost at sea. If that was the case, it was a short walk to continue

life as a 'merry widow' on Zeedijk. Prostitution was often the female equivalent of joining the navy: the last economic option.

In this century, Zeedijk was sparked with cultural diversity. In the 1930s the first openly gay establishments appeared. At the closed Café Maandje (Zeedijk 65) there is still a window shrine to legendary owner Bet van Beeren (1902-67), who must surely go down in history as the original Lesbian Biker Chick. In the 1950s all the jazz greats, from Chet Baker to Gerry Mulligan, came to jam and hang in the many after-hours clubs. Unfortunately, this marked the street as a place where heroin could be scored. By the 1970s, the street was crowded with dealers, junkies and indifferent cops, and most of the restaurants and cafés rented their tables to dealers. The magic number aspired to by junkies was 27 – ƒ25 for the stuff and ƒ2 for a drink that the owners insisted on to retain the establishment's façade. Amsterdam's reputation was littered with needles and bits of foil.

In recent years, police claim to have cleaned the street up. And indeed, the scene is much less intimidating. New businesses flourish: the famed dance, ambient and easy tune label **Outland Records** has its store at number 22, **Demask** offers its posh line of leathers and latexes at number 64. Excellent cheap Chinese food can be found at the New King, number 115-117.

Nieuwmarkt

Where Zeedijk ends at the broad square of Nieuwmarkt, your view will be captured by the huge and menacing castle-like **De Waag** – 'the Weighing House'. And if what motivates your walk through this area is to meditate on humankind's darkest sides, you can imagine the body parts that used to garnish the Waag's southeast side as a baleful warning. This is where public executions took place. Here people were tortured, hung, shot, or when Napoleon held influence, guillotined. There were always plenty of corpses for the medical guild to dissect, or Rembrandt to study and paint. One assumes none of the leftovers were sold at the open air market that has always existed here. To get truly depressed, imagine how in the dark days of the Nazi occupation this square was surrounded by barbed wire and used to gather those from the nearby Jewish quarter who were to be shipped off to concentration camps.

The **Nieuwmarkt** was also the site of many riots around 1980 when the city was busy demolishing housing to build the Metro. The prefab police station that blocks the Kloveniersburgwal canal's view to the south is a souvenir of this time. The streets leading west contain Amsterdam's small Chinatown, while the side streets lead into the reddest part of the Red-Light District.

The Bijlmer

On 25th November 1968, Alderman Elsenburg handed a bouquet of flowers and some keys to a middle-aged, professional couple, the first Amsterdam family to move into 'the city of the future'. These urban pioneers had moved out of their cramped apartment in the city centre to enjoy their dream in the Bijlmer, an experiment in social engineering and urban planning that had excited city planners all over the world.

Their spacious six-room apartment had all the new amenities: central heating, connections for a washing machine, and loads of room. The ten-storey apartment buildings with open walkways were arranged in a symmetrical honeycomb pattern typical of post-war architecture. Only 15 minutes away from the city centre by the not-yet-completed metro, the high-rises of the Bijlmer were located in a lush parkland of grass, trees and acres of space not found in the city centre. The new neighbourhood was going to be a great place to raise the kids.

Swiss architect Le Corbusier envisioned such communities in the 1930s. The idea was to separate work, living, shopping, recreation and traffic. His plan for a new urban space with cement high-rise apartments and plenty of green spaces coincided with the post-war optimism of the 1950s and the social agenda of the 1960s. The result was the Bijlmer which, like so many similar projects in the western world's sprawling cities, with hindsight now seems doomed to messy failure.

But there is more to the story of the Bijlmer (officially the Southeast, or Zuidoost), and there is a (reasonably) happy ending. Of course it is easy to see the failures. The concrete slabs are ugly. There is some crime. In the 1970s, immigrants from Africa and the last Dutch colony, Surinam moved in: real social problems coupled with white fears accelerated the flight of the early professionals. The inhuman sociology of the large apartment blocks offered little to slow the exodus.

But the Bijlmer is no slum. Crime in the Bijlmer as a whole is no worse than the Amsterdam average, even if some areas are dodgy at night. Its inhabitants are poorer than those in the old city, but there has not been the social breakdown as in similar neighbourhoods near Paris, for instance.

Furthermore, the past 30 years have seen construction and renewal in the Bijlmer, including many suburban-style developments in the '80s and '90s. Large shopping centres, futuristic glass office buildings, and the Academic Medical Center help the region to provide employment for over 45,000 people. The area is filled with excit-

ing modern architecture, including the new Ajax football stadium and a luxury multiplex cinema. Some of the high-rises are being demolished and replaced with more traditional housing. And beautiful Lake Gaasperplas and its surrounding parks are a peaceful retreat and recreation area.

However, on October 4, 1992, tragedy struck the Bijlmer. Around 6.30pm, an El Al cargo plane crashed into an apartment building. A huge, hot explosion destroyed much of the building and ignited the rest. People in flames jumped from their burning apartments. With no leaves on the autumn trees, thousands of nearby residents had unobstructed views of the tragedy.

There is a memorial to the victims of the crash: an unglamorous, unofficial, but nonetheless moving, community tribute to the 40 residents and the three flight crew who died in the accident. Built around a leafy tree, it consists of plaques, pictures and poetry from friends and family members.

By going to the Bijlmer you'll see a part of town that is foreign to many Amsterdammers. To get there, take the metro in the direction of Gaasperplas from any station in the city centre. Even better, rent a bike and take it on the metro. Look for the blue 'bikes here' square on one train door in every six. Your bike pays half price.

If you don't have much time, ride through the Bijlmer all the way to Gaasperplas, which is about 20 minutes from Waterlooplein station. Walk to Lake Gaasperplas, enjoy an ice cream on the shore and head back. If you make the trip within an hour you only have to pay for the metro once.

If it's Saturday afternoon, and you have time to kill, get off at Ganzenhoef and walk through the thriving market. When you get to the end of the market, turn left and head south along the metro tracks towards the plane crash memorial.

Boom Chicago gives tours of the Bijlmer from May to September (*see chapter* **Theatre**).

'De Wallen'

The canals Oudezijds Voorburgwal and Oudezijds Achterburgwal, with their interconnecting streets, are where carnal sin screams loudest. You are in the heart of the hole when you find the **Oude Kerk**, a rambling church with parts that date back to 1300. It is as if the church's famous large organ has played pied piper to all that is sleazy. The inscription over the bridal chamber, which translates as 'Marry in haste, Mourn at leisure', reflects the church's jaded location.

The Oudezijds Voorburgwal was known in the sixteenth century as the 'Velvet Canal' because it had the wealthiest of residents. Now the velvet has been replaced by red velour. Irony mounts as one notes the density of churches, chapels and orders on this canal. The **Museum Amstelkring**, formerly a clandestine attic church, can be found at number 40, the former convent Agnietenkapel is at number 231, while reps from the Salvation Army seem to lurk at every corner. On the Spinhuissteeg, opposite the **Cannabis Museum**, one encounters the Spinhuis, another former convent that used to set 'wayward women' to work spinning wool as penance. The male equivalent was at Heligstraat 9, where audiences watched prisoners being branded and beaten with a bull's penis. In a further historical foreshadowing of this neighbourhood's contemporary SM scene, the entrance gate sports a statue resembling a scolding dominatrix.

Warmoesstraat

It's hard to believe that Amsterdam's oldest street was once the finest of lanes, providing sharp contrast to its then evil and rowdy twin, Zeedijk. The poet Vondel ran his hosiery business at Warmoesstraat 101, Mozart's dad would be trying to scalp tickets at the posh bars for his young son's concerts, and Marx would later come here to write from one of the many inns. But with the influx of sailors, the laws of demand dictated a fall from grace. Adam and Eve in their salad days can still be seen etched in stone at number 25, but for the rest, this street has fallen to accommodating the low-end traveller. No shame, and the recent appearance of a few stores, galleries, and especially the **Condomerie** are bringing some brighter colours back to the strip.

Waterlooplein

To the south-east of the Red-Light District, the Waterlooplein and its immediate surroundings are a peculiar mix of old and new architectural styles. If you leave the Nieuwmarkt along St Antoniebreestraat you will pass several bars, coffeeshops and chic clothes shops, making it a good escape route out of the throbbing Red-Light District. The modern yet tasteful council housing which lines this street was designed by local architect Theo Bosch. Crossing the bridge at the end of St

'Shop at **Waterlooplein market** or the photographer gets it!'

Antoniebreestraat you arrive at the **Rembrandt-huis**; or take an immediate right down the steps to the **Waterlooplein** market.

The city council decided in 1931 to widen the streets between the Nieuwmarkt area, Weesperplein and the Plantage to cope with increasing traffic. World War II put these plans on hold, but afterwards they were adapted and carried out with greater alacrity, largely because of the depopulation of what had previously been the Jewish Quarter. By the 1960s almost all reminders of the old Jewish Quarter had been erased. Jodenbreestraat, Rapenburg and Muiderstraat were all widened to accommodate traffic and residential buildings were saved only along one side of these roads.

All these commuting routes join at Mr Visserplein. Apart from the **Portuguese Synagogue** and the **Joods Historisch Museum** (Jewish Historical Museum), Mr Visserplein is home to little more than a roundabout where five main roads conjoin. The section of the IJ tunnel route which was laid under Mr Visserplein is soon to be closed for good and filled with sand, removing a hang-out for drug addicts while at the same time reducing the flow of traffic.

If you leave Mr Visserplein from the west side you will arrive at the nineteenth-century Mozes en Aäronkerk. This church, covered in political murals, has been used as a social and cultural centre since 1970. Squashed in between that and the **Stadhuis-Muziektheater** (Stopera) complex is the **Waterlooplein market**.

The area where the Stopera now stands was once a Jewish ghetto. Jews settled in Amsterdam from about 1600, when they came to escape persecution throughout Europe, and there are several reminders of the area's past (*see chapter* **Sightseeing**). Demolition work to make room for the Stopera, the road and the Metro destroyed the

The **Joods Historisch Museum.**

sixteenth- and seventeenth-century buildings. The Muziektheater complex now dominates the view over the Blauwbrug (Blue Bridge) which used to be the main route into the city from the east. The current bridge was built in 1873, but a plaque depicting the original (taken from a demolished house) has been placed at the entrance of the Muziektheater car park.

The Plantage

The area known as the Plantage lies south east of Mr Visserplein and is reached via Muiderstraat, with the Portuguese Synagogue on the right. The Plantage has barely altered since its initial foundations were laid, mainly because it has always been residential. The wide, attractive Plantage Middenlaan winds past **Hortus Botanicus**, **Artis Zoo** and towards the **Tropenmuseum**. The last two were built on land that was part of an eighteenth-century plan to create a garden city for rich citizens who did not have a house on a canal. The Jews settled here too and the area was redeveloped on nineteenth-century diamond money (diamond cutting was one of the few trades open to Jews). The splendid headquarters of the diamond cutters' trade union still stands on Henri Polaklaan and other extant buildings such as the Gassan, the Saskiahuis and Coster stand as reminders that Amsterdam's most profitable trade was based in this area.

The brightly coloured Van Eyck's **Moedershuis**, a mother and child refuge – where children were smuggled to safety during World War II – is on Plantage Middenlaan and on the other side of the road is the attractive Huize St Jacob, an old people's home, rebuilt on the site of an earlier one, using the original stone portal.

The Plantage is still wealthy, with a somewhat faded charm. Its graceful buildings and tree-lined streets provide a residential area much sought after by those who want to live centrally, but away from the tourists. The area has already undergone extensive redevelopment and work is still continuing. Past the Muiderpoort city gate, the old army barracks and dockside warehouses have been turned into luxury housing association flats and houses.

Rembrandtplein

Over the Blauwbrug on the other side of the Amstel is Rembrandtplein. Not much to look at now, this used to be called Reguliersmarkt, where Amsterdam's butter market was found. In 1876 the square was renamed in honour of Rembrandt and there is a statue of the Dutch master in the centre of the gardens here, gazing in the direction of the Jewish Quarter. Although there is no market, it is probably the centre of more commercial activity

Museumplein – *anonymous sculpture still protesting the 1991 Van Gogh exhibition.*

now than ever before, with neon signs and loud music blaring out of the cafés, bars and restaurants on all sides. Two bars particularly worth visiting on this square are **Café Schiller**, for its sumptuous art deco interior, and Ritz, for its massive murals of Fred Astaire, Ginger Rogers and Richard Burton, among other film celebs.

Leidseplein

Tourists and Amsterdammers pack Leidseplein to drink at pavement cafés, listen to the buskers and soak up the atmosphere. It lies on the southwest edge of the *grachtengordel* and although called a square, it is in fact an L-shape, running from the end of Leidsestraat to the bridge over Singelgracht.

In the current climate of city-centre traffic reduction schemes, this square is a reminder that such ideas are not new. During the Middle Ages, carts and wagons were banned from the centre of Amsterdam. People heading for the city had to leave their vehicles in *pleinen*, or squares. At the end of the road from Leiden was a 'cart park', surrounded by warehouses and establishments catering for this captive clientèle.

Leidseplein has always been a centre for one reason or another. Artists and writers used to congregate here in the 1920s and 1930s and it was the scene of pre-war clashes between Communists and Fascists. During the war it was a focus for protests which were ruthlessly broken up by the occupying Nazis; there's a commemorative plaque on nearby Kerkstraat where a number of people were killed. More recently, Leidseplein is the venue for celebrations whenever Ajax win any-

thing (which is quite often) and the mini-riots which usually ensue and which the police take in their stride.

The café society associated with Leidseplein began in earnest with the city's first bar to incorporate a terrace: the Café du Théâtre. It was demolished in 1877, 20 years before Kromhout's impressive **American Hotel** – now a prominent meeting place – was completed at the south-west end of the square. Opposite the American is a building (dating from 1882) which reflects Leidseplein's transformation into its current state as architectural billboard. The enormous illuminated Drum and Hitachi adverts add nothing to the building's former grandeur.

The overriding feature of the square is the people who gather there. During the summer at least 1,000 seats are available on café terraces. The tolerant attitude of the Amsterdam authorities means that there's always plenty going on: Leidseplein is one of the few legal open-air stages for street performers (this does not necessarily mean many are very good) and a market for hawkers of trinkets.

On leaving Leidseplein you are likely to take either Leidsestraat or Weteringschans. The first choice is the one to take for any kind of shopping expedition and the latter leads past the **Paradiso** and eventually to the **Rijksmuseum** and the canal boat departure point.

Before you get that far, you will no doubt notice Max Euweplein, which backs onto the canal. There is a grand entrance with pillars forming a portal, on which is inscribed a Latin motto, roughly translating as 'Man does not piss against the wind'. The architects designed it to resemble an Italian *piazza*, with its shallow waterfall and steps. Initially it was crammed with exclusive shops and cafés, but many had to close leaving mostly tack and souvenir shops behind. It is still a pleasant alternative route to the **Vondelpark**. If you're going to stop for a drink, check out the interior of Café Max, the terrace of the Leidsebocht or the **Lido Complex**, which comprises a café, a restaurant, a casino and a theatre. Behind the Leidseplein, off the Leidsestraat, are numerous restaurants, cafés and snack bars of every description, so that's where to head if you're in need of sustenance.

The Museum Quarter

Part of the *Oud-Zuid* (Old South), one of the wealthiest areas in the city, the Museum Quarter's border runs along the Rijksmuseum and Vondelpark in the north, down Emmastraat to Reijnier Vinkeleskade and up along the Hobbemakade in the east.

A century ago this area was still officially outside the city limits and consisted of little more than vegetable patches. There were seven windmills and a candle factory which, because of the horrible smell it produced, had been built far from the centre of Amsterdam. Towards the end of the century the city expanded rapidly, and the city fathers saw the need to build an upper-class neighbourhood between the working-class areas to the west and south.

*Lizards lounging at **Leidseplein**.*

Most of the beautiful mansions, with their characteristic Art Deco gateways and stained glass windows, were built around the turn of the century. The exclusive shopping streets PC Hooftstraat and Van Baerlestraat are known throughout the country for their élite selection of designer shops and deliciously expensive restaurants. The heart of it all is Museumplein, the city's largest square, bordered by the **Rijksmuseum**, the **Stedelijk Museum**, the **van Gogh Museum** and the **Concertgebouw**.

Museumplein is not really an authentic Amsterdam square, either in shape or character: its irregular oblong shape has been causing the city problems since its development in 1872. It originally served as a location for the World Exhibition of 1883 and was then rented out to the Amsterdam ice-skating club between 1900 and 1936. During the Depression, the field was put to use as a sports ground, and during World War II the Germans built four bunkers and a concrete shelter on it, which remained until 1952. In 1953 Museumstraat, the large road that divides the square in two, was completed; it is now known as the shortest motorway in the world and can be extremely dangerous at times. However, plans are afoot to make the square more pivotal for the city, with better facilities. The local borough will be investing millions in restyling Museumplein to make it a more visitor-friendly green open space without the thoroughfare. It is planned that the motorway will eventually be closed off, an underground car park constructed and the van Gogh and Stedelijk museums expanded.

Roemer Visscherstraat is a quiet street leading into Vondelpark and one could easily pass it by. But for those interested in architecture it is worth taking a look at the houses from numbers 20 to 30. Each represents a different country built in the appropriate 'national' style. Russia comes complete with a miniature dome, Italy has been painted pastel pink and Spain's candy stripes have made it one of the street's favourites.

The Pijp

The colourful area of the Pijp (pipe) is the best known of the working-class quarters built in the late nineteenth century, when a population boom burst the city's seams.

To make the most of the highly priced land, every square metre was utilised, resulting in standard long, narrow streets. Thus the official name of 'Area YY' was soon dropped in favour of a nickname, 'De Pijp'. Because rents were still too high for many tenants, they were forced to let rooms to students and it was they who gave the area its bohemian character, together with the numerous Dutch writers who lived here, such as Heijermans, De Haan and Bordewijk. Many painters (including

Sarphatipark – *the Pijp's miniature answer to the Bois de Boulogne.*

Mondriaan) had studios here too, and the area was swarming with brothels and pubs.

At the turn of the century, the Pijp was a radical socialist area. Although the area has lost much of its radicalism since then, the students remain; families with children have all fled to suburbia. The number of cheap one- or two-bedroom apartments, combined with the almost central location, make the area very attractive to students, young single people and couples. The area also has the densest gay population in Amsterdam.

Over the last 35 years many immigrants have also found their way into the area and set up shop. The Pijp now houses a mixture of nationalities, providing locals with plenty of Islamic butchers, Surinamese, Spanish, Indian and Turkish delicatessens and grocery stores selling exotic food. Restaurants offer authentic Syrian, Moroccan, Surinamese, Pakistani, Chinese and Indian cuisine. They are all reasonably priced (which makes up for the often extraordinary interior décor) and most offer a take-away service.

The largest daily market in the Netherlands, **Albert Cuypmarkt** is the main focus for the area and attracts thousands of customers every day. It's the core of the Pijp streetlife and generally spills into the adjoining roads: the junctions of Sweelinckstraat, Ferdinand Bolstraat and Eerste Van der Helststraat, north into the lively Gerard Douplein and south towards Sarphatipark. This small but pleasant park was designed by Samuel Sarphati as a miniature Bois de Boulogne and, on a sunny day, you can just about see what he meant. During 1994

the park was entirely renovated and restored.

On the corner of Stadhouderskade and Ferdinand Bolstraat stands the **Heineken Brewery**. Production was stopped in 1988 but there are still tours around the building. Only the museum part of the brewery has been preserved, the rest was demolished and new luxury apartments were built on four levels, including high street shops on the ground floor. Since the beginning of 1996 this has been called Marie Heinekenplein after the painter (1844-1930) – in keeping with the other street names in the Pijp. Marie Heineken was also related to the founder of the brewery, Weinand Heineken, so using her name kills two birds with one stone. Her work can be seen at the **Amsterdam Historisch Museum**. Opposite the new building, at Ferdinand Bolstraat 4, is Visser barber's shop, where about ten hairdressers line up to cut hair in formation, at the bargain rate of *f*16.

Beyond the stall-filled Albert Cuypstraat, across Ferdinand Bolstraat, is the coach-party attraction of **van Moppe's Diamond factory**. This building dominates the Ruysdaelkade junction, the Pijp's red-light district.

Over 250 artists live in the vicinity of the Pijp and although it is no Greenwich Village, the area's creative community is active and gaining status in a district where most streets are named after their illustrious forebears (Jan Steen, Ferdinand Bol, Gerard Dou, Jacob van Campen). The *Kunstroute De Pijp* is a yearly exhibition of local work, displayed in the windows of shops, cafés and offices. Beyond the market and its environs

Postmodern pillars at **Max Euweplein.**

There is always a queue outside the little shop, no matter what time of day. Hidden halfway down Eerste Jan Steenstraat is a rather special bric-a-brac shop, **Nic-Nic**, which is a paradise for 1950s and 1960s freaks.

Running parallel to Albert Cuypstraat, the Ceintuurbaan has little of note for the visitor, with the exception of the buildings at 251-255: there are few other houses in the city that incorporate giant green gnomes with red hats in their wooden façades.

The Jordaan

The Jordaan area is roughly sock-shaped with its often-disputed borders at Brouwersgracht, Leidsegracht, Lijnbaansgracht and Prinsengracht. A good way to view its streets and canals is to climb the tower of the **Westerkerk**. At 85 metres high, one of the tallest structures in Amsterdam, it also makes a useful landmark. It's also to be avoided by anyone with vertigo.

The Jordaan emerged when the city was extended in the early part of the seventeenth century and was originally designated for the working classes, as well as providing a haven for victims of religious persecution, such as Jews and Huguenots. In keeping with the modest economic circumstances of the residents, the houses tend to be small and densely packed compared to the rather magnificent dwellings along the adjacent *grachtengordel.*

The area is a higgledy-piggledy mixture of old buildings (many of them listed monuments), bland modern social housing, and the occasional eyesore that has somehow sneaked past city planning. There are also odd, contemporary contributions such as the large, yellow tap 'sculpture' that protrudes from a house at Tuinstraat 157.

Despite its working class associations the property is now highly desirable and although the residents are mainly proud, community-spirited Jordaaners, the *nouveaux riches* are slowly moving in, many of them artists and musicians. Brouwersgracht, arguably the most beautiful canal in the area, with its trendy converted-warehouse apartments, is one obvious example.

There are several ideas as to the origin of the name Jordaan: some believe it to be a corruption of *joden*, Dutch for Jews, or the French word for garden, *jardin*. The latter seems more plausible: the area was formerly a damp meadow, and many streets have been named after flowers or plants. Many streets are also named after animals whose pelts were used in tanning, one of the main industries in the Jordaan in the seventeenth century. Looiersgracht (Tanner's Canal) is surrounded by streets such as Hazenstraat (Hare Street), Elandsgracht (Elk Canal) and Wolvenstraat (Wolf Street).

Part of the Jordaan's charm is what is hidden from the uninformed eye: the area has the highest

the Pijp is mostly residential, but a diverse range of coffeeshops, cafés and small restaurants characterise the area.

On a summer's day it is well worth finding a seat on the terrace of Café 't Paard on Gerard Douplein, overlooking the square with its recently renovated houses and a small part of Albert Cuypmarket. The café is dark and dingy inside, but while sipping a cappuccino on the terrace you can observe the locals and the recently erected sculpture comprising three pillars which are illuminated at night. You may even encounter the café-owner's huge but friendly dogs. They are usually chewing away on a humungous bone – part of their daily diet, donated by one of the many neighbouring butchers.

Crossing the Albert Cuypmarket from Gerard Douplein is Eerste van der Helststraat: this little square, with its cafés, coffeeshops, chip shops and authentic Italian ice cream parlour, turns into one big terrace during the summer. **Café De Duvel** serves international cuisine and many young locals and students gather here in the evenings. On the corner of Eerste van der Helststraat and Govert Flinckstraat is the area's best bakery, **Bakkerij Runneboom**. It not only sells a huge variety of Dutch bread (including 'Rembrandt' bread) and pastries, but also various typical Turkish, Moroccan and even Irish (buttermilk) breads.

concentration of *hofjes* (hidden garden courtyards) in the city. The better known ones in the area are **Claes Claesz Hofje** (Eerste Egelantiersdwarsstraat 3), which is mainly inhabited by music students, and **Linden Hofje** (Lindengracht 94-112), the oldest in Amsterdam.

The Jordaan has no major sights as such (apart perhaps from Hendrik de Keyser's rather unremarkable Noorderkerk, undergoing renovation until 1998), but is more of an area where you just stumble across things. It provides a welcome, relaxing break from the crowded tourist areas: it is constantly surprising to wander through its streets and hardly see a soul. In general, the area north of the Rozengracht (formerly a wide canal, now filled in) is more interesting and picturesque; the area to the south is more residential and commercial.

The district contains a number of interesting shops such as a doll makers/repairers (Eerste Egelantiersdwarsstraat 2); curio-shop, het Winkeltje (Prinsengracht 228); **Back Beat** (Egelantiersstraat 19), a record shop which specialises in 1950s and 1960s jazz, soul and blues; the English bookshop (Lauriergracht 71); and De Belly (Nieuwe Leliestraat 174-176) which sells organic food and snacks, as well as candles and other eco-friendly household goods. Rozengracht, Westerstraat and Elandsgracht are all lined with a mixture of shops that cater to every need.

The **Stalhouderij** is a tiny former stable that puts on English theatrical productions as well as holding workshops. Just around the corner from the theatre is where Rembrandt lived from 1659

until he died ten years later. All that remains of his former home at Rozengracht 184 is a plaque on the first floor bearing the inscription *Hier Stond Rembrandts Woning 1410-1669* (Here Stood Rembrandt's Home 1410-1669). The Jordaan's association with art is still alive with its many art galleries and resident artists.

This area contains some of the best vegetarian restaurants in the city. The most noteworthy are **De Bolhoed**, and **De Vliegende Schotel**. De Koophandel (Bloemgracht 49) is a late-night drinking bar which doesn't start filling up until around midnight and 't Smalle (Elandsgracht 12), set on this small, picturesque canal, was where Peter Hoppe (of Hoppe & Jenever, the world's first makers of gin) founded his distillery in 1780. For a more unique, local experience try the kitsch **Café Nol**. If you're not in drinking mode, Kunst en Koffie (Tweede Laurierdwarsstraat 64), a stylish coffeeshop/art gallery (in that order) is a great place to wile away the afternoon playing chess.

The area also boasts some of the best of the smaller and indoor markets: the **Noordermarkt** and the **Boerenmarkt** share the same site on different days; the remains of a former livestock market next to the Boerenmarkt can be a disturbing sight with cages crammed with tropical birds, ducks and even kittens. Adjacent to the Noordermarkt is Westerstraat general market and another general market fills the Lindengracht on Saturday mornings. Going south of the Rozengracht are two indoor markets, **De Rommelmarkt** and **De Looier**, both of which have cafés.

*The **Westerkerk** looms above the densely packed streets of the Jordaan.*

'Hé gabber, I saw it first!' – scrambling for bargains at the **Noordermarkt**.

The Waterfront

Amsterdam's historical wealth owes a lot to the city's waterfront: it was here that all the goods were unloaded and weighed, ready for storage in the many warehouses still found in this area. During Amsterdam's trading heyday in the seventeenth century, most maritime activity was centred east of Centraal Station, along Prins Hendrikkade and on the artificial islands east of Kattenburgerstraat. The VOC's wharf was here; a small naval base still is and the Admiralty has been converted into the **Scheepvaart Museum** (maritime museum), which dominates the area. It's an impressive Venetian-style building, designed by Daniel Stalpaert and completed in 1657. It houses a collection second only to London's National Maritime Museum in Greenwich. Nearby is another nautical museum, **Werf 't Kromhout**, a nineteenth-century shipyard.

The old harbour is now virtually disused and the IJ-Oevers (docklands) are undergoing massive redevelopment, a big issue within the city, concerning both locals and environmental groups. It is said to be the country's only remaining up-market area for new housing and office development. Plans for development – estimated to cost ƒ6 billion – are continually subject to alteration because of the lack of financial backing, pressure from local residents and new *stadsdeelraden* (local councils) and the ever-changing traffic-control plans. It seems likely that the squats, cheap housing and artists' studios presently found in this area will shortly be replaced with new low-cost housing, office buildings and

business premises, together with a Metro extension and a dual carriageway.

The Westelijke Eilanden (Western Islands), north-west of Centraal Station, are artificial islands, created in the seventeenth century for shipping-related activities. There are now trendy, converted warehouse flats and a yacht basin on Realeneiland, Prinseneiland and Bickerseiland, where there were once shipyards, tar distillers, fish-salters and smokers.

KNSM Island was originally where the KNSM shipping company docked their boats and unloaded cargo. In recent history it has been transformed from a squatters' paradise to a newly developed residential (for the most part) area which features some striking architecture and some new bars and venues, such as **Kanis & Meiland** and the AMP Studios. As for the squatters, many of them have made the transition to legal tenants and homeowners.

While Rotterdam is by far the world's largest port, Amsterdam and the nearby North Sea Canal ports of Zaanstad, Beverwijk and IJmuiden together rank among the world's 15 largest ports, handling 45 million tonnes per year. Amsterdam is now the centre of Nissan's European distribution and is still the world's largest cocoa port. Since 1876 access to the sea has been via the North Sea Canal, running west from Amsterdam, and because the working docks are also to the west there is little activity on the IJ behind Centraal Station beyond a handful of passenger ships and the free ferry that runs across to Amsterdam Noord.

Canals

A feature of Amsterdam's expansive Golden Age and a staple of its modern tourist brochures, these watery concentric circles are still well worth a wander.

Canals, drugs and commercial sex; commercial sex, drugs and canals. Amsterdam's image abroad is more or less defined by these three city icons, although only one of them is worthy of a postcard back home to grandma full of fascinating facts. Such as, the Dutch call them *grachten*. Or, they stretch 75.5 kilometres and reach an average depth of three metres. Or, they function to keep the sea and the surrounding bog at bay.

About 10,000 bicycles, 100 million litres of sludge and grunge, and on average 52 corpses (usually tramps who trip while pissed and pissing) are dredged from their murky depths each year. Perhaps you will be able to say that you saw police rescue a car with specially designed inflatables, or a barge full of summer job students scooping up condoms and tin cans with specially designed nets.

Or perhaps you can tell of feeling totally at one with the whole interconnectedness of these watery concentric circles that not only provide tranquil and scenic transport but that also cleanse and purge the scum off the street. But then the feeling subsides, and you remember how Albert Camus observed that these concentric rings resemble the circles of hell, and that if you follow this analogy inward to the central pit of damnation, you will find yourself back at the cheap hostel you are staying at in the Red-Light District.

It's important not to get bogged down in Amsterdam's inner pit. The major canals and their radials are where the real city exists and where its unique past is most evident. What they lack in specific sights, they make up for as a locus for scenic cappuccino slurping, quirky shopping, random walks and meditative gable gandering. The **Singel** was the original medieval moat of the city while the other three major canals that follow its line outward were part of a Golden Age urban renewal scheme that ended up quadrupling the city's size. The **Herengracht** (named after the gentlemen who initially invested in it), the **Keizersgracht** (named after the Roman Emperor Maximillian I) and the **Prinsengracht** (named after William, Prince of Orange) are the canals where originally the rich lived, and though still often residential, much has been given over to corporate office, hotels and museums. The radially connecting canals and streets, originally built for workers and artisans, have the higher density of cosy cafés and smaller speciality shops. It is also interesting to note that the major shopping stretches of Rozengracht, Elandsgracht, Leidsestraat and Vijzelstraat are all former radial canals, filled in to deal with the advent of motor traffic

BOGGED DOWN

Trade and imperialist plunder provided the financial impetus for Amsterdam's Golden Age. And even though 85 per cent of the population could not even afford the three-guilder tax for proper burial, by the end of the sixteenth century Amsterdam was one of the richest and most powerful cities in the world. It was bustling and dense – a boomtown constricted only by the bog from whence it came. In 1607 four men were commissioned to initiate a scheme that would stretch the city 541 hectares beyond its medieval borders of the Singel and Kloveniersburgwal canals. The goal of master carpenter Henrik Staets, ex-mayor Frans Oefgens, surveyor Lucas Sinck and architect Daniel Stalpaert was not only to increase housing and provide conditions for the continued growth of sea trade, but also to reflect the shining achievements of this capital, then the commercial focal point of the known universe. Of course this glory had to be dug, and dug it was with pick and shovel by legions of muck-sogged workers, mostly refugees from nearby Spanish-occupied towns.

Another less romantic edge was that these canals were to be the city's open sewer. But here engineering ingenuity saved the Golden Age from turning shit-brown. Several dozen locks were installed. These were closed at high tide to prevent floods and opened at low tide to flush the canals clean of waste. This delicate balancing of drainage, rainwater and tide remained functional with few modifications until the building of the huge Afsluitdijk in 1932 which transformed the Zuider Sea into the fresh water Ijsselmeer. Now sluice gates are closed every night, while millions of gallons of fresh water are pumped through the canals, a process that nightly replaces about a third of the water in the city.

Probably the best way of seeing the main canals, if not by boat (*see chapter* **Sightseeing**), is through random wandering. It may be helpful to note that these canals begin west of Centraal Station, along the beautifully shaded and warehoused Brouwersgracht, as do the house numbers. Similar numbers are vaguely parallel to each other on each of the canals.

Singel

One of the few clues to the Singel's past as the protective moat surrounding the city's medieval wall is the bridge that crosses at Oude Leliestraat. It's called the Torensluis and did indeed once have a look-out tower, while the space under the bridge was supposedly used as a lock-up for medieval drunks. But besides the **Bloemenmarkt** (*see chapters* **Sightseeing** *and* **Shopping**) by day and perhaps the **RoXY** (*see chapters* **Clubs** *and* **Gay & Lesbian**) by night, there are few specific sights. Perhaps you may want to join the debate on whether Singel 7 or Singel 166 is the smallest house in Amsterdam. There is a **House with Noses** at Singel 116, and Banning Cocq, the principal figure of Rembrandt's *Nightwatch*, used to live at Singel 140-142. If you're a pussy lover, then check out the **Poezenboot** (cat boat) at Singel 40, where stray and abandoned cats are looked after by the owner.

Herengracht

As the first canal to be dug in those glory days, the Herengracht attracted the richest of merchants. Here is where the houses and gable work get the most stately and overblown, especially in the stretch known as the 'Golden Bend' between Leidsestraat and Vijzelstraat. Excess defines the Louis XVI style of Herengracht 475, while tales of pre-rock 'n' roll excess are told of **Herengracht 527** whose interior was completely trashed by Peter the Great. You can annoy the current mayor by tying up your boat on his personal and pleasantly scenic dock in front of his official residence at **Herengracht 502**. If you are caught, you can try using the excuse that you are visiting the **Kattenkabinet** (Herengracht 497), a museum dedicated to cats. A yet more virtuous excuse but further away is the **Bible Museum** (Herengracht 366, *see chapter* **Museums**) which packs its collection behind a four-gabled and highly tendrilled façade. Stone masons were also very busy at **Herengracht 380**, an exact copy of a Loire Mansion, complete with coy reclining figures on the gable and frolicking cherubs and other mythical figures on its bay window.

Keizersgracht

Starting at the western, Brouwersgracht end of Keizersgracht, you will soon encounter the **'House with the Heads'** (Keizersgracht 123), a classic of pure Dutch Renaissance. The official story has these finely chiselled heads representing classical gods, but the real scoop is supposed to be that these were burglars' heads chopped off by a vigilante and a lusty maidservant. She decapitated six and married the seventh. So it goes.

Another classic is at **Keizersgracht 174**, an art nouveau masterpiece by Gerrit van Arkels and currently the headquarters of Greenpeace International. A yet more radical offering is the **Ferdinand Domela Nieuwenhuis Museum** (Keizersgracht 264). With a life motto that translates vaguely as 'I do not mind rotting, as long as I am young', one can understand Nieuwenhuis' position as patron saint of Amsterdam's rich history of anarchists. The **Felix Meritis Building** (Keizersgracht 324) is hard to ignore, a neo-Classical monolith with 'Happiness through Achievement' chiselled over its door. And achieve it did: after housing a society of Arts and Sciences in the 1800s, it went on to house the Communist Party and is now a foundation for experimental art and theatre. As if to counter this canal's radical tendencies, the **van Loon Museum** (Keizersgracht 672, *see chapter* **Museums**) presents aristocratic life as it was in the eighteenth century. This stretch was also the site in that time of the 'Slipper Parade' every Sunday, where the posh-footed rich strolled about to see and to be seen.

Prinsengracht

Prinsengracht is the most charming of the canals; especially around the Jordaan (*see chapter* **By Area**), the pompous façades have been mellowed with shady trees, cosy cafés and some of the funkier houseboats in town. The radiating streets of Prinsenstraat, Reestraat, Berenstraat and Runstraat offer a diversity of smaller, artier speciality shops. If it's a Monday morning and you are doing the weekly rummage market at the **Noorderkerk**, stop for coffee at the nearby **Papeneiland** (Prinsengracht 2), a café that remains unchanged after over three centuries of service. A tunnel from there used to go under the canal to a Catholic church during the Protestant uprising. The **Anne Frank House** (Prinsengracht 213, *see chapters* **Sightseeing**, **World War II** *and* **Museums**) and the scenic tower of **Westerkerk** are also nearby.

Puss in boat: Singel 40.

Singel 7 – Arguably the smallest house in Amsterdam.

Eating & Drinking

Restaurants

Amsterdam's restaurants cater for all cuisines and budgets, as long as you don't mind satay sauce with (almost) everything.

The Dutch are not exactly renowned for their cuisine, so if you ask anybody in Amsterdam what is the most typical meal you can eat here, you will probably be directed to an Indonesian restaurant. The former colony's cooking methods have been adopted to such an extent that the cuisine is almost considered a national speciality, to the extent that satay sauce comes with practically everything.

But this is a city where the visiting gourmand is positively spoilt for choice. The high concentration of non-nationals in this small corner of the world is reflected in the variety of restaurants. The most highly favoured restaurants tend to be those serving French food – and many Dutch chefs have been working under this influence ever since the Napoleonic occupation. The influx of 'guest workers' after World War II has since given birth to a multitude of Chinese, Filipino and Mediterranean eating places and more recently, travellers returning from India and Thailand have made a significant contribution to the internationalisation of menus.

Many brown cafés also serve decent food at reasonable prices: *see chapter* **Cafés & Bars**. And for fast food fiends, Amsterdam is heaven on earth, as fast food outlets are everywhere. The best bets are falafels and shoarmas (something like a doner kebab).

LEISURELY DINING

Dining in Amsterdam is a leisurely affair, although the Dutch tend to eat early, between 6.30pm and 9pm, and it is frustrating for the uninitiated to discover most restaurant kitchens shut at 10pm. However, once the meal is ordered and underway, customers are welcome to linger over coffee and dessert until after midnight. Bills include 17.5 per cent tax and 15 per cent service charge. It is customary to leave some small change, as well, if the service merits it, which you hand directly to your server. If you have any special requirements, such as high chairs or disabled access, it's best to phone the restaurant before setting out. For more places to take the kids, *see chapter* **Children**.

Credit cards are only accepted where specified and the **average price** given is based on the cost of a starter and a main course without any drinks. You could spend less – or more – depending on what you order and how much you drink. **If you want to find a restaurant in a particular area,** *see page 110* **Area Index.**

*A taste of **Oud Holland**. Page 100.*

City Landmarks

Café Americain
Leidseplein 28 (624 5322). Tram 1, 2, 5, 6, 7, 10, 11.
Open 7am-1am daily (non-guest breakfast from 10am); *kitchen open* 11am-11.30pm. **Average** ƒ45; breakfast buffet ƒ29,50. **Credit** AmEx, DC, EC, MC, V.
The glorious art deco interior of the Café Americain is a listed monument decorated with murals and marbled amber lampshades. Theatrical personalities, the pre- and *après*-theatre crowd and tourists meet under the high, vaulted roof.

De Blauwe Parade
Hotel Port van Cleve, Nieuwezijds Voorburgwal 178-180 (624 4860). Tram 1, 2, 4, 5, 9, 11, 14, 16, 17, 24, 25.
Open noon-midnight daily. **Average** ƒ40. **Credit** AmEx, MC, V, JCB.
Wholesome Dutch food in this centrally located restaurant named after the antique Delft Blue tiles that adorn the place.

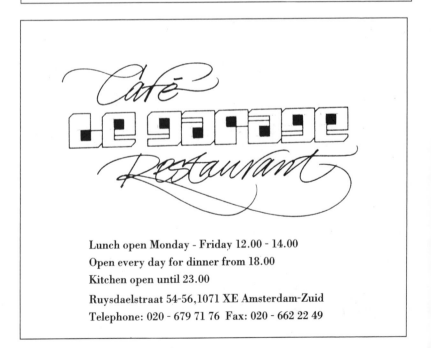

*Lovers of fine French food should make their way tout suite to **Tout Cort**.*

Halvemaan

Van Leyenberghlaan 20, Buitenveldert (644 0348). Bus 63, 64. **Open** noon-2pm, 6-10pm, Mon-Fri. **Average** *f*125. **Credit** AmEx, DC, EC, MC, V.

The 'half moon' name is reflected in the layout of this restaurant: a fascinating interior provides the stage for one of Amsterdam's most renowned chefs. The pastoral setting is perfect for a summer lunch or dinner. French, Caribbean, Italian and Dutch cuisines mix together for an interesting menu.

La Rive

Amstel Hotel, Prof Tulpplein 1 (622 6060). Tram 6, 7, 10/Metro Weesperplein. **Open** *breakfast* 6.30-10.30am Mon-Fri; 6.30-11.30am Sat, Sun; *lunch* noon-2pm Mon-Fri; *dinner* 6.30-10.30pm daily. **Average** *dinner f*125; *lunch f*49. **Credit** AmEx, MC, DC, V.

This elegant waterside restaurant in the Amstel Hotel is the home of Robert Kranenborg, one of the most famous chefs in the Netherlands. The lunch menu is an ideal introduction to his refined, regional French cuisine.

Pier 10

De Ruijterkade, Steiger 10 (624 8276). Tram 1, 2, 5, 9, 11, 13, 14, 16, 17, 24, 25, 26. **Open** 6.30-11pm daily. **Average** *f*50. **Credit** AmEx, MC, V.

One of Amsterdam's most surprising restaurants. An unusual combination of functional décor, candlelight, shipside vistas, innovative food and a casual atmosphere attracts a regular following.

't Swarte Schaep

Korte Leidsedwarsstraat 24 (622 3021). Tram 1, 2, 5, 6, 7, 10, 11. **Open** noon-11pm daily. **Average** *lunch f*48; *dinner f*68. **Credit** AmEx, DC, MC, JCB, EC, V.

Based in the same 300-year-old building since 1937, this restaurant is noted for its excellent wines (especially reds),

authentic antiques and subtle blend of classic, nouvelle and post-modern cuisine.

Tout Court

Runstraat 13 (625 8637). Tram 7, 10. **Open** noon-11.30pm Mon-Fri; 6-11.30pm Sat, Sun. **Average** *set menu f*39 (daytime only) *f*49. **Credit** AmEx, DC, MC, V.

A nouvelle-based menu changes every four to five weeks and a range of set menus offers good value. Service can be slow. *Wheelchair access with assistance.*

Belgian

Van Vlaanderen

Weteringschans 175, (622 8292). Trams 6, 10, 7, 24, 25. **Open** 6.30pm-10.30pm Mon-Sat. **Average** *f*56. **Credit** AmEx, EC, MC, V.

Hearty Flemish fare, heavy on rich sauces and large hunks of meat. Excellent service and wine list.

Chinese

Dynasty

Reguliersdwarsstraat 30 (626 8400). Tram 1, 2, 5, 11. **Open** 6-11pm Mon, Wed-Sun. **Average** *f*70. **Credit** AmEx, DC, MC, V.

This restaurant offers a mix of Oriental food: Vietnamese, Thai and Chinese dishes are served like works of art. But don't worry, the portions are also huge.

Hoi Tin

Zeedijk 122-124 (625 6451). Metro Nieuwmarkt. **Open** noon-12.30am daily. **Average** *f*35.

Busy but with patient and helpful service, Hoi Tin is worth

*Beautifully cooked and presented food and fine wines at **Bordewijk**. Page 100.*

a visit. Its menu is written in five languages and lists over 200 dishes, including vegetarian options. It's also possible to make your own variations on existing dishes.

Nam Kee
Geldersekade 117 (624 3470). Metro Nieuwmarkt. **Open** noon-12.30am daily. **Average** *f*35.
Small with greasy tiles covering floor and walls and service slow enough to put many people off. But Nam Kee's customers come back again and again because it's cheap and the fish dishes are supreme.

Oriental City
Oudezijds Voorburgwal 177-179 (626 8352). Tram 4, 9, 14, 16, 24, 25. **Open** 11.30am-10.30pm daily. **Average** *f*35. **Credit** AmEx, DC, MC, EC, V.
With views overlooking the Damstraat, the Royal Palace or the canals and some of Amsterdam's best, most authentic dim sum, Oriental City is deservedly popular with Chinese locals as well as tourists.

Dutch

Few restaurants serve exclusively Dutch food, but local dishes are real winter warmers (and fatteners) and include *boerenkool met rookworst* (potatoes, sausage and curly kale), *stamppot* (meat and vegetable stew) and *erwtensoep* (thick pea soup). The best dessert is usually *vlaai* or *vruchttaart* (fruit pie); if you're sure you've enough belly space, plump for a *pannekoek* (pancake).

De Blauwe Hollander
Leidsekruisstraat 28 (623 3014). Tram 6, 7, 10, 11. **Dinner served** 5-10pm daily. **Average** *f*22.
The four big tables – there's no separate seating – are always busy, but small parties seldom have to wait long to be seated. One of the few decent restaurants in a very touristy area, serving rich and tasty food.

Dorrius
Nieuwezijds Voorburgwal 5 (420 2224). Tram 1, 2, 5, 11. **Open** 5.30-11pm daily. **Average** *f*45. **Credit** AmEx, DC, JCB, MC, V.
Reincarnation of 1890 Amsterdam restaurant with the original interior. Wide selection of traditional Dutch food and products. Treat yourself to Dutch wine and spirits to complete the experience.

Hollands Glorie
Kerkstraat 220-222 (624 4764). Tram 16, 24, 25. **Open** 5-10pm daily. **Average** *f*27. **Credit** AmEx, EC, V.
The staff at Hollands Glorie serve up traditional, thoughtfully prepared fare in a cosy, intimate atmosphere. The garlic mussels starter should not be missed.

Keuken van 1870
Spuistraat 4 (624 8965). Tram 1, 2, 5, 11. **Open** 12.30am-8pm Mon-Fri; 4-9pm Sat, Sun. **Average** *f*11. **Credit** AmEx, DC, EC, MC, V.
Eating at this former soup kitchen not only brings you in touch with the Dutch populus, as you often have to share a table, it also serves nothing but authentic Dutch standards such as endive with rashers of bacon or rib of steak. Soup starts at *f*3, the dish of the day costs *f*8,50 and all other dishes are *f*11-*f*16,50.

Oud Holland

Nieuwezijds Voorburgwal 105 (624 6848). Tram 1, 2, 5, 11. **Open** noon-9.30pm Mon-Sat. **Average** ƒ25. **Credit** AmEx, DC, EC, MC, V, JCB.

The building dates from 1649 and the café was a regular meeting place for journalists in the 1920s. The present proprietors have had it since 1978 and serve traditional Dutch dishes such as pea soup, smoked eel and herring.

Pancake Bakery

Prinsengracht 191 (625 1333). Tram 13, 17. **Open** noon-9.30pm. **Average** ƒ15. **Credit** AmEx, MC.

Claiming 'the best pancakes in town', this is a quaint restaurant in the basement of one of Prinsengracht's lovely old houses. The pancakes are large, so you can eat your fill of typically Dutch fare with a variety of toppings for less than ƒ15.

De Rode Leeuw

Damrak 93-94 (555 0614). Tram 4, 9, 14, 16, 24, 25. **Open** noon-9.30pm daily. **Average** ƒ45. **Credit** AmEx, DC, EC, MC, V.

This brasserie is housed in one of the oldest heated terraces in Amsterdam. It specialises in all Dutch fare and even has a selection of Dutch wine on offer.

Witteveen

Ceintuurbaan 256-258 (662 4368). Tram 3, 12, 24, 25. **Dinner served** 5-11pm daily. **Average** ƒ37,50. **Credit** AmEx, DC, MC, V.

Deeply Dutch, but this popular, traditional café-restaurant attracts all ages. Its lengthy menu and set dishes are supplemented by Cajun dishes from the Cajun Louisiana next door.

Ethiopian

Lalibela

Eerste Helmerstraat 249 (683 8332). Tram 1, 3, 6, 12. **Open** kitchen 5-11pm daily. **Average** ƒ20.

This restaurant claims to be the most authentic Ethiopian restaurant in Amsterdam and it is certainly popular. Reservations are recommended, especially at the weekend, as the place gets packed quickly.

Fish

Albatros

Westerstraat 264 (627 9932). Tram 10. **Open** 6-11pm Mon, Tue, Thur-Sun. **Average** ƒ40. **Credit** AmEx, DC, MC, V.

Great fishy cuisine in a lovely setting. All dishes are cooked to perfection.

Julia

Amstelveenseweg 160 (679 5394). Tram 6/bus 146, 147, 170, 171, 172, 173. **Open** 5-10pm daily. **Average** ƒ35. **Credit** AmEx, MC, V.

For a real neighbourhood Dutch dinner, head out of town to Julia's. The special menu of ten different kinds of fish for ƒ32,50 is excellent value, as is the salmon trout at ƒ27,50 for the whole fish.

Lucius

Spuistraat 247 (624 1831). Tram 1, 2, 5, 11. **Open** 5pm-midnight Mon-Sat. **Average** ƒ47. **Credit** AmEx, DC, MC, V.

Lucius is a fish-eater's paradise, serving a dinner of fresh ocean fish (as opposed to the normal North Sea variety), poached, grilled or fried, and shellfish when in season. Lobster should be ordered in advance.
Wheelchair access.

Le Pêcheur

Reguliersdwarsstraat 32 (624 3121). Tram 1, 2, 5, 11. **Open** lunch noon-3pm Mon-Fri; dinner 6-11pm Mon-Sat. **Average** ƒ60. **Credit** AmEx, DC, MC, JCB, EC, V.

Choose from the à la carte or the menu of the day, both of which are provided in Dutch, French and English. The service is friendly but formal and the clientele are mature and worry more about the quality of the food than the price.

Sluizer

Utrechtsestraat 45 (626 3557). Tram 4. **Open** 5pm-midnight daily. **Average** ƒ35. **Credit** AmEx, DC, EC, V.

With interior design inspired by Charles Rennie Mackintosh and a top-floor luxury terrace, this is a chic yet unpretentious restaurant. An extensive menu of grilled, baked or poached fish. Children's dishes are available.

French

Beddington's

Roelof Hartstraat 6-8 (676 5201). Tram 3, 5, 12, 24. **Open** 6-10.30pm Mon; noon-2pm, 6-10.30pm, Tue-Fri, 6-10.30 Sat. **Average** ƒ100. **Credit** AmEx, DC, EC, MC, V.

French cuisine is complemented by original touches gleaned from long trips through the Far East. The menu includes beautifully presented fish dishes.

Belhamel

Brouwersgracht 60 (622 1095). Tram 1, 2, 5, 11, 13, 17. **Open** 6-10pm daily. **Set menus** ƒ45 and ƒ49,50. **Credit** AmEx, MC, DC, V.

A fresh approach to French cuisine and brilliant value for money characterise this beautiful art nouveau place. Ask for a table overlooking the canal.

Bonjour

Keizersgracht 770 (626 6040). Tram 4. **Open** 5-11pm Wed-Sun. **Average** ƒ50. **Credit** AmEx, MC, V.

Bonjour is a cosy, candlelit restaurant offering straightforward French home cooking. Set menus change every night and at ƒ27,50 they represent good value. The service is especially friendly and children are welcome.

Bordewijk

Noordermarkt 8 (624 3899). Tram 3. **Open** 5.30-10.30pm Tue-Sun. **Average** set menus ƒ59,50, ƒ69,50, ƒ79,50. **Credit** AmEx, MC, V.

This is a perfectly balanced restaurant which offers the very best of original food and excellent wines in a designer interior. Service and atmosphere are relaxed. Recommended.

Café Roux

Hotel Grand, Oudezijds Voorburgwal 197 (555 3111). Tram 9, 14, 16, 24, 25. **Open** 5.30am-11am, noon-3pm, 6-11pm, daily. **Average** ƒ40. **Credit** AmEx, DC, JCB, MC, V.

The same food is served in Café Roux as in the Grand Hotel itself and, naturally enough, is supervised by head chef Albert Roux. Despite the superstar status, a meal here is good value.

Crignon Culinair

Gravenstraat 28 (624 6428). Tram 1, 2, 5, 11, 14, 16, 24, 25. **Dinner served** 6-9.30pm Tue-Sat. **Average** ƒ30.

Cheese shop by day, restaurant by night. This small establishment, which specialises in fondues, is run by Adriaan Jaspers, an award-winning chef whose cuisine has a distinct emphasis on cheese. Meat and fish dishes are also on the menu.

Gorgeous food and a sumptuous art nouveau interior at **Belhamel**.

Le Garage

Ruysdaelstraat 54-56 (679 7176). Tram 3, 5, 6, 12, 16.
Open noon-2pm, 6pm-11pm, Mon-Fri; 6pm-11pm Sat,
Sun. **Average** ƒ57,50. **Credit** AmEx, DC, MC, V.
Dress up to eat in this trendy brasserie which is great for
people-watching and enjoying authentic French regional
food.

Jean Jean

*Eerste Anjeliersdwarsstraat 12-14 (627 7153). Tram 13,
14, 17.* **Open** 5.30-10.30pm daily. **Average** ƒ35.
Located in the Jordaan, this restaurant is mainly frequented
by locals. The kitchen staff are French, the waiters Dutch
and not over-solicitous. The restaurant itself is very simple
and the food is served in the traditional French style (you
won't leave hungry).

Kikker

*Egelantiersstraat 128-130 (627 9198). Tram 10, 13, 14,
17.* **Open** *dinner* 6-11pm daily. **Average** ƒ30. **Credit**
AmEx, DC, MC, V.
This two-storey restaurant is tucked away in the Jordaan
and is the perfect setting for an intimate French/Portuguese
meal. The brasserie is small, has friendly waiters, a tasteful
art deco interior and the opportunity to dine outside under
the ivy. Weekend nights offer entertainment in the form of
music, cabaret or comedians.

Luden

Spuistraat 304-306 (622 8979). Tram 1, 2, 5, 11. **Open**
noon-3pm, 6-11pm, Mon-Fri; 6-11pm Sat-Sun. **Average**
ƒ42,50. **Credit** AmEx, DC, MC, V.
A busy restaurant popular with people who appreciate the
excellent three-course set menu at an extremely affordable
ƒ42,50. All dishes are beautifully prepared and presented,
and the desserts are fabulous.

Taddy Zemmel

Prinsengracht 126 (620 6525). Tram 13, 14, 17. **Open**
6-10.30pm Tue-Sun. **Average** ƒ55. **Credit** AmEx, DC,
MC, V.
Great atmosphere in a theatrical interior. This busy place offers
good value French (and Dutch) food with interesting touches.

D'Theeboom

Singel 210 (623 8420). Tram 1, 2, 5, 11, 13, 14, 17.
Open 6-10.30pm Mon-Sun. **Average** *set menu* ƒ47,50; *à
la carte* ƒ60. **Credit** AmEx, DC, MC, V.
The three-course menu at ƒ47,50 gives d'Theeboom the best
quality-to-price ratio in town. The generous portions of classical French cooking and the strange absence of crowds must
make this one of Amsterdam's best kept secrets.

Het Tuynhuys

Reguliersdwarsstraat 28 (627 6603). Tram 1, 2, 5.
Open noon-2pm, 6-10.30pm, Mon-Fri; 6-10.30pm Sat,
Sun. **Average** ƒ65. **Credit** AmEx, DC, MC, V.
Het Tuynhuys serves eclectic food with a French accent in
either the elegant, garden-style interior, or the beautiful real
garden.

La Vallade

Ringdijk 23 (665 2025). Tram 9. **Open** noon-1am daily.
Average ƒ34,50.
La Vallade offers one of the best value menus in town: five
courses, including cheese, for ƒ34,50. The secret to doing it so
cheaply is that the restaurant only offers one menu per evening.

Le Zinc... et les Dames

Prinsengracht 999 (622 9044). Tram 16, 24, 25. **Open**
5.30-11pm Tue-Sat. **Average** ƒ40. **Credit** MC, V.
Provincial French cooking in a rustic setting. Wines are recommended for each dish. Very popular, but service can be
irritatingly slow.

Zuidlande

Utrechtsedwarsstraat 141 (620 7393). Tram 4. **Open**
6pm-10.30pm Mon-Sat. **Average** ƒ45. **Credit** AmEx,
EC, V.
An atmospheric little restaurant; subtle lighting and plenty
of candles combine with a warm and simple décor to create
a typically Gallic feel. Food is perfectly cooked and presented and for such a high standard of cuisine, prices are relatively low.

Zuid Zeeland

*Herengracht 413 (624 3154). Tram 4, 9, 14, 16, 20, 24,
25.* **Open** 6-10.30pm daily. **Average** ƒ55. **Credit**
AmEx, EC, MC, V.
A perennial favourite with Amsterdammers, Zuid Zeeland
specialises in fish dishes and the menu has a strong
Mediterranean slant. You can order à la carte or opt for a
set menu (ƒ52,50, ƒ62,50 or ƒ72,50) which you compile
yourself. The two women chef-owners, Riet Kint and
Sandra Derijker, really care about what they cook, and you
can taste it.

Indian

Akbar

*Korte Leidsedwarsstraat 33-35 (624 2211). Tram 1, 2,
5, 6, 7, 10, 11.* **Open** 5-11.30pm daily. *Set menu for two*
ƒ70; *vegetarian menu* ƒ30 per person. **Credit** AmEx, DC,
EC, MC, V.
The best of the Indian restaurants near the Leidseplein. A
good place to go, whether you want a meal to raise a sweat
or milder, creamier dishes.

Balraj

Binnen Oranjestraat 1 (625 1428). Tram 3. **Open** 4-
10pm daily. **Average** ƒ20.
Balraj is a small, cosy eating house just off
Haarlemmerdijk. Food is reasonably priced and particularly well done, with vegetarians generously catered for:
highly recommended.

Himalaya

Haarlemmerstraat 11 (622 3776). Tram 1, 2, 5, 11.
Open 5-11pm daily. **Average** ƒ30. **Credit** AmEx, DC,
MC, V.
Excellent Indian cuisine at reasonable prices. The staff can
make any dish more or less spicy than usual and the service is invariably welcoming and friendly. Less pretentious
than most, despite the wonderful art and designs on the
walls.

The India Cottage

Ceintuurbaan 111 (662 8873). Tram 3, 12, 24. **Open** 5-
11pm daily. **Average** ƒ35. **Credit** AmEx, DC, MC, V.
Just out of the centre of town, the India Cottage is a real find,
particularly if you are a fan of balti dishes. The restaurant
is warm and traditionally decorated. Service is friendly without being over-attentive.

Shiva

*Reguliersdwarsstraat 72 (624 8713). Tram 9, 14, 16,
24, 25.* **Open** 5-11pm daily. **Average** ƒ30. **Credit**
AmEx, DC, MC, V.
Air-conditioning keeps the heat down in the relaxed and elegant interior. The menu holds a careful selection of fairly
varied dishes ranging from the classics to a few specialities.

Swaagat

*Lange Leidsedwarsstraat 76 (638 4702). Tram 1, 2, 5,
11.* **Open** 12.30-3pm, 5-11pm, daily. **Average** ƒ32,50.
Credit AmEx, DC, MC, EC, V.
Decent Indian with good vegetarian options, and there's a
delivery service.

Italian

L'Angoletto

Hemonystraat 18 (676 4182). Tram 3, 4, 6, 7, 10. **Open**
5.45pm-11.30pm Fri-Sun. **Average** ƒ40. **Credit** V.
The most authentic trattoria in town with a Fellini-esque
atmosphere. It gets very busy, but the food makes the
wait for a table worthwhile.

Casa di David

Singel 426 (624 5093). Tram 1, 2, 5, 11. **Open** 5-
11.30pm daily. **Average** ƒ45. **Credit** AmEx, DC, EC,
MC, V.
A popular dark-wooded and beamed restaurant, that is perfect for romantic meals. The pasta is made on the premises
and is first-rate; the excellent crusty pizzas are made in a
wood-fired oven.

The Breakfast Club

The Dutch traditionally eat breakfast cold. A
typical Dutch breakfast (*ontbijt*) consists of
boterhammen, buttered slices of selected
breads with something on top – it may be
cheese, cold cuts or jam. Warm breakfasts
come in the shape of the *uitsmijter* – a 'throw-
outer' – due to it having in the past been served
at the end of an evening party as a cue for the
guests to sod off. Eggs are fried sunny-side up
splattered with ham, roast beef, veal or cheese,
and served on toast. If you want one of those
or a simple *broodje kaas* (cheese roll) with coffee, it is just a matter of walking into one of the
hundreds of brown cafés that litter the city.
More formal – British – breakfasts are harder
to find but do exist.

One of the best examples of a traditional
brown-stained wood affair is **Café Prins** in the
Jordaan. It is perfect for a date with a newspaper, especially when the sunny canalside patio
is open. The place is frequented by students and
a wide mix of neighbourhood types. For ƒ11,50,
you can get the full standard Dutch *ontbijt*, complete with toasted white bread, nut and raisin
bread, *ontbijtkoek* (gingerbread), a boiled egg,
ham, cheese, jam and a glass of freshly squeezed
juice. *Uitsmijters* and omelettes with choices
start at ƒ8.50.

Not too far away, and also equipped with a
scenic canalside patio, is **Greenwoods** where the
menu is more British in its emphasis: scones and
crumpets and a plethora of teas. For ƒ15, you can
tuck into a proper English fry-up of eggs, bacon,
onions, tomatoes, Heinz beans on toast with
orange juice and a choice of coffee and tea.

Café Paradox describes itself as a 'unique
blend of wholesome food, atmospheric smoke
and spacious mind-art interior'. It's on a charming sidestreet off Bloemgracht near the minis-
cule Stalhouderij Theatre. The food is excellent
and there is space to breathe (albeit air mingled
with marijuana) and nowhere in Amsterdam
can you get a better English breakfast (ƒ12,50).

Barney's Breakfast Bar on
Haarlemmerstraat is an expat place with its finger on the crusty/techno pulse. They serve up a
fine and filling fry-up (ƒ13,50 large/ƒ10,50 small)
with what is hyped to be the best sausage in
town. The emphasis is on both grease to gel the
stomach after a long night and a smoking menu
to mellow the mind and open the taste buds. The
normal menu (as in food) is also diverse, from a
mixed grill (ƒ15) for the protein junkies to a vegetarian breakfast (ƒ12,50) which replaces flesh
with a veggie burger.

Mono Ontbijt & Alcohol is a small cafe-
bar at the scenic beginning of Oudezijds
Voorburgwal. During the day, Mono is a mellow
zone blasting 1960s punk, surf and garage, and
serving an obsessive array of breakfasts. There
is an emphasis on hangover recovery with its
Ontbijt Radicaal (ƒ6,50) consisting of coffee,
aspirin, and a pack of smokes, and its surefire
Kater Ontbijt (ƒ10) which includes pickled herring, ham, sour cream, horseradish and a shot
of hair of the dog. Sundays cross into the realm
of the decadent as a Champagne breakfast (ƒ25)
is presented with roast beef, salmon mousse,
devilled eggs, assorted cheeses, toasts and
breads.

Barney's Breakfast Bar

Haarlemmerstraat 102 (625 9761). Tram 18, 22.
Open 9am-9pm daily. **Breakfast served** until
8.30pm daily.

Café Paradox

1e Bloemdwarsstraat 2 (623 5639). Tram 13, 14, 17.
Open 9am-8.30pm daily. **Breakfast served** until
2pm daily.

Café Prins

Prinsengracht 124 (624 9382). Tram 13, 14, 17.
Open 9.30am-1am Mon-Thur, Sun; 9.30am-2am Fri,
Sat. **Breakfast served** until 4pm daily.

Greenwoods

Singel 103 (623 7071). Tram 1, 2, 5, 11. **Open**
9.30am-7pm Mon-Fri; 11am-7pm Sat, Sun. **Breakfast
served** until 7pm daily.

Mono Ontbijt & Alcohol

*Oudezijds Voorburgwal 2 (625 3630). Tram 1, 2, 5,
11.* **Open** 10am-1am Mon-Thur, Sun; 10am-2am Fri,
Sat. **Breakfast served** until 6pm daily.

Hostaria

Tweede Egelantiersdwarsstraat 9 (626 0028). Tram 10, 13, 14, 17. **Open** 6-10.30pm Tue-Sun. **Average** ƒ40.
Owners Marjolein and Massimo Pasquinoli serve up a wonderful selection of classic Italian dishes including salmon carpaccio and a spectacular insalata di polipo. Excellent, unpretentious food at a good price.

Panini

Vijzelgracht 3 (626 4939). Tram 6, 7, 10, 16, 24, 25. **Open** 9.30am-9.30pm daily. **Average** ƒ22,50. **Credit** (minimum ƒ45) AmEx, DC, MC, V.
An Italian restaurant based in an old Amsterdam canal house. Great, Italian-style sandwiches are served at lunchtime; the evening menu is more robust.

Prego

Herenstraat 25 (638 0148). Tram 1, 2, 5, 11, 13, 17. **Open** 6-10.30pm Mon-Sat. **Average** ƒ55. **Credit** AmEx, MC, V.
A small comfortable restaurant frequented by local residents, where the imaginative chefs change the Mediterranean-based menu daily.

Toscanini

Lindengracht 75 (623 2813). Tram 3, 10. **Open** 6-11pm daily. **Average** ƒ50.
Authentic Italian food is prepared in an open kitchen, with a bustling atmosphere. Book early (from 3pm) if you want to guarantee a table.

Tartufo

Singel 449 (627 7175). Tram 1, 2, 5, 11. **Open** 5.30-11pm daily. **Average** ƒ35. **Credit** AmEx, DC, EC, MC, V.
Split over two floors, a two-in-one eating establishment: cheapish, wholesome pasta is served downstairs; more sophisticated fish and meat dishes upstairs.

Yam-Yam

Frederik Hendrikstraat 90 (681 5097). Tram 3. **Open** 6-10.30pm Tue-Sat. **Average** ƒ22.
Yam-Yam calls itself 'the first trattoria for world cuisine', with the menu consisting not only of wonderfully tasty Italian dishes, but also Thai and even sushi dishes.

Japanese

An

Weteringschans 199 (627 0607). Tram 6, 7, 10. **Open** 6-10pm Wed-Sun. **Average** ƒ35.
If you're going to eat at An, buy your drink beforehand, as there is no alcohol license in the restaurant. Good Japanese home cooking in café surroundings.

Docksider

Entrepodok 7-10 (626 9349). Tram 7, 9, 14/bus 22, 28. **Open** 5.30-10.30pm daily. **Average** ƒ35. **Credit** AmEx, DC, EC, MC,V.
A roomy Japanese restaurant in a charming waterside location behind Artis Zoo. The sushi and sashiui are fresh and delicious.

Kaiko

Jekerstraat 114 (662 5641). Tram 12, 25. **Open** 6-10pm Mon-Wed, Fri, Sat. **Average** ƒ50. **Credit** AmEx, DC, EC, MC.
Cross the Noord Amstelkanaal to find the best sushi in town. An elegant, if pricey, experience.

Morita-Ya

Zeedijk 18 (638 0756) Tram 1, 2, 5, 11, 13, 17. **Open** 6pm-10pm Mon, Tue, Thur-Sun. **Average** ƒ32,50. **Credit** AmEx, MC, V.

Cheap and cheerful place with erratic opening hours that serves fantastic sushi and sashimi.

Shizen

Kerkstraat 148 (622 8627). Tram 1, 2, 5. **Open** 5.30-10pm Tue-Sun. **Average** ƒ35. **Credit** AmEx, DC, EC, MC, V.
Shizen is a classy and convincing Japanese restaurant that justifiably takes great pride in producing affordable, macrobiotic food. There's no meat on the menu, but the fish is varied and excellent, and the vegetable dishes unbeatable.

Teppan-Yaki & Yamazato

Okura Hotel, Ferdinand Bolstraat 333 (678 7111). Tram 12, 25. **Lunch served** noon-2pm Mon-Fri. **Dinner served** 6.30-10.30pm daily. **Average** ƒ75; *set menus from* ƒ90. **Credit** AmEx, DC, JCB, MC, V.
These sister restaurants are among the finest purveyors of Japanese food. Customers at the Teppan-Yaki are treated to amazing showmanship by master Japanese chefs, while at the Yamazato, chefs sliver fish with the same dexterity. *Wheelchair access.*

Korean

Mokkalie

Utrechtsestraat 42 (625 9251). Tram 4. **Open** 11am-10.30pm daily. **Average** *set menu* ƒ25. **Credit** AmEx, DC, MC, V.
There are beer pumps affixed to four of the tables where you can have a go at pulling your own beers. The set menu is good value too, incidentally.

Mexican

Alfonso's

Korte Leidsedwarsstraat 69 (627 0580). Tram 1, 2, 5, 6, 7, 10, 11. **Open** 5pm-midnight Mon-Fri; noon-midnight Sat, Sun (noon-3am Thur-Mon in the summer). **Average** ƒ35. **Credit** AmEx, DC, EC, MC, V.
One of the few Mexican restaurants which acknowledges that vegetarians cannot live on bread alone. Otherwise the dishes served are pretty standard fare. *Wheelchair access.*

Pacifico

Warmoesstraat 31 (624 2911). Tram 4, 9, 14, 16, 20, 24, 25. **Open** 5.30-10pm Mon-Thur, Sun; 5.30-11pm Fri, Sat. **Average** ƒ40. **Credit** AmEx, MC, V.
The most authentic Mexican-style bodega in Amsterdam. The crowded bar and cramped eating area add to the effect, and the food has enough of a genuine edge to keep this place ahead of the rest. *Wheelchair access.*

La Margarita

Lange Brugsteeg 6 (624 0529). Tram 1, 2, 4, 5, 9, 11, 13, 14, 16, 17, 24, 25/Metro Centraal Station. **Open** 5-11pm Tue-Sun. **Average** ƒ35. **Credit** AmEx, DC, EC, MC, V.
Take along a large appetite as the portions are massive, though inexpensive. The extensive menu caters for all palates, with decent seafood, vegetarian and meat choices.

Rose's Cantina

Reguliersdwarsstraat 38-40 (625 9797). Tram 1, 2, 5, 11, 16, 24, 25. **Open** *dinner* 5.30-11pm Mon-Thur; 5.30-11.30pm Fri, Sat; 5-11pm Sun. **Average** ƒ30. **Credit** AmEx, MC, DC, V.
Definitely not the place for a quiet night out, and not particularly authentic either; but the ingredients are good enough and the portions more than generous. I

Take the **Road to Manila** for Philippine food.

International

Bern
Nieuwmarkt 9 (622 0034). Metro Nieuwmarkt. **Open** *bar* 4pm-1am Mon-Thur, Sun; 4pm-2am Fri, Sat. **Dinner served** 6-11pm daily. **Average** *f*22.
A popular brown café-restaurant with a reputation for its delicious cheese fondue made, of course, to a secret recipe. Bern's peppered steak is also recommended.

Café Cox
Marnixstraat 429 (620 7222/6846). Tram 1, 2, 5, 6, 7, 10, 11. **Open** 10am-1am Mon-Thur, Sun; 10am-2am Fri, Sat. **Lunch served** 12.30-2.30pm, **dinner served** 5.30-11.30pm, daily. **Average** *f*40. **Credit** AmEx, MC, EC, DC, V.
Imaginative French and modern Dutch cooking in a lively environment. Prices are reasonable.

De Impressionist
Keizersgracht 312 (627 6666). Tram 13, 14, 17. **Open** *dinner served* 6-10.30pm Mon-Thur, Sun; 6-11pm Fri, Sat. **Average** *set menus f*42,50-*f*62,50. **Credit** AmEx, DC, MC, V.
A team of British cooks produces English, American, Chinese, Japanese and Italian dishes, along with imaginative vegetarian selections.

Leg Af
Oude Leliestraat 9 (624 6700). Tram 1, 2, 5, 13, 14, 17. **Open** 6pm-10pm daily. **Average** *f*30.

Great fondues and at weekends, freshly-made sushi and sashimi too.

Lulu
Runstraat 8 (624 5090). Tram 1, 2, 5, 7, 10. **Open** 6-11pm daily. **Average** *f*45. **Credit** AmEx, DC, EC, MC, V.
This small French-Indonesian restaurant offers a *f*49 menu that is of such a high standard it makes you wonder how they do it. The fish dishes are especially well-prepared.

Piet de Leeuw
Noorderstraat 11 (623 7181). Tram 16, 24, 25. **Open** noon-midnight Mon-Fri; noon-11pm Sat; 5-11pm Sun. **Average** *f*29,50. **Credit** AmEx, DC, MC, V.
Most of the customers at this small, friendly steakhouse are here for the inexpensive steaks and french fries (cheap, but the quality's not bad). People tend to mix and mingle (they may ask to sit at your table if there's space).

Le Rendez-vous
Weteringschans 75 (623 4017). Tram 6, 7, 10. **Open** 11am-11pm daily. **Average** *f*30. **Credit** AmEx, DC, MC, V.
French onion soup, salmon on toast and pâté are accompanied by one of the excellent salads that give the place its name. Robust evening dishes include steaks, lamb cutlets and trout.

Small Talk
Van Baerlestraat 52 (671 4864). Tram 3, 5, 12, 16. **Open** *café* 8am-7pm Mon-Sat; 9am-6pm Sun; *restaurant* 11am-9.30pm Mon-Sat; 11am-8pm Sun; *traiteur* 11am-

9pm Mon-Fri; 9am-6pm Sat. **Average** *f*35. **Credit** AmEx, DC, MC, V.
Two cafés, side by side, offer some of the most pleasant people-watching opportunities in town. Small Talk attracts a fairly well-heeled clientele but the lunches and snacks remain reasonably priced. Dinners upstairs carry rather steeper tariffs.

Spanjer en van Twist
Leliegracht 60 (639 0109). Tram 13, 14, 17. **Open** *kitchen* 6-11pm daily; *café* 10am-1am Mon-Fri, Sun; 10am-2am Fri, Sat. **Average** *f*25. **Credit** MC, V.
Split-level, spacious, with a simple, minimalist interior and a shaded outdoor terrace. The menu is basic but varied with imaginative dishes as well as soups and specials which change every week.

De Smoeshaan
Leidsekade 90 (627 6966). Tram 1, 2, 5, 6, 7, 10, 11. **Open** *restaurant* 5.30-10pm Tue-Sat; *café* 11am-1am Mon-Thur, Sun; 11am-2am Fri, Sat (last orders 10pm). **Average** *restaurant* *f*40. **Credit** AmEx, EC, V.
There's an old Dutch café-bar downstairs, which is usually busy, and a slightly more formal restaurant upstairs, with a more varied menu (and higher prices). Both serve tasty Franco-Dutch food, with lots of fresh vegetables and salads, and both attract a young, lively crowd.

Trez
Saenredamstraat 39 (676 2495). Tram 6, 7, 10, 16, 24, 25. **Open** 6-11pm daily. **Average** *f*42.
A beautiful place in the Pijp with pretty tables and chairs, distinctive decorative themes, stylish glassware and an exposed kitchen in the middle of the restaurant. Excellent light French menu and good value for money.

Brasserie van Baerle
Van Baerlestraat 158 (679 1532). Tram 3, 5, 12, 16. **Open** noon-11pm Mon-Fri; *brunch* 10am-11pm Sun. **Average** *lunch* *f*45, *dinner* *f*55. **Credit** AmEx, DC, MC, V.
The media crowd has been hanging out at this turn-of-the-century townhouse brasserie since it opened about ten years ago. The food is strictly modern: oriental salads and homemade soups. On warm days, the garden is delightful.

Van Beeren
Koningsstraat 54 (622 2329). Metro Nieuwmarkt. **Open** 4pm-1am daily; *dinner* 5.30-10.30pm daily. **Average** *f*35.
An atmospheric and welcoming *eetcafé*. Dish of the day is *f*15, succulent sole or steaks cost *f*20 plus. It has a spacious and stunning back garden.
Wheelchair access with assistance.

Woeste Walmen
Singel 46-48(638 0765). Tram 1, 2, 5, 13, 14, 17. **Open** 6pm-late Sat, Sun.
A squat restaurant that exudes a glowing charm. Entrance is gained by ringing a bell on the bolted door. There are usually two menu options – one meat/fish and the other vegetarian, each with a starter, main course and pudding – all attractively presented.

North African

Hamilcar
Overtoom 306 (683 7981). Tram 1, 6, 11. **Dinner served** 5-11pm Wed-Sun. **Average** *f*30; *couscous* *f*19,50-*f*34. **Credit** DC, MC, V.
Just outside the centre of town, Hamilcar is definitely worth the walk up Overtoom. Delicious dishes, including couscous, are prepared by owner-chef Kamoun and served by his Dutch wife in a relaxed and spacious setting.

Philippine

A Road to Manila
Geldersekade 23 (638 4338). Metro Nieuwmarkt. **Open** 6-11pm daily. **Average** *f*34. **Credit** AmEx, MC, DC, V.
A restaurant popular with Amsterdammers, serving little-known Philippine dishes. Since it opened in 1995, A Road to Manila has attracted much attention and has quickly built up a band of enthusiastic regulars.

Portuguese

Girassol
Weesperzijde 135 (692 3471). Tram 6, 7, 10. **Open** 6-10pm Mon, Wed-Sun. **Average** *f*25. **Credit** EC, MC.
One of the best Portuguese restaurants in town, with a lively atmosphere and highly competent cooking. Specialities are seafood and swordfish.

Spanish

Centra
Lange Niezel 29 (622 3050). Tram 4, 9, 14, 16, 24, 25. **Open** 8am-11pm daily. **Average** *f*20.
Known for good, wholesome, homely cooking. The cafeteria tables and fluorescent lighting aren't very atmospheric, but you know you're in the right place because of the large, satisfied Spanish clientele.

Duende
Lindengracht 62 (420 6692). Tram 3. **Open** 4pm-1am Mon-Thur, 2pm-1am Sun; 4pm-2am Fri, 1pm-3am Sat. **Average** *f*12; *tapas* *f*3-7,50.
Good varied selection of tapas. The goat's cheese is very potent. Order at the bar and be prepared to share your table with an amorous couple or a flamenco dancer.

El Naranjo
Boomstraat 41a (622 2402). Tram 3, 10. **Open** 5pm-midnight daily. **Average** *f*30.
A warm atmosphere, enhanced by the friendly staff. Huge menu with over 26 tapas to choose from, Spanish beers and a wine card which also serves as a map, so you can see where your wine was harvested.

Tapas Bar
Spuistraat 299 (623 1141). Tram 1, 2, 5, 11. **Open** 4pm-midnight Mon, Wed-Fri; noon-1am Sat, Sun (closed Sept). **Average** *f*17; *tapas* *f*4 to *f*30.
The most straightforward name for the most pleasurable introduction to true Spanish cuisine. Choose the perfect accompaniment for your drink from a delicious array of Catalan dishes or combine a few into a substantial meal.

Tapas Cantina
Van Limburg Stirumplein 18 (688 1337). Tram 10. **Open** 6-10.30pm daily. **Average** *f*35; *tapas f* 5-*f*13.
A wonderfully atmospheric tapas bar complete with all the saints staring down at you from the walls. The tapas are as plentiful and rich as the seafood dishes are fresh and tasty.

Thai

Pathum
Willemsstraat 16 (624 4936). Tram 3/Bus 18, 22. **Open** 5-10pm daily. **Average** *f*20. **Credit** AmEx, MC, V.
A cheap and healthy place in the Jordaan, offering excellent Thai food at low prices. Ask the waiters for advice on how hot the dishes are if you don't like food too spicy.

Turkish

Lokanta Ceren
Albert Cuypstraat 40 (673 3524). Tram 4, 16, 24, 25.
Open 6pm-midnight daily. **Average** *f*25. **Credit**
AmEx, DC, EC, MC, V.
A small, friendly restaurant in the heart of a busy market
street in the Pijp. The numerous starters (*meze*) are displayed
on a huge tray and quickly disappear when accompanied by
fresh, warm Turkish bread and a glass of Raki. Round off
your feast with some fresh fruit.

Kilim
Lindengracht 248 (639 3167). Tram 3, 10. **Open** 3-
11pm daily. **Average** *f*20.
Turkish carpets and brass ornaments lend a cosy atmosphere to this Jordaan restaurant. Simple but decent Turkish
dishes such as kebabs and aubergine salads are highly recommended.

Vegetarian

Ambrosia
*Frederick Hendrikstraat 111-114 (684 9115). Tram 3,
12, 13, 14.* **Open** 5.30-9pm Tue-Sat. **Average** *f*12.
Laid-back atmosphere, eccentric but comfortable décor, and
cooks who merrily sing along to Abba and assorted 1970s

disco classics abet an eclectic vegetarian and fish menu with
a notable Indonesian influence.

De Bolhoed
Prinsengracht 60 (626 1803). Tram 13, 14, 17. **Open**
noon-10pm daily. **Average** *f*30.
Choose hearty vegan dishes à la carte or from the daily-
changing set-price menu at this great little place. The
restaurant is licensed and there's a sumptuous selection of
pastries; the banana cream pie is a *tour de force*, properly
tackled by two. The interior is a pleasantly eccentric mix
of folk, new age and modern.

Sisters
Nes 102 (626 3970). Tram 4, 9, 14, 16, 20, 24, 25.
Open 5-9.30pm daily. **Average** *f*17.
Even committed carnivores are converted by the Sisters'
range of wholesome, value-for-money food and by the infor-
mal, friendly atmosphere. Culinary influences run from
Italian to eastern and there's no skimping on portions.
Wheelchair access.

Vliegende Schotel
Nieuwe Leliestraat 162 (625 2041). Tram 13, 14, 17.
Open 5.30-10.15pm daily. **Average** *f*17,50.
Popular with locals and a mixed, arty crowd. A particularly
good place to go if you want to get away from it all, read
newspapers or swing the resident cat. A wide choice of delicious vegetarian food is served in huge portions.

Indonesian for beginners

Nowhere else in the world, excepting Indonesia
itself, will you find as many Indonesian restaurants as in the Netherlands. This has everything
to do with Indonesia's former status as a Dutch
colony. When Dutch rule over Indonesia ended
in 1948, people were left with a choice: either stay
and become Indonesian citizens, or go to Holland
and remain Dutch citizens. The ones that decided to go introduced Indonesian cuisine to the
Netherlands.

Before walking into the first Indonesian
restaurant you see, check if it describes itself as
'chin-ind'. If so, avoid it. Their menu has gone
through the same migration process as their proprietors – from China via Indonesia, finally to
settle down in the Netherlands. These places
serve neither Chinese nor Indonesian food, but
rather a Dutch-oriental hybrid. It can be OK but
it's not the real thing.

As you can imagine, being an archipelago of
more than 1,000 islands and being influenced
by Chinese, Arabs, Portuguese and Dutch, has
had its effect on Indonesia's choice of dishes.
Most restaurants have solved this problem by
putting the famous *rijsttafel* (rice table) on their
menu. Rijsttafel consists of small portions of
various dishes accompanied by plenty of rice
and is, if well prepared, a feast for stomach and
eye. The basis is always rice. Usually white

rice, but for special occasions like weddings or
funerals *nasi kuning* (yellow rice) is prepared.
Coloured with *kunir* (turmeric) and perfumed
with a leaf called *pandan*, it's a treat even without the side dishes.

Meat served includes beef, lamb, chicken and
pork. Indonesia is an Islamic state, so pork does
not enjoy the popularity it once had, but the non-
Muslims certainly know how to make a pig taste
great. There are also plenty of fish dishes ranging from shrimps and squid to mackerel and herring. Almost every vegetable we are familiar
with is used but lesser known ones are *taugé*
(bean sprouts) and *pak choi* (Chinese cabbage).
All these are prepared with herbs and spices and
other ingredients that give it the typical
Indonesian touch. The most important ones are:
onions, garlic, coriander, cumin, kecap (sweet
soy ketchup), coconut milk, Javanese sugar and
red hot chilli peppers.

Indonesian food can be very spicy and if you
are not used to it, beware. Consult the waiter and
build up to the most spicy dishes so your palate
can get used to it. If things are too hot, don't
drink. This just makes it worse. Instead have a
bit of plain rice or bread to put out the fire.

If you still feel like dessert after your *rijsttafel*,
most places have ice cream and tropical fruits on
the menu and offer a wider choice of Indonesian

Cheap Eats

't Balkje
Kerkstraat 46-48 (622 0566). Tram 1, 2, 5, 11. **Open**
9am-9pm daily. **Average** ƒ20.
Generous sandwiches, cheeseburgers, calamares, quiches
and Dutch treats such as *uitsmuiters* at low prices. A perfect
place to refuel, just off the Leidsestraat. The staff are very
friendly and have even been known to burst into song from
time to time.

Het Beeren
Koningstraat 54 (622 2329). Metro Nieuwmarkt. **Open**
5.30-9.30pm daily. **Average** ƒ12,50.
Quite simply the best *dagschotel* (dish of the day) in town;
ƒ12,50 gets you a fantastic spread, especially in winter when
traditional Dutch dishes such as *hutspot* (stew) and *stamppot* (mashed potato and cabbage) are served up in gigantic
portions.

Einde van de Wereld
Sumatrakade 15 (no phone). Bus 28. **Open** 6pm-late
Wed, Fri. **Average** ƒ8.
Not quite at the end of the world as its name suggests, but
it is a bit of trek (or a short bike ride) to this comfortable
squat restaurant overlooking the IJ. But it's worth thr trip
to sample huge servings of vegetarian and meat dishes that
only costing between ƒ8 and ƒ12. The drinks are cheap too.
Go early before the food runs out.

New King
Zeedijk 115-117 (625 2180). Metro Nieuwmarkt. **Open**
11am-11.30pm daily. **Average** ƒ25. **Credit** AmEx, MC,
DC, V.
Over 500 Chinese dishes of which more than half are under
ƒ15. There is a wide choice of rice, noodles, meat, chicken,
fish and vegetarian dishes. Portions are so big that one plate
serves three hungry people.

Rimini
*Lange Leidsedwarsstraat 75 (622 7014). Tram 1, 2, 5,
11.* **Open** 11am-11pm daily. **Average** ƒ15. **Credit**
AmEx, MC, DC, V.
Rimini is one of those places that defy economics by producing large and flavoursome pizzas and pastas at silly
prices (everything always seems to be half price). For ƒ15
you can get just about any pizza on the menu.

Silo
Westerdoksdijk 51 (no phone). Tram 3. **Open** 6pm-late
Tue, Fri, Sun. **Average** ƒ7,50.
Wonderful squatters' restaurant situated at the end of the
old Silo building overlooking the river IJ. Large wholesome
portions of vegan food (Tue) and vegetarian food (Fri, Sun).
Names are put on a list and called out when food is ready.
Arrive early (around 6pm) to ensure there is space on the
list. The Silo's future is uncertain at time of writing, but it's
a well-known place, so ask a local if it's still open before setting out there.

sweet snacks like *spekkoek* (cinnamon and clove-
flavoured cake) or *kueh lapis* (a kind of multi-lay-
ered jelly) that go very well with after-dinner
coffee. If you're a smoker try a *kretek*, the
Indonesian clove cigarette, to really put the
crown on your Indonesian banquet.

Bojo
*Lange Leidsedwarsstraat 51 (622 7434). Tram 1, 2, 5,
11.* **Open** 4pm-2am Mon-Fri; noon-2am Thur, Sun;
noon-4am Fri , Sat. **Average** ƒ20.
One of the few restaurants open into the small hours, this
is exceptionally good value for the touristy Leidseplein
area. A whole range of large-portioned, tasty Indonesian
dishes, including all the classics, such as gado gado and
cummi cummi (squid). The vegetarian special (including
a bit of everything meat-free) is both massive and delicious.

Kantjil & de Tijger
Spuistraat 291-293 (620 0994). Tram 1, 2, 5, 11.
Open 4.30-11pm daily. **Average** ƒ50. **Credit** AmEx,
DC, EC, MC, V.
Well-cooked, authentic food at fairly reasonable prices.
The service can be rather too relaxed at times and the
interior is bare and bright, but the food makes it worth-
while.

Mas Agung
Kinkerstraat 304 (689 3994). Tram 7, 17. **Open** 9am-
6.30pm daily. **Average** ƒ28.
Deliciously exotic delicacies in a small but impeccable
take-away where the friendly owners give their customers
a warm reception. The fine Indonesian Bintang beer is
available.

De Orient
Van Baerlestraat 21 (673 4958). Tram 2, 3, 5, 12.
Open 5-9.15pm daily. **Average** ƒ40; *rijsttafel buffet,
Wed* ƒ37,50 per person. **Credit** AmEx, DC, MC, V.
A beautiful, cosy restaurant with a dauntingly large menu
that has four pages of dishes for vegetarians to choose
from. The food is wonderfully varied, with subtle and
understated use of spices.

Puri Mas
Lange Leidsedwarsstraat 37-41 (627 7627). **Open** 5pm-
12.30am daily. **Average** ƒ35. **Credit** AmEx, DC, MC, V.
Impeccable service and excellent food characterise this
classy restaurant. Everything from light meals to full
meals with vegetarian meals and rijsttafels as well.

Sama Sebo
*Pieter Corneliszoon Hooftstraat 27 (662 8146). Tram
2, 3, 5, 12.* **Open** noon-3pm, 6-10pm, Mon-Sat.
Average ƒ30. **Credit** AmEx, DC, MC, V.
A comfortable and spacious restaurant with tables outdoors for fine days. If you're not familiar with Indonesian
dishes, the staff are more than willing to help out and will
also adapt any set menu for non-meat eaters. There is no
minimum charge and the atmosphere is refreshingly
relaxed, so if you just fancy a snack rather than a full meal,
this is a good choice.

Tempo Doeloe
Utrechtsestraat 75 (625 6718). Tram 4, 6, 7, 10.
Open 6-11.30pm daily. **Average** ƒ40. **Credit** AmEx,
DC, MC, V.
This upmarket restaurant is adorned with fresh linen
tablecloths and flowers. A spiciness-rating is given next
to the dishes on the menu and, be warned, the hot dishes
are just that. One of Amsterdam's best.

Area index

The Red Light District

CAFES & BARS: De Buurvrouw, p112; De Hoogte, p112; Mono, p112; Café 't Loosje, p114; Café de Sluyswacht, p114; Droesem, p114; Engelbewaarder, p119; G-Force, p119; Frascati, p121; Durty Nelly's, p121; Fiddlers, p121.
RESTAURANTS: Hoi Tin, p97; Nam Kee, p98; Oriental City, p98; Café Roux, p100; Pacifico, p104; Morita-Ya, p104; Bern, p105; Van Beeren, p107; A Road to Manila, p107; Centra, p107; New King, p109.

Waterlooplein

CAFES & BARS: Het Kantoor, p112; De Druif, p113; Tisfris, p116; Dantzig, p116.

The Plantage

CAFES & BARS: East of Eden, p116; Bierbrouwerij 't IJ, p122.
RESTAURANTS: Agora, p228.

Rembrandtplein

CAFES & BARS: De Jaren, p116; De Kroon, p116; L'Opera, p117; Mulligan's, p121; Schiller, p119; Backstage, p119; Huyschkaemer, p120.
RESTAURANTS: Dynasty, p97; Le Pêcheur, p100; Sluizer, p100; Zuidlande, p102; Shiva, p102; Panini, p104; Rose's Cantina, p104; Adobo, p108; Kantjil & de Tijger, p109; Tempo Doeloe, p109.

Leidseplein

CAFES & BARS: Café Ebeling, p112; Café de Koe, p112; Reynders, p114; Land van Walem, p116; Morlang, p116; The Lido Complex, p117; De Balie, p119; Gary's Muffins, p119; Metz, p119.
RESTAURANTS: Café Americain, p95; 't Swarte Schaep, p97; De Blauwe Hollander, p99; Hollands Glorie, p99; Akbar, p102; Swaagat, p102; Shizen, p104; Alfonso's, p104; Café Cox, p105; De Smoeshaan, p107; Rimini, p109; Bojo, p109; Puri Mas, p109.

The Museum Quarter

CAFES & BARS: Wildschut, p117; PC, p120
RESTAURANTS: Le Garage, p101; Mirafiori, p101; El Mareton, p102; Le Rendez-vous, p105; Small Talk, p105; Brasserie van Baerle, p107; De Orient, p109; Sama Sebo, p109.

De Pijp

CAFES & BARS: Carel's Café, p112; O'Donnells, p121.
RESTAURANTS: Beddington's, p100; The India Cottage, p102; L'Angoletto, p103; Teppan-Yaki & Yamazato, p104; De Waaghals, p106; Trez, p107; Lokanta Ceren, p108.

The Jordaan

CAFES & BARS: Café Soundgarden, p112; SAS, p113; Koophandel, p114; Nieuwe Lelie, p114; Orangerie, p114; De Reiger, p114; 't Smackzeyl, p114; De Tuin, p114; Twee

Prinsen, p114; Thijssen, p117; Café Nol, p119; Twee Zwaantjes, p119; Vergulde Gaper, p120; Café Cox, p120.
RESTAURANTS: Witteveen, p100; Semhar, p99; Jean Jean, p102; Kikker, p102; Balraj, p102; Yam-Yam, p104; Hostaria, p104; Toscanini, p104; Lulu, p105; Duende, p106; El Naranjo, p107; Pathum, p107; Kilim, p108; Vliegende Schotel, p108.

Centraal Station

CAFES & BARS: OIBIBIO, p116; Blarney Stone, p121.
RESTAURANTS: Pier 10, p97; Bordewijk, p100; Himalaya, p102; Barney's Breakfast Bar, p103; Silo, p109.

Canals and Centre

CAFES & BARS: Twin Pigs, p113; Vrankrijk, p113; Aas van Bokalen, p113; De Doffer, p113; 't Gasthuis, p113; Hoppe, p114; De Prins, p114; Het Molenpad, p114; Van Puffelen, p114; De Tap, p114; Café Dante, p114; Kapitein Zeppos, p116; Du Lac, p117; Café Luxembourg, p117; Scheltema, p119; Berkhoff, p119; Café Esprit, p119; Greenwoods, p119; Lanskroon, p119; Noord Zuid Hollands Koffiehuis, p120; Ovidius, p120; Pompadour, p120; Café Het Schuim, p120; Seymour Likely, p120; Felix Meritis, p121; O'Reilly's, p121; Tara, p121; De Beiaard, p122; Gollem, p122; De Wildeman, p122; De Admiraal, p122; De Drie Fleschjes, p122.
RESTAURANTS: De Blauwe Parade, p95;Van Vlaanderen, p97; Pancake Bakery, p100; Albatros, p100; Belhamel, p100; De Poort, p95; Tout Court, p97; Dorrius, p99; Keuken van 1870, p99; Oud Holland, p100; De Rode Leeuw, p100; De Schutter, p97; Taddy Zemmel, p102; Lucius, p100; Bonjour, p100; Excelsior, p100; Crignon Culinair, p100; Luden, p102; D'Theeboom, p102; Het Tuynhuys, p102; Zuid Zeeland, p102; Le Zinc...et Les Dames, p102; Casa di David, p103; Café Paradox, p103; Café Prins, p103; Café Prins, p103; Greenwoods, p103; Mono, p103; Prego, p104; Tartufo, p104; Vasso, p102; La Margarita, p104; An, p104; De Impressionist, p105; Piet de Leeuw, p105; Woeste Walmen, p107; Tapas Bar, p107; Ambrosia, p108; De Bolhoed, p108; Sisters, p108; Het Balkje, p109; Het Beeren, p109.

Amsterdam South

RESTAURANTS:
Halvemaan, p97; Genet, p99; Julia, p100; De Jonge Dikkert, p100; Kaiko, p104.

Amsterdam East

CAFES & BARS: De IJsbreker, p116.
RESTAURANTS: La Rive, p97; La Vallade, p102; Girassol, p107; Docksider, p104;.

Amsterdam West

CAFES & BARS: Café West Pacific, p113; Hellen's Place, p119.
RESTAURANTS: Lalibela, p100; Hamilcar, p107; Mas Agung, p109.

Cafés & Bars

From poky smoky brown bars to great gleaming grand cafés: the best places in which to give yourself a hangover.

In much the same way as political history, the grand scheme of European drinking has the Netherlands occupying something of an unfortunate position; sandwiched between the Belgians, who to all intents and purposes invented beer, and the Germans, who are reputed to drink most of it. Accordingly, the Dutch tend to find themselves squeezed out of boozing folklore, but the truth could not be more different. Until the appearance of Mr Gullit on English shores, England's most popular Dutchman was arguably Mr Heineken, closely followed by Mr Grolsch, whilst Amstel is one of the most popular brands in Europe. And who could forget that Oranjeboom is a beer and not, in fact, a tune? Advocaat, the famous egg-nog of yore, needs no explanation and jenever, Dutch gin, packs a mule-like kick.

With alcoholic credentials beyond any dispute – even Monty Python once featured 'The Bols Story... the history of Holland's most famous aperitif' – it will come as no surprise that Amsterdam is one of Europe's premier towns for drinking. For a relatively small city, there is a seemingly unfeasible amount of bars. And even these don't seem sufficient. For much of the the the year, the clientele overflow on to the street – not because the weather's nice, there just ain't no more room in the inn.

As a rule of thumb, if you are looking to supplement your liquid diet with a few solids then a café is the best bet. Bars tend to be dedicated to the art of quaffing rather than scoffing, although snacks are generally available. The grand cafés, to be found mainly around the tourist honeypots of the Leidseplein and Rembrandtplein, are larger than normal cafés and generally also less intimate, which may or may not be a bad thing. Prices are invariably higher. There are also certain cafés of the more genteel variety that don't serve spirits but do serve some of the best confectionery in Europe, more austere than the Germanic death-by-chocolate-and-cream affairs but no slouches in the flavour stakes. Indeed, it is often remarked upon that Amsterdam has a tremendous affection for tarts.

Amsterdam's famous brown cafés are the last bastion of what's left of Dutch culture. They are so named because, well, they are brown – darkened

Café West Pacific *and it's a gas, gas, gas. Page 113.*

down the years by industrial deposits of nicotine (there's no such thing as a no-smoking area in Dutch drinking culture). One rather perverse touch is the provision of carpets. On the tables. Which probably makes hoovering a bit of a chore.

GOING DUTCH

Getting a drink here is a piece of piss; or rather it isn't, because Dutch beers are much more potent on their home territory than the insipid namesakes sold abroad. Which probably explains why it is not, as a rule, consumed in pint quantities. Beer in Amsterdam is, without exaggeration, fantastic – a brew that both warms during winter and hits the spot in the summer months. Aside from the aforementioned Dutch brands, the better bars also serve a comprehensive selection of Belgian beers which range from strong to debilitatingly strong. Many of these are brewed by Trappist monks with an apparently perverse sense of humour: one rejoices in the name of Mort Subite (Sudden Death). Variants on the Dutch theme are *Witbier* (Dentergem, Raaf, Hoegaarden), a light beer popular in summer with a slice of lemon, and *Bokbier*, a cousin of traditional English ale that appears in the autumn and is particularly popular around Christmas.

Of matters more spiritual, jenever drinking is an education in itself, although detention frequently continues throughout the next day. Dutch gin is made from molasses and, in its natural state, only flavoured with juniper berries. It comes in a variety of ages, and its flavour mellows progressively up the scale with its maturity. It also comes in different flavours, such as lemon and blackcurrant.

For many, the best part about drinking in Amsterdam is not the booze or the venue, it's the fact most cafés and bars stay open well into the wee small hours. They will probably outlast the endurance of all but the die-hard drinker.

For more bars and cafés *see chapters* **Gay & Lesbian**, **Music**, **Students** *and* **Women**. Amsterdam's cinemas often have bars worth visiting even if you're not going to see a film; check out those at Kriterion, Movies, Rialto, Tuschinski and Vertigo (*see chapter* **Film**). Unless indicated otherwise, the bars and cafés listed don't accept credit cards.

For a list of bars, restaurants, shops and sights by area, *see page 110* Area Index.

Alternative Bars

De Buurvrouw

St Pieterpoortsteeg 29 (625 9654). Tram 4, 9, 14, 16, 24, 25. **Open** 8pm-2am Mon-Thur, Sun; 8pm-3am Fri, Sat.
Typical of bars in this area, De Buurvrouw, on a small side street off the Nes, plays loud, vaguely alternative rock and plays host to loud, vaguely alternative people. Prone to get very crowded, but definitely lively. (*See also chapter* **Music: Rock, Folk & Jazz.**)

Carel's Café

Frans Halsstraat 76 (679 4836). Tram 16, 24, 25. **Open** 10am-1am Mon-Fri; 10am-2am Fri, Sat; 11am-1am Sun.
In the Albert Cuyp area, this is a typical large neighbourhood café. Although frequented by all manner of locals, the atmosphere is essentially 'family', with a comprehensive lunch and dinner menu.
Branches: Saenredamstraat 32 (676 0888); Voetboogstraat 6 (622 2080).

Café Ebeling

Overtoom 52 (689 1218). Tram 1, 3, 6, 11, 12. **Open** 11am-1am Mon-Thur; 11am-2am Fri-Sun.
In the premises of an old bank, Ebeling is a well laid out, split-level bar which aims itself at the young and trendy without being snobby or needing to have the music so loud you can't think. The toilets are worth seeing – they're in the old vaults (safe doors and all) – while Ebeling is one of the few non-Irish bars in town that serves Guinness.

De Hoogte

Nieuwe Hoogstraat 2a (626 0604). Metro Nieuwmarkt. **Open** 10am-1am Mon-Thur; 10am-2am Fri, Sat; noon-1am Sun.
Small but characterful drinking-joint close to the Red-Light District catering to an alternative, hippyish crowd. Especially popular in the afternoons as a haven from the bustle of the tourist trap that is Nieuwe Hoogstraat.

Kanis & Meiland

Levantkade 127 (693 2439). Bus 28, 32, 59. **Open** noon-1am Mon-Thur, Sun; noon-3am Fri, Sat.
Situated on KNSM island (hence the name), Kanis & Meiland is well out of the centre, in the middle of Amsterdam's redeveloping docklands. A bright and spacious café with a pool table and a waterfront terrace. Perfect for summer.

Het Kantoor

Waterlooplein 123 (622 3553). Tram 9, 14/ Metro Waterlooplein. **Open** 8am-1am Mon-Sat; noon-6pm Sun.
'The Office' is a first-floor bar with a great view over the bustling market below. It gets enjoyably exuberant around 6pm when market traders finish for the day and head there to drink their takings.

Café de Koe

Marnixstraat 381 (625 4482). Tram 7, 10, 17. **Open** 4pm-1am Mon-Thur, Sun; 1pm-2am Fri, Sat.
A friendly upstairs bar decorated in a theme to suit its name (cows), along with a Scalextric track over the pool table. Staff are available for pinball competitions, if it's not too busy, and the chef of the café/restaurant downstairs serves great food for reasonable prices. One of the best bars in Amsterdam.

Mono Ontbijt & Alcohol

Oudezijds Voorburgwal 2 (625 3630). Tram 4, 9, 14, 16, 24, 25. **Open** 10am-1am Sun-Thur; 10am-2am Fri, Sat.
The reason this place opens so early is that it specialises in breakfast as well as alcohol. There are 11 different breakfasts, ranging from the traditional to the bizarre (tomatoes cooked in tea). Also the place to go for 1960s psych/garage sounds although whether this is what you need to accompany your ham and eggs is open to question. *See chapter* **Restaurants**.

Café Soundgarden

Marnixstraat 164-166 (620 2853). Tram 10, 13, 14, 17. **Open** 1pm-1am Mon-Thur; 1pm-2am Fri, Sat, 3pm-1am Sun.
Popular with a grungey, alternative crowd and with music to match. The pool table, darts board, pinball machine and table football provide hours of boozy fun and, if all that palls, you can always spend time seeing who has the most body piercings. It also has one of the best terraces in Amsterdam, recently revamped, overlooking the canal at the rear and perfect for summer nights.

*You won't get browned off at **De Druif**.*

SAS

Marnixstraat 79 (420 4075). Tram 7, 10, 17. **Open** 1pm-1am Mon-Thur; 1pm-2am Fri, Sat.
Comfortable sofas and chairs sit among the wonderfully cluttered, arty interior of this café. The decor changes whenever the owner feels like a change. Good, homely meals at very low prices (and in very large portions) are served downstairs and on the canalside terrace. Candlelit, casual and charmingly romantic. Occasional live music. A great little Amsterdam bar.

Twin Pigs

Nieuwendijk 100 (420 6822). Tram 1, 2, 4, 5, 9, 13, 17, 24, 25. **Open** noon-2am daily.
Twin Pigs is the newest, one of the biggest, and most certainly the loudest live music bar in Amsterdam. Its central location has made it a bustling place with a young Hard Rock Café-type and backpackers crowd. Beware the house wine, though.

Vrankrijk

Spuistraat 216 (no phone). Tram 1, 2, 5, 11, 13, 14, 17. **Open** 10pm-2am Mon-Thur, Sun; 10pm-3am Fri, Sat.
Amsterdam's premier squat bar attracts a largely international crowd of squatters (and their dogs). Cheap, wide range of drinks, a pool table and a wall of impenetrable noise music. Regular benefit nights, as well as a disco every Saturday. Ring the doorbell to get in.

Café West Pacific

Haarlemmerweg 8-10 (597 4458). Tram 10. **Open** bar 11.30am-1am Tue-Sun; 11.30am-2am Fri, Sat; restaurant 6-10.30pm daily.
A large bar with a huge fire, a dancefloor and a decent menu. A mixture of music plays, but from 11pm the emphasis is on dance music and the place fills up quickly. There's occasional live music, such as jazz, on Sundays. The café's in the Westergasfabriek, a former gas factory, where exhibitions and dance parties are held as well as occasional offbeat performances and plays.

Brown Cafés

Brown cafés come in shapes and sizes: the only thing they have in common is the nicotine stained walls which earned them their name. We've listed a selection of our favourites, but you'll find brown cafés all over the city.

Aas van Bokalen

Keizersgracht 335 (623 0917). Tram 1, 2, 5, 11. **Open** bar 4pm-1am daily; kitchen 4-10.30pm daily.
A stunningly unpretentious little bar serving some of the best-value food in town. It has a fine collection of 1970s tapes and a varied, young clientele.

De Doffer

Runstraat 12 (622 6686). Tram 1, 2, 5, 11. **Open** bar 11am-2am Mon-Thur; 11am-3am Fri, Sat; noon-2am Sun; kitchen noon-2.30pm, 6-10pm, daily.
A scruffy, friendly, down-to-earth bar with billiards at the back and cheap, filling food from ƒ16. Patronised by students.

De Druif

Rapenburgerplein 83 (624 4530). Tram 1/Metro Waterlooplein/bus 22, 31. **Open** 11am-1am Mon-Thur, Sun; 11am-2am Fri, Sat.
A little-known bar of immense charm, on the water's edge behind the harbour. If you make it out there you'll be the only non-local – but they're a very friendly bunch.

't Gasthuis

Grimburgwal 7 (624 8230). Tram 4, 9, 11,14, 16, 24, 25. **Open** 11am-1am Mon-Thur, Sun; 11am-2am Fri, Sat.
Most of the clientele here are students: it's just around the corner from the city's biggest university building. The lunchtime snacks – a large selection of rolls and sandwiches – are recommended, while the interior is far larger than it at first appears.

Hoppe

Spui 18-20 (623 7849). Tram 1, 2, 4, 5, 9, 11, 14, 16, 24, 25. **Open** 8am-1am Mon-Thur, Sun; 8am-2am Fri, Sat.
An Amsterdam institution, Hoppe allegedly dates from 1670. Always popular, it becomes impossibly crowded from 5pm to 6pm, when it's filled with stripey shirts and braces on their way home from the office.

Koophandel

Bloemgracht 49 (623 9843). Tram 10, 13, 14, 17. **Open** 10pm-3am Mon-Thur, Sun; 10pm-4am Fri, Sat.
A late-night bar for the very dedicated. In a former warehouse beside the Jordaan's prettiest canal, it remains virtually empty until midnight, when things get steadily livelier. Closing time is flexible but isn't usually before dawn.

Café 't Loosje

Nieuwmarkt 32-24 (627 2635). Tram 4, 9, 14, 16, 24, 25/Metro Nieuwmarkt. **Open** 9am-1am daily.
An outdoor terrace and old wooden interior make this a great place for late breakfasts, late nights and sunny afternoons. The walls are adorned with well-preserved tableaux of tiles dating from the beginning of the century.

Het Molenpad

Prinsengracht 653 (625 9680). Tram 1, 2, 5, 7, 10, 11. **Open** *bar* noon-1am Mon-Thur, Sun; noon-2am Fri, Sat; *kitchen* noon-3.30pm Mon-Fri; noon-4.30pm Sat, Sun.
One of the pleasures of Prinsengracht, this place is long, dark and narrow with a large reading table at the back, good tapes, changing art exhibitions and exceptionally fine food.

Nieuwe Lelie

Nieuwe Leliestraat 83 (622 5493). Tram 10, 13, 14, 17. **Open** 2pm-1am Mon-Thur; 2pm-2am Fri, Sat.
A charming split-level Jordaan brown bar, one of the few where you can be sure of a table until quite late in the evening. It's very quiet and relaxed, and chess boards are often unoccupied.

Orangerie

Binnen Oranjestraat 15 (623 4611). Tram 3/bus 18, 22, 44. **Open** 4pm-1am Mon-Thur, Fri; 3pm-2am Sat; 3pm-1am Sun.
A delightful, relaxed and very brown bar indeed, a stone's throw from Brouwersgracht and its converted warehouses; good for quiet evenings and private conversations.

Van Puffelen

Prinsengracht 377 (624 6270). Tram 1, 2, 5, 7, 10, 11. **Open** *bar* 3pm-1am Mon-Thur, Sun; 3pm-2am Fri; noon-2am Sat; noon-1am Sun; *kitchen* 6-11pm daily.
Recently merged with the neighbouring Paris Brest to become the biggest brown café in Amsterdam, yet it still retains its charm. A haunt of the beautiful people, particularly on summer evenings when you can sit on a barge moored outside.

De Prins

Prinsengracht 124 (624 9382). Tram 13, 14, 17. **Open** *bar* 9.30am-1am Mon-Thur, Sun; 9.30am-2am Fri, Sat; *kitchen* 6-10pm daily.
Not to be confused with De Prinses, a little way down the canal, De Prins is usually full of students and a good bet if you're young and in need of company. The pretty setting is matched by excellent food.

De Reiger

Nieuwe Leliestraat 34 (624 7426). Tram 10, 13, 14, 17. **Open** *bar* 11am-1am Mon-Thur, Sun; 11am-2am Fri, Sat; *kitchen* 6-10.30pm daily.
The style-conscious alternative to the Nieuwe Lelie (*see above*) down the street, this is a light and airy brown bar and one of the most popular in the Jordaan. Get there early, particularly if you want to eat.

Reynders

Leidseplein 6 (623 4419). Tram 1, 2, 5, 6, 7, 10, 11. **Open** 8.30am-1am Mon-Thur, Sun; 8.30am-2am Fri, Sat.
With its neighbour Eylders, probably the only bar worth considering on Leidseplein. Both are survivors of a bygone era, with white-aproned waiters and high-ceilinged interiors.

Café de Sluyswacht

Jodenbreestraat 1 (625 7611). Tram 9, 14/Metro Nieuwmarkt. **Open** 11am-1am Mon-Thur, Sun; 11am-2am Fri, Sat.
One of the most peaceful settings in Amsterdam. Directly opposite the Rembrandthuis, this former warehouse, built in 1695, now has a spacious terrace surrounded by the water of the Oude Schans on three sides. Inside, the décor is simple and the staff are friendly.

't Smackzeyl

Brouwersgracht 101 (622 6520). Tram 1, 2, 5, 11, 13, 17. **Open** 11.30am-1am Mon-Thur, Sun; 11.30am-2am Fri, Sat.
About as brown as you could wish for, this perfectly situated bar on the corner of two canals is one of the few to serve draught Guinness.

De Tap

Prinsengracht 478 (622 9915). Tram 1, 2, 5, 6, 7, 10, 11. **Open** 4pm-1am Mon-Thur, Sun; 4pm-2am Fri, Sat.
A long, narrow, wood-panelled bar not far from the frantic Leidseplein, serving abundant pre-dinner snacks – mainly of unshelled peanuts. It's popular for student reunions and office parties.

De Tuin

Tweede Tuindwarsstraat 13 (624 4559). Tram 3, 10, 13, 14, 17. **Open** 10am-1am Mon-Thur; 10am-2am Fri, Sat; 11am-1am Sun.
A classic Jordaan bar frequented by slightly alternative locals, 'the garden' is stone-floored, dark and always lively. Excellent apple tarts are served in the afternoons and there's always a partner for a game of chess or backgammon.

Twee Prinsen

Prinsenstraat 27 (624 9722). Tram 3, 10. **Open** 10am-1am Mon; 11am-1am Tue-Thur, Sun; 11am-2am Fri; 10am-2am Sat.
Opposite the Vergulde Gaper (*see below* under **Trendy**), this is an exceptionally friendly bar full of young and vaguely offbeat locals. The outdoor terrace is heated on chillier evenings.

Café-Gallery

Café Dante

Spuistraat 320 (638 8839). Tram 1, 5, 11. **Open** 11am-1am Mon-Thur, Sun; 11am-2am Fri, Sat.
Monthly exhibitions, organised by owner Rob Schut and collaborator Barbara van der Linden, hang all around the drinking area as well as on the walls of the balcony above. The staff are accustomed to their customers wandering around the premises as though they're in an art gallery.

Designer Bars

Droesem

Nes 41 (620 3316). Tram 4, 9, 14, 16, 24, 25. **Open** 5pm-1am Mon-Thur, Sun; 5pm-2am Fri, Sat.
Tucked away in the Nes, wine café Droesem claims to be the first bar of its kind in Amsterdam. House wine is served in

Café Thijssen: *the piano ain't a grand, but the café is. Page 117.*

carafes filled from barrels and the fine selection of cheese, breads, fish and meats are presented on wooden chopping boards. The quantities served depend entirely on your appetite. Less than five minutes' walk from the Dam.

East of Eden
Linnaeusstraat 11 (665 0743). Tram 9, 10, 14. **Open** 11am-1am Mon-Thur, Sun; 11am-2am Fri, Sat.
A pleasant, relaxed café on a corner overlooking the Tropenmuseum. The atmosphere is an odd mix of colonial splendour combined with the obvious James Dean fixation. At its best in the summer when the comfortable interior is augmented by a spacious terrace with a hedge killing much of the noise from the busy street.

De IJsbreker
Weesperzijde 23 (668 1805). Tram 3, 6, 7, 10. **Open** *bar* 10am-1am Mon-Thur, Sun; 10am-2am Fri, Sat.
The bar at this contemporary music centre (*see chapter* **Music: Classical & Opera**) is well worth the bike or tram ride for its ultra peaceful terrace on the Amstel, off-beat clientele and good music. Food is available all day and it's one of the few places open for breakfast on Sunday.

Kapitein Zeppos
Gebed Zonder End 5 (624 2057). Tram 4, 9, 14, 16, 24, 25. **Open** *bar* 10.30am-1am Mon-Thur; 10.30am-2am Fri, Sat; *summer* 4-10pm Sun, *winter* 4-9pm Sun; *kitchen summer* 6-10pm daily; *winter* 6-9pm daily.
Tucked away at the end of a cul-de-sac, this bar has a cobbled courtyard for summer evenings and loud music (live on Sunday afternoons). The tortilla chips have flavour, the menu is interesting and wide-ranging (from ƒ20).

Land van Walem
Keizersgracht 449 (625 3544). Tram 1, 2, 5, 11. **Open** *bar* 9am-1am Mon-Thur, Sun; 9am-2am Fri, Sat; *kitchen* 9.30am-10.30pm daily.
Land van Walem is one of the earlier designer bars: long, narrow and bright. The seriously self-important clientele is worth braving for the food; although it can be pricey (from

ƒ17) it's good and comes in large portions. Excellent vegetarian quiches and big salads are among the dishes.

Morlang
Keizersgracht 451 (625 2681). Tram 1, 2, 5, 11. **Open** *bar* 10am-1am Mon-Thur, Sun; 10am-2am Fri, Sat; *main kitchen* 5.30-11pm daily; *snack kitchen* 10am-11pm daily.
Next door to Land van Walem (*see above*) and a competitor in the style stakes. There's an awesome selection of foreign spirits and good food downstairs (from ƒ18).

OIBIBIO
Prins Hendrikkade 20-21 (553 9355). NS/Metro CS/Tram 1, 2, 4, 5, 9, 11, 13, 17, 24, 25. **Open** *bar* 9am-1am Mon-Thur, Sun; 9am-2am Fri, Sat; *restaurant* 5.30pm-10pm daily.
Near Centraal Station, this aesthetic and airy bar has a wonderfully relaxed atmosphere and serves good, healthy snacks and meals. It is overlooked by a gourmet vegetarian restaurant. Also in the building is a Japanese-style tea garden.

Tisfris
St Antoniesbreestraat 142 (622 0472). Tram 9, 14/Metro Nieuwmarkt. **Open** *bar* 10am-1am daily; *kitchen* 5.30-10pm daily.
A modern, trendy but undaunting split-level café decorated with paintings by Fabrice, a street artist whose works pop up with monotonous regularity all over town. The food is good and wholesome (from ƒ16), the clientele largely young and arty; a good place to put your feet up if you've been wandering around the flea market on nearby Waterlooplein.

Grand Cafés

Dantzig
Zwanenburgwal 15 (620 9039). Tram 9, 14/Metro Waterlooplein. **Open** 10am-1am Mon-Thur, Sun; 10am-2am Fri, Sat.
Right by the Stopera building, this café/resturant is a popular meeting place for performance-goers. It's spacious, with

*The **Schiller** has seen better days, but it's still the best bar on the block. Page 119.*

Oompah pah party

Aside from the obvious geography, there is no logical reason why Britain should be the only land of North-Western Europe that has escaped the curse of the 'oom-pah-pah' drinking song. Wherever you go, from Scandinavia through the Low Countries and down to Bavaria, this fundamentally Germanic form of entertainment will be encountered wherever people are boozing.

This includes Amsterdam where, in certain more traditional quarters, they get almost obsessive over their multi-verse communal dirges which go hand in hand with the perpetual search for the ultimate *gezelligheid* (translates roughly as matey, beery, smoky, dark-type atmosphere). These old Amsterdam songs which, unsurprisingly, seem mainly to concern boats and harbours, are the staple entertainment of many a dark winter's night. Well, it sure beats Dutch

TV. And if you find yourself in one of these traditional bars, mainly in the Jordaan area, it is not unknown for an unwitting spectator to end up as the evening's involuntary star turn, egged on to sing by a crowd of beery blokes with some of the most eccentric facial hair imaginable.

It may upon first impression appear that what is going on is little more than a German karaoke theme night, with much clinking of glasses and that bend-ze-knees rhythm so popular in the land of *Lederhosen*. You may or may not have a point, but under no circumstances remark upon any sort of similarity between Amsterdam folk songs and their German counterparts. For in spite of a strong physical resemblance and a mutual fondness for minimalist humour, there isn't much love lost between the two populations. And Dutch folk songs are unmistakably different, *right?*

old-fashioned library décor, complete with librarian's stepladder and pillars that emanate light from their Corinthian capitals. The large terrace has a supreme view across the River Amstel.

De Jaren

Nieuwe Doelenstraat 20 (625 5771). Tram 4, 9, 14, 16, 24, 25. **Open** *bar* 10am-1am Sun-Thur; 10am-2am Fri, Sat; *kitchen* 5.30-10pm daily.
A beautifully restored old building overlooking the Amstel, with exposed brickwork and a tiled mosaic floor. De Jaren serves snacks downstairs and a full restaurant menu upstairs (main courses from *f*20). With sunny balconies on both floors, down-to-earth service and an impressive range of beers and spirits, it's the most elegant and unpretentious of Amsterdam's new grand cafés.

De Kroon

Rembrandtplein 17/1 (625 2011). Tram 4, 9, 14. **Open** 10am-1am Mon-Thur, Sun; 10am-2am Fri, Sat.
Several local TV companies and radio stations are housed in the same building as De Kroon, hence the media types to be found here. Huge, high-ceilinged, spacious and airy.

Du Lac

Haarlemmerstraat 118 (624 4265). Bus 18, 22, 44. **Open** 4pm-1am Mon- Wed, Sun; 4pm-2am Thur- Sat.
A beautiful grand café fitted out in a quirky Art Deco style that includes heaps of greenery. At peak times, it packs in trendies by the hundred, each of whom has their favourite spot, be it one of the cosy snugs, the raised gallery, or the glass-walled conservatory. Live jazz on Sunday afternoons.

The Lido Complex

Leidsekade (626 2106). Tram 1, 5, 6, 7, 10, 11. **Gauguin Restaurant** *(622 1526).* **Open** 5.30-10.15pm Wed-Sun.
De Gouwe Ouwe Zender *(626 2106).* **Open** 11am-1am Mon-Thur; 11am-2am Fri-Sat; 11am-1am Sun.
The Lido Complex, which was first built in the 1930s as a homage to the Lido in Venice, appears to be just one huge outdoor café overlooking the Singelgracht but on closer inspection reveals itself to be a restaurant, café-diner and theatre, where anything from concerts to fashion-shows are held.

Café Luxembourg

Spuistraat 22-24 (620 6264). Tram 1, 2, 5, 11,13, 17. **Open** *bar* 10am-1am Mon-Thur, Sun; 10am-2am Fri, Sat; *kitchen* 10am-11pm daily.
Still going strong as *the* place to be seen for the trend-conscious and generally monied Amsterdammer, the Luxembourg is elegant, high-ceilinged and serves an excellent range of high-quality snacks till midnight (the dim sum are delicious, the club sandwiches colossal).

L'Opera

Rembrandtplein 27 (627 5232). Tram 4, 9, 14. **Open** 10am-1am Mon-Thur, Sun; 10am-2am Fri, Sat; *kitchen* 11am-10pm daily. **Credit** AmEx, DC, MC, V.
The interior is imposing and vaguely Parisian, with lots of mirrors and gilt. Unfortunately the overall sense of style is not matched by the service, which is slow. There's a good range of hot snacks served till late (from *f*10).

Thijssen

Brouwersgracht 107 (623 8994). Tram 3. **Open** 9.30am-1am Mon-Thur, Sun; 9.30am-2am Fri; 7am-2am Sat.
Thijssen is a relatively new café in the Jordaan, owned by three local barflys, and it blends in perfectly with the neighbouring cafes. Most of its clientele live in the area.

Wildschut

Roelof Hartplein 1-3 (676 8220). Tram 3, 5, 12, 24, 25. **Open** *bar* 9am-2am Mon-Thur, Sun; 9am-3am Fri, Sat; *kitchen* noon-3.30pm, 6-10.30pm daily.
Café/restaurant famous for its Art Deco interior and one of the city's hot spots; in summer it is practically impossible to find a space on the terrace that overlooks the Roelof Hartplein, a square surrounded by Amsterdam School architecture.

Jordaan Cafés

Two traditional cafés where the locals like to accompany the loud, oom-pah-pah music. A night out in these bars is guaranteed to be a raucous and rowdy affair.

Café Nol

Westerstraat 109 (624 5380). Tram 10. **Open** 8pm-2am
Mon-Thur, Sun; 8pm-3am Fri, Sat.
An over-the-top Jordaan bar which is always crowded with
lustily singing locals and the occasional lost tourist.
Something of an institution and not to be attempted unless
you're happy to lose every inhibition you ever had.

Twee Zwaantjes

Prinsengracht 114 (625 2729). Tram 13, 14, 17. **Open**
3pm-1am daily.
A slightly (but only just) less rowdy version of the Café Nol,
this is a tiny bar usually crammed to bursting point with
accordion playing, yodelling Jordaaners.

Literary Cafés

De Balie

*Kleine Gartmanplantsoen 10 (624 3821). Tram 1, 2, 5, 6,
7, 10, 11.* **Open** *July, Aug* noon-1am Tue-Thur, Sun; 5pm-
2am Fri, Sat; *Sept-June* 11am-1am Tue-Thur, Sun; 11am-
2am Fri, Sat.
Part of the cultural/political centre of the same name, the
Balie is a slightly sterile, marbled place full of more-or-
less active activists watching the riff-raff of Leidseplein
from large windows. Reasonably good food upstairs (from
ƒ17).

Engelbewaarder

Kloveniersburgwal 59 (625 3772). Metro Nieuwmarkt.
Open noon-1am Mon-Thur; noon-2am Fri, Sat; 2pm-1am
Sun.
A 'literary café' featuring Sunday live jazz, this is a scruffy
but attractive dive whose clientele (students, retired
American hippies and perspiring writers) will welcome
you providing you have something intelligent to say.
There is additional outdoor seating on a barge moored out-
side.

Scheltema

*Nieuwezijds Voorburgwal 212 (623 2323). Tram 1, 2, 5,
11, 13, 17.* **Open** 8am-11pm Mon-Fri; 9am-9pm Sat;
11am-7pm Sun.
Once thronged with journalists from the national dailies
based down the road, this bar has become quieter now
they've all moved out to the concrete wilderness. It retains
an attractive, slightly highbrow atmosphere.

Schiller

Rembrandtplein 26 (624 9846). Tram 4, 9, 14. **Open** *bar*
4pm-1am Mon-Thur, Sun; 4pm-2am Fri, Sat; *kitchen* 6-
10pm daily.
This beautiful, if rather faded, bar is a reminder of how things
were on Rembrandtplein before neon was invented. A great art
deco Amsterdam bar, it belongs to the hotel of the same name.

Sex Cafés

G-Force

*Oudezijds Armsteeg 7 (420 1664). Tram 1, 2, 4, 5, 9, 11,
13, 17, 24, 25/Metro CS.* **Open** 2pm-midnight daily.
A friendly café in the Red-Light District which is welcoming
to all who are interested in finding out more about SM. Plenty
of magazines for perusal, SM videos and artwork on show.

Hellen's Place

Overtoom 497 (689 5501). Tram 1, 6. **Open** 8pm-1am
Mon-Thur, Sun; 8pm-2am Fri, Sat.
An 'erotic' café which is welcoming to everyone, whatever
their sexual persuasion. There's a downstairs cellar, complete with darkroom and a special area for SM.

Tea Rooms

Backstage

Utrechtsedwarsstraat 67 (622 3638). Tram 4. **Open**
10am-6pm Mon-Sat.
Friendly café-boutique run by Greg and Gary, the eccentric
Christmas twins, who'll amuse you with gossip while you
eat cake or one of their famous mega tuna sandwiches. The
psychedelic décor matches the range of knitwear on sale
(which includes woollen bras) designed by one twin and knitted by the other. Possibly the most unusual afternoon tea
you will ever experience.

Berkhoff

Leidsestraat 46 (624 0233). Tram 1, 2, 5, 11. **Open**
10am-6pm Mon; 9am-6pm Tue-Sat.
Still one of the best for chocolate- and calorie-laden pastries
and cakes, the Berkhoff has a small salon attached. It's usually full of little old ladies.

Café Esprit

Spui 10a (622 1967). Tram 1, 2, 4, 5, 9, 14, 16, 24, 25.
Open *café* 10am-6pm Mon-Wed, Fri, Sat; 10am-10pm
Thur; *kitchen* 10am-4pm Mon-Wed, Fri, Sat; 10am-9.15pm
Thur. **Credit** AmEx, MC, V.
Owned by the neighbouring fashion store of the same
name, this ultra-modern café serves a full menu of
Californian food as well as classy rolls and salads. It's at
its best in summer, when the terrace catches the sun and
provides a welcome break from traipsing up Kalverstraat
looking for bargains.

Gary's Muffins

Prinsengracht 454 (420 1452). Tram 1, 2, 5, 11. **Open**
8am-6pm Mon-Sat; 10am-6pm Sun.
Marnixstraat 121 (638 0186) Tram 3, 10 **Open** 8am-
6pm Mon-Sat , 10am-6pm Sun.
Not quite your exclusive tea room but the best place in
town for genuine American muffins and bagels, all with
a wide range of fillings and flavours.The atmosphere is
both friendly and relaxed, although it can become very
cramped, especially at lunchtimes. The newer branch on
Marnixstraat, although way off the beaten track, is much
bigger. Also sells different kinds of fruit juices and big
mugs of coffee and tea (including herbal). *See chapter*
Early Hours.

Greenwoods

Singel 103 (623 7071). Tram 1, 2, 5, 11. **Open** 9.30am-
7pm Mon-Fri; 11am-7pm Sat, Sun.
This basic high-tea room serves cakes, scones and muffins
that are freshly baked on the premises, as well as a traditional English breakfast that is available all day. *See chapter* **Restaurants**.

Lanskroon

Singel 305 (623 7743). Tram 1, 2, 5, 11. **Open** 8am-
5.30pm Tue-Fri; 8am-5pm Sat. **Credit** DC, MC, V.
For many people's money the most refined *banketbakkerij*
(patisserie) in town, Lanskroon makes mouth-watering fruit
pies and chocolate cakes. Devour them on the premises in
the rather cramped tearoom.

Metz

Keizersgracht 455 (624 8810). Tram 1, 2, 5, 11. **Open**
11am-6pm Mon; 9.30am-6pm Tue, Wed, Fri, Sat; 9.30am-
9.30pm Thur. **Credit** AmEx, DC, MC, V.
A postmodern café on the sixth floor of the famous department store, offering one of the best views of Amsterdam.
Pricey food includes smoked salmon on toast and pastrami
on rye, plus soups and for larger appetites (and wallets)
entrecôte, Metzburgers and so on. Metz claims to serve
English afternoon tea; we've yet to be convinced.

Café Cox: *the relaxed face of Leidesplein.*

Noord Zuid Hollands Koffiehuis

Stationsplein 10 (623 3777). Tram 1, 2, 4, 5, 9, 11, 13, 16, 17, 24, 25. **Open** *café* 9am-9pm Mon-Sat; 10am-9pm Sun; *kitchen* 10am-8pm daily. **Credit** AmEx, DC, MC, V.
Most people shoot straight past this on their way out of Centraal Station – a shame because it's pleasantly relaxed, has a fine waterside terrace and serves reasonably priced, light food.

Ovidius

Spuistraat 139 (620 8977) Tram 1, 2, 5, 11, 13, 14, 17. **Open** 10.30am-1.00am Sun, Mon, 9.30am-2am Tues-Sat
The place to get a coffee in Amsterdam – they seem to have almost every conceivable bean – plus sandwiches which, although not cheap, redefine the very essence of the word.

PC

PC Hooftstraat 83 (671 7455). Tram 2, 3, 5, 11, 12. **Open** 10am-7pm daily.
A relaxed coffee shop, with wicker furniture, serving a good-value range of rolls, cakes and toasted sandwiches.

Pompadour

Huidenstraat 12 (623 9554). Tram 1, 2, 5., 11. **Open** 9am-6pm Tue-Fri; 9am-5pm Sat.
Chocolatiers of distinction in a remarkable gilt and mirrored interior: your chance to follow Marie Antoinette's instructions in appropriate period surroundings.

Trendy

Huyschkaemer

Utrechtsestraat 137 (627 0575). Tram 4. **Open** *bar* 3.30pm-1am Mon-Thur, Sun; 3.30pm-2am Fri, Sat; *kitchen* 6-10pm daily.
Transformed from its former existence as an old-style brown bar, the Huyschkaemer is now all rag-rolled pastels and intricate mosaics. Popular with the gilded youth of the up-and-coming Utrechtsestraat, it serves excellent food (from *f*20). *See chapter* **Gay and Lesbian.**

Café Het Schuim

Spuistraat 189 (638 9357). Tram 1,2, 5, 11. **Open** 10am-1am Mon-Thur; 10am-2am Fri, Sat; 2pm-1am Sun.
A student haunt by day, in the evenings arty thirtysomethings take over. Art is hung on the long, high walls with exhibitions changing every six weeks. A recently installed big screen makes it an unexpectedly good place to watch the footy, bizarre because most of the punters seem to hate it.

Seymour Likely

Nieuwezijds Voorburgwal 250 (627 1427). Tram 1, 2, 5, 11, 13, 17. **Open** 5pm-1am Mon, Tue, Thur, Sun; 9am-1am Wed; 5pm-2am Fri; 9am-2am Sat.
Hang-out of a young, snobby and self-consciously trendy crowd – listen to the conversation stop as you walk through the door as Amsterdam's idea of the beautiful people all pause to give you the sartorial once-over. The drinks are nothing special, service is fashionably aloof and you'll never find a seat because it's always packed. Just over the road is the equally asinine Seymour Likely 2. *See chapter* **Clubs.**

Vergulde Gaper

Prinsenstraat 30 (624 8975). Tram 3, 10. **Open** 10am-1am Mon-Thur, Sun; 10am-2am Fri, Sat.
An upmarket and larger version of the Twee Prinsen (*see above* **Brown Cafés**), the Vergulde Gaper is much reviled by the locals of the former as the 'yuppie pub across the road'. All that can truthfully be said is that the skirts are shorter and the braces more colourful. It also has a heated terrace.

Theatre Cafés

Café Cox

Marnixstraat 427 (620 7222). Tram 1, 2, 5, 6, 7, 10, 11. **Open** 10am-1am Mon-Thur, Sun; 10am-2am Fri, Sat.
Pleasant split-level bar and restaurant serving reasonably priced food. In the same building as the Stadsschouwburg, it invariably attracts quite a theatrical crowd, especially at night. *See chapters* **Restaurants** *and* **Theatre.**

Irish bars

The way of the Emerald Isle, as repackaged for European consumption, has never been so popular. It goes way further than the upward mobility of the ubiquitous pint of Guinness. The new style Irish bar aims to bring, as far as is possible, an idealised slice of Dublin into the heart of foreign cities. Just how many Dublin bars still have wizened old crones hammering away on a drum while their mate screeches away about the bastard English is debatable but they do here. A lot. And the natives love it; Amsterdam has surrendered to the legendary whimsical Gaelic charm as readily as any other city in Europe.

There are now six Irish bars more or less in the centre of town and several more tucked away in the suburbs, most boasting drearily obvious names. There is some debate going on as to whether the next bar to open here will be called O'Clichés. The atmosphere in the newer bars is deceptively old; it is not beyond the imagination to picture Pearse and O'Connell plotting away in one corner. This contrasts sharply with the raucous atmosphere when major sporting events are being televised (most bars have satellite dishes).

The televising of these events illustrates just how important the Irish bars have become as a focal point to the English-speaking community. Crowd-pullers such as the FA Cup final or the All-Ireland Hurling matches see almost every bar packed to the rafters while the everyday clientele consists also largely of native English speakers.

The success of the Irish bars has started to ruffle a few feathers; Dutch breweries are being hit where it hurts. Perhaps the most glaring example of this is on the recently opened Heinekenplein behind the Heineken brewery. Heineken, apparently miffed at the success of O'Donnells (tourists are heading there straight from the famous brewery tour to have a Guinness) are supposedly considering opening an Irish-style bar nearby. Imitation may well be the sincerest form of flattery but in this case it only compounds the notion that modern Dutch culture is singularly lacking in any form of originality.

Blarney Stone
Nieuwendijk 29 (623 3830). Tram 1, 2, 5, 11, 13, 17.
Open 10am-1am Mon-Thur, Sun; 10am-3am Fri-Sat.
Not the biggest Irish bar in town, nor the most lavishly furnished, but its location means that it is often crowded and pretty lively.

Durty Nelly's
Warmoesstraat 115-117 (638 0125). Tram 4, 9, 14, 16, 24, 25 **Open** 9am-1am Mon-Thur, Sun; 9am-2am Fri, Sat.
One of the larger establishments, Durty Nelly's is in the heart of the Red-Light District but doesn't reflect the seedy nature of its surroundings. The atmosphere is fairly relaxed but it gets packed at weekends.

Fiddlers
Warmoesstraat 55 (624 4974). Tram 4, 9, 14, 16, 24, 25. **Open** 3pm-1am Mon-Thur, Sun; noon-2am Fri, Sat.
Fiddlers is a noisy if compact joint in the Red-Light District and very much in tune with the local vibe. Judging from the photos on the wall, this place has seen some parties.

Mulligans
Amstel 100 (622 1330). Tram 4, 9, 14, 16, 24, 25. **Open** 4pm-1am Mon-Thur; 4pm-2am Fri; 2pm-2am Sat; 2pm-1am Sun.
Renowned above all other Irish bars in Amsterdam for its music: it has a regular live programme every week. They even have a monthly musical workshop to spread the gospel of traditional Irish music to a wider public.

O'Donnells
Marie Heinekenplein (676 7786). Tram 16, 24, 25. **Open** 10am-1am Mon-Thur; Sun 10am-3am Fri, Sat.
The newest bar in town, and one of the biggest; the interior is almost Tardis-like in its proportions although the inclusion of several secluded snugs mean that the atmosphere remains intimate even when crowded.

O'Reillys
Paleisstraat 103-105 (624 9498). Tram 1, 2, 5, 11. **Open** noon-1am Mon-Thur, Sun; noon-2am Fri, Sat.
Open for a couple of years, O'Reillys is the daddy of them all; truly cavernous and hugely popular, with an especially large proportion of Dutch people drinking here. Its central location works against a real atmosphere as people meet here but don't tend to stay long.

The Tara
Rokin 89 (421 2654). Tram 4, 9, 14, 16, 24, 25. **Open** 11am-1am Mon-Thur, Sun; 11am-3am Fri-Sat
Large, newish bar already renowned for its food and as a venue for live Irish music. The interior is more spacious than it seems at first glance and the decor and layout more adventurous than the rest.

Felix Meritis
Keizersgracht 324 (623 1311). Tram 13, 14, 17. **Open** 10am-5pm Mon, Sun; 10am-8.30pm Tue-Fri; 3-8.30pm Sat.
Huge, high-ceilinged and spacious, Felix Meritis attracts a theatrical crowd, as well as a student contingent, but the drinking public varies according to what performance is being held. There's an adjoining restaurant where you can eat prior to the show. *See chapter* **Theatre**.

Frascati
Nes 59 (624 1324). Tram 4, 9, 14, 16, 24, 25. **Open** *bar* 4pm-1am Mon-Thur, Sun; 4pm-2am Fri, Sat; *kitchen* 5.30-10.30pm daily.
The Frascati is more Victorian purple than brown, with a large mirror behind the bar and excellent, cheap food. Popular with students and theatrical types from the numerous fringe venues in the street. *See chapter* **Theatre**.

A good place to lose the plot: **Frascati**, *in the middle of fringe theatreland. Page 121.*

Speciality

Beer

De Beiaard
Herengracht 90 (625 0422). Tram 1, 2, 5, 11, 13, 14, 17.
Open 4pm-1am Mon-Thur, Sun; 4pm-2am Fri, Sat.
A high-ceilinged bar with a 1950s atmosphere and a huge
assortment of draught and bottled beers.

Bierbrouwerij 't IJ
Funenkade 7 (622 8325). Tram 6, 10. **Open** 3pm-8pm
Wed-Sun.
A brewery within a beautiful old windmill that sells seasonal
beer, such as *Bokbier*, but also their own 'home-brewed' *IJ*
which appears towards the end of the year, and their spring
beer aptly named *Easter IJ* (a play on the word *ij* which
sounds the same as *ei*, the Dutch word for egg).

Gollem
Raamsteeg 4 (626 6645). Tram 1, 2, 5, 11. **Open** 4pm-
1am Mon-Thur, Sun; 4pm-2am Fri, Sat.
An unbelievably wide range of lethal bottled beers explains
this small, crowded bar's popularity. Early evening is the
time to go if you want anything resembling conversation.

De Wildeman
Nieuwezijds Kolk 3 (638 2348). Tram 4, 9, 14, 24, 25.
Open noon-1am Mon-Thur; noon-2am Fri, Sat.
Around 200 bottled brews from various countries are always
available here, and if you're missing your favourite pint, this
is where it's most likely to be found: of the 18 draughts always
on tap, most are a regularly-changing selection of international beers. The place is usually packed with a noisy and

friendly mix of locals and visitors. Unusually for this tobac-
co-infused city, the quieter side bar is strictly non-smoking.

Proeflokalen

Generally little larger than a wardrobe, *proeflokalen* or tasting houses were originally tap-
house annexes where a distiller or importer would
serve potential clients a selection of his flavoured
jenevers and liqueurs before persuading them, several hours later, to buy a bottle. Unfortunately the
free sample element disappeared long ago, but
proeflokalen remain a feature of early-hours drinking. Most close at around 8pm: probably a good
thing given the potency of their wares.

De Admiraal
Herengracht 319 (625 4334). Tram 1, 2, 5, 11. **Open**
4.30pm-midnight Mon-Fri; 5pm-midnight Sat.
A large *proeflokaal* offering – uniquely – sofas and armchairs
so you can get sozzled in comfort. Bizarre-sounding liqueurs
from Amsterdam's only remaining independent distillery, De
Ooiyevaar, line the bar. Unusually, it stays open till midnight.

De Drie Fleschjes
*Gravenstraat 16 (624 8443). Tram 1, 2, 4, 5, 9, 11, 13,
16, 24, 25.* **Open** noon-8.15pm Mon-Sat; 3-7pm Sun
There's virtually nowhere to sit here: just knock back your
liqueur (ask for the barman's recommendation) and come
back for more in the company of large numbers of locals, the
odd student and office workers – some of whom have their
own reserved casks on the wall.

Coffeeshops

Where to weed out the finest coffeeshop comestibles, and tips on how not to make a hash out of purchasing it.

Let's face it, many of those visiting the historic city of Rembrandt and Van Gogh do so with but one thing in their minds – getting stoned. Amsterdam remains the one city in the world where people can stroll into what is ostensibly a café and purchase, over the counter and in full view of everyone, substances that would lead to arrest and possible criminal charges elsewhere in the world. Bizarrely, were the letter of Dutch law applied then the same fate would also await the reefer smokers of Amsterdam, for in fact da 'erb is not as legal as everyone seems to assume. But, then, neither is it illegal. The official term for this perplexing anomaly is 'decriminalised' but to all intents and purposes, recreational smokers needn't bother their fuddled heads with the ins and outs of Dutch legislation. Leave the paranoia and shifty glances at home. Not everything you've heard is true, but enough of it is.

THE HIGH LIFE

The official state of play is that it is illegal to sell soft drugs but possession is 'decriminalised' up to a limit of 30 grams. That many coffeeshops offer bulk deals of 50 grams would indicate something is awry; they are openly selling almost twice the permitted amount, breaking the law on all counts and implicating the purchaser.

Such open flouting of the law might indicate either imminent trouble or a convenient loop-hole, but in truth no one really pays the law that much attention, including the police and the city council, from whom the coffeeshops have to obtain a licence to operate. That local councils are ultimately responsible for overseeing coffeeshops means that Amsterdam is almost unique in the Netherlands; in parts of the bumpkin lands to the South they are banned completely. It's not only foreign tourists who are drawn to Amsterdam's narcotic honeypot.

The attitude of the locals is, as with most things, a mixture of apathy and amused tolerance. In the height of summer the odd comment might be passed about the great quantity of long-haired pimply adolescents who congregate around Dam Square or the Vondelpark to get stoned and play bad versions of 'Stairway to Heaven', but coffeeshops are used by locals and tourists alike. There are exceptions, though, such as the gaudier establishments in the centre, which are almost exclusively frequented by foreigners, probably because they are the only ones within stumbling distance of the hotel.

Which is where this chapter comes in. If tight-arse deals and high-volume 2 Unlimited is what whets the appetite then there are places aplenty. However, relaxed and friendly establishments with individual character are equal in number and not always way off the beaten track.

The whole Amsterdam weed phenomenon is celebrated in the annual 'Nederwiet Festival', not just a red eyed, mutual back-slapping get together of collected pot-heads, but a truly amazing show of strength from a much-maligned but increasingly vocal section of society. Amongst other things the festival has played host to a hemp fashion show, an exhibition of hemp's medicinal uses and musical offerings from pop's finest frazzled nobility; last year's line-up was headlined by Cypress Hill. Held every November, the main attraction and some would say the *raison d'etre* of the Nederwiet Festival is the Highlife Cup: a competition to find

Sense and sensimelia.

the best weed. A panel of experts (and there are no end of volunteers), award marks for flavour, appearance and effect. It is a prize much coveted by coffeeshop owners – a high ranking is prized in much the same way as a Michelin star is trumpeted by a restaurant. Several recent winners of the Highlife Cup are within easy reach and many more of a similar nature can be found by consulting *Highlife*, the magazine which presents the award and is on sale in many coffeeshops around town.

REEFER MADNESS

What all coffeeshops have in common is the manner in which hashish/marijuana is sold. First, note that it is illegal openly to advertise drugs by name. The abundance of palm leaves in coffeeshop décor is not some sort of signwriter's Caribbean fetish: the palm leaf closely resembles the marijuana leaf, the depiction of which is prohibited, as is the mention of anything druglike in the name of a coffeeshop. So don't be disconcerted if, upon entering one of these places, it appears that you can smell it and see it but not buy it. Almost all coffeeshops have a menu card either on the bar or just behind it and asking to see it is the work of a moment. Most hash/weed is sold per gram or in bags of *f* 25 or larger. Prices are generally much of a muchness, but quality and variety can vary enormously.

Good coffeeshops often have a bewildering array of comestibles. The hash side of things is fairly clear, as varieties are generally named after the country of origin. The exception is Pollem – compressed weed resin and suitably potent. Weed is a bit more complicated. It divides roughly into two categories: bush weeds naturally grown, such as Thai; and Nederwiet or Skunk, indigenous product of Holland, grown under UV lights for maximum toxi-hydro carbons (THC – the active ingredient). Just as with Guinness in Ireland, the Skunk here is worlds away from anything available elsewhere and a modicum of caution is advisable if you are at all interested in remembering more than brief flashes of your Amsterdam visit. You might see locals getting into a gigantic cone-shaped, pure-weed spliff. Think carefully about doing likewise. Dutch smokers have built up a tolerance to the stuff, although trying to engage one in conversation will usually reveal a somewhat altered perspective on life. The same caution should be exercised for most of the space cake on offer – re-entry and eventual return to the planet can be a protracted affair.

But the dos and don'ts are up to the indiviudal. This is a town where almost anything goes. The only don't that needs to be stressed is that you should never, ever buy anything from street dealers. Amsterdam's liberal drugs stance also means that junkies proliferate in certain areas of town, and if a street deal is not a precursor to a mugging then it will be for a shit time. Common sense is all that's needed – there are coffeeshops everywhere.

That being so it is nevertheless important to bear in mind that there are places where smoking is frowned upon. Not everyone in Amsterdam is going to smile and wave a peace sign because you have a joint in your hand. But the nature of any given situation will be fairly clear. You don't skin up in a restaurant in much the same way as you wouldn't crack open a bottle of beer. If in doubt don't be afraid to ask, the worst you will get is a 'no' – no one's going to call the police. Just be considerate and a little discreet and leave the Led Zep back catalogue well alone.

Coffeeshops

Borderline

Amstelstraat 37 (622 0540). Tram 4, 9, 14. **Open** 11am-midnight Mon-Thur, Sun; 11am-2.30am Fri, Sat.
Right opposite the iT club, Borderline is very much a clubbers' coffeeshop; the sounds are house, but not at such a volume that you can't hear your own cool slang. Borderline sells all manner of smart drugs as well as possessing a good menu, including possibly the best Pollem in the city.

Bulldog

Leidseplein 13-17 (627 1908). Tram 1, 2, 5, 6, 7, 10, 11. **Open** 9am-1am daily.
One of Amsterdam's oldest coffeeshops, the Bulldog is big, brash, loud and full of tourists. The bouncers are, well... bouncy in the extreme. The Bulldog at Night, at Korte Leidsedwarsstraat 45, is open way into the early hours.

Fatal Flower

Stadhouderskade 46 (679 4296) Tram 6, 7, 10, 16, 24, 25. **Open** 11am-10pm daily.
Part of the pre-fab that is Fatal Flower recently burnt down; they have re-opened without any obvious signs of renovation but it remains one of the most vibrant coffeeshops around. Because of its location near the ramp thing on Museumplein, it is populated largely by pimply adolescents of the skateboarding fraternity. Art lovers from the Rijkmuseum tend to steer clear.

Free City

Marnixstraat 233 (625 0031) Tram 6, 7, 10. **Open** noon-1am Mon-Thur, Sun; noon-2am Fri, Sat.
The interior of this cavernous establishment is done up, if that's the phrase, in a pseudo-cyberpunk style; *Mad Max*, *Total Recall*, you get the picture. The mainly Dutch clientele certainly do, tending to be ever so slightly on the eccentric side, lending an unworldly feel to the place that may not be to everybody's taste.

Free I

Reguliersdwaarstraat 70 (622 7727) *Tram 4, 9, 14, 16, 24, 25.* **Open** 11am-2am Mon-Thur, Sun; 11am-3am Fri, Sat.
Opposite Amsterdam's only specialist hip hop cafe, The Duivel, Free I is an oddball place, with the tiny interior done out to resemble some sort of African mud hut. Its especially good weed selection is complimented by almost non-stop hip hop music, making it popular with da homies from across the way.

Global Chillage

Kerkstraat 51 (639 1154). Tram 1, 2, 5, 11. **Open** 11am-1am daily.
Amsterdam's own little piece of Goa, tucked away in a side street near the Leidseplein. Very friendly and relaxed, so much so that everyone lies around on the floor – there are seats but the ground's, like, cool, maaan.

Greenhouse – *twice winner of the Highlife Cup, the weed-purveyor's Michelin star.*

Grasshopper
Oudebrugsteeg 16 (626 1529). Tram 4, 9, 16, 24, 25.
Open 10.30am-1am Mon-Thur, Sun; 8am-2am Fri,-Sat.
By the waterside on the edge of the Red-Light District and often a first stop for visitors. Atmosphere and décor are a lot less tacky than many of the surrounding coffeeshops.

Greenhouse
Tolstraat 4 (673 7430). Tram 4. **Open** 10am-1am Mon-Thur, Sun; 10am-2am Fri, Sat. *Waterlooplein 345 (622 5499). Tram 9, 14/Metro Waterlooplein.* **Open** 9am-1am Mon-Thur, Sun; 9am-2am Fri, Sat.
Winner of the Highlife Cup in both 1994 and 1995, the Tolstraat Greenhouse is a little out of town but well worth a visit. Your chosen smoke is weighed out in front of you, the atmosphere is relaxed and there are comfy sofas galore. The food, which is of the burger and chips variety, is a cut above the usual fare. A second, smaller Greenhouse has recently opened near the Waterlooplein for those too lazy or too stoned to attempt travelling by tram.

Homegrown Fantasy
Nieuwezijds Voorburgwal 87a (627 5683). Tram 1, 2, 5, 11. **Open** 11am-11pm Mon-Thur, Sun; 11am-midnight Fri, Sat.
Stockist of one of the widest selections of weed in Weedsville, with a central location that makes it a popular smoking venue.

Kadinsky
Rosemarijnsteeg 9 (624 7023). Tram 1, 2, 5, 11. **Open** 10am-1am Mon-Thur, Sun; 10am-2am Fri, Sat.
Kadinsky can be found in a small side street just off Spuistraat and is one of the best coffeeshops to be found in the centre of Amsterdam. The wide selection of weed and hash available is weighed out in front of the customer and the chocolate chip cookies are a sheer delight, guaranteed to satisfy the severest of munchies.

Katsu
Eerste van der Helstraat 70 (657 2617). Tram 16, 24, 25. **Open** 11am-11pm Mon-Thur; 11am-midnight Fri, Sat; noon-11pm Sun.
Another former Highlife Cup-winner slightly out of the cen-

tre, Katsu is just off the bustling Albert Cuypstraat market and can be almost as bustling at times. Laid back and ultra-relaxed, as is the service.

Paradox
Eerste Bloemdwarsstraat 2 (623 5639). Tram 13, 14, 17. **Open** 9am-7pm Mon-Sat; 11am-7pm Sun.
A light but rather cramped establishment which dishes up healthy food. A change from the usual dingy pit-in-Marrakesh atmosphere that pervades many coffeeshops.

Siberië
Brouwersgracht 11 (623 5909). Tram 1, 2, 4, 5, 11, 13, 17. **Open** 11am-11pm Mon-Thur, Sun; 11am-midnight Fri, Sat.
A small, welcoming place with a large selection of board games and regular exhibitions by local artists.

Stones
Warmoesstraat 91 (624 1406) Tram 4, 9, 14, 16, 24, 25. **Open** 9.30am-1am Mon-Thur, Sun; 9.30am-3am Fri, Sat.
If, having travelled all the way to Amsterdam, you find all this foreign rubbish a bit too much then Stones is the only place to be. Run by English blokes, it's a big, dark, noisy, weed-fuelled slice of Blighty in the heart of the Red-Light District. It's also equipped with a big screen which shows all live English footy, just like home, except that at home you can probably focus better.

Tweede Kamer
Heisteeg 6 (627 5709). Tram 1, 2, 5, 11. **Open** 10am-1am Mon-Thur, Sun; 10am-2am Fri, Sat.
A tiny brown place, in a tiny street off the Spui, much used by locals.

Yo-Yo
2e Jan van den Heydenstraat 79 (664 7173). Tram 3, 4. **Open** noon-8pm daily
A popular neighbourhood coffeeshop near the Sarphatipark, Yo-Yo also has regular art exhibitions. On Saturdays you can have personal horoscope readings, which will accurately predict that if you stay there you will have live music on Sundays. Because there is.

Shops & Services

Shopping

From ready-to-wear to rubbers to wear, from haute couture to cheap and cheerful, the shopkeepers of Amsterdam have got you covered.

That weekend feeling begins on Thursday evening in Amsterdam, and what kicks it off are the longer shopping hours: most businesses are open until 8.30 or 9pm, and after that bars and cafés are packed with weary shoppers enjoying a restorative glass of the national beverage (which could also be milk, but in this case is definitely beer) and snacks like *osseworst* (like steak tartare) or *bitterballen* (don't ask what's in them, but they're delicious with mustard).

Thursday evenings are known as *koopavonden* (buying evenings), but they can also be thought of as 'cope evenings', because without them, consumers wouldn't be able to cope with the shopping hours. This is less true today than it was a few years ago, because of the gradual shift toward longer opening times. While most businesses are open from 9 or 10am to 5.30 or 6pm, there are some shops in the city centre, notably the Albert Heijn at Koningsplein and the chemist Lillian on Leidsestraat, that are open late most nights.

The bustle of Thursday evenings is in stark contrast to the calm of Sunday mornings, which can be either soothing or eerie, depending on whether or not you've already got coffee and breakfast makings to hand. This is a dark hour for the consumer in need, because night shops (*avondwinkels*), don't open until early afternoon. Should you find yourself in such a jam, head for Leidseplein or Rembrandtplein, where the cafés tend to open earlier to serve the needs of either eager tourists or else those who haven't gone to sleep at all – the only people likely to be out and about at such an hour.

CONSUMER CULTURE

Generally speaking, conspicuous consumption is frowned upon in the Netherlands. The standard of living is high and people certainly spend lots of money, but it's not cool to let it show. It's fairly rare to see a status symbol like a Louis Vuitton handbag, and such items may even be viewed as *ordinaire* (common). Travel abroad has more cachet than designer doo-dads. This notwithstanding, shopping is indeed a favourite activity here, as attested to by the huge variety of shops and huge numbers of shoppers. When it comes to spending, the Dutch credo is 'value for money', and by and large that is indeed what they get.

WHERE TO SPEND IT

Amsterdam's strong suit is small speciality shops: olive oil, vitamins, bottled water, beer, rubber and leatherwear, clubwear, household goods from distant lands – you name it. But there's more to the shopping horizon than that, naturally. What follows is a 'cheat sheet' giving the general characteristics of the main shopping districts.

Damstraat: Running from the Dam to the Nieuwmarkt, this street is heavily laden with souvenir shops, élitist clothes shops and head shops, but has more than its fair share of drop-outs and pickpockets. It is a lively street with plenty going on but you need to ensure that your belongings aren't playing a major part of the action.

The Jordaan: Packed with shops run by artists who've turned their hands to commerce. If you're looking for special clothing, jewellery, household goods or gifts, it's a good bet you'll find them here. Also, keep a look out for some of the best bakeries and take-away joints in town. Less pricey antiques can be found around Looiersgracht, along with things which could easily be classified as junk.

Kalverstraat/Nieuwendijk: These two streets, which are divided by Dam Square, are the most popular shopping areas in Amsterdam. While there are some high quality stores here, many just offer downright junk. Unless you've been in solitary confinement for the last three years and desperately crave the sight, sound and smell of your fellow humans, avoid this strip on Saturdays. The Kalverstraat was named after the cattle *(kalver)* market which used to be held here in the late fourteenth century, and on busy days, humans carry on the tradition. Mid-week shopping, however, especially after the street's renovation several years ago, can be quite convenient and enjoyable.

Ground has been broken here for the building of a multi-storey shopping and apartment complex, to be known as the Vendex Triangle. The remains of a sixteenth century convent have been discovered on the site.

Magna Plaza: It's hard to believe that this fairy-tale of a building, just behind Dam Square, used to be a post office. This is the closest thing Amsterdam has to a stadium-sized atrium mall. Its five floors house a wide variety of well-known shops, and Café Ristretto on the second floor serves a mean espresso.

The Pijp: In some senses similar to the Jordaan but rather less arty and more ethnic – especially when it comes to food shops. Famous for the bustling Albert Cuyp market, which sells everything from pillows to prawns.

Leidsestraat: Connecting Koningsplein and Leidseplein, this was formerly one of the city's poshest streets. If you cast your eyes above the signs for burgers and souvenirs, you can still see architectural evidence of this, but most of the really fancy shops, with a few exceptions such as Cartier, have disappeared, leaving a few travel agents, and a passel of very good shoe shops and better clothes shops. Watch out for cyclists and trams, who compete for space with pedestrians and delivery lorries on this very lively street. It's officially forbidden to cycle here, but nobody, including officials, takes any notice.

PC Hooftstraat: If money's no object, this should be your destination. The PC Hooftstraat caters to dedicated followers of fashion who won't bat an eyelid at spending ƒ500 on a shirt and who can give a shop assistant with an attitude a good run for their money. Top designer labels are the street's bread and butter, whether for men, women or children. Shop windows have beautiful displays and many of the smart interiors are worth a visit in themselves. Most businesses on the street offer tax-free shopping to tourists from outside the EC and it's worth taking advantage of this; remember that the tax is included in the price tag.

Spiegelkwartier: Across from the Rijksmuseum and centred on Spiegelgracht, this area is famous for antique shops which offer authentic treasures at accordingly high prices.

Unless otherwise stated, credit cards are not accepted by the shops listed below.

Art Supplies

Peter van Ginkel
Bilderdijkstraat 99 (618 9827). Tram 3, 7, 12, 17. **Open** 10am-5.30pm Mon-Fri; 10am-4pm Sat. **Credit** EC.
The biggest art supplier in Amsterdam sells something for every creative persuasion. The rows of shelves are stacked with an inspiring range of paints and pigments, rolls of canvas, stretcher parts and many types of paper, including rolls of Fabriano as well as their own cheaper brand. The doorway notice board is a good place for finding models and studio spaces as well as occasional exhibitions and competitions.

J Vlieger
Amstel 52 (623 5834). Tram 4, 9, 14, 16, 24, 25. **Open** noon-6pm Mon; 9am-6pm Tue-Fri; 10am-5pm Sat. **Credit** AmEx, DC, EC, MC, V.
Separated into two parts, the ground floor specialises in papers and cards of every description, weight and colour. These include tissue, Fabriano and corrugated card. They also have a good variety of glues and tapes. Upstairs is a limited but quality selection of paints, pens and inks as well as small easels and hobby materials such as fabric paint and calligraphy sets.

Van Beek
Stadhouderskade 62-65 (662 1670). Tram 6, 7, 10, 16, 24, 25. **Open** 1-6pm Mon; 9am-6pm Tue-Fri; 10am-5pm Sat. **Credit** AmEx, EC, MC, V.
A large, well stocked shop for everything from oil paints to ready-cut wood and pre-made stretchers. There is always something on special offer if you are prepared to take a quick look around. The shop also runs a discount scheme for regular customers. The branch on Weteringschans is more specialised in graphic art equipment.
Branch: Weteringschans 201 (623 9647).

Auctions

Sotheby's (627 5656) and Christie's (664 2011) each have a branch in Amsterdam.

Veilinghuis De Nieuwe Zon
Overtoom 197 (616 8586). Tram 1, 6, 11. **Open** 9am-5pm Mon-Fri; 10am-4pm Sat, Sun when viewing days.
Auctions various times and dates, phone for details.
Art, antique and household goods are auctioned off once a month, except in the summer, when sales are less frequent. The organisers claim that the household auction is unique: antiques are mixed with house clearance items, with furniture to utensils sold off in boxed lots. Goods to be sold are on show the weekend before the auction.

Books

General Bookshops

The Netherlands has two weeks in the calendar that are devoted to books. One is the third week in March, which celebrates Dutch literature with assorted events and special offers. The other is the second week in October, when bookshops focus their displays on children's books. If you spend more than a certain amount of money on books during these weeks, you receive a book as a present. For book markets *see below* **Markets**. For other bookshops, *see chapters* **Theatre**, **Gay & Lesbian**, **Women's Amsterdam** *and* **Students**.

The American Book Center
Kalverstraat 185 (625 5537). Tram 4, 9, 14, 16, 24, 25. **Open** 10am-8pm Mon-Wed, Sat; 10am-10pm Thur; 11am-6pm Sun. **Credit** AmEx, EC, MC, V.
Since 1972 this shop has specialised in English-language books and magazines from the UK and the US. Four floors packed with titles on every conceivable subject. Special order service is available with CD-ROM search, and students receive a ten per cent discount.

Athenaeum Nieuwscentrum
Spui 14-16 (bookshop 623 3933/news centre 624 2972). Tram 1, 2, 5, 11. **Open** *bookshop* noon-6pm Mon; 9am-6pm Tue, Wed, Fri; 9am-9pm Thur; 9.30am-5.30pm Sat; *news centre* 8am-10pm Mon-Sat; 10am-6pm Sun. **Credit** AmEx, EC, MC, V.
A favourite hang-out for highbrow browsers, Athenaeum stocks newspapers from all over the world, as well as a wide choice of magazines, periodicals and quality books in many languages.

The Book Exchange
Kloveniersburgwal 58 (626 6266). Tram 4, 9/Metro Nieuwmarkt. **Open** 10am-6pm Mon-Fri; 10am-5pm Sat.
An Aladdin's cave where second-hand English and

*Superior bric-á-brac at **Nic-Nac**. Page 131.*

American books, mostly paperback, are bought and sold. The owner is a shrewd buyer but he will do trade deals and gives a ten per cent discount to anyone carrying a copy of the *Time Out Amsterdam Guide*.

The English Bookshop
Lauriergracht 71 (626 4230). Tram 7, 10, 17. **Open** 1pm-6pm Tue-Fri; 11am-5pm Sat.
English books, including fiction, non-fiction, children's books and cookbooks, are temptingly displayed. The proprietor knows his stuff and can offer good reading tips.

Martyrium
Van Baerlestraat 170-172 (673 2092). Tram 3, 5, 12, 24. **Open** 9am-6pm Mon-Fri; 9am-5pm Sat.
A high percentage of English-language hardbacks and paperbacks, including literature, art and photography, history and philosophy. Forty per cent of the books are remaindered, so there are real bargains to be found.

De Slegte
Kalverstraat 48-52 (622 5933). Tram 4, 9, 14, 16, 24, 25. **Open** 11am-6pm Mon; 9.30am-6pm Tue, Wed, Fri; 9.30am-9pm Thur; 9.30am-6pm Sat. **Credit** AmEx, EC, V.
One of the city's largest bookshops, De Slegte carries a vast number of volumes in English, Dutch and other languages (including textbooks, children's books, fiction and non-fiction). A mixture of antiquarian, remaindered and new, prices are low and the odd treasure can be found.

Scheltema, Holkema en Vermeulen
Koningsplein 20 (523 1411). Tram 1, 2, 5, 11. **Open** 1-6pm Mon; 9.30am-6pm Tue, Wed, Fri; 9.30am-9pm Thur; 10am-5pm Sat. **Credit** (minimum ƒ100) AmEx, EC, MC, V.
Six wonderful floors of books with specialist areas in medicine, law, economics and science.

WH Smith
Kalverstraat 152 (638 3821). Tram 4, 9, 14, 16, 24, 25. **Open** 11am-6pm Mon; 10am-6pm Tue; 9am-6pm Wed, Fri; 9am-9pm Thur; 10am-6pm Sat; 11am-5pm Sun. **Credit** AmEx, MC, V.
A large, attractive establishment where you can choose from thousands of titles, all in English. It sells newspapers and board games and has a good children's section on the top floor, as well as videos including classic BBC sitcoms.

Specialist Bookshops

Architectura & Natura
Leliegracht 44 (623 6186). Tram 13, 14, 17. **Open** noon-6.30pm Mon; 9am-6.30pm Tue-Fri; 9am-6pm Sat.
The name says it all: architecture and nature. The stock includes photographic books on architectural history, field guides and animal studies. Many of the books are in English.

Au Bout du Monde
Singel 313 (625 1397). Tram 1, 2, 5, 11. **Open** noon-6pm Mon; 10am-6pm Tue, Wed, Fri; 10am-9pm Thur; 10am-5pm Sat.
A friendly and relaxed bookshop that opened 25 years ago. Although it specialises in eastern philosophy and religion, there is a daunting selection of titles, all clearly marked, on subjects ranging from psychology to sexuality. Classical music plays in the background and a large table in the centre of the shop invites you to relax and browse. Au Bout du Monde also sells incense, cards and a handful of specialist magazines, as well as over 100 different tarot packs (well displayed on big cards that can easily be flipped over).

Intertaal
Van Baerlestraat 76 (671 5353). Tram 3, 5, 12, 16. **Open** 9.30am-6pm Mon-Wed; 9.30am-9pm Thur; 9.30am-6pm Fri, Sat. **Credit** AmEx, EC, MC.
As the name suggests (to anyone with a smattering of Dutch), this shop deals exclusively in language books, records and teaching aids. Whether grappling with basic Dutch or advancing your knowledge of English, you'll be well catered for here.

Jacob van Wijngaarden (Geographische Boekhandel)
Overtoom 97 (612 1901). Tram 1, 6, 11. **Open** 1-6pm Mon; 10am-6pm Tue, Wed, Fri; 10am-9pm Thur; 10am-5pm Sat. **Credit** AmEx, EC, MC, V.

Every part of our planet comes up for inspection in the geography books, nautical charts, maps and travel guides sold at Wijngaarden. A great deal of the stock is in English. You can also find cycling maps of the Netherlands and Europe.

De Kookboekhandel
Runstraat 26 (622 4768). Tram 1, 2, 5, 7, 10, 11, 17. **Open** 1-6pm Mon; 11am-6pm Tue, Wed, Fri; 11am-9pm Thur; 11am-5pm Sat.
This shop sells every conceivable cookery book, with good 'fresh' and 'green' sections. Largely English language.

Lambiek
Kerkstraat 78 (626 7543). Tram 1, 2, 5, 11. **Open** 11am-6pm Mon-Fri; 11am-5pm Sat. **Credit** AmEx, DC, MC, V.
Lambiek claims to be the world's oldest comic shop (established in 1968) and has thousands of comic books from all over the world. Some are collector's items. There's a cartoonists' gallery with a new exhibition of comic art for sale every two months. Free brochure.

Pied-a-Terre
Singel 393 (627 4455). Tram 4, 9, 14, 16, 24, 25. **Open** 10am-6pm Mon-Fri; 10am-5pm Sat; *Apr-Aug* 11am-9pm Thur.
A wonderful little shop with helpful staff, supplying international guides and maps (including Ordnance Survey) for active holidays – especially good for adventurous walkers and travel books.

Bric-a-Brac

Fifties-Sixties
Huidenstraat 13 (623 2653). Tram 1, 2, 5, 11. **Open** 1-6pm Tue-Fri; 1-5.30pm Sat.
Every available inch of space in this shop is packed with authentic period pieces – toasters, blenders, lamps and even vacuum cleaners – all in good working condition (220 volts). Non-electrical goods include floor-standing chrome ashtrays.

Nic-Nac
Eerste Jan Steenstraat 131 (675 6805). Tram 16, 24, 25. **Open** 6-9pm Thur; 10am-5pm Sat.
There is certainly no shortage of shops of this ilk in Amsterdam, but this definitely has the best selection of 1950s and 1960s furniture, lamps, ashtrays and kitchenware – most in mint condition. It is sometimes open at times other than those mentioned above, but that depends on the owner's mood.

Children

See also chapter **Children.**

Babies

Geboortewinkel Amsterdam
Bosboom Toussaintstraat 22 (683 1806). Tram 3, 7, 10, 12. **Open** 1-5.30pm Mon; 10am-5.30pm Tue-Fri; 10am-5pm Sat.
Beautiful maternity and baby clothes (including premature sizes) in cotton, wool and linen, baby articles, cotton nappy systems and ethnic woven baby slings, as well as birth information and childbirth videos.

Prénatal
Kalverstraat 40-42 (626 6392). Tram 4, 9, 14, 16, 24, 25. **Open** 1-6pm Mon; 9.30am-6pm Tue, Wed, Fri, Sat; 9.30am-9pm Thur. **Credit** AmEx, MC, V.
Four floors of goods for expectant mothers and small children (new-borns to five-year-olds). There are stacks of clothing, toys and furniture, plus cotton nappies for babies.

Baby Boutique de Concurrent
Bos en Lommerweg 363 (681 3298). Tram 12, 14. **Open** 9.30am-5.30pm Tue, Wed, Fri; 9.30am-9pm Thur; 9.30am-5pm Sat. **Credit** AmEx, DC, MC, V.
This handy shop sells baby items including car seats, buggies and highchairs.

Children's Books

De Kinderboekwinkel
Nieuwezijds Voorburgwal 344 (622 7741). Tram 1, 2, 5, 17. **Open** 1-6pm Mon; 10am-6pm Tue-Fri; 10am-5pm Sat.
The large selection of books in English and other languages is attractively displayed and arranged according to age. **Branch:** Rozengracht 34 (622 4761).

Children's Clothes

't Schooltje
Overtoom 87 (683 0444). Tram 1, 2, 5, 6, 11. **Open** 1-6pm Mon; 9am-6pm Tue, Wed, Fri; 9am-9pm Thur; 9.30am-5pm Sat. **Credit** AmEx, DC, MC, V.
The well-heeled, well-dressed child is fitted out here. The clothing and shoes for babies and children aged up to 16 are attractive but expensive.

Second Time
Frans Halslaan 31, Amstelveen (647 3036). Bus 66. **Open** 10am-5pm Tue-Sat.
Wonderful bargains in second-hand clothes for babies and children can be unearthed at this shop. Outfits are top brands and in good condition.

Children's Shoes

't Klompenhuisje
Nieuwe Hoogstraat 9a (622 8100). Tram 4, 9/Metro Nieuwmarkt. **Open** 10am-6pm Mon-Sat. **Credit** AmEx, DC, MC, V.
A delightful selection of well-made and reasonably priced shoes, traditional clogs and handmade leather and woollen slippers from baby sizes up to size 35.

Warmer Kinderschoenen
Bilderdijkstraat 134 (616 9627). Tram 3, 12. **Open** 1-6pm Mon; 9.30am-6pm Tue, Wed, Fri; 9.30am-9pm Thur; 9am-6pm Sat. **Credit** AmEx, EC, V.
Very pretty, soft leather shoes for children in Mediterranean designer styles, at reasonable to expensive prices.

Toys

De Zeiling
Ruysdaelstraat 21-23 (679 3817). Tram 2, 3, 5, 12, 16. **Open** noon-6pm Mon; 9am-6pm Tue-Fri; 9am-5pm Sat. **Credit** AmEx, DC, JCB, MC.
This gem of a shop is stocked with Rudolf Steiner-inspired artefacts, including hand-made wooden toys, rattles, puzzles, music boxes and night lights, baby clothes in natural materials and dyes, doll-making materials, cards and candles.

Department Stores

De Bijenkorf
Dam 1 (621 8080). Tram 1, 2, 4, 5, 9, 11, 13, 14, 16, 17, 24, 25. **Open** 11am-6pm Mon; 9.30am-6pm Tue, Wed, Fri; 9.30am-9pm Thur; 9.30am-6pm Sat. **Credit** AmEx, DC, MC, V.

Ornaments a-plenty at **Abracadabra**. *Page 135.*

De Bijenkorf is to Amsterdam what Harrods is to London and Bloomingdale's to New York. It has good clothing – both designer and their own label – kidswear, jewellery, cosmetics, shoes, accessories and a wonderful household goods department. Restaurant La Ruche is a good place for lunch. The new 'Chill Out' department on the fifth floor features street and clubwear as well as 1950s-style kitchenware and American food products like Campbell's soup and marshmallow cream. Their Sinterklaas (5 Dec) and Christmas displays and windows are traditionally extravagant and much-visited.

Hema

Reguliersbreestraat 10 (624 6506). Tram 4, 9, 14, 16, 24, 25. **Open** 11am-6pm Mon; 9.30am-6pm Tue, Wed, Fri; 9.30am-9pm Thur; 9am-6pm Sat.
A slightly upmarket version of the American five-and-dime store. Prices are low and the quality is amazingly high. Good buys are casual clothes, kids' clothing, swimwear, underwear, household items, stationery and accessories. Hema also sells pastries, bread, delicatessen foods and reliable mixed wines. There are ten branches scattered around town.

Maison de Bonneterie

Rokin 140-142 (626 2162). Tram 4, 9, 14, 24, 25.
Open 1-5.30pm Mon; 10am-5.30pm Tue, Wed, Fri, Sat; 10am-9pm Thur. **Credit** AmEx, EC, DC, MC, V.
At this venerable institution you'll find men's and women's clothing of the highest quality. By and large, things here are pretty conservative: the Ralph Lauren boutique within the store is about as wild as it gets. They also have a fine household goods department. By appointment to Her Majesty Queen Beatrix.

Metz & Co

Keizersgracht 455 (624 8810). Tram 1, 2, 5, 11. **Open** 11am-6pm Mon; 9.30am-6pm Tue, Wed, Fri; 9.30am-9pm Thur; 9.30am-6pm Sat. **Credit** AmEx, DC, MC, V.
Reminiscent of London's Heals, this is a good place to shop for special gifts. Designer furniture, glass and Liberty-style

fabrics and scarves. The top-floor restaurant is popular for business lunches and has a terrific view of the city. At holiday time, their Christmas shop puts even the weariest consumer back into the spirit of the season. *See also chapter* **Cafés & Bars.**

Vroom & Dreesmann

Kalverstraat 203 (622 0171). Tram 4, 9, 14, 16, 24, 25. **Open** 11am-6pm Mon; 9.30am-6pm Tue, Wed, Fri; 9.30am-9pm Thur; 9.30am-6pm Sat. **Credit** AmEx, DC, MC, V.
V&D stands for good quality at reasonable prices. Since its recent remodelling, this branch has taken on a new, snazzy look to go with new, snazzy merchandise. You can find an impressive array of toiletries, cosmetics, small leather goods and watches, clothing and undergarments for the whole family, kitchen items, suitcases, CDs and videotapes. Their ground floor bakery, Le Marché, sells excellent bread, ready-made quiches and sandwiches, and their La Place restaurant offers a salad and soup bar and just about every other thing you might want to put in your mouth. Prices are a step up from Hema (*see above*).

Fashion

Accessories

Abracadabra

Sarphatipark (676 6683). Tram 3, 12, 16, 24, 25. **Open** 10am-6pm Tue-Fri; 10am-5pm Sat. **Credit** AmEx, EC, V.
This charmingly decorated shop is the place to find treasures from India – jewellery in particular, but also a wide variety of bedspreads, lamps, masks, cards, beads, perfume and incense.

Body Sox

Leidsestraat 35 (627 6553). Tram 1, 2, 5, 11. **Open** noon-6pm Mon; 9.30am-6pm Tue, Wed, Fri; 9.30am-9pm Thur; 9.30am-5.30pm Sat. **Credit** AmEx, MC, V.

Step out in the latest designer tights from Mary Quant, Pierre Cardin and others: there's a large assortment of socks, tights, body stockings and lingerie, although the prices tend to be quite high.

De Grote Tas D'Zaal

Oude Hoogstraat 6 (623 0110). Tram 4, 9, 14, 16, 24, 25. **Open** 12.30-6pm Mon; 9am-6pm Tue, Wed, Fri; 9am-9pm Thur; 9am-5pm Sat. **Credit** AmEx, DC, JCB, MC, V.

Two floors filled with an extensive collection of suitcases, handbags, satchels and briefcases, including designs by Samsonite and Rimowa. Mainly sombrely coloured practical designs in hardwearing materials.

De Hoed Van Tijn

Nieuwe Hoogstraat 14 (623 2759). Tram 4, 9, 14, 16, 24, 25. **Open** 11am-6pm Tue-Fri; 11am-5pm Sat. **Credit** DC, MC, V.

More a curiosity than a hat shop, this old-style establishment stocks a vast collection of headgear including sombreros, homburgs, bonnets and caps. The range includes period hats dating from 1900 as well as many second-hand, new and handcrafted items.

Hoeden M/V

Herengracht 422 (626 3038). Tram 1, 2, 5. **Open** 1-6pm Mon; 10am-6pm Tue, Wed, Fri; 10am-9pm Thur; 10am-5pm Sat. **Credit** AmEx, DC, EC, V.

Supergrass

Cannabis, a plant which (to the dismay of many residents) tends to be associated with Amsterdam, has been infiltrating an area far removed from the lungs of those who smoke it: fashion. Hemp, the part of the cannabis sativa plant which doesn't get you high, can be made into cloth. Hemp cloth has assumed some new forms in recent years, some of which are remarkably silky, while others are durable and grow comfortable over time, like a pair of jeans. Trouble is, clothing made from hemp tends to be expensive. On the other hand, hemp can be easily grown in many developing countries, and for that reason is seen as a potential contributor to those economies by some shop owners. Sadly, many items of hemp fashion are blighted by marijuana leaf logos, which range in size from tiny to too darn big. Perhaps if these logos were eradicated once and for all, the wealthy who can afford this stuff would start buying it by the bale. At any rate, the range of hemp products is surprising and amusing.

Greenlands, Hemp Eco Store

Utrechtsestraat 26 (625 1100). Tram 4. **Open** 11am-6pm Tue-Fri; 11am-5pm Sat. **Credit** AmEx, DC, EC, JCB, V.

Greenlands' stock includes clothes, food and a small selection of stationery. Raw or roasted hempseeds can be used in cooking, and are high in protein and nonsaturated fats. The shop's cheesy, spicy vegetarian burgers substitute hempseed for soy, and they're delicious. The clean-cut designs on sale show that textiles are still the main use for hemp. Clothing made by the Hmong tribe in Thailand uses natural hues plus basic blue and red, and there is cloth from China of a yellowy-beige hue. Shirts, waistcoats, and jackets cost around ƒ150, while jeans and chinos are around ƒ200. The rough-looking weaves soften to a silky linen feel after a dozen washes. Chunky knitted jumpers are expensive (ƒ595), but with the claim of lifelong durability, just might be worth it.

Hemp Works

Nieuwendijk 13 (421 1762). Tram 1, 2, 5. **Open** noon-6pm Mon-Wed, Fri, Sat; noon-9pm Thur. **Credit** AmEx, DC, EC, JCB, MC, V.

More than 25,000 products can be made with hemp, and

Hemp on hangers at **Hemp Works**.

quite a few are in evidence here: the bricks in the 'exposed' brick wall are made of it, and of course the clothing – classic, basic pieces in the ƒ50 to ƒ300 range. The texture of the fabric ranges from rugged for work shirts and jeans, to something comparable to a silk/cotton blend. There are also tiny backpacks, shoes, cat litter, face creams and perfumes, healthy snacks and more.

KGB Hempire State Building

Droogbak 1 (627 1646). Tram 1, 2, 5. 11, 13, 17. **Open** 3-6pm Mon; by appt Tue; noon-6pm Wed-Sat.

Only slightly off the beaten track, and worth a visit for hemp/cannabis aficionados or wannabes. Seeds which produce smokable, edible, and (ultimately) sewable varieties of the plant are on sale here. While it would be wise to check before bringing seeds across any international borders, the rule of thumb is that within the EC it's legal – with the exception of France – and that it's illegal when entering the US or Australia. They also sell hemp fabric in bulk, and dispense information on drugs regulations and coffeeshops in Amsterdam.

This is the place if you want to find a hat that'll make you look like a member of the congregation in 'Four Weddings and a Funeral'. Top quality from well-known international designers such as Philip Treacy, Sandra Phillips, Patricia Underwood, Mirjam Nuver, Katja Langeveld and, for men, lids from Borsalino.

Reach Out – Mode Accessories
Kloveniersburgwal 46. Tram 4, 9, 14, 16, 24, 25. **Open** *summer* 10am-9pm daily; *winter* 10am-6pm daily.
Affordable fashion accessories such as hair bands, jewellery, sunglasses, bags, hats, watches and lighters.

Bespoke Tailoring

Paul Neve
Bilderdijkkade 40 (618 1129). Tram 3, 7, 12, 13, 14, 17. **Open** 10am-5pm Tue-Sat. **Credit** AmEx, EC, JCB, V.
Paul Neve has been making trousers at this site for 25 years and he believes he's the last tailor in Amsterdam to specialise in them. Denim trousers cost around ƒ175 and mohair between ƒ300 and ƒ350. Everything is made to the client's specifications.

Clubwear

Clubwear-House
Herengracht 265 (622 8766). Tram 1, 2, 5, 11,13, 17. **Open** 11am-7pm Mon-Wed, Fri; noon-9pm *(winter)*; 11am-5pm Sat. **Credit** (minimum ƒ75) AmEx, MC, V.
Amsterdam's biggest clubwear shop has a wide selection of groovy clothes from around the world plus its own clothes label, Wearhouse 2000, and can make special outfits to order. If it's club information, flyers or pre-sale tickets you want, the staff of enthusiastic clubbers are helpful and know what they're talking about. A good selection of local and international DJ tapes are available and occasionally DJs play in the shop on Saturdays. *See also chapter* **Clubs.**

ZX Fashion
Kerkstraat 113 (620 8567). Tram 1, 2, 5, 11. **Open** noon-6pm Mon-Wed, Fri; noon-9pm *(winter, 7.30pm)* Thur; 11am-5pm Sat. **Credit** AmEx, JCB, MC, V.
ZX stocks comfortably styled, street clubwear and accessories made in the Netherlands as well as imports from the US and England. Party tickets are occasionally distributed here. The Hair Police are based in the back of the shop and specialise in alternative hairstyles such as dread perms and extensions. *See chapter* **Services.**

Designer Fashion

Most of the shops selling designer labels and haute couture are to be found dotted in and around PC Hooftstraat.

Cora Kemperman
Leidsestraat 72 (625 1284). Tram 1, 2, 5, 11. **Open** noon-6.30pm Mon; 10am-6.30pm Tue, Wed, Fri, Sat; 10am-9pm Thur; noon-6pm Sun. **Credit** EC, V.
After 18 years designing Mac & Maggies's women's collection, Cora Kemperman decided to strike out on her own. Here the discerning but budget-minded customer will find designer clothes at high street prices. If you're after a fur bolero jacket and hip huggers, this is the place for you. Ditto for a super simple long black evening dress.

Puck and Hans
Rokin 66 (625 5889). Tram 4, 9, 14, 16, 24, 25. **Open** 1-5.30pm Mon; 10am-6pm Tue-Fri; 10am-5pm Sat. **Credit** AmEx, EC, V.
One of the best-known designer fashion shops in town,

popular with a youngish trendy crowd who want to look good without breaking the bank. There is a small collection including items from Jean-Paul Gaultier as well as clothes designed by Puck and Hans themselves.

Reflections
Stadhouderskade 23a (612 6141). Tram 2, 5. **Open** 1-6pm Mon; 10am-6pm Tue-Wed, Fri; 10am-9pm Thur; 10.30am-5.30pm Sat. **Credit** AmEx, DC, EC, MC, V.
Top-of-the-range designer clothes for those with the money to pay for it. Set within the Byzantium centre, this airy shop houses some of the giants in designer fashion including Donna Karan and Karl Lagerfeld.

Reflections Casuals
PC Hooftstaat 66 & 68 (664 0040). Tram 2, 3, 5, 12. **Open** 1-6pm Mon; 10am-6pm Tue, Wed, Fri; 10am-9pm Thur; 10am-5.30pm Sat. **Credit** AmEx, DC, EC, V.
Just around the corner from its mother shop, here the collection is for those more casual occasions, including denim by Calvin Klein and socks by Paul Smith.

Fetish

For specialist fetish shops such as RoB Gallery, *see chapter* **Gay & Lesbian.** Similar outlets: **Nothing Shocking,** Kloveniersburgwal 40 (420 2386); **Wrapped,** Singel 434 (420 4022).

Demask
Zeedijk 64 (620 5603). Tram 4, 9, 14, 16, 24, 25. **Open** 10am-7pm Mon-Wed, Fri; 10am-9pm Thur; 10am-7pm Sat. **Credit** AmEx, EC, MC, V.
This is a stockist of mainly leather and rubber fetish clothing for both sexes but also some PVC. High heels, bondage wear and SM accessories are available. Pre-sale tickets can be bought here for the parties they organise.

Haute Couture

Edgar Vos
PC Hooftstraat 132 (662 6336). Tram 2, 3, 5, 12. **Open** 1-6pm Mon; 9am-6pm Tue, Wed, Fri; 9am-9pm Thur; 10.30am-6pm Sat. **Credit** AmEx, DC, MC, TC, V.
Many of Mr Vos' customers are fashionable, international businesswomen. His handsome suits are often heavily tailored, made in gorgeous natural fabrics.

Frank Govers
Keizersgracht 500 (622 8670). Tram 1, 2, 5, 11. **Open** 10am-6pm Tue-Fri; 10am-5pm Sat. **Credit** AmEx, DC, MC, V.
Given the prices of the clothes here, Mr Govers attracts a surprisingly wide variety of clients, ranging from a priestess wanting vestments to a diamond heiress after a million-guilder, diamond-embroidered wedding dress. Ready-to-wear starts from ƒ1,000 and haute couture from ƒ3,000.

High Street Fashion

America Today
Magna Plaza ground floor (638 8447). Tram 1, 2, 5, 11, 13, 17. **Open** 11am-6pm Mon; 9.30am-6pm Tue, Wed, Fri; 9.30am-9pm Thur; 10am-6pm Sat; noon-6pm Sun. **Credit** AmEx, DC, EC, V.
What started out as a tiny venture is now making millions: this shop sells new American classics (Converse, Levi's, Timberland) at lower prices than anywhere else because it imports stuff straight from the States under a special tax agreement. It also has its own clothing brand.
Branch: Sarphatistraat 48 (638 9847).

Esprit

Spui 10 (626 3624). Tram 1, 2, 4, 5, 9, 11, 14, 16, 24, 25, 26. **Open** 11am-6pm Mon; 10am-6pm Tue, Wed, Fri; 10am-9pm Thur; 10am-5.30pm Sat. **Credit** AmEx, DC, MC, V.

Esprit caters for the whole family's clothing needs and is popular both with Dutch and international shoppers. It sells classic, time-tested casual and sporty clothing made from natural fabrics. Similar to Benetton but without the ad campaign or the racing team.

Exota

Hartenstraat 10 (620 9102). Tram 1, 2, 5, 11. **Open** 11am-6pm Mon; 10am-6pm Tue, Wed, Fri; 10am-9pm Thur; 10am-5.30pm Sat. **Credit** AmEx, EC, MC, V.

Exota is the shop for those who appreciate a more original selection of simple yet stylish clothes and accessories which cross the borders between high street and street fashion.

Hennes & Mauritz

Kalverstraat 125 (624 0624). Tram 4, 9, 14, 16, 24, 25. **Open** noon-6pm Mon; 10am-6pm Tue, Wed, Fri; 10am-9pm Thur; 9.30am-5.30pm Sat. **Credit** AmEx, DC, EC, V.

Fashion chainstore for men, women, teenagers and kids. Price range: reasonable to jaw-droppingly low. Quality: reasonable to jaw-droppingly low. Lots of items to appeal to trend-conscious guys and gals of all ages, plus updates of timeless standards. Both branches listed below have 'Big is Beautiful' departments.

Branches: Kalverstraat 114-118 (624 0441); Nieuwendijk 141 (639 2021).

Khymo

Leidsestraat 9 (662 2137). Tram 1, 2, 5, 11. **Open** noon-6pm Mon; 10am-6pm Tue, Wed, Fri; 10am-9pm Thur; 10am-6pm Sat. **Credit** AmEx, DC, MC, V.

Trendy fashion for twenty- to fortysomethings, both male and female. Famous labels include Katharine Hamnett, Jean-Paul Gaultier, and Marithé & François Girbaud.

Large Sizes

Big Shoe

Leliegracht 12 (622 6645). Tram 13, 14, 17. **Open** 10am-6pm Tue-Fri; 10am-5pm Sat. **Credit** AmEx, DC, MC, V.

Need a pair of red stilettoes one foot long? Big Shoe specialises in fashionable footwear for large sizes only. Every shoe on display is available in sizes 46 to 50 for men, 42-46 for women. Designs include modern, sporty, classical and chic styles in the latest colours; high heels, sandals, boots and gym shoes are all available.

G&G Special Sizes

Prinsengracht 514 (622 6339). Tram 1, 2, 5, 11. **Open** 9am-5.30pm Tue, Wed, Fri; 9am-5.30pm, 7-9pm Thur; 9am-5pm Sat. **Credit** AmEx, DC, MC, V.

A full range of men's clothing from size 58 up to 75 is stocked by G&G. Staff also tailor garments to fit, although this service costs a bit extra.

Lingerie

Hunkemöller

Kalverstraat 162 (623 6032). Tram 1, 2, 4, 5, 9, 11, 14, 16, 24, 25. **Open** 11am-6pm Mon; 9.30am-6pm Tue, Wed, Fri; 9.30am-9pm Thur; 9.30am-5.30pm Sat. **Credit** AmEx, DC, EC, MC, V.

Hunkemöller is a women's lingerie chain store with eight branches in and around Amsterdam. It deals in attractive but simply designed underwear, very good quality and reasonably priced.

Branch: Ferdinand Bolstraat 61 (662 2020).

Robin's Bodywear

Nieuwe Hoogstraat 20 (620 1552). Tram 4, 9, 14, 16, 24, 25. **Open** 1-6pm Mon-Wed; 11am-6pm Thur-Sat. **Credit** AmEx, MC, V.

Sizeable for a women's lingerie shop, Robin's Bodywear has an extensive selection of reasonable and more expensive items of underwear, swimwear and hosiery by Naf-Naf, Calvin Klein, Aubade, Lou and others.

Tothem

Nieuwezijds Voorburgwal 149 (623 0641). Tram 1, 2, 5, 11, 13, 17. **Open** 9.30am-5.30pm Tue, Wed, Fri; 9.30am-9pm Thur; 9.30am-5pm Sat. **Credit** AmEx, DC, MD, V.

This men's underwear shop sells mainly designer items by Hom, Calvin Klein and Body Art.

Shoes

For the best selection of shoes, head for Leidsestraat or Kalverstraat. The best bargains in second-hand shoes are to be had at Waterlooplein and the Noordermarkt on Mondays. *See below* **Markets**.

Antonio

Gasthuismolensteeg 12 (627 2433). Tram 1, 2, 5, 11, 13, 14, 17. **Open** 1-6pm Mon; 10am-6pm Tue, Wed, Sat; 10am-8pm Thur. **Credit** AmEx, DC, MC, V.

Antonio will fit your feet with boots and shoes by designers Lola Pagola, produced in a diversity of materials including snake, suede and crocodile as well as good old leather. For both men and women.

Free Lance Shoes

Rokin 86 (420 3205). Tram 4, 9, 14, 16, 24, 25. **Open** 1-6pm Mon; 10am-6pm Tue, Wed, Fri; 10am-9pm Thur; 10am-6pm Sat. **Credit** AmEx, MC, V.

The imaginative façade and interior décor immediately set this apart from other similar retailers. All the footwear is created by two French designers. Styles are both classic and trendy.

Jan Jansen

Rokin 42 (625 1350). Tram 4, 9, 14, 16, 24, 25. **Open** 11am-6pm Tue-Fri; 11am-5pm Sat. **Credit** AmEx, DC, MC, V.

Jan Jansen brings out two collections a year, and has fashionable footwear in the finest leather specially produced in Italy. Comfortable walking shoes have been his best-seller for years but well-fitted shoes ideal for special occasions are also available.

Kenneth Cole Shoes

Leidsestraat 20 (627 6012). Tram 1, 2, 5, 11. **Open** noon-6pm Mon; 9.30am-6pm Tue, Wed, Fri; 9.30am-9pm Thur; 9.30am-5pm Sat. **Credit** AmEx, DC, MC, V.

Although the stock is much the same as in Sacha, it changes frequently so bargains are to be found during sales. Kenneth Cole also stocks its own brand of more conservatively styled shoes as well as a good range of boots, including Timberlands and Doctor Martens.

Sacha

Kalverstraat 161 (627 2160). Tram 1, 2, 4, 5, 9, 11, 14, 16, 24, 25. **Open** noon-6pm Mon; 9.30am-6pm Tue, Wed, Fri; 9.30am-9pm Thur; 10am-5pm Sat. **Credit** AmEx, MC, V.

The Dutch branch of the English shoe shop stocks a good selection of affordable shoes and boots for men and women, often in outrageous styles and colours.

Branch: Van Baerlestraat 12 (673 1345).

Street Fashion

Punch

*St Antoniesbreestraat 73 (626 6673). Tram 4, 9,
14/Metro Nieuwmarkt.* **Open** 1-6pm Mon; 11am-6pm
Tue, Wed, Fri; 11am-9pm Thur; 11am-5.30pm Sat.
Credit AmEx, DC, EC, V.
Just about everything made by Doctor Martens is to be found
here; boots, shoes, T-shirts and sweatshirts alongside
Harrington jackets, Lonsdale wear, and sporty goods from
Fred Perry and Ben Sherman. There is also a selection of
'Directions' alternative hair colourants in vibrant shades.

RMF Streetwear

*Oudezijds Voorburgwal 189 (626 2954). Tram 4, 9, 14,
16, 24, 25.* **Open** 10pm-6pm Mon-Sat. **Credit** AmEx,
DC, MC, V.
Featuring a selection of American brands that until recently have been difficult to find here such as OG Wear,
Menace, No Joke, Top Dawg, South Pole, and Capheads.
Not a bargain hunter's paradise, but the clothing is of good
quality and you can be pretty confident that the next time
you go out you won't meet three other people wearing the
same shirt.

Rodolpho's

*Magna Plaza top floor (623 1214). Tram 1, 2, 5, 11,
13, 17.* **Open** 11am-6pm Mon; 9.30am-6pm Tue, Wed,
Fri; 9.30am-9pm Thur; 10am-5pm Sat; noon-6pm Sun.
Credit AmEx, DC, EC, V.
A rollerblade and skateboard outlet selling all accessories
necessary to look the part. The best place to buy the coolest
items currently fashionable on the streets. There's a large
selection of T-shirts as well as the latest in trainers.

Stillet

Damstraat 14 (625 2854). Tram 1, 2, 5, 11, 13, 17.
Open 10am-8pm(ish) Mon-Sat; 10am-8pm(ish) Sun
(summer only).

Stillet sells a huge collection of T-shirts with imaginative
logos and designs, including ecological and political themes
as well as cartoon images and club style. Some are designed
and printed here while others are imported from Britain.
Opening times depend on the owner's mood.

Vibes

Singel 10 (622 3962). Tram 4, 9, 14, 16, 17, 24, 25.
Open 11am-6pm Mon-Wed, Fri; 11am-6pm, 7-9pm,
Thur. **Credit** AmEx, DC, EC, MC, V.
The brainchild of two veteran skaters, this shop at the
Centraal Station end of Singel caters for every aspect of the
dedicated skate and snowboarder's obsession. Labels include
Stüssy, X-large, Inc and Haze, among others. Also sells comic
books, magazines, and other hip-hoppy accessories, and has
a large range of decks and snowboards on display.

Vintage and Second-hand

Donald E Jongejans

Noorderkerkstraat 18 (624 6888). Tram 3, 10. **Open**
11am-6pm Mon-Sat.
A great little shop in the Jordaan, which specialises in frames
for glasses and sunglasses dating from the mid-1800s to the
present day. The owner, Mr Jongejans, is very
particular about the fact that he sells not second-hand
frames, but vintage frames which have never been worn.
Well worth visiting.

Lady Day

Hartenstraat 9 (623 5820). Tram 1, 2, 5, 11. **Open**
11am-6pm Mon-Sat; 11am-9pm Thur. **Credit** AmEx,
MC, V.
Lady Day stocks highly fashionable designs including beautifully tailored second-hand and period suits and sportswear
classics, such as a fantastic selection of swimming costumes
from the 1940s and 1950s. Also period wedge shoes, pumps
and other accessories.

Bulbs at the **Bloemenmarkt**. *See page 140.*

Laura Dols

Wolvenstraat 7 (624 9066). Tram 1, 2, 5, 11. **Open**
11am-6pm Mon-Wed, Fri, Sat; 11am-9pm Thur.
Small shop packed with period clothing mainly from the 1940s
and 1950s. Well crafted dresses are available in sumptuous
materials. The emphasis is on women's clothing, although
there is a limited selection of menswear.

Zipper

Huidenstraat 7 (623 7302). Tram 1, 2, 5, 11. **Open**
11am-6pm Mon-Fri; 11am-9pm Thur; 11am-6pm Sat.
Credit AmEx, MC, V.
Excellent selection of jeans of various sorts as well as 1970s
hipsters and flares and some clubwear.
Branch: Nieuwe Hoogstraat 8 (627 0353).

Fabrics & Trimmings

Capsicum

*Oude Hoogstraat 1 (623 1016). Tram 4, 9, 16, 24,
25/Metro Nieuwmarkt.* **Open** 10am-6pm Tue, Wed, Fri;
10am-9pm Thur; 10am-5pm Sat. **Credit** AmEx, MC, V.
Capsicum is dedicated to natural fibres and splendid
textures: cotton woven in India and Thai silk in glowing
shades. Always an elegant window display.

Copenhagen 1001 kralen

Rozengracht 54 (624 3681). Tram 10, 13, 17. **Open**
10am-6pm Tue-Fri; 10am-5pm Sat.
Create your own designer jewellery or decorate a garment
from thousands of different beads. They provide all the bits
you need for self-assembly. Both conventional and uncon-
ventional work is sold here: the collection includes an awesome array of colour, size and shape.

Het Kantenhuis

Kalverstraat 124 (624 8618). Tram 4, 9, 14, 16, 24, 25.
Open 11.45am-6pm Mon; 9.15am-6pm Tue, Wed, Fri;
9.15am- 9pm Thur; 9.15am-6pm Sat. **Credit** AmEx, DC,
MC, V.
In business for 98 years. The 'Lace House' sells reasonably
priced tablecloths, place mats, doilies and napkins that are
embroidered, appliquéd or printed with Delft blue designs.
There are also lace curtain materials and kits to make cross-
stitch pictures of Amsterdam canal houses.

HJ van de Kerkhof

Wolvenstraat 9 (623 4084). Tram 1, 2, 5, 11. **Open**
9am-6pm Mon-Fri; 11am-5pm Sat. **Credit** MC, V.
Trimmings (*passementerie* in Dutch) of every type are
Kerkhof's speciality – stock includes lace collars, feather
boas, fringes and satin rosettes.

Kniphal

Albert Cuypstraat 162 (679 5831). Tram 4, 16, 24, 25.
Open 11am-5.30pm Mon; 9.30am-5.30pm Tue-Fri;
9.30am-5pm Sat.
Sizeable shop selling just about everything: zippers, poppers,
ribbons, pins and needles. The enormous range of textiles is
clearly displayed and includes beautiful natural, hand-woven
fabrics, extravagant sequined and crocheted textiles as well
as simple cottons and wools.
Branch: Knip Exclusief Tesselschadestraat 1B-C (612 2426)
deals, as the name suggests, in stuff of the fanciest sort.

Knopen Winkel

Wolvenstraat 14 (624 0479). Tram 1, 2, 5, 11. **Open** 1-
6pm Mon; 11am-6pm Tue-Fri; 11am-5pm Sat.
This button specialist is reputedly the only shop of its kind in
Holland. The vast selection of buttons – one-third old and two-
thirds new – comes from all over the world, including Spain,
Istanbul and Italy. They've been fashioned from
raffia, coral, horn, bone and wood as well as the usual plastic.

Kunst Leder

Elandsgracht 107 (623 0986). Tram 7, 10. **Open**
10.30am-6pm Mon-Fri; 10.30am-5pm Sat.
Friendly atmosphere with chaotic product display. A limited but unusual selection of furnishing and clothing materials, many plastic-coated. While they also sell sheets of plastic
and foam which they will cut to your specifications, their
main trade is in artificial leather.

McLennan's

Hartenstraat 22 (622 7693). Tram 1, 2, 5, 11. **Open** 1-
6pm Mon; 10.30am-6pm Tue-Fri; 10.30am-5.30pm Sat.
Silks from China, India, and Thailand are sold by the metre
at McLennan's. They also come ready made as kimonos,
scarves, lingerie or ever-blooming tulips (*f*3,50 each).

Flowers

It's tempting to bring home packets of bulbs from
Amsterdam, where bouquets and blooms are a
part of everyday life. Unfortunately, import regulations often either prohibit the entry of bulbs
entirely or require them to have a phytosanitary
(health) certificate.

No certificate is, however, currently needed to
take bulbs into the UK, and an unlimited amount
of bulbs can be carried into the USA, Canada and
the Irish Republic, as long as they have the appropriate phytosanitary certificate(s). Australia and
New Zealand allow no import of bulbs whatsoever and Japan allows the import of no more than one
hundred certified bulbs. Some bulb packaging is
marked with national flags, indictating the countries into which they can safely be taken.

You are allowed to take an unlimited quantity
of cut flowers back to the UK, as long as none are
gladioli or chrysanthemums. In the US, regulations
on cut flowers vary from state to state. Dutch
wholesale dealers know the regulations and can
ship bulbs to your home. This can be arranged at
the annual Keukenhof flower show (late March to
late May) or by mail order from the Frans Roozen
Nurseries (02502 47245) where the minimum order
varies, depending on where you live (*see chapter*
Excursions in Holland). For details of florists
see chapter **Services**.

At Schiphol Airport, you can buy your flowers
and bulbs at **Bloemenzaak Fleurtiek** (653 1702),
where staff claim to know all about the various regulations and health certificates. You have to buy a
minimum of ten bulbs and prices are much higher
here than at shops in the city.

If you're short of cash but want to impress someone with a bunch of flowers, head for the Albert
Cuyp Market (*see below* **Markets**). Just off the
corner of Van der Helststraat and Albert
Cuypstraat is a little stall which sells three bunch-
es of the flowers of your choice for a mere *f*6.

Naturally, no Danish Beaver cheese at **Kef,
French Cheesemakers**. *See page 141.*

Bloemenmarkt (Flower Market)

Singel, between Muntplein and Koningsplein. Tram 1, 2, 4, 5, 9, 11, 14, 16, 24, 25. **Open** 9am-6pm Mon-Sat.
Amsterdam boasts the world's only floating flower market. It is a fascinating collage of colour, stretching four blocks along the southern side of the Singel, with 15 florists and garden shops permanently ensconced on large barges. Although the market is right in the town centre, attracting busloads of tourists, it has a reputation for selling plants and flowers that last and are worth the money. Locals may find the prices a bit expensive, but the goods on sale here are still much cheaper than in most other countries. Plans are currently underway to upgrade the market, replacing the iron, roll-down shutters with transparent ones, so that shops' contents can be seen from both sides of Singel. The aim is to give this section of the canal a pleasant ambience that continues into the evenings, after all the flower shops have shut. A fountain is also planned.

Plantenmarkt (Plant Market)

Amstelveld, on Prinsengracht between Utrechtsestraat and Vijzelstraat. Tram 4, 6, 7, 10. **Open** 9.30am-6pm Mon.
This is the only other market in Amsterdam entirely devoted to botanical life. Although the emphasis is on plants, vases and pots, some flowers can be bought here too. In spring, most plants on sale are intended for the balcony or living room. Later in the year there are more garden plants and bedding plants for flower boxes.

Food & Drink

Dutch cuisine may seem to consist of nothing but meat and potatoes, but as far as snacking goes, there aren't many cities to rival Amsterdam in terms of variety, exoticism and, most of all, sensible prices. The ubiquitous *broodje*, or sandwich, is available on nearly every street corner. In the past 20 years, the quality of bakers has improved, and most snack shops offer freshly baked French and Italian rolls for sandwiches. Those wanting kosher sandwiches should ask the maker to hold the butter, as it is slapped on nearly every sandwich.

How the Dutch maintain their smooth, peaches-and-cream complexions is a mystery considering their favourite snack is chips munched with great dollops of mayonnaise. The best stall is Vlaamse Frites at Voetboogstraat 33, off Spui and Lange Leidsedwarsstraat 5. Fresh raw herring is almost as popular: this is served with raw onions and purists down the fish in just one gulp, head first, dangling the thing by the tail. Amsterdam's best herring stall is Bloemburg Vis Specialiteiten (*listed under* **Fish**).

For late-closing shops, *see box below* **In the Wee Small Hours**.

Bakeries

There are two kinds of bakeries. For bread, rolls and packaged biscuits, go to a *warme bakker*; for pastries and wickedly delicious cream cakes, you need a *banketbakker*. *See also below* **Chocolate**.

JG Beune

Haarlemmerdijk 156-158 (624 8356). Tram 18, 22, 28, 35. **Open** 8am-6pm Mon-Sat.
In business for more than 100 years, this bakery carries a full range of cakes and chocolates, plus some speciality items like chocolate tulips or *Amsterdammertjes* (those short poles branded with the city's triple-x symbol which keep people from parking on the pavements). Both can be gift-wrapped. They also have the technology to take a photo and transfer the image to a cake. The results will have you both smiling and licking your lips.

Mediterrané

Haarlemmerdijk 184 (620 3550). Tram 3. **Open** 8am-6pm Mon-Fri; 9am-5pm Sat.
French, Morroccan and Dutch baking traditions are all practised under one roof here, and the results are delicious. Famous for the best croissants in town. The café in the back serves espresso and cappucino.

Multi-Vlaai

Beethovenstraat 40A (671 1260). Tram 5, 24. **Open** noon-6pm Mon; 8.30am-6pm Tue-Fri; 8.30am-5pm Sat.
At its best, *vlaai*, a traditional pie from Limburg, in the south of the Netherlands, should be sweet but not *too* sweet. This shop has 22 varieties brought in fresh daily from Limburg. Flavour fads are fickle in the world of *vlaai*, but the most popular at this shop is currently apple crumble. Branches throughout Amsterdam.

Oldenburg

PC Hooftstraat 97 (662 8363). Tram 2, 3, 5, 12. **Open** 9am-6pm Mon-Wed, Fri; 9am-9pm Thur; 9am-5pm Sat.
This is one of two Oldenburg *banketbakkerijen* in Amsterdam, specialising in fancy dessert cakes, bavarois and chocolate mousse tarts. You can also buy home-made chocolates and marvellous marzipan confections in winter and chocolate eggs at Easter. Every month, a different theme is featured in the window.
Branch: Maasstraat 84 (662 2840).

Paul Anneé

Runstraat 25 (623 5322). Tram 1, 2, 5, 7, 10, 11. **Open** 8.45am-6pm Mon-Fri; 9am-5pm Sat.
Everything here is freshly baked daily from organically grown grains. Try the cakes and popular sour-dough bread. There is a display of (non-edible) bread decorations for which the shop is famous. There are also health food products such as soy milk, organic jam and apples, and sweets made without sugar.

Puccini, coffeeshop & dessertwinkel

Staalstraat 21/hs (626 5474). Tram 9, 14/Metro Waterlooplein. **Open** 9am-6pm Tue-Fri; 9am-5.30pm Sat.
This highly regarded bakery specialises in bon-bons and gorgeous desserts made on the premises without artificial ingredients. It is close to the Muziektheater and the Waterlooplein flea market, which makes it a great place to relax after shopping or to stop for a pre-performance pick-me-up.

Hartog's Volkorenbakkerij

Ruyschstraat 56 (665 1295) Tram 6, 7, 10/Metro Wibautstraat. **Open** 7am-5.30pm Mon-Fri; 6.30am-4pm Sat.
Volkoren means 'whole grain', and the variety of bakery items available at this venerable family-owned business, which recently celebrated its hundredth anniversary, are exclusively that – even the croissants. There is no fat in this bread, yet it tastes great and is even better for you. Get there early on Saturdays to avoid the queues.

Runneboom

Eerste van de Helststraat 49 (673 5941). Tram 16, 24, 25. **Open** 7am-5.30pm Mon-Fri; 7am-5pm Sat.
A tiny bakery in the Pijp which is a favourite with locals, and after just one bite, you'll know why. An enormous selection of French, Russian, Greek and Turkish loaves is on offer, with rye bread as the speciality of the house. Also delicious cakes and pastries.

Cheese

Every Dutch adult consumes about 13kg (6lb) of cheese per year. There is plenty to choose from. In general, the younger (*jong*) the cheese, the creamier and milder it will be. Riper cheeses (*belegen*) will be drier and sharper-tasting. Driest and sharpest of all is old (*oud*) cheese. The most popular cheeses are called Goudse (from Gouda), followed by Leidse, flavoured with cumin seeds, and Edammer, with its red crust.

Four interesting cheeses to get you started are: Friese *nagelkaas*, a ripe cheese whose sharp flavour is enhanced by cumin seeds and cloves; Kernhem, a good dessert cheese; and Leerdammer and Maaslander, which are both mild with holes. If you are interested in making a trip to a cheese-producing town, *see chapter* **Excursions in Holland**.

Kef, French Cheesemakers

Marnixstraat 192 (626 2210). Tram 3, 10. **Open** 10am-6pm Tue-Thur; 9am-6pm Fri; 9am-4pm Sat.
French cheesemaker Abraham Kef set up shop over 40 years ago and his shop still imports the finest selection of French cheeses – up to 70 – in Amsterdam. The range of goats' cheeses is particularly good. The shop looks its age in the nicest possible way: it's tiny, dark and wood-furnished, with tastings available at oak tables until an hour before closing time. You'll receive expert advice.

Wegewijs

Rozengracht 32 (624 4093). Tram 13, 14, 17. **Open** 8.30am-6pm Mon-Fri; 8.30am-5pm Sat.
This authentic Dutch cheese emporium has been run by the Wegewijs family at the same address for the last hundred years. Once upon a time, when the Rozengracht was still a canal, the cheese was delivered by boat. On offer are 50 foreign cheeses and over 100 domestic varieties, including *gras kaas*, a grassy-tasting cheese only available in summer. You can sample the Dutch cheeses before making your selection.

Chocolate

The Dutch are a nation of chocolate consumers: their cocoa is famous all over the world and makes description-defying delicious chocolate. Although considerable rivalry exists between Belgian and Dutch chocolatiers, Amsterdam offers enough shops utilising both recipes to let chocoholics sample and decide for themselves. Schiphol Airport also has good chocolate outlets. Try some and you'll want to stay forever.

Bon Bon Jeannette

Centraal Station (421 5194). Tram 1, 2, 4, 5, 9, 11, 13, 16, 17, 24, 25. **Open** 9am-9pm Mon-Sat; 9am-9pm Sun. AmEx, DC, EC, JCB, V.
Bon Bon Jeannette's chocolatiers manufacture their delicious wares right here in the shop's own atelier. The chocolate is all natural, without any additives or preservatives, and is so low in sugar and carbohydrates that many diabetics are able to enjoy it. For example, three of the bon-bons here are equivalent in calories to one apple or one slice of bread. They leave a delicious after-taste, almost like a fine wine does.
Branch: Europaplein 87 (664 9638).

Hendrikse Le Confiseur

Overtoom 448-450 (618 0260). Tram 1, 6. **Open** 8.45am-6pm daily.
Hendrikse specialises in the finest hand-made chocolates. Try *gianduja*, a fudge-like chocolate log made with ground hazelnuts and almonds. Marzipan and chocolate figures are also a speciality (and can be designed to order), as are delicious fruit preserves.

Huize van Wely

Beethovenstraat 72 (662 2009). Tram 5. **Open** 10am-6pm Mon; 9am-6pm Tue-Fri; 9am-5pm Sat.
Undoubtedly the most upmarket chocolatier in Amsterdam, Huize van Wely has been making chocolates, pastries and deluxe ice creams by hand at its factory in Noordwijk since 1922. The Amsterdam shop also boasts the largest selection of sauternes grand cru in the Netherlands. It also runs the chocolate concession at Schiphol Airport, offering a more limited selection of delicacies duty-free. Worldwide mail-order service.

Pompadour

Huidenstraat 12 (623 9554). Tram 1, 2, 5, 7, 11. **Open** 8am-6pm Tue-Fri; 8.30am-5.30pm Sat.
This small bonbonnerie and tea room with eighteenth-century interior imported directly from Liège is likely to bring out the little old lady in anyone. The handmade bon-bons, truffles and pastries are not only inspired by traditional Belgian, French and German recipes, but also offer the best price/quality ratio in town.

Delicatessens

Eichholtz

Leidsestraat 48 (622 0305). Tram 1, 2, 5, 11. **Open** 10am-6.30pm Mon; 9am-6.30pm Tue, Wed, Fri; 9am-9pm Thur; 9am-6pm Sat. **Credit** (minimum ƒ50) AmEx, EC, V.
This is the place where Yanks can find chocolate chips and Brits their Christmas puddings. Lots of imported foods, notably from the US and Britain, plus Dutch souvenirs (chocolate tiles and so on).

Loekie

Prinsengracht 705a (624 4230). Tram 1, 2, 5, 11. **Open** 9am-6pm Mon-Fri; 9am-5pm Sat.
Premium sandwiches at premium prices. Whether it's Parma ham, parmesan or pesto, Loekie will serve it in distinctive combinations on French bread, fresh ciabatta or just plain rye. Also a small selection of wines, sauces, and flavoured cooking oils. Catering service.

Renzo

Van Baerlestraat 67 (673 1673). Tram 3, 5, 12, 16. **Open** 11.30am-8.30pm Mon-Fri; 10.30am-6.30pm Sat; 10am-6.30pm Sun.
Don't let the trendy, tiled décor frighten you away or you'll miss the best tiramisu in town. No gourmet brand names here: fresh pastas, sauces, desserts, salads and sandwiches are all made on the premises. For those who wish to eat on the spot, there are multi-coloured tiled tables outside in summer, and rustic wooden tables inside during the rest of the year.

Traiteur Ricardo Food & Wine

Van Baerlestraat 16 (675 5138). Tram 3, 5, 12, 16. **Open** 10am-8pm Mon-Wed, Sat; 10am-9pm Thur-Fri; 11am-5pm Sun.
Chef Ricardo van Ede, veteran of some of the Netherlands' finest restaurants, is making it easier to get a little taste of heaven with his new shop specialising in Italian and French takeaway meals of the more robust, countrified sort, pastas imported direct from small manufacturers in Italy, plus oils, spices, coffee, tea, wine, Champagne, bon-bons and exotic fruits.

Ethnic

Besides Surinamese and Indonesian food stores, there is a wide variety of Spanish, Latin American and Asian shops. The Dutch love to cook at home and in cosmopolitan Amsterdam that means ingredients are available from all ends of the earth. Most markets have stalls offering authentic foreign snacks such as Vietnamese or Indonesian egg rolls (loempia), filled Indian pancakes (roti) and Surinamese chicken pasties (kippepasteitje). Favourite takeaway snacks include Chinese-Indonesian rice (nasi) and noodle (bami) dishes, Indonesian skewered meat with spicy peanut butter sauce (satay) and pizza (both continental and New York style).

Casa Molero
Gerard Doustraat 66 (676 1707). Tram 16, 24, 25.
Open 9am-6pm Tue-Sat.
Smaller selection of spices and packaged foods than La Tienda (*listed below*), but greater choice of Spanish hams and sausages. Casa Molero is the exclusive Dutch distributor for several Spanish and Portuguese wines, hence its vast Iberian wine collection. There's also a fine assortment of olive oils.

Hellas
Hobbemastraat 26A (662 7238). Tram 6, 7, 10. **Open** 9am-6pm Mon-Fri; 9am-5pm Sat.
Greek delicacies and wines, freshly-made snacks and salads, cheeses, filo pastry and vine leaves fill the shelves here.

J&J
Eerste Sweelinckstraat 20 (673 4309). Tram 3, 4, 16, 24, 25. **Open** 10am-6pm Mon-Sat.
Fantastic selection of Filipino food: from shrimp fry to coconut vinegar to dried salted fish. Sweets include cassava cookies and halo-halo (mixed fruits in crushed ice, milk and ice cream) on hot summer days.

Mario Pasta
Overtoom 248 (618 5639). Tram 1, 6, 11. **Open** noon-7pm Mon-Sat.
Sauces and seven different types of fresh pastas and salads made by Mario, who runs this one-man show of a shop. Wine, olive oil, cheeses, tiramisu and other Italian deli standards.

Meidi-Ya
Beethovenstraat 18-20 (673 7410). Tram 5. **Open** 10am-6pm Mon-Wed, Fri; 10am-9pm Thur; 9am-5pm Sat.
A Japanese speciality market with every food and condiment necessary for Japanese food, including fresh greens, flown in specially, and sake. Snacks can be eaten at the sushi bar plus hot dishes and snacks to take away. Catering service.

Oriental Commodities
Nieuwmarkt 27 (638 6181). Tram 4, 9, 14, 16, 24, 25/Metro Nieuwmarkt. **Open** 9am-6pm Mon-Sat.
The largest Chinese food emporium in Amsterdam covers the full spectrum of Asian foods and ingredients. One-stop shopping for shrimp and scallop-flavoured egg noodles, fried tofu balls, spicy chips, fresh vegetables, plus Chinese cooking appliances and utensils. Also a selection of Chinese-language videos and compact discs.

Smeraglia
Kinkerstraat 21 (616 6895). Tram 7, 17. **Open** 11am-6pm Tue-Fri; 10am-5pm Sat.
The friendly staff here can provide you with northern and southern Italian foods, wines and spirits.

De Thai Shop
Koningsstraat 42 (620 9900). Metro Nieuwmarkt. **Open** 10am-6pm Mon-Wed, Fri, Sat; 10am-9pm Thur.
A small shop which stocks a selection of exclusively Thai ingredients, including eight different types of curry, imported salted fish, plus fresh ingredients such as lemongrass and other herbs.

La Tienda
Eerste Sweelinckstraat 21 (671 2519). Tram 3, 4, 16, 24, 25. **Open** 9am-6pm Mon-Sat.
Open since 1936, this dusty old food shop looks like something off the set of a Spanish Civil War movie. Besides stocking manchego cheese, jamones serranos and chorizo from Spain, La Tienda offers the full gamut of spices and essences for Latin American cooking from Mexico to Surinam. Italian ingredients also on hand.

Toko Ramee
Ferdinand Bolstraat 74 (662 2025). Tram 16, 24, 25. **Open** 9am-6pm Tue-Fri; 9am-5pm Sat.
All the spices and ingredients used in Indonesian cooking are sold here, plus Chinese and Thai ingredients and takeaway dishes.

Fish

Bloemberg Vis Specialiteiten
Van Baerlestraat, across from Concertgebouw and between Stedelijk Museum and the corner. Tram 2, 3, 5, 12, 16. **Open** 9am-5pm Tue-Sat.
This famous stall is a must for anyone wishing to sample Dutch herring or mackerel. The owner is a recipient of the coveted 'Golden Herring of Amsterdam' award for his delicious cured fish and fish sandwiches.

Viscenter Volendam
Kinkerstraat 181 (618 7062). Tram 7, 17. **Open** 7.30am-6pm Mon-Sat.* **Credit** AmEx, MC, V.
The family that runs this popular shop commutes from Volendam, a major fishing village. It offers a large selection of freshwater and sea fish, shellfish, cured fish (try the smoked eels – *gerookte paling*), takeaway snacks and seafood salads.

Health Food

De Aanzet
Frans Halsstraat 27 (673 3415). Tram 16, 24, 25. **Open** 9am-6pm Mon-Fri; 9am-5pm Sat.
De aanzet is a cooperative stocking vegetables and fruit, freshly baked bread and pastries as well as eco-friendly household goods.

Biologische Boerenmarkt
Noordermarkt. Tram 3, 10. **Open** 10am-4pm every Sat.
This weekly market is the most interesting place to find healthy, organic foods. Stalls purvey fresh bread and cakes, organic fruit and vegetables produced without pesticides, organic dairy products, vegetarian cheese and paté, and grains and pulses by the sackful. It's not particularly cheap, though (*see below* **Markets**).

Deshima Freshop
Weteringschans 65 (625 7513). Tram 6, 7, 10, 16, 24, 25. **Open** 10am-6pm Mon-Fri; 10am-5pm Sat.
This basement macrobiotic shop sells only foods that contain no dairy products, meat or sugar. It also has some homemade and Japanese specialities. Courses in macrobiotic cookery are run as part of the Kushi Institute. Above the shop is a restaurant serving macrobiotic lunches from noon through to 2pm.

Gimsel

Huidenstraat 19 (624 8087). Tram 1, 2, 5, 11. **Open**
9.30am-6.30pm Mon-Fri; 9am-5pm Sat.
A popular and central health food shop with organic vegetables and fruit and excellent freshly baked bread, cakes
and savouries.

De Natuurwinkel

Weteringschans 133-137 (638 4083). Tram 6, 7, 10.
Open 7am-8pm Mon-Wed; 7am-9pm Thur; 7am-7pm Sat;
11am-5pm Sun.
The largest health food supermarket in Amsterdam with six
smaller branches scattered around the city (note that each
branch has its own opening times). You'll find everything
here from organic meat, fruit and veg (all delivered fresh
daily) to sugar-free chocolates and organic wines and beers.

Off-Licences (Slijterijen)

The legal age for buying or being served beer is
16; for wine and spirits it's 18. Beer *(pils)* and Dutch
gin *(jenever)* are the most popular alcoholic drinks.
Wines often cost less at an off-licence than at the
airport tax-free shopping centre.

De Bierkoning

*Paleisstraat 125 (625 2336). Tram 1, 2, 5, 11, 13, 14,
16, 17, 24, 25.* **Open** 1-6.30pm Mon; 11am-6.30pm Tue,
Wed, Fri; 11am-9pm Thur; 11am-6pm Sun.
'The Beer King', named for its location behind the Royal
Palace, stocks approximately 850 different brands of beer
from around the world, as well as all the matching glasses.

Chabrol, adviseurs in wijnen en gedistilleerd

Haarlemmerstraat 7h (622 2781). Tram 1, 2, 5, 11.
Open 9am-8pm Mon-Sat.
Offering wine, beer and spirits from all over the world as
well as expert advice, this shop provides the very best value
for money. There's a large selection of wines, some at very
reasonable prices indeed. Delivery within Amsterdam is free
of charge, and it is possible to borrow glasses for large parties. Staff are always attentive and helpful.

De Cuyp

Albert Cuypstraat 146 (662 6676). Tram 4, 16, 24, 25.
Open 9am-6pm Mon-Sat.
Specialising in miniature and giant bottles, De Cuyp stocks
more than 3,000 miniatures. Huge bottles include an eight-
litre bottle of jenever and a 21-litre bottle of Champagne.
There is a large international assortment of wines and spirits, including drinks from the Dominican Republic, Brazil,
and Surinam, as well as the owner's favourite, *pisco*, from
Chile. Free delivery within Amsterdam and rental glasses.

Wijnkoperij Woorts

Utrechtsestraat 51 (623 7426). Tram 4. **Open** 1-6pm
Mon; 9am-6pm Tue-Fri; 9am-5pm Sat.
A wine-lover's paradise, offering over 600 varieties, with
an emphasis on Italy. Tasting sessions are held on request
for groups of up to 12 (reservations necessary). Some of the
bottles have unique labels depicting the work of contemporary Dutch artists and are becoming collectors' items.
Free delivery Monday-Friday within Amsterdam.

Tea & Coffee

Geels & Co

*Warmoesstraat 67 (624 0683). Tram 4, 9, 14, 16, 24,
25.* **Open** 9am-5.45pm Mon-Sat.
Although not as old as some of its rivals, Geels & Co does

offer lower prices for the same coffee beans and bulk teas.
There is a large stock of contraptions for brewing and
utensils for serving.

Levelt

Prinsengracht 180 (624 0823). Tram 13, 14, 17. **Open**
noon-6pm Mon; 9am-6pm Tue-Fri; 9am-5pm Sat.
This is *the* tea and coffee specialist. In the wonderful shop,
which dates from 1839 and which still has much of the original tiled décor in place, Leefveld carries everything and anything to do with brewing and serving. For about *f*20 you can
buy a decorative tile made of pressed tea.

Supermarkets

That the Netherlands is one of the world's most
densely populated countries is perhaps most
apparent on Saturday afternoons at the supermarket – *any* supermarket. Thankfully, because
Amsterdam is a city that stays up late, Saturday
mornings are a different story, so this is a good
time to get out there and get the goods. If such
optimistic plans should not come to pass, be prepared to brave crowded aisles and long queues at
the cash registers. A few tips: unless a per piece
(per stuk) price is given, fruits and vegetables must
be weighed by the customer. Put your produce on
the scale, press the picture of the item, and press
the BON button to get the receipt. No matter how
many impatient people are standing in line behind
you, cashiers do not hesitate to ask for correct
change, so it's a good idea to have some handy.
You must pack your groceries yourself. If you
want a plastic bag (usually 35 cents), ask for it.
Otherwise, bring one from home.

Albert Heijn

Koningsplein 4 (624 5721). Tram 1, 2, 5, 11. **Open**
11am-8pm Mon; 9.30am-8pm Tue, Wed, Fri; 9.30am-9pm
Thur; 9.30am-8pm Sat.
The hours at this branch are an exception to those of most
other Albert Heijn stores, which generally close at 5.30pm.
Branch: Nieuwmarkt 18 (623 2461).

Dirk van den Broek

Heinekenplein 25 (611 0812). Tram 16, 24, 25. **Open**
11am-7.30pm Mon; 9.00am-8.30pm Tue, Wed, Fri; 9am-
9pm Thur; 8.30am-8pm Sat.
A perfectly good grocery store which offers less selection
and luxury than Albert Heijn, but beats them by a country
mile when it comes to low prices.
Branch: Wittenburgerstraat 18 (620 0070).

Hema

Nieuwendijk 174 (623 4176). Tram 1, 2, 5. **Open** 11am-
6pm Mon; 9.30am-6pm Tue-Sat.
Not the place for weekly basics, since it doesn't sell milk, but
it stocks everything you need for a picnic, and has lots of
good cheap snacks for parties.

Marks and Spencer

*Kalverstraat 66 (620 0006). Tram 4, 9, 14, 16, 24, 25,
26.* **Open** 11am-6pm Mon; 10am-6pm Tue, Wed, Fri;
10am-9pm Thur; 9.30am-6pm Sat. **Credit** EC, MC, V.
Full of the food, clothing and underwear you already know
and love, albeit at higher prices than in the UK. The food
range was extended in 1995, and many ex-pats can be found
there stocking up their cupboards, particularly during
Thursday late-night shopping hours.

In the wee small hours

The issue of shop opening hours stirs deep feelings in Amsterdam. Some feel that, for reasons of workers' rights and the health and happiness of the family, shops shouldn't be open past 5pm, with the exception of the Thursday *koopavond*. Others favour a more consumer-friendly economy, even though it means that a family member or friend will have to work at some ungodly hour. To compete with the new, longer opening hours of the bigger grocery stores, the night shops *(avondwinkels)* have had to alter their opening times. Joe Consumer has won a qualified victory: these shops are handy, but you pay a pretty penny for the convenience.

Avondmarkt
De Wittenkade 94-96 (686 4919). Tram 10. **Open** 4pm-midnight daily.
The Avondmarkt is the biggest and best night shop in town. Basically a supermarket where you can buy anything you need. Recommended – well worth a tram ride.

Dolf's Avondverkoop
Willemsstraat 79 (625 9503). Tram 3. **Open** 4pm-1am Mon-Sat; 11am-1am Sun.
One of the best nightshops in the Jordaan. It stocks all the urgent products you might suddenly need late at night, including toilet paper, toothpaste and bread. As pricey as most night shops.

Big Bananas
Leidsestraat 73 (627 7040). Tram 1, 2, 5, 11. **Open** 3pm-1am Mon-Fri; 11am-1am Sat, Sun.
A reasonable selection of wines, some dubious-looking canned cocktails and a variety of sandwiches are available. Expensive, even for a night shop.

Heuft's First Class Night Shop
Rijnstraat 62 (642 4048). Tram 4, 25. **Open** 5pm-1am Mon-Sat; 3pm-1am Sun. **Credit** AmEx, DC, EC, MC.
Go in person, or phone for a delivery of anything from Champagne and oysters to full meals, because Heuft's has it all – if you're willing to pay the price. Definitely the most classy nightshop in Amsterdam.

Mignon
Vijzelstraat 127 (420 2687). Tram 16, 24, 25. **Open** 5pm-1am Mon-Fri; 11am-1am Sat, Sun.
Part of a chain of night shops, this branch has friendly staff, and stocks drinks, snacks, sweets and other foods in abundance. A mix between a delicatessen and a self-service shop.

La Noche
Linnaeusstraat 24 (665 0440). Tram 3, 6, 9, 10, 14. **Open** 5pm-midnight Mon-Sat; 2pm-midnight Sun. **Credit** AmEx, EC, MC, V.
Carries basics like beer, wine, coffee, milk and biscuits. They have a good selection of take-away meals, and some quite good bon-bons, which they'll wrap in a cute little box for you.

Sterk
Waterlooplein 241 (626 5097). Tram 9, 14. **Open** 9am-2am daily. **Credit** AmEx, EC, MC, V.
More a delicatessen than a night shop, with a vast selection of mouth-watering goodies. The tantalizing quiches, many tasty pastries and imaginative salads are freshly made on the premises. Caters well for vegetarians, selling tofu and a full range of fresh fruit and veg. Good bet for a decent bottle of plonk and quality confectionery. Don't be shocked at the antics of some of the staff, who seem to be perfecting their stand-up comedy routines at their day jobs. Be prepared to ask for what you want (English is never a problem), because there is no self-service here.

Games and Models

Compendium
Hartenstraat 14 (638 1579). Tram 13, 14, 17. **Open** 1-6pm Mon; 10am-6pm Tue, Wed, Fri; 10am-9pm Thur; 10am-6pm Sat. **Credit** AmEx, DC, MC, V.
Come here for games galore, including fantasy role-playing from the USA and Britain, tin soldiers, chess sets, computer games and the Japanese board game 'Go'. The latest card games are also available.

Miniature Furniture
Prinsengracht 293 (622 1113/626 7863 private number, please ring at reasonable time). Tram 13, 14, 17. **Open** noon-4pm Sat and by appointment.
The remarkable assortment of diminutive furnishings is made on a one-twelfth scale by Dutch craftspeople. Ring Mrs Louise Meertens for an appointment to see them.

Scale Train House
Bilderdijkstraat 94 (612 2670/fax 612 2817). Tram 3, 7, 12, 13, 14, 17. **Open** 1-5.30pm Mon; 9.30am-5.30pm Tue-Fri; 9.30am-5pm Sat. **Credit** AmEx, DC, MC, V.
With a do-it-yourself kit you can build yourself a replica of St Peter's Basilica or the Arc de Triomphe. The ready-made parade includes electric trains (with steam or diesel engines and all kinds of rolling stock) plus tracks, European railway stations, houses and scenery. There is also a huge variety of modern and vintage vehicles in various sizes.

Schaak En Go Het Paard
Haarlemmerdijk 147 (624 1171). Tram 1, 2, 5, 11, 13, 17. **Open** 10.30am-6pm Tue-Fri; 10.30am-6pm Sat. **Credit** EC, MC, V.
A fine selection of beautiful and exotic chess sets which range from African to ultra-modern, as well as sets for the Japanese game Go.

Gifts and Handicrafts

C-Cedille
Lijnbaansgracht 275, near Spiegelgracht (624 7178). Tram 6, 7, 10. **Open** *Mar-Dec* 1-6pm Mon; 11am-6pm Tue-Sun; *Jan-Feb* 11am-6pm Tue, Thur-Sat; 1-6pm Sun. **Credit** AmEx, DC, JCB, MC, TC, V.
On one side C-Cedille sells designer jewellery, mostly handmade in the Netherlands. The other half has wooden toys, mobiles, glove puppets, music boxes and hand-made dolls in traditional Dutch costume. Also good-value etchings and aquarelles of typical Amsterdam scenes.

Holland Gallery De Munt
Muntplein 12 (623 2271/fax 638 4215). Tram 4, 9, 14, 16, 24, 25. **Open** 9am-6pm Mon-Sat. **Credit** AmEx, DC, MC, V.
Stockists of antique Delftware, royal and Makkumer pottery, plus other hand-painted objects such as traditional tiles and beautifully decorated wooden trays and boxes. Other highlights include miniature ceramic canal houses and dolls in traditional Dutch costumes. You'll find De Munt in the Munttoren (*see chapter* **Sightseeing**).

Poppette Doll Studio
WG Plein 425 (683 8862). Tram 1, 3, 6, 12. **Open** by appointment.
Jonette Stabbert is an American designer producing unique handmade gifts. Her speciality is teddy bears, some of which have appeared in Disney films, as well as ethnic cloth dolls.

Silverplate
Nes 89 (624 8339). Tram 4, 9, 14, 16, 24, 25. **Open** 11am-6pm Mon-Fri; 11am-5pm Sat. **Credit** AmEx, DC, MC, V.
Wine coolers, cocktail shakers, trays, serving dishes, candlesticks, and photo frames all in silver plate. There are also damask napkins and made-to-measure tablecloths.

Tesselschade – Arbeid Adelt
Leidseplein 33 (623 6665). Tram 1, 2, 5, 6, 7, 10, 11. **Open** 10am-6pm Tue-Fri; 10am-5pm Sat.
Toys and dolls, decorations and more utilitarian items (including tea-cosies, embroidered tea-towels and decorated clothes-hangers) are crafted and sold on a non-profit basis by an association of Dutch women – Arbeid Adelt, which roughly means 'work ennobles', and was founded in 1871.

Glass and Crystal

Royal Leerdam, one of the oldest glassworks in the Netherlands, is world-famous for its contemporary – and remarkably inexpensive – collections of glassware. Its 'Guild' wine goblet, created in co-operation with the Association of Dutch Wine Merchants in 1930, is still one of the company's most popular products. Amsterdam's better gift shops, such as Focke & Meltzer, carry Leerdam's lead crystal 'Unica' one-of-a-kind pieces. Cheaper glassware can be found at household furnishing stores throughout the city. An especially good choice from among these is Xenos, Kalverstraat 228 (622 9984), and at other locations around town.

Glasgalerie Kuhler
Prinsengracht 134 (638 0230). Tram 13, 14, 16. **Open** noon-6pm Tue-Sat; 1-4pm first Sun in month. **Credit** AmEx, DC, MC, V.
A large collection of contemporary European glass and crystal. Most pieces are unique, dated and signed by well-known artists, including five from the Netherlands. Glass-blowing is well represented, along with pate verre and cold laminated sculptures. Prices range from ƒ85 to ƒ15,000.

Health and Beauty

Body and Nature Care
Prinsengracht 420 (624 0203). Tram 1, 2, 5, 11. **Open** 1pm-5pm Tue-Fri; noon-4.30pm Sat.
Alice Versloot runs this specialist in make-your-own cosmetics, ranging from shampoos to creams and lotions for the body and face. There are essential oils and ready-made fragrances but you can also make your own perfume or eau de toilette. Courses cost ƒ150 for four two-hour sessions.

The Body Shop
Kalverstraat 157-159 (623 9789). Tram 4, 9, 14, 16, 24, 25. **Open** 11am-6pm Mon; 9.30am-6pm Tue, Wed, Fri; 9.30am-9pm Thur; 10am-5.30pm Sat. **Credit** AmEx, MC, V.
The usual wonderful array of shampoos, lotions and soaps for pampering your body as well as gift-wrapping and refill services. Prices are higher than in Britain.

Erica
Centraal Station – middle tunnel (626 1842). Tram 1, 2, 4, 5, 9, 11, 13, 17, 24, 25/Metro Centraal Station. **Open** 8am-8pm Mon-Sat.
An atypical setting for such a shop (amid newsagents and various food stalls in the main tunnel of Centraal Station), but Erica is definitely worth a visit, even if you're not embarking on a train journey. The shelves are crammed with an orderly array of homeopathic remedies, essential oils, cruelty-free cosmetics, herbs, herbal teas and vitamins.

Kruiderij 'De Munt'. *See page 147.*

Jacob Hooy & Co

Kloveniersburgwal 10-12 (624 3041). Tram 4, 9, 14, 16, 24, 25/Metro Nieuwmarkt. **Open** noon-6pm Mon; 8.30am-6pm Tue-Fri; 8.30am-5pm Sat.

Established in 1743, this old-fashioned chemist's sells around 600 kitchen and medicinal herbs, spices, natural cosmetics, health foods and homeopathic remedies. Jacob Hooy also has a huge array of different types of liquorice (*drop*).

Kruiderij 'De Munt'

Vijzelstraat 1 (624 4533). Tram 4, 9, 14, 16, 24, 25. **Open** 10.30am-6pm Mon; 10.30am-6pm Tue, Wed, Fri; 10.30am-9pm Thur; 10.30am-6pm Sat; 2pm-6pm Sun.

This tiny, picturesque store is chock-a-block with all it takes to turn your bathroom into a spa: a wide range of essential oils and treatment products from Neal's Yard, Kiehl's of New York and Weleda. If you've got a taste for herbs you can't find in coffee shops, they carry the full line of Celestial Seasonings teas, as well as Solgar Vitamins, and two or three different sorts of bee pollen in capsule form.

Lillian

Leidsestraat 74-76 (627 1900). Tram 1, 2, 5, 11. **Open** 9am-10pm Mon-Sat; 11am-10pm Sun. **Credit** AmEx, EC, V.

This recent arrival to the bustling Leidsestraat makes up for its unusually harsh fluorescent lighting with convenient opening times. All the big name cosmetics lines and vitamin brands, homeopathic products from Dr. Vogel, VSM and Pflüger, as well as a large selection of body and haircare products and beauty aids.

Palais des Parfums

Van Baerlestraat 74 (662 5781). Tram 2, 3, 5, 12. **Open** 1-6pm Mon; 9am-6pm Tue, Wed, Fri; 9am-9pm Thur; 9am-5pm Sat. **Credit** AmEx, DC, MC, £$TC, V.

A large perfumerie in the upmarket Van Baerlestraat stocking all the top brands of cosmetics and perfumes for both men and women. Upstairs there are five salons where you can be pampered with the products of your choice. A one-hour facial costs *f*60, a manicure *f*30, and a full-body massage *f*60.

Household Articles

Kitsch Kitchen

Eerste Bloemdwarsstraat 21(622 8261). Tram 13, 17. **Open** 11am-5.30pm Mon-Fri; 10am-5pm Sat.

A staggering range of kitsch imported from Mexico, Guatemala, India, China and parts of Africa. Culinary objects are represented in various designs and degrees of gaudiness. Choose from several materials: plastic, natural or tin. There are salt and pepper pots made from old Mexican beer cans, lamps from powdered milk tins and buckets made from sheet metal rejected for slight imperfections in the printed design. Although recycled, the articles are skilfully made and extremely intriguing. There are also Guatemalan religious lucky charms and tablecloths bearing outrageous motifs.

Trunk

Rosmarijnsteeg 12 (638 7095). Tram 1, 2, 5. **Open** 1-6pm Mon; 11am-6pm Tue-Sat. **Credit** Amex, DC, EC, MC.

Started in 1994 by two Art Academy graduates who sussed that after the sleek, clean 1980s, people were hankering for all things warm, cosy, cheerful and affordable, this shop stocks household treasures from Morocco, India, Mexico and other far-flung spots.

World of Wonders

Surinamekade 6 (463 4067). Bus 32, 28S. **Open** 10am-6pm Mon-Fri; 11am-6pm Sat; and by appointment. **Credit** EC, MC.

In a former warehouse on the KNSM Island, this shop resembles a treasure room from 'The Arabian Nights'. Cushions from Pakistan and Bangladesh – embroidered, appliquéd and studded with tiny mirrors – are piled up high; patterned sheets are stacked and draped; candelabra glisten in a distant corner. This is the place to find those exotic items you've been admiring at big department stores at an excellent saving and in a relaxed, friendly atmosphere.

Xenos

Kalverstraat (622 9984). Tram 4, 9, 14, 16, 24, 25. **Open** 11am-6pm Mon; 9.30am-6pm Tue, Wed, Fri, Sat; 9.30am-9pm Thur.

If you're setting up house on a tight budget or for a short period of time, this is the place to find much of what you'll need at very low prices.

Markets

The biggest and best market of all is held on Queen's Day and covers the city (*see chapter* **Amsterdam by Season**).

Amsterdam's numerous neighbourhood markets are the best places to find cheap food and clothes, particularly the Albert Cuyp and the Dappermarkt. For second-hand aficionados, the Noordermarkt on a Monday morning is a must.

Albert Cuypmarkt
Albert Cuypstraat. Tram 3, 4, 16, 24, 25. **Open** 9am-5pm Mon-Sat

Amsterdam's biggest general market, selling everything from pillows to prawns at prices worth knowing about. This is probably the best place to get your money's worth and is also worth noting for the material stalls – a firm favourite with painters who can pick up untreated canvas from around *f*3,95 a metre. Clothes tend to be run-of-the-mill cheapies but the odd bargain can be found.

Boerenmarkt
Westerstraat/Noorderkerkstraat. Tram 3, 10. **Open** 10am-3pm Sat.

Every Saturday the Noordermarkt transforms into the organic farmers' market. Products include organic fruit and vegetables (with opportunities for food and wine tasting) as well as essential oils, herbs, candles and the like. Groups of singers or medieval musicians can make the trip more of an outing than a shopping chore.

Dappermarkt
Dapperstraat. Tram 3, 6, 10, 14. **Open** 9am-5pm Mon-Sat.

This is a true locals' market, far less touristy than its famous counterpart and the prices reflect this, particularly on Saturdays, when Albert Cuyp's prices rise in accordance with the amount of extra people coming to the market.

Looier
Elandsgracht 109. Tram 7, 10. **Open** 11am-5pm Mon-Thur; 9am-5pm Sat.

The Looier is more upmarket than the Rommelmarkt (*listed below*), selling mainly antiques, with plenty of collectors items. It is hidden behind a façade of several shop fronts and the deceptive entrance appears at first to be that of a rather smart antique shop. However, once inside, it is easy to get lost in the quiet, warehouse-like premises and find yourself standing alone by a stall crammed with antiquated clocks eerily ticking away. De Looier has both a café and a bar serving alcohol.

Noordermarkt
Noorderstraat. Tram 3, 10/bus 18, 22, 44. **Open** 7.30am-1pm Mon.

A bargain-hunter's paradise. Tagged on to the end of the utilitarian Westermarkt, the Noordermarkt is compact and intended for the serious market shopper. Piles upon piles of new and (mainly) second-hand clothes, shoes, jewellery and hats which need to be sorted through with a grim determination to sift the dross from the delights. Prices can be laughably low, but if you don't arrive early the best will be already have been snaffled.

Oudemanhuis Book Market
Oudemanhuispoort (off Oudezijds Achterburgwal). Tram 4, 9, 14, 16, 24, 25. **Open** 10am-4pm Mon-Sat.

People have been buying and selling books, prints and sheet music on this charming arcade since the nineteenth century. English-language books appear from time to time. When the alley was first built, in 1601, it was the entrance to homes for the elderly, hence the name.

Rommelmarkt
Looiersgracht 38. Tram 7, 10. **Open** 11am-5pm Mon-Thur; 11am-5pm Sat, Sun

A flea market where, among household junk, you are likely to come across such bargains as a boxed set of Demis Roussos or every Nana Mouskouri album you weren't aware she'd ever made. There is a café to aid recovery from shock brought on by more impulsive purchases.

Stamp & Coin Market
Pedestrian island in front of Nova Hotel, Nieuwezijds Voorburgwal 276. Tram 1, 2, 5, 11, 13, 17. **Open** 11am-4pm Wed, Sat.

A specialist market for collectors of stamps and coins, old postcards and commemorative medals.

Waterlooplein
Waterlooplein. Tram 9, 14/Metro Waterlooplein. **Open** 9am-5pm Mon-Sat.

Top tourist market but no less entertaining for that. Basically a huge flea market, it's great for clothes (though it can be a bit pricey) with the usual selection of jeans, leather jackets and batik T-shirts as well as the odd excellent second-hand stall. Genuine bargains can be had if you are prepared to search, but they are often hidden among defunct toasters and down-at-heel shoes.

Westermarkt
Westerstraat. Tram 3, 10. **Open** 9am-5pm Mon-Sat.

A general market for utilitarian needs. The amount of people packing the aisle stands as proof to the prices and the range of goods, most of which seem to be made of plastic and come in a range of colours.

Everything but the girl at **Lillian.**

Parties

Christmas World
Nieuwezijds Voorburgwal 137-139 (622 7047). Tram 1, 2, 5, 11, 13, 17. **Open** 10am-6pm Mon-Fri; 10am-5pm Sat. **Credit** AmEx, MC, V.
Cheery Yuletide decorations from around the world are sold here all year round. The selection includes personalised stockings for Santa to fill and Delft blue ornaments. If you're looking for out-of-season bargains, you won't find them here. Opening hours are unreliable: a phone call will confirm definite times on any given day.

Party House
Rozengracht 93b (624 7851). Tram 7, 13, 14. **Open** 10am-6pm Tue, Wed, Fri; 10am-9pm Thur; 10am-5pm Sat. A multitude of masks hangs from the ceiling in this shop. There are also costumes and accessories for sale or hire and a profusion of practical jokes. Their motto: 'Everything for every party.'

Photographic Stores

Capi-Lux Vak
Basisweg 42 (586 6333). Tram 12/NS Amsterdam Sloterdijk Station. **Open** 8.30am-5.30pm Mon-Fri. **Credit** AmEx, V, MC.
The most comprehensive photography store and laboratory in Amsterdam – well, in its suburbs actually. Equipment is available for rental and computers can be hired for photography manipulation. The stock in the Amsterdam branch is not as broad but good for most professional and amateur needs. **Branch**: Nassaukade 361 (612 8223).

Music

Boudisque
Haringpakkerssteeg 10-18 (623 2603). Tram 1, 2, 4, 5, 9, 11, 13, 14, 16, 17, 24, 25. **Open** 1-6pm Mon; 10am-6pm Tue, Wed, Fri; 10am-9pm Thur; 10am-5pm Sat. **Credit** AmEx, MC, V.
A wide selection of pop, rock, heavy metal, ambient house, jungle and world music as well as T-shirts, CDs and CD-Roms.

Charles Klaasiek en Folklore
Weteringschans 193 (626 5538). Tram 6, 7, 10, 16, 24, 25. **Open** 1-6pm Mon; 9.30am-6pm Tue, Wed, Fri; 9.30am-6pm, 7-9pm, Thur; 9.30am-5pm Sat. **Credit** AmEx, DC, EC, MC, V.
As the name suggests. a specialist shop dealing in classical and folk. A good place to find some of the smaller German and French labels, and, bucking trends, they also still carry some vinyl.

Concerto
Utrechtsestraat 54-60 (626 6577/624 5467/623 5228). Tram 4. **Open** 10am-6pm Mon-Wed, Fri; 10am-9pm Thur; 10am-6pm Sat. **Credit** AmEx, MC, V.
New and second-hand records and CDs of all types – this is where to look for historic Bach recordings, odd Beatles items, or that favourite Diana Ross album that got lost in the move. There's also a large section of second-hand 45s and new releases for slightly less than the usual prices. You can listen before buying.

Get Records
Utrechtsestraat 105 (622 3441). Tram 4 . **Open** noon-6pm Mon; 10am-6pm Tue, Wed, Fri, Sat; 10am-9pm Thur; noon-5pm Sun.
The space liberated by clearing out much of the vinyl selection has been filled with a considerable selection of alternative and independent label CDs. The back of the shop is deceptive; a little corner to the left is partially dedicated to cheapies and well worth investigating.

Jazz Inn
Vijzelstraat 7 (623 5662). Tram 6, 7, 10, 16, 24, 25. **Open** 11am-6pm Mon; 10am-6pm Tue, Wed, Fri; 10am-9pm Thur; 10am-5pm Sat. **Credit** AmEx, EC, MC, V.
Unsurprisingly, jazz is the speciality here: the full spectrum, from 1930s stompers through to modern and Afro jazz.

Midtown
Nieuwendijk 104 (638 4252). Tram 1, 2, 5,11. **Open** 10am-6pm Mon-Sat; 10am-9pm Thur. **Credit** AmEx, EC, MC, V.
Specialises in house of all sorts: hardcore, gabber, trance, club, mellow and garage. Also a good source of information and tickets for hardcore parties.

Outland
Zeedijk 22 (638 7576). Tram 1, 2, 4, 5, 9, 11, 14, 16, 24, 25. **Open** 10.30am-6pm Mon-Wed, Fri; 10.30am-9pm Thur; 10.30am-5.30pm Sat. **Credit** AmEx, MC, V.
Bang in the middle of the Zeedijk, this shop specialises in house music. The décor is distinctly unusual, with a selection of paintings by Dadara and Herman Brood brightening the interior.

Virgin Megastore
Nieuwezijds Voorburgwal 182, Magna Plaza (622 8929). Tram 1, 2, 5, 11, 13, 17. **Open** 11am-6pm Mon; 9.30am-6pm Tue, Wed, Fri, Sat; 9.30am-9pm Thur; noon-6pm Sun. **Credit** AmEx, DC, EC, V.
The megastore is in one of the biggest mall projects the city has ever seen: Magna Plaza. Looking firmly to the future, Virgin doesn't stock vinyl – but it does have one of the largest selections of CDs, videos and computer games in the city, and T-shirts too.

Speciality Shops

Amsterdam has hundreds of specialist shops – usually small, fascinating places where the owners can indulge an obsession. Here we list a selection of the more interesting stores, but there are plenty; try, for example, wandering around the Jordaan (*see chapter* **Amsterdam by Area**) and the area around Utrechtsestraat.

Bangla Klamboe
Prinsengracht 232 (622 9492). Tram 13, 14, 17. **Open** *April-Oct* 1-5.30pm Thur, Fri; 11am-5pm Sat.
This little shop sells mosquito nets in two basic designs and a variety of colours. Take note: mosquitos are a real problem in summer and many Amsterdam residents have nets.

De Condomerie Het Gulden Vlies
Warmoesstraat 141 (627 4174). Tram 4, 9, 14, 16, 24, 25. **Open** 11am-6pm Mon-Fri; 11am-5.30pm Sat.
Opened in 1987, De Condomerie was the first shop of its kind in the world. It's still the only shop in the Netherlands to specialise in condoms. They come in all shapes, colours, textures and sizes with different kinds of lubrication. There are also novelty sheaths (luminous or flavoured) and others packaged as sweets, nuts and animals. The illustrated English-Dutch catalogue costs ƒ10. All regular condoms on sale in the shop have been laboratory-tested.

Dela Rosa's Vitamins
Staalstraat 10 (421 1201). Tram 4, 9, 14. **Open** 10am-6pm Mon-Fri; 10am-5pm Sat. **Credit** AmEx, DC, EC, JCB, V.

Kitsch Kitchen. *See page 147.*

Owner Susan Dela Rosa has 11 years' experience working with vitamins, and she'll take the time to help you find the supplement that's good for what ails you.

Ego-Soft

Nieuwe Kerkstraat 67 (626 8069). Tram 6, 7, 10/Metro Weesperplein. **Open** noon-6pm Tue-Fri; noon-5pm Sat. **Credit** EC, MC, V (over *f*200).

A small shop dealing with the more modern/hi-tech aspects of New Age. Brain machines (with free demonstrations) and psycho-active software are on display alongside meditational CDs, and self-awareness cassettes and videos. Stimulants on sale include guarana and the aphrodisiac Prime Time, and there are numerous books on psychedelia and drugs and how the brain works. Magazines such as *MONDO 2000* and *Gnosis* are also stocked. Every Wednesday in De Roos (*see below*) Ego-Soft gives free demonstrations of brain machines between 6pm and 7.30pm.

Fort van Sjakoo

Jodenbreestraat 24 (625 8979). Tram 9, 14/Metro Waterlooplein. **Open** 11am-6pm Mon-Fri; 11am-5pm Sat.

Radical politics of the kind championed in the squat heydays of the 1960s, 1970s and early 1980s is the lifeblood of this shop. It stocks books, pamphlets, badges, iconography and other paraphernalia of interest to activists, squatters and right-on browsers.

Harrie van Gennip

Govert Flinckstraat 402 (679 3025). Tram 16, 24, 25 **Open** 1-6pm Tue; 11am-4pm Sat; and by appointment.

Harrie van Gennip searches Europe for old gas-burning heaters in various states of disrepair, then brings them home and beautifully restores them. His collection contains about 100 of these, dating from 1870-1935.

Himalaya

Warmoesstraat 56 (626 0899). Tram 1, 2, 4, 5, 9, 16, 17, 24, 25/Metro Centraal Station. **Open** 1-6pm Mon; 10am-6pm Tue, Wed, Fri, Sat; 10am-8.30pm Thur; 1-5pm Sun. **Credit** AmEx, EC, MC, V

Shop/gallery/teahouse Himalaya is a haven amid seedy, bustling surroundings. The shop, established nine years ago,

stocks an extensive range of books and magazines (including many international ones), crystals, tarot cards and jewellery as well as a large number of New Age CDs and tapes (including the latest releases). The light and airy teahouse/gallery is a cosy place to relax, though views are limited to the somewhat murky canal at the back. There are daily changing readings in the shop in the afternoons such as Mahabote (Burmese astrology), tarot and Sacred Path Cards. Contact Himalaya for details.

Kramer/Pontifex

Reestraat 18-20 (626 5274). Tram 13, 14, 17. **Open** 10am-5pm Mon-Sat.

Mr Kramer is an old-fashioned doll and teddy doctor who has held his surgery on these premises for 25 years and fixes anything from a broken Barbie to a battered teddy bear. Actually two shops joined together, Pontifex on the other side sells a multitude of candles in all shapes and sizes.

Marañon Hangmatten

Singel 488-490, at the flower market (420 7121). Tram 1, 2, 5, 11. **Open** 10am-6pm Mon; 10am-6pm Tue-Fri; 10am-5pm Sat; 11am-5.30pm Sun. **Credit** AmEx, DC, MC, V.

Europe's biggest collection of hammocks for inside and out are available in a variety of colours and designs, with the most expensive and colourful hand-woven in South America and Mexico (from *f*60). Plus incense and oils to enhance your relaxation pleasure.

OIBIBIO

Prins Hendrikkade 20-21 (553 9355). Tram 1, 2, 4, 5, 9, 11, 13, 17, 24, 25/Metro Centraal Station. **Open** *café* 9am-midnight Mon-Thur, Sun; 9am-1am Fri, Sat; *restaurant* 5.30-10pm daily; *shop* noon-6.30pm Mon; 10am-6.30pm Tue, Wed, Fri; 10am-9pm Thur; 10am-6pm Sat; noon-5pm Sun; *sauna* 11am-midnight daily; *tea garden* 1pm-8pm daily. **Credit** AmEx, DC, EC, JCB, MC.

This impressive centre is home to many resident therapists and there is a diverse range of workshops and lectures (mainly in Dutch with a handful in English), *see chapter* **Sport & Fitness**. A huge, designer bar on the ground floor is overlooked by a gourmet vegetarian restaurant under one of the building's two towering skylights. There's also a

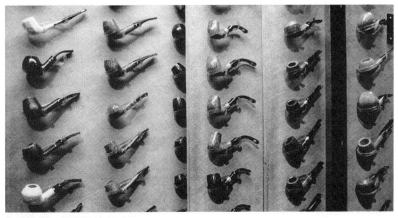

Hot pipes at **PGC Hajenius**.

Japanese-style tea garden, complete with waterfall and live fish, which serves oriental delicacies. The Passage, a shop selling only eco-friendly clothing, vitamins and minerals, including a wide variety of Neal's Yard products, runs between Nieuwendijk and Prins Hendrikkade; while the basement bookshop stocks a huge selection of books, CDs and videos. *See also chapter* **Cafés & Bars**.

Olivaria

Hazenstraat 2a (638 3552). Tram 7, 10. **Open** 11am-6pm Tue-Sat.
Carries a wide variety of olive oils from France, Spain, Italy, Greece, and Portugal, as well as vinegars, mustards and olives. You can sample the oil before buying, and if you're looking for a special gift, they offer beautiful (but expensive) Colle oil and vinegar sets.

Palm Music

's Gravelandse Veer 5 bg (422 0445). Tram 4, 9, 14/Metro Waterlooplein . **Open** noon-7pm Tue-Fri; 10am-5pm Sat. **Credit** AmEx, DC, JCB, MC, V.
Buys and sells second-hand and antique musical instruments; hires instruments to film, TV, and photography studios, prop agencies, theatres and professional musicians; provides certified valuations to private individuals for trade and insurance purposes; repair of acoustic and electric instruments. Upon request, the owner will send a catalogue of his current stock.

PGC Hajenius

Rokin 92-96 (625 9985). Tram 4, 9, 14, 16, 24, 25. **Open** 9.30am-6pm Mon-Wed, Fri-Sun; 9.30am-9pm Thur. **Credit** AmEx, DC, MC, V.
Hajenius was established as a tobacconist's in 1826 but is now owned by Swiss tobacco giants Burger. The interior of the shop dates from the 1920s. Famed for its own brand of cigars, Hajenius also stocks a splendid variety of pipes including the traditional Dutch clay version with either a 14" or 20" (35cm or 50cm) stem. The staff will organise the shipping of gifts worldwide.

De Roos

Vondelstraat 35-37 (689 0081/shop 689 0436/Het Ving 616 7826). Tram 1, 2, 3, 5, 6, 11, 12. **Open** *centre* 8am-11pm Mon-Fri; 9am-6pm, 7.30-11pm, Sat; 9am-6pm Sun; *shop* 10am-9.30pm (only for people on courses after 6.30pm) Mon-Fri; 11am-5pm Sat; *tea house* 10am-10pm Mon-Sat; 10am-5pm Sun

De Roos is a modest size compared to OIBIBIO and has a more intimate atmosphere. As you walk through the doors a sense of calm pervades the incense-laced air. A ground-floor shop offers a range of books on esoteric subjects as well as magazines, candles, crystals, herbs, tarot cards and incense. There is a delightful tea shop with a leafy garden at the back and a friendly resident cat. As well as regular workshops and lectures it is also possible to join daily open sessions in yoga, zen meditation and healing. Details of all activities can be found in De Roos' own, free programme. Het Ving is the information centre of De Roos: a small room crammed with a mind-boggling choice of leaflets. Advice and help is available when choosing a course or workshop.

A Taste of Ireland

Herengracht 228 (638 1642). Tram 13, 14, 17. **Open** 1-7.30pm Mon; 10am-7.30pm Tue-Fri; 10am-6pm Sat.
This shop stocks many of the goodies that you might miss from back home; fresh sausages, bacon and puddings are flown in fresh from Ireland every week and there is also an extensive selection of British and Irish beers and ciders on sale.

Waterwinkel

Roelof Hartstraat 10 (675 5932). Tram 3, 12, 24. **Open** 9am-6pm Mon-Fri; 9am-9pm Thur; 9am-5pm Sat.
Owner Jan Willem Bakker boasts of stocking 100 bottled mineral waters from around the world (from Britain to China). Customers are encouraged to sample before buying and bottles can be gift-wrapped and shipped.

De Witte Tandenwinkel

Runstraat 5 (623 3443). Tram 1, 2, 5, 11. **Open** 1-6pm Mon; 10am-6pm Tue-Fri; 10am-5pm Sat. **Credit** AmEx, DC, MC, V.
The White Teeth Shop has all you need for a dazzling smile, from junior-sized toothbrushes emblazoned with Mickey Mouse to interdental brushes and toothpicks.

Wooden Shoe Factory/De Klompenboer

Nieuwezijds Voorburgwal 20 (623 0632). Tram 1, 2, 5, 11. **Open** *1 Apr-15 Sept* 10am-9pm daily; *16 Sept-31 Mar* 10am-6pm daily. **Credit** AmEx, DC, MC, V.
Wooden shoes (*klompen*) may not be the height of fashion but they do make a tasteful souvenir of your stay in the Netherlands. Buy them large enough to wear over heavy socks. Plus, you can brush up on your clog history at the exhibition in the back of the shop.

Services

Champagne for breakfast, a belly-button piercing or non-chemical haircare? Amsterdam is at your service.

Amsterdam is not the most service-orientated of cities, although most needs can be catered for with a little insider knowledge and a degree of persistence. As most Amsterdammers adhere to the Dutch saying, 'I work to live, not live to work,' you'll find it harder to get things done when the sun comes out. But the good news is that, no matter what you need doing, it can usually be done in English.

SERVICE INFORMATION

Generally the more expensive the shop, the greater the number of services it has to offer. Every department store (*see chapter* **Shopping**) has a customer service division (*klantenservice*) which will advise on packaging and shipping arrangements.

Business-related services are listed in our *chapter* **Business**. For emergency services and car hire companies, *see chapter* **Survival**; for bicycle hire *see chapter* **Getting Around**.

Unless otherwise stated, services listed can not be paid for with credit cards.

Beauty Services

GM van Heusden
Stromarkt 45 (624 2408). Tram 1, 2, 5 ,11, 13, 17. **Open** 8.30am-5.30pm Mon-Fri by appointment.
A licensed chiropodist who takes care of all foot problems. Basic footcare costs *f*65 per session.

AYK Suncentre
Tesselschadestraat 1e (618 3347). Tram 1, 2, 5, 6, 7, 10. **Open** 8am-10pm Mon-Fri; 8am-8pm Sat; 10am-8pm Sun.
The sun-beds at AYK offer safer exposure and more natural skin colour due to the combination of protector lamps and turbo filters. For *f*5 you get between three and five minutes, depending on your type of skin.

Camera, TV & Radio Hire

Capi-Lux Vak
Basisweg 42 (586 6333). Tram 12/Bus 42, 44, 82/NS Amsterdam Sloterdijk. **Open** 8.30am-5.30pm Mon-Fri. **Credit** AmEx, MC, V.
Camera and lighting equipment rental at the most comprehensive photography store in Amsterdam.

Ruad BV
Overtoom 371 (669 8336). Tram 1, 5. **Open** 9.30am-6pm Tue-Fri; 9.30am-5pm Sat. **Credit** AmEx, MC, V.
Camcorders, televisions and video recorders are hired out on a short- or long-term basis. A steep security deposit is required (*f*1,000 for a video recorder, for example). Book in advance and take a passport.

Cheap Flights

KLM Call & Go
(023 5674 567). **Open** 1-10.30pm daily.
This last-minute KLM phoneline gives information on cheap European and intercontinental flights. After recorded information in Dutch, you are automatically put through to reservations. There's a minumum stay of two nights and a maximum stay of four weeks.

Clothing Care

Clean Brothers
Jacob van Lennepkade 179 (618 3637). Tram 3, 12, 17. **Open** 8am-8pm Mon-Fri; 9am-5pm Sat.
A same-day service-wash is available at this launderette. If you prefer to wash your own things or need some dry-cleaning, try the Kerkstraat branch, open daily 7am-9pm. The Westerstraat branch offers an ironing service for *f*3 per item and is open 8am-8pm daily.
Branches: Kerkstraat 56 (622 0273); Westerstraat 26 (627 7376).

Cleaning Shop Express
Huidenstraat 22 (623 1219). Tram 1, 2, 5, 11. **Open** 9am-6pm Mon-Fri; 9am-5pm Sat.
A full range of services, including: dry-cleaning; laundering; leather and carpet cleaning; repairs; alterations and invisible mending. Staff will also hand-launder and press shirts and sheets. Two-day service on request.

Het Strijkpaleis
(665 6606). **Open** 9.30am-5pm Mon-Fri.
This ironing service collects your items anywhere in town and delivers them back within 24 hours. Prices range from 25c for a handkerchief to *f*2,75 for a shirt.

Costume Hire

Party House
Rozengracht 93B (624 7851). Tram 13, 14, 17. **Open** 10am-6pm Mon-Wed; 10am-9pm Thur; 10am-5pm Sat.
A multitude of masks hangs down from the ceiling. There are also costumes and accessories for sale and hire and an abundance of practical jokes.
Branches: Utrechtsestraat 90 (620 8304); Rozengracht 65 – balloon specialists (420 1272).

Contact Lenses and Glasses

Prins Brillen
Ferdinand Bolstraat 130 (662 5476). Tram 25, 24. **Open** 1-5.45pm Mon; 9am-5.45pm Tue-Fri; 9am-5pm Sat. **Credit** AmEx, MC, V.
Both glasses and contact lenses are reasonably priced, and there are some interesting frames.

Schmidt Optiek

Rokin 72 (623 1981). Tram 4, 16, 9, 24, 25. **Open** 1-5.30pm Mon; 9.30am-5.30pm Tue, Wed, Fri; 9.30am-5.30pm, 6.30-9pm, Thur; 9.30am-5pm Sat. **Credit** AmEx, MC, V.

While not the cheapest, this is the most fun shop for selecting glasses, built in 1906 and with hundreds of drawers to hold its stock – currently comprising over 2,000 frames.

Hans Anders

Ferdinand Bolstraat 118 (06 0075). Tram 25, 24. **Open** 9am-5pm Mon-Fri; 9am-3pm Sat. **Credit** AmEx, MC, V.

The cheapest contact lenses in town. For ƒ75 you'll get a pair of contacts that'll last about six months.

Florist

Johan Licher

Herengracht 369 (627 6328). Tram 1, 2, 5, 11. **Open** 8am-6pm Mon-Fri; 8am-5pm Sat.

This tiny corner florist shop is bursting with colour. As well as a good selection of flowers and plants, it stocks a range of terracotta and painted pots. It also offers the full Interflora service. *See also chapter* **Shopping**.

Food Delivery

American Style Pizza

(676 1476/615 6775). **Open** 4-11pm daily.

A standard pizza costs ƒ11,50 with extra toppings at ƒ1,50 each. Free delivery.

Bel Menu

(669 3834/fax 669 3495). **Open** 5-9pm daily.

Ideal for the comsopolitan or pernickety eater, as you can choose from Greek, Chinese, Argentinian, French, Italian, Dutch and Surinamese menus.

Bojo Rijsttafel Express

(694 2864). **Open** 4-9pm daily.

Rice tables start at ƒ29,50 for which you get rice, two meat dishes, two vegetable dishes, egg, chicken, satay and prawn crackers. Your order must come to at least ƒ25 for delivery, which then costs an additional ƒ2,50.

Hans Sluiman Oesters

(tel/fax 675 3996). **Open** 24 hours daily.

Sluiman arrives at your door wearing a spotless apron and carrying an enamel bucket, a pepper mill, a bottle of Tabasco sauce, and a big silver bowl, filled with seaweed and oysters. There are three types of oysters: De Creuses at ƒ3 each, Fine de Claire at ƒ3 each, and Imperial at ƒ5 each. The cost of delivery and opening is included in the per-piece price. Place your order a day in advance.

Ontbijt Service

(616 1613). **Open** 10am-4.30pm Tue-Fri for ordering, delivery daily.

Three standard breakfasts include bread rolls, various cheeses and cold sliced meats, a boiled egg, fresh orange juice, tea or coffee and a fruit salad. Prices are ƒ29, ƒ39 and ƒ79, with extra meat and cheese and a small bottle of Champagne added to the ƒ39 meal and more of everything, plus fish and a big bottle of Champagne, for the de luxe version. Treat yourself.

Two in One

(612 8488). **Open** noon-midnight daily.

Surinamese and Indian food at reasonable prices. Chicken roti with potatoes, curry and egg costs ƒ8,50; with lamb it's ƒ10,50. Delivery, in west, south and central Amsterdam only, costs ƒ2,50.

Pieces for piercing at **Body Manipulations**. *See page 153.*

Formal Dress Hire

Joh Huijer

Weteringschans 153 (623 5439). Tram 6, 7, 10. **Open** 9am-6pm Mon-Fri; 9am-6pm, 7-9pm Thur; 9am-4pm Sat. **Credit** AmEx, V, MC, DC.

Men's formal dress hire: all clothing is from the German label, Lacerna, in British sizes 34 to 50. A complete outfit, including cuff-links and bow tie, can be hired for about ƒ150.

Maison Van Den Hoogen

Sarphatipark 88-90 (679 8828). Tram 3. **Open** 9am-6pm Mon-Wed, Fri; 9am-8.30pm Thur; 9am-4pm Sat.

A formal dress-hire outlet where you'll find a choice of women's cocktail and evening dresses in British sizes 8 to 12 as well as suits and tuxedos for men.

Hairdressers

Nederlandse Kappers Academie

Weteringschans 167 (626 3430). Tram 6, 7, 10. **Open** 9am-5pm Mon-Fri.

Inexpensive haircuts are available at this hairdressers' training institute. Cuts are done by advanced students and cost ƒ21,50 for men and ƒ17 for men. No appointment necessary.

The Hair Company

Sint Antoniesbreestraat 124 (420 3845). Metro Nieuwmarkt. **Open** 9.45am-6pm Tue, Wed; 9.45am-9pm Thur; 10am-6.30pm Fri; 9.30am-5.30pm Sat.

Only chemical-free products used in this simply designed store. Customers are of all ages, the service is good and the prices are reasonable (ƒ52,50 for women and ƒ45 for men).

Hair Police

Kerkstraat 113 (420 5841). Tram 1, 2, 5, 11. **Open** noon-6pm Mon-Sat.

This innovative hair salon celebrated its tenth year in business in 1996. Cuts start at ƒ50, as do colouring treatments.

Extensions start at ƒ10 for two strands to ƒ800 for a full head of long braids. Free consultations.

Kinki Kappers

Utrechtsestraat 34 (625 7793). Tram 4. **Open** 1-6pm Mon; 9.30am-6pm Tue, Wed, Fri, Sat; 9.30am-9pm Thur.
In this trendy, lively shop you can get a wash, cut and blow-dry for ƒ55.

Toni & Guy

Magna Plaza, Nieuwezijds Voorburgwal 182, second floor (620 0662). Tram 1, 2, 4, 5, 9, 13, 14, 16, 17, 24, 25. **Open** 11am-6pm Mon; 9.30am-6pm Tue, Wed; 9.30am-9pm Thur; 9.30am-6pm Fri, Sat; noon-6pm Sun.
Toni & Guy promise you a haircut to fit your face and personality. Consultations are free, and prices for a cut and blow-dry range from ƒ55-ƒ75.

Online Service Providers

NLnet

(024 3653653/e-mail: info@nl.net). **Open** 8.30am-5.30pm Mon-Fri.
Internet access and an e-mail address with NLnet costs ƒ20 for a start-up set and thereafter ƒ15 a month plus ƒ3 per on-line hour.

CompuServe

(sales 06 022 49 68/free support 06 022 59 91/e-mail 70006.101@compuserve.com). **Open** 9am-9pm Mon-Fri; 10am-5pm Sat. **Credit** AmEx, MC, V.
There is no start-up cost, and in the first month you get 10 hours free. Once you're signed on, you can either pay ƒ16,50 per month for five free hours and ƒ4,90 for each subsequent hour, or ƒ42 per month for 20 free hours, then ƒ3,20 per hour thereafter. Provides (sluggish) Internet access as well a huge variety of CompuServe's own forums and services. If you're already a member, the number to dial to log on in Amsterdam for 28,800 access is: 688 0085.

Euronet

(625 6161). **Open** 9am-6pm Mon-Fri.
A start up set costs ƒ99 and that includes the first month on-line. After that it's ƒ45 a month for unlimited hours or ƒ37,50 a month if you decide to commit for one year.

Xs4all

(620 0294). **Open** noon-8pm Mon-Fri.
An Internet access company: getting connected costs ƒ30, therafter it's ƒ30 a month for unlimited hours or ƒ360 for one year's unlimited netsurfing.

Watch and Jewellery Repairs

Elke Watch Company

Kalverstraat 206 (624 7100/623 6386). Tram 1, 2, 4, 5, 9, 11, 14, 16, 24, 25. **Open** 9am-5.30pm Mon-Fri. **Credit** AmEx, DC, MC, V.
Besides selling them, Elke carries out quick repairs to watches and some jewellery and offers a service for simple jobs.

Packing and Removals

De Gruijter

Industrieweg 11-13, 2382 NR Zoeterwoude (071 89 9313). NS Zoeterwoude. **Open** 8.30am-5pm Mon-Fri.
Accustomed to dealing with fragile and expensive items, De Gruijter will package and send your purchases or household belongings anywhere in the world by sea or air and also offer storage facilities.

Photocopying

Printerette

Spuistraat 128 (624 8520). Tram 1, 2, 5, 11, 13, 14, 17. **Open** 9am-5.30pm Mon-Wed, Fri; 9am-9pm Thur.
The cheapest copy shop in town: 6c per sheet for do-it-yourself copying.

Kinko's

Overtoom 62 (589 0910). Tram 1, 2, 5, 6. **Open** 24 hours daily.
An inspiring range of services, from copies on paper, business cards and even T-shirts, to faxing and printing. Underground car park and delivery are free, as are the paperclips, glue and correction fluid at each copier.

Photo Processing

Capi-Lux

Leidsestraat 77 (623 3019). Tram 1, 2, 5, 11. **Open** 9am-6pm Mon-Fri; Thur 9am-9pm;9am-5pm Sat. **Credit** AmEx, DC, MC, V.
This central shop offers a dependable one-hour colour film service. Slides take three days and black and white processing takes five.

"S" Color

Singel 356 (624 9102). Tram 1, 2, 5, 11. **Open** 24 hours Mon-Thur; noon-10pm Fri; 1-6 pm Sat; 4pm-midnight Sun.
The film laboratory used by top professional photographers will push, pull, and clip test all formats of film, and are quick and reliable.

Shoe Repairs

Luk's Schoenservice

Prinsengracht 500 (623 1937). Tram 1, 2, 5, 11. **Open** 1-5.30pm Mon; 8.30am-5.30pm Tue-Fri; 9am-1pm Sat.
A complete repair and cleaning service: Luk does quick, professional and top-quality work which can usually be completed in a day. You can trust him with your satin evening shoes.

Tattoos and Body Piercing

Body Manipulations

Oude Hoogstraat 31 (638 4639). Metro Nieuwmarkt. **Open** 1-6pm Mon; noon-6pm Tue, Wed, Fri, Sat; noon-9pm Thur.
Rates begin at ƒ15 for an earlobe to ƒ50 plus jewellery for any other hole, aside from face piercing which is more expensive. No appointment necessary.

Hanky Panky

Oudezijds Voorburgwal 141 (627 4848). Tram 4, 9, 16, 20, 24, 25. **Open** *summer* 11am-9pm, *winter* 11am-6pm, Mon-Sat.
The drummer of Pearl Jam and ex-Take Thatter Robbie Williams are among the many rock stars to have been tattooed here. *See also chapter* **Museums**.

Skin Deep

Tweede Goudsbloemdwarsstraat 3 (638 8590). Bus 18. **Open** 11am-7pm Mon-Sat.
Specializing in Celtic, modern and primitive designs, Skin Deep will tattoo or pierce any part of your body. Charges start at ƒ100 an hour for tattoos.

SCULPTURE

MALEVICH
MONDRIAN
JOHNS
WARHOL
OLDENBURG
MONET CEZANNE
KLEIN SCHOONHOVEN

DRAWINGS

PICASSO CHAGALL
KOUNELLIS MERZ FABRO
VAN GOGH MATISSE

POSTERS

APPEL LUCEBERT FONTANA

STEDELIJK
MUSEUM
OF MODERN ART
AMSTERDAM

VIDEO

SCHOLTE   KOONS

DANIËLS

PRINTS

LICHTENSTEIN
KIEFER POLKE
RYMAN ANDRE DIBBETS
VAN ELK NAUMAN DE MARIA

PAINTING

KIRCHNER
KANDINSKY

INDUSTRIAL DESIGN

APPLIED ART

Paulus Potterstraat 13

telephone 020 5732911

Open daily from 11 a.m. to 5 p.m.
From April 1 ▶ September 30
11 a.m. to 7 p.m.

PHOTOGRAPHY

Galleries & Museums

Galleries

Sculpture, ceramics, photography, jewellery and common or garden paintings: art is everywhere in Amsterdam.

Art is part of everyday life here: many Dutch people hang original works in their homes and there are schemes to help everyone afford gallery art. Out on the streets and in the parks there is a huge variety of public art; many are works commissioned by the local government, but there is almost as much uncommissioned and unofficial art which appears discreetly overnight and, as a rule, is as eagerly accepted by the locals as the official monuments. In addition to the regular galleries many bars, shops and cafés also hold regularly changing exhibitions. The Netherlands is one of the few European countries which still actively supports the arts and the effect is obvious: over 250 commercial galleries in Amsterdam alone, as well as three world-class art museums. For many, knowledge of Dutch art begins and ends with the great luminaries – Rembrandt, Van Gogh, possibly Mondriaan – but the contemporary art scene here is vast and incredibly diverse. Gone are the days when native modernist art fell either into the clean lines of De Stijl or the violent abstraction of CoBrA. Today, thanks partly to the growing international community of artists, there is everything and the wonderfully non-elitist galleries are more influenced by personal taste than fashion.

THE GO-BETWEENS
Some confusion arises about the difference between a gallery and a *kunsthandel*. A *kunsthandel* (art dealer) is more likely to buy and resell art, to carry multiples of paintings as prints and to go for established names. A gallery, strictly speaking, acts as a sort of agent to the artist, exhibiting and selling art and taking a commission, though not buying the art outright. But to complicate matters, many *kunsthandels* decided to call themselves galleries when 'gallery' became fashionable in the sixties.

SUPPORTING THE ARTS
Since World War II art has been strongly supported, notably in subsidies to individual artists. Artists were thus guaranteed a market: the government. This was more a social programme – to keep the artists off the street – than a subsidy to the arts. In the mid-1980s there were over 3,500 artists on this programme, about half of them in Amsterdam.

Those days are now over and an enormous reshuffling is taking place. The massive artists' support programme was discontinued at the end of the eighties, while caution and consolidation prevailed.

Artists no longer had a secure market. Initially there was an inevitable sense of panic, but now a keener sense of the world outside the studio has developed. That official subsidies provided so many artists with the opportunity to 'discover themselves' for so long is unique and has lent a special quality to the art now in Amsterdam's galleries. Business and industry continue are slowly warming to the idea of sponsoring and buying art.

MUSEUMS VS GALLERIES?
Relationships between museums and galleries are always convoluted. In the Netherlands, the art world is dominated by five of the world's best museums: the Haags Gemeentemuseum (The Hague, *see chapter* **The Randstad**), Amsterdam's Stedelijk Museum (*see chapter* **Museums**), the Rijksmuseum Kröller-Müller (Otterlo, *see chapter* **The Provinces: Gelderland**), the Groningen Museum (Groningen, *see chapter* **The Provinces**) and the Van Abbe Museum (Eindhoven, *see chapter* **The Provinces: Noord Brabant**). All 'discover' relatively new artists and are known for their 'eye' for art likely to be in demand. They provide a standard and sometimes a market for privately-owned art galleries, but they are a very hard act for the galleries to follow without access to public funding.

The Amsterdam gallery guide, *Alert* (available at galleries and some newsagents) is in Dutch but it has maps of all districts, with the gallery locations clearly marked and is very helpful when finding your way around. Custom-made guided tours of the galleries are run by Amsterdam Gallery Guide, *see chapter* **Sightseeing**. Many of the galleries listed below close for a month, either in July or August, so it's best to phone before setting out to visit one in these months. Unless otherwise specified, the galleries listed below do not accept credit cards.

Galleries

ABK/Amsterdams Beeldhouwers Kollektief
Zeilmakerstraat 15 (625 6332). Tram 3. **Open** noon-5pm Thur-Sun.
Amsterdam's sculptors' collective is a partly subsidised organisation with members' fees making up the shortfall.

The best in contemporary sculpture can be seen at **Galerie Fons Welters**, *Page 160.*

Every kind of three-dimensional work is exhibited in both solo and group shows. The standard of exhibitors varies, with figurative work often the best on show.
Wheelchair access.

Galerie Akinci

Lijnbaansgracht 317 (638 0480). Tram 16, 24, 25. **Open** 1-6pm Tue-Sat.
Akinci is a reliable, exciting gallery located within a war-ren-like complex which opened in 1993 to help seven local gallery members fight the recession together. The shows are very mixed, combining the known with the unknown, the local with the far-flung. High quality guaranteed, though some shows may be a little daunting for the unini-tiated.
Wheelchair access.

Galerie Paul Andriesse

Prinsengracht 116 (623 6237). Tram 10. **Open** 10am-12.30pm, 2-6.30pm Mon-Fri; 2-6pm Sat; 2-5pm 1st Sun of month.
When Paul Andriesse takes you on to his books you know you've made it. This is one of *the* galleries for experimental and truly avant-garde work by artists who have already got something of a reputation. Names include Marlene Dumas and Pieter Laurens Mol.

Animation Art

Berenstraat 39 (627 7600). Tram 1, 2, 5, 11. **Open** 11am-6pm Tue-Fri; 11am-5pm Sat. **Credit** AmEx, DC, MC, V.
Entirely devoted to animation, with original Disney and other animators' 'cels' – outlines or line drawings of car-toon characters which are then painted on to cellulose acetate – and limited editions of hand-inked originals on display are often for sale. A must for all cartoon fans.

De Appel

Nieuwe Spiegelstraat 10 (625 5651). Tram 16, 24, 25. **Open** noon-5pm Tue-Sun.
An Amsterdam institution and the first gallery in the coun-try to recognise video art. Now housed in the former ICAA building, the gallery holds varied exhibitions of often very new contemporary art, favouring young and unknown artists.
Wheelchair access.

Art Affairs

Lijnbaansgracht 316 (620 6433). Tram 16, 24, 25. **Open** 1-6pm Wed-Sat; 2-5pm 1st Sun of month. **Credit** AmEx, MC, DC, V.
Art Affairs presents an international program of art leaning towards the conceptual. The gallery holds various exhibi-tions including paintings, printing, photography, sculpture and performance art, with artists like Morellet, Baldwin Romberg and Jan Smejkal.
Wheelchair access.

ArCAm

Waterlooplein 213 (620 4878). Tram 9, 14/Metro Waterlooplein. **Open** 1-5pm Tue-Sat.
Devoted to the promotion of contemporary Dutch architec-ture, with particular focus on Amsterdam and its environs. The centre organises exhibitions of architectural drawings and models, lectures and discussion forums. Relevant English-language publications are also available.

Aschenbach

Bilderdijkstraat 165C (685 3580). Tram 3, 7, 12, 13, 17. **Open** 1-6pm Wed-Sat..
Aschenbach was the first Amsterdam gallery to show Russian artists but it also concentrates on showing new, rel-atively unknown artists from across Europe. Its lack of con-cern about being 'established' gives the gallery added charm.
Wheelchair access with assistance.

Galerie Binnen

Keizersgracht 82 (625 9603). Tram 1, 2, 5, 11, 13, 17. **Open** noon-6pm Tue-Sat. **Credit** EC, MC.
The city's foremost gallery for industrial and interior design and the applied arts (*binnen* means 'inside' or 'indoors'). The owners have a great roomy space to show new work by Dutch designers, including installations and spatial projects, plus glass, ceramics and jewellery.
Wheelchair access.

Bloom

Bloemstraat 150 (638 8810). Tram 13, 14, 17. **Open** 1-6pm Tue-Sat; 2-5pm 3rd Sun of month.
Founded in 1992, Bloom is one of Amsterdam's most excit-ing young galleries, regularly exhibiting ground-breaking artists and switching easily between traditional media and conceptual and installation works. The quality of the shows is always high: recent names include Sally Mann, Mark Madel and Karel Goudsblom.
Wheelchair access.

Boomerang

Boomstraat 12 (420 3516). Tram 3. **Open** noon-6pm Mon, Thur-Sun.
Hidden away behind the Noordermarkt, Boomerang is a haven for both art lovers and anthropologists. Dedicated to the promotion of Australian art – mainly Aboriginal, but also with occasional shows from European Australians – most of the exhibitions here are wonderful, opening uneducated eyes to the wealth of different styles in traditional crafts.
Wheelchair access.

Clement

Prinsengracht 845 (625 1656). Tram 16, 24, 25. **Open** 11am-5.30pm Tue-Sat.
Galerie Clement (previously called Printshop) is the grand-daddy of printmakers' studio-galleries – it has been an ate-lier since 1958, a gallery since 1968. Artists do their own prints and the gallery also exhibits their drawings and paint-ings. Standards are mixed.

Collection d'Art

Keizersgracht 516 (622 1511). Tram 1, 2, 5, 11. **Open** 1-5pm Wed-Sat.
An old gallery (founded 1969) which corners the market for good, established Dutch artists: Armando, Constant, and a stable of big names.

Conscious Dreams

Kerkstraat 117 (626 6907). Tram 1, 2, 5, 11. **Open** 10-6.30pm Mon-Sat. **Credit** AmEx, DC, MC, V.
Young, trendy gallery promoting aspiring artists from in and around the Amsterdam club scene. Past shows have includ-ed computer art, cyberspace collages and virtual reality.
Wheelchair access.

Gallery Delaive

Spiegelgracht 23 (625 9087). Tram 6, 7, 10. **Open** 11am-5.30pm Tue-Sat; noon-5pm Sun. **Credit** AmEx.
Internationally acclaimed, Delaive is an upmarket, high-qual-ity gallery, though the emphasis on names rather than tal-ent occasionally backfires, resulting in the occasional less than impressive exhibition. Generally a safe bet for excellent shows by artists with international reputations.

Galerie Van Wijngaarden

Lijnbaansgracht 318 (626 4970). Tram 16, 24, 25. **Open** 1-6pm Tue-Sat
This is essentially a gallery exhibiting young Dutch talent

Mosey to the **Melkweg** *for excellent photgrapy shows. Page 160.*

from amongst others the Rietveld Akademie and the artists studio's the Jan van Eyck Akademie. The work exhibited is mainly figurative, with the emphasis being on new developments in the art world.

D'Eendt

Spuistraat 272 (626 5777). Tram 1, 2, 5, 11. **Open** noon-6pm Thur-Sat.
Once a trendsetter, D'Eendt has had its ups and downs in recent years. The gallery features paintings and installations by young international artists. Shows are of variable quality: modern and naïve figuratives are the strongest work.

Espace

Keizersgracht 548 (624 0802). Tram 1, 2, 5, 11. **Open** 1-5.30pm Wed-Sat; 2-5pm 1st Sun of month, (during Sept '96, 2nd Sun of month).
Based in Amsterdam since 1960, Eva Bendien is one of Amsterdam's *grande dames* of art. Her gallery shows Lucassen, Lucebert and Pierre Alechinsky. Co Westerik's popular, odd, Dutch realism is another highlight.
Branch: Kerkstraat 276 (638 6034).

De Expeditie

Leliegracht 47 (620 4758). Tram 13, 14, 17. **Open** 1-6pm Wed-Sat.
The one-man shows at De Expeditie take months of preparation. Siguidur Gudmunsson, Barry Flanagan and a number of Dutch artists have all worked and exhibited here.

Barbara Farber

Keizersgracht 265 (627 6343). Tram 13, 14, 17. **Open** 1-6pm Tue-Sat.
A top gallery and an absolute phenomenon in Amsterdam. Barbara Farber shows new avant-garde work and has an eagle-eye for unlaunched artists, particularly young Americans.

Galerie Fons Welters

Bloemstraat 140 (622 7193). Tram 13, 14, 17. **Open** 1-6pm Tue-Sat; 2-5pm 1st Sun of month.
One of the top galleries in the city, with a preference for sculpture but exhibiting everything – provided it is top quality, innovative and prepared to push the boundaries a little further than the mainstream. A must for any lover of contemporary art.

Galerie van Gelder

Planciusstraat 9a (off Haarlemmerplein) (627 7419). Tram 3. **Open** 1-5.30pm Tue-Sat; 1-5.30pm 1st Sun of month
One to watch: Van Gelder regularly picks up on bright young talent that is just making its mark around the world. A truly international collection of artists can be expected in the group shows, which are almost consistently excellent. .
Wheelchair access.

Lumen Travo

Lijnbaansgracht 315 (627 0883). Tram 16, 24, 25. **Open** 1-6pm Tue-Sat. 2-5pm 1st Sun of month.
Another member of the Lijnbaansgracht gallery complex, Lumen Travo is a reliable bet for good, well-thought out conceptual art as well as a generally impressive selection of other international contemporary art. The changing exhibitions are always worth seeing.
Wheelchair access.

Melkweg

Lijnbaansgracht 234a (624 1777). Tram 1, 2, 5, 6, 7, 10. **Open** 2-7pm Wed-Sun.
The Melkweg is equally important in the Amsterdam art world as it is in the music. Artistic director Suzanne Dechart is open to anyone with good ideas and the exhibitions – always photographic – can be excellent.
Wheelchair access.

Mokum

Nieuwezijds Voorburgwal 334 (624 3958/625 8025/fax 624 3958). Tram 1, 2, 5, 11. **Open** 11am-6pm Wed-Sat; 1-5pm 1st Sun of month. Also by appointment.
Mokum specializes in Dutch realism, an extremely well-developed school of its own here. Magic (or fantastic) realists are also represented.
Wheelchair access to ground level only.

Montevideo/TBA & Réné Coelho

Spuistraat 104 (623 7101). Tram 1, 2, 5, 11. **Open** 10-5pm Tue-Sat.
Montevideo is a media artists' organisation; its gallery puts on solo shows of work related to electronic media, photography, sculpture and installations.
Wheelchair access.

Nanky de Vreeze

Keizersgracht 22 (627 3808). Tram 1, 2, 5, 11. **Open** 10.30-6.30pm daily.
One of the largest and most attractive commercial galleries in Amsterdam. Aims to show a broad range of works, with the emphasis on sculpture and two-dimensional art rather than conceptual or installation pieces.
Wheelchair access.

De Opsteker

Noorderstraat 61 (638 6904). Tram 16, 24, 25. **Open** 1.30-5.30pm Thur-Sun, also by appointment..
Opened originally as a photo gallery for new, young artists in 1992, De Opsteker's tiny gallery is now home to mixed exhibitions of photography, painting and small-scale sculpture. A second exhibition space opened in 1994 in Durgerdam's old village church.
Wheelchair access.

Oude Kerk

Oudekerksplein (625 8284). Tram 4, 9, 14, 16, 24, 25. **Open** 1-5pm Mon-Fri; 11-5pm Sat; 1-5pm Sun.
Admission *f*5 adults; *f*3,50 concessions; free under-12s.
Amsterdam's oldest church, situated in the heart of the Red Light District is one of the most beautiful – and bizarre – exhibition spaces. Since the spaces are openly available for rent, the shows vary enormously in quality.
Wheelchair access.

Ra

Vijzelstraat 80 (626 5100). Tram 4, 9, 14, 16, 24, 25. **Open** noon-6pm Tue-Fri; 11am-5pm Sat. **Credit** AmEx, MC, V.
Although Ra isn't the only place for jewellery, it's the one everyone will send you to. There's a thin line between sculpture and jewellery these days, as a look around this gallery will show – you may prefer putting these works on your mantelpiece to wearing them.

Reflex Modern Art Gallery

Weteringschans 79A (627 2832). Tram 6, 7, 10. **Open** 10.30am-5.30pm Tue-Sat; *Weteringschans 83.* **Open** 10.30am-5.30pm Thur-Sun. Credit AmEx, DC, MC, V.
As well as a new exhibition changing each month, featuring top international artists such as Arman, Ben and Kriki, the gallery always has an excellent selection of graphics and lithos by Corneille and Appel.
Branch: Spiegelgracht 8 (639 1917).
Wheelchair access at all branches.

Scheltema Holkema Vermeulen

Koningsplein 20 (523 1411). Tram 1, 2, 5, 11. **Open** 1-6pm Mon; 9.30am-6pm Tue-Fri; 9.30am-9pm Thur; 10am-5pm Sat.. **Credit** AmEx, MC, V.
Although actually a bookshop, Scheltema regularly shows excellent photography along its staircase, with travel photos and more experimental photography all finding a place.

Carrying a torch for modern art: **Torch Gallery**. *Page 162.*

Galerie Foundation for Indian Artists

Fokke Simonszstraat 10 (623 1547). Tram 16, 24, 25. **Open** 1-6pm Tue-Sat.

Devoted to the promotion of contemporary Indian art in the Netherlands, Galerie Foundation for Indian Artists' exhibitions are of reliably high quality and incredible diversity. Successful international artists such as Dilip Sur, Bhupen Khakhar and Jaya Ganguly are regular exhibitors as are many artists as yet unknown in the West.
Wheelchair access.

Stedelijk Museum Bureau Amsterdam

Rozenstraat 59 (422 0471). Tram 12, 14. **Open** 11am-5pm Tue-Sun.

Opened in October 1993, the Stedelijk's latest venture promotes young Amsterdam-based artists. It holds eight solo and group exhibitions a year in the main gallery area, a regular series of lectures to accompany the shows and a changing selection of artists' videos.
Wheelchair access.

Steendrukkerij

Lauriergracht 80 (624 1491). Tram 13, 14, 17. **Open** 1-5.30pm Wed-Sat; 1-5pm 1st Sun of month. (Closed July and August).

Steen is stone, *drukker* is printer, and the *drukkerij* is the place where printers print. The gallery, not surprisingly, shows lithos, woodcuts, and experimental prints. It has a straightforward approach.
Wheelchair access.

Steltman

Spuistraat 330 (622 8683). Tram 13, 14, 17. **Open** 11am-6pm Tue-Sat. **Credit** AmEx, DC, MC, V.

A light, airy gallery with shows which range from the wonderfully playful three-dimensional glass and ceramic designs of Borek Sipek to the photo realism of Peter Handel's female nudes.
Wheelchair access to ground level only.

Swart

Van Breestraat 23 (676 4736). Tram 2, 3, 5, 12, 16, 24, 25. **Open** 3-6pm Wed-Sat.

Riekje Swart is the undisputed *grande dame* and godmother of the Amsterdam art scene. She began in 1964 with constructivism and didn't show women because they weren't aggressive enough for her (she does show them now, occasionally). She is critical, opinionated and is looking for young people because 'no one buys expensive artists here'. Artists love her and galleries admire her.
Wheelchair access.

Taller Amsterdam

Keizersgracht 607 (624 6734). Tram 16, 24, 25. **Open** 1-5pm Tue-Sat.

An artists' collective, still producing inspirational work some 30 years after its creation, with founders and lynchpins, Armando Bergallo and Hector Vilche still very much involved. Situated in a beautifully converted former coach-house, the gallery space is large and accommodating.
Wheelchair access.

Torch

Lauriergracht 94 (626 0284). Tram 7, 10. **Open** 2-6pm
Thur-Sat. **Credit** AmEx, DC, MC, V.
One of the classier and more prestigious galleries, court-
ing impressive international names such as Cindy
Sherman. Group exhibitions are owner Adriaan van der
Have's speciality, with particular emphasis on current
developments in the art world and fabulous themed shows,
such as 1994's Elvis extravaganza. Reliable and highly rec-
ommended.
Wheelchair access.

2 1/2 x 4 1/2

Prinsengracht 356 (626 0757). Tram 13, 14, 17. **Open**
1-5pm Tues-Sat.
The sole survivor of a number of (exclusively) photo galleries, including the Canon Image Center which, sadly, was
transformed into a shoe shop in 1994. Its survival has something to do with the invariably high quality of its work; the
solo shows can be excellent.

Vromans

*Gebouw Atrium, Strawinskylaan 3101 (642 7295). Bus 48,
51, 63.* **Open** 9am-5pm Mon-Fri, 12-3pm Sat and 1st Sun
of month.
Situated a little way out of the centre and housed in a fine
example of modern office architecture, Vromans is an unusual gallery. Devoted almost entirely to sculpture, with the
main exhibition space at the base of a huge glass atrium
tower, the work shown is variable but the setting always a
pleasure to walk around. Worth the tram ride.
Wheelchair access.

De Witte Voet

Kerkstraat 149 (625 8412). Tram 1, 2, 5, 11. **Open**
noon-5pm Wed-Sat.
Though some still think the term ceramics means pots rather
than scuplture, this is *the* ceramics gallery, mounting solo
shows of predominantly Dutch artists. The work on display
varies from the traditional to the outlandish and the market
is still said to be growing.

W139

*Warmoesstraat 139 (622 9434). Tram 4, 9, 14, 16, 24,
25.* **Open** noon-6pm Wed-Sun.
A gigantic, airy gallery (by Amsterdam standards), which
invariably produces excellent shows. With close links to the
art schools and a positively welcoming attitude to all young
innovators, W139 is at the leading edge of avant-garde art
in the city.
Wheelchair access.

XY

Tweede Laurierdwarsstraat 42 (625 0282). Tram 10.
Open noon-5pm Tue-Fri; 12.30-4pm Sat. **Credit** AmEx,
MC, DC, V.
One of the most exciting of the small Jordaan galleries, reg-
ularly producing excellent shows and the innovator of the
Supermart – the first supermarket devoted entirely to afford-
able fine art. Manager Oscar van der Voorn switches happi-
ly between local artists and international stars.

Artists' Books

Boekie Woekie

Berenstraat 16 (639 0507). Tram 1, 2, 5, 11, 13, 14, 17.
Open noon-6pm Tue-Fri; noon-5pm Sat.
Boekie Woekie exhibits and sells graphics and books by
artists. Graphics is a broader term in Dutch than in English
– it includes all forms of printmaking – so if Dutch artists
say they make graphics (as a huge number will) don't
assume they're layout people at an advertising firm.

Events

Art Fairs

Amsterdam's annual art fair is called the **KunstRai**
(the Rai is Amsterdam's congress centre) and it
takes place at the end of May or early June. So much
art in one place at one time can be overwhelming,
but everything is there – at least as far as the
'accepted' gallery circuit is concerned. You may buy
art at the KunstRai or simply go to admire it. *See
also chapter* **Amsterdam by Season**.

Open Ateliers

Neighbourhoods with large artist populations
and artists' studio complexes hold open days,
often in the spring or autumn. Recent open days
have been held at Prinseneiland, in the Jordaan
and at WG Terrein. Dozens of studios are open to
the public for a weekend or more; most present a
group show.

Artoteeks

In Amsterdam you can borrow works of art as
you would books from a library – for a week,
a month or a year. The *artoteek* (a play on the
Dutch word *bibliotheek* – meaning library) and
the *kunstuitleen* (*kunst* means 'art', *uitleen*
means 'lend out') works on the same principle
as a library. The main difference between the
two is that the *kunstuitleen* is subsidised,
rather than run by the city. At both, borrow-
ers can take a work of art home on loan, with
the option to buy. Because of the astounding
over-supply of artists and the cautious market, *artoteeks* and *kunstuitleens* carry huge
numbers of artists. They provide a good cross-
section of art, within the restrictions of size,
and durability to withstand frequent transport. All have exhibition spaces for solo shows
and have hundreds of works in stock. As for
kunstuitleens, only the **SBK** has maintained a
semi-independent structure and high standards. It contains 10,000 works, by 900 artists
and also represents foreign artists.

SBK Kunstuitleen
(Fine Arts Foundation)

*Nieuwe Herengracht 23(623 9215). Tram 1, 2, 5,
11.* **Open** 1-8pm Tue and Thur; 1-7pm Fri; 9am-
5pm Sat; 1-5pm 1st Sun of month. **Hire cost**
between *f*8-*f*40 per month.
When borrowing for the first time, three months' hire
fee must be paid in advance plus *f*10 to sign in. Of each
hire fee paid, 60 per cent is 'banked' by the SBK
(Stichting Beeldende Kunst) and this money may later
be used towards the purchase of a painting.

Museums

**Sex, drugs, torture, tattoos and a whole heap of Van Goghs –
Amsterdam's exhibits are far from conventional.**

The Netherlands has a daunting 830 museums. In Amsterdam alone the collections are incredibly diverse. Thematically, one can be found to fit the purpose of just about anybody's visit, whether that be an intake of Dutch culture, art and history, or a dose of sex, drugs and alcohol. Rock 'n' roll is as yet uncatered for, unless you count the **Tattoo Museum** – the artwork of whose instigator, Henk Schiffmacher, can be seen sported on the skins of such luminaries as Cypress Hill and The Red Hot Chili Peppers.

Virtually all the museums are within walking distance of one another. If you plan your route in advance, there will be ample time to combine another great national pastime, hanging out and drinking coffee – many museums have wonderful cafés or restaurants, apart from those you'll find in nearby streets. A more leisurely alternative, and a great way to view the city, is to relax into a seat on the **Museumboot**.

Holland has produced some of the best-known and most prolific artists in the world. Many of the finest works of Rembrandt, Vermeer and Frans Hals are part of the national heritage and are housed in the **Rijksmuseum** (*see page* 164); while the life and works of Van Gogh are documented in the **Van Gogh Museum** (*under* **Art**). Apart from Amsterdam's **Rembrandthuis**, (*under* **Art**), there are two art museums further afield which particularly worth visiting: the **Frans Hals Museum** in Haarlem, housing some fine work by Hals and his contemporaries; and the **Boymans-Van Beuningen** in Rotterdam, which displays canvasses by Van Eyck, Rembrandt, Bosch and others (*both under* **Further Afield**).

As the Rijksmuseum, the Van Gogh and the **Stedelijk** are all about a minute's walk from each other, many people tend to make a beeline for them, overdose on the first day and miss out on the numerous other extremely rewarding collections. Both the **Technologie Museum** (*under* **Technology**) and the **Tropenmuseum** (*under* **Ethnography**) are highly informative and excellent fun. Even the most reluctant museum-goer will enjoy some hands-on scientific experiments or a chance to try the instruments you saw the Peruvians busking with at Leidseplein.

Several museums offer a detailed account of the Netherlands' history, the largest and most general being the **Amsterdams Historisch Museum**.

All aboard the **Museumboot**.

Others deal more specifically with the experience of Netherlanders during the Nazi occupation. One of these, the **Anne Frankhuis**, is a major tourist attraction and the queues are often dauntingly long. If your time is limited then choose the **Vertzetsmuseum** (Museum of the Resistance) which provides a fascinating, comprehensive documentation of the occupation (*see* **Historical**).

A few of Amsterdam's museums have recently undergone expansion, refurbishment or re-housing and some new ones have opened. The south wing of the Rijksmuseum was re-opened in 1996, restored to its former glory with original features uncovered. The generous *f*37,5 million donation of one Japanese society has enabled the Van Gogh Museum also to start work on a new wing. Designed by Japanese architect Kisho Kurokawa, who created the Hiroshima City Museum of Contemporary Art, the new wing is due for completion in 1998. The

The Rijksmuseum

If you've been to Amsterdam's Centraal Station, you might think you are seeing double when you glimpse the Rijksmuseum. Both of these splendid neo-Renaissance buildings were designed by PJH Cuypers. Opened in 1885, the museum is backed by a small quaint garden with sculptures, a pleasant end to what could be an exhausting visit. The museum gets over one million visitors every year – almost twice as many as its closest rivals, the Van Gogh Museum and the Stedelijk, which have around 600,000 and 500,000 per year respectively. The collection has expanded considerably since the eighteenth century, when William V first started acquiring pieces for his private amusement.

As this is the largest museum in the Netherlands, a map or guide book is useful. The shop stocks a comprehensive book called *Treasures of the Rijksmuseum* for ƒ35 and foldout floor plans to help you along your way. There is a fabulous selection of paintings from the fifteenth century until around 1850 as well as decorative and oriental arts. Quarterly exhibitions are held in the print room and during the winter months there are other special exhibitions.

If you only have limited time, head for the Dutch Masters on the first floor. Here is Rembrandt's *Night Watch*, recently cleaned and now accompanied by an exhibition showing this process and offering a discussion as to why this painting was so innovative. Here also are *The Kitchen Maid* and *The Young Woman Reading a Letter* by Johannes Vermeer, each capturing a moment in the lives of two women from totally different backgrounds.

Pieter de Hooch was another painter of seventeenth-century domestic life, while Jan Steen focused on the lower classes for his moralistic genre scenes. Together with the landscapes of Jacob van Ruisdael and Paulus Potter, the winter landscapes of Hendrik Avercamp and Jan van de Capelle and the maritime scenes of Willem van de Velde, this section offers an excellent insight into life in the Netherlands during the Golden Age.

Other attractions include superb examples of Delftware, porcelain, pottery, silverware and oriental art. The Gallery Room is devoted to seventeenth- and early eighteenth-century dolls' houses which are furnished and decorated in the materials which would originally have been used in the life-sized equivalents.

Although part of the Rijksmuseum building, the South Wing has its own entrance. The admission fee covers the entire museum and it is possible to access the main building internally, but complicated – better to go out and come back in again through the other entrance. Re-opened in 1996, after a three-year renovation programme, the South Wing now provides a home for eighteenth- and nineteenth-century paintings, the Asiatic art objects – 53 statues, 80 statuettes, 341 artefacts (lacquer work, ceramics, jewellery, weaponry, bronze and jade) and 30 paintings – and the Textile and Costume collection.

Rijksmuseum

Stadhouderskade 42 (06 88981212). Tram 2, 5, 6, 7, 10/bus 63, 170. **Open** 10am-5pm daily; 1-5pm Sun, public holidays. **Admission** ƒ12,50; ƒ5 under-18s, CJP card holders; ƒ7,50 over-65s; free with Museum Card; group discounts (min 20 persons).
Café. Educational department. Films and slide shows. Guided tours by prior arrangement. Wheelchair access with assistance.

Rijksmuseum South Wing

Hobbemastraat 19 (573 2911/Dutch recorded information 573 2737). Tram 2, 3, 5, 11, 16. **Open** 10.00-17.00. daily, (closed Jan 1). **Admission** ƒ12,50; ƒ5 6-18s, CJP card holders; ƒ7,50 over-65s; free with Museum Card; group discounts (min 20 persons).
Shop and garden. Wheelchair access and toilets for the disabled.

---

most major new development will hopefully be completed early in 1997 when the existing Technologie Museum NINT (*under* **Technology**) is scheduled to be relocated near Centraal Station as a world-class science centre. Just outside Amsterdam, in Amstelveen, the **CoBrA Museum of Modern Art** (*see box*), opened in 1995, displays some of the finest works by CoBrA group members. 1996 saw the opening of the world's only Tattoo Institute, part of which is the **Tattoo Museum** (*under* **Miscellaneous**) detailing many aspects of this art form. Lastly, the familiar and striking façade of the

Torture Museum (*under* **Miscellaneous**) left the Leidsestraat to reappear in a less brutal manner on the Rokin.

We list below a few of the major art collections but for more museums outside Amsterdam *see below* **Further Afield** *and chapters* **Excursions in Holland**, **The Randstad** *and* **The Provinces**. A guide brought out by the Museum Card foundation containing listings (in Dutch) of some 830 museums can be bought from various bookshops. The VVV tourist offices (*see chapter* **Essential Information**) are also helpful.

MUSEUM BOAT

The Museumboot is remarkably good value, even for tourists on a tight budget. Tickets entitle holders to get on and off at any of seven stops serving 16 of the capital's 40-odd museums located on or near one of the concentric canals or by the River IJ near Centraal Station. Bearing in mind that the larger museums such as the Rijksmuseum and the Stedelijk demand at least half a day each, the Museumboot would be better used to take in more of the smaller ones which are not so easily accessible via public transport. Tickets also give up to 50 per cent discount on admission prices; *see below* **Tickets & Discounts**.

Museumboot

Office and main boarding point: Stationsplein 8 (625 6464/622 2181). Tram 1, 2, 4, 5, 9, 11, 13, 14, 16, 17, 24, 25. **Departs** every 30 mins (summer), 45 mins (winter), 10am-5pm daily. **Stops** at seven points: Prinsengracht (Anne Frankhuis, Theatermuseum); Singel (Museumplein, Rijksmuseum, Van Gogh Museum, Stedelijk Museum); Herengracht/Leidsegracht (Bijbels, Amsterdams Historisch, Allard Pierson); Amstel/Zwanenburgwal (Rembrandthuis, Joods Historisch, Hortus Botanicus, Tropenmuseum); Oosterdok/Kattenburgergracht (Scheepvaart Museum,

Werf 't Kromhout); Centraal Station (Madame
Tussauds, Museum Amstelkring). **Day tickets** ƒ22;
ƒ18 under-13s; ƒ16 Museum Card-holders. Tickets can
also be bought from the office opposite Rijksmuseum.

TICKETS & DISCOUNTS

Most museums are reasonably priced, between
around ƒ5 and ƒ10. If you're thinking of taking in
more than a few – in Amsterdam or elsewhere in
the country – the **Annual Museum Card**
(Museumjaarkaart) is a good buy. Costing ƒ45
(ƒ32,50 for under-18s and pensioners), the ticket
offers free or reduced admission to almost 400
museums throughout the Netherlands. Special
exhibitions are normally not covered by the ticket,
but you may be entitled to a reduction. The card
can be purchased at one of the participating museums (check the listings below) or at the VVV tourist
offices. Reductions can often also be obtained with
a valid student identity card, or a CJP under-26
card, available at the AUB Uitburo (*see chapter*
Essential Information).

Top of the list for good value is the national
museum weekend (held around the second week
of April each year) – two days on which some 350
museums throughout the country are open free of
charge (*see chapter* **Amsterdam by Season**).
But it's only really worthwhile if you're on a shoe-
string budget, since you'll have to vie with all the
locals taking advantage of this popular freebie.

This doesn't mean that the Dutch steer clear of
museums the rest of the year, but they are choosy.
Temporary exhibitions at the major museums are
often popular at weekends. It's also wise to avoid
Wednesday afternoons if you're going to a museum that may be popular with children, as most primary schools have that afternoon off. Many
museums are closed on Monday with the notable
exception of the Museum Van Loon (*under* **Golden
Age**), which is only open on Sunday and Monday.

Museums do not always have captions and
explanations in English, but many sell reasonably
priced English guidebooks. Enquire when you buy
your ticket. Several museums also offer guided
tours in English for groups; always phone to
enquire or to make a booking.

Many museums are closed on public holidays
(*see chapter* **Essential Information**). Always
phone to check.

Tropical treats at the **Tropenmuseum**.

storey house (built 1606) where he lived for almost 20 years.
The museum has an intimate atmosphere enhanced by the
low-level lighting, used to preserve the etchings. Visitors can
trace Rembrandt's development as an etcher and the fasci-
nation which biblical stories and human emotions held for
him. The only paintings here are by Rembrandt's teacher,
Pieter Lastman, and those painters who worked under
Rembrandt in his studio. Don't miss Rembrandt's amusing
drawings in the basement, depicting the men's and women's
toilets, and the miniature self-portraits on the first floor.
There are also temporary exhibitions on the top floor.
Guided tours and etching demonstrations by arrangement.

Stedelijk Museum of Modern Art

*Paulus Potterstraat 13 (Dutch recorded information 573
2737). Tram 2, 3, 5, 12, 16.* **Open** 11am-5pm daily;
11am-4pm public holidays; *April-Oct* 11 am-7pm Mon-
Sun **Admission** ƒ8; ƒ4 under-17s, CJP card holders; free
with Museum Card, under-7s. **Credit** (shop only) AmEx,
EC, MC, V.
The best collection of modern art in Amsterdam exhibited
in spacious, well-lit rooms. Alongside the permanent displays, the regularly changing temporary exhibitions, drawn
from the collection, tend to focus on particular trends or specific artists and the works. After occupying various locations
around the city, the Stedelijk finally settled in its present neo-
Renaissance abode, designed by A W Weissmann in 1895. In
time, the building became too small for the ambitions of its
directors and an ugly new wing was tacked on in 1954.
Highlights include paintings by Monet, Cézanne, Picasso,
Matisse, Kirchner and Chagall. The museum also has a
prized collection of paintings and drawings by the Russian
artist, Kasimir Malevich. The Dutch De Stijl group, of which
Piet Mondriaan is probably the most famous, are also well
represented along with other post-1945 artists including De
Kooning, Newman, Ryman, Judd, Stella, Lichtenstein,

Art

Rembrandthuis

*Jodenbreestraat 4-6 (638 4668). Tram 9, 14/Metro
Nieuwmarkt.* **Open** 10am-5pm Mon-Sat; 1-5pm Sun,
public holidays. **Admission** ƒ7,50; ƒ6 over-65s; ƒ5 10-
15s, CJP card holders; free with Museum Card, under-9s;
group discount (min 15 persons) ƒ5, ƒ3,50 10-15s.
Rembrandt may not have signed everything he painted, nor
is everything that bears his signature painted by his hand,
but the controversial Dutch master must have had his hands
full just working on the legacy of etchings that he left behind.
About 250 of these are on display at the charming three-

Warhol, Nauman, Middleton, Long, Dibbets, Van Elk, Kiefer, Polke, Merz and Lounellis. Interior design buffs will enjoy the extensive collection of furniture by Gerrit Rietveld. The Nieuwe Vleugel Stedelijk Museum (New Wing) is used as a temporary exhibition space, often focusing on design and applied art. The Appelbar and restaurant are both decorated with the designs of CoBrA artist, Karel Appel. The restaurant has a terrace overlooking the sculpture garden, and is a lovely place to sit on a sunny day.

Café and restaurant. Guided tours f65 (book at least two weeks ahead). Occasional lectures with special exhibitions (f7-f10). Library (open to library card-holders only, phone for details), closed July and August. Art History courses, f75 for 8 sessions, advance booking essential. Shop. Wheelchair access and toilets for the disabled.

Van Gogh Museum

Paulus Potterstraat 7 (570 5200). Tram 2, 3, 5, 12, 16. **Open** 10am-5pm daily. **Admission** f12,50; f5 under-18s; f7,50 over- 65s; free with Museum Card; group discount (min 20 persons).

The exterior may be bland but the collection is remarkably colourful and cleanly displayed. Apart from the bright colours of his palette, Van Gogh is also known for his productivity, and both are clearly reflected in the 200 paintings and 500 drawings that form part of the permanent collection. An exceptionally good selection of works by Van Gogh's contemporaries, such as Toulouse-Lautrec and Gauguin, is also on view. A selection of Van Gogh's Japanese prints are on display on the second floor, while his artistic development is further illustrated by changing exhibitions created from the museum's archives and private collections.

Library. Restaurant. Shop. Wheelchair access and toilets for the disabled.

Archaeology

Allard Pierson Museum

Oude Turfmarkt 127 (525 2556). Tram 4, 9, 14, 16, 24, 25. **Open** 10am-5pm Tue-Fri; 1-5pm Sat, Sun, public holidays. **Admission** f6; f4,50 over-65s, CJP card-holders, students; f3 12-15s; free with Museum Card, under-12s.

Established in 1934, the Allard Pierson Museum claims to now hold the world's richest university collection of archeological exhibits – gathered from Egypt, Greece, Rome and other ancient civilisations. Although these are highly interesting, the building has a disappointingly subdued atmosphere and many statues, sculptures, clay tablets and ceramics are unimaginatively presented. There is a more creative, if limited, selection of scale maquettes (of the pyramids, Olympia and so on), as well as a full-scale model of a Greek chariot and sarcophagi, but often the accompanying English text is minimal and not very enlightening. The temporary exhibitions held on the first floor usually draw larger crowds and also have a separate entrance fee, usually around f5.

Guided tours at f35 must be booked three days in advance. Wheelchair access with assistance.

Botanical

Bosmuseum

Koenenkade 56, Amsterdamse Bos (643 1414). Bus 70 (Sunday afternoons, between Easter and November only). **Open** 10am-5pm daily. **Admission** free.

Recounts the history and use of the Amsterdamse Bos, the extensive forest built in the 1930s to provide Amsterdammers with work and a place to spend their days off. Its mock woodland grotto, which turns from day to night at the flick of a switch, is wonderful for children, but it's not really worth making a special trip for the museum alone.

Guided tours in the forest (call for information). Shop. Restaurant. Wheelchair access.

Hortus Botanicus (University of Amsterdam)

Plantage Middenlaan 2A (625 8411). Tram 7, 9, 14. **Open** *Apr-Sept* 9am-5pm Mon-Fri; 11am-5pm Sat, Sun; *Oct-Mar* 9am-4pm. **Admission** f7,50; f4,50 5-14s; free under-5s.

You don't have to be the green-fingered kind to enjoy these beautiful gardens, established in 1682, when ships from the East India Company brought back tropical plants and seeds, originally intended to supply doctors with medical herbs and shrubs. A new greenhouse has recently been constructed, with three differing but extraordinarily hot climates. The terrace is one of the nicest in Amsterdam, with only the distant sounds of the city to remind you of where you are. There is one shop selling small plants, seeds and bulbs and another specialising in environmental books. *See also chapter* **Sightseeing**.

Café. Wheelchair access.

Hortus Botanicus (Vrije Universiteit)

Van der Boechorststraat 8 (444 9390). Tram 5/bus 51, 76, 170, 171, 162. **Open** 8am-4.30pm Mon-Fri. **Admission** free.

The horrors of city planning: this small garden is wedged between the high buildings of a university and a hospital. It was built in 1967, so doesn't have the charm of its counterpart in the city centre (*above*), but it's pleasant for a stroll if you're in the neighbourhood – the city limits near Amstelveen. The fern collection is one of the largest in the world, while the Dutch garden shows the great variety of flora originally found in this country.

Cinema

Nederlands Filmmuseum (NFM)

Vondelpark 3 (589 1400/library 612 3021). Tram 1, 2, 3, 5, 6, 11, 12. **Open** *box office* 10am-9.30pm Mon-Fri; 1-9.30pm Sat, Sun; *library* (no loans) 10am-5pm Tue-Fri; 11am-5pm Sat; *film screenings* 8.30pm or 7.pm and 9.30pm daily; 1pm and 3pm matinée Sun. **Tickets** *cinema* f10; f8 CJP card holders, over-65s, groups (min 10 persons); f5 members. **Membership** f30.

A great three-in-one visit for the real film buff, the NFM is a cinema, a museum, and has an extensive library devoted to film immediately next door. Housed in a grand former nineteenth-century tea room on the edge of the Vondelpark, the NFM, like some other Amsterdam cinemas, is a museum in itself. Although actual exhibitions are only sporadically held here, (it's always advisable to check directly with the NFM about these) the two-screen cinema is furnished with original period artefacts acquired from an old broken-down cinema. The museum vaults hold some 35,000 national and international films which are screened in thematic blocks. In late 1992 the museum hit world headlines with the discovery of some unique, early Disney footage. The library (Vondelstraat 69-71) houses the country's largest collection of film books and mags, scripts, photos, archives, videos and biographies – it's a perfect place for film students to study. All film screenings are announced in the newspapers (Wednesday afternoon or Thursday morning) and in their own brochure (*see also chapter* **Film**). The NFM occasionally holds temporary exhibitions.

Assistance for wheelchairs available, preferably with prior arrangement

Ethnography

Tropenmuseum (Tropical Museum)

Linnaeusstraat 2 (568 8215). Tram 9, 10, 14. **Open** 10am-5pm Mon-Fri; noon-5pm Sat, Sun, public holidays. Kindermuseum (children's museum) has different opening hours (*see chapter* **Children & Parents**).

Admission ƒ10; ƒ5 6-18s, CJP card-holders, students, over-65s; free with Museum Card, under-5s.

The Tropenmuseum, hugely enjoyable for both adults and children, takes an honest look at daily life and problems in the tropical and sub-tropical regions of the Third World. Ironically the vast three-storey building was originally designed and erected in the 1920s to glorify the colonial activities of the Dutch. Now it is host to a stimulating, imaginatively presented and colourful collection of articles, including costumes, musical instruments, puppets and domestic utensils. Visitors are encouraged to experience the exhibitions by smelling samples of tree barks, herbs and spices as well as walk-through lifesize reproductions of bazaars (including an African compound and an Indian village) accompanied by tapes of street sounds and music. Excellent temporary exhibitions are creatively mounted in the large hall on the ground floor. The shop has a good selection of souvenirs and books from or dealing with Third World countries. Attached to the main Tropenmuseum is the Tropenmuseum Junior, for children aged between six and 12 (*see chapter* **Children & Parents**).

Café. Guided tours ƒ60 per hour (max 25). Wheelchair access and lifts.

Seek out **Our Lord in the Attic**.

Golden Age

Museum Amstelkring: Ons' Lieve Heer op Solder (Our Lord in the Attic)

Oudezijds Voorburgwal 40 (624 6604). Tram 4, 9, 14, 16, 24, 25. **Open** 10am-5pm Mon-Sat; 1-5pm Sun. **Admission** ƒ7,50; ƒ5 under-19s, over -65s and CJP; free with Museum Card,under 5s. Groups (min 10 persons) ƒ5.

One of the most surprising of the smaller museums in Amsterdam, the Amstelkring is undeservedly neglected by most visitors. In the heart of the Red-Light District, this building houses the only remaining attic church in Amsterdam (built 1663). It was saved from demolition in the late nineteenth century by a group of historians who called themselves the Amstelkring (Amstel Circle). The lower floors of the house include furnished living rooms that could have served as the setting for one of the seventeenth-century Dutch masters. Upstairs, the chaplain's room has a small cupboard bed. The pilgrimage upwards leads visitor to the highlight of the museum: the beautifully preserved attic church, the altarpiece of which features a painting by eighteenth-century artist, Jacob de Wit. The church is sometimes used for services and a variety of other meetings.

Guided tours by prior arrangement.

Museum Willet-Holthuysen

Herengracht 605 (523 1870). Tram 4, 9. **Open** 10am-5pm Mon-Fri; 11am-5pm Sat, Sun. **Admission** ƒ5; ƒ2,50 under-16s.

Originally built in 1689, the interior of this pleasant patrician's mansion is more reminiscent of a French château than a Dutch canal house. Both Louis XV and neo-Louis XVI styles are very much visible. The latter was mainly introduced by the Willet-Holthuysens, the family who acquired the house in 1860 and gave it its name. Their passion for over-embellishment is also apparent in their legacy of rare *objets d'art*, glassware, silver, fine china and paintings. There are no English texts to accompany the exhibits, but there is an English-language video that explains the history of the house and the canal system. A view from the veranda into the eighteenth-century garden almost takes you back in time, but the illusion is sadly disturbed by the adjoining modern buildings.

Guided tours for groups by prior appointment.

Museum Van Loon

Keizersgracht 672 (624 5255). Tram 16, 24, 25. **Open** 11am-5pm Mon; 1-5pm Sun. **Admission** ƒ7,50; ƒ5 over-65s and groups (min 10, max 40 persons); free under-12s.

Behind the classical façade of this canal house lies a classically furnished interior, showing how wonderful it was to be a wealthy resident of Amsterdam in the seventeenth century. Designed by Adriaan Dortsman, the same architect who designed the New Lutheran Church on Singel (*see chapter* **Sightseeing**), the patrician's house was the home of Ferdinand Bol, one of Rembrandt's former pupils. Apart from the Louis XV décor, the museum has an unusually large collection of family portraits from the seventeenth and eighteenth centuries, added after the purchase of the house in 1884 by Hendrik van Loon. The eighteenth-century garden, laid out in the French style, contains a coach house from the same period (now a private home).

Guided tours (min 10 persons) by prior arrangement.

Historical

Amsterdams Historisch Museum

Kalverstraat 92 (523 1822). Tram 1, 2, 4, 5, 9, 14, 16, 24, 25. **Open** 10am-5pm Mon-Fri; 11am-5pm Sat, Sun. **Admission** ƒ8; ƒ4 under-17s, groups of min 15 persons; free with Museum Card.

The courtyard of the Amsterdam Historical Museum is a welcome oasis of peace in the Kalverstraat, Amsterdam's main shopping thoroughfare. The main entrance is hard to find: look for a tiny alley and a lop-sided arch bearing the three crosses of the city's coat of arms. The museum is in a former convent and orphanage dating from the sixteenth century. The development of the city from the thirteenth century to the present day is illustrated through various *objets d'art*, archeological finds and interactive displays. The best view of the Civic Guard Gallery – a covered street gallery with several massive group portraits commissioned by wealthy burghers in the sixteenth and seventeenth centuries – is from the second floor of the museum. Another attraction is the adjacent Begijnhof (*see chapter* **Sightseeing**). The Amsterdams Historisch Museum is also the starting point for Mee in Mokum tours (*see chapter* **By Area: the Jordaan**). Tours leave at 11am (Tue-Thur, Sun), last around two hours, and cost only ƒ4 (which includes a series of money-saving coupons entitling you, among other things, to a 50 per cent reduction on admission to the Amsterdams Historisch Museum). You need to phone up at least one day in advance to guarantee an English-speaking guide (for reservations call 625 1390, 1-4pm Mon-Fri). If you're the sort of person who hates stuffy, long-winded tours then this is the trip for you.

Library open 1-5pm Mon-Fri. Restaurant; many parts not accessible with wheelchair.

Anne Frankhuis

Prinsengracht 263 (556 7100). Tram 13, 14, 17. **Open**
Sept-May 9am-5pm Mon-Sat; 10am-5pm Sun, public
holidays; *June-Aug* 9am-7pm Mon-Sat; 10am-7pm Sun,
public holidays. **Admission** ƒ8; ƒ4,50 10-17s, over-65s,
CJP card-holders; free under-10s; group discounts (min 10
persons).
The Anne Frankhuis is one of the city's most visited sights,
attracting about half a million people every year. Having
already fled from persecution in Germany in 1933, Anne
Frank, her sister Margot, her parents and four other Jews
went into hiding on 5 July 1942. Living in an annex behind
Prinsengracht 263, they were sustained by friends who
risked everything to help them. A bookcase marks the
entrance to the sober, unfurnished rooms which sheltered
the eight inhabitants for two long years. Eventually, on 4
August 1944, the occupants of the annex were arrested and
transported to concentration camps, where Anne died along
with Margot and their mother. Her father, Otto Frank, survived and decided that Anne's moving and perceptive diary
should be published. The archive here contains a photo
album of Mr Dussel, one of the Jews in hiding with Anne,
which was found in 1978 at Waterlooplein Flea Market.
There's also an exhibition on the Jews, and their persecution
in the war, and a display of different editions of the diary.
Exhibitions chart current developments in racism, neo-
Fascism and anti-semitism; there are explanatory texts in
English. The museum is managed by the Anne Frank
Foundation, which aims to combat prejudice, discrimination
and oppression. A statue of Anne Frank by Mari Andriessen
(1977) stands at the corner where Westermarkt and
Prinsengracht meet.
*Bookshop. Documentation department (Keizersgracht
192, tel 556 7100). Educational department. Guided
tours by prior arrangement. Videos.*

Verzetsmuseum Amsterdam

Lekstraat 63 (644 9797). Tram 4, 25. **Open** 10am-5pm
Tue-Fri; 1-5pm Sat, Sun, public holidays. **Admission** ƒ5;
ƒ2,50 under-15s, CJP card-holders, over -65s; free with
Museum Card,under-8s.

This collection is housed in a former synagogue in the
Rivierenbuurt, the part of town where Anne Frank lived
between escaping the Nazi Germans in 1933 and hiding in the
attic on Prinsengracht. The permanent collection holds artefacts, documents and interactive displays explaining matters
such as sabotage, espionage and the February Strike. You can
hear radio broadcasts, look around a mock-up of a hiding place
and see a bicycle-powered machine used to print illegal papers.
Much of today's Dutch press started underground, namely:
Het Parool (The Password), *Vrij Nederland* (Free Netherlands)
and *Trouw* (Loyalty) (*see chapter* **Media**). Early editions of
these are on display. Exhibitions on the first floor highlight
contemporary developments such as extreme right-wing
Dutch political parties. Only basic information is supplied in
English. Built in the southern part of the city, the museum is
surrounded by early twentieth-century architecture typical
of the Amsterdam School. There are other Resistance
Museums in Leeuwarden in Friesland (*see chapter* **The
Provinces**) and Gouda (*see chapter* **The Randstad**).
*Guided tours (min 8, max 15 persons; ƒ2,50 per person,
by prior arrangement). Library.*

Hollandsche Schouwburg

Plantage Middenlaan 24 (626 9945) Tram 7, 9, 14.
Open 11am-4pm daily. **Admission** free.
A small but very impressive exhibition about the tragic historical role of this theatre building. During World War II it
functioned as a collection point for Jews that were to be sent to
camps. Strangely the façade of the Schouwburg has been left
intact while most of the main structure was removed to serve
as a memorial monument. A guide in English is available.

Maritime

Nederlands Scheepvaart Museum

Kattenburgerplein 1 (523 2222). Bus 22, 28. **Open**
10am-5pm Tue-Fri; noon-5pm Sun; *14 June-13 Sept* also
10am-5pm Mon. **Admission** ƒ12,50; ƒ8 6-12s; free with
Museum Card, under-6s; ƒ27,50 family ticket. Group
discounts.

The beautiful **Museum van Loon**, *home of Rembrandt's pupil Ferdinand Bol. Page 168.*

Get up early to join the daily scrum outside the **Anne Frank Huis**. *Page 169.*

It takes some time to see the whole collection based in this monumental building, dating from 1656. Originally used as a warehouse for the upkeep of the city's fleet of ships, it stands in what was the sea arsenal of the United Provinces, in the heart of Amsterdam's nautical district. The history and techniques of navigation and overseas trade from its very simple beginnings are shown with the use of wooden models, old paintings, drawings and ship parts. The many explanations about naval combat, for instance, are informative, clear and interesting, even for people without any real knowledge of nautical matters. The best part of this polished exhibition is the full-size replica of the seventeenth-century East India Company ship, harboured right behind the museum. You can mingle with over-acting 'sailors' on the decks and in the holds, and they'll happily tell anything you want to know about the ship. One of the largest museums of its kind in the world.
Restaurant. Shop. Wheelchair access.

Museumwerf Werf 't Kromhout

Hoogte Kadijk 149 (627 6777). Bus 22, 28. **Open** 10am-4pm Mon-Fri. **Admission** ƒ2,50; ƒ1,50 under-15s, ƒ1,75 over-65s.
This nostalgic museum is full of old, silent ship engines and tools. The shipyard is obviously very proud of the fact that it's one of the few remaining original yards still in use, but its eighteenth-century heritage is no longer very apparent, nor is the yard as active as it once was.
Bar. Guided tours by arrangement.

Religion

Bijbels Museum

Herengracht 366 (624 7949). Tram 1, 2, 5, 11. **Open** 10am-5pm Mon-Sat; 1-5pm Sun. **Admission** ƒ5; ƒ2,50 under-16s; ƒ3,50 CJP card-holders, over-65s; free with Museum Card. ƒ4 groups (min 10 persons).
Many tourists visit the Biblical Museum for the two adjoining patricians' houses that accommodate it. Built in 1660-62 by the renowned Dutch architect Philip Vingboons, the houses feature stunning early eighteenth-century ceiling paintings by Jacob de Wit. The emphasis of the permanent exhibition is on life in biblical times. It is illustrated by archeological finds from Egypt and the Middle East, a reconstruction of a Palestinian house, models of Solomon's temple and various audio-visual displays. There is also a fine collection of Bibles. The exhibition does have a religious atmosphere, which may bother or bore non-believers. Some explanations are in English and there is an English guidebook for borrowing.

Joods Historisch Museum

Jonas Daniel Meijerplein 2-4 (626 9945). Tram 9, 14. **Open** 11am-5pm daily; closed Yom Kippur (mid-end Sept). **Admission** ƒ7; ƒ3,50 10-16s, over 65s, ISIC card holders; free under-10s, Museum Card holders; group discounts (50 per cent, min 10 persons). ƒ9 combined with a visit to Bijbels Museum.

The museum was housed in De Waag (*see chapter* **Sightseeing**), near the Red-Light District until 1987, when it was moved to this former high German synagogue which appropriately stands in the heart of the former Jewish quarter of Amsterdam, only a short walk from both Waterlooplein market and the Muziektheater (*see chapter* **Music: Classical & Opera**). The permanent exhibition is full of interesting articles from past and present, illustrating many aspects of Judaism in the Netherlands and concentrating on personal history, religion and the influence of Dutch culture on Jewish culture. Worth going just to see the series of lively autobiographical paintings by Berlin-born Jew, Charlotte Salomon, who was killed at Auschwitz at the age of 26. The museum organises walks around the neighbourhood and visits to the nearby Portuguese Synagogue. The shop and kosher café can be found in the narrow Shulgass, which links up with the synagogue.
Guided tours by prior arrangement (min 25 persons).

Technology

Technologie Museum
Tolstraat 129 (570 8111). Tram 3, 4. **Open** 10am-5pm Mon-Fri; noon-4pm Sat-Sun. **Admission** *f*8; *f*5,50 6-12s; free under-6s.
You're not meant to keep your hands in your pockets here – most exhibits are big on interaction. You can build a dam and change the water flow or see the inside of a steering mechanism move to your directions. On the upper floor, the exhibition becomes digital. Computers, scanners, CD-I and other products of modern technology are still at your command but explanations of how they function are more limited. The museum is due to relocate to a spot near the entrance of the IJ tunnel (*see above* **Introduction**), adjacent to the

Scheepvaart Museum in Amsterdam's harbour, at some time in 1997. Amsterdammers have great expectations of this new museum, designed by Renzo Piano who was responsible for the Pompidou Centre, which will then be known as IMPULS. Bear in mind that this project is already one year behind schedule and that even the name of the street on which it will stand was still undecided at the time this was published. Also that the entrance fee is due to rise to *f*17,50 for adults. *Restaurant. Shop.*

Theatre

Theatermuseum
Herengracht 168 (623 5104). Tram 13, 14, 17. **Open** 11am-5pm Tue-Fri. **Admission** *f*5; *f*3 students, CJP card-holders, over-65s; free with Museum Card.
The Theatermuseum was undergoing extensive renovations at time of writing, and is scheduled to re-open in summer 1997. Possessing the first neck gable in Amsterdam, the Theatermuseum (built in 1638 by Philip Vingboons) is an architectural gem and provides an opportunity to step behind one of Amsterdam's many beautiful façades. Inside, the eighteenth-century plasterwork, the ceiling paintings by Jacob de Wit and the spiral staircases are simply magnificent and alone make this museum worth a visit. Both permanent and temporary exhibitions relate the story of Dutch theatre, both front and backstage. As well as viewing the costumes, prints and set drawings, the visitors are invited to operate the working maquettes of set designs and create wind and rain with the special machines on display. Tea and cakes in the lovely old garden behind the house is a treat in summer. The museum also boasts an extensive library.
Café. Guided tours by prior arrangement (f 4, min 15). Library.

Lair of the CoBrA

In 1948, a group of like-minded artists combined the initial letters of the cities in which they worked – Copenhagen, Brussels and Amsterdam – to come up with CoBrA. For three years this striking label described the efforts and collaborations of such now individually famed artists as Asger Jorn, Karel Appel, Eugene Brands, Doutrement, Constant, Corneille and Lucebert. While their Surrealist forebears had embraced Freud, CoBrA artists were more inspired by those who seemed directly wired into Jung's collective unconscious: primitives, children and the mentally deranged. Vaguely humanoid monsters, both happy and scary, became the CoBrA trademark. The goal was to express immediate sensual urges and the key was spontaneity. Ragged excess drips of paint (with poetry often scrawled in) was a common technique; the action always transcended the product. CoBrA's brand of revolutionary thought did not call for art for the masses, but rather art by the masses.

And so, with all due irony, the CoBrA Museum of Modern Art recently opened in the posh peo-

ple's suburb of Amstelveen. The original CoBrA exhibits and publications tended to cause outrage rather than cultural pride. But time and hindsight have had their effect. From inspiring the Provo happenings of the 1960s (*see chapter* **Post-War**) to explaining the escalating market prices of 'Outsider Art' in the 1990s, CoBrA has proved to be the most relevant art movement in Holland this century. If museum funding had been available back in those heady post-war days, perhaps crayons would have been freely distributed on every street corner. But since this money arrived almost 50 years after the fact, a colourful representative collection is now permanently housed in Amstelveen and all the various strands of CoBrA are finally given their due.

CoBrA Museum of Modern Art
Sandbergplein 1, Amstelveen (547 5038). Tram 5/Bus 51. **Open** 11am-5pm Tue-Sun. **Admission** *f*5; *f*2,50 under 16s; *f*3,50 CJP card-holders, over-65s; group discount (min 15 persons).
Cafe (open 10am-5.30pm). Shop. Wheelchair access and toilets for the disabled.

Transport

Aviodome
Schiphol Centre (604 1521). Train to Schiphol airport.
Open *Apr-Sept* 10am-5pm Mon-Sun; *Oct-Mar* 10am-5pm Tue-Fri; noon-5pm Sat, Sun. **Admission** *f*8,50; *f*7,50 over -65s; *f*6 4-12s; free under-4s.

Aeroplane enthusiasts will loop-the-loop over the dislays in this exhibition. Follow the signs from Schiphol train station to the Aviodome, where over 30 historic aircraft are neatly parked or suspended from the dome ceiling. The exhibition starts with the first motorised plane: the Wright Flyer from 1903, and the Spider, designed by the Dutch pioneer Anthony Fokker. You don't always have to stay behind the lines: kids enjoy playing Biggles and clambering into a cockpit, while adults may prefer the more realistic flight-simulator demonstrations (on prior request). Also popular is the Space Department, which contains the American Mercury capsules. The aluminium dome shows films and has a larger collection of models, photos and aeroplane parts. The Aviodome also organises markets and fairs as well as occasional theme weekends, focusing on subjects such as restoration (check with the VVV, local press or at the museum). However, if you see an aeroplane as just another means of transport, the informative but somewhat perfunctory Aviodome is unlikely to raise your interest levels.
Bar. Group discounts (max 20). Guided tours f35 (max 25 persons). Shop. Wheelchair access.

Tram Museum Amsterdam
Amstelveenseweg 264 (673 7538). Tram 6, 16. **Open** *Apr-July, Oct* 10am-5.30pm Sun; *July-Sept* 10am-5.30pm Tue-Sun. Trams depart every 20 mins. **Admission** *f*5; *f*2,50 4-11s, over-65s, CJP card holders; free under-4s.

When open, the Electric Tram Museum is almost always on the move. Some of the antique trolleys, collected from cities throughout Europe, are still in use. Kids in particular love going for a 30-minute ride in one of the museum's colourful conveyances through the nearby – and surprisingly rural – Amsterdamse Bos (*see chapters* **Sightseeing** and **Children & Parents**).
Café at Haarlemmermeer station.

Schipholscoop
South Terminal, Schiphol Airport (601 2000). **Open** 10am-6pm Mon-Fri; 10am-5pm Sat, Sun.

The new visitors' centre at Schiphol Airport opened in June 1994 and appears to be a PR success. The Schipholscoop has interactive exhibitions which provide information about Schiphol's economic and environmental significance, as well as details on noise pollution and job opportunities. There are already plans to expand it further.

University History

Universiteitsmuseum De Agnietenkapel
Oudezijds Voorburgwal 231 (525 3341). Tram 4, 9, 14, 16, 24, 25. **Open** 9am-5pm Mon-Fri; only open weekends on National Museum Weekend (*see above* **Tickets and Discounts**) and every second weekend in October for National Day of Science. **Admission** free; special exhibitions *f*2,50.

The Agnietenkapel, built in 1473 and part of the University since its foundation in 1632, is one of the few Gothic chapels to have escaped the demolisher's hammer. It has a sober, Calvinistic beauty, with lovely stained glass windows and old wooden beams and benches. The chapel is more stimulating than the collection, which focuses on the history of education, research and student life at the University of Amsterdam. One of the most interesting exhibits is the Grote Gehoorzaal (Large Auditorium), where respected seventeenth-century academics Vossius and Barlaeus gave their first lectures. It has a beautiful wooden ceiling, decorated with soberly painted, ornamental Renaissance motifs such as angels, masks, flowers and a portrait of Minerva, the Roman goddess of Science and Arts. The Auditorium is now used for symposia, the presentation of certificates and occasional lectures.

Zoological

Artis Zoologisch Museum
Plantage Kerklaan 40 (623 1836). Tram 7, 9, 14. **Open** 9am-5pm; buildings close at 4.30pm. **Admission** *f*20; *f*13 under-12s. Group discount *f*2,50 per person, min 20 persons.

This zoo, planetarium and zoological museum make a great outing for children. Apart from the usual range of animals there is a special section for nocturnal creatures and a fascinating aquarium. The 150-year old Artis Zoo contains a small but interesting museum featuring thematic exhibitions and a collection of stuffed animals. The narration in the planetarium is in Dutch but a short English translation is available. The feeding ground for humans is ideally situated between the pond with flamingoes and a popular children's playground. *See also chapters* **Children & Parents** *and* **Sightseeing**.
Café. Restaurant. Shop. Guided tours by prior arrangement. Wheelchair access.

Miscellaneous

Erotic Museum
Oudezijds Achterburgwal 54 (624 7303). Tram 4, 9, 14, 16, 24, 25. **Open** 11am-1am daily. **Admission** *f*5.

The Erotic Museum is little more than five floors of complete tack. You are initially welcomed by a lifesize model of a man with an unfeasibly large tongue in a dirty old raincoat and a female mannequin on a bicycle, being lifted on and off a dildo attached to the seat as she pedals. This pretty much sets the tone for the rest of the exhibits. The exact use of the large selection of sexual toys, tool, photos and artworks on display are left to the imagination as there is little in the way of explanation for the less enlightened. One floor is devoted to all things SM and includes some of the original photos taken of the queen of SM, Betty Page. Still, it's only *f*5 and is worth the admission fee just to see a series of original erotic sketches by John Lennon done during their Bed In in Amsterdam in 1969 depicting him and Yoko in various erotic positions.

Hash Mariihuana Hemp Museum
Oudezijds Achterburgwal 148 (623 5961). Tram 4, 9, 14, 16, 24, 25/Metro Nieuwmarkt. **Open** 11am-10pm daily. **Admission** *f*6.

Where else but Amsterdam would you expect to find the world's only permanent cannabis information museum? It gives you a whirlwind cultural tour of cannabis in history, as well as a growing marijuana garden, and a selection of clothes, carpet and paper made with the hemp plant. The process of making hashish is described and the uses of marijuana as medicine explained along with details of different smuggling, rolling and smoking methods. A visit to the museum makes for an interesting half-hour, although when it gets too worthy and educational, it's a little dull. Next door is a 'head shop', which sells all the accoutrements for home growing. Recently a number of shops have opened in the city selling various hemp products, from clothes to cat litter: *see chapter* **Shopping**. You see old examples of hemp products here, including a Bible. *Wheelchair access with assistance.*

Sex Museum
Damrak 18 (627 7431). Tram 4, 9, 14, 16, 24, 25. **Open** 10am-11.30pm daily. **Admission** *f*3,95.

Museum is a rather pretentious title for this unsurprisingly popular and highly commercial enterprise: a lot of sex toys

Stone me! It's the **Hash Marihuana Hemp Museum**. *Page 173.*

and erotica in the form of photos, etchings and videos. It doesn't really offer much more than you would learn from a look inside the shops and prostitutes' windows in the Red-Light District. The dated photos displaying unusual sexual antics and a handful of etchings are the only things you may not have seen before, although the tacky pictures showing women involved in sexual acts with eels, donkeys and dogs always seem to be popular. And the depiction of a tart and her pimp using 1970s mannequins is quite the most un-PC thing you've ever seen. Save your money for an ice-cream to eat as you wander down Oudezijds Achterburgwal instead.

Tattoo Museum

Oudezijds Achterburgwal 130 (625 1565). Tram 4, 9, 6, 20, 24, 25. **Open** noon-5pm Tue-Sun. **Admission** *f5.* Groups by appointment.

Henk Sciffmacher, the force behind the world's only official tattoo institute, is a renowned figure in the tattoo world. Not only has he run the famous tattoo parlour Hanky Panky (*see chapter* **Services**), in the heart of the Red-Light District, for some 16 years, he is also responsible for organising the annual Tattoo Convention, as well as appearing on numerous TV programmes about the art form. Housed in a former liquor factory, the tattoo institute (open since May 1996) is a non-profit making venture. It includes a museum, a public library, an archive and an information centre. The exhibition detailing the history of tattoos includes hundreds of ancient and ethnographical tools, thousands of drawings, photos and prints and even some preserved pieces of tattooed skin. Internationally renowned tattoo artists also make guest appearances. *Guided tours by prior arrangement.*

Torture Museum

Damrak 20-22 (639 2027). **Open** 10am-11pm daily. **Admission** *f7,50; f4 under 13s; f5,50 students.*

A must for the macabre-minded, the Torture Museum has around 60 instruments of agony to wince at. Despite the exhibition elevating through a three-storey building, the rooms, connected by a confusing arrangement of doors, are definitely dungeonesque. The atmosphere is enhanced by lighting which endows everything with a sinister deep-brown tinge. The gruesome antiques, gathered from all over Europe, are each accompanied by a historical poster showing how it was used. Items include the guillotine and the chair of nails from the Spanish Inquisition as well as painful punishments for homosexuality, blasphemy and witchcraft. Expect to spend most of your time here cringing, crossing your legs and holding various bits of your body as you imagine these instruments of torture being put into practice.

Further Afield

Catherijneconvent

Nieuwegracht 63, Utrecht (030 231 7296). Bus 2, 22 from Utrecht Central Station. **Open** 10am-5pm Tue-Fri; 11am-5pm Sat, Sun,public hols. **Admission** *f7; f3,50 under-18s;* CJP card-holders; free with Museum Card; *f5* over-65s, groups (max 20 persons); free under-6s.

In this fifteenth-century convent the history of Dutch Christian culture is illustrated. The exhibition contains the biggest collection of medieval paintings, sculpture, gold and silver, textiles and manuscripts in the Netherlands. The *bogenkelder* (vaulted cellar) with its many old Bibles with silver cast covers and the beautiful stained glass windows in the adjoining church should not be missed. An English guidebook is available. *Café. Shop. Wheelchair access.*

Boymans-Van Beuningen, Rotterdam

Museumpark18-20 (010 441 9400). Tram 5/Metro from Rotterdam Central Station. **Open** 10am-5pm Tue-Sat; 11am-5pm Sun, public holidays. **Admission** *f7,50; f4* children under 16, CJP card-holders, Museum Card-holders; free under-4s; group discount (min 15 persons).

This large museum has exceptionally high-quality canvasses displaying gems by Van Eyck, Rembrandt, Bosch and other masters. A lot of the best French and surrealist art is here too, along with modernist paintings and sculpture, industrial design and major exhibitions. *Guided tours by prior arrangement. Wheelchair access.*

Frans Hals Museum Haarlem

Groot Heiligland 62, Haarlem (023 516 4200). Bus 1, 2, 3, 4, 5, 71, 72 from Haarlem Central Station. **Open** 11am-5pm Mon-Sat; 1-5pm Sun. **Admission** *f*6,50; *f*3,50 10-17s; *f*3 under-11s, CJP card-holders; free with Museum Card, under-10s. *f*4,75 Groups (min 20 persons).

Some of Hals' finest canvasses are here, plus paintings by his illustrious contemporaries. There are reconstructed rooms illustrating the building's original use as the Oudemannenhuis (an almshouse for elderly men). Hals is famous for his group portraits of civic and almshouse regents; two of the eight displayed here depict the regents of the Oudemannenhuis itself. There is also a modern and contemporary art collection, including outstanding examples of artists from Haarlem and surrounding areas. Most explanations are in English. *Café. Guided tours in English (Sept-May), 1.30pm Sun. Shop. Wheelchair access.*

De Lakenhal, Leiden

Oude Singel 28-32 (071 516 5360). **Open** 10am-7pm Tue-Fri; noon-7pm Sat, Sun and public holidays. **Admission** *f*5; *f*2,50 6-18s, CJP card-holders; free with Museum Card, under-6s.

An awe-inspiring collection combining local history with decorative arts and paintings of just the right proportions. Don't overlook the extraordinary *Last Judgement* by Lucas van Leyden, the landscapes of Jan van Goyen and the wonderful genre scenes of Jan Steen.

Guided tours (f1,50 for groups of 20). Library (10am-12.30pm Tue, Thur, Fri; 2-5pm Wed).

Mauritshaus, The Hague

Korte Vijverberg 8 (070 346 9244). **Admission** *f*10; *f*5 over-65s, under-18s, CJP card-holders; groups (max 20 persons) *f*8 per adult; *f*4 under-18s and over-65s; free with Museum Card.

This is one of the country's finest Golden Age houses (recently restored) and holds magnificent masterpieces by Rubens, Van Dyke, and the Flemish School. There are also rooms devoted to Rembrandt, Jan Steen, Holbein and Vermeer. It is a museum of ideal proportions; not too large to tire you out and not too small to begrudge the admission charge.

University and Specialist Collections

Amsterdam has a variety of small, specialised collections, dealing with subjects ranging from the life and times of famous Dutch authors (whose names you might come across on street street signs) to embryological specimens. Museum is too grand a word for some of the smaller collections, which are only really interesting for connoisseurs. The collections listed below can only be visited by appointment and are free unless otherwise stated.

Anatomy

Museum Vrolik

Entrance on south side of AMC medical faculty, Meibergdreef 15 (566 9111). Bus 59, 60, 61, 120, 126/Metro Holendrecht. **Open** 2-5pm Tue, Wed. Closed between Christmas and New Year. **Admission** *f*1 each group tours (min 12); visiting at other times with prior arrangement.

The museum (an anatomical embryological laboratory) contains eighteenth and nineteenth-century specimens of human embryos, human anatomy and congenital malformations collected by Professor Gerardus Vrolik and his son, Professor Willem Vrolik.

Gas & Electricity

Bedrijfsmuseum ENW Amsterdam

Spaklerweg 20 (597 3107). Bus 46, 169/Metro Spaklerweg. Open by appointment only, call between 8am and 4pm. Industrial artefacts relating to gas and electricity production and distribution.

Literary

Bilderdijkmuseum

De Boelelaan 1105 (645 4368). Bus 8, 23, 26, 48, 49, 64, 65, 67, 158, 173, 197. **Open** by appointment made at the Oude Drukken room on first floor of the Vrij University.

The life and times of the Dutch writer/academic Willem Bilderdijk (1756-1831) is illustrated by displays of his manuscripts, etchings and personal belongings.

Multatuli Museum

Korsjespoortsteeg 20 (638 1938/624 7427). Tram 1, 2, 5, 11, 13, 17. **Open** 10am-5pm Tue; noon-5pm Sat, Sun; other days by appointment only.

The life of the nineteenth-century writer, Eduard Douwes-Dekker (who wrote under the pseudonym Multatuli) is illustrated by photos and other objects. There's also a library.

Railway

Werkspoormuseum

Oostenburgergracht 77 (625 1035). Bus 22, 28. Open by appointment only, call between 9am-5pm Mon-Fri. Paintings, prints, models and other objects illustrate the history of the Dutch railroad.

Religious

Historisch Documentatiecentrum van de Vrije Universiteit

De Boelelaan 1105 (548 4648). Bus 8, 23, 26, 49, 64, 65, 67, 68, 158, 173, 197. **Open** 9am-5pm Mon-Fri.

The history of the Dutch Protestant University and its founder Abraham Kuyper is explained with the help of documents, photos, and artefacts.

Social History

Ferdinand Domela Nieuwenhuis Museum

Herengracht 266 (673 2820). Tram 13, 14, 17. **Open** 10am-4pm Wed, public holidays closed. By appointment only.

Documents focusing on the life of Ferdinand Domela Nieuwenhuis (1846-1919, *see chapter* **Between the Occupations**) and the labour movement.

Instituut voor Sociale Geschiedenis

Cruquiusweg 31 (668 5866). Tram 6, 10/bus 22. **Open** 9.30am-5pm Mon-Fri, 9.30am-1pm Sat.

An international library specialising in the social history of the world, run by the Institute for Social History. The library contains original writings by Karl Marx and Friedrich Engels.

Vakbonds Museum

Henri Polaklaan 9 (624 1166). Tram 7, 9, 14. **Open** 11am-5pm Tue-Fri; 1-5pm Sat, Sun.

A recently opened trade union museum, home to a permanent exhibition showing aspects of the Labour Union in Dutch history. The building was designed by Berlage to house the offices of the Netherland's first trade union (*see also chapter* **Between the Occupations**).

Arts & Entertainment

Media

The text might be Dutch, but Amsterdam's print media has a reputation for fine typography and design, while the 'Rotterdam of the Internet' has more cool web sites than you can shake a modem at.

Ever since the Golden Age Amsterdam has been an important media centre, its liberal tolerance ensuring a large printing and publishing community. Today, global publishing giants such as Elseviers and VNU are based here, and European editions of *Time* and *The Economist* are printed in the suburbs. But the fundamental thing about the local media is of course that it's in Dutch – and let's face it, you don't speak it and are unlikely to learn in the forseeable future.

The good news for media addicts is that you don't need to be able to pronounce *scheepvaart-maatschappij* to enjoy a local fix. The language might be user-unfriendly, but the Dutch flair for the visual remains as strong as ever. Amsterdam has an international reputation for graphic design and typography, while a small but creative local multimedia and online industry is emerging. The city has been fully cabled for years now, and the state-owned phone company is one of Europe's more progressive and efficient. Together with an international outlook and historically strong distribution skills, these factors ensure Amsterdammers a rich and varied media diet.

Print

The Dutch newspaper business is as much the product of historical religious as political divisions, but as with elsewhere in the world, concentration of media ownership has tended to bland out the differences. *De Telegraaf*, once a collaborationist and still a right-wing daily, is Holland's largest-selling paper and the nearest the country has to a *Sun*-style tabloid, despite the pretension of broadsheet size. *Het Parool* (*The Password*) was the largest underground wartime journal and has spent the last few years sloughing off its socialist past to reposition itself as a cosy Amsterdam evening local. Its sister morning paper, *De Volkskrant* (*People's Paper*), was established as a Catholic organ. Censored during the war, it later turned leftwards and enjoys a relatively young, progressive readership. *Trouw* (*Faith*), the other Amsterdam-published mainstream national daily, began life as a Protestant paper, also went underground during the war, and is today owned by the same company as *Het Parool* and *De Volkskrant*.

Perhaps the most well-regarded national daily, the *NRC Handelsblad*, is published in Rotterdam, albeit with significant Amsterdam input. For some strange socio-religious reason, Sunday papers have never taken off here.

Moving on to news you can actually use, the stunningly dull *Financiele Dagblad* has a daily half-page business summary in English and on Saturdays the *International Herald Tribune* has a weekly English pullout, *The Netherlander* (ƒ5). *What's On In Amsterdam* (ƒ3,50) is a turgid fortnightly guide to the city available in and published by the VVV tourist office. Free, and with the same dates and gigs listed, is the Dutch *Uitkrant*, available from AUB city council ticket offices. Also free, distributed in shops, bars and coffee shops, is *To The Point*, a fold-out brochure of current events.

A wide selection of native periodicals are available, from earnest political weeklies (*De Groene Amsterdammer*, *Vrij Nederland*) through tawdry sensation-mongers (*Panorama*, *Nieuwe Revue*), to Dutch versions of *Cosmo* and *Elle*. As with the daily newspapers, there is a formidable language barrier – although the latter can be worth a glance, along with their male equivalent, *Man*, if only to see the fashion, interior decor and lifestyle to which young Amsterdammers are encouraged to aspire.

But wherever the Dutch press is available, there will generally also be a wide selection of foreign magazines (though not always newspapers). Particularly good selections can be found at Athaeneum and WH Smith. The American Discount Book Center round the corner from Smith's has everything from *Whole Earth Review* to obscure rap 'zines, plus four floors of US and British books. For all three places *see chapter* **Shopping**. Also try Centraal Station, or assorted branches of Bruna and AKO.

There are a number of Dutch magazines which merit a look for their excellent design, styling and photography alone. Post-*Wired* start-ups *Blvd.* and *Wave* (see its website, *http://www.riv.net/heatwave*), which aim a cool mix of music, media, technology and fashion at Dutch Generation X-ers, are well worth a flick through on the plane home, as are *Dutch* (culture, fashion and design, also at *http://www.dag.nl/dutch*), *ArtView* (visual culture from advertising to design and fine art) and *Hype*,

The International Herald Tribune's Saturday editon has a special pullout on Amsterdam.

(quarterly showcase of fashion, photography and cartoons, with minimal English text). The quarterly *View On Colour*, though outrageously expensive, is a useful tool for anyone working professionally with colour. Amsterdam's sporadically published, hard-to-find, but internationally influential journal *Mediamatic* (*see also below* **New Media**) is a classy critique of new media and the wired revolution in Dutch and English. Recent issues came with free award-winning CD-ROMs, and it's worth hunting down while you're here. Occasional good 'zines come and go – *Tofu 666* was a cool one at time of press. Fort van Sjakoo (Jodenbreestraat 24, 625 8979, above ultra-alternative record store Staalplaat, is a good place to find these as well as international anarcho-squatter tracts, while local comix and cartoonists can best be tracked down in the excellent Lambiek or Athaeneum Nieuwscentrum. *See chapter* **Shopping**.

Broadcast

A unique system of airtime allocation and strictly limited commercialisation came to an end in 1992, following a period of airwave attack from neighbouring Luxembourg. Before that, the three state channels (Nederland 1, 2 and 3) had their hours divided among a number of stations (again, originally based on religious as much as political differentiation) according to the numbers of 'members' they have (determined by newsstand and subscription sales of each station's weekly TV and radio guides). Worthy, dull and with hopelessly outmoded continuity and graphics, only the lefty-artsy VPRO managed to produce anything of real merit from within the insular broadcasting enclave of Hilversum, 30 minutes out of town.

This cosy arrangement began to crack when RTL4 started broadcasting commercial TV, in Dutch, from Luxembourg. Reform has produced a number of new stations in recent years: Veronica and SBS6 (glitzy, youth-oriented), TV10 (old repeats like *The Onedin Line* and *The Persuaders!*), and RTL5 (more US series and films). Others (such as Eurosport) have been lost to pay-per-view or subscription. By the time you read this some may have switched back and it's a full time job for channel-hoppers to keep up; the best bet is simply to surf. Uncertainty was increased both by the sale of the publically-owned local cable network (KTA) to a consortium led by Philips and the Postbank in 1995, and the privatisation of the phone system in 1996 in preparation for full EC-mandated telecoms competition. With several interactive TV and pay-per-view systems being given trials in the Netherlands (and we haven't even mentioned the Internet yet), the much-vaunted 'media convergence' cannot be too far away in Amsterdam, although not before even greater turbulence for consumers as rival systems slug it out.

Cable radio relies on a collection of national stations, MOR pop, jazz and classical channels, the world services of Britain, America and Holland, and a couple of local channels.

New Media

Holland is the third busiest European country for Internet activity after Germany and the UK, and Amsterdam's role in cyberspace perhaps looms even larger than its geographical position. Dubbed the 'Rotterdam of the Internet', the city is a major connection and distribution node for European transatlantic phone traffic. In the 1980s, a skilled, even infamous, group of hackers and phone phreakers grew up here by taking advantage of the fact. Hacktic's international get-togethers – The Galactic Hackers Conference in 1989 and its follow-up in a field outside town in 1994, have become legendary 'flesh meets' for the digital underground.

As the legal net around such activities tightened, Hacktic established XS4ALL (access for all, geddit?), a low-cost Internet access point for the masses. Hacktic's members mostly went legit, working in multimedia and computer security or building impressive Web sites, and a golden age of electronic pranks (they once hacked the Amsterdam cable system to flash porno during the opening ceremony of the Olympics) has been replaced by the more responsible 'digital rights watchdog' role they now share with other Net access providers.

Initially set up as a pilot project funded by the City Council and built by programmers from Hacktic, Amsterdam's Digitale Stad (Digital City,

http://www.dds.nl) has been a great success as a new electronic suburb (*see chapter* **Amsterdam Today**). Based on the US Freenets, it offers access to city councillors, information about the city in Dutch and English, electronic art and chat rooms, and hundreds of citizens' home pages. Other Dutch and European cities have since copied the idea, creating a network of virtual cities.

There are a number of public terminals (such as in the Balie and Waterlooplein post office) where the Digital City can be accessed. To check your e-mail while in town, there are a few cybercafés springing up. The first, **Freeworld**, is a coffee shop on Korte Nieuwendijkstraat 30, open 10am-1am. They charge *f*2,50 per 20 mins (e-mail: *visitor1/2@cafe.euronet.nl*). Also, **Coffeeshop Internet** at Prinsengracht 480 (638 4108). **Mystere 2000**, Lijnbaansgracht 92 (620 2970/ e-mail: *myster@net.info.nl*), is more of a 'New Edge' centre with regular lectures and workshops, and also Net access points, open Tue-Fri 11am-5pm and Thur 5-9pm.

While you're surfing, there are other Amsterdam Web pages worth checking out. VPRO (*http://www.vpro.nl*) is an innovative site maintained by the eponymous TV station. The website of *Mediamatic* (*http://www.mediamatic.nl*; *see also above* **Print**) includes electronic copies of the last three issues, plus transcripts of talks given at the Doors of Perception conferences they co-organised with the Dutch Design Institute (*http:www.design-inst.nl*). Home Page of the Netherlands (*http://www.eeb.ele.tue.nl/netherlands.html*) provides links to all other sites in Holland. The Red-Light District came online (so to speak) in 1996, when Casa Rosa introduced a members-only Web site featuring live sex shows, 24-hour films and chat rooms (*http://www.fun.nl*).

A number of clubs have either their own web site or at least run a home page, such as Mazzo (*http://www.xs4all.nl/~mazzo*), Zilch (*http://www.xs4all.nl/~zilch/*), Devils Jam (*http://www.channels.nl/devilsjam.html*) and the Melkweg (*http://www.knoware.nl/melkweg/melkweg.htm*).

The *Time Out* website includes up-to-date listings on events in Amsterdam, as well as New York, Berlin, London, Madrid, Paris, Budapest and Prague (*http://www.timeout.co.uk*).

Before we leave cyberspace, note that in the summer of 1996, following trials in Arnhem, Holland is set for the introduction of a nationwide digital cash scheme. Using special microchip-implanted cards, it will be possible to use digidosh for small cash transactions such as feeding parking meters, using vending machines and paying small amounts in certain shops, and then refill your card from a home PC. Amsterdam's DigiCash (*http://www.digicash.com*) has also developed one of the world's most sophisticated network e-cash systems.

Clubs

Where to mellow out, go gabber or rock the house. Plus, the DJs who'll delight and the places to avoid like the plague.

Amsterdam has a stable club scene in which house music predominates. Hip hop, funk, soul or acid jazz can be found here and there, but only on certain nights in music venues or clubs that otherwise play still more house.

House is split between mellow club house and gabber or hardcore house. The gabber scene revolves around huge, more or less monthly events for up to 10,000 speed-crazed punters. This can be something to behold: a cavernous industrial space with laser beams and strobes going wild while video screens flash natural disasters and other macabre footage. Pogoing furiously on the main dance floor are thousands of teenaged boys sporting gaudy shell suits and shaven heads. As 200bpm techno shudders through the hall, they jump up and down, wiggling and kicking their feet at top speed as they do their trademark chicken dance. Though still decidedly male-dominated, there are increasing numbers of gabber girls – similar to their male counterparts, except with heads shaved only at the back and sides.

The mellow parties are more frequent and smaller, with attendances ranging from 200 to 2000 people. Expect to pay between ƒ30-ƒ50 for a mellow party and ƒ60 upwards for a gabber rave. Parties finish around 6am but flyers for after-hours events will be given out during the night. The best advice on which parties and DJs to listen to will come from the local ticket outlets listed below.

Although Amsterdam is a small city, the enthusiasm generated by a local crowd never fails to impress. People are free spirited and the liberal attitude towards soft drugs and sex often surprises visitors. Everyone knows there are coffeeshops, but often polite tourists ask if they may smoke joints in clubs. The answer is yes. Tales of ubiquitous ecstasy taking are, however, somewhat exaggerated. Once it was more prominent in the whole scene, but these days ecstasy is only found at the very largest events.

The illegal party scene in Amsterdam has all but died, although a couple of good venues do still exist. Look out for flyers for parties at squatted venues like the Silo or the Vrieshuis Amerika. All parties now require a licence from the council/police and most must operate from a venue that already has an alcohol licence.

In clubs the average entry price is pretty cheap, but if you want to leave and return to the club on

Tip this bouncer ƒ5 – or else!

another day, you are expected to tip the doormen (around ƒ5). If you don't, they won't let you in again next time.

It's also obligatory to pay for the toilets (50 cents) in most clubs and parties. The drinks aren't usually overpriced and even if the beers are small, they are stronger than in most countries. Opening hours are 10pm to 4am with an extra hour from Thursday to Saturday. Dressing up can be a good idea if you're planning to visit the iT or RoXY, but for most other clubs there is no strict dress code.

Club RoXY Singel 465 1012 WP Amsterdam Holland t +31(0)20 620 0354 f +31(0)20 6269454

The Clubs

Amnesia

Oudezijds Voorburgwal 3 (638 1461). Tram 4, 9, 14, 16, 24, 25. **Open** 11pm-4am Thur, Sun; 11pm-5am Fri, Sat. **Admission** ƒ7,50-ƒ15.

Amnesia is a small club on the ground floor of a youth hostel/hotel in the heart of the Red-Light District. It attracts mainly a young crowd and tourists. Most nights are based around hardcore gabber, which makes this a good place to catch Amsterdam's hardest DJs when there are no big raves on in town.

April's Exit

Reguliersdwarsstraat 42 (625 8788). Tram 1, 2, 4, 5, 9, 11, 14, 16, 24, 25. **Open** 11pm-4am Mon-Thur, Sun; 11pm-5am Fri, Sat. **Admission** free.

This is a male gay club (although women are admitted) that attracts a trendy crowd. The dancefloor is reached through a comfortable bar. Spectacular lights and a good mix of current upbeat dance music make this small club worth checking out. Very cruisey at the weekends.

Arena

's Gravesandestraat 51 (694 7444). Tram 3, 6, 7, 10. **Open** 12.30pm-5.30am Fri; 11pm-5.30am Sat. **Admission** ƒ5.

Refurbished international youth hostel with regular parties and bands. All kinds of dance music is played, including hip hop and house on Friday and Saturday nights. The venue is also used by private party organisers. The building used to be a convent and the parties are in what used to be the chapel. (*see also chapters* **Music: Rock, Folk & Jazz** *and* **Accommodation**).

Cash

Leidseplein 12 (627 6544). Tram 1, 2, 5, 6, 7, 10, 11. **Open** 10pm-4am Thur-Sun. **Admission** ƒ10.

Well at least they're honest: the name says it all. This is a fairly small, unashamedly commercial disco that plays top-40 music, complete with tacky décor, thick pile carpets and plastic palm trees. Smart attire is essential and you're supposed to be over 21 to get in. Definitely one for the local white stiletto, dance-around-your-handbag crowd.

Cockring

Warmoesstraat 96 (623 9604). Tram 4, 9, 14, 16, 24, 25. **Open** 11pm-4am Sun-Thur; 11pm-5am Fri, Sat. **Admission** free.

Daily, free and very popular men-only disco in the leather area of the Red-Light District. This small strictly gay club attracts a mixed crowd from tourists to trendies in leather. The music is along garage and hi-nrg house lines, and the sound system is excellent. Resident DJ Misja plays very fine trance. *See also chapter* **Gay & Lesbian**.

Dansen bij Jansen

Handboogstraat 11 (620 1779). Tram 1, 2, 5, 11. **Open** 11pm-4am Mon-Thur, Sun; 11pm-5.30am Fri, Sat. **Admission** ƒ3,50-ƒ4.

If you want to meet the town's student population, then this is the place. It gets packed on most term nights, although the music selection is very safe. Officially this is a student-only club and you need a student card to get in. No dress restrictions, though.

Escape

Rembrandtplein 11 (622 3542). Tram 4, 9, 14. **Open** 10pm-4am Mon-Thur, Sun; 10pm-5am Fri, Sat. **Admission** ƒ20.

Until quite recently this was the most commercial tacky club in Amsterdam. Now it has been transformed into the venue for the city's biggest Saturday night club, Chemistry. The Escape is a cavernous venue (capacity upwards of 2,000), but

DJs from A-Z

A run-down of Amsterdam's major mixing maestros and top turntable artistes.

Angelo

Amsterdam's rising star plays mellow but upbeat house. Excellent late-night DJ.

Clyde

One of Amsterdam's best hip hop DJs.

Dano

The number one gabber DJ in Holland.

Dimitri

Amsterdam's number one export DJ. Resident at RoXY on Thursdays, he also plays his trademark mellow, soulful house in Chemistry at the Escape once every six weeks.

100% Isis

The most successful female club house DJ in Holland.

Joost van Bellen

RoXY DJ who plays mainly disco and mellow house.

Marcello

Very mellow DJ who used to play in the iT and now plays parties and at Chemistry.

Paul Jay

One of the first DJs to push the Amsterdam house scene by organising parties and the underground magazine *Wild!*. Plays progressive house.

Per

Found fame playing the beat club parties at the beginning of Amsterdam's house scene. Plays mellow house, good for big crowds. Now host of Timemachine in the Melkweg – once every six weeks.

Remy

Club house DJ who gets the younger crowd moving.

Spacecake

Ambient, Amsterdam-style.

Vandy

Founder and DJ of After Hour Power, an Ibiza-style after-hours club every first Sunday of the month in various venues.

Zen

Amsterdam's best trance DJ.

you still may have to queue to get in. On a good night the DJs are of a high calibre, such as Dimitri or Marcello and some international guests.

Havana

Reguliersdwarsstraat 17 (620 6788). Tram 1, 2, 5, 11. **Open** 11pm-1am Mon-Thur, Sun; 11pm-2am Fri, Sat. **Admission** free.

Early closing, free-entry gay/mixed bar, with a small dance floor upstairs. It's right on the main drag of the trendy gay area and tends to get totally packed at the weekend before other clubs open.

iT

Amstelstraat 24 (625 0111). Tram 4, 9, 14. **Open**
11pm-4am Wed, Thur, Sun; 11pm-5am Fri, Sat.
Admission ƒ10-ƒ15.
Amsterdam's biggest and most famous gay club has suffered an image problem since the death of its flamboyant
owner, Manfred Langer. Now the door policy is much more
open than it used to be, but the iT has retained some of its
glamorous, exhibitionist atmosphere. This is where you can
see Amsterdam's most extravagant transvestites. Busy
Thursdays and Sundays attract a mixed (gay and straight),
trendy crowd, who are among the best-dressed clubbers in
Amsterdam. Saturdays are strictly gay-only and are always
heaving. The music ranges from mellow to garage to pumping, hi-nrg house.

Korsakoff

Lijnbaansgracht 161 (625 7854). Tram 10, 13, 14, 17.
Open 11pm-4am Mon-Thur, Sun; 11pm-5am Fri, Sat.
Admission usually free.
An alternative grunge club where live bands are featured on
Wednesdays. Sounds include hip hop, metal and even main-
stream rock. Small but friendly: the ideal place to get ham-
mered if you want to keep drinking until late.

Marcanti Plaza

Jan van Galenstraat 6-8 (682 3456). Tram 3. **Open**
11pm-4am Mon-Thur, Sun; 11pm-5am Fri, Sat.
Admission ƒ10.
This huge (2,000-capacity) white elephant never really took
off as planned. It was supposed to be a large multi-media
and entertainment centre; instead on Saturdays it is the
venue for a tackily dressed, can't-get-in-anywhere-else
crowd. Give it a miss.

Mazzo

Rozengracht 114 (626 7500). Tram 13, 14, 17. **Open**
10pm-4am Mon-Thur, Sun; 10pm-5am Fri, Sat.
Admission ƒ7,50-ƒ12,50.
One of the most relaxed clubs in town: no dress restrictions
and the door personnel are friendly to foreigners. Busy on
Fridays and Saturdays, with international guests and resident DJs. Eery kind of underground house music is catered
to, from experimental to progressive and trance. A good time
is nearly always guaranteed.

Melkweg

*Lijnbaansgracht 234 (624 8492). Tram 1, 2, 5, 6, 7, 10,
11.* **Membership** ƒ3,50. **Admission** times and prices
vary according to programme.
This big multi-media centre functions mainly as a live venue,
but at weekends after the bands finish, a varied mix of dance
music is played. This is the host for frequent theme nights
that range from hip hop to house. The entrance price is
always low and there are no dress restrictions. The new Max
hall has significantly raised the standard of the Melkweg as
a venue. Look out for Timemachine parties with DJ Per. *See
also chapters* **Music: Rock, Folk & Jazz, Film, Art
Galleries** *and* **Theatre**.

Odeon

Singel 460 (624 9711). Tram 1, 2, 5, 11. **Open** 10pm-
4am Mon-Thur, Sun; 10pm-5am Fri, Sat. **Admission** ƒ5-
ƒ12,50.
Large non-trendy club on three floors, with a mix of all kinds
of commercial dance music. Popular with students, shop-
assistants and office clerks.

Paradiso

*Weteringschans 6-8 (623 7348). Tram 1, 2, 5, 6, 7, 10,
11.* **Membership** ƒ4. **Admission** times and prices vary
according to programme.
No trip to Amsterdam is complete without visiting the
Paradiso. Every Friday night at midnight the VIP Club puts

on DJs and sometimes live acts. The best nights are those
done in association with the young upcoming party organisers. The best venue in Amsterdam to see a live band. *See
also chapter* **Music: Rock, Folk & Jazz**.

Richter (36 Op De Schaal Van)

Reguliersdwarsstraat 36 (626 1573). Tram 1, 2, 5, 11.
Open 11pm-4am Mon-Thur, Sun; 11pm-5am Fri, Sat.
Admission ƒ7,50-ƒ10.
A small club on two floors that caters for an older crowd.
The music varies from soft house and garage to funk and
soul. Unfortunately the crowd can sometimes be a little bit
on the dodgy side, but it's good for a boogie mid-week when
a lot of the other clubs are closed.

RoXY

*Singel 465 (620 0354). Tram 1, 2, 4, 5, 9, 11, 16, 24,
25.* **Open** 11pm-4am Wed, Thur, Sun; 11pm-5am Fri, Sat.
Admission ƒ7,50-ƒ12,50.
An old converted cinema with a large dancefloor and
upstairs balconies. A loud, high-quality sound system just
about combats the acoustic problems created by the high
ceiling. This is the home of the Amsterdam in-crowd so only
ambitious and dedicated clubbers should attempt to get in.
Wednesday is raunchy gay 'hard' night, which attracts a
mainly male fashion-conscious crowd, and a handful of
women. The key night is Thursday which features Dimitri,
the Netherlands' most famous DJ.

Seymour Likely 2

*Nieuwezijds Voorburgwal 161 (420 5062). Tram 1, 2, 5,
11, 17.* **Open** midnight-4am Thur, Sun; midnight-5am
Fri, Sat. **Admission** ƒ5 Thur, Sun; ƒ10 Fri, Sat.
No house music is allowed: just jazz-dance, soul and hip-hop
for an older (25-35), trendy and artistic crowd. Some of the
best non-house DJs can be seen here and the interior is interesting enough to make the entry price worthwhile.

Soul Kitchen

Amstelstraat 32. Tram 4, 9, 14. **Open** 11pm-5am Fri,
Sat. **Admission** ƒ7,50-ƒ12,50.
For lovers of soul music this spacious club plays a truly varied selection of funky music, from 1960s soul through to
1970s disco.

Out of Town

Distances from Amsterdam are so small that many
people regularly make the effort to travel out to these
clubs, depending on DJs and special theme nights.

Stalker

Kromme Elleboogsteeg 20, Haarlem (023 314652).
Open 11pm-3am Thur; 11pm-5.30am Fri, Sat; 10pm-3am
Sun. **Admission** free Thur, Sun; ƒ5 Fri, Sat.
Hidden down a dark alley in this picturesque town is this
small but ambitious club. Lots of guest DJs and acts from
Amsterdam perform here. The club has an excellent sound
system and attracts a lively crowd.

De Waakzaamheid

Hoogstraat 4, Koog a/d Zaan (075 285829). **Open** *café*
7pm-2am daily; *disco* 7pm-5am Fri, Sat. **Admission**
ƒ7,50-ƒ15.
In the middle of a sleepy village just outside Zaandam, this
adventurous venue attracts a mixed crowd from the surrounding towns. Housed in a beautiful old wooden building,
it claims to have staged one of the last concerts by Billie
Holiday in the 1950s. Nowadays you get a surprisingly
upfront dance mix from a variety of local DJs and the occasional guest from the UK. A good range of different beers,
excellent bar food and a separate salsa/jazz room are also
big attractions.

*Have a flaming good time at the **Melkweg**, where dance music follows live acts.*

Tickets and Information

The places to pick up flyers and tickets for the best clubs and parties in Amsterdam:

Clubwear-House

Herengracht 265 (622 8766). Tram 1, 2, 5, 11, 13, 17. **Open** 11.30am-6.30pm Mon-Wed, Fri; 11.30am-8.30pm Thur; 11.30am-6pm Sat.
Large clubwear shop with flyers and tickets for almost all mellow and underground events.

Conscious Dreams

Kerkstraat 117 (626 6907). Tram 1, 2, 5, 11. **Open** 10am-6.30pm Mon-Sat.
Occasional ticket outlet with some flyers. Sells smart drinks and mushrooms.

Dance Tracks

Nieuwe Nieuwstraat 69 (639 0853). Tram 1, 2, 5, 11. **Open** noon-6pm Mon; 10am-6pm Tue; Wed; 10am-9pm Thur; 10am-6pm Fri, Sat; 1pm-6pm Sun.
Record shop with flyers and some tickets for the more hardcore house scene.

Groove Connection

Sint Nicolaastraat 41 (624 7234). Tram 1, 2, 5, 11. **Open** 2pm-6pm Mon, 11am-6pm Tue, Wed; 11am-9pm Thur; 11am-6pm Fri; 11am-5pm Sat; 2pm-6pm Sun.
Record shop with some underground tickets and flyers.

Midtown Records

Nieuwendijk 104 (638 4252). Tram 1, 2, 5, 11, 13, 17, 24, 25. **Open** 10am-6pm Mon-Wed; 10am-9pm Thur; 10am-6pm Fri-Sun.
Record shop with tickets and flyers for the hardcore and gabber scene.

Outland Records

Zeedijk 22 (638 7576). Tram 1, 2, 5, 11, 13, 17, 24, 25. **Open** 10.30am-6pm Mon-Wed, Fri; 10am-9pm Thur; 10am-5pm Sat.* **Credit** AmEx, MC, V.
Very popular record shop with tickets for mellow house events. Flyers only with record purchase.

ZX Fashion

Kerkstraat 113 (620 8567). Tram 1, 2, 5, 11. **Open** noon-6pm Mon-Sat.
Some flyers and occasional tickets. Sells clubwear.

Dance

Mixing home-grown talent with the best the world has to offer, Amsterdam is the centre of Holland's thriving dance scene.

The Netherlands' traditional role as link between countries across the ocean with those at its European back door is clearly reflected in the current dance scene. Dutch choreographers and dancers form a definite minority within the rich selection of dance on offer throughout the year. Foreign work regularly seen in Amsterdam includes that of William Forsythe, Anne Teresa De Keersmaeker, Pina Bausch, Lloyd Newson, Saburo Teshigawara and Trisha Brown. Whether it be a touring company passing through, a guest choreographer or lead dancer invited for a limited engagement, choreographies imported from repertoires abroad, or the core of the larger companies and schools being made up of foreign dancers, the dominant theme in Dutch dance is strikingly non-Dutch.

A contributing factor is flux in the financial structure upon which local dancers and choreographers depend. From top to bottom – government subsidy and policy organs to individual independent practitioners – a new form is being furiously sought with which to greet the new millennium. The tendency seems to be toward bundling resources – space, administrations, pools of dancers and so on. The question remains as to whether this will serve the majority of those involved. Who will be left by the wayside? Most likely young, inexperienced dancers just finishing their studies.

Having said that, the established generation has not fared too well since the implementation of the new Art Plan in the beginning of the 1990s. Only two companies retained their structural subsidies – **Dansgroep Krisztina de Châtel** and **Studio's Onafhankelijk Toneel**. Everyone else has been left to scrabble for the few places available at one of the collective platforms or for one of the handful of available project subsidies.

Veterans to look out for (apart from the top two companies, **Nederlands Dans Theater** and **Het Nationale Ballet**) are Beppie Blankert, Shusaku Takeuchi, Jacqueline Knoops, Lisa Marcus, Bianca van Dillen and Truus Bronkhorst. Emerging names to watch for are Suzy Blok & Chris Steel, Maria Voortman, Paul Selwyn Norton, Marcello Evelin, Harijono Roebana, Feri de Geus, Anouk van Dijk and Ron Bunzl.

Tickets for performances can be reserved and purchased at the specific venues or for a surcharge purchased from the AUB Uitburo or the VVV offices (*see chapter* **Essential Information**). To find out which companies are currently performing in the city pick up the latest edition of *Uitkrant*.

FESTIVALS AND EVENTS

In July each year the Amsterdam Stadsschouwburg (*see chapter* **Theatre**) hosts **Julidans**, a month-long showcase of international dance. The **International Concours for Choreographers** in Groningen is a competition for the new generation of choreographers where prizes are awarded for ensemble choreographies. Information about festivals, competition events, performances, courses and workshops is available from the Theater Instituut Nederland, Herengracht 168 (623 5104). Open 11am-5pm Mon-Sat.

<h2 style="background:black;color:white">Venues</h2>

Here we list venues which are specifically for dance performances; for other venues, *see chapter* **Theatre**. Unless otherwise stated, credit cards are not accepted at the venues listed.

Dans Werkplaats Amsterdam
Arie Biemondstraat 107 (689 1789). Tram 1, 11, 17. **Open** *information and reservations* 10am-5pm Mon-Fri; Ticket prices vary.
The dance studio at Danswerkplaats stages performances once a month, either here or at venues elsewhere in the city or country. Often at the top of the bill are modern dancers who studied at one of the Amsterdam academies.

Muziektheater
Amstel 3 (625 5455). Tram 4, 9, 14, 16, 24, 25/Metro Waterlooplein. **Open** *box office* 10am-6pm or start of performance daily. **Tickets** ƒ35-ƒ110; concessions for CJP card holders. **Credit** AmEx, DC, MC, V. **Backstage tours** every Wed and Sat at 3pm, ƒ8,50.
The new Muziektheater is Amsterdam at its most ambitious. The plush crescent-shaped building opened in 1986, seats 1,596 and is home to both the Nationale Ballet (*see below* **Companies**) and the Nederlands Opera. The big stage is also used by visiting companies such as the Royal Ballet and the Martha Graham Company. The panoramic glass walls of the three-level lobbies give an impressive view of the River Amstel by night.
Wheelchair access and toilets for the disabled.

Soeterijn
Linnaeustraat 2 (568 8500). Tram 9, 10, 14, 22. **Open** *reservations and information* 10am-4pm Mon-Fri; box office one hour before performance. **Tickets** ƒ15-ƒ22,50; concessions for CJP card-holders.
Located in the Tropen Instituut, this theatre holds regular non-western dance programmes, as well as musical, theatrical and children's events.
Wheelchair access.

Het Nationale Ballet – *one of Amsterdam's top companies, here seen swanning about.*

Het Veemtheater
Van Diemenstraat 410 (626 0112). Tram 3/Bus 35.
Open reservations and information 10am-4pm Mon-Fri.
Tickets *f*15; *f*12,50 CJP, over-65s.
A former warehouse next to the port, which specialises in mime and movement theatre.
Café (open 6pm-1am).

Out of Town

AT&T Danstheater
Schedeldoekshaven 60, 2511 EN Den Haag (070 360 4930). **Open** *box office* 10am-6pm Mon-Sat; until curtain time on performance days; from one hour and 15 min beforehand for matinées. **Tickets** *f*30-*f*45; concessions for CJP card holders. **Credit** AmEx, DC, EC, MC, V.
This has been the home of the Nederlands Dans Theater (*see below* **Companies**) since 1987. The building's design, by leading Dutch architect, Rem Koolhaas is both daring and handsome. It's considered a better venue than Amsterdam's Muziektheater, as it was designed exclusively for dance.
Wheelchair access by arrangement.

Rotterdamse Schouwburg
Schouwburgplein 25, 3012 CL Rotterdam (010 411 8110). **Open** *box office* 11am until performance Mon-Sat; from 1 hour before curtain time Sun; phone bookings until 7pm. **Tickets** *f*20-*f*90; concessions for CJP, over-65s. **Credit** AmEx, DC, EC, MC, V.
This large theatre first opened in 1988. Because of its square shape it has been nicknamed the 'Kist van Quist' (Quist's box), after its architect. It plays host to the bigger national companies as well as dance troupes from abroad.
Bar. Café. Shop. Wheelchair access; toilets for the disabled.

Toneelschuur
Smedestraat 23, 2011 RE Haarlem (023 5312 439).
Open *box office* 3-6pm Mon-Thur; 3-10pm Fri, Sat.
Tickets *f*17,50; *f*14 CJP; concessions for CJP.
Many dance and theatre lovers from Amsterdam go to Haarlem (15 minutes by train, *see chapter* **The Randstad**) to congregate at the Toneelschuur. This theatre has two halls and is nationally renowned for its programmes of theatre and modern dance.
Bar. Café. Wheelchair access.

Companies

Nationale Ballet
Information from Muziektheater (see above **Venues**).
This is the largest company in the Netherlands and has over 20 Balanchine ballets in its repertoire, the largest collection outside New York. Since moving to the Muziektheater in 1986, its repertoire has had to include more classical ballet to fill the 1,600 seats every night. Toer van Schayk and Rudi van Dantzig have been instrumental in developing this company's distinctive style within contemporary ballet. Canadian Wayne Eagling is the new artistic director.

Nederlands Dans Theater
Information from AT&T Danstheater (see above **Venues: Out of Town**).
The design of the Nederlands Dans Theater's base suits the repertoire of the company; the black stage walls direct all the attention towards the quality of the movement. The work of Hans van Manen and Jiri Kylin forms the core of the programming. Live music is incorporated into every performance. Apart from the main company there is also NDT2, consisting of novices, and NDT3, made up of veterans.

Dansgroep Krisztina de Châtel
An outstanding modern dance company created in 1976 by Hungarian-born Krisztina de Châtel. Her choreographies are an impressive example of minimalist modern dance. Performances in Amsterdam usually take place in the Bellevue (*see chapter* **Theatre**).

Folkloristisch Danstheater
Kloveniersburgwal 87-89 (623 5359 box office; 623 9112 information 10am-4pm Mon-Fri). Tram 9, 14/Metro Nieuwmarkt. **Open** *box office* one hour before performance. **Tickets** *f*12,50; concessions for CJP, over-65s.
This Amsterdam-based company performs original dance from all over the world. The corps of 23 dancers works with guest choreographers from the specific countries where the folk dances originate.

Stichting Dansers Studio Beppie Blankert
Entrepotdok 4 (638 9398).
Unique within the world of modern dance, Beppie Blankert offers a platform for a shifting group of freelance dancers and choreographers.

Out of Town

The Amsterdam performances of these companies usually take place in the Stadsschouwburg (*see* chapter **Theatre**).

Djazzex

In 1983 Djazzex started in The Hague as a middle-of-the-road, jazz-cum-showdance company, but it soon developed its own style: a mixture of jazz and modern dance. The company has been a pioneer in the Netherlands and abroad, promoting jazz dance as more than pure entertainment.

Introdans

Primarily a touring company, Introdans, based in Arnhem, tries not to be too highbrow. Productions vary from easy-going dramatic ballet to innovative work by Dutch choreographers. In keeping with the increasing internationalisation of dance, the company has recently collaborated with choreographers from abroad.

Raz

This new, large modern dance company, based in the southern city of Tilburg, has recently been making waves under the artistic leadership of Hans Tuerlings.

Reflex

Based in Groningen and founded in 1986, Reflex has built up a modern dance repertoire that is both varied and tasteful. The artistic leadership was taken over in 1990 by Patricia Tuerlings, who suffuses her work with an air of the absurd.

Rotterdamse Dansgroep

Information from Rotterdamse Schouwburg (see above **Venues: Out of Town**).
The Rotterdamse Dansgroep is one of the most vigorous exponents of New York modern dance in the Netherlands. Imported dance routines are mixed with work by young Dutch choreographers.

Scapino Ballet

Information from Rotterdamse Schouwburg (see above **Venues: Out of Town**).
The oldest dance company in the country. Until recently the company's work was more oriented towards youth dance and 'family' programmes, but under the leadership of Nils Christe and Ed Wubbe the company's image is more in line with current trends.

Movement Theatre

Cloud Chamber

A collaboration which incorporates different nationalities from across the globe, Cloud Chamber provides the best Dutch example of 'the postmodern multi-media spectacle'.

Griftheater

On the international mime scene, Griftheater is a veritable giant. The company produces both location movement theatre as well as productions for existing theatre spaces. Under the leadership of Frits Vogels, the work is an excellent combination of modern mime with the plastic arts.

Lisa Marcus

In recent years the work of this transpanted New Yorker has become increasingly controversial thanks to her extreme images and eroticism.

Shusaku and Dormu Dance Theatre

A veteran choreographer in Holland, Japanese Shusaku Takeuchi has been producing fascinating work for over 20 years. Specialising in huge location spectacles, often on or near bodies of water, Shusaku's work usually incorporates live music. Huge constructions, fire and impressive lighting typify his outdoor work. Shusaku's indoor work is highly influenced by his plastic arts background.

Tender

Information: call Tenderline 624 4257.
You never know where this innovative group may pop up: in the supermarket or on a café terrace. The unannounced arrival of strange characters up to bizarre things in otherwise normal settings usually heralds a performance.

Events

Spring Dance

Information and bookings Keistraat 2, HV 3512 Utrecht (030 332032).
Held every year in Utrecht in late April/early May, this festival attempts to give an overview of recent developments in modern dance, film and music from around the world.

Holland Festival

Bookings (from February) Nederlands Reserverings Centrum, Postbus 404, 2260 AK Leidschendam (070 320 2500/bookings 621 1211). **Tickets** *f20-f120.*
Dutch dance companies premiére at this annual festival of performing arts (in June). Major companies from abroad also appear. Direct ticket sales (from May) from AUB Uitburo and VVV tourist offices and individual theatres.

Uitmarkt

Information 626 2656.
Dance, music, theatre and cabaret are performed alfresco in the last weekend of August every year on the Museumplein.

Holland Dance Festival

Information and bookings (070) 361 6142/fax (070) 365 0509.
Every two years in October (the next is in 1997), this festival takes place in The Hague's Danstheater. Many of the world's larger companies are attracted to the event and the quality of work is consistently high. De Nederlands Dans Theater usually represents Holland.

Cadans

Information from Korzo Theater (070) 363 7540.
The Hague's exciting international festival of contemporary dance takes place in November on even-numbered years. Festival policy requires each piece to be made specifically for the occasion. Exclusive premieres from around the world.

Courses and Workshops

Trainingsfonds Moderne Theaterdans

Danswerkplaats Amsterdam Arie Biemondstraat 107b (689 1789). Tram 1, 6, 7, 11, 17. **Classes** 10am-12.30pm Mon-Fri. **Cost** *f8,50-f12,50* per class.
Daily modern dance classes offered include barre lessons, advanced and intermediate technique.

Singel Dans en Theater

Eerste Nassaustraat 7 (681 0067). Tram 10. **Classes** 10am-noon, 6pm-midnight, Mon-Sat. **Cost** *f5-f12.*
Classes in both the morning and evening offered by a collective of eight members.

Dansstudio Cascade

Koestraat 5 (623 0597/689 0565). Metro Nieuwmarkt. **Classes** 6-10pm Mon-Fri. **Cost** *f11-f20.*
Modern dance technique, yoga, and capoeira to stretching and contact improvisation. Most teachers here work within the 'new dance' technique. Costs vary.

Film

Amsterdam's cinemas might not show much home-grown product, but they do have art deco interiors and beer on tap.

Films aren't one of Holland's greatest exports and sadly are often even passed over in Dutch cinemas in favour of US family flicks and thrillers (more popular with the already reluctant Dutch film goers). Not to say that what's on offer isn't worth the effort. Names worth noting include the documentary film-maker Jos de Putter (*Solo, de wet van de favela*); George Sluizer (*The Vanishing*); Dick Maas, who is riding on the success of his *Flodder* films, though most will remember him through his 1988 cult hit *Amsterdamned*; and Marleen Gorris, whose film *Antonia* won an Academy Award for Best Foreign Language Film in 1995.

Dutch filmmakers are particularly successful abroad. Director Paul Verhoeven has become a national hero after his successes with *Robocop*, *Total Recall* and *Basic Instinct* (*see* **Paul Verhoeven** *page 189*); cameraman Robby Muller is the regular choice of German director Wim Wenders; screenwriter Menno Meyes (*The Color Purple*) and a small army of editors and technicians are all in regular Hollywood demand. Cameraman turned director Jan de Bont (*The Jewel of the Nile, Ruthless People, Black*

Rain) is hot property in Tinseltown. His directorial debut, *Speed*, was one of the highest-grossing films in 1994. Director Peter Greenaway shoots many of his films in the Netherlands using local crews, most recently *The Baby of Mâcon*, which was shot at the Oude Kerk. In front of the camera, Rutger Hauer (*Blade Runner, The Hitcher*) lost ground to Jeroen Krabbé (*The Living Daylights, Kafka, Prince of Tides*) as the most visible Dutch actor worldwide.

The best way to bone up on Dutch film is to attend one of Holland's three main film festivals (*see below* **Film Festivals**), in which many entries are by home-grown directors and producers.

THE CINEMAS

Although few in number, Amsterdam's cinemas offer as balanced and substantial a filmic diet as any other European city, from Hollywood blockbuster junk food to the indigenous flavours of home grown produce.

Cinemas can be divided into two main categories – first run/mainstream and art-house (*filmhuizen*). Amsterdammers have a healthy

Huub Stapel searches for an insane killer in cult hit 'Amsterdamned'.

appetite for foreign and art-house fare (mainstream venues are outnumbered two to one). The Dutch translate the words art-house literally. Not only do the venues offer a cosmopolitan mix of art films, documentaries and retrospectives as well as an informed selection of the more intelligent Hollywood flicks, but each also has a unique personality and charm. With the exception of the **Uitkijk**, all have marvellous cafés and **The Movies**, especially notable because of its lavish art deco interior, also has an enchanting restaurant.

Of the mainstream cinemas, the **Tuschinski** is a marvel in itself with sumptuous original art deco architecture and fittings. All, however, even the largest, **City**, have a certain cosiness, seemingly obligatory in every Dutch establishment. By 1997 Pathé expect to have installed Dolby CP50 SR in all of its cinemas which in layman's terms means a wicked all-round sound sytem.

TICKETS AND INFORMATION

Cinema programmes in the multiplexes change each Thursday. Weekly listings of the main venues are prominently displayed in virtually every café, bar and cinema. Other reliable sources include *Uitkrant,* the Wednesday edition of *Het Parool* and the *Amsterdams Stadsblad*. There is also an excellent monthly Dutch film mag, *De Filmkrant*, which has comprehensive free information. Although these listings are in Dutch they can easily be understood by the non-native.

In mainstream houses be prepared for an obligatory 15-minute *pauze* (interval), slapped into every main picture. None of the art houses operate the dreaded *pauze*, except in films longer than two-and-a-half hours. The publicised starting time in multiplexes allows fifteen minutes' grace while pre-film commercials are shown; art houses go straight into the movie.

A ticket can be reserved in advance at most venues for a nominal charge of 50c. Credit cards are not accepted. As noted by John Travolta in *Pulp Fiction*, you can drink a beer (and from a glass, no less) in many Amsterdam cinemas. Smoking is invariably forbidden, however.

Café life at the Kriterion. Page 119.

All films are shown in the original language (predominantly English) with Dutch subtitles. Films in Dutch are indicated by the words *Nederlands Gesproken* after the title.

First Run & Mainstream

Alhambra
Weteringschans 134 (623 3192). Tram 4, 6, 7, 10. **Tickets** *f8,50; f15 evenings Fri-Sun. (2 screens).*
A small and rather drab Pathé theatre. Its bold metallic 1970s exterior suggests more glorious days long past. The films are usually transfers from the City or Tuschinski (*below*) and tend to run and run until well and truly exhausted.
Wheelchair access with assistance to screen 2.

Calypso/Bellevue Cinerama
Marnixstraat 400 (623 4876). Tram 1, 2, 5, 7, 10, 11. **Tickets** *f11; f15 evenings Fri-Sun. (2 screens each).*
Two separate and glitzy complexes, next to each other and sharing a common box office. Also home to the occasional first-run or European première.
Wheelchair access to all screens with assistance.

City
Leidseplein (623 4579). Tram 1, 2, 5, 6, 7, 10, 11. **Late shows** midnight Fri, Sat. **Tickets** *f10; f15,50 evenings Fri-Sun. (7 screens).*
The large frontage and huge electronic advertisement hoarding dominate the Kleine Gartman Plantsoen (a small road off the Leidseplein) and a bank of TV sets in the foyer runs a constant diet of trailers. Much frequented by tourists and loud youngsters. The fare is family-orientated mainstream, and predictably, trade is heavy all week with long queues at weekends. There are also occasional premières. For special screenings, the City 1 and City 7 theatres are combined into one theatre and City 1 is also available for hire for conferences and parties.
Wheelchair access with assistance to screens 1-4.

Tuschinski
Reguliersbreestraat 26 (626 2633). Tram 4, 9, 14, 16, 24, 25. **Tickets** *f11; f15 evenings Fri-Sun; f15-f20 balcony seats; f27,50 eight person box (with glass of champagne).*
The Tuschinski was built in 1922 by Polish tailor-turned-architect Abraham Tuschinski, originally as a variety theatre for rich merchant families. It is now Amsterdam's most prestigious cinema, which inevitably means long box-office queues spilling out into the street at evenings and weekends. It is home to regular premières and occasional royal screenings and offers a lively and occasionally inspired film choice. As the building's stunning art deco alone attracts so many visitors, tours are organised in July and August every year. These are at 10.30am on Mondays and Sundays; tickets (*f7,50*) are available from the box office.
Wheelchair access with assistance to all screens except Screen 5.

Revival & Art Houses

Alfa
Hirschgebouw, Leidseplein (627 8806). Tram 1, 2, 5, 6, 7, 10, 11. **Tickets** *f8-f11; f15-f20 evenings Fri-Sun. (4 screens).*
A Pathé art house. The décor is sober in comparison to the independents but the film choice is reliably intelligent, with many movies in English. There are also kids' matinées most afternoons and the **IDFA** *(see* **Film Festivals***)* each winter. Weekends are busy.
Wheelchair access to all screens with assistance.

Film

Paul Verhoeven

Has sex made this man a national hero?

There is little about sex that can still shock an Amsterdammer. But Dutch director Paul Verhoeven has made a pretty big impact with it elsewhere. Even though he was forced to cross the ocean to receive the acclaim and funds he warranted, he took with him this little piece of home. His first leap into international recognition, *Turks Fruit* (*Turkish Delight*) – Oscar nominee for Best Foreign Language Film in 1973 – was a love/sex/death porno exercise. Bringing him full circle in 1996, *Show Girls*, which explicitly focused on a dancer in a seedy club, caused a storm with the press, who regarded it as little more than soft porn, if less stimulating.

Even before this, he raised more than just eyebrows with Sharon Stone's leg-crossing routine in *Basic Instinct*. Exchanging flesh for futuristic fantasy, his other two major international hits, the sci-fi blockbusters *Robocop* and *Total Recall*, are equally unforgettable.

After six years at university Verhoeven pinballed his way through the world of the moving image, getting an extra ball each game. Beginning as a documentary film-maker for the Royal Dutch Navy he then did a highly successful stint in Dutch television before breaking into feature films and being swept away to Tinseltown. The rest is celluloid history. Provocative he is. Talented he is. And of course that makes him a national hero.

Cinecenter

Lijnbaansgracht 236 (623 6615). Tram 1, 2, 5, 6, 7, 10, 11. Tickets *f13,50-f16.* (3 screens).
The Cinecenter is a novel and welcoming venue with *commedia dell'arte* prints adorning walls and stairways. Each screen has its own name and décor – Coraline, Peppe Nappa, Pierrot and the tiny 52-seat Jean Vigo. The programme offers an international choice of films with around 60 per cent French to 40 per cent English/US, with Spanish, Russian and Chinese screenings also common. A pleasant café sells toasties and apple pie. In summer the lack of air conditioning can make the place unpleasantly warm.
Café. Wheelchair access to all screens with assistance.

Desmet

Plantage Middenlaan 4A (627 3434). Tram 7, 9, 14/Metro Waterlooplein. Tickets *f10 Sun-Wed; f14 Thur-Sat.* (2 screens)
The Desmet has a striking art deco design with an ornate downstairs café. The film choice is imaginative and wholly international. Mini-festivals, 'Desmet favourites', focus on a particular director or genre each month. Often thrown in are the odd horror film and Dutch premières. Sundays are regularly used to stage special events such as lectures, documentaries and public interviews with directors, actors and producers. The weekend gay screenings are well attended (*see also chapter* Gay & Lesbian).
Café/bar. Wheelchair access with assistance by prior arrangement.

Kriterion

Roetersstraat 170 (623 1708). Tram 6, 7, 10/Metro Weesperplein. Late shows 12.15am Fri, Sat. Tickets *f10 Mon-Thur, Sun; f12,50 Fri, Sat. f8,50 sneak preview.*
This friendly, neighbourhood venue, run entirely by volunteer students, screens a broad and interesting film choice. Children's matinées are on Wednesday, Saturday and Sunday. Mini-festivals are a speciality, and recently they have resurrected the yearly Cinestud student film festival. Late-night, weekend screenings centre on cult American or erotic French movies. Every Thursday evening there is a sneak preview at a reduced price. The downstairs bar is lively in the evenings and at weekends is open all day, even to those not attending a screening.
Café/bar. Wheelchair access to Screen 1.

The Movies

Haarlemmerdijk 161 (624 5790). Tram 3. Late shows 12.15am Fri, Sat. Tickets *f13,50.*
Perhaps the most aesthetically pleasing of all the city's art houses, The Movies dates from 1928. The café, worth a visit even if you don't also intend to partake of the fine film programme, has been restored to its full 1930s charm. The films themselves are predominantly international, from obscure to near-mainstream, but almost always featuring something worthwhile. Negative points: if you are taller than 5'5" (170cm), it will be hard for you to sit comfortably in their small chairs.
Café. Restaurant. Wheelchair access with assistance.

Rialto
Ceintuurbaan 338 (662 3488). Tram 3, 12, 24, 25.
Tickets *f*12,50-*f*17; five-visit cards *f*50.
A stylish alternative cinema just a short journey from the
centre of town. It offers a mixed diet of new and old inter-
national flicks and the occasional European première.
Thematic blocks change monthly and there will always be
at least one all-time classic. The membership packages
include ticket discounts and permanent seat reservations.
Café/bar. Wheelchair access to Rialto 2 downstairs.

Riksbioscoop
*Reguliersbreestraat 31 (624 3639). Tram 4, 9, 14, 16,
24, 25.* **Tickets** *f*2,50.
Formerly the Cineac, this cinema is now what the Americans
call a Dollar Cinema (in Holland's case this is a *f*2,50 coin or
rijksdaalder). The idea is to take last year's top films and put
them on a near constant loop. Films change every Thursday
and it's proving a massive success.

De Uitkijk
*Prinsengracht 452 (623 7460). Tram 1, 2, 5, 6, 7, 10,
11.* **Tickets** *f*12,50.
Amsterdam's oldest cinema, the staunchly independent De
Uitkijk dates from 1913 and is a charming, 158-seat converted canal house. Films that prove popular tend to stay
put. The owner's 'movies over ice-cream' policy means there
are no refreshments.
Wheelchair access with assistance.

Multi-media Centres

Melkweg
*Lijnbaansgracht 234A (624 1777). Tram 1, 2, 5, 6, 7,
10, 11.* **Late shows** 12.30am Fri, Sat. **Tickets** *f*11,50.
Membership *f*3,50 (included in admission price).
Though better known as a rock venue, the Melkweg runs a
consistently imaginative film programme in its cosy first-
floor cinema, running from mainstream action/adventure
through cult films to art house movies. Can be noisy if the
film coincides with a concert. *See also chapter* **Music: Rock,
Folk & Jazz.**
Café/bar.

Soeterijn
Linnaeusstraat 2 (568 8500). Tram 9, 10, 14.
Tickets *f*10.
Right next to the Tropenmuseum (*see chapter* **Museums**),
the Soeterijn stages regular ethnic music, theatre and, occasionally, documentaries and feature films from developing
countries. Film night is Monday, with one show at 8.30pm.
During occasional festivals celebrating the Third World,
films are shown throughout the week.

Film Museum

Nederlands Filmmuseum (NFM)
*Vondelpark 3 (589 1400/library 612 3021). Tram 1, 2,
3, 5, 6, 11, 12.* **Open** *library* 10am-5pm Tue-Fri; 11am-
5pm Sat; *film screenings* 8.30pm or 7pm and 9.30pm; 2pm
Wed. **Tickets** *cinema f*10; *f*8 CJP card holders, over-65s,
groups of min 10 people; *f*5 subscribers. **Yearly
subscriptions** *f*30.
This government-subsidised film museum was established
in the 1940s and has a staggering 35,000 films in its vaults,
culled from every period and corner of the world. Many, if
missed here, you will be lucky ever to see again. Sunday is
the day for Dutch film screenings and children's matinées.
Silent movies are accompanied by live piano music. On
balmy summer Saturday evenings there are outdoor screenings on the first-floor terrace. Part of the Filmmuseum's

On the terraces at the NFM.

unique archive can be watched on video here too. Café
Vertigo in the basement has one of Amsterdam's most
charming terraces (*see also chapters* **Cafés & Bars** *and*
Museums).

Film Festivals

Nederlandse Film Festival
Festival office *'t Hoogt 4-10, 3512 GW Utrecht (030
322 684).* **Open** 10am-6pm Mon-Fri.
An all-Dutch affair aimed at the Dutch public and film industry, running in the third week of September. The festival features around 100 feature films in a variety of venues, plus
shorts, documentaries and a selection of TV programmes.
Each new Dutch production is shown here, along with a
selection of students' efforts from the Amsterdamse Film
Academie. There are also lectures from guest speakers and
student workshops on technique. The festival presents its
own awards to the year's best films and holds an annual ret-
rospective of a Dutch film personality.

Rotterdam Film Festival
PO Box 21696, 3001 AR Rotterdam (010-4118080).
Tickets phone for details. **Credit** AmEx, MC, V.
The Rotterdam Film Festival, which has been going on for
over 25 years, is the biggest film festival in the Netherlands
and is international in scope, with around 90 films in its
main programme and up to 100 others compiled in retrospectives. There's also an accompanying series of lectures
and seminars by guest directors, actors, producers and
other industry figures, plus afternoon workshops on film
technique. The festival is non-competitive (no awards)
with an emphasis on 'art' movies, and runs in late January
and early February.

International Documentary Filmfestival Amsterdam
(627 3329). **Tickets** phone for details. **Credit** AmEx, MC,
V.
As the name suggests, documentaries are the staple of this
annual festival. A *f*10,000 prize is awarded to the best film
in the name of the late Dutch documentary maker Joris Ivens.
Every afternoon there is an opportunity to pose your questions to a few of the directors. 1997 is the tenth anniversary
of this wonderful event.

Exploding Cinema
(Information on 616 5580/668 4252)
Exploding cinema sporadically organise alternative events
where self-produced VHS, 8mm and 16mm films are
screened. The evenings often include live performances,
installations, exhibitions, VJs and DJs, as well as a forum for
the directors to field questions from the viewers.

Music: Classical & Opera

Amsterdam has a buzzing interest in all kinds of classical music and offers an international agenda of aural delights.

Classical music in in Amsterdam covers all bases, from the daring production in 1996 of Schoenberg's massive 'Moses and Aaron' by the **Concertgebouw Orchestra** to twelfth-century Gregorian chants. However, the **Concertgebouw** remains a world-famous temple of standard 'classical' fare, an illustrious and well-loved venue for many world-famous artists and performers, as well as a dedicated public.

At the Beurs van Berlage, the **Netherlands Philharmonic**, directed by Hartmut Haenchen, plays a symphonic series alongside its regular productions at the **Netherlands Opera**. The **Rotterdam Philharmonic Orchestra** has been taking great steps since the arrival of Valery Gergiev as chief conductor. Semi-staged operas and choral concerts are being planned in collaborations with the phenomenal Kirov Opera in St Petersburg, which he also directs. The Radio Philharmonic Orchestra based in the broadcasting town of Hilversum, continues to work at the highest levels

under the skilled baton of the internationally acclaimed Edo de Waart.

The **Netherlands Opera** has consolidated its international status under the artistic direction of Pierre Audi, whose contract remains indefinite. Following the success of his Monteverdi trilogy, with authentic accompaniment and minimalistic modern staging, the next few years will see the build-up to the staging of Wagner's mammoth 'Ring' cycle.

ENSEMBLES

The '95-'96 season was fittingly fêted as the '**Year of the Ensemble**' in celebration of the city's twenty professional groups, whose repertoires range from baroque through to contemporary and improvised. On the period front, there are as many chamber consorts as orchestras. Dutch musicians were the founders of authentic performance practice (performances using authenthic period instruments, a phenomenon which only really took off in the 1970s) and now their students are spread-

The Nederlandse Opera's 1996 production of 'La Bohème'.

ing their skills and techniques around the globe. Ton Koopman still holds the torch as harpsichordist and 'director who doesn't conduct' of the **Amsterdam Baroque Orchestra**, founded in 1979. Along with his newer **Amsterdam Baroque Choir**, he has just embarked on a sixty-CD project for Erato to record JS Bach's complete cantatas. Since 1993, Marc Minkovski has led the **Amsterdam Bach Soloists**, formed by members of the Concertgebouw Orchestra. Recorder-player and director Frans Brüggen extends authentic practice into the classical era with his **Orchestra of the 18th Century**, whose daring tempi, brilliant strings, and valveless natural horns make for exciting performances.

The number of specialist new music ensembles is quite remarkable for a city the size of Amsterdam. From the 20 or so based here, the **Asko** and **Schoenberg Ensembles** are the most interesting, and are usually directed by Reinbert de Leeuw and Oliver Knussen. Their repertoire is challenging and revealing, including regular world premières. In choral concerts they often collaborate with the flexible professionals of the **Netherlands Chamber Choir**. Ed Spanjaard's **Nieuw Ensemble**, founded in 1980, provides the popular Proms at the **Paradiso** (*see chapter Music: Rock, Folk & Jazz*), again a contemporary concert series, and Lev Markiz conducts the strings of the **Nieuw Sinfonietta** in both classical and modern repertoire.

The cross-over scene is also thriving. This includes the minimalist emphasis of **Orkest De Volharding**, as well as the jazz-based flexibility of the **Willem Breuker Kollektief** and the **Maarten Altena Ensemble**, who mix composed and improvised material and meet equal success on both the classical and jazz circuits.

The Netherlands still benefits from the subsidy of the Arts which makes much of this adventurous activity possible: a treat for composers, performers and audiences alike. The hard-hitting timbres of Dutch minimalism, introduced by Louis Andriessen, have impressed a whole generation of young British and American composers, such as Steve Martland, Graham Fitkin and Michael Torke.

WHAT'S ON & BOOKING IT

Ticket prices in Amsterdam are reasonable in comparison with other European cities. With the predominance of subscription sales, it is sometimes tricky to get hold of tickets, but it's always worth trying for returns on the day of a concert. Most venues also hold weekly lunchtime concerts free of charge (*see* **Lunchtime Menus** *below*). To find out what's on where, get a copy of the free Dutch listings paper *Uitkrant* published by the cultural information centre, **AUB Ticketshop** (621 1211), or surf to *Time Out Amsterdam*'s weekly website (http//:www.time-out.nl). For details of where to get both magazines *see chapter* **Media**. The VVV (*see chapter* **Essential Information**) can give details of forthcoming concerts. The only discounts are for students, over-65s (and some venues only accept Dutch ID) and CJP card-holders (*see chapter* **Essential Information**).

Concert Halls

Where a telephone number is given in the listings below, tickets will be available from the venue's box office. Tickets are also available from the booking agency, **AUB Ticketshop** (621 1211), which accepts all major credit cards.

Beurs van Berlage: AGA Zaal and Yakult Zaal

Damrak 213 (627 0466). Tram 4, 9, 14, 16, 24, 25. **Open** *box office* (mid-Aug-June) 12.30-6pm Tue-Sat; 75 mins before performance for ticket sales and collection. **Tickets** *f*15-*f*35; concessions for CJP card holders. This former stock exchange is now a cultural centre, housing a large exhibition hall, two concert halls, one of Holland's dedicated classical radio stations, the **Concertzender**, and the offices of the resident orchestras: the **Netherlands Philharmonic** and the **Netherlands Chamber Orchestra**. Entered from the Damrak, the medium-sized Yakult Zaal offers comfortable seating, a massive stage and controllable but not ideal acoustics. The 200-seat AGA Zaal is a free-standing glass box within the walls of a side room, sometimes referred to as the 'diamond in space'. *See also chapters* Architecture *and* Sightseeing: Heritage. *Wheelchair access and toilets for the disabled.*

*The classical **Concertgebouw**. Page 193.*

Muziektheater: *home of the Netherlands Ballet, Opera and Ballet Orchestra.*

Concertgebouw

Concertgebouwplein 2-6 (reservations 671 8345 10am-5pm daily/24-hour information in Dutch 675 4411). *Tram 2, 3, 5, 12, 16.* **Open** *box office* 10am-7pm daily; 40 mins before performance for ticket sales and collection. **Tickets** *f25-f100* depending on the programme; concessions for CJP card holders, students. **Credit** AmEx, DC, MC.

The Concertgebouw is the favourite venue of many of the world's top soloists and orchestras, including their own **Concertgebouw Orchestra**. The acoustics of the **Grote Zaal** (Great Hall) are second to none and a seat anywhere in the house provides great listening. The **Kleine Zaal** (Small Hall) is less comfortable, but features top-class chamber groups and soloists, including the resident Borodin Quartet. Visiting stars push prices up, but for 75 per cent of the remaining concerts, tickets cost less than *f30*. The VARA-Matinées on Saturdays at 3pm are renowned for concert performances of opera, and the Sunday morning concert is a bargain at *f20; f10* for concessions (including half-price entry to museums on the same day). Special themes for the 96-97 season are the Britten-Shostakovich coupling, and 'Schubert Plus' in celebration of his 200th anniversary. Throughout July and August, the **Robeco Group Summer Concerts** offer subsidised ticket prices (f25; f15 for concessions) for high profile artists and orchestras during the usual 'off-season'.

Wheelchair access and toilets for both halls by arrangement.

IJsbreker

Weesperzijde 23 (box office 693 9093/admin 668 1805). *Tram 3, 6, 7, 10/Metro Weesperplein.* **Open** *box office* 9.30am-5.30pm daily; *café* 10am-1am Mon-Thur, Sun; 10am-2am Fri, Sat. **Tickets** *f12,50-f22,50; f12,50-f20* CJP card holders.

This is the world-famous international centre for contemporary music, run by director Jan Wolff. The venue co-produces several new music concerts with both the Holland Festival and the VARA-Matinée. Many of the concerts feature obscure and avant-garde Dutch works and musicians. Every Friday there is a free lunchtime concert (*see above* **Lunchtime Menus**). The innovative electro-acoustic concerts take place in the space of the **Artis Planetarium**

dome (*see chapter* **Sightseeing**). The IJsbreker's café boasts one of the best outdoor terraces in town with a fantastic view of the Amstel; open all day and after the concerts (*see chapter* **Cafés & Bars**).

Wheelchair access with assistance.

Opera

Muziektheater (Stopera)

Waterlooplein 22 (625 5455). *Tram 9, 14/Metro Waterlooplein.* **Open** *box office* 10am-6pm Mon-Sat; 11.30am-6pm Sun, or until start of performance. **Tickets** *f35-f110*; concessions for CJP card holders, over-65s. **Credit** AmEx, DC, MC, V.

The modern Muziektheater is home to the **National Ballet** and the **Netherlands Ballet Orchestra** (*see chapter* **Dance**) as well as the **Netherlands Opera**, and visiting guest productions. High-quality opera and dance productions at reasonable prices. The auditorium, inside floor to ceiling glass and marble-faced pillars, giving a wonderful view of the Amstel river. The stage's spaciousness invites particularly ambitious ideas from world-famous stage directors such as Willy Decker (Wozzeck and Werther) and Harry Kupfer (Die Frau ohne Schatten) and Peter Sellars (Pelléas et Mélisande). Free lunchtime concerts are held between September and June in the Boekman Zaal (*see* **Lunchtime Menus**). Tours of the building are given on Wednesdays and Saturdays at 4pm, costing *f8,50*. If you book in advance, the guide will be prepared with English translations.

Wheelchair access and toilets for the disabled.

Stadsschouwburg

Leidseplein 26 (624 2311). *Tram 1, 2, 5, 6, 7, 10, 11.* **Open** *box office* 10am-start of performance Mon-Sat, one and a half hours before performance, Sundays and Holidays **Tickets** *f15-f45*; concessions for CJP card holders, over-65s.

With productions designed for portability, the **Nationale Reisopera** (National Travelling Opera) receives less attention than it deserves. There are usually two or three performances of each production in the red velvet surroundings of this municipal theatre. Recent musical directors include young Lawrence Renes and Marc Minkowski in Gluck's 'Orfeo ed Euridice.'

Koninklijk Theater Carré
Amstel 115-125 (622 5225). Tram 4, 6, 7, 10. **Open** *box office 10am-7pm Mon-Sat; 1-7pm Sun.* **Tickets** *f25- f100; concessions for CJP card holders, over-65s.*
This former circus theatre hosts large-scale musicals such as 'Cats' and 'La Cage aux Folles' alongside reputable opera and ballet companies on tour from the former Eastern bloc with popular classics.

Churches

Many performances take advantage of the monumental churches around the city, also offering the chance to see their interiors. During the summer, the city's many bell-towers resonate to the intricate tinkling of their carillons: thumping the 'keyboard' mechanism triggers a whole array of smaller bells into surprisingly rapid renderings of tunes. But churches are not reserved for organ and carillon recitals. The recently refurbished **Amstelkerk** and **Lutherse Kerk**, and the intimate **Bethanienklooster** are also used for concerts. Most churches have no box office, but tickets and information are available from the **AUB Ticketshop**, Leidseplein (621 1211), which accepts all major credit cards.

Engelse Kerk
Begijnhof 48 (624 9665). Tram 1, 2, 4, 5, 9, 11, 14, 16, 24, 25.
Nestled in an idyllic courtyard, the Academy of the **Begijnhof** (*see chapter* **Sightseeing**) arranges weekly concerts of baroque and classical music at the English Reformed Church, with particular emphasis on using authentic period instruments in performances. The series of free lunch-time concerts in July and August features young players and new ensembles. The acoustics are vibrant and clear.
Wheelchair access.

Nieuwe Kerk
Dam (Nieuwe Kerk foundation 626 8168). Tram 1, 2, 5, 9, 11, 13, 14, 16, 17, 24, 25. **Open** 10am-5pm daily. **Tickets** *f7,50; f5 CJP card holders, students.*
Performances 8pm.
The Nieuwe Kerk has a magnificent sixteenth-century organ and hosts organ concerts by top Dutch and international players. Gustav Leonhardt, grandfather of baroque performance practice, is the resident organist. There's no regular programme, but it's a popular venue for organ series. *See also chapter* **Architecture**.
Wheelchair access with assistance.

Oude Kerk
Oudekerksplein 23 (625 8284). Tram 4, 9, 14, 16, 24, 25. **Open** *15 Apr-15 Sept* 11am-5pm Mon-Sat; *16 Sept- 14 Apr* 1-5pm Mon-Sat. **Tickets** *f7,50-f15; f6-f12,50 CJP card holders, over-65s.* **Performances** June-Aug. Carillon concerts every Saturday at 4pm.
Jan Sweelinck, the Netherlands' most famous seventeenth-century composer, was organist here. Concerts include organ and carillon recitals, choral and chamber music. The Oudekerk organises a summer 'wandering' concert series (three pieces in three venues, with promenades and coffee breaks) together with the Amstelkring Museum. *See also chapter* **Sightseeing**.
Wheelchair access with assistance.

Waalse Kerk
Oudezijds Achterburgwal 157. Tram 4, 9, 16, 24, 25. Information from Organisatie Oude Muziek (030 236 2236) **Tickets** *f22,50; f18,50 concessions.*
Small, elegant and intimate, this was the Huguenot church for Amsterdam. It is now a favourite location for chamber music, early music and choral concerts.

Out of Town

Anton Philipszaal, Den Haag
Spuiplein 150 (box office 070 360 9810/information 070 360 7927). **Open** *box office* 10am-6pm; 75 mins before performance. **Tickets** *f30-f80; concessions for CJP card holders, over-65s.* **Credit** AmEx, DC, MC, V.
Home of The Hague's Residentie Orchestra since 1987, situated amidst the modern architecture of the city centre. Inside it's a soundly designed hall with excellent acoustics.
Wheelchair access and toilets for the disabled.

De Doelen, Rotterdam
Kruisstraat 2 (010 413 2490). **Open** *box office* 10am-6pm Mon-Thur, Sat, Sun; 10am-9pm Fri. **Tickets** *f20- f150; concessions for CJP card holders, students.* **Credit** AmEx, DC, MC, V.
The Doelen is home to the **Rotterdam Philharmonic Orchestra** (RPO) directed by Valery Gergiev, and contains a large and small concert hall. The acoustics of the large hall are one of the reasons why the Rotterdam Philharmonic sounds so wonderful on tour: it has to work hard for a warm, expressive sound at home. The Doelen hosts about two dozen series a year, ranging from contemporary orchestral work to jazz and just about everything in between, including the RPO's own season.
Wheelchair access and toilets for the disabled.

Vredenburg Music Centre, Utrecht
Vredenburgpassage 77 (box office 030 2314544; 24-hour concert information 030 231 3144). **Open** *box office* noon-5pm Mon; 9am-5pm Tue-Sat; 45 minutes before performances. **Tickets** *f15-f45; concessions for CJP, over-65s.* **Credit** AmEx, DC, EC, MC, V.
Worth the half-hour train ride from Amsterdam, as many performers make their only Dutch appearances here. Acoustically it's a favourite among musicians, even though it sits within the ugly concrete structure of a shopping mall, and is regularly used for recordings. Vredenburg remains 100 per cent government subsidised, which makes for cheaper ticket prices than in Amsterdam. Also used for pop concerts.

Lunchtime Menus

Many of Amsterdam's lunchtime concerts are free and run throughout the standard September to June season: these include the **Boekmanzaal** at the **Muziektheater** with a recital each Tuesday at 12.30pm. Most famous is the lunchtime concert at the **Concertgebouw**, on Wednesdays at 12.30pm, with up-and-coming ensembles or soloists and even previews of evening concerts by a visiting world-famous orchestras. Get there early to fight your way in. The NCRV records a recital at the **IJsbreker** each Friday, at 12.30pm, usually of intriguing unknown works.

The **Stedelijk Museum** (*see chapter* **Museums**) stages occasional concerts, often of innovative contemporary music, on Thursday and Saturday afternoons at 3pm.

*Watching the world go by on the terrace at the **IJsbreker**.*

Festivals and Organisations

The AUB Uitburo and the VVV (*see chapter* **Essential Information**) can give further details on the events listed below.

Holland Festival

Various venues in Amsterdam. Enquires to Kleine Gartmanplantsoen 21, 1017 RP Amsterdam (627 6566). **Dates** June. **Admission** *f*25-*f*110.
The most important arts festival in Holland mixes the best of local musical, theatrical and dance ensembles with international tours and co-productions, as well as film. 1997 is the festival's 50th anniversary. Daring productions and premières always abound. *See also chapter* **Amsterdam by Season**.

International Gaudeamus Music Week

Postal and telephone enquiries Stichting Gaudeamus, Swammerdamstraat 38, 1091 RV, Amsterdam (694 7349/fax: 694 7258/e-mail gaud@xs4all.nl/website at http://www.xs4all.nl/~gaud/ **Dates** 1st week in September
Annual competition for young composers organised by the Centre for Contemporary Music. A whole week of intense discussion of the state of the art plus performances of selected entries and work by already established composers. Also of interest is the International Gaudeamus Interpreter's Competition (1st week of March, in De Doelen, Rotterdam), a similar competition for performers of contemporary repertoire. Two feasts for contemporary music devotees.

Uitmarkt

Dates third week in August. **Admission** free.
Held in August in Amsterdam's town centre, this annual event is a hugely popular open-air 'music market'. Musicians and ensembles play on temporary stages, previewing concerts scheduled for the coming season. The public can buy series tickets and other music-related bargains. One of the most popular events is the Prinsengracht concert, held on a float in the canal opposite the Pulitzer Hotel. *See also chapter* **Amsterdam By Season**.

Utrecht Early Music Festival

Various venues in Utrecht. Enquiries to: Stichting Oude Muziek, Postbus 734, 3500 AS Utrecht (030 236 2236). **Dates** last week Aug-first week Sept. **Admission** *f*15-*f*35.
Top baroque and classical artists and ensembles from around the world, performing in churches and concert halls throughout the city. A specialist's treasure trove, there are always some novel finds, and the reputed specialists to perform them.

Offbeat

Network for Non-Western Music

Pauwstraat 13a, 3512 AG, Utrecht (030-233 2876).
Indonesian, Turkish, African and Middle Eastern culture is brought to the Netherlands by this organisation. In Amsterdam, they present concerts at the **Soeterijn** (*see chapter* **Theatre**) at the Tropeninstituut (568 8500).

STEIM (Stichting for Electro-Instrumental Music.)

Achtergracht 91, 1017 WL, Amsterdam (622 8690/e-mail: steim@xs4all.nl; website at http://www.xs4all.nl/~steim
Amsterdam's electronic music institution is a unique research team examining the interface between man and music. Prototype MIDI controllers (Michel Waisvisz' gloved 'Hands' have the biggest claim to fame), novel sensors and hard- and software packages to convert any manner of signals into MIDI data. The five annual Rumori concerts at the **Theater Frascati** (626 6866) (*see chapter* **Theatre**) and their own intimate concerts give technophobes an intriguing glimpse into the future.

Taller Amsterdam

Keizersgracht 607, 1017 DS Amsterdam (624 6734)
Founded by two visual artists, Taller is a 'total-theatre cooperative' which stages in workshop productions. The results most resemble music-theatre with a political edge, created by themselves or contemporary composers.

Music: Rock, Folk & Jazz

Dutch music may be a bit dodgy, but Amsterdammers are spoilt for choice when it comes to live music from around the world.

For a two-bit town that you can walk across in less than an hour, Amsterdam packs a cultural wallop. There are a lot of world-renowned venues providing international music along these ancient and soggy streets. This is where troubadours roamed, Chet Baker played and died, and Lee 'Scratch' Perry spent his most eccentric years. The minstrel tradition continues to entertain and annoy in the form of busking. From strumming, numbing guitar to the celestial farting of the didgereedoo, street entertainment is at its densest at Centraal Station, the Dam, Leidseplein and Vondelpark on a Sunday. Now you know.

Zeedijk was the groovy hepcat strip of the 1950s. After making their bread at the Concertgebouw earlier in the evening, jazz legends like Gerry Mulligan, Count Basie and the tragic Chet would gather and jam at one of the many after-hour places around here. The most famous is the former Casablanca, whose void has been filled by the **Bimhuis**, a place to catch current jazz legends in intimate confines. The multimedia centres, the **Melkweg** and the **Paradiso**, both came to be in the heady and revolutionary 1960s, erupting respectively from a milk factory and an imposing stained-glassed church. Thanks to massive council subsidies, they have been able to chart every new trend ever since; from hippy to punk to techno to easy tune. The **Arena** is a more recent and smaller but nevertheless innovative venue. It is understandable that Amsterdam's crowds sometimes come across as jaded. They are spoilt.

With some of the world's best bands clamouring to play here, it is easy to forget the many local bands working hard to be heard. Besides opening slots at the aforementioned venues, there are fewer small places since the general demise of squats for them to strut their stuff. And except for the crassly commercial (such as 2 Untalented), few ever get beyond the Dutch club circuit. This is perhaps understandable when an act's lyrics are sung in Dutch, as with such top acts as the intense Raggende Manne (granted that the singer's vocal chords do regularly stretch beyond language) and the hip hop Osdorp Posse (who can give you a quick lesson in the depths of Dutch slang). But most Amsterdam-based bands choose either to remain instrumental (like Jazz, the ambient-metal of Kong, or latest surf sensations, the Treble Spankers) or opt for the more malleable and universal tongue of English. The international respect garnered by the likes of Urban Dance Squad, Bettie Serveert, and the Ex, and the appearance of many promising new bands, seems to hint that there is a renaissance occurring in the often slighted homegrown music scene.

Intrepid travellers who wish to jump head first into truly authentic Dutch musical culture should investigate the small brown bars in the Jordaan, where there are any number of crooners, accompanied by the crowd singing along, belting out trad tunes of lost love and spilt beer.

Full listings of all musical genres are on *Time Out Amsterdam*'s Internet site (*www.timeout.nl*), in the *Uitkrant* and rock music magazine, *Oor*.

Venues

Akhnaton

Nieuwezijds Kolk 25 (624 3396). Tram 1, 2, 5, 11, 13, 17. **Open** 11pm-5am Fri, Sat. **Admission** ƒ10-ƒ15.
Akhnaton is renowned for its world music, hosting regular African dance nights and salsa parties, as well as providing recording studios and rehearsal facilities. Not exactly on the palatial side, the club is prone to bursting at the seams, so prepare to make like a sardine.

AMP Studios

KNSM laan 13 (638 0019). Bus 28. **Open** noon-midnight daily. **Admission** free-ƒ15.
Starting out as rehearsal space for bands in a remote part of the city's harbour area, AMP Studios now offer regular concerts and parties, full recording facilities both analogue and MIDI, and a fully-licensed bar/café. Slowly but surely the building's location is changing: from being in the middle of nowhere to being in the middle of Amsterdam's newest urban development project on KNSM island.

Arena

's Gravesandestraat 51 (694 7362). Tram 3, 6, 14/Metro Weesperplein. **Open** 9.30pm-2am Mon-Thur, Sun; 9.30pm-4am Fri, Sat. **Admission** ƒ7,50-ƒ15.
Recently re-structured architecturally and aesthetically, the former Sleep-In hostel is now a sparkling new multi-media cultural centre called the ARENA (and still also a hostel – *see chapter* **Accommodation**). There is an excellent alter-

Jazz in a subdued and reverent atmosphere at the **Bimhuis.**

native party venue in the old nuns' quarters high in the rafters, but after lowering the ceiling to improve sound quality below, the outcome is worse sonically with a slightly cramped atmosphere both onstage and on the dancefloor. Nevertheless, with the constant flux of a predominantly transient crowd, you're always guaranteed to see new faces and if it all gets too much there's always the coffeeshop next door. Proud of its reputation for swaying towards the underground contingent of international bands, ARENA provides a refreshing chance to see the more obscure names at the cutting edge of new music.

De Buurvrouw

Pieterpoortsteeg 9 (625 9654). Tram 4, 9, 14, 16, 24, 25. **Open** *8pm-2am Mon-Thur, Sun; 8pm-3am Fri, Sat.* **Admission** free.
Imaginative décor, frequent live performances and a particularly eclectic record collection make this pocket-sized watering-hole stand out from the multitude of little bars that saturate the city. Attracting a predominantly alternative rock clientèle, Rage Against The Machine blasts out along with early Buzzcocks and Sonic Youth. Local rock bands play occasionally. *See also chapter* **Cafés & Bars**.

Caneçao

Lange Leidsedwarsstraat 68 (638 0611). Tram 1, 2, 5, 11. **Open** *10pm-4am Mon-Thur, Sun; 10pm-5am Fri, Sat.* **Admission** free.
A buzzing little bar that swings to the summery sounds of salsa and samba, transporting you from the mundanity of Amsterdam life to far-off tropical beaches. Catering for a large South American and tourist clientèle, the drinks are a tad pricey but worth the extra guilder to drift off to foreign climes with a tequila sunrise or four.

Cruise Inn

Zeeburgerdijk 272 (692 7188). Tram 6, 10. **Open** *9pm-3am Fri, Sat.* **Admission** usually free.
James Dean clones twist the night away in this gloriously pink wooden club house: DJs and visiting bands often appear on Saturday nights. Brothel-creepers abound as do vintage clothes and quiffs and even more vintage motorbikes.

Maloe Melo

Lijnbaansgracht 163 (420 0232). Tram 7, 10, 13, 14, 17. **Open** *8pm-2am Mon-Thur, Sun; 8pm-3am Fri, Sat.* **Admission** *ƒ5.*
A cosy hang-out for budding musos and punters escaping the chaotic revelry of the Korsakoff next door.

Escape

Rembrandtplein 11 (622 3542). Tram 4, 9, 14. **Open** *10pm-4am Thur; 10pm-5am Fri, Sat.* **Admission** *ƒ10 Thur, Fri; ƒ12,50 Sat.*
A huge, cavernous, commercial disco, situated amongst a profusion of tourist bars and sex theatres, that is mainly host to hip hop and soul acts: both Method Man and Jocelyn Brown have played here. A plastic and glitzy atmosphere but good quality sound and effective lights and lasers. *See also chapter* **Clubs**.

Last Waterhole

Oudezijds Armsteeg 12 (624 4814). Tram 4, 9, 16, 24, 25/Metro Centraal Station. **Open** *noon-1am Mon-Thur, Sun; noon-3am Fri, Sat.* **Admission** free.
Hidden down a small sidestreet in the heart of the Red-Light District, this largish, well-known bar caters mainly for the Amsterdam chapter of the Hell's Angels and other meaty grebos. Don't let this deter you though. Many residents of the adjoining youth hostel venture in to play pool and listen to all sorts of native rockers getting up and jamming live, almost every night.

Marcanti Plaza

Jan van Galenstraat 6-8 (682 3456). Tram 3. **Open** *10pm-5am Sat.* **Admission** *ƒ15.* **Membership** *ƒ10.*
With a capacity of 3,000 and a relatively lax dress code, there is definitely no entrance discrimination here. Marcanti Plaza is not as spangly as the Escape but similarly doubles as a great live venue and attracts the same teenybop ravers who high-school house crowd on Saturdays. Live performances

are relatively infrequent, and are usually a pretty heavy affair, involving artists from the hardcore rap, swingbeat or ragga fraternity. *See also chapter* **Clubs**.

Café Meander
Voetboogstraat 5 (625 8430). Tram 1, 2, 5, 11. **Open** 8.30pm-3am Mon-Thur; 8.30pm-4am Fri-Sun. **Admission** free.
Live perfomances are held daily, varying from jazz and funk to soul and blues.

Melkweg (Milky Way)
Lijnbaansgracht 234 (624 8492). Tram 1, 2, 5, 6, 7, 10, 11. **Open** 7.30pm-late Tue-Sun; disco 1-5am Fri, Sat. **Admission** ƒ7,50-ƒ25; includes admission to disco, theatre and cinema. **Membership** (compulsory) ƒ4 per month.
Once a dairy (hence the name), the Melkweg opened in the 1960s and is still run on a cooperative basis. Completely remodelled in '95 with the construction of the additional Pepsi-sponsored 'Max' hall, the multi-media centre is now able to play host to a double helping of well-known international acts, plus the usual theatre, dance and film events. Thanks to the canny stepped design of the Max this is now the only venue in town where people of normal height can see over the infamously lofty Netherlanders, and sound quality is extremely decent to boot. Access to both halls is restricted whilst concerts are in progress, but the whole building is utilised for the ever popular Dance Arena on Saturday nights and the other specialised club nights. Keep your eyes peeled for their posters or pick up one of the monthly information sheets from the foyer. *See also chapters* **Cafés & Bars**, **Clubs**, **Film**, **Galleries** *and* **Theatre**.

Mulligan's
Amstel 100 (622 1330). Tram 4, 6, 7, 10. **Open** 4pm-1am Mon-Fri; 4pm-3am Sat; 2pm-1am Sun. **Music** Fri, Sat, Wed. **Admission** free.
In the centre of town on the Amstel, this smoky little bar is bursting with character and sets itself apart from some of the other tackier Irish theme bars. A predictable, but no less entertaining, collection of folk singers and storytellers perform most weekends cramming themselves into the small wooden interior. *See also chapter* **Cafés & Bars**.

Naar Boven
Reguliersdwarsstraat 12 (623 3981). Tram 1, 2, 5, 11. **Open** 10pm-4am Mon-Thur, Sun; 10pm-5am Fri, Sat. **Admission** free Mon, Tue, Sun; ƒ7,50 Wed, Thur; ƒ10 Fri, Sat.
Industrial metal furnishings meld with black and white chequered walls and coordinated plastic bar stools with nice comfortable living-room chairs. In firing distance from swinging local party den, the Richter, this home of funk, hardcore and popular Amsterdam painter Herman Brood, fills up with Italian suits and high heels: load on the sovereign rings and thick gold chains.

OCCII
Amstelveenseweg 134 (671 7778). Tram 2, 6. **Open** 10pm-3am Fri, Sat; 9pm-2am Sun. **Admission** prices range from free-ƒ10.
A former squat venue, this cosy and friendly bar-cum-music hall immediately makes you feel at home and invites you to pull up a chair and take in some great local talent. Comfortably tucked away at the end of a delightful cycle ride through Vondelpark, it's a fine excuse to escape the hubbub of the city centre and catch an eclectic mix of quirky cabaret acts and earthy new bands. *See also chapter* **Gay & Lesbian**.

O'Donnell's
Ferdinand Bolstraat 5 (676 7786). Tram 16, 24, 25. **Open** 11am-1am Mon-Thur; 11am-3am Fri, Sat; 10.30am-1am Sun. **Admission** free.
A welcome new addition to the Irish contingent, O'Donnell's is a friendly and classic-looking bar perched proudly on the corner of the Heinekenplein, and is in stark contrast to its somewhat cold surroundings. Musically there's no need to fear dodgy 'Wild Rover' renditions by a one-stringed Albert

For the refurbished **Paradiso***, the writing is on the wall.*

Cuyp virtuoso, instead prepare to be drenched in lore as some seriously nimble-fingered fiddlers skip through a righteously puritanical Irish repertoire. *See also chapter* **Cafés & Bars**.

O'Reilly's

Paleisstraat 103-105 (624 9498). Tram 1, 2, 4, 5, 9, 11, 14, 16, 17, 24, 25. **Open** 11am-2am Mon-Thur, Sun; 11am-3am Fri, Sat. **Admission** free.

One of the larger Irish haunts, chock-full most nights and with an extra vat of merrymakers on Fridays and Saturdays. A lively atmosphere is provided by the mixture of resident Guinness-lovers and rowdy tourists on the quest for a decent pint. The décor is home-from-home cosy, with a living room style area at the back complete with log fire and bookcase, which provides a comfortable backdrop when visiting artists pull up a chair and strum good old Irish folky tunes. *See also chapter* **Cafés & Bars**.

Paradiso

Weteringschans 6-8 (623 7348). Tram 1, 2, 5, 6, 7, 10, 11. **Open** 9pm-5am-ish various days, phone for details. **Admission** *f*8,50-*f*30. **Membership** (compulsory) *f*4 per month.

Like the Melkweg, the Paradiso has recently undergone extensive refurbishments; there's no extra concert hall, but the toilet has been moved downstairs, and the cloakroom is now thoughtfully positioned by the front entrance. The exterior is also somewhat less aesthetically goth-like, with the sooty brickwork has been cleansed, and now the old church takes on a slightly more angelic appearance. The weekly programme caters for a wide range of musical tastes, from local band nights to bigger names on tour – the Rolling Stones and the artist formerly known as Prince have both graced the Paradiso with their presence. Tickets can be bought at the door on the evening of the concert, but are also available from the AUB ticket office, VVV tourist offices (for both *see chapter* **Essential Information**) and major record shops. *See also chapter* **Clubs**.

PH 31

Prins Hendriklaan 31 (673 6850). Tram 2. **Open** 9pm-2am Mon-Thur. **Admission** *f*7,50.

This ex-squat bar, now a one-room venue with a small stage and separate theatre room, is in an unlikely residential area of town, beyond Vondelpark. Local residents seem to tolerate noisy comings and goings, which is lucky as the sound system is powerful. Politically motivated local bands are regular performers.

Soeterijn Theatre

Linnaeusstraat 2 (568 8500). Tram 9, 10, 14. **Open** information and reservations 10am-4pm Mon-Fri; box office one hour before performance. **Admission** *f*12,50-*f*22,50.

A small theatre attached to the Tropenmuseum, which exhibits artefacts from all over the world (*see chapter* **Museums**). The Soeterijn follows the same policy in its music programming, featuring international folk musicians. A formal, all-seater venue, it's not necessarily the best context for some performances. *See also chapter* **Theatre**.

Twin Pigs

Nieuwendijk 100 (624 8573). Tram 4, 9, 16, 24, 25/Metro Centraal Station. **Open** 8pm-3am Mon-Thur, Sun; 8pm-4am Fri, Sat. **Admission** free.

Attracting a potent mix of afternoon drinkers and potheads, this relaxed but lively bar hosts a collection of loud local bands generally in the blues/rock vain. The rather imposing PA system keeps the emphasis on live music rather than mere drinking and chatting.

Winston Kingdom

Warmoesstraat 123-129 (625 39120). Tram 4, 9, 16, 24, 25. **Open** 8pm-3am Mon-Thur, Sun; 8pm-4am Fri, Sat. **Admission** free.

Part of the Winston Hotel (*see chapter* **Accommodation**), this recently renovated bar attracts a mixture of residents, locals and wandering tourists. At the weekends the pool

Amsterdam in song

While the preference of famous artists for both playing and living in Amsterdam is well documented, the artists themselves have more often than not chosen to immortalise the Venice of the North in song. Lyrical references to the Dutch capital crop all over the place, a tribute to the evocative spirit of a city that down the years has been a firm favourite with people of an artistic bent.

It's a good even bet that almost every speaker of English will have heard or sung a ditty featuring Amsterdam in title or text. Whether the writer of 'A Windmill in Old Amsterdam' was dabbling in modern-day Amsterdam's most famous attraction is not recorded but the song most certainly caught on with children the world over, no matter how improbable the idea of rodents wearing small wooden shoes might appear. Arguably even less credible was the concept of two self-important long-hairs booking themselves into the Amsterdam Hilton for a

week and then spending the whole time in the sack while claiming it was all for world peace; but this really did happen and was duly documented in the Beatles' final UK number one 'The Ballad of John and Yoko'.

Amsterdam has for some reason proved popular with the more highly strung stars; Scott Walker and David Bowie have both recorded versions of Jacques Brel's 'Amsterdam'. And of course they don't come much more highly strung than the genius of Max Bygraves whose 1950s hit 'Tulips from Amsterdam' was a pop classic of its day.

But Amsterdam references are by no means the sole property of pop ballads. There is also a hipper quotient. The Stone Roses referred to Amsterdam as Sodom and Gommorah in their song 'Daybreak' while English cult psychedelic band Tomorrow dedicated a whole song to Amsterdam's Provo movement when they penned 'My White Bicycle' in 1967.

Bettie Serveert – *one of the few Dutch bands to achieve any respect abroad.*

tables make way for a mixture of up-and-coming musicians, poets and certifiably loony thespian types. Frequent performances from the Knitting Factory stable.

Vondelpark
Tram 1, 2, 3, 5, 6, 7, 10, 11, 12. **Open** dawn-dusk daily.
One of the most pleasant ways to spend a hot summer afternoon or dusky evening is to wander down to the park and spy on some of the more unusual examples of artistry and musicianship or just plain mad people. Buskers appear all over the place, ranging from accomplished string quartets and African drummers to jazz singers and jugglers. There is an organised agenda of entertainment for the permanent outdoor podium and flyers and posters are usually plastered over various trees and gates in the park. *See also chapters* **Architecture, By Area** *and* **Sport & Fitness.**

Jazz

In summer, the Netherlands comes alive to the sound of jazz, with outdoor festivals in the centre of Amsterdam, as well as the North Sea Jazz Festival in The Hague (*see below* **Festivals**). Throughout the year, there are venues playing host to big international stars while local groups and jam sessions sneak into the early hours in snug bars on most nights of the week. *See also chapter* **Cafés and Bars.**

Alto Jazz Café
Korte Leidsedwarsstraat 115 (626 3249). Tram 1, 2, 5, 6, 7, 10, 11. **Open** 9pm-3am Mon-Thur, Sun; 9pm-4am Fri, Sat. **Admission** free.
Popular with Americans, this cosy and relaxed traditional brown bar is in an otherwise commercialised tourist area just off Leidseplein. Live jazz is played every night of the week by the in-house musicians and guests.

Bamboo Bar
Lange Leidsedwarsstraat 115 (624 3993). Tram 1, 2, 5, 6, 7, 10, 11. **Open** 9pm-3am Mon-Thur; 9pm-4am Fri-Sun. **Admission** free.
A small bar with a friendly crowd of regulars enjoying Brazilian and world music. Squeeze in for local blues and jazz every night except Sunday.

Bimhuis
Oudeschans 73 (623 1361). Tram 9, 14/Metro Nieuwmarkt/Waterlooplein. **Open** box office 8-9pm Thur-Sat. **Admission** ƒ15-ƒ25.
Opened in 1974, the city's major jazz venue stages a mixture of well-known international artists as well as avant-garde local talent in a subdued and reverent atmosphere. It's often hard to get a seat, so arrive early. There are free sessions on Monday through Wednesday from 9pm. Tickets cannot be booked, but are available on the day from the AUB or VVV tourist offices (*see chapter* **Essential Information**) or on the door one hour before performances.

Bourbon Street
Leidsekruisstraat 6 (623 3440). Tram 1, 2, 5, 6, 7, 10, 11. **Open** 9pm-3am Sun-Thur; 9pm-4am Fri, Sat. **Admission** free.
Spacious bar with a podium for jazz most nights of the week and a very late licence. Friendly staff and customers will make you feel at home. Performances can border on the poetic.

De Engelbewaarder
Kloveniersburgwal 59 (625 3772). Tram 4, 9, 14, 16, 24, 25/Metro Nieuwmarkt. **Open** noon-1am Sun-Thur; noon-3am Fri, Sat. **Admission** free.
Come here for a meal from the mid-price, varied menu and jostle with rowdy musicians who use the café as an office. The Sunday afternoon session draws an informed crowd of heavy drinkers restoring their alcohol balance from the previous night.

IJsbreker

Weesperzijde 23 (668 1805). Tram 3, 6, 7, 10/Metro Weesperplein. **Open** *box office* 9.30am-5.30pm Mon-Fri; *café* 10am-1am Mon-Thur, Sun; 10am-2am Fri, Sat. **Admission** *f*15-*f*22,50.

This venue is on the picturesque banks of the Amstel and is especially pleasant on summer evenings. The programming concentrates on contemporary classical music and experimental jazz. It's worth a visit for the bar alone even when there's no live performance. *See also chapter* **Music: Classical & Opera.**

Joseph Lam Jazz Club

Van Diemenstraat 8 (622 8086). Tram 3. **Open** 9pm-3am Sat; 9pm-2am Sun. **Admission** *f*7,50 Sat; free Sun.

A little off the beaten track, in an old harbour area to the west of Centraal Station. The crowd is an older group of jazz enthusiasts who go there to hear traditional and Dixieland jazz. Sunday night is the open stage session.

Festivals

It may be because of the geography or the Netherland's peculiarly festival-friendly narcotics legislation; it certainly isn't the weather. Whatever the reasons, Holland is host to a myriad music festivals catering for tastes ranging from the musical cabbage stew of **Racism Beat It!** through to the haute cuisine of the **North Sea Jazz Festival**. Many of the festivals take place in Amsterdam. Events such as the annual **World Roots Festival**, **Drum Rhythm** and **Tegentonen** head the field for the lesser publicised subsidiary events held throughout the year (*see also chapter* **Amsterdam By Season**). Tickets for most festivals are available from VVV offices and the AUB (*see chapter* **Essential Information** for both).

A Campingflight To Lowlands Paradise

Date last weekend in August. **Information** and tickets from VVV tourist offices and AUB ticket office. **Tickets** about *f*120 for three days.

About half an hour from Amsterdam by train, hidden in deepest Polderland near Dronten, these spacious scout jamboree pastures host a different kind of camp fire extravaganza every August when a horde of international artists takes a trip out to the countryside. Renowned for keeping the cleanest and most efficient facilities in the festival world, Lowlands is equipped with a supermarket, fully operational toilets and showers, and an appealing variety of sit-down restaurants and bars. Expect a heavy-duty line-up during the day with the likes of Biohazard, dEUS and Radiohead, followed by a nighttime fiesta of dance with DJs and bands lasting into the early hours.

Drum Rhythm Festival

Date about one week, usually in May/early June. **Information** and tickets: Jazz Inn record shop and AUB ticket office. **Tickets** *f*20-*f*40.

The Drum Rhythm Festival is all over the place both in terms of music and venues. Artists in 1995 included Dreadzone, the Skatalites, Soul Coughing and David Byrne. Venues range from the Beurs van Berlage and the Paradiso (*see above* **Venues**) to the cavernous Escape club and enormous hall of the RAI Congresgebouw.

Dynamo Open Air Festival

Date early to mid June. **Information** and tickets from VVV tourist offices and AUB ticket office. **Tickets** about *f*58 for three days.

Indisputably the loudest weekend in a field you're ever likely to experience. And, with a turnout of roughly nine billion stagediving, skateboarding adolescent devotees of MTV culture, it may give the distinct impression that the Dutch language contains at least 50 per cent American slang. Also, if you rely on the use of all major limbs it's probably not wise to head for front stage centre when Machine Head are due on. Previous highlights have also included Dog Eat Dog, NOFX and Biohazard.

Halfway Amsterdam

Date early to mid June. **Information** and tickets from VVV tourist offices and AUB ticket office. **Tickets** about *f*60.

A great day out to get you in full festival swing, this event takes place halfway between Amsterdam and Haarlem (hence the name), at the Recreatieterrein Spaarnwoude. Local talent such as Bettie Serveert and De Dijk groove along with the likes of Sheryl Crow, Galliano and Paul Weller. Organisers have resisted strong public pressure to rename the festival 'Mudbath Amsterdam'.

North Sea Jazz Festival

Date 3 days in mid-July. **Information** Festival organisers: PO Box 87840, 2508 DE Den Haag. **Tickets** from *f*95 per day, *f*225 for three-day pass, available in Amsterdam from Uitburo and VVV tourist offices.

Their policy of levying extra fees for individual performances makes this thing pricey to the point of being elitist, but on the other hand it is undoubtedly one of the best jazz festivals anywhere. Founded in the early 1970s, the festival (held in The Hague's Congresgebouw) showcases an astonishing list of international performers, from celebrated veterans such as Oscar Peterson and Lionel Hampton to the triumphant croonings of Tony Bennett and James Brown. The playlist is always eternal and everyone is catered for regardless of musical persuasion.

Parkpop

Date one day in late summer. **Information** and tickets available in Amsterdam from VVV tourist offices and AUB ticket office. **Admission** free.

The biggest of the numerous free, one-day festivals held each year in Holland, Parkpop is one of the few festivals that caters for both Dutch and international music in equal amounts. It's mainly second division acts on the bill, although this throws up the odd gem; last year saw great performances from both Sparks and Dick Dale. The crowd is very mixed, Parkpop is more a family day with a bit of music for good measure.

Pink Pop

Date one day in late May/early June. **Information** and tickets available in Amsterdam from VVV tourist offices and AUB ticket office. **Tickets** approx *f*60.

Held near Landgraaf, a small village in the south within spitting distance of both Belgium and Germany, this major outdoor pop festival usually has an impressive line-up of famous Dutch and international stars and is getting more and more popular every year. Expect to find a diverse mixture of artists such as Sinead O'Connor, Teenage Fanclub, Bad Religion and, of course, Biohazard on the bill. But be warned, it always seems to rain on the day.

Racism Beat It!

Date early September. **Information** from VVV tourist offices and AUB ticket office. **Admission** free.

Representatives from the world of sport, television, radio and music join hands and make their own contribution to the festival's theme. It's mainly a day for the Dutch media task force, with bands such as 2 Unlimited, The Scene and Lois Lane, plus assorted lesser purveyors of corporate schlock, all making a self-righteous stand. Generally a pretty tame affair.

Sport & Fitness

Skate on the canals, watch Ajax at home, play cricket in the Amsterdamse Bos, or take up korfball.

Besides their obvious passion for football, the Dutch are obsessed by the skate and the cycle. The Dutch landscape makes for ideal cycling terrain while the chill of the Dutch winter ensures that there's no end of suitable ice for sliding on, whether it be on your feet or on your arse.

In terms of individual fitness the Dutch tend to be horribly healthy; they probably have to be in order to compensate for the industrial amounts of tobacco and fried food that they consume. Accordingly there are excellent sports facilities in Amsterdam, from hi-tech gymnasia through to determined individuals dragging their unwilling frames around the city's various parks.

Leisure facilities are as equally developed, as befits one of the richest nations in the world. When they tire of their umpteen television channels, the Dutch are especially fond of saunas and have an almost perverse preoccupation with their suntans, hence the proliferation of sunbed centres. For further information on sports and leisure facilities and events in Amsterdam, phone the city's Sport and Recreation Department (552 2490). For all sorts of keep-fit and yoga courses, contact the local *buurtcentrum* (community centre).

Spectator Sports

Baseball

Pirates
Jan van Galenstraat Sportpark, Jan van Galenstraat (616 2151). Tram 13/Bus 19, 47. **Season** Apr-Oct.
Admission free.
Although recently relegated from the top flight, Amsterdam Pirates are still the city's top team. The good news for fans of what in Holland is known as 'honkbal', is that following relegation, admission is now free. The same applies for the women's team who are still in their respective top division. Matches are every Saturday at 2.30pm, with more matchday information available from the club secretary (684 8143).

Cricket

KNCB (Dutch Cricket Board)
Nieuwe Kalfjeslaan 21B, Amstelveen (645 1756/fax 645 1715). Bus 8, 26, 65, 146, 147, 170, 171, 172, 173.
Open 10am-5pm Mon-Thur. **Admission** free.
Cricket is still a minority sport, although the Dutch did compete in the last cricket World Cup, at last giving the English a chance to beat them at something. The Dutch team has also competed in English domestic cup competitions in the last couple of seasons. Amsterdam's premier club, the Amsterdam Cricket Club, plays its matches on Sundays from 10.30am in the peaceful surroundings of the Amsterdamse Bos (*see chapter* **Sightseeing**).

*Tackle some hockey with **Amsterdam** – the region's strongest club. Page 204.*

Cycling

Despite the terrain, the Netherlands has a tradition of producing professional cyclists who have excelled in the French Alps during the Tour de France. The most renowned is Joop Zoetemelk, runner-up six times before winning in 1980. In 1985, he finally became the world champion at the age of 38.

Most Dutch people follow the Tour de France avidly on TV and also watch the many *criteriums* (road races) all over Holland, in which their Tour de France heroes ride circuits around a village. Although on the decrease, these sometimes attract crowds of over 50,000. For further information, contact the Koninklijke Nederlandsche Wielren Unie (Dutch Cycle Federation), PO Box 136, Polanerbaan 15, 3447 GN Woerden (03480 11544).

If you want to cycle in the Netherlands, contact the Nederlandse Toer Fiets Unie (Netherlands Cycle Touring Union), Landjuweel 11, 3905 DE Veenendaal (08385 21421). For both cycle hire and for cycle touring, *see chapter* **Getting Around**.

Van Chaam

Chaam, Noord Brabant (016149 491503 – private number, please ring at reasonable times). **Dates** first Wed after Tour de France. **Admission** ƒ15.
The biggest and oldest *criterium* in the Netherlands attracts thousands of spectators. A hundred professional riders and twice as many amateurs cycle 12 times around the 8km (5 mile) circuit of this village in the south of the country.

Football

The big three excepted, professional football in Holland is still pretty much at grass roots level. Even in the Eredivisie, equivalent of the English Premier league, facilities border on the amateur. Few clubs entertain thoughts above their station; the usual highlight of their season being a trouncing from Ajax. Getting to see Ajax themselves will prove to be tricky; the opening of their new 50,000-seat stadium has coincided with an upsurge in their popularity – Ajax matches are almost entirely given over to season ticket holders. Meanwhile, on Sunday afternoons during the warmer months the Vondelpark tends to be one big footie game and most people are only too happy to let you join in. Highlights of the Dutch league are shown on TV every Sunday evening, usually at 6.45pm.

Ajax

(information on 691 2906). **Matches** *Sept-June* 2.30pm Sun.
See opposite **"Que sera, sera..."**.

Feyenoord

De Cuyp, Olympiaweg 50, Rotterdam (010 492 9499). **Admission** ƒ37, ƒ47, ƒ52. **Matches** *Sept-June* 2.30pm Sun.
Feyenoord have been the least sucessful of the big three over the last few years, but remain the best-supported club in the Netherlands. De Cuyp is the only stadium in Holland which can regularly boast an atmosphere. An additional plus is that matches are rarely sold out (capacity is 52,000).

PSV

Frederiklaan 10A, Eindhoven (040 250 5505). **Admission** ƒ25-ƒ65. **Matches** *Sept-June* 7.30pm Sat; 2.30pm Sun.
Following PSV's near domination of the domestic scene at the end of the 1980s, the Eindhoven club have fallen upon comparatively lean times although last season saw something of a renaissance, spearheaded by Dutch player of the year Luc Nilis and the gifted Brazilian, Ronaldo.

Hockey

Amsterdam

Wagener Stadium, Nieuwe Kalfjeslaan (640 1141). Bus *125, 170, 171, 172, 173, 194.* **Admission** league games free; *internationals* ƒ10-ƒ25. **Matches** *Sept-late May* 12.45pm Sun *(women)*; 2.30pm Sun *(men)*.
The strongest club in the region. Their 7,000-capacity stadium also hosts most of the national teams' home matches.

Korfball

As far as indigenous sports go, korfball is as good as the Dutch have been able to come up with. A shotgun marriage of netball and volleyball, korfball has caught on swiftly and the national federation now has more than 90,000 members. The season has three stages: from September to mid-November and from April to June matches are played outdoors; from mid-November to mid-April the game goes indoors.

Blauw Wit

Joos Banckersweg (Barbara Geeredzen 614 1614; private number, please ring at reasonable times). Tram *12, 14/Bus 15, 21.* **Admission** free. **Matches** 2pm Sun.

Rhoda

Sportpark Ookmeer, Willinklaan, Osdorp (611 0416). Bus *19, 68.* **Admission** usually free; *finals* ƒ5; free under-16s, over-65s. **Matches** 2pm Sun; occasionally 2pm Sat.

Motor Sports

TT Races

De Haar Circuit, Assen (05923 55000/fax 05923 56911/race day information 05923 313800). Exit Assen South off motorway A28, then follow signs. **Admission** grandstand ƒ85; circuit ƒ65; circuit ƒ50.
More than 100,000 people come to this week-long June event, which culminates in the Grand Prix races for sidecars and 125, 250 and 500cc bikes on the final Saturday. The European championships are run for all classes of bike on the Tuesday and the TT Formula One and historic TT races are on the Thursday. Real fanatics go along on the days in between to watch the practice laps. Tickets can be booked in advance from TT Assen, PO Box 150, 9400 AD Assen.

Zandvoort

Stichting Exploitatie Circuit Park, Burgermeester Van Alphenstraat (02357 18284). Train to Zandvoort from *Centraal Station.* **Admission** paddock ƒ35; grandstand ƒ17,50.
This car-racing track, about 30km (19 miles) from Amsterdam (*see chapter* **The Randstad**), was once a venue for Formula One racing and Zandvoort's administration still hope to persuade motorsport's top echelon to return. Meanwhile a programme of international races, including some nostalgic events, runs roughly every other weekend between March and October. Tickets are available at the door from 8am on the day.

"Que sera, sera..."

Just at the moment, Dutch football in general and Ajax Amsterdam in particular are very much in vogue. Dutch players are one of the most valued commodities in football, the jewel in the crown of many ambitious European clubs, while Ajax and their pragmatic if rather dull coach, Louis van Gaal, are headed toward apparent demi-god status. They also have a brand-new 50,000-seat stadium which, in terms of facilities if not atmosphere, is far and away the best in Europe, finally giving the club a stadium befitting their status. Previously, Ajax had played most of their games in 'De Meer', with a capacity of less than 20,000, while big games were played in the Olympic stadium.

Fans here, meanwhile, have to be some of the least vociferous in the world. Their chants are usually nicked from *Match of the Day* and their misinterpretations are, well... strange. ('Que sera, sera, we're coming from Amsterdam'?). Ajax supporters are the worst of the lot. They start hurling abuse at their own team if the score is still 0-0 after five minutes and, apart from at big matches, rarely manage much more than polite applause.

This changes when any two of Dutch football's ruling trimuvirate (Ajax, Feyenoord and PSV Eindhoven) come up against each other. Insults roll off the terraces (there are still standing areas in most Dutch stadia) but most of the fans' energy goes into beating the shit out of each other. This should not deter potential visitors. The mere presence of the Dutch riot police, known as the ME, is usually enough to quell all but the most

fanatical hooligans (although the ME are not above the odd pre-emptive strike, as England fans who were here in 1993 can confirm).

On the pitch the action (and the word is used loosely) is of a high technical standard but uniformly lacking in passion. The two teams trot out, Ajax score as many as they feel like and everyone goes home. Only in Europe do Ajax come up against consistently good opposition, and it is then that the superlatives heaped upon them become understandable. They play in exactly the same manner against the cream of Europe as they do when they turn out against FC Nobody in the Dutch league, seemingly intent on taking the piss right from the kick-off. Their tactic is to play keep-ball *ad infinitum*, at little more than snail's pace, then suddenly lurch into a lightning move which usually ends up with the ball in the back of the net. This can take anything from the first five minutes to the last five as it did against AC Milan in the 1995 European Cup Final. They then go back to playing their keep-ball game and there is usually precious little that the opposition can do about it.

When victories against the best in Europe come so easily the routine of domestic football can well be imagined. That the Dutch league has been won only twice in the last 20 years by teams outside of the top three doesn't add to the suspense either. In a good year it is never more than a two-horse race, which must leave Feyenoord supporters wondering how the hell they keep managing to come fifth.

*Close encounters of the **Ajax** kind – and even the roof lifts off.*

Basketball & Skateboarding

Basketball and skateboard devotees can dunk or skate for free on Museumplein, near the Rijksmuseum. There are several basketball courts, two skate ramps and usually a small crowd of teenage fashion statements in attendance.

Golf

Golf has become quite popular but is still considered élitist by most Dutch people. If you're a member of a British club, you are allowed to play on any Dutch course. Otherwise, you can only play on public courses.

Sloten

Sloterweg 1045 (614 2402). Bus 176, 179. **Open** *golf course* 8.30am-dusk Mon-Fri; *driving range* 8.30am-5.30pm Mon-Fri. **Cost** *golf course* ƒ18,50 per day; *driving range including hire of 60 balls* ƒ6,50.
A public course with nine holes and friendly staff. A half-set of golf clubs can be hired for ƒ10.

Spaarnwoude

Het Hogeland 2, Spaarnwoude (023 5385599). **Open** *summer* 7am-9pm daily; *winter* 8.30am-4pm daily. **Cost** *18-hole course* ƒ36 per round; *12-hole course* ƒ8 per round; *9-hole course* ƒ16 per round.
An 18-hole course with water and wind hazards. There are also 12- and 9-hole courses. No advance reservations but you can book by phone for the same day from 8.30am.

Health and Fitness

The Garden Gym

Jodenbreestraat 158 (626 8772). Tram 9, 14/Metro Waterlooplein. **Open** 9am-11pm Mon, Wed, Fri; noon-11pm Tue, Thur; 11am-6pm Sat; 10am-7pm Sun. **Admission** *1-day* training and shower; ƒ22,50 *training and sauna;* ƒ17,50 sauna only.
The cheapest all-in-one price in town gives you the choice of high and low impact and step aerobics, bodyshape, callisthenics and stretching. The floor isn't sprung.

Splash

Looiersgracht 26 (624 8404). Tram 7, 10. **Open** 10am-10pm Mon-Fri; 11am-6pm Sat, Sun. **Admission** *1-day pass* ƒ25; *1-week pass* ƒ50; *2-week pass* ƒ75; *1-month pass* ƒ150. **Credit** AmEx, V.
Facilities include a weights room, a Turkish bath, a massage service and sauna. Eight aerobics classes daily. Everything is free once you have paid admission.

Sporting Club Leidseplein

Korte Leidsedwarsstraat 18 (620 6631). Tram 1, 2, 5, 6, 7, 10, 11. **Open** 9am-midnight Mon-Fri; 10am-6pm Sat, Sun. **Admission** 1-day pass ƒ25.
A central health club with a weights room and a sauna.

Horseriding

De Amsterdamse Manege

Nieuwe Kalfjeslaan 25 (643 1342). Bus 63, 170, 171, 172. **Open** 9am-10pm Mon-Fri; 9am-5pm Sat; 9am-3pm Sun. **Cost** ƒ27,50/hr; ƒ21/hr 8-18s.
Outdoor rides with supervision in the Amsterdamse Bos (*see chapter* **Sightseeing**) with indoor rides also available. Take your own boots and riding hat. Booking essential.

Nieuw Amstelland Manege

Jan Tooropplantsoen 17 (643 2468). Bus 63, 170, 171, 172. **Open** 9am-midnight Mon-Fri; 9am-7pm Sat, Sun. **Cost** *adults* ƒ27,50/hr; *children* ƒ20/hr 6-16s.
Indoor rides only. Individual lessons cost ƒ65 per hour. Take your own boots and riding hat. Booking essential.

Saunas

Dutch saunas are mixed, so shed inhibitions along with clothes. Some health clubs (*see above* **Health and Fitness**) also have saunas. For women-only saunas *see chapter* **Women**; for saunas for gays and lesbians *see chapter* **Gay & Lesbian**.

Deco Sauna

Herengracht 115 (623 8215). Tram 1, 2, 5, 11, 13, 14, 17. **Open** 11am-11pm Mon-Sat; 1-6pm Sun. **Cost** *Mon-Fri before 2pm* ƒ16,50; *other times* ƒ24 for up to 5 hours. Quiet children tolerated: half-price for under-12s before 8pm.
The most beautiful sauna in town, with art deco glass panels and murals. Facilities include a Turkish steam room, a Finnish sauna, a cold plunge bath, footbaths, a solarium and a juice and snack bar. Soothing massages by appointment.

Oibibio

Prins Hendrikkade 20-21 (553 9311). Tram 1, 2, 4, 5, 9, 11, 14, 16, 17, 24, 25/Metro Centraal Station. **Open** 11am-midnight daily. **Cost** ƒ22 before 5pm; ƒ26 after 5pm; *(quiet) children* ƒ17,50.
The sauna in this New Age centre has all usual facilities plus such luxurious extras as mud baths, individually filled bubble baths with added essential oils (ƒ10 extra) and massages.

Snooker and Carambole

There are several halls where you can play snooker or pool fairly cheaply, although there are no tables in bars. When it comes to *biljart* (billiards), carambole, played on a table without pockets, is still the major variation. Below are some snooker and carambole centres where drinks are also sold.

Biljartcentrum Bavaria

Van Ostadestraat 97 (676 4059). Tram 3, 12, 16, 24, 25. **Open** 11am-1am Mon-Thur, Sun; 11am-2am Fri, Sat. **Cost** *snooker 11am-2pm* ƒ10/hr; *2pm-1am* ƒ15/hr; *carambole* ƒ10/hr.
Famous in Amsterdam for its billiards team, which plays in the first division of the league. There are four floors here: the third and fourth devoted to carambole and billiards, the second floor to snooker and the first to pool. Phone before turning up, as some evenings are for members only.

Snookercentrum de Keizer

Keizersgracht 256 (623 1586). Tram 13, 14, 17. **Open** 1pm-1am Mon-Thur, Sun; 1pm-2am Fri, Sat. **Cost** *1-7pm* ƒ8,50; *7pm-1am* ƒ15/hr; half-price if playing alone.
This place has eight snooker tables, all in separate rooms. There are telephones in all the rooms so players can phone orders down to the bar and have drinks sent up. Members pay a reduced rate but anyone is welcome to play here.

Snookerclub Overtoom

Overtoom 209 (618 8019). Tram 1, 6, 11/Bus 171, 172. **Open** 10am-1am Mon-Thur, Sun; 10am-2am Fri, Sat. **Cost** *10am-6pm* ƒ10/hr; *6pm-1am* ƒ15/hr. **Membership** ƒ50 per year.
The atmosphere in this former church is quiet, making it a club for the serious snooker player. While anyone can play here, members pay ƒ2,50 less per hour.

Horses for courses on the Amsterdamse Bos – **De Amsterdamse Manege***. Page 206*

Skating

When temperatures drop to freezing, the Dutch put on Walkmans and go skating on the iced-over polders, keeping warm with hot chocolate and alcoholic drinks bought from stalls on the banks. Although Amsterdammers skating on their own canals make a great spectacle, bear in mind that the canal water is dirty and the waterways hardly ever freeze completely in winter. Avoid areas around the edges and under bridges as these thaw first, and if there isn't another soul on the ice you'd be well advised not to venture out. A good place to skate in town is the Oosterpark pond which seems to stay frozen for longer than any other body of water, or the Grote Vijver and Bosbaan in the Amsterdamse Bos (*see* chapter **Sightseeing**) on the edge of town.

Jaap Edenhall

Radioweg 64 (694 9652). Tram 9/Bus 8, 69, 120, 169. **Open** *mid-Oct-early Mar* 8.30am-5pm, 7.30-9.30pm, Mon, Wed; 8.30am-5pm Thur; 8.30am-4.30pm, 8-10pm Tue, Fri; 2-4pm Sat; 10.30am-4.30pm Sun. **Admission** ƒ6; ƒ4 under-15s and OAPs. **Skate hire** ƒ6,50.
Though skate hire is only ƒ6,50, the staff will ask for a deposit of a passport, a driver's licence or ƒ100. The rink is open from the middle of October until the end of March.

Sports Centre

Borchland

Borchlandweg 8-12 (696 1441/1444). Metro Strandvliet. **Open** 7.30am-midnight Mon-Sat; 8.30am-midnight Sun. **Credit** AmEx, DC, MC, V.
The only big *omni-sportcentrum* (sports centre) in

Amsterdam, offering squash, outdoor and indoor tennis, tenpin bowling, badminton and a restaurant. Rates are higher in the evening and at weekends.

Squash

Dickysquash

Karel Lotsylaan 16 (646 2266). Metro Zuid/Bus 48, 63. **Open** 9am-midnight Mon-Sat; 9am-11pm Sun. **Cost** *court hire* ƒ15/30 mins, ƒ25/1 hour. **Membership** ranges from ƒ365 to ƒ595 per year.
Caters for the more experienced player.

Squash City

Ketelmakerstraat 6 (626 7883). Bus 18, 22. **Open** 8.45am-11.15pm Mon-Fri; 8.45am-9pm Sat, Sun. **Cost** court hire ƒ35/45 mins (2 people inc sauna and gym). **Credit** AmEx, MC, V.
The place to head for if you see squash as more of a hobby than a battle. You can use the sauna and weights room at no extra charge.

Swimming: indoor pools

As the indoor pools have different hours for different groups (fitness swimming for adults, swimming for all ages, family swimming and so on), it's best to phone for information. They usually have special times reserved for swimming lengths, in the early morning, mid-afternoon and evening.

Marnixbad

Marnixplein 9 (625 4843). Tram 3, 7, 10. **Admission** ƒ4,25, 12 sessions ƒ42,50; under-18s ƒ3,75, 12 sessions ƒ37,50.
As well as a 25m (82ft) indoor pool, with water slides and a whirlpool, Marnixbad also boasts a sauna.

*Sub-tropical aquatic fun at the **Mirandabad**.*

De Mirandabad
De Mirandalaan (644 6637). Tram 15, 69, 169.
Admission *f5,75; f4,50 4-17s; f4 over-65s.*
The only sub-tropical pool in Amsterdam, De Mirandabad
is very clean, with a stone beach and a wave machine that's
switched on every half hour. It's not good for swimming
lengths, but there's plenty of fun to be had on the waterslide,
and in the whirlpool and outdoor pool.

Zuiderbad
*Hobbemastraat 26 (679 2217). Tram 1, 2, 5/Bus 26, 66,
67, 170, 179.* **Admission** *f4,50; f4 under-18s; f2,50
over-65s.*
The Zuiderbad was built in 1912, making it one of the country's oldest pools. Extensively renovated in 1994, it still
retains its original, picturesque detail. There's nude swimming between 4pm and 5pm on Sundays.

Swimming: outdoor pools

During summer, open-air pools offer a good means
of escaping the city heat. The best ones are
Brediusbad (682 9116), a 1950s-style pool with
high diving boards, children's pools and sunbathing area; **Flevoparkbad** (692 5030), which

has two huge pools with kids' areas, playground
and sunbathing area. They're open daily (sometimes as late as 9pm) from around May 14 until
September 5. Phone for times and prices.

Table Tennis

Tafeltennis Centrum Amsterdam
Keizersgracht 209 (624 5780). Tram 13, 14, 17. **Open**
4pm-1am Mon-Sat; 1pm-1am Sun. **Cost** *f10 table/hr (inc
bats and balls). Booking essential.*
One of the only places where you can ping pong in town.
Showers and bar.

Tennis

There are four busy open-air courts at Vondelpark
(*see chapter* **Sightseeing**).

Amstelpark
*Karel Lotsylaan 8 (644 5436). Bus 26, 48, 63, 158/Metro
Zuid.* **Open** 8am-midnight daily. **Cost** *f35/hr; racket hire
free.* **Membership** *Oct 1-March 31 f500 Apr 1-Sept 30
f125.*
The Amstelpark has 36 courts in all. During the summer
there are ten indoor courts, and in the winter six of the outdoor courts are covered over, giving a total of sixteen indoor
courts. Reservations may be made by phone.

Kadoelen
Kadoelenweg – opposite 290 (631 3194). Bus 92. **Open**
9am-midnight daily. **Cost** *mid Sept-mid Apr Mon-Fri
9am-4pm f30/hr; after 4pm f40; summer f25/hr.*
Kadoelen is subsidised by the local council, so the nine indoor
courts cost less to hire than elsewhere. Tennis lessons can
be arranged in advance.

Watersports

Holland has serious amounts of water and watersports are accordingly very popular: sailboards are
considered normal holiday luggage for the Dutch.
If you want to go sailing, visit Loosdrecht
(25km/15 miles south east of Amsterdam) or go to
the IJsselmeer. In Muiden (20km/12 miles east of
Amsterdam) catamarans can be rented. For information about canoeing phone the Dutch Canoe
Federation on 033 62 2341. Most watersports
schools ask for a deposit when you rent a boat; a
passport usually suffices.

Duikelaar
*Sloterpark, Noordzijde 41 (613 8855). Tram 13, 14/Bus
19.* **Open** 9am-6pm Mon-Fri; 11am-5pm Sat, Sun. **Cost**
*sailing boat f15/hr; 1 and 2-person canoes f7,50/hr per
person; sailboard and wetsuit f15/hr.* **Deposit** *f100 plus
passport.*
On the banks of the Sloterplas lake (in the western suburbs),
you can rent small sailing boats, canoes and sailboards. The
season runs from May to October; from November to April
only canoes are available for hire. The Sloterparkbad indoor
and open-air (summer) swimming pools are here too.

Park Gaasperplas
Metro Gaasperplas/Bus 59, 60, 158, 174. **Open** 24 hours
daily.
Tucked away behind the Bijlmermeer in Amsterdam South-
East, this park's large lake is a centre for watersports and
windsurfing. There's also a campsite.

Theatre

Since the 1960s, when anti-establishment thespians hurled tomatoes at the old élite, Amsterdam theatres have been enjoying enormous international input.

The wide variety of theatre in the Netherlands is reflected in the range and number of venues offering quality work. Small, off-the-beaten-track theatres are just as likely to be home to interesting productions as the larger, more established, subsidised venues.

The Dutch theatrical tradition dates back to the middle ages and developed through the seventeenth-century when theatre companies used to perform all over Europe. In the Golden Age, Dutch was the international language of trade. Hooft, Bredero and Vondel were the most popular playwrights of the time and their plays are still performed, both in classic rendition as well as modern.

Throughout the eighteenth and nineteenth centuries, theatre was still by and for the people. It was not until the end of the nineteenth century that it became an élitist affair, something for those with an 'education' – actors and public alike. This attitude is still fairly entrenched, though in general not reflected in ticket prices – which tend to be very reasonable, compared, say, with London.

TOMATO SAUCE

In the late 1960s young actors and directors who wanted to introduce new ideas and forms into the theatre started the 'tomato action' – hurling tomatoes during performances at their older, established colleagues. At the time, Dutch theatre was controlled by a small, exclusive group of actors and directors. The aim of the tomato-throwing was to provoke discussion and it was obviously successful, since – as is the way of these things – the throwers themselves now form the Dutch theatre establishment.

They have begun to use works and acting styles from other parts of the world, influenced by the influx of information and talent from eastern Europe, and there has been an increasing number of co-productions and exchanges. It's striking how few original Dutch-language productions are currently being staged. However, all but a few productions in Amsterdam are performed in Dutch and this includes the work from the many avant-garde companies. The most innovative fringe groups are Nieuw West, Orkater, De Trust, Art & Pro and the Mexicaanse Hond. The forte of Dutch theatre is design: sets, lighting and costumes are often striking and innovative, while Dutch acting,

Dutch comedy features at **Kleine Komedie.**

certainly in the more commercial, mainstream companies, tends towards the declamatory.

CUTBACKS

In the mid-1980s the government started a programme of drastic cut-backs in arts support. Like some of the major orchestras, several companies have been forced to merge, and a few have disappeared altogether. And, as so often happens in these situations, 'serious' theatre loses out to more popular forms of entertainment, such as cabaret and musicals.

DRAMATIC EVENTS

Many of the larger Dutch cities host their own theatre festivals (*see below* **Festivals and Events**). Location theatre is another new development: venues such as fortresses, warehouses, factories

Look out for performances by the innovative **Tonnelgroep Amsterdam**.

and stables form an integral part of performances. Look out for upcoming performances by Griftheater, which operates between mime and the plastic arts; Dogtroep and choreographer/theatre-maker Shusaku Takeuchi (*see chapter* **Dance**).

ENGLISH-LANGUAGE THEATRE

Because virtually everyone in Amsterdam speaks English, there is a large potential audience for English-language theatre in the capital. However, there is quite a fast turnover of companies. In addition to the **Stalhouderij**, which has its own playing space, and **Theater de Bochel** which has converted a bathhouse into a playing space (for both, *see below* **Venues**), there are several other companies. Panache, for example, typically co-produces or manages two or three productions a season, usually in the summer. There is also a handful of groups – The Amsterdam Chamber Theatre (ACT), the Euro-American Theatre and Yell Theatre – who, though they produce plays less frequently, help keep the flow of English-language theatre constant. Stand-up

English-language comedy is increasingly popular in the in the capital. **Boom Chicago** and **Downstage West** best represent this fast-paced form of entertainment (*see below*).

INFORMATION AND BOOKINGS

Uitkrant is a monthly freesheet (*see chapter* **Essential Information**), with listings for almost every venue in Amsterdam. It's available in most theatres, bookshops and tourist information centres. For information (not reservations) on performances and concerts, phone 621 1211 (9am-9pm Mon-Sat). *What's On in Amsterdam* (ƒ3,50 from VVV tourist offices) gives details of selected events in English, and consult the *Time Out Amsterdam* web site at http://www.timeout.nl.

Tickets can be bought or reserved direct from theatre box offices, or from the **AUB Uitburo**, from 10am to 6pm Mon to Sat (until 9pm on Thur; *see chapter* **Essential Information**). There is a ƒ2 booking charge, ƒ5 for credit card booking by phone. You can also reserve or purchase tickets from one of the **VVV** tourist offices, or through their telephone reservation service (06 34034 066 – 50c per minute extra phone charge); there is a ƒ3,50 surcharge on the price of tickets. Unless otherwise stated, credit cards are not accepted at the venues listed. For details on the CJP card (a discount card for under-26s), go to the **AUB Uitburo**.

Venues

Amphitheater

Paviljoen 1, Marius van Bouwdijk Bastiaanstraat 54 (entrance opposite 1e Helmerstraat 115) (616 8942 noon-5pm Mon-Fri). Tram 1, 3, 6, 11, 12. **Open** *box office* one hour before start of performance. **Tickets** ƒ15; ƒ7,50, ƒ12,50 CJP, over-65s. **Performances** 8.30pm or 9pm.
The complex where this alternative theatre workshop is housed used to be a hospital, but the smell of disinfectant has long gone now. It provides a stage for smaller (co)productions, often of an experimental nature.

De Balie

Kleine Gartmanplantsoen 10 (623 2904 2-8pm Tue-Fri, 5-8pm Sat). Tram 1, 2, 5, 6, 7, 10, 11. **Open** *box office* 5-8.30pm Tue-Sat. **Tickets** ƒ10-ƒ17,50; ƒ2,50 off CJP, over-65s. **Performances** at varying times.
This centre of international culture, including theatre, music and literature also stages lectures, debates, discussions and special projects, all of which informally influence Amsterdam's sometimes controversial political opinions and lifestyle. *Café. Wheelchair access.*

Bellevue

Leidsekade 90 (624 7248). Tram 1, 2, 5, 6, 7, 10, 11. **Open** *box office* 11am-6pm Mon; 11am-8.30pm Tue-Sun times vary. **Tickets** ƒ17,50, ƒ15; ƒ5 discount CJP card holders. **Performances** 8.30pm as well as lunchtime shows. **Credit** AmEx, DC, EC, MC, V.
Bellevue hosts serious spoken theatre by state-subsidised companies such as the Ro Theater; lesser-known interesting companies like Het Volk; physical comedy by the likes of Carver and dance. It's here you'll find new Dutch cabaret artistes as well as modern dance companies such as Krisztina de Châtel and Reflex (*see chapter* **Dance**). *Café. Wheelchair access by arrangement.*

Badhuis Theater De Bochel

Andreas Bonnstraat 28 (668 5102). Tram 3, 6, 7, 10. **Open** *box office* 7pm-start of performance. **Reservations** taken until 30 mins before showtime. **Tickets** ƒ17,50, ƒ12,50. **Performances** at varying times.
Once a public bathhouse, Theater De Bochel now plays host to a variety of guest artists and performers who often work in English. As well as reworking established scripts, these guests tend to produce a lot of their own off-beat creations. The atmosphere is relaxed and friendly, usually seen by a mixed bunch of nationalities. East European work can often be seen here. *Café.*

Boom Chicago

Lijnbaansgracht 238 (639 2707). Tram 1, 2, 5, 6, 7, 10, 11. **Open** *box office* noon-8pm daily; *dinner and seating* from 7pm daily; *show* 8.15pm daily. **Tickets** ƒ25 (4th person free). **Credit** AmEx, MC, V.
Funny, fast-paced American improvised (mainly) comedy show in a laid-back setting. Some of the sketches are rehearsed, others are based on suggestions (a lot of them predictable Amsterdam clichés such as dope and sex, but it's none the worse for that) from the audience. Dinner and drinks are served throughout the show, and it all adds up to a great evening out. Runs from May to late September.

De Brakke Grond

Nes 45 (626 6866/624 0394). Tram 4, 9, 14, 16, 24, 25. **Open** *box office* 1-6pm, or 8.30pm if there is a performance; until 7.30pm if performance in the Frascati, Mon-Sat; 12.30pm-start of performance Sun. **Tickets** *Rodezaal* ƒ17,50; *Expozaal* ƒ20; *studio* ƒ12,50, reductions for CJP cardholders and over-65s. **Performances** 8.30pm. Also Sunday matinées and lunchtime shows.
Operating on a similar artistic basis to its neighbour, the **Frascati**, with which it shares a box office (*see below*), De Brakke Grond places more emphasis on Flemish productions. Exhibitions are also regularly held here. *Café.*

Cosmic Theater

Nes 75 (622 8858 2-5pm). Tram 4, 9, 14, 16, 24, 25. **Tickets** ƒ15, no concessions. **Performances** 8.30pm.
Cosmic Theater is a relatively new arrival on the theatre boulevard, with programming geared towards the new, multicultural Europe. *Café.*

Felix Meritis

Keizersgracht 324 (623 1311). Tram 1, 2, 5, 11, 13, 17. **Open** *box office* 10am-5pm Mon; 10am until time of last performance Tue-Sat. **Tickets** ƒ16,50, ƒ20; ƒ12,50, ƒ16,50 concessions for CJP, over-65s. **Performances** usually at 8.30pm.
This beautiful, early nineteenth-century building was the centre of fringe theatre in the early 1970s. A multicultural programme covers theatrical performances, dance, music, video and seminars. Some of the best Dutch dance has been premièred here, including the work of the first lady of Dutch dance, Truus Bronkhorst. Budget cuts in recent years have changed programming policies and the theatre doesn't operate on the scale it used to. *Café.*

Frascati

Nes 63 (626 6866/623 5723). Tram 4, 9, 14, 16, 24, 25. **Open** *box office* see **Brakke Grond** above. **Tickets** *Zaal 1* ƒ17,50; *Zaal 2* ƒ15; *Zaal 3* ƒ7,50; concessions for CJP cards holders and over-65s. **Performances** times vary.
One of the better venues for interesting new work, with one large auditorium and two smaller ones. *Café.*

Koninklijk Theater Carré

Amstel 115-125 (622 5225). Tram 4, 6, 7, 10. **Open** *box office.* **Tickets** ƒ25-ƒ100; concessions for CJP, over-65s (only on day of performance). **Performances** 8.15pm. **Credit** AmEx, DC, EC, MC, V
Once home to a circus, Carré now hosts some of the best Dutch comedians and cabaret artistes. It is also the traditional venue for Dutch versions of popular British and North American musicals. Other offerings include folk dance and revues. The theatre has just undergone major refurbishment. Backstage tours take place at 3pm on Wednesdays and Saturdays. A tour costs ƒ5 per person, phone for reservations.

Melkweg

Lijnbaansgracht 234A (624 1777). Tram 1, 2, 5, 6, 7, 10, 11. **Open** *box office* 1-5 pm Mon-Fri; from 7.30pm Wed-Sun; 4-6pm Sat, Sun; phone reservations 10am-8pm daily. **Tickets** ƒ10 plus membership; concessions for CJp, over-65s. **Membership** 1 month ƒ4; 3 months ƒ6; year ƒ20.
This multi-media centre behind the Stadsschouwburg (*see below*) opened its doors in 1970 on the site of a former milk factory. The symbol of Amsterdam liberalism and tolerance in the 1970s, the Melkweg has managed to retain its worldwide reputation as a cultural meeting place. In 1983 it became a founder member of Transeuropehalles, an international network of multi-media cultural groups. It is also one of the few places where 'new dance' can be seen and foreign touring

companies, of both dance and movement theatre, often make a brief stop here. *See also chapters* **Galleries, Film, Music: Rock, Folk & Jazz** *and* **Clubs.**
Café.

De Nieuw Amsterdam
Spuistraat 2 (627 8672/8699). Tram 1, 2, 5, 14, 17. **Open** *box office* 10am-5pm Mon-Fri; also 7.30pm-start of performance. **Tickets** *f*15; *f*12,50 CJP card holders, over-65s.
De Nieuw Amsterdam (DNA) is a network of artists of many nationalities producing 'non-western' productions both in their own space and on tour. This multicultural theatre also runs a school programme for youths interested in attending a theatre academy in the future. DNA is the brainchild of renowned director, Rufus Collins.

De Stadsschouwburg
Leidseplein 26 (624 2311). Tram 1, 2, 5, 6, 7, 10, 11. **Open** *box office* 10am-start of performance Mon-Sat; from one and a half hours before performances on Sundays and holidays. **Tickets** *f*14-*f*45; concessions for CJP card holders, over-65s. **Performances** 8.15pm.
Credit AmEx, EC, V.
The Stadsschouwburg (municipal theatre) is into its third incarnation: the first two buildings were destroyed by fire in the seventeenth and eighteenth centuries. The present theatre, opened in 1894, is a beautiful and impressive baroque building built in the traditional horseshoe shape and seating about 950. Director Cox Habbema is responsible for a policy which not only nurtures traditional Dutch theatre, but also stages a wide variety of contemporary national and international productions. There's also a space for small-scale productions here, called the Bovenzaal.
Café.

De Stalhouderij
1e Bloemdwarsstraat 4 (626 2282; 1-6pm). Tram 13, 14, 17. **Open** *box office* 8pm-start of performance. **Tickets** *f*15; *f*12,50 CJP card holders, over-65s, students. **Performances** 8.30pm.
This former livery-stable is the smallest theatre in Amsterdam – the size of an average living-room – and is unusually intimate. It is the one place where every performance played is in English.
Wheelchair access with help.

Studiotheater
Lijnbaansgracht 238 (behind Stadsschouwburg) (625 5454). Tram 1, 2, 5, 6, 7, 10, 11. **Open** *box office* times and prices vary with production.
This flexible 'black box' theatre hosts an assortment of usually smaller ad hoc productions, often in English. No programming policy, which means that just about anything goes. In the summer, the theatre is home to **Boom Chicago** (*see above*).

Vondelpark Theatre
Vondelpark (673 1499). Tram 1, 2, 3, 5, 7, 10, 11, 12. **Performances** Early June-early Sept, Wed-Sun. Free.
Throughout the summer months, the Vondelpark hosts a wide variety of theatre and music. The open-air theatre is in the middle of the park by the fountain. Cabaret, drama, concerts, kids' programmes and dance all feature. The atmosphere alone is worth experiencing. *See also chapter* **Music: Rock, Folk & Jazz.**

Westergasfabriek
Haarlemmerweg 8-10 (info and tickets from AUB: 621 1211). Tram 10/bus 18, 22. **Performances** 8.30pm. **Tickets** *f*25-*f*28.
This former gas factory complex has recently been turned into a theatrical breeding ground. On any given evening there might be up to five different performances, in just as many disciplines. Ideal for location projects and repertory theatre alike.

Bookshop

International Theatre & Film Books
Leidseplein 26 (in the Stadsschouwburg building, to the right of the main entrance) (622 6489). Tram 1, 2, 5, 6, 7, 10, 11. **Open** noon-6pm Mon; 10am-6pm Tue-Sat.
Credit AmEx, DC, EC, MC, V.
This shop offers a wide variety of international magazines and books on the stage and screen. There are books on everything from history to theatre management, often in English, as well as texts of current productions.

Festivals and Events

Holland Festival
Bookings (from February) *Nederlands Reserverings Centrum, Postbus 404, 2260 AK Leidschendam (070 320 2500/credit card bookings 020 621 1211).* **Tickets** *f*20-*f*100. **Direct sales** (from May) from AUB Uitburo and VVV offices and individual theatres. **Credit** AmEx, DC, EC, MC, V.
Amsterdam's most prestigious festival takes place throughout June every year and presents not only theatre, but also music and dance. Advance programme information is available from Holland Festival, Kleine Gartmanplantsoen 21, 1017 RP Amsterdam (627 6566; open 9am-6pm Mon-Fri).

Over het IJ Festival
Reservations and information 636 1083 (10am-5pm Mon-Fri) or from AUB: 621 1211.
A summer-long outdoor festival of larger location projects, this festival is one of the most exciting in Amsterdam. All performances take place across the IJ channel in Amsterdam North. Look out for productions by Traject Theater and Griftheater in particular. The festival kicks off in June with a month of indoor dance and movement theatre performances.

International Theatre School Festival
Reservations to be made at the specific venues.
Information *626 1241/638 3346.* **Tickets** *f*15; *f*12,50; reductions for CJP.
A festival of theatre school productions from all over the world takes place at the end of June in the Nes theatres, as they are called: De Brakke Grond; Cosmic Theater; De Engelenbak; Frascati, and at the Stadsschouwburg (*above*). The programme is quite varied, with productions from theatre schools based in the Netherlands as well as abroad.

Uitmarkt
Various locations: Museumplein, Dam, and sites along the Amstel. **Dates** last weekend in August.
In the last weekend of August every year, theatres, performing artists and companies preview and sell their programmes for the coming season. From Friday to Sunday, outdoor stages are set up in squares around Amsterdam's centre, with free music, dance, theatre and cabaret performances. *See also chapter* **Amsterdam By Season.**

Theatre Museum

Nederlands Theatermuseum
Herengracht 168-170 (623 5104). Tram 13, 14, 17. **Open** 11am-5pm Tue-Sun. **Admission** *f*5; *f*3 students, CJP card holders; free under-4s.
The museum forms part of The Netherlands Theatre Institute, which also houses an excellent library and a theatre bookshop. The building itself is an example of seventeenth-century splendour. The collection includes a fine eighteenth-century miniature theatre, modelled after the second Stadsschouwburg with working rain, thunder and wind machines. Also holds exhibitions. *See chapter* **Museums.**
Guided tours (min 15 people).

Early Hours

Shops, food and liquid fuel for night owls and early birds.

Those used to draconian drinking laws may well be happy with Amsterdam's closing times, but if you want to throw caution to the wind and carry on boozing all night, there are indeed places where you can continue to satisfy your thirst.

First things first: accidents do happen even in this comparatively safe corner of the world. In such an eventuality, ring 0611 for the emergency services, for less immediate medical emergencies *see chapter* **Survival** for a list of 24 hour casualty departments. If it is a late-night chemist or pharmacist that is required, ring 06 35032042 (24 hours) for the Centrale Dokters Dienst (Central Medical Service). Alternatively, check the daily newspaper *Het Parool*, which publishes details of which *apotheken* (pharmacies) are open late that week. Details should also be posted in the local *apothheek* window.

If you need to change money, the GWK bureaux de change in Centraal Station and Schiphol Airport are both open 24 hours daily. For night shops *see chapter* **Shopping**.

The city's public transport ceases to function after midnight; there are night buses but even they become sporadic in the smallest of the small hours. Nightbuses are numbered from 71 to 77, with numbers 73 to 76 running through the city centre. The relevant stops have a black square with the bus number printed on it, but you could be waiting for a while; between 2am and 4am on weekdays and 2.30am and 3.30am on the weekend there are no services whatsoever.

Which leaves taxis or your own two feet, and whether well oiled or just fatigued, the chances are you'll take a taxi. They can be found on ranks at Centraal Station, Dam, Rembrandtplein, Leidseplein and the junction of Kinkerstraat and Marnixstraat. They can be ordered by phoning the 24 hour central taxi control on 677 7777. If you are eccentric enough to be driving around Amsterdam in your own car, the main 24-hour petrol stations (*benzinestations*) within Amsterdam are: Gooisweg 10-11; Sarphatistraat 225; Marnixstraat 250 and Spaarndammerdijk 218.

Night Bars

Koophandel
Bloemgracht 49 (623 9843). Tram 10, 13, 14, 17. **Open** 4pm-very late.
What more do you want? A bar that is not too sure as to when it closes, except that it will probably be daylight. Koophandel is for the dedicated drinker and a popular haunt for bohemian arty types. Don't bother turning up before mid-

night because it will be virtually empty, and don't expect to stumble out before the next day dawns.

De Pieter
St Pieterspoortsteeg 29 (623 6007). Tram 4, 9, 14, 16, 24, 25. **Open** 11pm-3am Mon-Thur, Sun; 11pm-4am Fri, Sat.
Something of a student hang-out which resembles a typical brown café. This is a small, dark and noisy bar that gets even smaller and noisier when the owner decides to squeeze in a live band.

Riba
Marnixstraat 5 (623 3235). Tram 3. **Open** 7pm-1am Mon-Thur, Sun; 10pm-4am Fri, Sat.
They have chilli peppers on the bar here. Sliced and raw. The regulars, who are mainly of Turkish extraction and very friendly, eat them. They will encourage you to do the same. Under no circumstances should you do so. Follow this bit of advice and a splendid time is guaranteed for all; this is a great café in the finest Amsterdam singalong tradition.

San Francisco
Zeedijk 40-42 (623 2871). Metro Centraal Station. **Open** midnight-5am daily.
The décor in San Francisco would not look out of place in *Saturday Night Fever*, but the staff are friendly and genuine. This is a warm and accommodating venue despite its unaccomadating location.

De Waag
Zeedijk 130 (624 6449). Metro Nieuwmarkt. **Open** 12.30-6am daily.
Almost on the Nieuwmarkt and undeniably atmospheric, De Waag is smoky, dimly lit and overtly a hard-drinking bar. Slightly intimidating it may be, but this is a genuine Amsterdam night-café, warts and all.

Food

Most of the so-called night restaurants are in and around the Leidseplein and vary from okay to awful. Luckily for them the late-night gastronome tends to have taste buds anaesthetised by copious quantities of alcohol and they can get very busy after 1am. An alternative is Amsterdam's myriad snack bars. Many of these stay open late, the best bet being one of the Febo or Barbarella chains. Those around the Leidseplein are basically open around the clock; Barbarella are first off the mark with a greasy spoon type breakfast, available from 6.30am at weekends.

Bojo
Lange Leidsedwaarsstraat 51 (622 7434). Tram 1, 2, 5, 6, 7, 10, 11 **Open** 5pm-2am Mon-Thur, Sun; 5pm-3am Fri, Sat
An Indonesian restaurant of variable quality (although the vegetarian special is always good) in the middle of Amsterdam's late-night area. It's often crowded and noisy with often a long wait to get served, even by Amsterdam's snail's pace service standards.

In Focus

Business

Need a translator, a fax machine or somewhere to hold a conference? Amsterdam's business services at a glance.

Information

Many of the agencies listed below are in The Hague (Den Haag). For details of embassies, consulates and libraries, *see chapter* **Survival**.

American Chamber of Commerce
Van Karnebeeklaan 14, 2585 BB Den Haag (070 3659808). **Open** 9am-4pm Mon-Fri.

British Embassy, Commercial Department
Lange Voorhout 10, 2514 ED Den Haag (070 364 5800). **Open** 9am-1pm, 2.15-5.30pm, Mon-Fri.
This office co-operates with the British Department of Trade and Industry to assist British companies operating in the Netherlands.

British-Netherlands Chamber of Commerce
Bezuidenhoutseweg 181, 2594 AH Den Haag (070 347 8881). **Open** 9am-4pm (trade enquiries in person 10am-noon, 2-4pm; over the phone 10am-noon, 1.30-4pm) Mon-Fri.

Centraal Bureau voor Statistiek (CBS)
Prinses Beatrixlaan 428, 2273 XZ Voorburg (070 337 3800). **Open** 9am-noon, 2-5pm Mon-Fri.
The Central Bureau for Statistics provides statistics on every aspect of Dutch business, society and the economy.

Commissariaat voor Buitenlandse Investeringen Nederland (Netherlands Foreign Investment Agency)
Bezuidenhoutseweg 2, 2594 AV Den Haag (070 379 72333/fax 070 379 6322). **Open** 8am-6pm Mon-Fri.
Probably the most useful first port of call for business people wishing to relocate to the Netherlands.

Douane Amsterdam (Customs)
Leeuwendalersweg 21 (586 7511). Tram 12, 14/bus 21, 68, 80. **Open** 8am-5pm Mon-Fri.

Douane Rotterdam (Customs)
West Zeedijk 387, Rotterdam (010 478 7922). **Open** 8am-4.30pm Mon-Fri.

Economische Voorlichtingsdienst, EVD (The Netherlands Foreign Trade Agency)
Bezuidenhoutseweg 151, 2594 AG Den Haag (070 379 8933). **Open** 9am-4pm Mon-Fri.
A useful library and information centre for business people. It incorporates the Netherlands Council for Trade Promotion (NCH), another handy source of information.

Kamer van Koophandel (Chamber of Commerce)
De Ruijterkade 5 (523 6600). Tram 1, 2, 4, 5, 9, 11, 13, 16, 17, 24, 25. **Open** 8.30am-4pm Mon-Fri.
Amsterdam's Chamber of Commerce is a spanking new

building on the harbour front. Staff have lists of import/export agencies, government trade representatives and companies by sector. They will also advise on legal procedure, finding an office and hiring local staff. The bureaucracy can be baffling, but persevere: once you've found the right person, you can get all the information you need.

Ministerie van Economische Zaken (Ministry of Economic Affairs)
Bezuidenhoutseweg 30, 2594 AV Den Haag (070 379 8911). **Open** 9am-4pm Mon-Fri.
The information department of this ministry will try to provide answers to general queries concerning the Dutch economy. But you'll probably find detailed enquiries are referred to the EVD (Netherlands Foreign Investment Agency, *see above*).

Ministerie van Buitenlandse Zaken (Ministry of Foreign Affairs)
Bezuidenhoutseweg 67, Den Haag (070 348 6486). **Open** 9am-4pm Mon-Fri.
Staff at the Ministry's information department will answer general queries only. Detailed enquiries will probably be referred to the EVD (Netherlands Foreign Investment Agency, *see above*).

Banking

The branches listed below are head offices. Most do not have general banking facilities, but staff will be able to provide a list of branches that do. For information about foreign exchange, *see chapter* **Essential Information**.

ABN AMRO
Vijzelstraat 68 (629 2940). Tram 6, 7, 10, 16, 24, 25. **Open** 9am-5pm Mon-Fri.
ABN and AMRO, the Netherlands' two biggest banks, merged at the end of 1990 to be become one big super bank. This is their main office.

Citibank NA
Hoogoorddreef 54B (651 4211). Bus 62, 137, 158, 163, 164, 174-176, 187-189. **Open** 9am-5pm Mon-Fri.
Affiliated to the US Citibank, deals with business transactions only.

Credit Lyonnais Bank Nederland NV
Strawinskylaan 3093 (504 7070). Tram 5/NS railway from Schiphol Airport to RAI station. **Open** 9am-6pm Mon-Fri.
Deals with business transactions only – their consumer banking department has now been taken over by the Belgian Generale Bank.

Generale Bank
Buitenveldertselaan 3a (404 0510). Tram 5/Metro 51. **Open** 9am-4pm Mon-Fri.
The Generale Bank now also deals with the consumer banking department of the Credit Lyonnais Bank Nederland.

*The **ING** head office at Bijlmerplein.*

ING Group
Bijlmerplein 888 (563 9111). Bus 59, 60, 62, 137/Metro Bijlmer. **Open** 9am-4pm Mon-Fri.
Incorporates the 50 Amsterdam branches of the post office bank, offering full banking and exchange services.

Lloyds Bank
Leidseplein 29 (524 9300). Tram 1, 2, 5, 6, 7, 10, 11. **Open** 9am-5pm Mon-Fri.
Only business transactions can be carried out here.

Rabobank
Wilhelminaplantsoen 120 (569 0510). Bus 136. **Open** 9am-5pm Mon-Fri.
Rabobank has 29 Amsterdam branches.

Société Générale
Museumplein 17 (571 1500). Tram 3, 5, 12, 16. **Open** 9am-5pm Mon-Fri.
Only commercial transactions are undertaken by this bank.

Swiss Bank Corporation
Hoogoorddreef 5 (651 0595). Bus 62, 137, 158, 163, 164, 174-176, 187-189. **Open** 8.30am-5.00pm Mon-Fri.
Commercial transactions only.

Verenigde Spaarbank
Singel 548 (624 9340). Tram 4, 9, 14, 16, 24, 25. **Open** 9am-5pm Mon-Fri.
Full banking facilities in their 41 Amsterdambranches.

Exchanges

Effectenbeurs (Stock Exchange)
Beursplein 5 (523 4567). Tram 4, 9, 14, 16, 24, 25. **Open** 9.30am-4.30pm Mon-Fri.
Stock for officially listed Dutch companies is traded here.

Nederlandse Termijnhandel (Dutch Association of Futures and Options Traders)
Damrak 261 (638 2239). Tram 4, 9, 14, 16, 24, 25. **Open** 9am-5pm Mon-Fri.

The commodity exchange for trading futures in potatoes and pigs.

Optiebeurs (European Options Exchange)
Rokin 65 (550 4550). Tram 4, 9, 14, 16, 24, 25. **Open** 9am-5pm Mon-Fri.
The EOE opened in 1987 and is now the largest options exchange in Europe. Trading share, gold and silver options as well as bond and currency options, it books about 55,000 transactions daily: way ahead of the City of London. Tours around this impressive building are possible if you make a prior appointment. You can watch trading on the floor from a visitors' balcony. Phone to reserve a place.

Conferences

Amsterdam has established itself as an important congress and conference venue. Most major hotels offer full conference facilities and the city's main congress centre, the **RAI** (*see below*) hosts some 65 international events a year. A number of specialist conference organisers have sprung up to arrange these events.

Grand Hotel Krasnapolsky
Dam 9 (554 9111/fax 622 8607/telex 12262 KRAS NL). Tram 1, 2, 4, 5, 9, 11, 14, 16, 24, 25.
Bang in the centre of the city, the recently refurbished Krasnapolsky (*see chapter* **Accommodation**) now has the most comprehensive in-hotel meeting facilities, including a convention centre for up to 2,000 people. The largest meeting room is suitable for conferences of up to 700.

RAI Congresgebouw
Europlein (549 1212; exhibition centre and restaurant: fax 646 4469/telex for offices only 13499). Tram 4, 25/NS railway from Schiphol Airport to RAI Station. **Open** *office and enquiries* 9am-5pm Mon-Fri.
A self-contained congress and trade fair centre in the south of the city. The building contains nine halls totalling

63,000sq m/56,000sq yds of covered exhibition space and 19 conference rooms which can seat between 40 and 1,750 people. Full translation and business services are available.

Stichting de Beurs van Berlage (Berlage Exchange Foundation)
Damrak 277 (626 5257/fax 620 4701). Tram 4, 9, 14, 16, 24, 25. **Open** *office and enquiries* 9am-5pm Mon-Fri.
This stunning building was completed in 1903, to be used as a commodity exchange (*see chapter* **Architecture**). Later (1978-1987) it was the venue for the European Options Exchange. It is now used for cultural events and smaller trade fairs (up to 2,500 visitors can be provided with buffet dinners). Berlage Hall, within the building, provides a stylish conference venue for between 50 and 200 people.

World Trade Center
Strawinskylaan 1 (575 9111/fax 662 7255/telex 12808). Tram 5/NS railway from Schiphol Airport to RAI Station. **Open** *office and enquiries* 9am-5pm Mon-Fri.
Just about anything you might need to run a conference can be provided here. Facilities include an international press centre, small studios for top-level meetings and 14 business-class rooms seating from four to 40 people. A conference room seating up to 250 costs ƒ1,550 per full day of 8am-11pm (excluding VAT and services). Worldwide conference facilities and secretarial, translating and legal services can be supplied. *See also below* **Office Services**.

Conference Organisers

NOVEP (Netherlands Organization Bureau for Events and Projects)
Amaleastraat 7, 2514 JC, Den Haag (070 3421722/070 342 1707/fax 070 361 4461). **Open** 9am-5pm Mon-Fri.
VCO (Meeting and Congress Organisation, of NOVEP) will organise congresses or conferences to your specifications. This bureau was moving in September 1996. At the time of going to press the new address was not known, but their telephone number will be the same.

QTL Convention Services
Keizersgracht 782 (626 1372/fax 625 9574). Tram 4. **Open** 9am-5.30pm Mon-Fri. **Credit** AmEx, EC, V.
These specialists in teleconferencing will organize and supply the equipment for congresses and seminars.

Business Services

You can send faxes from some district post offices and from Telehouse 24 hours daily, but some commercial outfits, such as Telecenter, are less expensive. For details, *see chapter* **Survival**. Lots of tobacconists and copy shops have fax facilities too. Major hotels have fax services for guests (and sometimes non-guests, if the hotel is not too busy), but prices are high. The World Trade Center (*listed under* **Office Hire**) also has full reception and transmission facilities.

Couriers and Shippers

Fedex
Berquetlaan 20-22, Oudemeer (06-0222333 free call).
Americans used to Fedex's overnight service will be happy to know that even from Amsterdam their package can be delivered to the US by 10.30 the next morning, albeit with a slightly steeper price tag. Your package will be picked up by a multilingual driver who will even fill out the form for you.

International Couriers Amsterdam
Coenhavenweg Loods 8, Pier Asia (686 7808/7805). Bus 40. **Open** 24 hours daily.
This worldwide courier service will transport packages across Amsterdam within an hour for ƒ19,50. Rates for London (up to 0.5kg/1.1lb, arriving before noon the following day) start at ƒ80.

XP Express Systems
Parellaan 14, 2132 WS Hoofdorp (06 099 1234/fax 023 5627901). **Open** 8.30am-9pm Mon-Fri.
Documents of up to 250g/9oz can be delivered to London within 24 hours for ƒ106 (ƒ141 for parcels up to 1kg/2.2lb). Overnight delivery to destinations throughout the Netherlands costs ƒ40 plus ƒ1,50 per kilogram.

Forwarding Agents

Geytenbeek BV
De Rutherfordweg 150, 3542 CN Utrecht (030 2412416/fax 030 2415181). **Open** 8.30am-5.30pm Mon-Fri.
A business removals and exhibition delivery service, Geytenbeek deals with all customs formalities.
Branch: RAI Congresgebouw, Europaplein 8 (644 8551).

Mailing services

Mail & More
Nieuwezijds Voorburgwal 86 (638 2836/fax 638 3171). Tram 1, 2, 5, 11. **Open** 9am-5.30pm Mon-Fri.
Mail & More will deal with your mail requirements, such as mailouts, as well as providing a message service, fax and photocopying services and word processing.

Printing and Duplicating

Grand Prix Copyrette
Weteringschans 84A (627 3705). Tram 16, 24, 25. **Open** 9.00am-6pm Mon-Fri.
There are a number of branches of this firm around the city. Each offers both monochrome and colour copying, ring binding, fax services and laser printing. The Amsteldijk branch is also open 11am-4pm Sat.
Branch: Amsteldijk 47 (671 4455).

Multicopy
Weesperstraat 65 (624 6208/620 4922). Bus 31/Metro Waterlooplein. **Open** 8am-7pm Mon-Fri; noon-4pm Sat.
Typical of Amsterdam's slickly run photocopy shops, the machines here are metered, so rather than annoying staff by asking for change, you pay a total on your way out. You can make colour and monochrome copies in A4, A3 and A2 sizes, on white or coloured paper.

Translations (Vertalingen)

Berlitz Language Center
Rokin 87 (622 1375/fax 620 3959). Tram 4, 9, 14, 16, 24, 25. **Open** 8.15am-9pm Mon-Thur; 8.15am-6pm Fri; 9am-1pm Sat.
Specialists in commercial, technical, legal and scientific documents. All European languages translated, plus Japanese and Arabic. English/Dutch translation from ƒ40 per 100 words.

Creative Translations
Oosterpark 72-4 (692 1637).Tram 6, 9, 10, 14/Bus 22. **Open** 9.30am-5pm Mon-Fri.
Dutch/English, copywriting and editing, specialists in advertising, culture, theatre, film, song lyrics and poetry. English native speaker. ƒ30 per 100 words.

Krasilovsky and Sons
Haarlemmerplein 8 hs (638 5854/fax 620 4033).Tram 3/Bus 22, 18. **Open** 10am-5.30pm Mon-Fri.
Copy and translations, Dutch/English. Specalities are film, television, theatre and the arts. Other services available are copywriting, scriptwriting and editing.

Mac Bay Consultants
PC Hooftstraat 15 (662 0501/fax 662 6299). Tram 2, 3, 5, 12. **Open** 9am-5pm Mon-Fri. Phone line is open 24 hours.
Specialises in translating financial documents. Dutch/English translations cost ƒ172,50 an hour. Other languages are also translated and there is a copywriting service.

Tibbon Translations
Utrechtsedwarsstraat 18 (420 1007/fax 420 0047). Tram 4. **Open** 9am-5pm Mon-Fri.
Dutch/English, English/Dutch and all EC languages are translated at a reasonable price. Tibbons Translations also offers a copywriting and editing service.

Interpreters (Tolken)

Congrestolken – Secretariaat
Prinsengracht 993 (625 2535/fax 626 5642). Tram 4, 16, 24, 25. **Open** 9am-5.30pm Mon-Fri.
Highly specialised staff for conference interpreting. Languages offered include Arabic, Japanese, Cantonese and all European languages.

Randstad Uitzendburo
World Trade Center, Strawinskylaan 69 (662 8011). Tram 5. **Open** 8.30am-5.30pm Mon-Thur; 8.30am-6pm Fri. This branch of the employment agency (*see below* **Office Services: Staff**) has a number of freelance interpreters and translators on its books. Costs vary widely.

Office Services
Equipment Hire
Avisco
Stadhouderskade 156 (671 9909). Tram 6, 7, 10. **Open** 7am-5pm Mon-Fri.
Slide projectors, video equipment, screens, cameras, overhead projectors, microphones and tape decks hired out or sold.

Decorum Verhuut
Jarmuiden 21 (611 7905). Bus 44, 82. **Open** 8am-5pm Mon-Fri.
Office furniture can be hired from this firm.

MiniOffice
Singel 417 (625 8455). Tram 1, 2, 5, 11. **Open** 10am-6pm Mon-Fri. **Credit** (minimum ƒ50) AmEx, DC, EC, MC, V.
Use a Macintosh or Compaq computer with all the latest design, spreadsheet and word-processing software at hourly rates for in-office use. Laser prints, scans, disk conversions between Mac and DOS also available. Photocopying is not cheap.

Office Hire
Euro Business Center
Keizersgracht 62 (520 7500/fax 520 7510). Tram 13, 14, 17. **Open** 8.30am-5.30pm Mon-Fri. **Credit** AmEx, DC, MC, V.
Fully equipped offices for hire (long- or short-term) which include the use of telex, fax, photocopier, phone and mailbox services plus multilingual secretaries. For a minimum of

three months, fully-equipped offices cost between ƒ1,550-ƒ4,775 per month. Private offices come at around ƒ125-ƒ200 per day.

Jan Luyken Residence
Jan Luijkenstraat 58 (5730 730/fax 676 3841/telex 16254 HTLIJNL). Tram 2, 3, 5, 11, 12. **Open** *office* 9am-5pm Mon-Fri. **Credit** AmEx, DC, EC, MC, V.
Three fully equipped offices for hire, long- or short-term. Projectors, videos, phones, telex, fax and mailbox are among the many services that can be provided. Small temporary offices cost ƒ250 per day. Conference rooms with capacities of up to 55 people cost ƒ450 to ƒ600 per day.

World Trade Center
Strawinskylaan 1 (575 9111/fax 662 7255/telex 12808). Tram 5/NS railway from Schiphol Airport to RAI Station. **Open** *office and enquiries* 9am-5pm Mon-Fri.
Office space in the World Trade Center is let by the **Dutch Business Center Association** *Strawinskylaan 305 (571 1800/fax 571 1801)*
Over 200 companies work in the rather soulless, air-conditioned luxury of the Trade Center. Offices can be hired long- or short-term. Audio and projection equipment is also for hire. Secretarial services cost ƒ80 per hour, and telex, fax and photocopying facilities are offered. *See also above* **Conferences**.

Relocation

Home Abroad
Weteringschans 28 hs (625 5195/fax 624 7902). Open 10am-5.30pm Mon-Fri.
A company that assists in all aspects of setting up business in the Netherlands. There's a fixed hourly rate of ƒ95 for advice and assistance, but rates for other services, such as seminars on the Dutch way of doing business, are negotiable.

Formula Two Relocations
Jacob Obrechtstraat 70 (672 2590/fax 672 3023). Tram 11, 16. **Open** 8.30am-5.30pm Mon-Fri.
This is an independent company, established in 1983, offering a comprehensive relocation service to companies and individuals moving to The Netherlands.

Employment Agencies (Uitzendbureaus)

Content Uitzendbureau
Nieuwezijds Voorburgwal 156 (625 1061). Tram 1, 2, 5, 11, 13, 17. **Open** 8.30am-5.30pm Mon-Fri.
A firm with office, secretarial, medical and technical staff on their books. There are nine branches in Amsterdam; this is the head office.

Manpower
Van Baerlestraat 41 (664 4180). Tram 3, 5, 12. **Open** 8.30am-5.30pm Mon-Thur; 8.30am-6.30pm Fri.
A large employment agency with five branches in Amsterdam. Staff can be provided for general office, secretarial, computer and other work.

Randstad
Diemermeer 25 (569 5911). Metro Gaasperplas. **Open** 8.30am-5.30pm Mon-Fri.
There are 13 branches of Randstad in Amsterdam supplying office and secretarial staff, translators and data-entry staff.

Tempo Team
Rokin 118 (622 9393). Tram 4, 9, 14, 16, 24, 25. **Open** 8.30am-5.15pm Mon-Fri.
Secretarial, hotel and catering, medical, technical and academic staff are on Tempo's books.

Children & Parents

Amsterdam's friendly atmosphere, plentiful parks and abundant sights spell lots of fun for the whole family.

As a nation, the Dutch have a relaxed approach to parenting. This is especially true in the capital. Amsterdam kids are more spontaneous, more indulged and more boisterous than their counterparts elsewhere in Europe. Though small and accessible, Amsterdam wasn't built for kids – which city was? – but its hidden courtyards and many parks and canals give children the space and the opportunity to explore. In the summer months many free (or reasonably priced) activities are organised for school-age children in the city's parks and playgrounds.

Amsterdam is bursting with cultural events for children. For details of these check with the AUB ticket office on Leidseplein (621 1211) or look in *Uitkrant*. Listings (under *Jeugd*) are mostly in Dutch, but the guide provides telephone numbers, so you can investigate further.

For children's clothing, shoes, bookshops and toyshops, *see chapter* **Shopping**.

School holidays

Primary school children have every Wednesday afternoon free. The main school holidays for the Amsterdam region are as follows: **1996** 12-20 Oct, 22 Dec-5 Jan. **1997** 2-9 & 28-31 Mar, 30 Apr-11 May, 26 Jun-10 Aug, 12-19 Oct, 20 Dec-4 Jan. **1998** 21 Feb-1 Mar, 10-13 Apr, 26 Apr-5 May, 12 Jul-23 Aug, 12-19 Oct.

Transport

Amsterdam's size and layout make it easy to reach most interesting places for youngsters on foot, although manoeuvring a pushchair over the older cobbled sections can be frustrating. The fastest, most convenient way to get around is by tram, bus or metro, although some of the older vehicles can be difficult to board with a pushchair – remember that the bottom step on a tram must be pressed down to keep the doors open (*see chapter* **Getting Around**). For fun, go by water taxi or, with older children, rent a canal bike (*see chapter* **Sightseeing**). Remember to navigate on the right-hand side of the waterway. Pleasant, and free, is a trip on the River IJ ferry to Amsterdam North; boats leave from behind Centraal Station about every ten minutes.

Tram Museum Amsterdam

Haarlemmermeerstation, Amstelveenseweg 264 (673 7538). Tram 6, 16. **Open** First Sun in Apr-last Sun in Oct. **Departs** 10.30am, 11am, then every 20 mins till 5.40pm, Sundays only. During May and summer school holidays: 1pm, 2.30pm, 4pm Tue-Sun. **Return fare** *f*5 adult; *f*2,50 4-11s and over-65s; free under-4s.
Not so much a museum as a pleasure ride. The antique electric tram carriages come from cities all over Europe and the 60-minute round trip in one of the colourful old trolleys along the edge of the Amsterdamse Bos (*see below and chapter* **Sightseeing**) is particularly enjoyable.

Outdoor Entertainment

In winter, you can take the kids skating at the Jaap Edenhal rink (*see chapter* **Sport**), or if you visit when it's really freezing, you can join *tout* Amsterdam on the ice – canals and park ponds are transformed into Breugelesque scenes, with skaters of all ages and abilities.

Competent in-line skaters and skate-boarders off all ages can try their skills out on the free skate ramp on Museumplein behind the Rijksmuseum.

Parks

Parks (*see chapter* **Sightseeing**) are the best places for children's entertainment, and each park has a playground, usually with a sandpit and sometimes a paddling pool. Watch out, though, for unleashed pooches and their droppings.

Vondelpark (570 5411 for information) is famous for its summer programme of free afternoon entertainment, including children's theatre, musicians, mime artists and acrobats. It also has the best children's playground in town, where you can sit and drink a coffee while your offspring leap about. **Amstelpark** has a miniature train, a maze, a small children's farm and pony rides. **Flevopark** is the wildest and least used of the city's parks and is a good, peaceful spot for kicking a ball around or picnicking. The adjacent

Meet all the usual farm beasts at **De Dierenpijp**.

Flevoparkbad has two fantastic outdoor swimming pools and a toddlers' paddling pool in a spacious grassy recreation area (*see chapter* **Sport**).

Amsterdam's largest green areas are on the edge of town: the **Amsterdamse Bos** has boating lakes, an open-air theatre, large playgrounds and wild deer. Plane spotters will enjoy watching low-flying aircraft coming in to land at nearby Schiphol. It also has the magical Bos Museum (*see chapter* **Museums**) and Geitenhouderij Ridammerhoeve (645 5034), a goat farm with 120 milk goats and loads of goatlets. Open 11am-5pm Mon, Wed-Sun (it gets very busy on Sunday afternoons), it sells biodynamic goats' milk, cheeses and ice-cream, and has a small recreation area and sandpit. From April to September you can hire bikes with children's seats by the main Bosbaan entrance and pick up a map at the Bos Museum. **Gaasperpark** (*see chapter* **Sport**) has superb sport and playground facilities, including a paddling pool and lake for swimming.

Urban Farms

Smaller farms are listed in the telephone directory under *Kinderboerderijen;* admission is free.

Artis Zoo Children's Farm

Part of **Artis Zoo** (*see chapter* **Sightseeing**). Animals include pigs, calves, chickens, sheep and goats. The latter are small and frisky and will nibble bags and pushchairs, so it's best to park these outside the gate, removing valuables first. Artis also has a great (dog-free) play area, so you can have a full day out for one admission price.

De Dierenpijp

Lizzy Ansinghstraat 82 (664 8303). Tram 3, 12, 24, 25.
Open 1-5pm Mon, Wed-Sun.

Centrally located in the Pijp district. You can meet all the usual farm beasts here, but without the crowds of Artis Zoo. The resident sow produces regular litters of pink piglets and you can buy fresh farm eggs. On Wednesday afternoons there are children's activities and handicrafts, and kids can hold and stroke the smaller animals.

De Uylenburg

Staalmeesterslaan 420 (618 5235). Tram 7, 13, 17/bus 18. **Open** *Sept-Apr* 10am-4pm daily; *May-Aug* 10am-5pm daily.

A children's farm in Rembrandtpark. There is also a simple play-and-do area for children with pony rides and grooming.

Children's Films

There are a few special children's film shows at the **Kriterion**, **Rialto** and the **Filmmuseum** (*see chapter* **Film**). Most films for under-tens are dubbed into Dutch (indicated by the words *Nederlands gesproken* in the film listings). However, many family-oriented films are in English with Dutch subtitles. In the Autumn school holiday, many theatres and independent cinemas take part in **Cinekid** (624 7110), a children's film festival with quality films from all over the world, many in English. Call for details.

Museums

See chapter **Museums** for details of the **Nederlands Scheepvaart Museum** (maritime museum), where children can handle exhibits on the ships docked outside, including a reproduction of an eighteenth-century Dutch East Indies trading vessel. There are also guided tours of the

Greenpeace boat, Sirius, which is docked outside from Oct-Apr; the **Aviodome**, an aviation museum with an exciting flight simulator; and the **Allard Pierson** archaeological museum, which has a small but good mummy collection and regular exhibitions with an educational slant.

Some museums are now organising special children's days at the weekends. These are great fun and extremely popular with junior culture-vultures, particularly at the **Rijksmuseum**: check with the AUB ticket office (621 1211) for dates and times.

For **Artis Planetarium** and **Madame Tussauds Scenerama** *see chapter* **Sightseeing**.

Kindermuseum
Linnaeusstraat 2 (568 8233). Tram 9, 10, 14/bus 22. **Open** from 2pm Wed; from 12.30pm Sat, Sun. Phone for opening times during school holidays. **Admission** via main Tropenmuseum.

The Children's Museum is a part of the **Tropenmuseum** (*see chapter* **Museums**) designed specially for children between six- and 12-years-old. Long-running exhibitions introduce young people to the cultures of the developing world: the guided programmes last 75 minutes, after which parents and younger and older siblings are invited to take a look as well. Staff (who speak English on request) entertain their young visitors, telling stories and answering questions, with lots of participation. Up until May or June 1997 is the highly recommended interactive exhibition 'Stories to know where to go', about the culture and traditions of the Australian Aboriginals, brought to life with the use of music, painting, dance and performance. From around September 1997 is a new interactive exhibition about the indigenous cultures of Bolivia. (Phone for exact details, dates and times.) *Shop. Wheelchair access.*

NINT Museum of Science & Technology
Tolstraat 129 (570 8170). Tram 4. **Open** 10am-5pm Mon-Fri; noon-5pm Sat, Sun and public holidays. Closed 25 Dec, 1 Jan and 29 Apr. **Admission** *f*10 adults; *f*7 under-13s; free under-4s.

One of the few museums in which children are allowed to touch and handle objects, and where their needs are central: even the holograms are at kids' height. Test your reaction times, see your shadow frozen on the fluorescent wall or blow a giant bubble. Special activities at weekends, Wednesday afternoons and holidays. Children aged from six to 13 can celebrate their birthdays at the NINT (570 8114 for bookings). The NINT closes for good on 1 Dec 1996, and is scheduled to reopen in May 1997 in a prestigious new high-tech location near Centraal Station, under the name IMPULS Science and Technology Center. (Call the VVV tourist office for new address and opening times.)
Baby-changing facilities. Café & shop. Wheelchair access; toilets for the disabled.

Swimming Pools and Saunas

Good pools for kids are the Mirandabad (a subtropical pool with a wave machine, a whirlpool, a toddler pool and a slide), Zuiderbad and Marnixbad indoor pools and the Flevopark outdoor pool (*see chapter* **Sport**). For local pools, look in the phone directory under *zwembad* and check by phone for special children's hours. Don't be surprised to find mixed communal dressing rooms – the Dutch are pretty relaxed about stripping off in

public. As for saunas, most tolerate children if they keep a low profile, especially at off-peak hours (*see chapter* **Sport**).

Sportfondsbad Oost
Fronemanstraat 3 (665 0811). Tram 3, 9. **Open** *family swimming* 11.30am-1pm Sat; 11am-1pm Sun (the first hour on Sundays is for specially for families with children under 4); *family sauna* 11am-1pm Sun. **Admission** to sauna *f*14,50 adults, *f*12,50 under-12s. Price includes swimming in heated instruction pool.

Restaurants

As a rule, the cheaper restaurants and pizzerias are a good bet, as are the brown cafés which have a kitchen – but try these for lunch or an early evening meal around 6pm, as they can get smoky and crowded later on. Children are allowed in to licensed bars and cafés, as long as they don't run amok. *See chapters* **Cafés & Bars** *and* **Restaurants**.

Enfant Terrible
De Genestetstraat 1 (612 2032). Tram 1, 3, 6, 12. **Open** 9.30am-8pm Mon-Fri; kitchen open 6-8pm Wed-Fri.

This little café-restaurant attached to the Birth Centre is specially designed for parents and under-5s, although older kids are welcome. You can either eat here with your child, or eat in peace while a play-leader keeps your tot amused (*f*2,50 per hour, half-price for second child). There is a simple, tasty set meal with vegetarian alternative for *f*17,50, with child's portions of *f*7,50. You can also leave your child in safe hands and nip off into town on your own (*f*10 per hour, *f*25 for three hours). All in all, a terribly civilised idea.

KinderKookKafé (Children's café)
Oudezijds Achterburgwal 193 (625 3257). Tram 1, 2, 4, 5, 9, 11, 14, 17, 24, 25/Metro Nieuwmarkt. **Open** 6-8pm Sat; 5-7pm Sun.

This small restaurant is entirely run by children: they cook, serve, present the bill and wash up, with a little help from the friendly grown-up staff. There is a simple set menu of main course and dessert, with a vegetarian alternative. Ingredients are fresh and healthy and prices are very low: *f*5 1-4s; *f*10 5-12s; *f*15 13-99s, *f*2,50 drinks. At weekends children can cook for their own guests: on Saturdays eight-12 year-olds can prepare dinner from 3.30 onwards, and on Sundays five-eight year-olds can prepare and serve an English-style high tea. Weekdays are reserved for prepare-it-yourself birthday parties and cookery courses for five-12s. Advance reservation is essential. Phone for details.

Pizzeria Capri
Lindengracht 63 (624 4940). Tram 3, 10/Bus 18, 22. **Open** 11am-10pm Mon, 4-10 pm Tue-Fri & Sun, 9am-10pm Sat; kitchen open from 6 pm.

Children are welcome at this friendly pizzeria-cum-gelateria with small pavement terrace. Both staff and customers remain remarkably unfazed by kids dropping pasta on the floor, and there's plenty of real Italian ice-cream on hand for blackmail purposes. This is also a good place to drop in to for a *cappuccino* and ice after a visit to the Noordermarkt on a Monday morning or the Boerenmarkt on a Saturday. (*See chapter* **Shopping**)
Highchair available.

Theatre and Circus

The children's theatre phoneline (622 2999) has recorded information in Dutch or check listings under *Jeugd* in the free weekly *Uitkrant*. For just

Clowning around at **Circustheater Elleboog**.

ƒ12,50 you can buy a reduction card valid for one season at six children's theatres. For information call Stichting Jeugdtheater Amsterdam (625 3284). Many theatres and music venues put on concerts and dance performances specially for children throughout the year: Check with the AUB ticket office (621 1211) for details.

Circustheater Elleboog

Passeerdersgracht 32 (626 9370). Tram 5, 7, 10/bus 67, 171, 172. **Open** *phone for activity and session times.* **Admission** non-members half day ƒ10; full day ƒ15; club membership ƒ125 per year, plus ƒ2 per visit. Booking essential (10am-5pm). For circus performances, check *Uitkrant* listings. **Admission** ƒ10 adults, ƒ7,50 under-17s.

At the Elleboog circus-theatre, kids aged from four to 17 can try out circus and clowning skills, learning conjuring tricks, make-up skills, unicycle riding, juggling and tight-rope walking. Activity days end in a small performance for parents and friends. Non-member sessions are always busy, mostly with Dutch kids, but the staff do speak English. The club has about 400 members, who attend sessions once a week and do regular performances.

Children's birthday parties (623 5326). Central hearing-aid system (in Dutch) for deaf children. Disabled children welcome. Wheelchair access.

De Krakeling

Nieuwe Passeerdersstraat 1 (625 3284/624 5123). Tram 7, 10. **Shows** 2pm Wed, Sat, Sun; 8pm Thur-Sat. **Admission** ƒ9 adults with child, ƒ16 unaccompanied; ƒ7 4-17s. Some performances ƒ3 extra.

De Krakeling has separate productions for over-12s and under-12s – phone to check what's on. For non-Dutch speakers, there are puppet and mime shows and sometimes musicals. Shows are listed in a programme available from the theatre and in *Uitkrant*.
Wheelchair access.

Out of Town

Children can enjoy trips to the windmills, castles, bulb fields, clog-makers and traditional towns near Amsterdam (*see chapter* **The Randstad**). The following places are especially suitable for kids.

Archeon, Alphen aan den Rijn

De Oude Wereld 200 (0172 447 777). By car 50km (31 miles) from Amsterdam, A4 to Leiden, N11 to Alphen a/d Rijn and follow Archeon signs; rail NS Rail Idee ticket (includes train, bus and admission). **Open** *Easter-31 Oct*

10am-5pm daily; Jun-Aug till 6 pm. **Admission** ƒ24,50 adults, ƒ17,50 4-11s, under-4s free. **Credit** EC, V.
This impressive and unusual archeological theme park offers visitors a trip back through history. This starts in the high-tech entrance building which acts as a giant time-machine, tracing life on earth from its primordial beginnings up to the Ice Age, complete with a life-size T-Rex. The vast outdoor area contains a Bronze Age settlement, a medieval market and a Roman town, with plenty of hands-on activities and games. Visitors can enjoy food cooked to ancient Roman or medieval recipes, watch a gladiator fight, or take a dip in the open-air plunge pool outside the Roman bath house (take swimwear). The Archeon experience gets the thumbs-up from young visitors – a great day out, with plenty of laughs.
Sightseeing boat. Wheelchair access; toilets for the disabled; wheelchairs for hire. Toy shops.

Efteling

Europalaan 1, Kaatsheuvel, Noord-Brabant (0416 288 111). By car 110km (68 miles) from Amsterdam, A27 exit Kaatsheuvel, N261 follow Efteling signs; rail NS Rail Idee ticket (includes train, bus and admission). **Open** *Easter-31 Oct 10am-6pm daily; Jul-Aug till 10 pm.* **Admission** ƒ30, under-4s free. **Credit** AmEx, DC, MC, V.

Brainchild of illustrator Anton Pieck, this original wonderland succeeds in delighting at child level without the hype or glitz of most major theme parks. Pieck designed an enormous fairytale forest (*sprookjesbos*) peopled with dwarves and witches, well-loved characters from Grimms' stories and the Arabian Nights, enchanted and haunted castles, and even talking rubbish bins. Efteling also has a vast amusement park with state-of-the-art thrills, as well as more traditional fairground rides for tinies. It's almost too much for one day – if you're flush, there's a hotel with a package deal, open all year (0416 282 000). Note: Efteling does get very busy in the holidays, especially at weekends, with interminable queues for the main attractions. Phone for accurate advice on off-peak visiting times.
Café and restaurant. Guide book and map in English, ƒ5. Pram hire. Shops. Wheelchair access; toilets for the disabled.

Linnaeushof

Rijksstraatweg 4, Bennebroek (023-5847624). By car 20km (13 miles) on A5 to Haarlem, then on N208 south; rail NS Rail Idee ticket (includes train, bus and admission). **Open** 10am-6pm daily Apr-Sept.
Admission ƒ11, under-1s free.
Between Haarlem and the Lisse bulb fields is this huge leisure park, formerly the estate of the Swedish botanist Carl von Linné. The pleasant grounds of woods, gardens and picnic spots accommodate some 300 attractions designed for children, including a Wild West train, cable cars, moonwalk, pedaloes, mini-golf, trampolines, a water play area (take swimwear) and go-karts (extra charge). There is also a large new play area for under-fives, with lots of imaginative safe-play ideas. A good day out for a budget price, especially for the under-tens.
Café and restaurant. Shops. Wheelchair access; toilets for the disabled.

Madurodam

Haringkade 175, The Hague (070 355 3900). By car 57km (35 miles) from Amsterdam on A4; rail NS Rail Idee ticket (train, bus and admission). **Open** *Easter-30 Sept 9am-10pm daily; 1 Oct-26 Mar 9am-5pm daily.* **Admission** ƒ19,50 adult; ƒ14 4-11s; under-4s free. **Credit** AmEx, DC, MC, V.

This 'largest miniature village in the world' is more popular with children than with grown-ups, who can succumb to back-ache from peering into the knee-high buildings. An odd jumble of the country's most famous features, it incorporates working models of Rotterdam's port, Schiphol airport and the ubiquitous windmills, all built to scale (1:25). Less pre-

dictably, it prides itself on keeping up with the latest architecture: the newest addition to this Lilliputian panorama is
a model of Rotterdam's Erasmus Bridge. The best time to go
is on a summer's evening, when the models are lit from inside
by a total of 50,000 tiny lamps.
*Café and restaurant. Shop. Wheelchair access;
wheelchairs for hire; toilets for the disabled.*

Nederlands Spoorwegmuseum and Museum van Speelklok tot Pierement

*Utrecht: By car 38km (24 miles) on A2; rail NS Rail Idee
ticket (train, bus and admission to both museums).* **Open**
all year 10am-5pmTue-Sat, 1-5pm Sun; closed 3 & 30 Apr,
25 Dec, 1 Jan. (Check opening times for other holidays by
phone).
Nederlands Spoorwegmuseum, *Maliebaanstation 16
(030 230 6206).* **Admission** ƒ11 adult; ƒ7 4-12s; under-
4s free.
The National Railway Museum is housed in an historic station, where over 60 old and new locomotives can be admired
from inside and outside. There are also rides on a miniature
Intercity and TGV line for under-12s.
Museum van Speelklok tot Pierement, *Buurkerkhof
10 (030 231 2789).* **Admission** ƒ7,50 adult; 4-12s ƒ4;
under-4s free.
A 20-minute walk from the Railway Museum, this has a
unique antique collection of mechanical music boxes, circus,
fairground and street organs and wondrous tin toys. A great
double day out for junior machine freaks.
*Café. Shop. Wheelchair access; wheelchairs for use; toilets
for the disabled.*

Parenting

Babyminders

If you want an evening out without kids contact
the service listed below. Babysitting in a hotel is
less comfortable than at home, so you'll be
charged a higher rate. A number of hotels also
have their own babysitting service. For babysitting services in the suburbs, look in the *Gouden
Gids* under *Oppascentrales.*

Oppascentrale Kriterion

Roeterstraat 170 (624 5848). **Book** by phone 5.30-7pm
daily. **Rates** 7pm-midnight ƒ5 per hour; midnight-3am
ƒ7 per hour; 3am-7pm ƒ10 per hour; ƒ5 administration
charge; ƒ7,50 supplement on total bill for Fri and Sat
evenings; ƒ20 minimum charge.
This reliable babysitting service has been running for 45
years and uses male and female students over 18 years of
age, all of whom are individually vetted. They're particularly
busy at weekends, so it's best to book in advance.

Childbirth

Amsterdam is probably the best place in the world
to have a baby. Over 40 per cent of births still take
place at home, and the city's midwife and health visitor system is second to none. Options include active
birth, water birth and Leboyer, as well as 'domino'
system hospital deliveries. Prenatal services, delivery and aftercare are all covered by *ziekenfonds*
(national health) or private health insurance policies.

Astrid Limburg Midwife Practice

Sarphatipark 97 (671 0650). Tram 6, 7, 10.
A radical and friendly midwife practice, centrally situated.
The midwives will also do water births at home.

The Birth Centre

De Genestetstraat 3 (685 3898). Tram 3, 7, 10, 12.
Phone for opening times of various services.
Midwife practice, baby clinic, courses, information centre
and shop.

Children's rights

Kinderrechtswinkel

Staalstraat 19 (626 0067). Tram 4, 9, 14, 16, 24, 25.
Open walk-in consultations 3-6 pm Mon, 2-5pm Wed,
Sat.
This children's rights office supplies under-18s with information about legal matters and the responsibilities of teachers, parents and employers. Kids may phone or visit; staff
will answer questions from adults, but prefer dealing with
the children involved.

Kindertelefoon (Childline)

(06-0432 freephone). **Open** 2-8pm daily.
Young people from eight to 18 are welcome to phone this line
to get information on something as innocent as a cake recipe,
as well as advice on serious issues like bullying, sexual
abuse, running away from home and so on. Staff do not give
information on children's entertainment.

Crèches and playgroups

Crèches take children aged from three months
to four years. There are long waiting lists for
both council crèches (*kinderdagverblijven*) and
playgroups (*speelzalen*). Private crèches have
shorter waiting lists but are more expensive. For
a list of childcare facilities in your area and a
registration form (register **early** in pregnancy),
contact your local Welfare Department office
(*Stichting Welzijn*).

Kinderbijslag (Family Allowance)

Parents from EEC countries who live and/or work in the
Netherlands are entitled to claim family allowance from the
Dutch state for their children. For information and an appli-
cation form call the SVB (560 0911).

Schools

Primary schooling is optional for children from
four years, and compulsory from five years. Most
schools are open from 8.45am-3.15pm, and primary schools have Wednesday afternoons free.
The state system includes Montessori, Dalton,
Jennaplan and Steiner/ Waldorf, as well as classical, denominational or special needs schools.
For more information about schools in your area,
contact your local council office (*stadsdeelkan-
toor*). For information on English-speaking or
international schools, contact The British
Council (622 3644).

Toy libraries

There are several toy libraries in Amsterdam,
where you can borrow toys large and small for
your children. There is a registration fee, and a
small borrowing charge. Look in the telephone
directory under *speel-o-theek.*

Gay & Lesbian

Sex, steam and every queer's dream: 'Europe's gay capital' (almost) offers it all.

Greased-up, black capped leather boys clink down the Warmoesstraat (dubbed the 'Rue de Vaseline); trendy boys hang out down the Reguliers-dwarsstraat; queens camp it up around the musical Amstel and lesbians walk around aimlessly searching for sapphic nightlife, invariably ending up at the sole women-only bar in Amsterdam, the **Saarein** (*see page 233* **Lesbian Bars**). For men the opportunities are endless in this veritable gay Mecca, where just about anything is tolerated (and indeed legal). For lesbians the scene is limited: barely a handful of lesbian-owned (but mixed) bars and clubs, and (currently) no lesbian-only clubs, just sporadic one-nighters at various venues. But still, Amsterdam's legendary tolerance makes it one of the most popular destinations in Europe for the lesbian or gay traveller.

AGE OF CONSENT TO MARRIAGE

The Netherlands originally decriminalised homo-sexuality in 1811. But in 1911, pressure from moralising Catholics and Calvinists led to Article 248-bis, which made the age of consent 16 for heterosexuals, but 21 for homosexuals. It wasn't until the high-profile gay and lesbian rights move-ment of the sixties and seventies which outraged moralists – but won tolerance – that article 248-bis was finally abolished: in 1971 the age of consent for gay men was lowered to 16.

Politics are now directed towards issues such as adoption, pension and inheritance rights for same-sex couples, raising awareness of people with HIV/AIDS and, of course, tackling homo-phobia which does still exist here, although to a lesser extent than in other European countries. However, one major Amsterdam-based organi-sation, the SAD-Schorerstichting, conducted a survey at the start of 1996 which showed increased intolerance towards gays and lesbians throughout the Netherlands, especially towards gay and lesbian teachers.

The beginning of 1996 saw a shift in opinion towards gay and lesbian marriage in parliament. The possibility of a same-sex marriage which included equal benefits to that of a heterosexual marriage (inheritance, pension rights and so on) was discussed. However, since that would mean that a married gay couple would also be able to adopt children, many of the politicians previously

in favour of the motion turned against it. This was largely because the Netherlands would be the first country to recognise adoption rights for same-sex couples and the Dutch parliament didn't want to cause any more controversy within the European Community than it already has done with its liberal stance on drugs.

Furthermore, the majority of gay groups also don't wish to introduce gay and lesbian marriages, as is the case in Sweden, because they see it as con-forming to a heterosexual lifestyle; they aim to find a better alternative. However, if gays and lesbians *would* like to attend some sort of ceremony, the Remonstrantse Broederschap (Remonstrants Brotherhood) on Nieuwegracht 27, 3512 LC Utrecht (030 316 970) is allowed to bless gay rela-tionships whether or not you are Dutch, or belong to their church.

Homomonument

Westermarkt. Tram 13, 14, 17.

The Homomonument is the world's first memorial to per-secuted gays and lesbians. Designed by Karin Daan, its three triangles of pink granite form a larger triangle that juts out into Keizersgracht. You can read about its history in a book by Pieter Koenders, *The Monument*. Those vic-timised in World War II are commemorated here every 4 May, but flowers are laid daily in memory of more private grief and especially on World AIDS Day (1 December). The monument is also a positive symbol for the homosexual community and a focus for demonstrations. The date of the monument's unveiling in 1987, 5 September, is celebrated as 'Coming Out Day' and parties are held here on occasions such as Queen's Day and Liberation Day (*see below* **Gay Calendar** *and chapter* **Amsterdam by Season**).

Pink Tolerance

Cruising

Cruising is generally tolerated: public expressions of affection and even discreet sex in open spaces are all allowed, within reasonable limits – in places where offence is unlikely to be taken. Particularly popular are both the Vondelpark (*see chapter* **Sightseeing**) and the wooded Nieuwe Meer in the south-west of the city. However over the last couple of years there has been an increase in less tolerant attitudes towards cruising areas. For example, plans are being drawn up to redesign the Nieuwe Meer, making the area more open – largely due to public concern over cruising.

Prostitution

The liberal prostitution laws here also apply to gays: there are several male brothels throughout the city and 'rent boy bars', mainly to be found in Paardenstraat, are legal. However this street is full of exploited, mainly Eastern European boys and can be a highly dangerous area in terms of both personal safety and unsafe sex. Caution is strongly advised.

Darkrooms

Darkrooms, found in several bars and clubs, must comply with strict regulations that enforce supplying safer sex information and ensure condoms are available for use. This trend for darkrooms is also on the increase on the lesbian scene.

SM

The practice of SM is legal here to the extent that there is even one SM bar open: G Force (Oudezijds Armsteeg 7, 420 1664; *see chapter* **Cafés & Bars**). Whilst G-Force is not exclusively gay and lesbian, you can get information about SM in general as well as forthcoming SM events here. There are many leather bars in and around the Warmoesstraat with well-equipped darkrooms.

Safer Sex

Since the advent of HIV/AIDS, the Dutch have developed a highly responsible attitude towards the practice and promotion of safer sex (*see below* **Help and Information**).

Condoms are easily available from most gay bars. Several years ago, as part of the 'Safe Service', bars were supplied with a bright pink neon light in the shape of a condom to 'subtly' notify customers that condoms were available there.

Queer Culture

Many gay and lesbian artists are popular in the Netherlands. Examples include Mathilde Santing (who also has a cult following in the UK), author Gerard Reve, drag queen Nicky Nicole (a household name here) and brazen media hog Paul de Leeuw.

Films such as *For a Lost Soldier* (based on the autobiographical novel by National Ballet choreographer, Rudi van Dantzig) and *The Fourth Man* (directed by Paul Verhoeven and based on the book by Gerard Reve) both enjoyed international success. *The Fourth Man* even gaining a cult following in the US.

Archives

Homodok

Oudezijds Achterburgwal 185 (525 2601). Tram 4, 9, 14, 16, 24, 25. **Open** 10.30am-4.30pm Wed-Fri.
The Documentation Centre for Lesbian and Gay Studies houses an extensive range of literature (books, journals, magazines, newspaper articles and theses). Visitors should write at least one month in advance, detailing their intended area of study. Homodok will then send a list of material available on that subject, with information about study times.

Lesbisch Archief

Eerste Helmersstraat 17 (618 5879). Tram 1, 2, 3, 5, 6, 11, 12. **Open** 1-4.30pm Mon-Fri.
The lesbian archives, housed in a building along with other gay and lesbian organisations, specialises mainly in audio-visual material but also includes a selection of books, magazines and photos. Every first Sunday of the month the Archief arranges a cultural afternoon with lectures, slide/video showings or a walking/boat tour of lesbian Amsterdam. For women's archives IIAV, *see chapter* **Women**.

Bookshops

Translated Dutch literature and other gay books and publications in English can be found at the specialist bookshops below, and at both the American Discount Book Center and WH Smith (*see chapters* **Students** *and* **Shopping**).

Intermale

Spuistraat 251 (625 0009). Tram 1, 2, 5, 11. **Open** 10am-6pm Mon-Wed, Sat; 10am-9pm Thur. **Credit** AmEx, MC, V.
Amsterdam's biggest gay bookstore stocks literature, porn, books on history and sexuality, as well as a large selection of cards, magazines and newspapers.

Vrolijk

Paleisstraat 135 (623 5142). Tram 1, 2, 5, 11, 13, 14, 17. **Open** 11am-6pm Mon; 10am-6pm Tue, Wed, Fri; 10am-9pm Thur; 10am-5pm Sat. **Credit** MC.
A wide range of new and second-hand gay and lesbian books, many in English, plus a huge stock of international magazines and details of events. They also stock T-shirts plus music videos and CDs by gay and lesbian artists.

Xantippe

Prinsengracht 290 (623 5854). Tram 1, 2, 5, 11. **Open** 1-6pm Mon; 10am-6pm Tue-Fri; 10am-5pm Sat. **Credit** AmEx, DC, MC, V.
Women's bookstore with a large number of lesbian titles and other merchandise. *See chapter* **Women**.

Gay Cinema

Gay & Lesbian Switchboard (*see below* **Help and Information**) has a list of cinemas and theatres with special gay and lesbian programmes. Smaller gay porn cinemas can be found in the centre of Amsterdam: for more information *see below* **Gay and Lesbian Publications**.

Desmet

Plantage Middenlaan 4 (627 3434). Tram 7, 9, 14/Metro Waterlooplein. **Open** box office 6.30pm-15 mins after last film starts.
This beautiful art deco cinema has a weekly gay and lesbian film repertoire on Saturdays at midnight, and Sundays at 4.15pm (*see chapter* **Film**). Details of programmes are listed in the bi-monthly *Queer Fish* (*see below*) and the weekly Filmladder found in the major Dutch newspapers.

Gay and Lesbian Publications

The comprehensive *Best Guide To Amsterdam & The Benelux* reviews gay and lesbian places in Amsterdam (as well as throughout the rest of the Netherlands, Belgium and Luxembourg) and is recommended. Britain's monthly magazine *Gay*

Lesbian Nightlife

There is currently no lesbian club in Amsterdam, only a number of one-nighters held at various venues across the city. Currently the most popular weekly night for women is Saturday night's women-only disco at the **COC** (*see* **Help and Information**) from 10pm-4am. The monthly Pussy Lounge held on the third Sunday of the month at the **RoXY** is enormously popular. Although most clubs are welcoming to women, particularly popular with lesbians are **Havana de Trut** on Sunday nights and **RoXY**'s 'Hard' on Wednesdays. The **Homolulu** (*see below* **Restaurants**) holds (fairly boring) women-only parties on the first Sunday and third Friday of each month from 8pm (but at 1am men are admitted). **Vive la Vie** women's bar also regu-larly organises huge lesbian-only parties at the nearby **iT**. The **Vrouwenhuis** (women's centre) occasionally organises one-off women-only parties (*see chapter* **Women**). **De Brug** (Het Bavohuis, Borneostraat 40, 694 0499) is a disco for over-35s, with music to match, held on the first Saturday of each month from 10.30pm until 2am (but closed over summer); you must show ID to prove your age and younger women are welcome only as guests. Because the lesbian scene changes so rapidly however, it is best to phone the Gay and Lesbian Switchboard (*above*) to check details of the latest initiatives and closures. Also watch out for flyers posted in women's bars for more underground and irregular events.

Living it up at **Vive la Vie**.

Times carries listings in English on Amsterdam for gays and lesbians. *Gay New Amsterdam*, written in both Dutch and English, comes out fortnightly and is distributed free in gay establishments. This newspaper caters for both tourists and locals, has some good news articles and always makes an interesting read. *Queer Fish,* a fortnightly under-ground 'zine written in English and distributed throughout Amsterdam, has extensive gay listings. The SAD-Schorerstichting also pro-duces a very useful *Gay Tourist Map* and a *Gay Tourist Info* safer-sex booklet (with a gay male bias) in English every year.

The following are in Dutch: *de GAY Krant*, the

country's fortnightly national gay newspaper; *sQueeze* (SUB-SIC) a monthly glossy similar to the British *Attitude*; *Homologie*, a cultural and intellectual magazine published every two months; *XL*, the COC's monthly; *Ma'dam*, a monthly women's magazine also produced by the COC; *WildSide*, a lesbian SM magazine, produced by the COC-based group of the same name; *Expreszo*, a widely read gay and lesbian youth magazine; *Uitklapper*, a two-monthly gay and lesbian listings paper. *De Regenbooggids* is a gay/gay-friendly equivalent of the Yellow Pages. All titles can be found at gay bookshops and some newsagents.

Media

On Dutch national TV gay and lesbian issues are frequently addressed, and gay and lesbian characters comfortably integrated in dramas and soaps (and no longer stereotyped as always camp and effeminate, or tragically dying of AIDS-related illnesses). Other programmes such as *All You Need is Love*, a heterosexual dating show, regularly includes gay and lesbian contestants and for *Prisoner Cell Block H* fans there is *Vrouwenvleugel (Women's Wing)*, the Dutch equivalent of the Australian soap. And although the Dutch have never been prudes when it comes to the subject of sex there has recently been a noticeable increase in the number of programmes blatantly showing jack-off parties, fist-fucking, and SM activities, both nationally and locally.

Every Tuesday between 6pm and 7pm Amsterdam's local cable TV station, Salto, broad-

casts gay and lesbian programmes. On the first Saturday of the month *Wilma-TV*, a lesbian magazine show, also appears on Salto. There are two gay and lesbian pages on Teletext, set up by GayLINC. One is nationwide on NOS Teletekst (page 447); the other has only Amsterdam-based information and can be found on SALTO Teletekst (page 601) or on AT5 Teletekst (page 710). For the gay and lesbian radio station MVS Radio (with programmes in English on Sundays), *see chapter* **Media**.

Help and Information

COC (National)
Nieuwezijds Voorburgwal 68-70 (623 4596). Tram 13, 14, 17. **Open** 9am-5pm Mon-Fri.
This is the head office of the COC (which is largely subsidised by the Dutch government) and can help with all matters relating to gays and lesbians. With just over 10,000 members and branches throughout the country, it's one of the world's biggest gay rights organisations and is concerned mainly with two aspects: social and activist.

COC (Amsterdam)
Rozenstraat 14 (information 623 4079/office 626 3087 1-5pm Wed-Sat). Tram 13, 14, 17. **Open** *office* 9am-5pm Mon-Fri; *information-coffeeshop* 1-5pm Wed-Sat; *café* 8pm-midnight Wed; 8pm-3.30am Fri, Sat. *HIV Café* 8pm-midnight Thur.
The Amsterdam branch deals with the COC's more social side. Many groups meet here such as the English Speaking Group and the lesbian SM group, WildSide; the regular HIV café is also held here (*see below* **HIV/AIDS**). The trendy information-coffeeshop is a useful place to get help with any enquiries you may have about the COC, or the gay scene in general: there's also a large noticeboard. COC weekly discos are very popular with people from all scenes and age groups. Discos are mixed (but with a male bias) on Fridays (10pm-

Is it a coffeeshop? Is it a meeting place? Is it a disco? It's the **COC** *and it's all three.*

4am) and lesbian-only on Saturday (10pm-4am), with admission at ƒ5 and a token system for buying drinks (a *strippenkaart* costs either ƒ5 or ƒ15).

Gay and Lesbian Switchboard
Postbus 11573, 1001 GN Amsterdam (623 6565). **Open** 10am-10pm daily.
The English-speaking men and women on this phoneline are specially trained in giving information and advice on all gay and lesbian matters, from scene news to safer sex.

HIV/AIDS

The Dutch government and local organisations are progressive in their approach towards HIV/AIDS with active research, a series of high-profile fund-raising events, and regular, visible safer sex campaigns (targeting cruising areas and darkrooms) such as the infamous Safe Sex Guerilla. This team of hunky young men regularly perform a sexy, cheeky safer-sex act, followed by the handing out of free condoms and lube.

There are also a number of organisations that deal specifically with HIV/AIDS (*see below*). Every Thursday evening the **COC** (*see above*) holds an HIV Café, often with informal, themed talks; there is also an HIV Café held at the HIV Vereniging *(see below)*. Stichting AIDS Fonds (Postbus 10845, 1001 EV Amsterdam; 626 2669/fax 627 5221) was specifically set up to channel money into research and safer sex promotion, as well providing grants for the more personal needs of people with AIDS. It also subsidises the Buddy Project at the SAD-Schorer Stichting. For HIV/AIDS phone lines *see chapter* **Survival**.

HIV Vereniging
Eerste Helmersstraat 17 (616 0160).Tram 1, 2, 3, 5, 6, 11, 12 **Open** *office* 9am-5pm Mon-Fri; *phone* 10am-4pm Mon-Fri
This, the Netherlands HIV Association, supports the individual and collective interests of all those who are HIV positive. They produce a two-monthly magazine *HIV Nieuws* (ƒ45 year only by subscription) as well as running the Internet service HIVNET (with the latest HIV/AIDS information) and the help phone line, HIVplusLIJN (*see chapter* **Survival**).

Gay Calendar

Gay celebrations on **Koninginnedag** (Queen's Day), held annually on **30 April**, are located around the Homomonument: there are drag acts, bands and stalls, and it ends with a huge open-air disco. It takes place between noon and 9pm. Many gay and lesbian bars and clubs also organise their own celebrations.

Remembrance Day takes place on **4 May** on the Dam. Although gay and lesbian victims from World War II are remembered at this important event, the NVIH/COC hold their own ceremony at the Homomonument (sometimes following a remembrance service at the COC). Also here on **May 5** there's an open-air party to celebrate **Liberation Day**.

AIDS Memorial Day takes place at the Beurs van Berlage on the last Saturday of May with performances of ballet, opera and classical music. Names of deceased loved ones are read out and candles lit. Afterwards everyone walks to the nearby Dam where symbolic white balloons are released.

The future of the annual **Roze Zaterdag** (Pink Saturday) held in a different town in the Netherlands each year on the last Saturday in June, was under discussion at time of writing. Check local press for details.

AmsterDAM diner is a huge exclusive HIV/AIDS fund-raising dinner (supplied free by almost all the city's five-star hotels) with quality entertainment. Held in a tent on the Dam in July, tickets cost ƒ275 per person, unsurprisingly attracting a commercial crowd (as well as a crowd of nosey onlookers).

Another impressive HIV/AIDS fund-raising event is **Rendez Vous**. This free open-air event was formerly held annually in Amsterdam. However the organisers are now holding it twice a year in other Dutch cities (Delft in **August** 1996, Den Bosch in **November** 1996). It encompasses art exhibitions, cabaret, and a wide range of live music from classical to pop.

The **Hollywood Party** has a reputation for bringing traffic on Reguliersdwarsstraat to a complete standstill as glitzy transvestite 'stars' leave their cocktails behind at the Havana and make their way to the iT in limousines. At the party there is a chance for the best lookalike to win a ticket to Tinseltown itself. It takes place on a weekend sometime in **August**.

New in 1996 is **Amsterdam Pride**. Organised by Gay Business Amsterdam, this is a three-day extravaganza including street parties, performances and a parade on boats around the canals. Grab anything that floats and get bouyant during the first week of **August**.

Various activities are organised by the Nationale Commissie AIDS-Bestrijding on and around **World AIDS Day** on **1 Dec**, though the main events may not be held in Amsterdam.

For more information on any of the above or any other events that take place in Amsterdam, phone the Gay & Lesbian Switchboard (*under* **Help & Information**).

Relax at the **Huyschkaemer**. *Page 233.*

SAD-Schorer Stichting

PC Hooftstraat 5 (662 4206). Tram 2, 3, 5, 6, 7, 10, 12.
Open 9am-5.30pm Mon-Fri.
This state-funded social agency offers gay and lesbian coun-selling, education and HIV prevention advice. One depart-ment is solely concerned with HIV/AIDS and related matters, including a Buddy Project. Phone for an appointment. The staff speak English. They also run a weekend clinic for men with gay sexual contacts: examinations and treatment of sex-ually transmitted diseases and tests for HIV (7-9pm Fri-Sun).

Groups

ACT UP!

ACT UP! Postbus 15452, 1001 ML Amsterdam (639 2522/fax 623 0680/e-mail HIV-net 6622866).
The Amsterdam branch of this AIDS action group meet every second and fourth Sunday of the month at Houtkopersburgwal 14-15.

Dikke Maatjes

c/o COC, Rozenstraat 14, Amsterdam
Chubby men's group that meet at the COC on the first Thursday of the month as well as organising other social evenings.

Groep 7152

Postbus 1402, 3500 BK Utrecht (021 5263040).
This is a countrywide organisation for lesbians and bisexu-al women. In Amsterdam they meet every third Sunday of the month (though not in the summer months) at the Crea Café (Turfdraagsterpad 17: *see chapter* **Students**.

Long Yang Club Holland

Postbus 58253, 1040 HG Amsterdam (695 7656).
The Dutch branch of this worldwide organisation for Asian/oriental gays and their friends meets regularly in Amsterdam.

Netherbears

c/o Le Shako, Postbus 15495, 1001 ML. Amsterdam (625 1400).
The hairy men's club, Netherbears, meets at the cultural Le Shako ('s Gravelandseveer 2) every second Sunday of the month (between 5pm and 9pm).

Remember Stonewall

Postbus 3762, 1001 AN Amsterdam.
A group of politically active, left wing *potten* (dykes) and *flikkers* (queers).

Sjalhomo

Postbus 2536, 1000 CM Amsterdam (023 312318 evenings only).
This national organisation for Jewish gays and lesbians has around 150 members and organises cultural, social and political activities on Jewish feast days.

Stichting Gay & Lesbian Games Amsterdam 1998

Postbus 2837, 1000 CV Amsterdam (620 1998/fax 626 1998/e-mail info@gaygames.nl).
Preparations are well under way for the 1998 games which Amsterdam is hosting – the first time they have been held this side of the Atlantic.

Stichting Tigertje

Postbus 10521, 1001 EM Amsterdam (673 2458).
Stichting Tigertje organise a variety of sports activities (including an HIV swimming group) for gays and lesbians.

WildSide

Postbus 16017, 2301 GA Leiden.
WildSide is a lesbian SM group that is based at the COC in Amsterdam. The group holds regular meetings every first Saturday of the month as well as regular 'play parties' at the COC.

Reguliersdwarsstraat: *home to Amsterdam's trendiest gay bars.*

Clubs and Bars

Camp Scene

Chez Manfred

Halvemaansteeg 10 (620 0171). Tram 4, 9, 14. **Open** 4pm-1am Mon-Thur; 4pm-3am Fri, Sat; 3pm-1am Sun. **Admission** free.

In this small but cosy bar, between Amstel and Rembrandtplein, an exuberant crowd gathers every night. The mixed clientèle of all ages sings along to chart music and Dutch songs. So called because it used to be owned by the late iT club entrepreneur, Manfred Langer. Happy hour is between 5.30pm and 7pm.

Le Montmartre

Halvemaansteeg 17 (620 7622). Tram 4, 9, 14, 16, 24, 25. **Open** 4pm-1am Mon-Thur, Sun; 4pm-3am Fri, Sat. **Admission** free.

A fun place if you enjoy the combination of Dutch camp sing-a-long with chart and dance music. There is a small dancefloor at the back where the young customers get rid of their inhibitions as they party. There are spontaneous Dutch cabaret and drag acts.

Macho Scene

Argos

Warmoesstraat 95 (622 6595). Tram 4, 9, 16, 24, 25. **Open** 10pm-3am Mon-Thur, Sun; 10pm-4am Fri, Sat. **Admission** free.

Argos is the oldest and most famous leather and denim bar in Amsterdam and most definitely the cruisiest. There is a basement darkroom with cabins, one of which has a hammock. On the first Monday of the month they hold 'Boot Black' with slave boys polishing clients' boots. And if your face fits you may be lucky enough to be personally invited to one of their monthly private parties 'Sex Train'. Men only.

The C'ring (Cockring)

Warmoesstraat 96 (623 9604). Tram 4, 9, 16, 24, 25. **Open** 11pm-4am Mon-Thur, Sun; 11pm-5am Fri, Sat. **Admission** free.

The C'ring nightclub is one of the few gay venues for which you need to queue to get in at weekends after 1am. It attracts all types of gays aged under about 40, despite its location in the leather-and-denim district. The dancefloor sounds are underground and hard house. Despite air-conditioning, the pulsating and gyrating masses raise the temperature. The C'ring's a cruisey place, with a darkroom reached through the industrial/hi-tech toilets. Men only.

De Spijker

Kerkstraat 4 (620 5919). Tram 1, 2, 5, 11. **Open** 1pm-1am Mon-Thur, Sun; 1pm-3am Fri, Sat. **Admission** free.

Spijker means 'nail' or 'tack' and there's a huge nail impaled into the counter of this friendly mixed American-style bar. It has recently become less leather-orientated (there is no dress code), but is still cruisey, with porno/cartoon videos and an upstairs darkroom. There is also a pool table and a daily happy hour between 5-7pm. Women welcome.

The Web

St Jacobsstraat 6 (623 6758). Tram 1, 2, 3, 5. **Open** 2pm-1am Mon-Thur, Sun; 2pm-3am Fri, Sat. **Admission** free.

Close to Centraal Station, this is one of the most popular leather bars: the dress code is butch (no perfume or pink sweaters). There is a small roof garden, a darkroom upstairs and porn videos in the downstairs bar. The Web has a reputation for throwing wild parties and for having the cleanest toilets of any leather bar in town. Men only.

Trendy Scene

A number of Amsterdam's clubs hold gay one-nighters, so *see also chapter* **Clubs**.

Café April

Reguliersdwarsstraat 37 (625 9572). Tram 1, 2, 4, 5, 9, 14, 16, 24, 25. **Open** 2pm-2am Mon-Thur, Sun; 2pm-3am Fri, Sat. **Admission** free.

Large and relaxed, with friendly staff who will serve you with snacks or cakes made at Downtown coffeeshop just along the street. Café April, Exit (*see below*) and Downtown (*see chapter* **Cafés & Bars**) merged in 1994 and are all owned by the same company. The décor is modern with photos on display; there's also a notice-board. Relatively quiet by day, it fills up around midnight: during 'peak hour', midnight-1am (2am Fri and Sat) beer is sold for *f*1,50 a glass and the place gets packed.

Exit

Reguliersdwarsstraat 42 (625 8788). Tram 1, 2, 4, 5, 9, 14, 16, 24, 25. **Open** *ba*r 4pm-5am Sun; *disco* 11pm-4am Mon-Thur, Sun; 11pm-5am Fri, Sat. **Admission** free.
A smart disco for trendy young gays. Reached via a comfortable bar area, the disco room was once a hay loft. The dancefloor is cruisey and overlooked by a balcony. State-of-the-art equipment pumps out the lights and latest music for the benefit of an enthusiastic crowd.

Havana

Reguliersdwarsstraat 17 (620 6788). Tram 1, 2, 5, 16, 24, 25. **Open** *bar* 4pm-1am Mon-Thur; 4pm-2am Fri; 2pm-2am Sat; 2pm-1am Sun; *disco* 10pm-1am Mon-Thur, Sun; 10pm-2am Fri, Sat. **Admission** free.
An early-closing free-entry bar with a separate dance area upstairs, Havana has become one of the most popular gay bars. A people-watcher's paradise – where Gaultier clashes with Dolce & Gabbana – it gets very busy from around 10pm, especially at weekends.

Huyschkaemer

Utrechtsestraat 137 (627 0575). Tram 4, 6, 7, 10. **Open** 4pm-1am Mon-Thur, Sun; 4pm-3am Fri, Sat; *kitchen* 6-10pm daily.
Attracts a mixed, mainly young and artistic gay and lesbian crowd. Food costs around ƒ25 for a main dish and includes a vegetarian selection.

iT

Amstelstraat 24 (625 0111). Tram 4, 9, 14. **Open** 11pm-4am Thur, Sun; 11pm-5am Fri, Sat. **Admission** ƒ12,50/free for gays Thur; ƒ17,50 Fri, Sat, Sun
Since the death of its manager Manfred Langer at the end of 1994, this converted cinema has definitely lost some of the glamorous, international appeal that made it famous. However, old visitors to the club won't find much changed except the inflated admission price at the weekend.

RoXY

Singel 465 (620 0354) Tram 1, 2, 4, 5, 9, 11, 14, 16, 24, 25. **Open** 11pm-4am Wed, Thur, Sun; 11pm-5am Fri, Sat. **Admission** average ƒ10-ƒ15
Host to the weekly gay 'hard' night which attracts a large,

mainly male fashion-conscious crowd and a handful of women as well as the monthly 'Pussy Lounge' for lesbians (*see box* **Lesbian Nightlife**).

La Strada

Nieuwezijds Voorburgwal 93-95 (625 0276). Tram 1, 2, 5, 11, 13, 17. **Open** 4pm-1am daily; *kitchen* 5-10pm daily.
This spacious and centrally located establishment attracts quite an artistic and cultural crowd. Each month the work of a different artist is displayed on the walls. Meals cost around ƒ22,50 and include a vegetarian selection.

De Trut

Bilderdijkstraat 165 (612 3524). Tram 3, 7, 12, 17. **Open** 11pm-4am Sun. **Admission** ƒ2,50.
Great squatter's club in a basement which attracts a good mixed crowd of gays and lesbians. Get there early as the door shuts around 11.30pm and it is *very* popular.

Lesbian Bars

Saarein

Elandsstraat 119 (623 4901). Tram 7, 10. **Open** 3pm-1am Tue-Thur, Sun; 3pm-2am Fri, Sat.
Amsterdam's notorious women-only bar frequented by Mathilde Santing. At time of writing, it's the only one in town. There is a pool table in the basement. *See chapter* **Women**.

Vandenberg

Lindengracht 95 (622 2716). Tram 3. **Open** 5pm-1am Mon-Fri, Sun; 5pm-2am Fri, Sat.
A decent neighbourhood eatery. *See chapter* **Women**.

Vive la Vie

Amstelstraat 7 (624 0114). Tram 4, 9, 14. **Open** 3pm-1am Mon-Thur, Sun; 3pm-3am Fri, Sat.
On the edge of the bustling Rembrandtplein (and not much quieter inside) this lively bar attracts a largely lipstick/femme clientèle (men welcome). There is a terrace outside in the summer. Owner Mieke Martelhof organises lesbian parties throughout the year as well as a women-only 'Steam Party' at Thermos Night Sauna (*see below* **Saunas**) on the first Sunday of the month.

Boys will be boys at **Mr. B**. *Page 234.*

Cafés

For more women-friendly cafés and bars, *see chapter* **Women**.

Downtown
Reguliersdwarsstraat 31 (622 9958). Tram 1, 2, 4, 5, 9, 14, 16, 24, 25. **Open** *summer* 10am-9pm daily; *winter* 10am-8pm.
Good-value light snacks, salads and cakes are served by pleasant staff. To a background of mellow music, you can peruse the art exhibitions and selection of magazines and newspapers (many in English). The outdoor terrace with its sculpture of a reclining male nude is, during the summer, one of the most popular gay haunts on this gay street.

Françoise
Kerkstraat 176 (624 0145). Tram 16, 24, 25. **Open** 9.30am-6pm Mon-Sat.
Charming lesbian-owned café-gallery serving good food at reasonable prices. There are also two apartments above the premises for rent with TV, bathroom and kitchen (ƒ125 for two people). *See also chapter* **Women**.

Coffeeshop

Otherside
Reguliersdwarsstraat 6 (625 5141). Tram 1, 2, 5, 11. **Open** 10.30am-1am daily.
Near the Flower Market on the Singel and on the same street as Havana and April, this is the only gay coffeeshop in the city. No alcohol is sold but they do have a small hash menu.

Restaurants

Hemelse Modder
Oude Waal 9 (624 3203). Metro Nieuwmarkt. **Open** 6pm-midnight Tue-Sun; *kitchen* 6-10pm Tue-Sun.
On the edge of the Red-Light District, by one of its more scenic canals, this mixed restaurant is highly recommended for its candle-lit meals, aesthetic interior and friendly, mostly gay and lesbian staff. Food is Mediterranean with vegetarian options always available.

Homolulu
Kerkstraat 23 (624 6387). Tram 1, 2, 5, 11. **Open** 10pm-4am Tue-Thur, Sun; 10pm-5am Fri, Sat.
Tacky and dated (seventies time-warp) lesbian-owned restaurant/nightclub with mixed straight and gay nights. Door policy can sometimes be uneccesarily strict.

Leather/Sex Shops

A few gay leather and rubber shops can be found in the heart of the leather district on the edge of the Red-Light District, such as **Master Leathers** at Warmoesstraat 32 (624 5573) and **Mr B** at Warmoesstraat 89 (422 0003), as well as, of course, as numerous sex shops. Rubber lovers should also pay a visit to **Black Body** at Lijnbaansgracht 292 (626 2553), a specialist rubber shop. *See also chapter* **Shopping**.

The Bronx
Kerkstraat 53-55 (623 1548). Tram 1, 2, 5, 6, 7, 10, 11. **Open** noon-midnight daily. **Credit** AmEx, MC, V .
A large selection of magazines, books, cards and toys is stocked and videos for hire or sale (plus viewing cabins).

Drake's
Damrak 61 (627 9544). Tram 4, 9, 14, 16, 24, 25. **Open** 9am-1am Mon-Thur, Sun; 9am-2am Fri, Sat.
A well-equipped, late-opening sex shop that also has a cruisey cinema on the premises, with lots of private booths.

RoB Gallery
Weteringschans 253 (625 4686). Tram 6, 7, 10. **Open** 11am-6.30pm Mon-Fri; 11am-5pm Sat. **Credit** AmEx, MC, V.
This international company sells leather and rubber clothing (also made to measure), posters, cards, videos and magazines. There's a gallery showing regular exhibitions .

Saunas

Fenomeen
Eerste Schinkelstraat 14 (671 6780). Tram 6. **Open** 1-11pm daily. **Admission** 1-6pm ƒ10; 6pm-closing time ƒ12,50.
Relaxed squat sauna, very popular with lesbians on Monday's women-only day. Open-plan and split level with sauna, steam bath, cold bath, chill-out room with mattresses, a café serving wholefood snacks and an outside area with showers. Thur, Sat and Sun no smoking is allowed. For other women-only saunas *see chapter* **Women**.

Thermos Day
Raamstraat 33 (623 9158). Tram 1, 2, 5, 7, 10. **Open** noon-11pm Mon-Fri; noon-10pm Sat, Sun. **Admission** ƒ27,50.
There's a steam room, dry-heat room, a small cinema showing porn, private cubicles, a bar and restaurant, and a gym.

Thermos Night
Kerkstraat 58-60 (623 4936). Tram 1, 2, 5. **Open** 11pm-8am daily. **Admission** ƒ27,50.
Thermos Night has similar facilities to Thermos Day (but no restaurant) and also has a small Jacuzzi and a darkroom.

Hotels

It is illegal for hotels to refuse accommodation to gays and lesbians. The **Gay & Lesbian Switchboard** (*see above*) can provide more information on hotels that are gay and lesbian friendly.

Centre Apartments
Heintje Hoeksteeg 27 (627 2503/fax 625 1108). **Rates** *apartments* ƒ165-175 (two person); ƒ45 (each additional person); *studios* ƒ135-145 (two person).

Centre Guesthouse
Tweede Leliedwarsstraat 4-6 (627 2503/fax 625 1108). **Rates** *single* ƒ105; *double* ƒ125.

Greenwich Village Hotel
Kerkstraat 25 (626 9746/fax 625 4081). Tram 1, 2, 5, 11. **Rates** *single* ƒ100; *double* ƒ125. **Credit** AmEx, MC, V.

Hotel New York
Herengracht 13 (624 3066/fax 620 3230). Tram 1, 2, 3, 5, 11, 13, 14. **Rates** *single* from ƒ150; *double* ƒ200; *luxury double (with bath)* ƒ250; *triple* f275. **Credit** AmEx, DC, MC, V.

Orfeo Hotel
Leidsekruisstraat 14 (623 1347/fax 620 2348). Tram 1, 2, 5, 6, 7, 10, 11. **Rates** *single* ƒ65-ƒ75; *double* ƒ92,50-ƒ105; *twin* ƒ97,50-ƒ110; *studio apartment* ƒ120-ƒ150 (one person), ƒ130-ƒ165 (two person); ƒ150-ƒ180 (three person). **Credit** AmEx, MC, V.

Students

Where to hang out, eat cheaply, learn Dutch, get your library card and purchase a text book or two.

Together with Groningen, Leiden and Utrecht, Amsterdam is one of the main student cities in the Netherlands. Almost ten per cent of its inhabitants devote their time to courses in higher education. The city's two major universities are **UvA** (Universiteit van Amsterdam) and **VU** (Vrije Universiteit). Many of the UvA buildings scattered across the city are historic and listed (you can recognise them by their red and black plaques) and you can also satisfy your hunger pangs for a few guilders in their refectories.

The biggest buildings are those of the Faculteit der Letteren (languages, literature and history) and the main college centre at Oudemanhuispoort. The Crea Organisation is based at nearby Turfdraagsterpad 17. This subsidised institution organises inexpensive creative courses, lectures and performances covering music, theatre, dance, broadcast media, photography and fine art. A course that suits your interest won't be too expensive as the Crea shows mercy on the student budget. And for meeting other students, the Crea Café is a good spot (*see below* **Cafés & Bars**).

THE ETERNAL STUDENT IS NO MORE

Dutch higher education is divided in two sectors: Institutes of Higher Vocational Education (HBO) and Universities. Courses span four years. Up until the 1980s students could continue in education for as long as they wanted, but the government decided to put a stop to the many 'eternal students' who were still happily studying well into their forties. Nowadays only people between the ages of 18 and 27 are granted the measly five-year grant, amounting to less than unemployment benefit and cut back every year.

Although students have the freedom to spread their studies over five years, to keep their scholarships they must annually achieve a passing grade in at least half of their courses. Those who want to continue their studies for longer than five years have to finance the extra years themselves. At the time of writing, the government is planning to cut scholarships back to three years, after which students will be obliged to take out a loan. This decision has already resulted in fewer university entrances.

Café Het Paleis: *deservedly popular for soups, sandwiches, sunlight and students.*

ASVA
*Spinhuissteeg 1 (union 622 5771/ 525 2818/
accommodation agency 623 8052); Binnengasthuisstraat
9, inside Service & Information centre. Tram 4, 9, 14,
16, 24, 25.* **Open** *union and accommodation agency*
12.30pm-4pm Mon-Fri; 12.30-4pm Thur.
ASVA offers assistance to foreign students. The accommodation agency can find you a room for about *f*350 per month,
charging a *f*10 deposit. The accommodation lottery is held
daily at 4pm and at 6pm on Thursday. Anyone with an
ASVA membership card (*f*25 for a year). can participate.

OBAS
Voetboogstraat 2 (525 2833). Tram 4, 9, 14, 16, 24, 25.
Open 11am-3pm Mon-Fri.
This UvA union is progressive, pragmatic and mostly con-
cerned with law students. There are no facilities here, but
foreign students can contact OBAS for help and information.

SRVU
*De Boelelaan 1115B (548 3600). Bus 8, 13, 26, 48, 49,
64, 65, 67, 173.* **Open** *July-mid Aug* irregular hours,
message in English on answerphone; *mid Aug-June* 12.30-
3.30pm Mon-Fri. Closed Christmas and Easter holidays.
The SRVU is the union for VU students. Its accommodation
service can also help foreign students find a place to stay, as
well as providing them with general help and advice.

Amsterdam nightlife is frequented most by its students. Although open to everybody, the bars listed below are essentially student hangouts.

Students are often entitled to discounts on admission at clubs, museums, attractions and places of
entertainment; presenting an ISIC card is often
enough but CJP cards (from the Uitburo, *see chapter* **Essential Information**) are more frequently
used. Nightclubs frequented by students include
Dansen bij Jansen, R*o*XY, Richter, Odeon, Escape
(*see chapter* **Clubs**) and the iT (*see chapter* **Gay
& Lesbian**). For discount travel agencies and
advice on hitchhiking, *see chapter* **Survival**.

Cafés and Bars

If you want to meet academic types somewhere
more conducive to conversation than the library,
the following are some of the bars to frequent.
Others worth checking out include Het Gasthuis,
Café Bruin, De Tuin and De Reiger (*see chapter*
Cafés & Bars).

Café Het Paleis
Paleisstraat 16 (626 0600). Tram 1, 2, 5. **Open** noon-1am
Mon-Thur; 1pm-1am Sun; noon-2am Fri, Sat; *kitchen* 6-
11pm daily.
Het Paleis has been deservedly popular with students for
several years. When the weather's good, its terrace is almost
constantly bathed in sunlight and the sandwiches and soups
are wonderful. In the evening Het Paleis has a kitchen serving everything from oriental dishes to Dutch *hutspot*.

Crea Café
Grimburgwal (627 3890). Tram 9, 14, 16, 24, 25. **Open**
9.30am-1am Mon-Fri; 10am-1am Sat; noon-7pm Sun.

Going Dutch

If you're feeling guilty about the excellent quality of English spoken by Amsterdammers, you
can get your own back by tackling the Dutch
language at any one of several institutions.
Below we list a reputable selection.

Volksuniversiteit Amsterdam
Ratenburgerstraat 73 (626 1626). Tram 1, 2, 5, 11.
Open *information* 10am-4pm Mon-Fri.
There are three levels of day and evening courses at the
Volksuniversiteit. Courses start in January and are given
in schools all over town. A course of 12 weekly lessons
costs *f*260. 24 lessons (twice a week) cost *f*490 and 36
lessons (three times a week) cost *f*685.

VU Department of Applied Linguistics
*De Boelelaan 1105, Room 9A21 (444 6398). Bus 8,
23, 26,48, 49, 64 ,65, 67, 173.* **Office** open 3pm-5pm
Mon. **Credit** AmEx, MC, V.
Anyone who is a student can enrol on the VU self-study
programme Nederlands Tweede Taal (Dutch Second
Language) and use the laboratory facilities. The six-
month programme starts in September and January.
Beginner's Dutch is an eight-week intensive course for
VU-students. Level I is five hours a day, four days a week.
Levels II, III and IV are eight-week courses with three-
hour lessons four times a week. Courses cost from *f*384.

British Language Training Centre
*Oxford House, Nieuwezijds Voorburgwal 328 (622
3634). Tram 1, 2, 5, 11.* **Open** *information* 8.30am-
5.30pm Mon-Fri.
Various courses in the Dutch language.The intensive course,
Nederlands 1, runs six hours a day for two weeks and costs
*f*930. There are five levels of evening courses running for
about three months. The foundation course starts at *f*860;
higher level courses cost *f*860. The centre can arrange tai-
lormade courses at a group rate (max 12 students).

Dutch Language Centre
Leidsestraat 32 IV.(422 1906) Tram 1, 2, 5, 11. **Open**
8am-10pm Mon-Fri; 10am-10pm Sat, Sun.
DLC offers a range of courses given by native speakers.
You can decide the topic and contents of your lesson.
Prices vary from *f*60 per hour for one person to *f*75 per
hour for three people.

Language Solution
(422 3121)
Language Solution offers individually-geared courses to
get you to the required level within the quickest time.
Group courses with a maximum of five people start every
first week of the month. A course of four hours a week
lasts ten weeks and is about *f*1500, materials included.
Private lessons are *f*75 an hour and if you bring someone
else, that second person pays half price.

Arty students gather at this café, which has a terrace overlooking the water.

Schutter Café
Voetboogstraat 13-15 (622 4608). Tram 1, 2, 5. **Open** *bar* 11am-1am Mon-Thur, Sun; 11am-3am Fri, Sat; *kitchen* 5.45-9.30pm daily.

A café frequented by both students and tourists. There are snacks and 40 different types of beer, including several British varieties. Meals are also available; there are two *dagschotels* (dishes of the day) for ƒ14,50, as well as vegetarian choices and a dish of the month. Lunch is served between noon and 2.45pm.

Mensae

Amsterdam has several large mensae (student restaurants) where the food is good and the prices are low. They are subsidised and open to the public, but are generally only patronised by students and a handful of budget-conscious civilians.

Agora
De Roetersstraat 11 (525 5270 college switchboard). Tram 7. **Open** noon-2pm, 5-7pm, Mon-Fri. **Average** ƒ8.

Agora is the new, stylish mensa at the Roetersstraat, serving reasonable food at affordable prices.

Het Trefcentrum Atrium
Oudezijds Achterburgwal 237 (525 3999). Tram 4, 9, 14, 16, 24, 25/Metro Nieuwmarkt. **Open** *lunch* noon-2pm, *dinner* 5-7pm, Mon-Fri. **Average** ƒ10.

Het Trefcentrum Atrium is a buffet/self-service restaurant where a starter and main course can be had from as little as ƒ8,25. The building once housed the university hospital and the original separate entrances for men and women can still be seen.

Mensa VU
De Boelelaan 1105 (444 5897). Bus 8, 23, 26, 48, 49, 64, 65, 67, 173. **Open** 10am-7pm Mon-Fri. **Dinner** served 5-7pm Mon-Fri. **Average** ƒ7,50.

Mensa VU is large, modern and spacious and offers a choice of three different meals.

Student Bookshops

Fortunately for the impecunious student, Amsterdam provides plenty of sources for cheap books. For second-hand academic texts, browse the stalls in Oudemanhuispoort – there are many volumes in English to be found. A principal outlet for new academic volumes is the Athenaeum Nieuwscentrum (*see chapter* **Shopping**).

Allert de Lange
Damrak 62 (624 6744). Tram 4, 9, 16, 24, 25. **Open** 1-6pm Mon; 9.30am-6pm Tue-Fri; 9.30am-5pm Sat. **Credit** MC, V.

Tomes concerning the language, literature, history and culture of France, Germany and England are the speciality at Allert de Lange. You will also find sections on philosophy, history, history of art, film, travel and photography.

The American Book Center
Kalverstraat 185 (625 5537). Tram 4, 9, 16, 24, 25. **Open** 10am-8pm Mon-Wed, Fri, Sat; 10am-10pm Thur; 11am-6pm Sun. **Credit** AmEx, DC, V.

This shop has an excellent book-ordering department. Students receive a 10 per cent discount on all book and study purchases.

VU Academic Bookshop
De Boelelaan 1105 (644 4355). Bus 8, 23, 26, 48, 49, 64, 65, 67, 173. **Open** 9am-7pm Mon-Fri; 10am-3.30pm Sat. **Credit** AmEx, DC, MC, V.

The VU Bookshop (VU Boekhandel) has a large selection of books relating to all sciences and a good collection of novels, tourist guides and children's books.

Study

For people wishing to study in Amsterdam, a number of UvA departments offer international courses and programmes for postgraduates, graduates and undergraduates which are all taught in English. Details are available from the Foreign Relations Office (Spui 25, 1012 SR, Amsterdam). Most postgraduate institutes of the UvA also take foreign students.

Amsterdam Summer University
Felix Meritis Building, Keizersgracht 324 (620 0225). Tram 1, 2, 5. **Courses** last week of July-end of first week of Sept.

ASU offers an annual summer programme of courses, workshops, training and seminars in the arts and sciences as well as international classes. All courses are taught in English, last between three days and four weeks and cater for postgraduates, graduates and undergraduates.

Foreign Student Service (FSS)
Oranje Nassaulaan 5 (671 5915). Tram 2. **Open** 9am-5pm Mon-Fri.

The FSS promotes the well-being of foreign students, providing personal assistance and general information on studying in the Netherlands. It also runs the International Student Insurance Service (ISIS) and organises a number of social and cultural activities.

UvA Main Library
Singel 425 (525 2301/information 525 2326). Tram 1, 2, 5, 11. **Open** *for study* 9am-11pm Mon-Fri; 9.30am-5pm Sat; *for book lending* 11am-5pm Mon; 9.30 am-8pm Tue, Thur; 9.30am-5pm Wed, Fri ; 9.30am-12.45pm Sat. Closed Jul 1-Aug 15.

Anyone can use this library to study, although to borrow books you need a UB library card (ƒ30). There's an online catalogue system and a good refectory where you can buy cheap sandwiches and drinks between 9.30am and 5pm. For details of the British Council and American Institute libraries, *see chapter* **Survival**.

UvA Service & Information Centre
Binnengasthuisstraat 9 (information 525 8080). Tram 4, 9, 16, 24, 25. **Open** 9am-4pm Mon-Wed, Fri; 9am-7pm Thur.

Personal advice on studying and everything that goes with it. The documentation centre stocks all the infomation you need to select a suitable course for you in Holland or abroad.

VU Main Library
De Boelelaan 1105 (444 5200). Bus 8, 23, 26, 48, 49, 64, 65, 67, 173. **Open** 10am-4pm Mon-Fri. **Membership** ƒ30 per year.

Anyone can apply for membership, which entitles you to study, borrow and use books for reference.

VU Student Information
(Office 444 7777/direct line 444 5000). **Open** 9am-4pm Mon-Fri.

The helpline for the Vrije Universiteit. They can provide help and advice on courses, studying and accommodation.

Women

The women's scene: from bookshelves to bars, hotels to healthcare.

Don't let the tall, blonde, lipstick-coated, big-breasted Dutch women wearing their jeans so far up their bums that they double as denim jackets disguise the fact that today's freedom hasn't been easily won. Although the feminist movement lost momentum after Dutch women won the right to vote in 1919, the radical Dolla Mina (Mad Mina) group founded in the 1960s took up the cause with a vengeance. It soon became notorious for colourful actions such as singing 'Faithful forever, but who will clean the kitchen sink?' to newly-weds outside City Hall, or invading a gynaecologists' conference displaying stomachs scrawled with 'Boss over our own bellies'.

Today's Dutch women are cool and independent, feminist yet domesticated, more often seen on bicycles laden with kids at either end. Any radical groups of women are to be found mainly within the squatter scene – continuing to fight for the rights of women, especially foreign women from oppressive regimes.

On the whole, Amsterdam remains both an attractive and relatively safe and hassle-free destination for the woman traveller.

The **Vrouwenfietsenmakerij**. *Page 240*.

the pavement terrace. Vegetarian meals are available – for between *f*11 and *f*22 – but the kitchen is shut on Saturdays. It's mainly frequented by women, but men are welcome too.

Going Out

For lesbian parties *see chapter* **Gay & Lesbian**.

Cafés and Bars

Café Saarein
Elandsstraat 119 (623 4901). Tram 7, 10. **Open** 3pm-1am Tue-Thur, Sun; 3pm-2am Fri, Sat.
Amsterdam's only café where men are refused admission at any time. Although the hub of the lesbian scene, the atmosphere is more that of a women's café. Darts, pool or pinball can be played in the basement where the resident cat often hangs out. There is also a general noticeboard filled with flyers for forthcoming events and desperate pleas for accommodation. Don't be intimidated by the locals all apparently knowing each other.

Françoise
Kerkstraat 176 (624 0145). Tram 16, 24, 25. **Open** 9.30am-6pm Mon-Sat.
At this lesbian-owned café and gallery you can get tea, coffee, home-made pastries and full meals (including vegetarian). Exhibitions of work by women artists change every month. Décor is traditional and music classical. They also offer accommodation. *See also chapter* **Gay & Lesbian**.

Vandenberg
Lindengracht 95 (622 2716). Tram 3. **Open** 5pm-1am Mon-Fri, Sun; 5pm-2am Fri, Sat.
A cosy place in the Jordaan for a good dinner or a coffee on

Saunas & Sports

Most sports centres, swimming pools and saunas have women-only sessions; *see chapter* **Sport & Fitness**. *See chapter* **Gay & Lesbian** for the formerly squatted **Sauna Fenomeen**.

Eastern Bathhouse Hammam
Zaanstraat 88 (681 4818). Tram 3. **Open** noon-10pm Tue-Fri, Sun; noon-8pm Sat. Closed Aug. **Admission** *f*15.
This unique bathhouse treats women to the pleasures of Eastern bathing. A thorough steaming, cleansing and washing is included in the admission and for an extra *f*25 you can enjoy a scrub or massage. A relaxation area and snacks are also available.

Kenau Women's Centre
Overtoom 270 (616 2913). Tram 1, 6. **Open** 10am-4pm Mon-Thur.
This centre offers a wide range of self-defence courses for women of all ages, including karate, aikido and tai chi chuan. There is also a special course offered for women who have experienced sexual or physical harassment.

Business Women

Mama Cash
Eerste Helmerstraat 17/2 (689 3634). Tram 1, 2, 3, 5, 6, 12. **Open** 9am-5pm Mon-Thur.
Launched in 1983, Mama Cash gives financial backing to women's business ventures. Founder Marjan Sax, who used her *f*2.5 million inheritance to set up the foundation, was spurred into action to counter 'a deep-rooted reluctance within the Netherlands to support career women.'

STEW
Oostenburgervoorstraat 172 (623 9369). Tram 10/Bus 22, 28. **Open** 9am-5pm Mon-Fri.
This association offers training and advice (in Dutch) for

women (and men) wishing to start their own small businesses or work as freelancers. Special women-only programmes are also offered.

Women's International Network
PO Box 15692, 1001 ND Amsterdam (662 0084). **Membership** Sept-June ƒ150.
This network of professional women offers support and a wealth of contacts and advice for career-orientated women. To join you should be over 25, of professional or entrepreneurial status, and have been employed for a minimum of five years. Associate membership is available for women temporarily out of work. There's an international mix and everything is in English: monthly meetings, guest speakers, lectures and workshops. Every first Wednesday of the month they host a 'Network Cocktail Hour'.

Women's Centres

Het Vrouwenhuis (The Women's House)
Nieuwe Herengracht 95 (625 2066). Tram 7, 9, 14/Metro Waterlooplein. **Open** *telephone enquiries* 11am-4pm Mon-Fri; *bar* opening times vary depending on evening courses; *library* noon-5pm Wed; noon-9pm Thur. Closed July to mid-Aug (during school holidays).
Besides offering a wide choice of classes and courses, the Vrouwenhuis also houses feminist magazines *Surplus* and *Vrouwen* and such organisations as NVB (Dutch Women's Movement) and ZAMI (Black/Immigrant Women's Centre, phone 639 3138). The women's library stocks some 3,000 titles by and about women and on the days when it is open, you can visit the Vrouwenhuis for information. There are new courses each season including chess, rock 'n' roll dancing, tap dancing, assertiveness and politics for beginners. The Vrouwenhuis also organises a celebration annually on International Women's Day (March 8) and occasional parties.

Xenia Intercultural Women's Centre
Klaas Katerstraat 2 (619 8765). Bus 19, 68. **Open** 9am-10pm Mon-Fri; 4-8pm Sun.
Classes and courses for women of all nationalities, including children's ballet, aerobics, sewing and hairdressing. On Sunday evenings women get together for dinner and a chat. No membership required but do sign up for the Sunday dinner beforehand.

Literature
Archives

For **Lesbian Archives,** *see chapter* **Gay & Lesbian;** for **Centraal Bibliotheek,** *see chapter* **Survival.**

IIAV
Obiplein 4 (665 0820). Tram 3, 6, 14. **Open** noon-5pm Mon; 10am-7pm Tue; 10am-5pm Wed-Fri.
The International Archives of the Women's & Lesbian Movement (IIAV) relate the history of the movement through books, documents, periodicals, press clippings and photographs. It's the best place for information about recent developments in the feminist movement and the position of women in Dutch society.

Bookshops

Opzij (ƒ6,50) is the leading feminist publication in The Netherlands and has comprehensive what's-on listings. *Savante* is a quarterly women's studies magazine (ƒ6,75). A wide range of international

women's titles can be picked up at **Xantippe** (*see below*) or English-language bookshops such as **WH Smith** or **The American Book Center** (*see chapter* **Shopping**). For books, the second-hand women's bookstores (*see below*) which also carry English titles can occasionally throw up a rare gem. For gay bookstore **Vrolijk**, which, like Xantippe, also stocks the latest novels in English, *see chapter* **Gay & Lesbian**.

Antiquariaat Lorelei
Prinsengracht 495 (623 4308). Tram 1, 2, 5, 7, 10, 11. **Open** noon-6pm Wed-Fri; noon-5pm Sat.
Stocks a huge selection of second-hand, old and rare books, including novels by and about women. Titles in English cover all subjects from biography and feminist theory to travel and sociology. Lorelei also has a notice-board for information on events and activities of interest to women.

Vrouwen in Druk
Westermarkt 5 (624 5003). Tram 1, 2, 5, 7, 10, 11, 13, 14, 17. **Open** 11am-6pm Mon-Fri; 11am-5pm Sat.
Close to the Homomonument, this shop stocks second-hand books (with dozens of shelves of English titles) by female authors, covering feminist theory, history and literature.

Xantippe
Prinsengracht 290 (623 5854). Tram 1, 2, 5, 7, 10, 11. **Open** 1-6pm Mon; 10am-6pm Tue-Fri; 10am-5pm Sat. **Credit** AmEx, EC, MC, V.
Claims to be the largest women's bookshop in Europe, stocking new titles, comics and magazines – many in English. The travel section is particularly good. Helpful staff can provide up-to-date information on what's on for women.

Delve into feminist history at the IIAV.

Shops

Bicycle Repair

Freewheel
Akoleienstraat 7 (627 7252). Tram 10, 13, 14, 17.
Open 9am-6pm Tue-Fri; 9am-5pm Sat.
Friendly women-run bicycle repair shop that also sells second-hand bikes and rents out *bakfiets* – bikes with large trolleys attacked. Rental costs ƒ7.50 (hour); ƒ35 (day); ƒ25 (night).

Vrouwenfietsenmakerij
Palembangstraat 67 (665 3218). Tram 3, 6. **Open** 9am-5.30pm Tue, Wed, Fri; noon-5.30pm Thur; 9am-5pm Sat.
A women-run bicycle repair shop in the east of the city which also sells second-hand bikes.

Erotica

Demask
Zeedijk 64 (620 5603). Tram 4, 9, 14, 16, 24, 25.
Open 11am-7pm Mon-Wed, Fri, Sat; 11am-9pm Thur.
Credit AmEx, EC, MC, V.
Popular shop offering a wide but pricey range of leather and rubber clothing for men and women.

Female & Partners
Spuistraat 100 (620 9152). Tram 13, 14, 17. **Open** 1-6pm Mon; 11am-6pm Tue- Sat. **Credit** AmEx, EC, MC, V.
Specialists in gear such as vibrators, dildoes, erotic lingerie, rubber and PVC clothing. The women who run the shop are friendly and will put you at ease if you feel awkward about such purchases.

Mail & Female
Prinsengracht 489 (623 3916). Tram 1, 2, 5, 11. **Open** 1-6pm Mon; 11am-6pm Tue-Sat. **Credit** AmEx, EC, MC, V.
Erotic paraphernalia ranging from massage oils to kinky clothing and the most innovative vibrators you're ever likely to come across. Check out the glossy catalogue too.

NVSH
Blauwburgwal 7-9 (623 9359). Tram 1, 2, 5, 11, 13, 17.
Open 11am-6pm Mon-Fri; noon-5pm Sat.
The Netherlands' Association for Sexual Reform sells rubber and leather items, books, sex toys and safe sex supplies.

Hotels

There are no women-only hotels, but the following are noted for being women-friendly.

Granada Hotel
Leidsekruisstraat 13 (623 6711). Tram 1, 2, 5, 6, 7, 10, 11. **Rates** single ƒ75; double ƒ110-ƒ125. **Credit** AmEx, EC, MC, V.
A relaxed, mixed hotel, much frequented by women and gays on a tight budget. Many rooms have shared facilities. There's a returnable deposit for keys and you won't be surcharged for overnight company.
Hotel services *Car park (enclosed) nearby. Sitting room.*

Quentin Hotel
Leidsekade 89 (626 2187). Tram 1, 2, 5, 6, 7, 10, 11. **Rates** single ƒ67,50-ƒ92,50; double ƒ87,50-ƒ145. **Credit** AmEx, EC, MC, V.
Particularly welcoming to lesbians, though not to small children. The English-speaking staff are friendly and have a useful knowledge of the cultural scene in Amsterdam.
Hotel services *24-hour bar. Car park (guarded) nearby. Snacks and drinks available 24 hours daily.*

Health and Safety

Amsterdam is a relatively unthreatening city for women, although it has places to avoid, particularly after dark. If you are raped or sexually abused call an appropriate help line (*see below*). Women's health and well-being is taken seriously here and any of the centres below will happily advise on contraception or the morning-after pill, or refer you to women-friendly doctors for other matters. For other health establishments and counselling services, *see chapter* **Survival**.

Aletta Jacobshuis
Overtoom 323 (616 6222, fax 685 1961). Tram 1, 6.
Open 9am-4.30pm Mon-Fri; 7.30-9pm Tue, Thur; emergencies Sat (*only* for the morning-after-pill).
Information and help on sexual problems and birth control. Make a phone appointment to get prescriptions for contraceptive pills, the morning-after pill or condoms.

Meldpunt Vrouwen Opvang Amsterdam
PO Box 67024, 1060 WA Amsterdam (611 6022).
Open 9am-5pmMon-Fri.
Institution encompassing numerous support groups including Stichting Vrouwen 40-60 for women in crisis situations, particularly those between the ages of 40 and 60; Vrouwen Opvang Leger Des Heils (the Salvation Army refuge for women) and De Roggeveen for homeless women.

MR '70
Sarphatistraat 620-626 (624 5426). **Open** 9am-4pm Mon-Thur; 9am-1pm Fri.
An abortion clinic which offers help and advice.

Vrouwen Gezondheidcentrum
Obiplein 4 (693 4358). Tram 3, 6, 14. **Open** 10am-1pm Mon, Tue; 7-10pm Thur; 1-4pm Fri.
Women working at the Women's Health Care Centre give information and advice on all health matters. They refer patients to *vrouwvriendlijke arts* (doctors, clinics and therapists sympathetic to women's specific needs) and run courses and evening classes on issues such as pregnancy, eating disorders and the menopause.

Helplines

AIDS-infolijn
06 0222220 (Dutch); 06 0223338 (Chinese); 06 0992255 (Moroccan); 06 0994488 (Turkish) **Open** 2-10pm Mon-Fri.
Free line for advice on all aspects of HIV and AIDS. English speakers should ring the Dutch number.

Blijf van Mij Lijf
(638 7638) **Open** 24 hours daily.
24-hour support line for abused women and their children.

De Eerste Lijn
(612 7576) **Open** 10.30am-11.30pm Mon-Fri; 3.30-11.30pm weekends.
Hotline for victims of sexual violence.

Meldpunt Vrouwen Opvang Amsterdam
(611 6022) **Open** 9am-5pm Mon-Fri.
Central helpline for women who have been sexually abused

Vrouwen Bellen Vrouwen
(625 0150). **Open** 9.30am-12.30pm Tue, Wed, Thur; 7.30-10.30pm, Tue, Thur.
Women can get advice and support by ringing this phone line, 'Women Call Women'.

Trips Out of Town

Beyond
Amsterdam

Venturing forth from the capital – the hows, whys and wherefores.

There's more to the Netherlands than just Amsterdam. The national borders enclose 12 distinctive provinces, each with their own spoken dialects that also vary from town to town. But the whole country covers just 41,864 square kilometres (16,000 square miles) and even the remotest corners are less than a day's drive or train ride away. Many towns and cities worth visiting are less than an hour from Amsterdam.

COMMON GROUND
More than almost any other, this country has been shaped by its inhabitants. Over half the land is below sea level, much of it laboriously reclaimed (*see chapter* **The Provinces: Fighting the Sea**). The vulnerability of their land fuels Dutch concern for the environment. One person's failure to maintain their part of a dyke could imperil an entire town. During the flood of 1995 when the river Maas rose far beyond its banks, part of the provinces Limburg and Brabant were flooded and whole towns had to be evacuated. A sense of community has become engrained in the Dutch nature: in the eighties, workers agreed to forego pay rises for five years until the economy could be revived.

WHERE IS HOLLAND?
Due to the importance of the region of Holland in Dutch history, the entire country has confusingly become widely known by that name, instead of the Netherlands. In fact, Holland accounts for just two of the 12 provinces: Noord (North) and Zuid (South). Amsterdam lies in the south of Noord Holland and is an easy day trip away from most of the classic Dutch attractions.

The contemporary face of Holland is represented by its ring of major cities called The Randstad (*see chapter* **The Randstad**). The cosmopolitan Randstad is sometimes considered by the provinces as a rather self-obsessed state within a state, yet it's not homogeneous. A popular piece of advice which summarises the differences quite well is 'Work in Rotterdam, party in Amsterdam and sleep in The Hague'. As high-speed road and rail links unify the country, regional customs and accents are being eroded, but the provinces are still fighting to preserve their identity.

Travel Information
The **Netherlands Board of Tourism** (Vlietweg 15, 2266 KA, Leidschendam; 070 3705 705) and branches abroad, can help with general information. For each centre of interest, we've listed the appropriate VVV tourist office, which will also suggest and reserve accommodation, as will **Nederlands Reservings Centrum** (Postbus 404, 2260 AK, Leidschendam; tel 070 320 2500). For all transport information and timetables (trains, buses and metros) contact the **OV Reisinformatie** information phone line (06 9292): calls are charged at 50 cents per minute. Lines are open 6am-midnight daily.

Roads
The Netherlands' extensive network of motorways and roads is well-maintained, and clearly signposted. *See chapter* **Survival** for advice on driving and for the motoring organisation ANWB, which offers a broad selection of maps and suggested excursions.

Buses and Coaches
The national bus service is reasonably priced, but not as easy to negotiate as the railway (*see below*). For bus information and timetables phone **OV Reisinformatie** (*above*). Private coach companies offering good value half and full-day excursions (from ƒ30 per person for local trips to ƒ60 per person to Belgium; ask at VVV for details). **Eurolines**, Rokin 10 (627 5151) covers destinations all over Europe: Brussels costs from ƒ35 one-way and from ƒ60 return.

Cycling
The Netherlands is flat (but windy) and cycle paths are plentiful; the VVV and ANWB sell cycle tour maps. Most major railway stations have bike hire depots. You'll need proof of identity and a cash deposit (usually around ƒ200). Rail ticket holders with a bike ticket bought at the station are entitled to a discount. Occasionally, it is also possible to

pay using a credit card. Bicycles cost around $f8$ per day and $f32$ per week; for mountain bikes the rent goes up to around $f20$ per day and $f80$ per week (while the deposit rises to around $f300$). During the summer months we recommend that you reserve a bike at least one day in advance. Bicycles can not be taken on Dutch trains at peak times (6.30-9am, 4.30-6pm, Mon-Fri) and it costs $f10$ one-way and $f17,50$ return to take them on board. Throughout July and August there are no time restrictions.

Netherlands Railway (NS)

The prices listed below are a rough guide: fares are updated in January each year.

The extensive NS rail network is efficient, clean, punctual and inexpensive. Services are frequent, so reservations are unnecessary, unless you are travelling on an international train. First class travel is one-and-a-half times the cost of second class. Credit cards are not accepted at ticket offices. Departure times are displayed on yellow station posters; a national timetable can be bought at stations and most newsagents, and the **OV Reisinformatie** (*above*) can help with any departure and arrival information. For information on international departures and arrivals phone **NS Internationaal Reisinformatie** on 06 9296; calls cost 50c per minute and lines are open 9am-5pm Mon-Fri.

As a rule, national tickets are valid for one day only; if you make a return journey over more than one day you must buy two single tickets. If you are returning on the same day you pay a cheaper rate if you specifically ask for a day-return ticket (*dagretour*). InterRail tickets are valid in the Netherlands, but a supplement is payable on Eurocity trains.

Any passenger who may need special assistance during their journey (such as wheelchair provision) can phone 030 355555 (8am-4pm Mon-Fri) at least one day before day of travel to ensure that help will be provided.

Children under four travel free; four- to 11-year-olds can pay a fixed fare of $f2,50$ (regardless of first or second class) with a **Railrunner** pass but must be accompanied by a fare-paying adult. Four- to 11-year-olds who travel alone pay 40 per cent of the standard fare.

Rail Rover passes offer unlimited travel anywhere in the country: a one-day pass costs $f66$ (2nd class) or $f99$ (1st class). For an extra $f7,50$ a **Link Rover** pass entitles you to travel on all trams, buses and metro trains nationwide. A five-day Rail Rover pass, valid on five consecutive days only, costs $f313$ (2nd class) or $f470$ (1st class); a Link Rover pass costs an extra $f25$.

A **Euro Domino Holland** ticket entitles you to unlimited travel on any three, five or ten days within the period of one month. Cost per adult (2nd class) is as follows: *three days* $f90$ (adult), $f65$ (under 26); *five days* $f140$ (adult), $f99$ (under 26); *ten days* $f250$ (adult), $f175$ (under 26). There is a Euro Domino Holland ticket for children between four and 11 but it's actually cheaper for them to travel on a Railrunner ticket.

During June, July and August the **Zomertoer** (Summer Tour) ticket, a special version of the Euro Domino Holland entitles you to three days of travel within ten consecutive days, for one or two passengers travelling together. Prices for one person are $f85$ (2nd class) and $f104$ (1st class); for two people $f115$ (2nd class) and $f155$ (1st class). A **Zomertoer Plus** ticket is also valid for travel by (interliner) bus, tram or on the metro at an extra cost of $f17$ for one person and $f25$ for two.

If you are under 19 then you can have unlimited travel within the Netherlands and Belgium for any four days over a ten-day period using a **TourTime** pass (2nd class). The cost is $f65$; an additional pass for buses, trams and the metro costs $f15$. TourTime is available only in June, July and August and during Dutch school holiday periods. Proof of age (passport) is required. You must show your passport in order to buy a seven-day Rail Rover, Euro Domino Holland, Zomertoer Plus or TourTime.

For group travel, the **Meermanskaar** (Multi Rover) offers unlimited travel on one day for up to six people (not before 9am Mon-Fri except during July and August when there is no restriction). Prices for 2nd class range from $f98$ for two people to $f168$ for six; first class travel costs from $f144$ for two people to $f246$ for six.

Other options ideal for longer stays are tickets offering a 40 per cent discount on standard fares which are valid for a year: the **Jongerenkaart** (under-26s); the **Rail-Aktief-Kaart** (26-59) and the **60+ Seniorenkaart** (over-60s); each cost $f99$. However they cannot be used between 4am and 9am Mon-Fri except in July and August. These tickets also entitle you to further savings on travel in the evenings and at weekends.

If travelling to the Frisian Islands it is wise to buy a special **Waddenbiljet** (Wadden ticket) which is a train, bus and boat ticket all in one. Its validity is unlimited so you can return whenever you wish. Prices from Amsterdam start around $f100,75$, depending on the island you visit.

Day Excursions

NS offers around 188 all-inclusive excursions (discount rail and other travel, admission to sights and occasional extras), to destinations all over the Netherlands. Details can be found in the (Dutch) handbook *Er-op-Uit!* ($f4,95$), available at tourist offices and railway stations.

Excursions in Holland

Cheeses, tulips, windmills, traditional costumes – there's a day trip to match every Dutch cliché.

Galloping in with the Gouda at a traditional cheese market.

The majority of the Netherlands' stereotypical sights are concentrated in the area around Amsterdam: Noord and Zuid Holland. Both of these provinces are small and many of the sights are close to each other and easily reached by public transport or special tours (*see chapter* **Beyond Amsterdam**).

Cheese

The Dutch export around 420,000 tonnes of cheese every year. For types of cheese, *see chapter* **Shopping**. The summer cheese markets, museums and traditional farms capture the flavour of how this commodity used to be made and sold. The most famous is at **Alkmaar**. A lesser-known but authentic farmers' cheese market is held every Tuesday throughout the year in the village of Bodegraven, between Gouda and Utrecht.

There are many thatched-roof *kaasboerderijen* (cheese farms) near Gouda, several of which are on the picturesque River Vlist. Look out for the sign '*kaas te koop*' (cheese for sale), indicating a farm shop where you may be able to look behind the scenes as well as buy freshly made Gouda, often laced with herbs.

Alkmaar

Getting there 37km (22 miles) north-west; *by train* direct from Centraal Station.
VVV *Waagplein 2 (072 5114284).* **Open** *Apr-Oct* 9am-5.30pm Mon-Wed; 9am-7pm Thur; 9am-6pm Fri; 9am-5pm Sat.

Alkmaar cheese market (*mid Apr-mid Sept* 10am-noon Fri) is as much a ritual for tourists as for members of the cheese porters' guild. Garbed in pristine white uniforms and straw hats with coloured ribbons denoting the competing guilds, they weigh the cheeses and carry them in wooden trays hung from their shoulders. Arrive by 9.30am to see the buyers testing a core of cheese from each lot. The ceremony, takes place at the *Waag* (weigh house). There's a Cheese Museum upstairs and craft stalls outside. The VVV also offers a written walking tour of the medieval centre, dating from 935AD, which often resounds to the sound of a carillon concert. The **Hans Brinker Museum** is dedicated to the boy who stuck his finger in the dyke to save Haarlem; the **Biermuseum** has a beer-tasting cellar and there is an impressive art and toy collection at the **Stedelijk Museum**.

Edam

Getting there 10km (5 miles) north; *by bus* 110, 112, 114 from Centraal Station.
VVV *Stadhuis, Damplein 1 (0299 371727).* **Open** *Apr-Oct* 10am-5pm Mon-Sat; *Nov-Mar* 10am-2pm.
This tiny town was a prosperous port during the Golden Age and has some exquisite façades and bridges. It suffers fewer tourist hordes than Volendam (*see below*), which is a bus-ride away. At the **cheese market** (*July-Aug* 10am-noon Wed), the famous red-skinned cheese arrives by various means, including boat and horse-drawn cart. **Grote Kerk**, rebuilt in 1602, has remarkable stained glass. The *speeltoren* (bell tower) of **Kleine Kerk** has one of the country's oldest carillons (1561). In the municipal museum on Damplein there are portraits of a 202kg (445lb) man and a 2.75m (9ft) tall woman, as well as a floating cellar.

Gouda

Getting there 29km (18 miles) south-west; *by train* direct from Centraal Station.
VVV *Markt 27 (0182 513666).* **Open** 9am-5pm Mon-Fri; 10am-4pm Sat.
Golden wheels of *kaas* are traded at the Thursday **cheese market** (*July-Aug* 10am-noon) in front of the 1668 **Waag** (weigh house) – whose gablestone depicts cheese-weighing – and the Gothic city hall of 1450. A general market runs throughout the year (9am-1pm Thur; 9am-5pm Sat). Gouda's other famous products include clay pipes and pottery (which are displayed in the **De Moriaan Museum**) and candles, some 20,000 of which illuminate the square during the Christmas tree ceremony. **St Janskerk** (entrance *f*3) boasts over half of Holland's antique stained-glass windows, 70 in all, and holds carillon concerts (*July-Aug* 12.30-1.30pm Thur, free). A hospice and hospital from 1320 to 1910, the Stedelijk Museum **Caterina Gasthuis** has Golden Age silver and modern art. The **Molen de Roode Leeuw** is a corn grinding windmill, around which you can take a special group tour (phone VVV for an appointment).

Purmerend

Getting there 26km (15 miles) north-east; *by train* direct from Centraal Station; *by bus* 100, 106 or 106 from Centraal Station.
VVV *Kerkstraat 9 (0299 425365).* **Open** 1-5pm Mon; 10am-5pm Tue-Fri; 9am-4pm Sat.
Purmerend has become an Amsterdam dormitory town. A population explosion over the last three decades has changed its character, but some authenticity can be found on Tuesday mornings from 7am until 10pm when the cattle and general markets take place; deals are sealed by a handclap. There are art exhibitions in **Museum Waterland** and local history in the **Purmerend Museum**. If you're driving, the most rewarding return route to Amsterdam is via the country roads through Den Ilp and Landsmeer.

Flowers

Since it arrived here 400 years ago, the tulip has become Holland's hallmark. When it blooms thousands of tourists make for the **Keukenhof Bulb Gardens** in Lisse (*see below* **Nurseries and Gardens**). Dutch blooms can be seen all year round in markets, botanical gardens, auctions and flower parades. For export rules on bulbs and flowers, *see chapter* **Shopping**.

Floral calendar

Spring: The flower trade's year kicks off in mid- to late February with the indoor **Westfriese Flora** (0228 5 11644) at Bovenkarspel, near Enkhuizen. From late March to late May, the **bulb district** from Den Helder to The Hague, is carpeted with blooms of the principal crops: daffodils, crocuses, gladioli, hyacinths, narcissi – and tulips.
Summer: In mid- to late May, golden fields of rapeseed brighten Flevoland, Friesland and Groningen (*see chapter* **The Provinces**). In The Hague, the Japanese Garden at **Clingendael Gardens** is in flower from early May to mid-June, and in **Westbroek Park** the rose garden (which contains 350 varieties) bursts into colour during July and August. In late June there's the **Floralia** exhibition at the Zuider Zee Museum, Enkhuizen (*see below* **Traditions: West Friesland**).
Autumn: Heather purples the landscape (especially in Gelderland's Veluwe, *see chapter* **The Provinces**) during August and September, when greenhouse flowers also emerge. This is the season of most flower parades (*see below*).
Winter: In November, the public and florists from all over the world view new varieties at the **Professional Flower Exhibition** at Aalsmeer Flower Auction (*below*). At Christmas there's the **Kerstflora** show at Hillegom, near Lisse in Noord Holland.

Flower parades

Noordwijk-Haarlem Parade (0252 434710). Noordwijk (10am) *via Sassenheim* (1pm) *to Haarlem* (7pm). **Date** Sat after April 19. Floats on show at Lisse and Hobahohallen all day for the two days preceding the parade.
Rijnsburg Parade (071 4055911). Rijnsburg (11am) *via Leiden* (1pm) *to Noordwijk* (4pm). **Date** first Sat in Aug. Floats on show at Boulevard, Noordwijk (Sat evening, Sun).
Aalsmeer-Amsterdam Parade (0297 325100). Aalsmeer (8.30am) *to Amsterdam* (4pm). **Date** first Sat in Sept.
The Aalsmeer-Amsterdam Parade is Europe's largest flower procession and floats can be viewed (3-10pm Fri; 9am-5pm Sun) in Aalsmeer Auction Hall (*see below* **Flower Auctions**). Highlights are the parade down Amstelveenseweg before lunch, the 4pm reception at Dam Square, Amsterdam (*see chapter* **Amsterdam by Season**) and the illuminated cavalcade through Aalsmeer (9-11pm). Be early.

Flower Auctions

Aalsmeer Flower Auction

Legmeerdijk 313 (0297 332185). **Getting there** 15km (9 miles) south-west; *by bus* 172 from Centraal Station to Aalsmeer Flower Auction. **Open** 7.30-11am Mon-Fri. **Admission** *f*5; under-12s free. Avoid visiting on Thursdays, as it's usually too quiet. On other days, you can catch the best action before 9am.
Each year more than 3.5 billion cut flowers and 400 million pot plants are handled, mostly for export, at the **Verenigde Bloemenveilingen Aalsmeer**, the world's biggest flower auction. To bid, dealers push a button to stop a 'clock' which counts from 100 down to one – bidders risk either overpaying or not getting the goods. This procedure gave rise to the English phrase 'Dutch auction'. Of growing importance is **Westland Flower Auction** at Naaldwijk, south of The Hague (0174 633333).

Broeker Veiling

Museumweg 2, Broek-op-Langerdijk (0226 313807). **Getting there** 36km (22 miles) north; *by train* to Alkmaar, then bus 155 or by train to Heerhugowaard and from there by taxi. **Open** *Apr-Nov* 10am-5pm Mon-Fri; noon-5pm Sat, Sun. **Admission** *auction and museum* *f*7,50; *f*4,50 under-15s; *incl boat trip* *f*12,50; *f*7 under-15s.
The oldest auction in the world is now strictly for tourists, who can buy small lots of flowers, fruit and vegetables. Bidding is done as at a professional auction. Admission

includes a museum of old farming artefacts and (for a small extra fee) a boat trip around the area. A visit is easily combined with a trip to Alkmaar (*see above* **Cheese**).

Nurseries and Gardens

Over a hundred botanical gardens serve as research centres for the industry, notably Hortus Botanicus, Leiden (071 275144) and Hortus Bulborum, Zuiderkerklaan 23a, Heiloo, which from mid-April to mid-May displays offshoots of the original tulips introduced from Turkey. For Flevohof farm, *see chapter* **The Provinces: Flevoland.**

Frans Rozen Nursery

Vogelenzangseweg 49, Vogelenzang (023 5847245). **Getting there** 25km (16 miles) west; *by train* to Heemstede, then bus 90 to Café Rusthoek. **Open** *late Mar-May* 8am-6pm daily; *July-Sept* 9am-5pm Mon-Fri. **Admission** *f*2; under-14s free.
The huge greenhouse and extensive fields of this 200-year-old nursery are open to the public. Here you can gain an insight into commercial cultivation and the meticulous development of new hybrids – and also purchase bulbs for export. There's a tulip show in April and May and a free summer show between July and September.

Keukenhof Bulb Gardens

Keukenhof, near Lisse (0252 419144). **Getting there** 27km (17 miles) south-west; *by train* from Centraal Station to Leiden, then bus 54. **Open** *21 Mar-22 May 1995* 8am-7.30pm daily; similar in 1996. **Admission** *f*16; *f*14 over-65s; *f*8 4-12s.
Keukenhof Bulb Gardens contain over 500 varieties of tulip and over six million bulbs bloom in the 28 hectares (70 acres) of this former royal 'kitchen garden', some under glass. The gardens and café get overrun, so arrive early with a picnic lunch. With the help of a VVV map, you can tour the bulb district (in bloom from March to late May), from which over half of the world's cut flowers and pot plants originate. The bulb district's history is covered at the **Museum voor de Bloembollenstreek** (02521 17900), also in Lisse. *Café. Wheelchairs and pushchairs for hire after reservation.*

Traditions

A few Dutch die-hards still wear local costume or keep to their old ways. Some make a genuine effort to preserve traditions, as at Staphorst (*see chapter* **The Provinces: Overijssel**), while others pander to tourists looking for the 'authentic' Holland by hauling out their lace caps and turning on windmills (*windmolens*) for special days.

Kinderdijk windmills

Getting there 60km (37 miles) south-west; *by train* from Centraal Station via Rotterdam to Dordrecht, then bus 152 to Alblasserdam, then bus 154.
VVV Alblasserdam , Cortgene 2, inside City Hall (078 6921200)
Open *Summer* 9am-5pm Mon-Sat; *Winter* 9am-1pm Mon-Fri. **Kinderdijk windmills** *Molenkade, Alblasserdam (078 6914300).* **Open** *Apr-Sept* 9.30am-5.30pm daily. **Admission** *f*3; *f*1,75 6-14s; under-6s free.
The sight of these 19 windmills under sail is spectacular, particularly when they're illuminated in the second week of September. To drain water from reclaimed land, windmills

were usually clustered in a co-ordinated group called a *gang* (a term adopted in English). This *gang* now operates just for tourists (July-Aug, 2.30-5.30pm Sat); you can look around inside Nederwaarde mill and it's also possible to go on a boat trip around the windmills.

Schoonhoven

Getting there 48km (30 miles) south; *by train* from Centraal Station to Gouda, then bus 197.
VVV *Stadhuisstraat 1 (0182 385009).* **Open** *May-Sept* 10am-12.15pm, 1.15-4.30pm Tue-Fri; 10am-3pm Sat; 1.30-4pm Sun. *Oct-Apr* 10am-noon, 2-4pm Tue-Fri; 10am-3pm Sat; 2-4pm Sun.
Schoonhoven has been famous since the Middle Ages for its silversmiths, who crafted such items as filigree jewellery, miniatures and ornaments for traditional costume. You can see antique pieces in the **Nederlands Goud- Zilver- en Klokkenmuseum** (Gold, Silver and Clock Museum) and the **Edelambachthuis** (Museum of Antique Silverware). There's an annual **silver market** on Whit Monday (late May), but silver shops are open all year round. Starting at *Silverhuys* (Silver House), Haven 1-3, is a row of buildings full of silver and pewter collectables, many of traditional design. **Klokkenhuys** (Clock House), Haven 9, stocks barometers and 500 extraordinary timepieces. At **Edelambachthuis**, Haven 13, a working silversmith gives demonstrations (Tue-Fri). This attractive town retains large sections of its ramparts. Olivier van Noort, the first Dutchman to sail around the world (1598-1601) and Claes Louwerenz Blom, who in 1549 first introduced the windmill to Spain, are buried in **St Bartholomaeus Kerk** (1354); there are great views from its tower, which leans 1.56m (5ft) off centre. The carillon of the 1452 **Stadhuis** has 50 bells made from the guns of Van Noort's ship.

Traditional costume

Bunschoten-Spakenburg 40km (25 miles) south-east; *by train* from Centraal Station to Amersfoort, then bus 116. **Dates** *mid July-mid Aug* Wed.
Schagen 48km (30 miles) north; *by train* direct from Centraal Station. **VVV** *Markt 22 (0224 298311).* **Dates** *July, Aug* Thur.
About a fifth of Bunschoten-Spakenburg residents still wear traditional dress on special market days (many of the older folk wear it every day). At Schagen, which has two medieval castle towers, costumed dancers entertain tourists, who also enjoy the cattle and craft markets and parades of horse-drawn carriages. Costumes are also worn at the markets in Hoorn and Medemblik (*see below* **West Friesland**), and sometimes on Sundays in Urk, Flevoland and on market day (July-Aug 10am-4pm Thur) in Middelburg, Zeeland (*see chapter* **The Provinces**). Also of interest is the **National Costume Museum** in The Hague (*see chapter* **The Randstad**).

Witches' Weigh House, Oudewater

Getting there 29km (18 miles) south; *by train* from Centraal Station to Gouda, then bus 180.
VVV *Markt 8 (0348 564636).* **Open** *Apr-Oct* 10.30am-4.30pm Tue-Sat; 1.30-4.30pm Sun; *Nov-Mar* 10.30-12.30pm Tue-Sat.
Witches' Weigh House *Leeuweringerstraat 2 (0348 563400).* **Open** *Apr-Oct* 10am-5pm Tue-Sat; noon-5pm Sun, public holidays. **Admission** *f*2,50; *f*2 CJP card holders, over -65s,Museum Card; *f*1,25 4-12s; free under -5s.
Dating from 1000AD, Oudewater (north of **Schoonhoven**, *see above*) was known for cheese, rope-making and its particularly honest merchants. Then in 1487 an epidemic of witch-hunting broke out, lasting until the beginning of the seventeenth century. Oudewater achieved fame for its honest weighing of suspected witches and warlocks in the *Heksenwaag* (Witches' Weigh House). This was after Charles V attended a witch trial in Polsbroek where the

(bribed) weighmaster declared that the woman suspect weighed only 2.5kg; at Oudewater she was found to weigh 50kg and was consequently acquitted. Each of the accused received a document, recognised throughout Europe, verifying that she was too heavy to travel by broom. Today's (free) certificate comes in six languages for the swarms of tourists who step on to the scales. The Weigh House also has a small, informative museum of witchcraft.

Waterland

Until the IJ tunnel was built in 1956, the Waterland district north of Amsterdam was accessible mainly by ferry and steam railway to Volendam. That isolation preserved much of the area's heritage, which is best enjoyed from the seat of a bicycle. For nearby **Edam** and the Museum Waterland in **Purmerend**, *see above* **Cheese**.

Broek-in-Waterland

Getting there 10km (6 miles) north-east; *by bus* 111 from Centraal Station.
For **VVV**, *see under* **Monnickendam**.
Full of eighteenth-century charm, this town has Waterland's greatest collection of old wooden buildings. Even rich Amsterdam merchants declined to build their country homes in stone, for fear of them sinking.

Marken

Getting there 15km (9 miles) north-east; *by train* NS *Rail Idee* ticket (including Volendam); *by bus* 110 from Centraal Station to Volendam and then boat to Marken; bus 111 direct to Marken or to Monnickendam and then by boat to Marken.
VVV, *see under* **Monnickendam** or **Volendam**.
Now reached by a causeway, this island was once full of fishermen, but is now bursting with costumes, souvenir shops and tourists. However, it's bearable out of season and is far more attractive and authentic than Volendam (*see below*), a boat ride away. The pristine wooden houses are painted green with white stripes and stand on stone piles to escape flooding. The **Marken Museum** explains the island's history. You can see *klompen* (clogs) being carved, and buy a souvenir pair at the shoemaker's, Kast 52 (9am-6pm daily).

Monnickendam

Getting there 12km (7½ miles) north-east; *by bus* 111 from Centraal Station.
VVV *De Zarken 2 (0299 651998).* **Open** *Sept-June* 9.30am-12.30pm, 1.30-5pm, Mon-Fri; 9.30am-5pm Sat; *July-Aug* 9.30am-5pm Mon-Fri; 9.30am-5pm Sat.
The remarkable thing about Monnickendam is the proportion of ancient buildings which have been preserved, whether Golden Age merchants' houses or herring smoke houses. The harbour fish restaurant, Stuttenburgh (Haringburgwal 2-5, 02995 1869), displays a collection of music boxes. On the *speeltoren* (bell tower) of the old town hall, now a museum, there's a delightful antique carillon, with two mechanical white knights parading as it plays.

Volendam

Getting there 18km (11 miles) north-east; *by train* NS *Rail Idee* ticket (*see* **Marken**); *by bus* 110 from Centraal Station.
VVV *Zeestraat 37 (0299 363747).* **Open** *mid Mar-Oct* 10am-5pm daily; *Oct* 10am-3pm Mon-Sat; *Nov-mid Mar* 10am-3pm Mon-Fri.
Volendam was such a successful fishing village that its flag flew at half-mast when the Zuider Zee was enclosed in 1932, cutting off access to the sea. The village's enterprise was soon applied to creating a theme park from its historic features but, unfortunately, the gaily garbed locals can barely be seen for the coachloads of tourists that are dumped there.

De Zaanse Schans

Near Zaandijk (information **Zaandam VVV** *Gedempte Gracht 76 (075 6162221).* **Open** 9am-5.30pm Mon-Fri; 9am-4pm Sat.
Getting there 14km (9 miles) north; *by train* NS *Rail Idee* ticket (includes cruise on River Zaan, admission to windmill museum, a pancake and a cup of coffee); *by bus* 89 from Marnixstraat.
De Zaanse Schans is a reconstructed museum village with a difference – people actually live in it. It sees around 800,000 visitors a year. The Zaan district was noted for industrial windmills (powering the manufacture of paint, flour and lumber), and you can buy mustard produced in one of the five working mills here. Amid the gabled homes, green with white trim, are an old-fashioned Albert Heijn grocery store, a former merchant's home and a cheese house. Boat trips on the adjacent Zaan River provide another perspective.

West Friesland

Facing Friesland across the northern IJsselmeer is West Friesland. Although part of Noord Holland for centuries, it has its own customs and slightly fewer visitors. One way to visit is to take a train to **Enkhuizen**, then a boat to **Medemblik** and on to Hoorn via the **Museum Stoomtram** (steam railway); there's an all-inclusive NS *Rail Idee* ticket for this route.

Enkhuizen

Getting there 45km (28 miles) north-east; *by train* direct from Centraal Station, NS *Rail Idee* ticket.
VVV *Tussen Twee Havens 1 (0228 313164).* **Open** *Apr-Oct* 9am-5pm daily; *Nov-Mar* 9am-5pm Mon-Fri.
Zuider Zee Museum *Wierdijk 18 (0228 310122).* **Open** *Binnenmuseum* 10am-5pm daily; *Buitenmuseum Apr-Oct* 10am-5pm daily. **Admission** *f*15; *f*10 4-12s, *f*12 over-65s.
This once-powerful fishing and whaling port has many relics of its past, but most people come for the remarkable **Zuider Zee Museum** (opened 1983). It comprises two separate sites: the indoor Binnenmuseum with its section on seafaring life and crafts, and an open-air reconstructed village, the Buitenmuseum. To make good use of the one-way crowd control system, start with the Buitenmuseum; it's reached by boat from the main jetty or the station jetty. Take a guided tour, or just wander around the hundred or so homes, shops and other buildings transplanted from towns around the Zuider Zee and authentically arranged.

Hoorn

Getting there 33km (20 miles) north-east; *by train* NS *Rail Idee*.
VVV *Veemarkt 4 (06 340 31055).* **Open** *Sept-June* 1-6pm Mon; 9.30am-6pm Tue, Wed, Fri; 9.30am-6pm, 7pm-9pm Thur; 9.30am-5pm Sat; *July-Aug* 1-6pm Mon; 9.30am-6pm Tue-Fri; 9.30 am-5pm.
Museum Stoomtram Hoorn-Medemblik Tickets from Van Dedemstraat 8, Hoorn (0229 214862), or any rail station. **Train times vary a lot, so call first**.
This pretty port dates from 1311 and grew rich on the Dutch East Indies trade; its success is reflected in grand architecture. Local costume and crafts can be seen in the weekly folklore celebrations called *Hartje Hoorn* (July-Aug 10am-5pm on most Wednesdays). The **Museum van de 20e Eeuw** (Museum of the Twentieth Century), Bierkade 4 (0229 214001) has a permanent exhibition of daily life in this century as well as special exhibitions. The baroque former Staten-College (council building) of 1632 now houses the **Westfries Museum**, which focuses on art and interior décor with a brief section on the region's past. Even older is the **hoofdtoren** (harbour tower) and **St Jansgasthuis**, a hospital from 1563 until 1922 and now an exhibition centre.

Medemblik

Getting there 45km (28 miles) north; *by train* NS *Rail Idee* (*see above*).

VVV *Dam 2 (0227 542852).* **Open** *Nov-Mar* 10am-noon, 2-4pm, Mon-Sat; *Apr-Oct* 10am-5pm daily.

An ancient port dating from 334AD and dominated by the Gothic St Bonifacius Kerk and **Radboud Kasteel**. Built in 1289, the castle is smaller than when it defended Floris V's realm, but still retains its knights' hall, towers, dungeon and a cellar tavern. Traditional costume is worn at the Saturday market (July-Aug), when goods are brought in by barges. Nearby is the circular village of **Opperdoes**, built on a *terp* mound (*see chapter* **The Provinces: Fighting the Sea**), and the 'long-village' of **Twisk**, with pyramid-roofed farm buildings.

Castles

The Netherlands is studded with 400 castles and many fortress towns retain large parts of their defences. Some of the best are within half an hour of Amsterdam; for those further afield, *see chapter* **The Provinces**. Eighty of the castles are open for tourists or business conferences; the fifteenth-century NJHC **Slot Assumberg** at Heemskerk, between Haarlem and Alkmaar, is a youth hostel (0251 232288). Or you can try the ultimate power lunch by flying from Schiphol to Maastricht on Air Excel (043 3650700) and booking a four-course lunch at either **Château Neercanne** in Maastricht (043 3251359) or **Kasteel Erenstein** in Kerkrade (045 5461333). Closer and cheaper is the castle tour you can do by driving, cycling or boating down the River Vecht.

De Haar

Kasteellaan 1, Haarzuilens, Utrecht (03407 71275). **Getting there** 30km (19 miles) south; *by train* direct to Utrecht, then bus 127. **Open** *Jan 1- mid Aug, 2nd Sun in Oct-mid Nov* 11am-4pm Mon-Fri; 1-4pm Sat, Sun (hourly tours: bookings 03407 3804). **Admission** *castle and grounds* ƒ10; children under-5 not permitted; *grounds only* ƒ2,50.

De Haar looks like the quintessential medieval castle although its romantic embellishments are relatively recent neo-Gothic re-creations. In 1887, the baron who inherited the ruins of De Haar married a Rothschild and together they recreated it on a majestic scale, commissioning the Rijksmuseum's architect, PJH Cuypers, and moving the entire village of Haarzuilens 2km (¾ mile) to make room for the outstanding formal grounds. The whole process took over 20 years. The castle (largest in the Netherlands) had previously been completed in 1391, was destroyed in 1482, rebuilt in 1505 and damaged again, by the French, in 1672-73. The lavish interior boasts tapestries, Louis XIV-XVI furniture and Far Eastern art, with spectacular stone carvings and stained glass in the hall.

Muiden (Rijksmuseum Muiderslot)

Herengracht 1, Muiden (0294 261325). **Getting there** 12km (7½ miles) south-east; *by bus* 136 from Amstel Station. **Open** *Apr-Oct* 10am-4pm Mon-Fri; 1-4pm Sat, Sun (tours hourly 10am-4pm); *Nov-Mar* 1pm-3pm Sat, Sun. **Admission** ƒ7,50 adults; ƒ5 under-12s, CJP holders, over-65s; free Museum Card holders; group discounts by arrangement.

Muiden is a moated rectangular castle strategically situated at the mouth of the River Vecht. It was originally built in 1280 for Count Floris V, who was murdered here in 1296 (*see chapter* **Early History**). Rebuilt in the fourteenth cen-

tury, the fortress has been through many sieges and frequent renovations. The seventeenth-century furnishings may seem out of context; they originate from the period of its most illustrious occupant, the Dutch poet and historian PC Hooft, who entertained the Muiden circle of writers, musicians and scholars in the castle's splendid halls. You can look round only on a guided tour (in English by arrangement).

Naarden

Getting there 20km (12 miles) south-east; *by train* direct from Centraal Station; *by train* 136 from Centraal Station.

Naarden VVV *Adriaan Dortsmanplein 1B (035 6942836).* **Open** *May-Sept* 9.15am-12.45pm, 1.30-5pm Mon-Fri; 10am-4pm Sat; noon-4pm Sun; *Easter and autumn holidays* 10am-12.45pm, 1.30-3pm, Mon-Fri; 10am-2pm Sat.

Vestingmuseum *Turfpoortbastion, Westvalstraat 6 (035 6945459).* **Open** *Easter-Oct* 10am-4.30pm Mon-Fri; noon-5pm Sat, Sun, public holidays. **Admission** ƒ5; ƒ4,50 over-65s; ƒ3,50 4-16s; free under-4s, Museum Card holders.

A double-moated, star-shaped stronghold with arrowhead-shaped bastions – one of Europe's most perfectly preserved fortified towns. It was in active service until 1926 and is currently being reconstructed. The defences are explained in the **Vestingmuseum**, located partly underground in the Turfpoort (Peat Gateway) bastion; admission includes a boat trip around the *vesting* (fortress). Cannons are fired by men in sixteenth-century soldiers' uniforms (2-4pm third Sun of month, May-Sept). The fortifications date from 1675, after the inhabitants were massacred by the Duke of Alva's son in 1572. The slaughter is depicted on the wall of the **Spaansehuis** (Spanish House), now a museum. Bach's St Matthew Passion is presented in the **Grote Kerk**, noted for its fine acoustics, on the Sunday (4.40pm), Thursday (7pm), Friday and Saturday (both 11.30am) before Easter.

River Vecht tour

Getting there 35km (22 miles) south-east; *by train* direct to Utrecht from Centraal Station.

Cruise Utrecht Canal Touring Co *Oudegracht, opposite number 85 (030 2720111/030 2319 377).* **Times** *Mid May-Sept* leaves Utrecht 9.30am on Tuesday and Friday to Loenen, returns to Utrecht 6pm. **Tickets** ƒ27,50 adults, ƒ22,50 under-13s over-65s.

Meandering upstream from Muiden (*see above*) into Utrecht province (*see chapter* **The Provinces**), you reach Loenen, a charming town of cobbled streets, with a leaning church spire and the restored castle of **Loenersloot**, with a thirteenth-century keep. Gracing the river banks are seventeenth- and eighteenth-century mansions, built as retreats by Amsterdam merchants. At Breukelen, which gave its name to Brooklyn, New York, is the elegant, classical house of **Gunterstein** (rebuilt in 1681). Beyond it, on the other bank, is **Nijenrode**, a medieval castle destroyed in 1672 and rebuilt, which fell into disrepair and was restored in 1907 in seventeenth-century style. Across the river is **Oudaen**, a country house partly dating from 1303. A detour east around the lake Loosdrechtse Plassen leads to castle museum **Sijpesteyn**. Built on the foundations of a manor house which was destroyed in about 1580, this castle was rebuilt at the turn of the century in medieval style (tours: *Easter-Oct* 10am-5pm Tue-Fri; noon-5pm Sat, Sun. ƒ7 adults, ƒ4 4-14s; call 035 5823208). Back on the Vecht, between **De Haar** castle (*see above*) and the city of Utrecht is **Slot Zuylen** at Maarsen. Surrounded by woods and a moat, it dates from about 1300, but has an eighteenth-century façade (tours: *mid-Mar-mid-May, mid-Sept-mid-Nov*, Sat, Sun; *mid-May-mid-Sept* Tue-Sun; ƒ7 adults, ƒ4 4-16s, ƒ5 over-65s; call 030 2440255).

Triumph of the mill – a stereotypical Dutch sight.

The Randstad

The circular sprawl of 'Edge City' contains 40 per cent of the Dutch population and most of its major cities.

The Randstad ('Edge City' – so-called because of its coastal location on the Netherlands' western edge) is essentially a ring-shaped conurbation bounded by Amsterdam, Delft, Haarlem, The Hague, Leiden, Rotterdam and Utrecht. In recent years Gouda (*see chapter* **Excursions in Holland**) and Dordrecht have also come to be considered part of the Randstad. This is one of the most densely populated areas in the world. Forty per cent of the Dutch population inhabit this urban sprawl. Although separately administered and fiercely independent, the individual towns work together by choice for their common good.

The road, rail and waterway networks are impressive even by Dutch standards and the area's strong economy accounts for at least half of the national turnover. The Randstad's importance is based on several factors: Rotterdam's port, which handles more tonnage than any other in the world; Amsterdam's Schiphol airport and the city's role as financial and banking centre; the seats of government and royalty at The Hague; and a huge agricultural belt.

Regarded with awe and sometimes resentment by the outlying provinces, the Randstad is often accused of monopolising government attention and funds, although it has no formally defined status and is still prone to bitter rivalries between cities and municipalities.

Delft

Delft is most famous for its blue and white pottery and tiles and there are still a few factories which are open to visitors (*see below*). For a historical perspective, the **Lambert van Meerten Museum**, a nineteenth-century mansion, houses fine pieces of tin-glazed earthenware, as well as a vast collection of magnificent ebony-veneered furniture. The enormous range of tiles – depicting everything from battling warships to copulating hares – compares startlingly with today's mass-produced trinkets.

Almost everything you might want to see in this compact city is located along the Oude Delft, as are the best views. Position yourself either on the Boterbrug (Butter Bridge) or on one of the floating cafés in the middle of the canal. Delft's loss in trade has been Rotterdam's gain, but it has meant that the city's centuries-old gables, hump-backed bridges

and shady canals remain unchanged. To get an idea of how little it has altered, go to the Hooikade, where Vermeer painted the *View of Delft* now hanging in the Mauritshuis (*see below* **The Hague**).

Museums in Delft have the air of private residences and are blessedly devoid of crowds. **Het Prinsenhof** on Sint Agathaplein has permanent exhibitions on William the Silent (assassinated here in 1584) and the building's role as the convent of St Agatha until 1572. Opposite, in another wing of the convent, are the ethnographic collection and exhibitions of the **Nusantara Museum**.

Delft also has two spectacular churches with soaring spires which can be seen for miles around. The **Nieuwe Kerk**, in the Markt opposite De Keyser's 1618 Stadhuis, contains the mausoleums of William the Silent and lawyer-philosopher Hugo de Groot. Not to be outdone, the Gothic **Oude Kerk**, with its picturesque tilting tower, is the last resting place of Vermeer (1632-75).

Transport and Information

Getting there 60km (37 miles) south-west on A4, then A13; *train* 53 mins direct; 1 hour, change at The Hague.
VVV Office *Markt 85 (0251 126100)*. **Open** 9am-6pm Mon-Fri, 9am-5pm Sat; *Apr-Sept* also 11am-3pm Sun.

Delftware Factories

Royal Delftware Factory 'De Porceleyne Fles' *Rotterdamseweg 196 (015 2569214)*. **Open** *Apr-Oct* 9am-5pm Mon-Sat, 10am-4pm Sun; *Nov-Mar* 9am-5pm Mon-Fri, 10am-4pm Sat.
Delft Pottery De Delftse Pauw *Delftweg 133 (015 2124920)*. **Open** *15 Apr-Oct* 9am-4pm daily; *16 Oct-Mar* 9am-4pm Mon-Fri, 11am-1pm Sat, Sun.

Eating and Sleeping

Restaurants Just out of Delft in the village of De Zweth on the River Vecht is Zweththeul, *Rotterdamweg 480 (010 470 4166)*; quiet and expensive, in a former farmhouse. In summer, delicious sandwiches are served on a canal barge at Klijwegs Koffiehuis, *Oude Delft 133 (015 2124625)*. **Hotels** De Ark, *Koommarkt 59-65 (015 2140552/2157999)* is up-market with single rooms at *ƒ140-ƒ175* and doubles at *ƒ175-ƒ235*; Dish, *Kanaalweg 3 (015 2569358)* is reasonably priced with singles at *ƒ125* and doubles at *ƒ170*; the cheapest is De Kok, *Houttuinen 15 (015 2122125)* where singles cost *ƒ95-ƒ125* and doubles *ƒ125-ƒ150*.

Museums

Museum Lambert van Meerten, *Oude Delft 199 (015 2602358)*. **Open** 10am-5pm Tue-Sat; 1-5pm Sun, public holidays.
Het Prinsenhof, *Sint Agathaplein 1 (015 2602358)*. **Open** 10am-5pm Tue-Sat; 1-5pm Sun, public holidays.

Nusantara Museum, *St Agathaplein 4 (015 2602358).*
Open 10am-5pm Tue-Sat; 1-5pm Sun, public holidays.

The Hague

Once the hunting area of the Counts of Holland, The Hague was founded in 1250 when William II built a castle on the site of the present **Binnenhof** parliament buildings. These retain a bastion-like appearance, complete with a water lily-filled moat and medieval **Ridderzaal** (Hall of Knights). Guided tours are organised daily when the buildings are not in use. An attractive modern hall was added to the complex in 1994. The only evidence of unruly days gone by is the **Gevangenpoort** (prison gate), across the Hofweg, where political prisoners were once jailed and outside of which the brothers De Witt were lynched after being accused of conspiring to kill William of Orange. Every year on Prinsjesdag (third Tuesday of September) the Queen arrives at the Binnenhof in a golden coach for the state opening of parliament.

Unfortunately you can no longer visit the palaces: Voorhuit Paleis and Paleis Noordeinde at either end of the fashionable Lange Voorhout avenue and Queen Beatrix's residence, Huis ten Bosch, at the far end of the Haagse Bos. Here there is only one guard on patrol, sometimes casually smoking a cigarette by the driveway entrance. The Mauritshuis (*see chapter* **Museums: Further Afield**), a former regal home, is now open to the public and houses an excellent art collection including works by Rubens, Rembrandt, Van Dyck, Vermeer and even Warhol.

As one of the greenest cities in Europe, The Hague has a number of parks: Clingendael has a Japanese garden and Meijendael, out of town, is part of the ancient forest. The Scheveningse Bosje which is big enough to get lost in, is flanked by the Madurodam miniature city (*see chapter* **Children and Parents**) and the **Haags Gemeentemuseum**. Notable for its magnificent art nouveau architecture and for housing works by Mondrian and other modern masters, the latter museum incorporates the Dutch costumes, clogs and caps of the **Kostuum Museum** (National Costume Museum), and is linked to the **Museon**, a hi-tech ethnological display, and the **Omniversum**, a planetarium with state-of-the-art projections. Between the Scheveningse Bosje and the city is **Vredes Paleis** – the Peace Palace – built in 1907 to host conferences, a role it still holds as the UN's Court of International Justice. More cultural diversions are the Anton Philipzaal concert hall (*see chapter* **Music: Classical & Opera**) and the North Sea Jazz Festival in early July (*see chapter* **Music: Rock, Folk & Jazz**).

Just beyond the park is **Scheveningen**, a former fishing village once linked to The Hague only by canal, but now a huge resort with high-rise hotels and, in summer, a boggling choice of beach cafés. Presiding over the beach is the 1887 **Kurhaus** (spa hotel), a legacy of Scheveningen's days as a bathing place for European high society. The main salon, with its humungous chandeliers and awesome glass cupola, is a wonderfully intimidating place to take tea. This was the venue for the Rolling Stones' first ever performance in the Netherlands; the gig was called to halt after 15 minutes because the audience were totally out of control. There is also a popular casino on the premises.

To stand any chance of recapturing the past head back into The Hague to the **Mesdag Museum**. This paintings of the Scheveningen coast by members of The Hague School. Around the corner is the **Panorama Mesdag**, where you can view HW Mesdag's remarkable 360-degree painting of Scheveningen village in 1880.

Transport and Information
Getting there 50km (31 miles) south-west on A4, then A44; *train* 50 mins to Den Haag CS, changing at Leiden if necessary.
VVV Office *Koningin Julianaplein, at Centraal Station (06 34035051).* **Open** *mid Apr-Sept* 9am-9pm Mon-Sat; 10am-5pm Sun; *Oct-mid Apr* 9am-6pm Mon-Sat; 10am-5pm Sun.

Eating and Sleeping
Restaurants Luden, *Frederikstraat 36 (070 360 1733)* serves expensive Dutch food with French panache. Schlemmer, *Lange Houtstraat 17 (070 360 8580)* has a medium-priced restaurant frequented by Dutch politicians and a trendy upstairs café. At Salvatore, *Deltaplein 605-606 (070 325 9635)* an Italian meal costs around ƒ30.
Hotels Des Indes Intercontinental, *Voorhout 54 (070 363 2932)* is the most luxurious hotel in town, with prices to match. City Hotel, *Renbaanstraat 1-3 (070 355 7966)* has singles for ƒ65 and doubles at ƒ115; the youth hostel NJHC Hostel Ockenburg, is at *Monstersweg 4 (070 397 0011)* and charges between ƒ26-ƒ31 per person.

Museums
Haags Gemeentemuseum, *Stadhouderslaan 41 (070 3381111).* **Open** 11am-5pm Tue-Sun.
Mesdag Museum, *Laan van Meerdervoort (070 3635450).* **Open** 10am-5pm Mon-Sat, noon-5pm Sun, public holidays.
Panorama Mesdag, *Zeestraat 65 (070 3642563).* **Open** 10am-5pm Mon-Sat, noon-5pm Sun, public holidays.

Haarlem

All trace of Haarlem's origins as a tenth-century settlement on a choppy inland sea disappeared with the draining of the Haarlemmermeer in the mid-nineteenth century. This doesn't mean that Haarlem has lost its appeal: the town centre is simply beautiful. Around the old market square you'll find old, wide canals lined with large and small houses full of character. Haarlem lies between Amsterdam and Zandvoort, a busy Dutch coastal resort attracting flocks of Amsterdammers and its fair share of Germans during the summer. Haarlem's most famous heritage is the St Bavo's Church which dates from around 1313. This was the subject of many Dutch paintings but suffered severe fire damage in 1328. Due to lack of funds, it took another 150 years and several master builders to complete the restoration work. The Gothic church still dominates the town's main square. Inside it is surprisingly bright, with cavernous, white transepts as high as the nave and choir stalls. Painter Frans Hals is buried here and it also houses the famous Müller organ (1738) which has 5,000 pipes and was once played by both Handel and the young Mozart.

Haarlem residents have given its Grote Markt the nickname 'living room of Haarlem', because it is so cosy. It is one of the loveliest squares in the Netherlands, surrounded by monumental architecture such as the Stadhuis which dates from 1300. A little further out, about 15 minutes by foot, is Groot Heiligland. This used to be the Oudenmannenhuis, a shelter for elderly men, but currently houses the Frans Halsmuseum. For ƒ10, Haarlem's VVV sells a City Walks book in English which contains two walking routes through Haarlem, one of which takes you to the most important almshouses. The **Provenniershuis** is the largest; its garden used to be part of St Michael's monastry on Grote Houtstraat. **Brouwershofje** on Tuchthuisstraat is one of the oldest (1472). The **Frans Halsmuseum** has a magnificent collection of seventeenth-century portraits, still lives, genre paintings and landscapes, including works by Pieter Claesz, Jacob van Ruisdael and Adriaan van Ostade. Frans Hals' eight group portraits of militia companies and regents form the highlight of the permanent exhibition. The museum also houses a large collection of period furniture, Haarlem silver and ceramics, an eighteenth-century apothecary with Delftware pottery, and a large modern collection. Works by artists from Haarlem and the surrounding areas are on show as well as examples of Dutch Impressionist, Expressionist, CoBrA and contemporary artists, including Appel, Corneille, Armando and Dekkers (*see chapter* **Museums: Further Afield**).

The **Teylers Museum**, founded in 1778, is the Netherlands' oldest museum. Fossils and minerals sit alongside antique scientific instruments in a passable imitation of an alchemist's workshop. Unexpectedly, it also has a superb collection of 4,000 drawings dating from the sixteenth to the nineteenth century by masters such as Rembrandt, Michelangelo, Raphael and Claude Lorraine.

Haarlem is more than a city of nostalgia, of course. The **Patronaat** at Zijlsingel 2 (023 5326010) is a venue where Dutch and international up-and-coming bands play, with ticket prices from ƒ10 to ƒ25. Patronaat is Haarlem's answer to the Melkweg in Amsterdam; although it doesn't have the resources to book the more famous bands, it is still worth checking what's on.

Transport and information
Getting there 20km (12 miles) west on A5; *train* 17 mins direct to Haarlem.

VVV Office *Stationsplein 1 (023 5319059).* **Open** *Apr-Sept* 9am-5.30pm Mon-Sat; *Oct-Mar* 9am-5.30pm Mon-Fri, 9am-4pm Sat.

Eating and Sleeping
Restaurants Alfonso's, *Oude Groenmarkt 8 (023 5317434)* serves Mexican food from ƒ19,75; Greek food is served at Zorba de Griek, *Smedestraat 47 (023 5315188)* starting at ƒ18,50; De Waag, *Damstraat 29 corner Spaarne (023 5311640)* serves French dinners is from ƒ35; Pamukkale, *Gedempte Oudegracht 29 (023 5326300)* is a Turkish restaurant, serving dishes from ƒ20,50 and offering live music Thur-Sun.
Hotels Carlton Square Hotel, *Baan 7 (023 5319091)* is as pricey as Haarlem gets (*single* ƒ225, *double* ƒ260, *triple* ƒ305); Waldor, *Jansweg 40 (023 5312622)* is reasonably priced at ƒ65 for a single room, ƒ75 for a double and ƒ125 for triples. NJHC Hostel Jan Gijzen, *Jan Gijzenpad 3 (023 5373793)* is a youth hostel, ƒ26,50 per night for non-members, ƒ21,50 per night for members (both including breakfast).

Museums
Teylers Museum, *Spaarne 16 (023 5319010).* **Open** 10am-5pm Tue-Sat; 1-5pm Sun.

Leiden

Leiden is home to the Netherlands' oldest university, founded in 1581 after the city bravely stood up to the Spanish during the Dutch Revolt in 1574 (*see chapter* **War and Reformation**). The siege almost starved the population into submission, but the city was rescued when William of Orange opened dykes to flood central Holland, enabling his ships to sail up to the town walls. *Leidens Ontzet* (The Relief of Leiden) is still celebrated with a carnival-like festival every October 3, when commemorative dishes, such as stew, herring and white bread, are consumed in vast quantities.

In the late sixteenth and seventeenth centuries, Leiden was the birthplace of many renowned figures. Rembrandt was born here, as were fellow painters Jan van Goyen and Jan Steen. Both Descartes and American president, John Quincy Adams studied at Leiden university. The main student quarter is around Sint Pieterskerk, also the home of the Pilgrim Fathers between 1609-1620 before they sailed to America via Plymouth on the Mayflower. Their leader and pastor, John Robinson, remained behind and is buried in the church. The **Pilgrims' Documentation Centre** is based at Vliet 45.

Leiden's **Museum van Oudheden** (National Museum of Antiquities) houses an extensive collection of Egyptian mummies which should not be missed; **Rijksmuseum voor Volkkunde** (National Museum of Ethnology) displays artwork from all over the world, focusing on many of the Dutch colonies; and **De Lakenhal** includes

Rotterdam Harbour – *both a lesson in imaginative modernism and a fine spot for a beer.*

paintings by famous Dutch artists in a building that once housed the clothmakers' guild (see also chapter **Museums: Further Afield**).

Also worth a visit is **Molenmuseum De Valk** (Windmill Museum) where you can explore the inside of a typical Dutch windmill and absorb the view of Leiden from the balcony. You can also see across the city's rooftops from the Burcht, a twelfth century fort on an ancient artificial mound. Reach it via the fifteenth-century Korenbeursbrug (corn exchange bridge), the only roofed bridge in Leiden. On the opposite side is the town hall, which was designed towards the end of the sixteenth century, but had to be rebuilt after a fire in 1929.

As the centre of Leiden is so small, an ideal way to get to know your way around is by embarking on one of the four walking tours which are marked out by a series of arrows on the streets. Guide maps of these tours are available at the VVV.

Transport and Information

Getting there 40km (24 miles) south-west on A4; *train* 35 mins direct.

VVV Office *Stationplein 210 (071 5146846)*. **Open** 9am-5.30pm Mon-Fri; 9am-4pm Sat.

Eating and Sleeping

Restaurants Annie's Verjaardag, *Hoogstraat 1 (071 5125737)* is a cosy café underneath a bridge and a pleasant spot for summer drinking with its boat deck and canal barge. The average price of a meal is ƒ40.
Hotels Golden Tulip, *Schipholweg 3 (071 5221121)* offers single rooms at ƒ145-ƒ215 and doubles at ƒ175-ƒ245; Mayflower, *Beestenmarkt 2 (071 5142641)* has singles at ƒ125-ƒ150 and doubles at ƒ170-ƒ200; Bik Hotel, *Witte Singel 92 (071 5122602*; closed Oct) is cheaper at ƒ40 for singles and ƒ80 for a double.

Museums

Museum van Oudheden, *Rapenburg 28 (071 5163163)*. **Open** 10am-5pm Tue-Sat; noon-5pm Sun.
Rijksmuseum voor Volkkunde, *Steenstraat 1 (071 5211824)*. **Open** 10am-5pm Tue-Fri; noon-5pm Sat, Sun.
Molenmuseum De Valk, *2e Binnenvestgracht 1 (071 5165353)*. **Open** 10am-5pm Tue-Sat; 1-5pm Sun.

Rotterdam

Practically the whole of Rotterdam's old city centre was destroyed by bombs in May 1940 and, with commendable daring, the authorities decided to start afresh rather than try to reconstruct its former maze of old canals. Perch on the busy Willemsbrug bridge for a magnificent view of the futuristic skyline, or, if you can stomach the expense and the height, go up the **Euromast** at Het Park for an overview of the immense Rhine-Maas delta.

Not every bomb-site was developed immediately after World War II, because the city first wanted to plan its future function. One success of this policy is the redeveloped **Old Harbour**. It's a lesson in imaginative modernism and has given the world Piet Blom's witty *Kijk-Kubus*. These tilted, cubic houses on stilts are nicknamed 'the bleak

woods', but are popular with tourists, who can visit number 70 *(010 4142285)*.

The few surviving original buildings have become icons. **St Lawrence Church**, built in 1646, has been heavily restored; a solitary row of merchants' houses survives on Wijnhaven; but best of all is **Schielandshuis**, Korte Hoogstraat, off Beursplein, a seventeenth-century mansion which doubles as an excellent city museum. It displays recreations of scenes in Rotterdam from its medieval times – when it was the village where Erasmus was born – to the construction of the Nieuwe Waterweg. Another architectural highlight is the former warehouse of the Holland-America Lijn. It's a bit off the beaten track but is well worth visiting as it has been renovated to house the fantastic Hotel New York.

The city's deep-water channel to the sea facilitated the creation of the world's biggest harbour, **Europoort**. Take one of the various SPIDO boat tours from Willemsplein (010 413 5400), or follow the *Havenroute* map (from the ANWB motoring organisation; *see chapter* **Survival**). Just downstream is **Delfshaven**, where genuinely old buildings are being restored. These include the former warehouses containing the **Museum de Dubbelde Palmboom**, which covers working life in the Meuse estuary. A plaque on the quay marks where the Pilgrim Fathers left for America in 1620, having held a final service at the nearby **Oude Kerk**, where they are also commemorated.

Without a doubt, the best museum in Rotterdam is the **Boymans-Van Beuningen** (*see chapter* **Museums: Further Afield**), but also try the **Prins Hendrik Maritime Museum** – a startling piece of architecture with stunning river views. It has comprehensive, if slightly exhausting displays on seafaring, plus interesting ships docked outside.

Transport and Information

Getting there 73km (45 miles) south on A4, then A13; *train* 1 hour direct.

VVV Coolsingel 67 *(010 402 3200)*. **Open** 9am-6.30pm Mon-Thur; 9am-9pm Fri; 9am-5pm Sat; *Easter-Sept* also 9am-5pm Sun. **Centraal Station** *(06 9292)*. **Open** 9am-10pm daily.

Eating and Sleeping

Restaurants Tropicana, *Maasboulevard 100 (010 402 0720)*, is an expensive revolving restaurant with great river views. The fine food at Zocher's, *Baden Powellaan 12 (010 436 4249)* averages ƒ50 a head. Café de Unie, *Mauritsweg 34 (010 411 7394)* is a reconstruction of a famous pre-war café; the well-presented (usually fish) dishes are medium-priced. De Tuin, *Plazoon 354 (010 452 7743)* is in the lovely Kralingse park and serves traditional dishes from ƒ40 and has an impressive wine list.
Hotels At Hotel New York, *Koninginnenhoofd 1 (010 486 2066)* you can stay in the wonderfully preserved boardroom for ƒ350-ƒ600; other double rooms cost from ƒ160. King's Garden *Westesinglaan 1 (010 4366633)* is more reasonable at ƒ85 for singles and ƒ150 for doubles; the NJHC youth hostel is at *Rochussenstraat 107-109 (010 436 5763)*; *see chapter* **Accommodation** for rates.

Museums

Museum de Dubbelde Palmboom, *Voorhaven 12 (010 4761533)*. **Open** 10am-5pm Tue-Sat; 1-5pm Sun.
Maritime Museum Prins Hendrik, *Leuvehaven 1 (010 4132680)*. **Open** 10am-5pm Tue-Sat, 11am-5pm Sun.

Utrecht

Utrecht is the fastest growing city in Europe in terms of population, but it still seems an oasis of tranquility compared to Amsterdam. The city takes its name from the *oude trecht* (old ford) which was founded by the Romans in 48AD as a strategic crossing over the Rhine. It later became an important Christian centre after the country's patron saint, St Willibrord, chose it as a base to convert the Netherlands to Christianity in around 700AD.

But there's more to Utrecht than just history and picturesque scenery. **Utrecht University** is the largest in the Netherlands. As a result the city centre has a young, relaxed atmosphere and plenty of cafés, but also a huge housing problem. Rents are even higher than in Amsterdam.

The city also boasts the largest shopping centre in Holland (and one of the country's biggest eyesores): the **Hoog Catharijne**. This is combined with Utrecht railway station and so large that you easily can get lost and spend a whole day in the building (adjacent buildings also host major trade fairs and exhibitions). For more luxurious designer goods, head for La Vie, the shopping centre opposite.

Utrecht's shops are a mixture of old and new, suitable both for bargain hunters and designer label shoppers. It's best to shop during the week as on Saturdays it can get extremely crowded, especially on the Oudegracht where all the main stores are located. There is a general market on Vredenburg on Wednesdays and Saturdays as well as a flea market in St Jacobsstraat on Saturday mornings and two flower and plant markets in Janskerkhof and Oudegracht, also on Saturday. Utrecht is very compact and everything is within easy walking distance.

A good place to start your visit is the **Domtoren** (Dom Tower). This imposing structure, the highest church tower in the country, dominates the cityscape, dwarfing everything around it. The views from the top of the fourteenth-century tower are breathtaking, but with 465 steps to climb, this is definitely not for those with weak hearts or an aversion to exercise – though there are several resting places.

From the tower you can see the **Domkerk**, which also dates from the fourteenth century, and the **Pandhof**, a cloister garden planted with many medicinal herbs. The herb garden, which has a decorative fountain at its centre, provides a quiet place to sit and contemplate before you continue on your travels.

Another good place to explore is the **Oudegracht** – the canal which runs through the centre of Utrecht. Its waterside footpaths and cellars are quite unique; unlike Amsterdammers who winch their goods up by a pulley into their houses, the residents of Utrecht had goods delivered across the quays into the basement of their canalside houses. Many of these cellars now house cafés and shops and are excellent places to get a snack and watch the boats navigate their way through the narrow bridges. There are regular boat trips and *waterfietsen* (water-bikes) can also be hired. Another way to explore Utrecht is by horse-drawn carriage (030 2710235 for details).

Of Utrecht's several museums, the magnificent **Rijksmuseum het Catharijneconvent** has the largest collection of medieval art in the Netherlands and gives a fascinating account of the country's religious history.

The **University Museum** displays the world of science, both past and present. There's a special laboratory where youngsters can do optical experiments. The Dutch Railway Museum, **Nederlands Spoorwegmuseum** is housed in buildings which date from 1874; the **Rijksmuseum van Speelklok tot Pierement** has a collection of automated musical instruments from the eighteenth century to the present day (for both, *see chapter* **Children and Parents**).

A short distance out of Utrecht is the fascinating **Rietveld-Schröderhuis** which was designed in 1924 by architect and furniture designer Gerrit Rietveld for a wealthy acquaintance, Truus Schröder. When she died in 1985, this expensive architectural commission was put into the hands of a foundation so that others would benefit from it. To visit you need to make an appointment well in advance (030 2362310).

Transport and Information

Getting there 40km (25 miles) south-east; *train* 30 mins direct.
VVV Office *Vredenburg 90 (06 34034085, fax: 030 2331417)*. **Open** 9am-6pm Mon-Fri; 9am-4pm Sat.

Eating and Sleeping

Restaurants Moustache, *Drieharingenstraat 18 (030 2318953)* is a fairly expensive French restaurant run by the well-known culinary Fagel family, with meals from ƒ35; Pancake Bakery de Oude Munt Kelder, *Oudegracht a/d werf 12 (030 2316773)* offers pancakes from ƒ6,50 along with a view on the canal.
Hotels Holiday Inn, *Jaarbeursplein 24 (030 2910555)* charges ƒ330 for doubles and ƒ295 for singles; the Parkhotel, *Tolsteegsingel 34 (030 2516712)* is a budget hotel with a swimming pool, double rooms cost from ƒ83-ƒ95, singles from ƒ57; Bunnik Youth Hostel, *Rhijnauwenselaan 14, Bunnik (030 6561277)* is only 10 mins from the centre by bus, ƒ28 without an international youth hostel card, ƒ23 with one, breakfast included.

Museums

Rijksmuseum het Catharijneconvent, *Nieuwegracht 63 (030 2317296)*. **Open** 10am-5pm Tue-Fri; 11am-5pm Sat, Sun, public holidays.

The Provinces

There are twelve provinces in the Netherlands and they're not all flat.

While urban life is mostly concentrated in the Randstad, the other regions of the Netherlands each have specific characters. We have listed the VVV tourist offices of each province (most accept only postal and phone enquiries), and for important regional centres; unless otherwise stated, they're open from 9am to 6pm Monday to Saturday. We've also stated if there's an appropriate NS rail excursion ticket (*see chapter* **Beyond Amsterdam**). There's a sketch map of the Netherlands at the back of this book; for a scale map, the Falk Plan tourist map has a useful place index.

PROVINCIAL CHARM

The people of the predominantly Protestant northern provinces – Friesland, Groningen and Drenthe – are renowned for loyalty and hard work. Friesland was once an independent tribal nation that reached along the coast from North Holland to eastern Germany and whose people were called 'unconquerable' by Pliny the Elder. Theirs is still the most individualistic province.

Famous for their costumes (now seldom worn) and breeds of cattle and dog, they still stick to their own distinct language and literature; even road signs are bi-lingual. Popular myth attributes the Frisians' greater than average height to constant flooding, which only the tall survived.

Neighbouring **Groningen**, a staid, rural and conservative area, has a surprisingly liberal university, although graduates don't usually stay around long.

The fens, moors and forests of **Drenthe** are a world apart, inhabited since the Palaeolithic age. Saxons initially occupied the slightly hillier **Overijssel**, an area due east of Amsterdam. Many traditions in this ultra-conservative area have survived tourism and the arrival of new industries.

The largest province, **Gelderland**, borders Germany and is sandwiched between north and south. Its terrain of wild countryside, orchards and commercial rivers has been fought over for centuries, while retaining its own character. Gelderland became land-locked when part of the Zuider Zee was drained to form **Flevoland**. Today, the enormous and impressive Afsluitbrug connects North Holland with Friesland.

Another victory over the sea was the building of the Delta Works flood barrier to protect the islands of **Zeeland**, once isolated in the river delta bordering Belgium. Increased tourism and industry is transforming this province's traditional way of life.

Caricatures of the Dutch come unstuck in the Catholic south, where there are even a few small hills. The relaxed and light-hearted people of **Noord Brabant** and **Limburg** celebrate carnivals in the streets. The entire Noord Brabant village of Eersel sometimes gathers for weddings in a large tent at the market-place, savouring milk and brandy with sugar. Wedged between Belgium and Germany, the rolling landscape of Limburg is also home to bon vivants, who thrive on its famous cuisine.

Drenthe

Drenthe's affectionate nickname – Het Oude Landschap (the old landscape) – goes back centuries, but human habitation dates back even further – about 50,000 years. This north-eastern province has tended to be neglected by the more vibrant west, which could explain why it has the reputation of being a dark, mysterious landscape haunted by its pagan past. It's certainly why the population took so long to abandon Catholicism and also partly why the area was, until recently, relatively backward economically. Even today, Drenthe is very rural. The best place to appreciate what much of the countryside looked like as little as 20 years ago is in Orvelte at the Oud Saksisch Kijkdorp (Old Saxon Village).

To find out more about the province's prehistoric, Roman and Merovingian past, start at the magnificent Drents Museum (open Tue-Sun) in **Assen**. The area is full of ancient sites. The most impressive monuments are the *hunebedden* (megaliths), towards the German border. Burials took place between 3400BC and 2300BC in this string of megalithic burial sites, constructed from boulders shed by the nearby *Hondsrug* (Dog's Back), a glacial moraine on which most of Drenthe is built. The history of the monuments is explained at the **National Hunebedden Information Centre** in Borger.

The Drenthe countryside is the perfect backdrop to the megalithic tombs. Rivulets run through peat cuttings (look out for villages ending in *veen* – peat bog) on huge silent heaths such as the Fochtelooer Veen near Assen and the Dwingeloose Heide and Uffelter Veen, either side of Uffelte. There's also a great forest near Uffelte, the Drentse Wold and another, Ellertsveld, west of the *hunebedden*. Near Ellertsveld is a more chilling reminder of the past, the Nazi transit camp at Westerbork (*see chapter* **World War II**).

Further Information

Drenthe province VVV *PO Box 10012, 9400 CA Assen (0592 351777).* **Open** 8.30am-5pm Mon-Fri.
Assen VVV *Brink 42, 9401 HV (0592 314324).* **Open** 9am-5.30pm Mon-Fri; 9am-1pm Sat; *Oct-Jan* 9am-5pm Mon-Fri; *Jun-Sept* 9am-5pm Mon-Fri; 9am-3pm Sat.
Emmen VVV *Marktplein 17, 7811 AM (0591 6613000).* **Open** *Apr-Sept* 9am-5.30pm Mon-Fri; 9am-4pm Sat; *mid Oct-Mar* 9am-5pm Mon-Fri; 9am-1pm Sat.
Nationaal Hunebedden Informatie Centrum *Bronnegerstraat 12, Borger (0599 236374).* **Open** *Feb-Dec* 10am-5pm Mon-Fri; 1-5pm Sat, Sun, public holidays.
Orvelte Saxon Village *Dorpstraat 3 (0593 322335).* **Open** *Apr-Oct* 10am-1pm, 2pm-5pm Mon-Sat; 2pm-5pm Sun, public holidays. **Admission** ƒ6; ƒ4 4-12s; ƒ5,50over-65s; free under-4s.

Flevoland

Just north-east of Amsterdam, Flevoland only became a province in its own right in 1986, when the polders (pieces of reclaimed land) of South Flevoland and East Flevoland were combined with the north-east polder (formerly in Overijssel, *see below*). It's the most recent stage in the Netherlands' massive, historic land reclamation process.

Drained between 1950 and 1957 to create more room for the burgeoning population, Flevoland offered little to entice new residents. Its capital, **Lelystad**, should have been a planner's dream. Development there is refreshingly low-level and it has an interesting community centre, the Agora, but it's tiresome to get to and sits hunched on the windy outer edge of the province. By contrast, the space-age city of **Almere**, intended as a satellite to Lelystad, is almost embarrassingly successful. Now an outpost of Amsterdam, with low-cost, low-energy housing, it attracts thousands of the capital's commuters.

There's a large bird sanctuary at the lake **Oostvaardersplassen**, south-west of Lelystad, and a brand new adventure park with a notorious rollercoaster at Walibi Flevo.

Reminders of Flevoland's recent past as a sea bed are periodically unearthed by archaeologists. Centuries-old remains, some Roman, of vessels, anchors and cannon balls are displayed in the **Schokland Museum** (open *Apr-Sept* daily, *Oct-Mar* Tue-Sun) and **Scheepsarcheologiemuseum** (Museum of Maritime Archaeology) in **Ketelhaven**.

Further Information

Provincial VVV *Stationsplein 186, 8232 VT Lelystad (0320 240500).* **Open** 9am-5pm Mon-Fri.
Almere-Stad VVV *Spoordreef 20, 1315 GP (036 5334600).* **Open** 9am-5.30pm Mon-Fri; 9am-2pm Sat; *May-Aug* 8.30am-9pm Thur.
Urk VVV *Wijk 2, 8321 EP (0527 684040).* **Open** *Apr-Oct* 9am-5pm Mon-Fri; 9am-1pm Sat.
Walibi Flevo *Spijkweg 30, Biddinghuizen (0321 331514).* **Open** *Mid Apr-Oct* 10am-6pm Mon-Sun. **Admission** ƒ28, free under-5s.
Rijksmuseum Scheepsarcheologie *Vossemeerdijk 21, Ketelhaven (0321 313287).* **Open** *Apr-Sep* 9am-5pm Mon-Sun. **Admission** ƒ3,50; ƒ1,50 under-14s; ƒ2,50 CJPcard holders, over-65s, groups .

Friesland

Friesland, in the far north, has always been regarded by southerners as a kind of windswept barbarian outpost. It has its own dialect, a highly unusual landscape and the nearest thing to provincial nationalism you're likely to find in the Netherlands. The region used to be literally cut off because of its vast network of lakes and canals.

In summer, the lakes are packed with yachts and motor cruisers. The town of **Sneek** is the boating focus. The best way to explore the waterways is to go on an excursion or rent a boat and stop off at lovely little fishing towns like **Grouw, Terhorne, Heeg** and **Sloten** or, towards the northern coast, **Dokkum**. Sloten's narrow cobbled streets, illuminated bridges and high-water warning cannon make it one of the most attractive villages in Friesland.

The best feature of the province is its landscape, but the capital, **Leeuwarden**, has a picturesque centre within a star-shaped moat. Like Groningen (*see below*), Friesland is dotted with beautiful brick churches, built on *terpen* (mounds) to escape flooding. The best examples, such as that at **Hogebeintum**, west of Dokkum, are at the far north of the province.

The five sparsely populated **Frisian Islands** (or Wadden Islands), and the sea around them, have become the symbol of the Dutch conservation movement. Even today they are reserved more for migrant birds and a diminishing grey seal colony than for human visitors. Sadly you can't island-hop, since each island's ferry only shuttles to and from the coast (two to five times per day). Between May and September, when the tide is out, you can cross to the nearer islands by foot, provided you're with a local guide and don't mind *wadlopen* – wading up to your ankles in mud.

Terschelling, with its sixteenth-century lighthouse and old fishing villages, is the most picturesque island. **Ameland** is good for walking and cycling tours, and has a nature reserve. The biggest island, **Texel**, is in fact administered by Noord Holland and reached via Den Helder. It has two bird reserves (De Slufter and De Muy) and a seal sanctuary at the resort of De Koog. On more remote **Schiermonnikoog**, further east, local accents are thicker and cars are banned. **Vlieland**, also car-free, is the most deserted island – not surprising since some of its beaches are reserved for bombing practice by the Dutch Air Force. The archipelago continues east as Germany's Ostfriesische Inseln; the resorts on **Borkum** island can be reached from Delfzijl in Groningen (*see below*).

Further Information

Provincial & Leeuwarden VVV *Stationsplein 1, 8911 AC (06 32024060).* **Open** 9am-5.30pm Mon-Fri; 10am-2pm Sat.
VVV NO Friesland *Grote Breedstraat 1, 9100 KH (05190 93800).* **Open** 1-5pm Mon; 9am-6pm, Tue-Thur; 9am-6pm, 7-9pm, Fri; 9am-5pm Sat. *Jul-Aug* 11am-5pm Mon.

Hindeloopen VVV *Postbus 4, 8713 ZG (05142 2550).*
Open 1-5pm Mon; 10am-5pm Tue-Sat.
Sneek VVV *Marktstraat 18, 8601 CV (05150 14096).*
Open 9am-5pm Mon-Fri; 9am-2pm Sat.

Frisian Islands

Ameland VVV *R. van Doniaweg 2, PO Box 14, 9163 ZL
Nes (0519 542020).* **Open** 8.30am-12.30pm, 1.30-6.30pm,
Mon-Fri; 8.30am-4pm Sat.
Schiermonnikoog VVV *Reeweg 5, PO Box 13 ZP
(0519 531233).* **Open** 9am-1pm, 2.30-6.30pm, Mon-Sat.
Terschelling VVV *Willem Barentskade 19a, PO Box 1,
8880 AA Terschelling-West (0562 44300).* **Open** *Jan-
Apr,Nov-Dec* 9am-5pm Mon-Fri; 11am-1pm, 4-5.pm Sat;
May-Oct 9am-5.30 Mon-Fri; 11am-1pm, 4pm-5.30pm Sat.
Also open Fri evenings after arrival of last ferry.
Texel VVV *Emmelaan 66, 1791 AV Den Burg (0222
314741).* **Open** 9am-6pm Mon-Fri; 9am-5pm Sat. *Apr-Nov*
closes half an hour later every day *Jul-Aug* also 11am-3pm
Sun.
Vlieland VVV *Havenweg 10, PO Box 1, 8899 ZN (0562
45111).* **Open** 9am-5pm Mon-Fri; when ferry arrives Sat,
Sun.

Gelderland

Gelderland, in the east, is the largest province.
Nearly a third is covered by the Veluwe (Bad Land),
a 4,600 hectare (11,400 acre) stretch of forest and
moorland. In the south of the Veluwe, near Arnhem,
is the Netherlands' biggest national park, the Hoge
Veluwe. In this park are bicycle racks, where visitors can borrow a white bike free of charge. Hidden
among the trees, near the park's Otterlo entrance, is
the fascinating Kröller-Müller Museum. Principally
housing a bequest by the art lover Hélène Kröller-
Müller, it holds an impressive collection, including
the most important Van Goghs outside Amsterdam
as well as works by Mondriaan and the Dutch sym-
bolists. There is a sculpture park outside including
pieces by Rodin, Moore, Hepworth and Giacometti.
  Not far from Hoge Veluwe is **Paleis Het Loo**,
which was originally built as a hunting lodge by
William III in 1685-92. It is the Netherlands' nearest approximation to the Palace of Versailles and
well worth a visit.
  The **Betuwe** (Good Land) is the south-west
region of fertile land sandwiched between the
River Waal, the River Maas and the River Lek further north. The countryside east and towards
Germany, dubbed Achterhoek (Back Corner), is
dominated by commercial waterways.
  The number of times you'll need to cross rivers
will make it obvious why Allied divisions found it
so difficult to stage a surprise attack on **Arnhem**,
the provincial capital, in 1944. The war cemetery
and **Hartenstein Villa**, now the Air Museum, are
in Oosterbeek, while the Bevrijdingmuseum
(Liberation Museum) is in Nijmegen. Arnhem and
Nijmegen, the province's biggest city, both have
several good museums, notably Arnhem's excellent Nederlands Openlucht Museum, an open-air
collection on folklore (open Apr-Oct daily; NS rail
excursion available). The best thing about both

cities are their imposing Gothic churches and river-
side views. Nijmegen's church survived the city's
almost total destruction by Allied bombs.

Further Information

Provincial VVV *PO Box 142, 6860 AC Oosterbeek (026
3332033).* **Open** 9.15am-1pm, 1.30pm-5pm Mon-Fri for
telephone and postal enquiries only.
Arnhem & Zuid Veluwe VVV *Stationsplein 45, PO
Box 552, 6811 KL (026 4420330).* **Open** *Apr-Sep* 11am-
5.30pm Mon; 9am-5.30 Tue-Fri, 10am-2.30pm Sat.; *Oct-
Mar* 1pm-5.30 Mon; 9am-5.30pm; 10am-1pm Sat.
Nijmegen VVV *St Jorisstraat 72, PO Box 175, 6500 AD
(024 3225440).* **Open** 9am-5pm Mon-Fri;
9am-4pm Sat; *May-Mid Sep* 10am-5.30pm Mon-Fri.
HogeVeluwe National Park *entrances at
Schaarsbergen, Otterlo and Hoenderloo (Visitors' Centre
0318 591627).* NS rail excursion/bus from Arnhem (late
Jun-early Aug). **Open** *park* 9am-5pm daily; *Visitors'
Centre* 10am-5pm daily. **Admission** *all-in tickets for park
and museum* ƒ8; ƒ4 6-12s; under-7s free; ƒ8 per car.
Kröller-Müller Museum *Hoenderloo, Nationaal Park
De Hoge Veluwe (0318 591041).* NS rail excursion. **Open**
10am-5pm Tue-Sat; 11am-5pm Sun *Sculpture park* closed
Nov-Mar. **Admission** *as for Hoge Veluwe.*
Paleis Het Loo *Amersfoortseweg, Apeldoorn (055
5212244).* NS rail excursion 51. **Open** 10am-5pm Tue-
Sun. **Admission** ƒ12,50; ƒ10 children, over-65s, CJP card
holders.

Groningen

All roads lead to the city of **Groningen**, the far north-
eastern province's capital and namesake. This isn't
surprising when you discover that it has generated
six centuries of local wealth, first as a member of the
Hanseatic League and then as the only grain market
for miles around. The province's history is explained
in the **Groningen Museum** (open Tue-Sun), also
noted for its exhibitions of modern art.
  The symbol of Groningen's good fortune is its fifteenth-century **Martinikerk**. The six-tiered church
tower has a carillon and can be climbed for fine
views. The lush agricultural landscape that you can
see from the Martini tower is sprinkled with eighteenth-century *kop-romp* (head-trunk) farmhouses,
a combination of tall, stuccoed villas and wide barns
built for heavy harvests. They can best be seen in
the Westerwolde district bordering Germany, particularly lining a five-kilometre (three-mile) street at
Bellingwolde, near **Winschoten**.
  The rural churches are the real glory of the
province. Unusual, beautifully proportioned and
generally with high, saddleback towers peeping over
a ring of trees, they're seen to best effect in the morning mist or under a thick blanket of snow. You can
see some wonderful examples in a 70-kilometre (44-
mile) loop north-east of Groningen city. Begin the
tour with the church at **Garmerwold**, which has
geometric designs outside and sixteenth-century
frescos inside. Move on past the chapel of a former
Benedictine monastery at **Ten Boer** to **Stedum**,
where the church sits astride a mound, surrounded
by a moat. The church at **Loppersum** has well-preserved frescos and the one at **Appingedam** sits in

the marketplace of the attractive town centre, next to an arcaded town hall of 1630. Skirt north up the coast, passing the churches at **Bierum**, **Spijk** and **Uithuizermeeden**, to **Uithuizen**. This town has a church with a twelfth-century tower and one of the loveliest, but least visited, country houses in the Netherlands, the fortified fifteenth-century **Menkemaborg** (Feb-Dec 10am-noon, 1-5pm, daily). Return to Groningen via **Het Hogeland** open-air museum at Warffum (Apr-Nov 10am-5pm Tue-Sat; 1-5pm Sun) or the circular villages of **Kantens** and **Middelstum**, each built round a *terp*.

Further Information

Provincial & Groningen VVV *Gedempte Kattendiep 6, 7911 PN (06 32023050; f 1/min).* Open 9am-5.30pm Mon-Fri; 9am-4pm Sat.
Appingedam VVV *Wijkstraat 38, 9901 AX (0596 624488).* Open 10am-5pm Mon-Fri; 2-5pm Sat, Sun.
Uithuizen VVV *Mennonietenkerkstraat 13, 9981 BB (0595 434051).* Open 10am-5pm Mon-Fri.
Winschoten VVV *Stationweg 21A, 6970 AC (0597 412255).* Open 9am-5.15pm Mon-Fri; 9am-12.45pm Sat.

Limburg

This southern spur of Dutch territory, wedged between Belgium and Germany, is the antidote to all those clichés about the Netherlands being flat. The valley of the **Geul**, a small stream which drives waterwheels and clatters past black and white half-timbered farmsteads, is dominated by **Valkenburg**, a fortified town with prehistoric caves and Roman catacombs, and dotted with picturesque villages. Nearby **Heerlen** has Roman baths in its **Thermen Museum** (closed Mon). Try not to miss the strangely peaceful, pink and white town of **Thorn** close to the Belgian border.

Maastricht, best known for European treaty-signing, is the provincial capital and notably un-Dutch in character. Its eleventh-century **Basilica of St Servatius** is built of stone and is reminiscent of Rhineland churches, with its vividly painted and gilded north portal. Walk the length of the remaining southern ramparts at Maastricht for a breathtaking view of the river and the city's oldest building, the Romanesque **Basilica of Our Lady**.

Maastricht is a wonderful town to explore; make for the tiny streets jostling around the Markt, many of whose shops sell *Limburgs vlaai*, a fruit tart often eaten around **carnival** time as a special treat before Lent (*see also below* **Noord Brabant**). The French influence has turned Maastricht into the gastronomic capital of the Netherlands, a fact celebrated in the last week of August, when restaurateurs set up tents and stalls on Vrijthof Square for public tastings, the so-called *preuvenement*.

Almost as rewarding, both gastronomically and culturally, is **Roermond**. The part-Romanesque, part-Gothic **Munsterkerk** was built in 1220; nine years later the impressive tombs of the Count of Gelderland and his wife were installed.

Further Information

Provincial VVV *Kerkstraat 31, Postbus 811, 6300 AV Valkenburg (043 6017321).* Open 9am-12.30pm, 1.30-5pm, Mon-Fri.
Heerlen VVV *Honingmanstraat 100, 6411 LM (045 5716200).* Open 9am-5.30pm Mon-Wed, Fri; 9am-8pm Thur; 9am-2pm Sat.
Maastricht VVV *Kleine Straat 1, 6211 ED (043 3252121).* NS rail excursion 39. Open 9am-6pm Mon-Fri; 9am-5pm Sat, public holidays.
Roermond VVV *Kraanpoort 1, 6041 EG (0475 333205).* Open April-Sep 9am-6pm Mon-Fri; 9am-4pm Sat; Oct-Mar 9am-5pm Mon-Fri; 10am-2pm Sat.
Valkenburg VVV *Dorrenplein 5, 6301 DV (043 6013364).* Open 9am-6pm Mon-Fri; 9am-5pm Sat; 10am-2pm Sun.

Noord Brabant

Noord Brabant, bordering Belgium in the south, was one of the last provinces to renounce support of Spain during the Dutch Revolt at the turn of the seventeenth century and one of the most reluctant to forget its Burgundian past. Consequently, its character has been shaped to a large extent by its Catholic population, who in 1867 commissioned PJH Cuypers and G van Swaay to build a replica of Rome's St Peter's Basilica in **Oudenbosch**, east of Breda. Five centuries earlier, and with a better result, the Cathedral of St Jan was built at **'s-Hertogenbosch**. It is the only real example of pure Gothic architecture in the country.

Den Bosch, as the provincial capital is known, was the birthplace of Hieronymous Bosch and there's a statue of the painter in the marketplace. It is one of the two main Dutch centres of **carnival** (the other is Maastricht) which takes place the weekend before Lent. The Mediterranean-style celebrations are slightly marred by the severe cold weather in this part of the world.

The city of **Eindhoven** is dominated by the industrial multi-national Philips. An electric bulb works was founded here in 1891 by Dr AF Philips, whose statue is on Stationsplein. The **Van Abbe Museum** (closed Mon) houses a collection of major modern art so large it can't all be exhibited at once. Art lovers should also head a few miles north to **Nuenen**. Van Gogh's family lived in the vicarage there and displays of memorabilia have made it something of a place of pilgrimage. Towards the German border are the nature reserve of **De Groote Peel**, and the National War and Resistance Museum at Overloon (*see chapter* **World War II**).

If you prefer to be out of doors, head west to the wilderness of the **Biesbosch** tidal estuary, north of **Breda**, a shopping town whose main sight is the Grote Kerk. You can take boat excursions through the Biesbos (reed forest) from the fortress town of **Geertruidenberg**. Vintage car enthusiasts would also enjoy the nearby **Nationaal Automobiel Museum** (01621 85400, open April to September). Downstream is another fortified city, **Willemstad**, built in 1565-83 by William the Silent to safeguard the choppy Hollandsch Diep waters.

Further Information

Provincial VVV *Postbus 3259, 5003 DG Tilburg (013 5434060).* **Open** 9am-5.30pm Mon-Fri;10am-4pm Sat for telephone and postal enquiries only.
Bergen Op Zoom VVV *Beursplein 7, 4611 JG (0164 266000).* **Open** 9am-6pm Mon-Fri; 9am-5pm Sat.
Breda VVV *Willemstraat 17, 4811 AJ (076 5222444).* **Open** 9am-6pm Mon-Fri; 9am-5pm Sat.
Eindhoven VVV *Stationsplein 17, 5611 AC (040 2449231).* **Open** 10am-5.30pm Mon; 10am-5.30pm Tue-Fri; 9am-4pm Sat.
's-Hertogenbosch VVV *Markt 77, 5211 JX (073 6122334).* **Open** 11am-5.30pm Mon; 9am-5.30pm Tue-Fri; 9am-4pm Sat.

Overijssel

Criss-crossed by long, winding rivers and 400 kilometres (249 miles) of canoe routes, the province of Overijssel is superb for watersports and is dotted with holiday homes and hikers' cabins; the VVV even provides self-drive, horse-drawn carts, which you can sleep in.

Most visitors head for the Lake District, comprising the **Weerribben** and **Wieden** districts. Between the two runs the road linking **Steenwijk** and **Blokzijl**, both fortified towns, the latter with a marina in its old harbour. Dominating Wieden is the huge **Beulaker Wijde/Belter Wijde** lake, bordered by **Vollenhove**, a Zuider Zee port until the North-east Polder was drained; **Zwartsluis**, where paintings dating from the seventeenth century, when it was Fortress Zwartsluis, still hang in the town hall; and the watersports centre of **Wanneperveen**, with its splendid thatched farmsteads and thousands of eager boaters.

Almost completely hidden among the reedlands are the villages of **Belt Schutsloot** and **Giethoorn**, where the residents get around mostly by boat, the buildings being individually marooned, with only boats and foot bridges to connect them. The Jazz Inn and Blues Inn music festivals are held on a platform in the lake every August, and a procession of flower-decked boats is staged the following Saturday.

Travelling up the IJssel you reach **Kampen**, which has a wealth of historic buildings and a particularly beautiful waterfront. Further on is **Zwolle**, which like Kampen was a Hanse town and retains its star-shaped moat and bastions. In the town hall, parts of which date from 1448, is an imposing *schepenzaal* (elders' meeting chamber), a feature found only in Overijssel. Boats leave for the lakes from Zwarte Water. Where the IJssel enters the province is the major city of **Deventer**, known for its domed tower of St Lebuinuskerk.

Almost every town in Overijssel has a summer carnival. **Raalte** holds its harvest festival in the third week of August (Wed-Sat); vehicles parade through **Lemelerveld** covered in flowers during

Bloemen Corso (early August); and sheepdogs herd sheep around **Hellendoorn** during its sheep market in mid-August. It's on special market days (Wednesdays, late July to early August) and on Sundays that you're most likely to see people in traditional costume at **Staphorst**, just north of Zwolle. Many of these strictly Protestant locals also inter-marry and shun the modern world, banning vaccinations, cars on Sundays – and cameras. This *lintdorp* (ribbon village) – or *weendorp* (peat village) – is nearly 12 kilometres (7½ miles) long; it swallowed up settlements along canals dug in peat, and incorporates farmhouses decorated in unique colour schemes. The community has retained a rigidly religious lifestyle centred on its countless Dutch Reformed Churches.

East along the River Vecht from Zwolle and surrounded by woods is the superb fishing centre of **Ommen**. Collect a fishing licence from the post office and ask about the best baits and fishing spots in the first-class tackle shop, Beste Stek (Vrijhof 1; 05291 54972). Hotel de Zon, on the river bank, is favoured by fishermen swapping angling stories. Stretching south are the **Salland Hills**, which rise to 81 metres (266 feet) at Holterberg, south of Nijverdal, where there's fun to be had at **Hellendoorn Adventure Park**.

The district stretching up to Germany is **Twente**, dominated by the province's biggest city, **Enschede**. Rebuilt after a fire in 1862, its main draws are Los Hoes, a textile industry museum, and the Rijksmuseum Twente, which displays modern art. Some of Twente's surviving Saxon farms can be seen on an NS day excursion (which includes travel in a horse-drawn covered wagon), or on a six-day cycle tour (March to October) organised by the provincial VVV, who can forward luggage from hotel to hotel. Some of the finest farms are concentrated around **Ootmarsum**, a knot of narrow streets lined with timber buildings, and **Denekamp**, with its thirteenth-century sandstone church and Natura Docet natural history museum. These two Catholic towns celebrate Easter with tree felling, street processions, ritual chanting and bonfires.

Further Information

Provincial VVV *Postbus 500, 7600 AM Almelo (0546 818767).* **Open** 10am-5.30pm Mon; 9.30am-5.30pm Tue-Fri.
Enschede VVV *Oude Markt 31, 7511 GB (053 4323200).* **Open** 10am-5.30pm Mon; 9am-5.30pm Tue-Fri; 9am-1pm Sat.
Giethoorn VVV *on a boat, Beulakerweg, 8355 AM (0521 361248).* NS rail excursion 48. **Open** Mar 2-Oct 31 9am-6pm, Mon-Sat; 9am-6pm Sun; *Nov 1-Mar 1* 10am-5pm, Mon-Fri; 10am-noon Sat.
Ommen VVV *Markt 1, 7731 DB (0529 451638).* **Open** *Jan-May and Oct-Dec* 1am-5pm Mon; 9am-5pmTue-Fri; 10am-5pm Sat; 2-5pm Mon. *May-Sep* 9am-5pm Mon-Fri; 10am-5pm Sat; 2-5pm Sun.
Zwartsluis VVV *Stationsweg 32, 8064 DG (038 3867453).* **Open** 8am-6pm Mon-Fri; 8am-5pm Sat.
Zwolle VVV *Grote Kerkplein 14, 8011 PK (038 42213900).* **Open** 9am-5.30pm Mon-Fri; 9am-4pm Sat.

Utrecht

If you go anywhere in the Netherlands by land, the chances are you'll go through the city of **Utrecht**, the country's main rail and road junction, just south of Amsterdam (*see chapter* **The Randstad**). Earlier travellers, who came down the Lek river, chose the province in 863AD as the location for Europe's largest trading post, **Dorestad**. It is the site of present-day **Wijk-bij-Duurstede**, which still has many ancient buildings. In either direction along the Lek, old towns such as **Rhenen**, **Amerongen** and **Culemborg** remain virtually unchanged.

Between Amsterdam and Utrecht are the 2,500 hectare (6,200 acre) **Loosdrechtse Plassen** and smaller **Vinkeveense Plassen**. These fan-shaped lakes have narrow strips of land radiating into them and are now used mainly for fishing and watersports. The area groans with private wealth, as the many villas dotted around the picturesque old villages of **Oud-Loosdrecht**, **Westbroek** and **Breukeleveen** testify. A few kilometres away in Noord Holland are **Hilversum**, home of Dutch television, and the mini-Hollywood at **Laren**. For a taste of more ancient privilege, wander down the Vecht, which flows north between the plassen. It's the Netherlands' prettiest navigable river, overshadowed by iron bridges, grand, decaying estates at **Loenen**, **Vreeland** and **Breukelen**, and the province's ubiquitous castles (*see chapter* **Excursions in Holland: Castles**).

In the east of the province, **Soestdijk** is home to the country's former queen, now Princess Juliana, and at **Austerlitz**, Napoleon's army built a huge sand pyramid purely because they had nothing else to do at the time. Best of all, though, is **Amersfoort**, a beautifully-preserved medieval town set in a ring of canals on the edge of the Leusder Heide.

Further Information

Amersfoort VVV *Stationsplein 9-11, 3800 RK (033 4635151).* **Open** *Sep-Sep* 9am-6pm Mon-Fri; 9am-noon Sat; *Oct-Apr* 9am-5.30 Mon-Fri; 9am-2pm Sat.
Utrecht VVV *Vredenburg 90, 3511 BD (06 34034085).* **Open** 9am-6pm Mon-Fri; 9am-4pm Sat.
Wijk-bij-Duurstede VVV *Markt 24, 3961 BC (0343 575995).* **Open** 10am-4.30pm Mon-Thur; 10am-9pm Fri, 9am-4pm Sat; noon-3pm Sun.

Zeeland

This collection of islands in the river delta bordering Belgium has a famous maritime past and distinctive Zeeland traditions which were preserved by its isolation. But in January 1953 massive storm floods swept away old buildings and farms, brutally launching the province into the twentieth century. Salt water damage and tide-marks, seen halfway up columns in the medieval churches of **Kruiningen** (on the isthmus to Beveland Island) and **Brouwershaven** (on

Schouwen Island), are the only reminders of the perennial threat of flooding – eliminated, the Dutch hope, by the **Delta Works**, the world's biggest flood barrier. It was completed in 1986, after 30 years of construction costing ƒ14 billion. The revolutionary technology is explained at **Delta Expo** on Neeltje Jans, an island halfway along the Ooster Schelde Dam.

Changes in tide movements have not affected the main activity of oyster and mussel catching. Seafood is available all over Zeeland, but the best hauls of the day usually find their way to restaurants in **Yerseke** (a town near Kruiningen named after the Dutch for oyster). In season (September to April) you can take a tour of the oyster beds.

In the Middle Ages, Zeeland grew fat on the cloth and wool trade with England and France. Indeed the English still know the port of **Vlissingen** as Flushing. It's the birthplace of the heroic Admiral de Ruyter (*see chapter* **Decline & Fall**), whose statue in the Rotunda surveys the dramatic seascape. Among the local artefacts in the Stedelijk Museum is a copy of De Ruyter's portrait by Ferdinand Bol; the original is in Zeeuws Museum in the provincial capital, **Middelburg**, alongside tapestries depicting local sea battles. Although bombed in 1940, Middelburg has a charming circular centre parcelled within star-shaped fortifications, now landscaped. Like **Goes**, it owed its prosperity to medieval trade with England.

Over the Westerschelde estuary is **Zeeland Vlaanderen** (Flanders). From there it's a short hop over the Belgian border to the beautiful cities of Antwerp, Ghent and Bruges (*see chapter* **Beyond Amsterdam**).

Just north of Middelburg is the most beautiful town in Zeeland, **Veere**, where elegant flèche spires and the towering Church of Our Lady can be seen across the flats for miles. The churches in the province are worth a tour in themselves. Many were used as lighthouses for ships at sea. The churches at **Kapelle**, **Zoutelande** and **'s-Heer Arendskerke** are among the biggest and best.

Further Information

Provincial & Middelburg VVV *Markt 65A, 4330 AC (0118 63300).* **Open** *Nov-Feb* 9.30am-5pm Mon-Fri; 10am-3pm Sat; *Mar-Oct* 9.30am-5pm Mon-Sat; 12pm-4pm Sun. NS rail excursion 4 (includes Walcheren miniature town).
Goes VVV *Stationsplein 3, 4461 HP (01113 220577).* **Open** noon-5pm Mon; 9am-5pm Tue-Fri; 9am-noon Sat.
Veere VVV *Oudestraat 28, 4351 AV (01181 501365).* **Open** *Sept-Nov* 11am-4.30pm Mon-Sat; *Nov-Apr* 1.30-4.30pm Mon-Sat; *Apr-June* 11.30am-4.30pm Mon-Sat; *July, Aug* 10am-5.30pm daily.
Vlissingen VVV *Nieuwendijk 15, 4381 BV (0118 412345).* *Sept-Jun* 9am-5pm Mon-Sat; *Jul, Aug* 9am-6pm Mon-Sat; 1-5pm Sun.
Yerseke VVV *Kerkplein 1, 4401 ED (0113 571864).* **Open** 9-4pm Mon; 10am-4pm Tue-Fri; 9am-noon Sat.
Delta Expo *Postbus 19, 4328 ZG Burghamsteede (0111 652702).* **Open** *Apr-Oct* 10am-5.30pm daily; *Nov-Mar* 10am-5.30pm Wed-Sun.

Survival

Whether it's dealing with wheel-clamps, contacting the embassy, or taking a bath – all you might need to know to live out your stay.

Communications

Telephones/PTT Telecom

Public phone boxes are scattered throughout the city. The kiosks are mainly glass with a green trim and have a green and white *ptt telecom* logo. There are both coin-operated and card phones. Coin boxes take 25c, ƒ1 and ƒ2,50 coins. Phonecards are available from post offices and phone centres (*see below*), priced ƒ5, ƒ10 (with 5 free units) or ƒ25 (15 free units). Many coin-operated public phones are being converted into card phones to prevent junkies from breaking into the cashboxes. It's best to buy a card. The procedure for **making a call** is as follows:
Listen for the dialling tone (a low-pitched hum), insert money – a minimum of 25c, or in some cases 50c – dial the appropriate code (none required for calls within Amsterdam), then dial the number. A digital display on public phones shows the credit remaining, but only wholly unused coins are returned. Phoning from a hotel room is more expensive.

International phone calls
Dial the code 00, then the country code. International calls can be made from all phone boxes. **Off-peak rates** apply between 8pm-8am Monday to Friday and all day on Saturday and Sunday. For more information on off-peak rates, ring international directory enquiries (*below*).

Telephone directories
can be found in post offices and phone centres (*see below*). When phoning information services, taxis or train stations you may hear the recorded message, '*Er zijn nog drie (3)/twee (2)/een (1) wachtende(n) voor u.*' This tells you how many people are ahead of you in the telephone queuing system.

The **emergency code is 06-11:**
In phoneboxes you don't have to insert coins or a card to dial this number. Emergency phonelines are listed under **Emergencies** (*see page 262*); help phonelines are listed under **Help and Information** (*see below*).

Directory Enquiries 06 8008 (7am-2am, 60c charge).

International Operator 06 0410 (24hrs, free).
International Directory Enquiries 06 0418 (24hrs, free).

Phone Centres

If you have a number of phone calls to make and little change, it's best to use a phone centre. They can be found in most tourist areas (for example Damrak and Kalverstraat) and some are more expensive than others. Telecenter is the largest.

Telecenter
Raadhuisstraat 48-50 (484 3654). Tram 1, 2, 5, 11, 13, 14, 17. **Open** 8am-2am daily. **Credit** AmEx, DC, MC, TC, V.

As well as being a convenient place to make international phone calls, Telecenter offers fax, telex and telegram services. The cost of sending a **fax** ranges from ƒ5,50 for one page (50c per additional page) to ƒ13,25 for one page (ƒ9,75 per additional page). You can arrange to have a fax sent to you at Telecenter on 626 3871 or 626 5326, at a cost of ƒ5. The sender must include your name and telephone number with their fax and Telecenter will phone to inform you of its arrival. The **telex** service costs 15c-ƒ5,30 per minute to send plus ƒ10 operator charges, and ƒ5 to receive. The number is 11101 TELEH NL. For **telegrams**, *see below*.

Telegrams, Telex and Fax

Telegrams can be sent from phone centres or post offices for a basic charge of ƒ23,50, plus 35c per word under 11 letters (including address and signature) inside the Netherlands; ƒ27,50 plus 85c per word under 11 letters elsewhere. If you don't have a Dutch phone number there's ƒ2,50 to ƒ5 surcharge. Information on 06 0409. For **telex** and **fax** facilities, *see below* **Phone Centres** and *chapter* **Business**.

Post/PTT Post

For post headed outside Amsterdam, use the *overige bestemmingen* slot in letter boxes. The logo for the national postal service is *ptt post* (white letters on a red oblong). **Post offices** open from 9am to 5pm, Mon-Fri and can be recognised by their red and royal blue signs. The **postal information phoneline** is 06 0417 (8am-8pm Mon-Fri; 9am-1pm Sat).

Stamps
At time of writing, it costs 80c to send a postcard from Amsterdam to anywhere in Europe (ƒ1 to the USA) and ƒ1 for letters weighing less than 20g. To send post elsewhere prices vary according to weight and destination. Stamps (*postzegels*) can also be bought with postcards from many tobacconists and souvenir shops.

Main Post Office
Singel 250 (556 3311). Tram 1, 2, 5, 11, 13, 14, 17. **Open** 9am-6pm Mon-Wed, Fri; 9am-8pm Thur; 10am-1.30 Sat.
In addition to usual services, facilities here include phones, directories, photo-booths, a wall-map of Amsterdam, stamp machines, counters where you can buy packaging for parcels and a counter for collectors' stamps and stationery.

Post Restante
Post Restante, Hoofdpostkantoor PTT, Singel 250, 1012 SJ Amsterdam, The Netherlands.
If you're not sure where you'll be staying in Amsterdam, people can send your post to the above address. You'll be able to collect it from the main post office (*above*) if you produce ID such as a passport or driving licence with photo.

Centraal Station Post Office

Oosterdokskade 3 (555 8911). Tram 1, 2, 4, 5, 9, 11, 13, 16, 17, 24, 25. **Open** *8.30am-9pm Mon-Fri; 9am-noon Sat.*
Only this and the main post office (*above*) deal with parcels. A five-minute walk east from Centraal Station.

Foreign Newspapers

For the American Book Center and WH Smith, *see chapter* **Shopping**. Most newsagents have foreign papers: the ones below are particularly well-stocked.

AKO

Rozengracht 21 (624 5369). Tram 13, 14, 17. **Open** 8am-8pm Mon-Fri; 10am-6pm Sat, Sun.
Kiosk *Centraal Station, Stationsplein 13 (627 4320). Tram 1, 2, 4, 5, 9, 11, 13, 16, 17, 24, 25.* **Open** 6am-11pm daily.
Two of the best-stocked branches of this large chain.

Athenaeum Nieuwscentrum

Spui 14-16 (623 3933). Tram 1, 2, 5, 11. **Open** noon-6pm Mon; 9am-6pm Tue, Wed, Fri; 9am-9pm Thur; 9.30am-5.30pm Sat, 8am-10pm Sun.

Bruna

Leidsestraat 89-93 (622 0578). Tram 1, 2, 5, 11. **Open** 8.30am-10pm daily.

Disabled

The most obvious difficulty people with mobility problems face in the Netherlands is negotiating the winding cobbled streets of the older towns. Poorly maintained and broken pavements are widespread and canal houses, with their narrow doorways and steep stairs, can also present access problems. But the pragmatic Dutch don't have preconceptions about people with disabilities and any problems are generally solved quickly and without fuss.

Most of the large museums have reasonable facilities for wheelchair users but little for the partially sighted and hard of hearing. Most cinemas and theatres also have an enlightened attitude and are accessible, some with assistance. In this *Guide* we list establishments that claim to have wheelchair access, but it's advisable to check in advance and to be specific about your needs.

The **metro** is accessible to wheelchair users who 'have normal arm function'. There is a **taxi service** for wheelchair users (*see chapter* **Getting Around**). Most **trams** are inaccessible to wheelchair users and the high steps may also pose problems. New trams on the following routes should be accessible by wheelchair: 1, 2, 5, 6, 11, 16 and 24.

NS (the rail network) produces a booklet called *Rail Travel for the Disabled*, available from all main stations or by telephone on 235 5555. Timetables in braille are also available. There is wheelchair access to refreshment rooms and toilets at all stations. If you need assistance to board a train, phone 235 5555 between 8am and 4pm Monday to Friday, if possible at least a day in advance and before 2pm.

The Netherlands' Board of Tourism (AUB) and the VVV (*see chapter* **Essential Information**) produce brochures listing accommodation, restaurants, museums, tourist attractions and boat excursions with facilities for the disabled.

Drugs

The Amsterdam authorities have a relaxed attitude towards **soft drugs**. Possession of up to 30g (1oz) of cannabis, though technically still an offence, is regarded as a misdemeanour for which you're unlikely to be prosecuted.

There are many coffeeshops (*see chapter* **Coffeeshops**) where cannabis is sold over the counter. It's unwise to buy drugs on the street – at best you'll get ripped off, at worst, made ill or poisoned. You can purchase the best hash in smaller, backstreet coffeeshops; some of these produce their own extra strong homegrown grass (skunk) or buy hash directly from importers.

Smoking is not acceptable everywhere in Amsterdam. Use some discretion. Many bars and cafés will not tolerate the practice and eject offenders. Outside Amsterdam, public consumption of cannabis is largely unacceptable.

Foreigners found with any amount of **hard drugs** – cocaine, speed, ecstasy, LSD and especially heroin – should expect prosecution. Organisations offering advice to users can do little to assist foreigners with drug-related problems, although the Drugs Prevention Centre (626 7176) is happy to provide help in several languages, including English. Visitors caught dealing in drugs are likely to be prosecuted and repatriated pretty swiftly.

If you are suffering from the ill effects of too much cannabis, go to a hospital outpatients' department or see a doctor, who will be well-acquainted with the symptoms. There are two **helplines** that offer advice and information on drug and alcohol abuse. They are both open between 9am and 5.30pm Mon-Fri (626 7176).

Embassies and Consulates

The VVV offices have lists of embassies and consulates; most are based in The Hague. We list the main ones for English-speaking countries.

American Consulate General

Museumplein 19, 1071 DJ Amsterdam (664 5661/679 0321). Tram 3, 5, 12, 16. **Open** 8.30-noon Mon-Fri.

Australian Embassy

Carnegielaan 4, 2517 KH Den Haag (070 310 8200). **Open** 9am-12.30pm, 1.15-5.15pm Mon-Thur; 9am-12.30pm Fri; *open for visa enquiries* 8.45am-12.30pm Mon-Fri.

British Consulate General

Koningslaan 44, 1075 AE Amsterdam (676 4343; visa enquiries 675 8121). Tram 2, 6. **Open** 9am-noon, 2-3.30pm Mon-Fri.

British Embassy
Lange Voorhout 10, 2514 ED Den Haag (070 364 5800). **Open** 9am-1pm, 2.15-5.15pm Mon-Fri.

Canadian Embassy
Sophialaan 7, 2514 JP Den Haag (070 361 4111). **Open** 9am-1pm, 2-5.30pm Mon-Fri.

Eire Embassy
Dr Kuyperstraat 9, 2514 BA Den Haag (070 363 0993). **Open** 9.30am-12.30pm, 2.30-5pm Mon-Fri.

New Zealand Embassy
Mauritskade 25, 2514 HD Den Haag (070 346 9324). **Open** 9am-12.30pm, 1.30-5.00pm Mon-Fri.

Health

For **emergency services and medical or dental referral agencies** *see* **Emergencies**.

In the case of minor accidents, try the outpatients' departments at the following hospitals (*ziekenhuis*), all of which are open 24 hours a day.

Academisch Medisch Centrum
Meibergdreef 9 (566 9111/566 3333). Bus 59, 60, 61, 62, 120, 126, 158/Metro Holendrecht.

Boven IJ Ziekenhuis
Statenjachtstraat 1 (634 6346). Bus 34, 36, 37, 39.

VU Ziekenhuis
De Boelelaan 1117 (444 4444).Metro 51. Bus 23, 48, 64, 65, 173.

Lucas Ziekenhuis
Jan Tooropstraat 164 (reception 510 8911; first aid 510 8164). Bus 19, 47, 80, 82, 97.

Onze Lieve Vrouwe Gasthuis
Eerste Oosterparkstraat 279 (599 9111). Tram 3, 6, 10.

Dentists

For a dentist (*tandarts*), phone the dentist administration bureau 06 8212230. This costs about ƒ0,40 per minute but somebody is available to find a dentist 24 hours, daily. The Central Medical Service may also be of help (*see* **Emergencies**).

AOC
Wilhelmina Gasthuisplein 167 (616 1234). Tram 1, 2, 3, 5, 6, 11, 12. **Open** 8.30am-4pm Mon-Fri. Emergency dental treatment.

Prescriptions

Chemists (*drogist*) sell toiletries and non-prescription drugs and usually open 9.30am-5.30pm Mon-Sat, although many close all day on Tue. For prescription drugs go to a pharmacy (*apotheek*), usually open 9.30am-5.30pm Mon-Fri.

Outside these hours phone the **Afdeling Inlichtingen Apotheken** on 694 8709 (24 hours daily) or consult the daily newspaper *Het Parool* which publishes details of which *apotheken* are open late that week. Details are also posted at local *apotheken*.

Special Clinics

AIDS Helpline
(freephone 06 022 2220). **Open** 2-10pm Mon-Fri.
A free national helpline with English-language advice, information and counselling for those concerned about AIDS and related problems. Booklets (in English) on safe sex are also available from COC (*see chapter* **Gay & Lesbian**).

GG en GZ
Groenburgwal 44 (555 5822). Tram 9, 14/Metro Waterlooplein. **Open** 8-10.30am, 1-3.30pm, Mon-Fri.
Free and confidential advice and treatment by appointment on sex-related problems and sexually transmitted diseases.

HIV Plus Lijn
(685 0055). **Open** 1-4pm Mon, Wed, Fri; 8-10.30pm Tue, Thur.
An opportunity to talk in confidence with others who are HIV positive .This telephone information and helpline also offers support to friends and family of those who are HIV positive.

HIV Vereniging Nederland
Eerste Helmersstraat 17 (616 0160). Tram 1, 3, 6, 7, 10, 11, 12. **Open** 9am-5pm Mon-Fri,7-9pm Fri, Sat; 2-3pm Sun. *Phonelines* **open** Mon-Fri 10am-4pm.
The HIV Vereniging has a regular weekend clinic offering VD and HIV testing for gay men. On other days consultation is by appointment only.

SAD Schorerstichting
PC Hooftstraat 5 (662 4206). Tram 6, 7, 10. **Open** 9am-5pm Mon-Fri; 7-9pm Fri-Sun for medical reasons only.
The Foundation for Additional Services (SAD) has a regular weekend clinic offering VD and HIV-testing for gay men. On other days, consultation is by appointment only.

Contraception and Abortion

MR '70
Sarphatistraat 620-626 (624 5426). Tram 6, 7, 10. **Open** 9am-4pm Mon-Thur; 9am-1pm Fri.
An abortion clinic which offers help and advice.

Polikliniek Oosterpark
Oosterpark 59 (693 2151). Tram 3, 6, 9. **Open** 9am-5pm for advice services. *Phonelines* **open** 24 hours a day.
Information and advice on contraception and abortion. Abortions are carried out (on Tue and Fri only) although non-residents without appropriate insurance will be charged from ƒ600 for the operation. The process is prompt and backed up by sympathetic counselling.

Rutgersstichting
Aletta Jacobshuis, Overtoom 323 (616 6222). Tram 1, 11. **Open** by appointment 9am-4.30pm Mon-Fri; 7.15-9pm Tue, Thur. **Consultation** fee ƒ37,50.
Besides giving information on health issues, the staff at this family planning centre can help visitors with prescriptions for contraceptive pills, morning-after pills and condoms, IUD fitting and cervical smear tests. Prescription costs vary.

Help and Information

There is a charge for all 06 numbers.
VVV (tourist office) *(06 340 340 66).* **Open** 9am-5pm daily. *See also chapter* **Essential Information**.
Transport information: GVB *(06 9292).* **Open** 6am-midnight Mon-Fri; 7am-midnight Sat-Sun. *See also chapter* **Essential Information**.
Time (06 8002).
Weather (06 8003).

Help Phonelines

Alcoholics Anonymous

(625 6057). **Open** 24-hour answerphone.
Phone and leave a message on the answerphone and a counsellor will ring you back.

Crisis Helpline

(675 7575). **Open** 9am-3pm Mon-Thur; 24 hours Fri-Sun.
A counselling service, comparable to the Samaritans in the UK and Lifeline in the US, for anyone with emotional problems, run by volunteers. English isn't always understood at first, but keep trying and someone will be able to help you.

Narcotics Anonymous

(662 6307). 24-hour answerphone message with direct numbers of counsellors you can contact.

Legal and Immigration

Bureau Voor Rechtshulp

Spuistraat 10 (626 4477). Tram 1, 2, 5, 11. **Open** 9am-12.30pm, 1.30pm-5pm Mon-Fri, by appointment only.
This legal advice centre has qualified lawyers who give free legal advice on matters of tenancy, social security, immigration, insurance, consumer complaints and disputes with employers. On the initial visit, staff will assess whether they can help you and then refer you to the nearest of their four offices.

Legal Advice Line

(444 6333). **Open** 9pm-5pm Mon, Wed, Thur; 9am-1pm Tue, Fri.
You can get free advice on this phoneline from student lawyers, who offer a relaxed, friendly service. They deal mainly with civil law queries and problems, but will occasionally be able to help with minor criminal law matters. Most speak excellent English.

ACCESS

Plein 24, 2511 CS Den Haag (070 3462525). **Open** 9.30am-3.30pm Mon-Fri (with answerphone service outside office hours).
The Administrative Committee to Coordinate English Speaking Services is a non-profit organisation, which provides assistance in English through a telephone information line, workshops and counselling.

Libraries

You'll need to present proof of residence in Amsterdam and ID if you want to join a library (*bibliotheek*) and borrow books. It costs *ƒ*34 (23-64yrs) or *ƒ*20,50 (18-23 yrs, 65+) per year and is free for under-18s. However, in the public libraries (*openbare bibliotheek*) you can read books, newspapers and magazines, without membership or charge. For university libraries, *see chapter* **Students**.

American Institute

Plantage Muiderstraat 12 (525 4380). Tram 7, 9/Metro Waterlooplein. **Open** 10am-4pm Mon, Wed, Fri.

British Council Library

Keizersgracht 343 (622 3644). Tram 1, 2, 5, 11. **Open** 1.30pm-4.30pm Wed, Thur.

Centrale Bibliotheek

Prinsengracht 587 (523 0900). Tram 1, 2, 5, 11. **Open** 1-9pm Mon; 10am-9pm Tue-Thur; 10am-5pm Fri,Sat; 1pm-5pm Sun (Mar-Oct only).

Anyone is welcome to use this, the main public library, for reference purposes. There is a variety of English-language books and newspapers and a small coffee bar. *Wheelchair access.*

Left Luggage

There is a staffed left-luggage counter at Schiphol Airport, open 7am-10.45pm daily. The charge is *ƒ*5 per item per day. There are also lockers in the arrival and departure halls, costing *ƒ*5 and *ƒ*8 per day. Inside Amsterdam, there are lockers at Centraal Station with 24-hour access, costing *ƒ*4 and *ƒ*6; maximum ten days storage.

Lost Property

For the sake of insurance, report lost property to the police as quickly as possible; for the central police phone number, *see below* **Police and Security**. If you lose your passport, inform your embassy or consulate as well. For anything lost at the Hoek van Holland ferry terminal or Schiphol Airport contact the company you're travelling with, as neither point has a central lost property depot. For lost credit cards, *see* **Emergencies**.

Centraal Station

NS Lost Property Information, Stationsplein 15 (557 8544). Tram 1, 2, 4, 5, 9, 13, 11, 13, 16, 17, 24, 25. **Open** 7am-11pm daily.
Items found on trains are kept here for four days and then sent to *NS Afdeling Verloren Voorwerpen, Tweede Daalsedijk 4, 3500 HA Utrecht (2-4pm Mon-Fri 030 2 353 923).*

GVB Head Office

Prins Hendrikkade 108-114 (551 4911). Tram 1, 2, 4, 5, 9, 13, 16, 17, 24, 25. **Open** 9am-4pm Mon-Fri.
Report here for any item lost on a bus, metro or tram. If reporting a loss from the previous day, phone after 2pm to allow time for the property to be sorted.

Police Lost Property

Stevensonstraat 18 (559 3005). Tram 9, 14. **Open** 9.30-3.30pm Mon-Fri. *Phonelines* **open** 12pm-3.30pm Mon-Fri.
Try here for items lost in the streets or parks. Also report any loss to the police station in the same district as they generally hold items for a day or so before sending them on here.

Police and Security

The Dutch police are under no obligation to grant a phone call to those they detain (they are entitled to hold people for up to six hours for questioning if the alleged crime is not too serious, 24 hours for serious matters), but they will phone the relevant consulate on behalf of a foreign detainee.

If you are a victim of theft or assault, report it to the nearest police station. In the case of a serious incident or an emergency, phone the **emergency switchboard** on **0611** and ask for police.

Hoofdbureau Van Politie (Police Headquarters)

Elandsgracht 117 (559 9111). Tram 7, 10. **Open** 24 hours daily.

Locksmiths

Amsterdam Security Center
Prinsengracht 1097 (671 6316). Tram 4. **Open** *for emergencies* 24 hours daily. **Credit** AmEx.
The cost of calling a locksmith varies depending on the area. To get into a car will cost around ƒ95; into a house ƒ85 to ƒ125. After midnight prices rise and you can expect to pay a minimum of ƒ135.

Religion

Catholic
St John and St Ursula *Begijnhof 30 (622 1918). Tram 1, 2, 4, 5, 11, 16, 24, 25.* **Open** 1pm-6pm Mon; 8.30am-6pm Tue-Sat. **Services** *Dutch* 10am Sun; *English* 12.15pm Sun; *French* 11.15am Sun.

Dutch Reformed Church
Oude Kerk *Oudekerksplein 1 (625 8284). Tram 4, 9, 16, 24, 25.* **Open** 11am-5pm Mon-Sat. 1pm-5pm Sun. **Services** *Dutch* 11am Sun.

Jewish
Liberal Jewish Community Amsterdam *Jacob Soetendorpstraat 8, (642 3562)). Tram 4.* **Open** *office* 9am-3pm Mon-Thur; 9am-3pm Fri. **Services** 8pm Fri; 10am Sat.Open *office rabbinate (644 2619)* 10am-3pm Mon-Fri.
Times may vary so phone first to check.
Orthodox Jewish Community Amsterdam *PO Box 7967, Van der Boechorststraat 26 (646 0046). Bus 69, 169.* **Open** 9am-5pm Mon-Fri by appointment only.
Information on orthodox synagogues and Jewish facilities.

Muslim
THAIBA Islamic Cultural Centre *Kraaiennest 125 (698 2526). Metro Gaasperplas.* **Prayer** 12.30pm, 3pm, 4.35pm, 6.35pm daily.
Phone first for details of prayer times and cultural activities.

Quaker
Religious Genootschap der Vrienden *Vossiusstraat 20 (679 4238). Tram 1, 2, 5, 11.* **Open** 11am-4pm Tue; on other days you can call *070-3632132.* **Service** 10.30am Sun.

Reformed Church
English Reformed Church *Begijnhof 48 (624 9665). Tram 1, 2, 4, 5, 9, 11, 16, 24, 25.* **Open** *May-Sept* 2-4pm Mon-Fri. **Services** *English* 10.30am Sun; *Dutch* 7pm Sun.
The main place of worship for the English-speaking community in Amsterdam.

Salvation Army
National Headquarters *Oudezijds Armsteeg 13 (520 8408). Tram 4, 9, 16, 24, 25.* **Open** 9am-5pm Mon-Fri.
Information on Salvation Army Citadels in Amsterdam.

Washing and Cleaning

A comprehensive list of launderettes (*wassalons*) can be found in the *Yellow Pages* (*Gouden Gids*). For dry-cleaners, *see chapter* **Services**.

Baths and Showers

Sportfondsenbad
Fronemanstraat 3 (665 0811). Tram 9. **Open** 4-8pm Mon, Fri; 10am-1pm Tue, Thur; **Cost** ƒ2,25 per shower.
Bring your own towel.

Marnixbad
Marnixplein 9 (625 4843). Tram 3, 10. **Open** for baths or showers 4-7.30pm Mon-Fri; 1pm-5pm Sat. **Cost** ƒ2,75 per shower; ƒ3 per bath.
The best place in town for a wash; there's also a bar.

Stichting De Warme Waterstaal
Da Costakade 200 (612 5946). Tram 3, 7, 12, 17. **Open** 1-6.30pm Tue; 10am-4.30pm Sat. Sauna **Cost** ƒ2,50 per shower; ƒ4,50 per bath. Bring your own towel.

Travel and Driving

For rail travel, *see chapter* **Getting Around**.

Driving and Breakdown

If you must bring a car to the Netherlands (and it's best not to) you should join a **national motoring organisation** beforehand. These provide international assistance booklets, which explain what to do in the event of a breakdown in Europe. To drive in the Netherlands you'll need a valid national driving licence, although the Dutch motoring club, **ANWB** (*see below*) and many car hire firms favour an **international driving licence**, available from branches of national motoring organisations. In Britain, take your full licence and a passport photo to a branch of the AA or RAC and they will process it in minutes.

Major roads are usually well-maintained and clearly sign-posted. Motorways are labelled 'A'; major roads 'N'; and European routes 'E'.

Emergencies

Emergency Switchboard (06 11)
24-hour switchboard for ambulance, fire and police.

TBB (570 9595)
A 24-hour service which refers callers to a dentist. Operators can also give details of chemists open outside normal hours.

Lost credit cards
Report lost or stolen credit cards on the following 24-hour numbers:
American Express (*504 8666*)
Diner's Club (*557 3407*)
Mastercard (*030 283 5555*)
Visa (*660 0611/660 0700/660 0600*)

Rape & Sexual abuse
TOSG *612 7576*) **Open** 10.30am-11.30pm Mon-Fri; 3.30-11.30pm Sat-Sun.
A helpline for women who are victims of rape, assault, sexual harassment or threats.
Meldpunt Vrouwenopvang (Women's refuge) (*611 6022*) **Open** 9am-5pm daily; answerphone between 5pm-9pm.
Women being abused will be referred to a safe house or safe address within Amsterdam.

Some points to note: the Dutch drive on the right; drivers and front-seat passengers must always wear seatbelts; speed limits are 50km an hour within cities, 70km an hour outside, and 100km an hour on motorways. Be wary of cyclists; trams will not give way to cars in most circumstances.

To bring your car into the Netherlands you'll need an international identification disk, a registration certificate, proof of the vehicle having passed a road safety test in its country of origin and insurance documents.

Royal Dutch Touring Club (ANWB)

Museumplein 5 (673 0844; 24-hour emergency line 06 0888). Tram 2, 3, 5, 12, 16. **Open** 9am-5.30pm Mon-Fri; 9am-4pm Sat. **Credit** foreign currency, EC , MC, TC, V.
If you haven't already joined a motoring organisation, you can enrol here for around ƒ140,75, which covers the cost of assistance should your vehicle break down. If you're a member of a foreign motoring organisation, you're entitled to free help providing you can present membership documents. You may find emergency crews don't accept credit cards or cheques at the scene.

Spare parts

If you think you can fix it yourself, try one of these. Phone first to check they've got the part you need.
Bergam Automaterialen *Kalfjeslaan 25, Amstelveen (643 0321).* **Open** 8.30am-6pm Mon-Fri; 9am-4pm Sat.
Dick's Car Clinic *Groenmarktkade 5 (626 3217). Tram 3.* **Open** 8.15am-5.30pm Mon-Fri.

Parking and Petrol

Parking in central Amsterdam can be rather a nightmare: if you are lucky enough to find a space, bear in mind that the whole of the town centre is metered between 9am-7pm and the meters are difficult to see. Meters will set you back ƒ4 an hour, which may seem steep but illegally parked cars get clamped or towed away without any caution. Car parks (*parkeren*) are indicated by a white 'P' on a blue square, but after 7pm parking at meters is free. Below we list a selection of central car parks where you're more likely to find a space during peak times. Wherever you park, first empty your car completely of all valuables and the radio since cars with foreign number plates are particularly vulnerable to break-ins. If you do find you've become the latest victim of car-crime, report it at the nearest police station.
De Bijenkorf *Beursplein, Damrak.* **Open** 8am-midnight Mon-Thur; 8am-noon Fri; 24hrs Sat, Sun. **Cost** ƒ1,25 per half hour for first three hours; ƒ2,25 per half hour following; ƒ1,25 per half hour at night.
Europarking *Marnixstraat 250 (623 6694).* **Open** 6.30am-12.30am Mon-Thur;.6.30am-1.30am Fri,Sat .**Cost** ƒ2,25 per hour, ƒ3 in Summer.
Kroon & Zn *Waterlooplein 1 (638 0919)* (covered, under the city hall/opera house). **Open** 24 hours daily. **Cost** ƒ2,50 per hour; ƒ45 for 24 hours.
Museumplein *(671 6418)* (uncovered). **Open** 8am-midnight daily. **Cost** ƒ4 per hour 8am-7pm; ƒ10 per hour 7pm-midnight; free parking midnight-8am.
Prinsengracht 540-542 *(625 9852).* **Open** 24 hours daily. **Cost** ƒ3 per hour; ƒ30 for 24 hours.

In the city limits the main **24-hour petrol stations** (*benzinestations*) are at:
Gooiseweg 10-11; Sarphatistraat 225; Marnixstraat 250; Spaarndammerdijk 218.

Fines & Clamps

If your car has been clamped or towed away,these are the places to retrieve your vehicle and pay the ƒ121 fine:
Bakkersstraat 13 *(639 2741/639 2469)* **Open** 8am-8pm Mon-Sat.
Cruquiuskade 25 *(553 0333)* **Open** 8.30am-5pm Mon-Fri. For towed cars only.
Korte Leidsedwarsstraat 2 *(523 3120)* **Open** 7.30am-11pm Mon-Sat.
Ceintuurbaan 159 *(553 0192/553 0193)* **Open** 8am-8pm Mon-Sat.
Nieuwe Zijdskolk (next to the garage) *(553 0190/553 091)* **Open** 8am-11pm Mon-Sat.
Weesperstraat 105A *(553 0300)* **Open** 8.30am-5pm Mon-Fri. Head office.

Clamping

Amsterdam's wheel-clamp (*wielklem*) teams are swift to act and show little mercy. A yellow sticker on the windscreen informs you where to go to pay the fine (ƒ121). Once you've paid, return to the car and wait for the traffic police (information on 523 3115) to remove the clamp. Happily, this service is prompt. For ƒ29 extra fee a courier service can do the job for you (call 620 3750). If you park illegally or fail to pay your parking fine within 24 hours, your car will be towed away. It'll cost at least ƒ300 (plus the parking fine) to reclaim it from the pound if you do so within 24 hours and ƒ55 for every six hours thereafter. The pound is at Cruquiuskade 25 (555 9800/555 9831). Take your passport, licence number and enough cash or personal cheques to pay the hefty fine. Credit cards are accepted.

Car Hire

Dutch car hire (*auto-verhuur*) companies generally expect at least one year's driving experience and will want to see a valid national driving licence and passport. All companies will require a deposit through an international credit card and you'll generally need to be over 21. Prices given below are for one day's hire of the cheapest car available at the time of writing, excluding insurance unless otherwise stated.

Adam's Rent-a-Car

Nassaukade 344-346 (685 0111). Tram 7, 10, 17. **Open** 8am-6pm Mon-Wed; 8am-9pm Thur-Sat. **Credit** AmEx, DC, MC, V.
Hire for a day costs from ƒ75; the first 100km are free, and after that the charge is 35c/km.

Dik's Autoverhuur

Van Ostadestraat 278-280 (662 3366). Tram 3, 4. **Open** 8am-7.30pm Mon-Sat; 9am-12.30pm, 8-10pm Sun. **Credit** AmEx, DC, MC, V.
Prices start at ƒ43 per day plus 41c/km excluding tax.

Hertz

Overtoom 333 (612 2441). Tram 1, 6. **Open** 8am-6pm
Mon-Thur; 8am-7pm Fri; 8am-4pm Sat; 9am-2pm Sun.
Credit AmEx, DC, MC, V.
Prices start at ƒ98 per day, including unlimited mileage and
insurance.

Ouke Baas

Van Ostadestraat 362-372 (679 4842). Tram 3, 4. **Open**
7am-8pm Mon-Fri; 7.30am-9pm Sat; 8am-1pm, 7-10.30pm
Sun.
Inclusive of VAT and the first 100km, Ouke Baas' cheapest
car costs ƒ70 per day. After the first 100km it costs 20c/km.
there is a student discount (take student card as proof).

Discount Travel

Budget Air

Rokin 34 (626 5227). Tram 4, 9, 14, 16, 24, 25. **Open**
8.30am-5.30pm Mon-Fri; 10am-4pm Sat. **Credit** AmEx,
DC, MC, V.
Low-cost fares to worldwide destinations with discounts for
students, young people and senior citizens.

Eurolines

Rokin 10 (627 5151). Tram 4, 9, 14, 16, 24, 25. **Open**
9.30am-5.30pm Mon-Fri; 10am-4pm Sat. **Credit** MC, V.
Bus tickets for Europe and Morocco; discounts for those
under 26.

NBBS

*Dam 17 (620 5071). Tram 1, 2, 4, 5, 9, 11, 13, 14, 16,
17, 24, 25/Leidsestraat 53 (638 1736). Tram 1, 2, 5. 11.*

Open *both branches* 9am-6pm Mon-Fri; 10am-4pm Sat.
Low cost flights to worldwide destinations, with discount
travel for students and young people, and a Eurotrain discount for under-26s.

Travel Express

Rokin 38 (626 4434). Tram 4, 9, 14, 16, 24, 25. **Open**
9.30am-5.30pm Mon-Fri.
Travel Express arrange bus travel to European destinations.
There are also 'bike' buses – buses with space allocated for
bicycles – to some locations in the summer, package trips to
London by air and citytrips by train.

Hitch-Hiking

International Lift Centre

*Nieuwezijds Voorburgwal 256 (622 4342). Information
line 06 88981515.* **Open** 10am-6pm Mon-Fri; 11am-3pm
Sat.
Helpful service based in the centre of town. It costs ƒ10 to
register for 12 months, about ƒ15 if a lift is found and then
a maximum of 6c/km payable to the driver. ILC-Reisburo
(6205121) is also based at this address; it provides for budget bus and air journeys. Phone for details.

Starting points

Direction The Hague and Rotterdam: at the access to
the motorway, between RAI rail station (terminus of tram 4)
and the RAI congress building on Europa Boulevard.
Direction Utrecht: by the corner of Rijnstraat and President
Kennedylaan (terminus of tram 25).
Direction Arnhem and Germany: Gooiseweg, close to
Amstel NS rail station.

Size conversion chart for clothes

Women's clothes									
British	8	10	12	14	16	•	•	•	•
American	6	8	10	12	14	•	•	•	•
French	36	38	40	42	44	•	•	•	•
Italian	38	40	42	44	46	•	•	•	•
Women's shoes									
British	3	4	5	6	7	8	9	•	•
American	5	6	7	8	9	10	11	•	•
Continental	36	37	38	39	40	41	42	•	•
Men's suits/overcoats									
British	38	40	42	44	46	•	•	•	•
American	38	40	42	44	46	•	•	•	•
Continental	48	50/52	54	56	58/60	•	•	•	•
Men's shirts									
British	14	14.5	15	15.5	16	16.5	17	•	•
American	14	14.5	15	15.5	16	16.5	17	•	•
Continental	35	36/37	38	39/40	41	42/43	44	•	•
Men's shoes									
British	8	9	10	11	12	•	•	•	•
American	9	10	11	12	13	•	•	•	•
Continental	42	43	44	45	46	•	•	•	•
Children's shoes									
British	7	8	9	10	11	12	13	1	2
American	7.5	8.5	9.5	10.5	11.5	12.5	13.5	1.5	2.5
Continental	24	25.5	27	28	29	30	32	33	34

Children's clothes

In all countries, size descriptions vary from make to make, but are usually based on age or height.

Further Reading

Literature

Boon, Paul Louis: *Chapel Road* (Dedalus, 1991)
Memories of life on a Belgian street by the left wing author.
van Dantzig, Rudi: *For a Lost Soldier* (Bodley Head, 1991)
Autobiographical story by Dutch choreographer. Set in the years following 1944, it tells the story of a man's search for the soldier who seduced him when he was twelve years old.
De Moor, Margriet: *First Grey, Then White, Then Blue* (Picador, 1994)
Compelling story of perception, love and mortality.
Joris, Lieve: *Back to the Congo* (Macmillan, 1992)
Historical novel about Belgium and its ex-colony.
Krabbé, Tim: *The Vanishing* (Random House)
A man's search for his vanished lover. Beautifully written and twice made into a feature film (NL & US).
Minco, Marga: *Bitter Herbs* (Penguin Books, 1991)
Succinct autobiographical masterpiece about a Jewish family falling apart during and after the war. Also by the same author is 'The Fall' (Peter Owen Ltd, 1990).
Morley, John David: *The Anatomy Lesson* (Abacus)
Very hip and trendy novel about two American brothers growing up in Amsterdam. One has cancer, the other's a drug-taking drop-out..
Mulisch, Harry: *The Assault* (Collins, 1985)
A boy's perspective of the last war and the catastrophic repercussions of a resistance attack on a Nazi outside his family's home.
Multatuli: *Max Havelaar: or the Coffee Auctions of the Dutch Trading Company* (Penguin, 1987)
One of the most famous and successful Dutch books. Set in the Dutch colony of Java in 1856, it tells the story of a colonial officer and his clash with the corrupt government.
Nooteboom, Cees: *The Following Story* (Harvill, 1994)
An exploration of the differences between platonic and physical love. Also by this important European author: 'Rituals', 'Philip and the Others', 'In the Dutch Mountains', 'The Knight has Died', 'A Song of Truth' and 'Semblance and Mokusei'.
Rubinstein, Renate: *Take It or Leave It* (Marijon Press; out of print, but worth hunting down)
Diary of one of the Netherlands' most renowned journalists and her battle against multiple sclerosis.
Welsh, Irvine: *The Acid House* (Jonathan Cape)
A book of short stories by the celebrated Scottish author, a resident of the city. One of the stories is set in Amsterdam's druggy underworld.
van der Wetering, Janwillem: *The Japanese Corpse* (Corgi, 1979).
The cosmopolitan underworld of Amsterdam is the setting for this off-the-wall police procedural. One of an excellent series.

Architecture

Ford, Charles: *Blue Guide Amsterdam* (A&C Black, 1993)
Fuchs, RH: *Dutch Painting* (Thames & Hudson World of Art Series, 1978)
Comprehensive guide to the history of Dutch painting.
Groenendijk, Paul: *Guide to Modern Architecture in Amsterdam* (010 Publishers)
Kloos, Maarten (ed): *Amsterdam, An Architectural Lesson* (Thoth Publishing House, 1988)
Six architects and town planners give their opinion on the development of the city. With wonderful illustrations and photographs.
Overy, Paul: *De Stijl* (Thames & Hudson World of Art Series, 1991)
Wit, Wim de: *The Amsterdam School: Dutch Expressionist Arcitecture* (MIT Press, 1983).
Early twentieth-century architecture examined, with good use of photographs and illustrations.

History

Andeweg, Rudy B, & Irwin, Galen A: *Dutch Government & Politics* (Macmillan Press, 1993)
An introduction to Dutch politics which assumes no prior knowledge.
Boxer, CR: *The Dutch Seaborne Empire* (Penguin, 1990)
The Netherlands' wealth and what happened to it.
Burke, Peter: *Venice and Amsterdam* (Polity Press, 1994)
A wonderfully succinct comparative history.
Gies, Miep and Gold, Alison Leslie: *Anne Frank Remembered* (Corgi, 1988)
The story of the woman who helped the Frank family during the war.
Israel, Jonathan I: *The Dutch Republic and the Hispanic World 1606-1661* (OUP, 1986)
How the Dutch Republic broke free.
Kussmann, EH: *The Low Countries 1780-1940* (OUP, 1978)
Good background reading.
Parker, Geoffrey: *The Thirty Years' War* (Routledge, 1993).
Parker, Geoffrey: *The Dutch Revolt* (Penguin, 1990)
The fate of the Netherlands and Spain in descriptive, analytical history.
Schama, Simon: *The Embarassment of Riches* (Harper Collins, 1987).
Lively, witty, social and cultural history of the Netherlands.
Schetter, William Z: *The Netherlands in Perspective: the Organizations of Society and Environment* (Martinus Nijhoff, 1987)
An essential book which goes beyond the usual stereotypes.
Wels, CB: *Aloofness & Neutrality* (Hes Publishers, Utrecht)

General interest

Dedalus Book of Dutch Fantasy (Dedalus Books)
Anthology of contemporary Dutch short stories.
Frank, Anne: The *Diary of Anne Frank* (Pan Paperbacks, 1954)
The war-time diary of the young Anne Frank. Immensely, compulsively readable.
Van Straaten, Peter: *This Literary Life* (Fourth Estate Books, 1990)
Collection of one of the Netherlands' most popular cartoonist's works, displaying his dry humour to full effect.
White, Colin & Boucke, Laurie: *The Undutchables* (White Boucke Books).
Everything you ever wanted to know about the Dutch (and they'd rather you didn't find out).

Index

Maps

Advertisers' Index

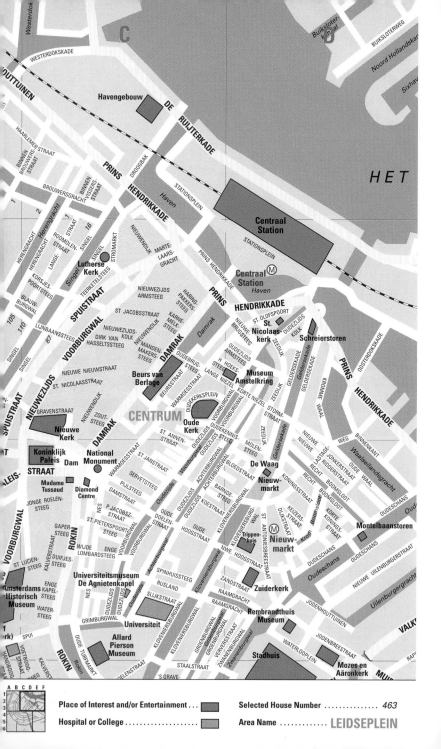

Place of Interest and/or Entertainment . . .

Hospital or College . . . .

Selected House Number *463*

Area Name . . . . **LEIDSEPLEIN**

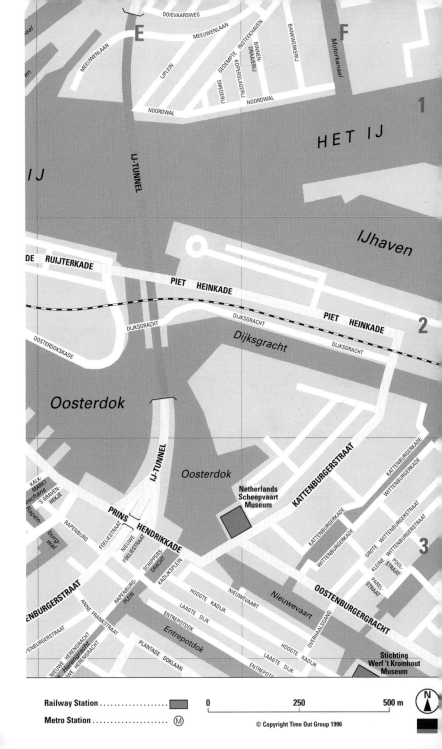

OOIEVAARSWEG

MEEUWENLAAN

E

F

MEEUWENLAAN

GEDEMPTE INSTEEKHAVEN

BINNEN-DRAAIERIJ

BANKWERKERIJ

Motorkanaal

MEEUWENLAAN

IJPLEIN

KOPERSLAGERIJ

SMEDERIJ

1

NOORDWAL

NOORDWAL

HET IJ

IJ-TUNNEL

I J

IJhaven

DE RUIJTERKADE

PIET HEINKADE

DIJKSGRACHT

PIET HEINKADE

2

DIJKSGRACHT

OOSTERDOKSKADE

Dijksgracht

DIJKSGRACHT

Oosterdok

IJ-TUNNEL

Oosterdok

KATTENBURGERSTRAAT

KATTENBURGERKADE

WITTENBURGERKADE

KALK-MARKT
schans

's GRAVEN-HEKJE

Netherlands
Scheepvaart
Museum

KATTENBURGERKADE

WITTENBURGERSTRAAT

GROTE WITTENBURGERSTRAAT

Rapen-

RAPENBURG

PRINS HENDRIKKADE

KATTENBURGERKADE

KLEINE WITTENBURGERSTRAAT

POOL-STRAAT

3

burg-wal

FOELIESTRAAT

NIEUWE

WITTENBURGERKADE

PAREL-STRAAT

FOELIESTRAAT

SCHIPPERS-GRACHT

KADIJKSPLEIN

NBURGERSTRAAT

ANNE FRANKSTRAAT

RAPENBURG-PLEIN

HOOGTE KADIJK

NIEUWEVAART

Nieuwevaart

OOSTENBURGERGRACHT

NBURGERSTRAAT

NIEUWE HERENGRACHT

Nieuwe Herengracht

NWE HERENGRACHT

ENTREPOTDOK

LAAGTE DIJK

Entrepotdok

PLANTAGE DOKLAAN

HOOGTE KADIJK

OVERHAALSGANG

Stichting
Werf 't Kromhout
Museum

LAAGTE DIJK

ENTREPOTD

Railway Station . . . .

Metro Station . . . . Ⓜ

0   250   500 m

© Copyright Time Out Group 1996

N

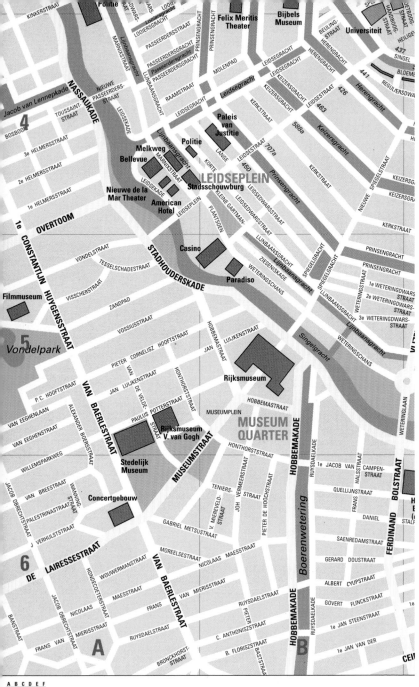

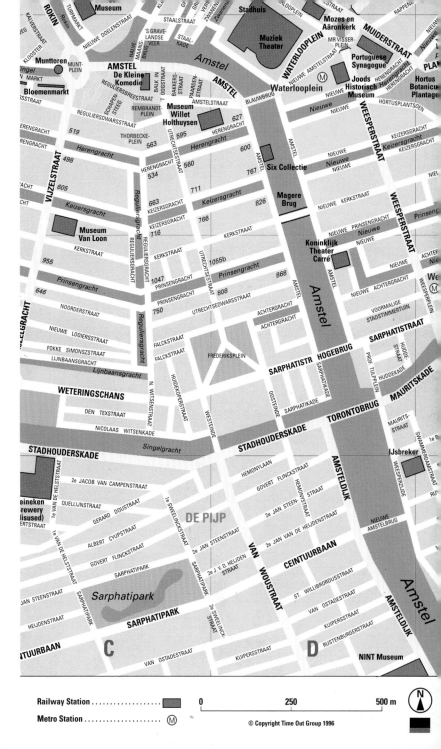

ROKIN
TURFMARKT
Museum
NIEUWE DOELENSTRAAT
STAALSTRAAT
KLOVENIERSBURGWAL
GRIMBURGWAL
VERVERSTRAAT
ZWANENBURGWAL
Zwanenburg
LOOIERSGRACHT
RAPPENBURG
Stadhuis
Mozes en
Aäronkerk
MUIDERSTRAAT
Nieuwe

KALVERSTRAAT
Munttoren
MUNT-
PLEIN
MAANS
BRUG
HALVE
'S GRAVE-
LANDSE
VEER
STAAL-
KADE
Amstel
Muziek
Theater
WATERLOOPLEIN
MR VISSER-
PLEIN
Portuguese
Synagogue
HERENGRACHT
HERENGRACHT
PLA

KLOOSTER
Singel
'N MARKT
AMSTEL
De Kleine
Komedie
REGULIERSBREESTRAAT
BALK IN
T OOGSTRAAT
BAKKERS-
STRAAT
PAARDEN-
STRAAT
AMSTELSTRAAT
AMSTEL
Waterlooplein
NIEUWE AMSTELSTRAAT
M
Joods
Historisch
Museum
Hortus
Botanicus
Plantage

Bloemenmarkt
SSTRAAT
REGULIERSDWARSSTRAAT
SCHAPEN-
STEEG
REMBRANDT-
PLEIN
Museum
Willet
Holthuysen
BLAUWBRUG
Nieuwe
HORTUSPLANTSOEN

ERENGRACHT
519
THORBECKE-
PLEIN
563
595
627
HERENGRACHT
Nieuwe
WEESPERSTRAAT
KEIZERSGRACHT
Keizersgracht
KEIZERSGRACHT

RENGRACHT
498
Herengracht
Herengracht
600
767
AMSTEL
NIEUWE
Nieuwe
NIEUWE

VIJZELSTRAAT
'ACHT
605
534
560
711
Six Collectie
Nieuwe

CHT
Keizersgracht
663
Keizersgracht
826
Magere
Brug
NIEUWE KERKSTRAAT
Prinseng

Museum
Van Loon
KEIZERSGRACHT
766
NIEUWE PRINSENGRACHT
Nieuwe
WEESPERSTRAAT
NIE
ACHTER
Nie

716
KERKSTRAAT
NIEUWE

955
KERKSTRAAT
KERKSTRAAT
1055b
Koninklijk
Theater
Carré
NIEUWE ACHTERGRACHT
We
WESPERPLEIN
M

Prinsengracht
1047
PRINSENGRACHT
Prinsengracht
868
AMSTEL
Amstel
VOORMALIGE
STADSTIMMERTUIN

646
750
808
ACHTERGRACHT
SARPHATISTRAAT

ELGRACHT
NOORDERSTRAAT
PRINSENGRACHT
UTRECHTSEDWARSSTRAAT
ACHTERGRACHT
HUDDE-
STRAAT
PROF. TULPPLEIN

NIEUWE LOOIERSSTRAAT
SARPHATISTR
HOGEBRUG
HUDDEKADE

FOKKE SIMONSZSTRAAT
FALCKSTRAAT
SARPHATIKADE
MAURITSKADE

LIJNBAANSGRACHT
Lijnbaansgracht
FALCKSTRAAT
FREDERIKSPLEIN
OOSTEINDE
SARPHATIKADE
MAURITS-
STRAAT
SWAMMERDAMSTRAAT

WETERINGSCHANS
N. WITSENSTRAAT
HUIDEKOPERSTRAAT
WESTEINDE
SARPHATIKADE
TORONTOBRUG
1e B

DEN TEXSTRAAT
IJsbreker

NICOLAAS WITSENKADE
Singelgracht
STADHOUDERSKADE
WESPERZIJDE

STADHOUDERSKADE
HEMONYLAAN
MAURITS-
STRAAT
RU

eineken
(rewery
(isused)
ERTSTRAAT
1e VAN DE HELSTSTRAAT
2e JACOB VAN CAMPENSTRAAT
QUELLIJNSTRAAT
GOVERT FLINCKSTRAAT
AMSTELDIJK

GERARD DOUSTRAAT
2e JAN STEEN-STRAAT
NIEUWE
AMSTELBRUG

ALBERT CYUPSTRAAT
1e SWEELINCKSTRAAT
DE PIJP
2e JAN STEENSTRAAT
2e JAN VAN DE HEIJDENSTRAAT

GOVERT FLINCKSTRAAT
VAN
WOUSTRAAT
CEINTUURBAAN

SARPHATIPARK
2e J. V. D. HEIJDEN
STRAAT
ST. WILLIBRORDUSSTRAAT
AMSTELDIJK

JAN STEENSTRAAT
Sarphatipark
SARPHATIPARK
VAN OSTADESTRAAT
Amstel

HEIJDENSTRAAT
SARPHATIPARK
2e SWEELINCK
STRAAT
KUIPERSSTRAAT
RUSTENBURGERSTRAAT

TUURBAAN
C
VAN OSTADESTRAAT
KUIPERSSTRAAT
D
NINT Museum

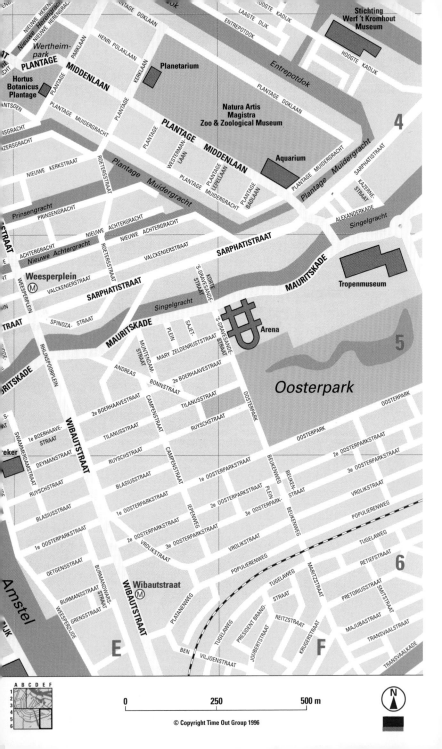

Stichting
Werf 't Kromhout
Museum

HOOGTE KADIJK

NIEUWE HERENG
NIEUWE HERENGRA
Nieuwe Herengrac
NIEUWE HERENGRACH

LAAGTE DIJK
ENTREPOTDOK

HOGTE KADIJK
LAAGTE DIJK

Wertheim-
park

PARKLAAN

HENRI POLAKLAAN

Entrepotdok

PLANTAGE

MIDDENLAAN

KERKLAAN

Planetarium

PLANTAGE DOKLAAN

Hortus
Botanicus
Plantage

PLANTAGE

4

ANTSOEN

PLANTAGE

PLANTAGE MUIDERGRACHT

Natura Artis
Magistra
Zoo & Zoological Museum

SGRACHT

PLANTAGE

PLANTAGE MIDDENLAAN

ZERSGRACHT

Plantage

WESTERMAN
LAAN

PLANTAGE MIDDENLAAN

Aquarium

SARPHATISTRAAT

NIEUWE KERKSTRAAT

ROETERSSTRAAT

Muidergracht

PLANTAGE
LEPELLAAN

PLANTAGE
MUIDERGRACHT

PLANTAGE MUIDERGRACHT

Plantage Muidergracht

KAZERNE-
STRAAT

PLANTAGE
BADLAAN

Prinsengracht

PRINSENGRACHT

NIEUWE ACHTERGRACHT

ALEXANDERKADE

Singelgracht

TRAAT

ACHTERGRACHT
Nieuwe Achtergracht

ROETERSSTRAAT

NIEUWE ACHTERGRACHT

SARPHATISTRAAT

MAURITSKADE

Weesperplein

VALCKENIERSTRAAT

VALCKENIERSTRAAT

KORTE
'S-GRAVESANDE-
STRAAT

Tropenmuseum

WEESPERSTRAAT

SARPHATISTRAAT

IN

SPINOZA- STRAAT

Singelgracht

'S-GRAVESANDE-
STRAAT

Arena

5

TRAAT

MAURITSKADE

PLEIN

SAJET

MUNTENDAM-
STRAAT

MARY ZELDENRUSTSTRAAT

RIJNSPOORPLEIN

RITSKADE

ANDREAS

BONNSTRAAT

2e BOERHAAVESTRAAT

Oosterpark

S-
AT

1e BOERHAAVE-
STRAAT

2e BOERHAAVESTRAAT

CAMPENSTRAAT

TILANUSSTRAAT

OOSTERPARK

OOSTERPARK

eker

WIBAUTSTRAAT

TILANUSSTRAAT

RUYSCHSTRAAT

OOSTERPARK

SWAMMERDAMSTRAAT

DEYMANSTRAAT

RUYSCHSTRAAT

CAMPENSTRAAT

1e OOSTERPARKSTRAAT

2e OOSTERPARKSTRAAT

BEUKENWEG

3e OOSTERPARKSTRAAT

RUYSCHSTRAAT

BLASIUSSTRAAT

1e OOSTERPARKSTRAAT

2e OOSTERPARKSTRAAT

PLEIN

VROLIKSTRAAT

BLASIUSSTRAAT

IEPENWEG

3e OOSTERPARK-

BEUKENWEG

POPULIERENWEG

1e OOSTERPARKSTRAAT

2e OOSTERPARKSTRAAT

3e OOSTERPARKSTRAAT

VROLIKSTRAAT

BEUKENWEG

TUGELAWEG

Amstel

OETGENSSTRAAT

BURMANSDWARS-
STRAAT

Wibautstraat

VROLIKSTRAAT

POPULIERENWEG

MAURITSSTRAAT

RETIEFSTRAAT

6

BURMANSTRAAT

WIBAUTSTRAAT

TUGELAWEG

STRAAT

PRETORIUSSTRAAT

SMITSSTRAAT

WEESPERZIJDE

GRENSSTRAAT

PLATANENWEG

TUGELAWEG

PRESIDENT BRAND-

REITZSTRAAT

KRUGERSTRAAT

MAJUBASTRAAT

TRANSVAALSTRAAT

IJK

BEN

VILJOENSTRAAT

JOUBERTSTRAAT

E

F

TRANSVAALKADE

Street Index

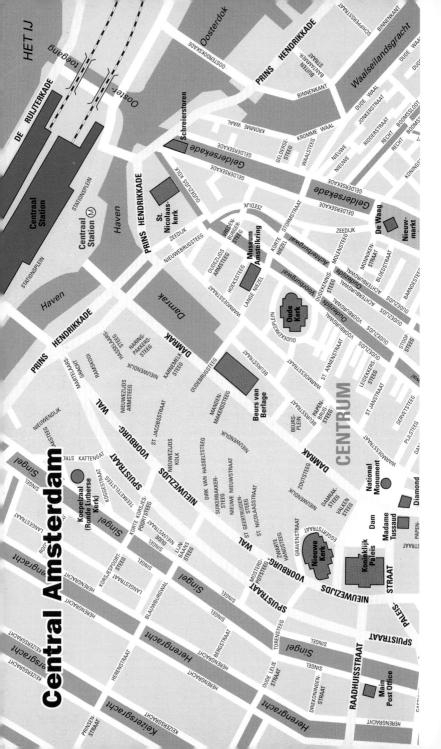

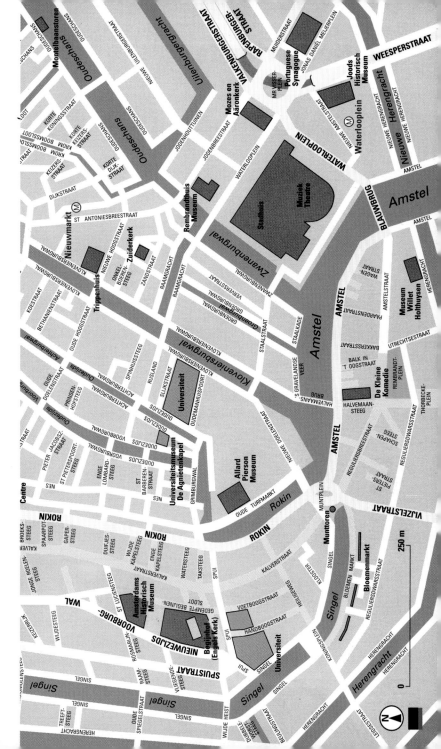

The Netherlands

0   25   50 km

Schiermonnikoog
Borkum
Ameland
Terschelling
Uithuizermeeden
Uithuizen
Warffum Spijk Bierum
Hoogebeintum Kantens Appingedam
Vlieland Dokkum Middlestum Stedum Loppersum
GRONINGEN Garmerwolde
LEEUWARDEN
Texel Harlingen Grouw Drachten Veendam Winschote
Sneek FRIESLAND Fochteloöerveen Assen Bellingw
Terherne
Heeg Heerenveen Stadskana
Den Helder Sloten Lemmer Uffelter Westerbork Orvelte Borger
Anna Veen Ellertsveld
Paulowna IJSSELMEER Steenwijk Dwingeloose
Schagen Opperdoes Medemblik Blokzijl Uffelte Heide Emmen
Twisk Enkhuizen Emmeloord Giethoorn Hoogeveen
Broek-op- Wanneperveen Meppel
Langedijk Hoorn Urk Vollenhove Staphorst
Heiloo Alkmaar Zwartsluis
Limmen MARKERMEER Kampen ZWOLLE Ommen
Beverwijk Pumerend Edam Lelystad Ketelhaven
Kennemer IJmuiden Zaanstad Volendam Oostvaarders- Flevohof OVERIJSSEL Oothmarsum
Duinen Nat.Pk. Monnickendam plassen Lemelerveld Denek
HAARLEM Broek in W FLEVOLAND Hellendoorn Almelo Oldenze
Zandvoort AMSTERDAM Harderwijk Raalte Nijverdal Hengelo
Vogelenzang Bennebroek Almerestad Deventer Holterberg ENSCHED
Keukenhof Hillegom Fort Bunschoten- APELDOORN 81m
Noordwijk Lisse Aalsmeer Naarden Laren Spakenburg Zutphen
Katwijk Rijnsburg Loenen Bussum Soestdijk
Breukelen Hilversum Hoge Veluwe Winterswijk
Scheveningen Oudaen Sijpesten Nat. Park
1. Oud-Loosdrecht Alphen Castle Amersfoort
2. Breukeleveen LEIDEN ZUID- Vreeland Ede
3. Westbrook Austerlitz Oosterbeek
DEN HAAG Zoetermeer HOLLAND De Haar Wijkbij ARNHEM Doetinchem
Naaldwijk DELFT Gouda Castle UTRECHT Duurstede
Hoek van Holland Oudewater Rhenen
Europoort ROTTERDAM Schoonhoven Tiel NIJMEGEN
Vlaardingen Culemborg
Stellendam Voorne Alblasserdam Gorinchem
Schouwen Putten De Biesbosch Oss
Brouwershaven Goeree- Hoeksche-Waard Nat. Park 's-HERTOGENBOSCH
Oosterscheldedam Overflakkee Drunen Uden
Delta Expo Zierikzee Oosterhout Waalwijk Overloon
Noord Oudenbosch BREDA Kaatsheuvel De Groote Peel
Middelburg Beveland TILBURG Nat. Reserve
Goes Yerseke Roosendaal NOORD - BRABANT Nuenen Helmond
Veere Kapelle Bergen op
Zoutelande Tholen Zoom EINDHOVEN Venlo
Vlissingen Kruiningen
Zeebrugge Zeeuws - Vlaanderen ZEELAND LIMBURG
Terneuzen Weert Thorn
BRUGGE ANTWERPEN Roermond
BRUGES ANVERS
GENT Sittard
GAND Geleen
BELGIQUE Valkenburg Heerlen
MAASTRICHT Schin AACHEN

NOORDZEE

WADDEN ISLANDS

DEUTSCHLAND

Where do you find out what's happening in London?

Time Out

London's biggest-selling weekly entertainment guide.
On sale at newsagents every Wednesday.

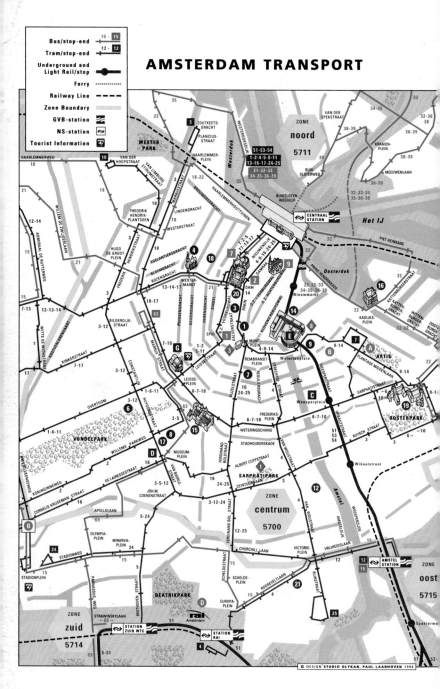

AMSTERDAM TRANSPORT

Bus/stop-end 15 - [15]
Tram/stop-end 12 - [12]
Underground and Light Rail/stop
Ferry
Railway Line
Zone Boundary
GVB-station
NS-station
Tourist Information

ZONE **noord** 5711

ZONE **centrum** 5700

ZONE **zuid** 5714

ZONE **oost** 5715

Het IJ

VONDELPARK

WESTER PARK

BEATRIXPARK

OOSTERPARK

ARTIS

CENTRAAL STATION

AMSTEL STATION

STATION ZUID WTC

STATION RAI

rai Amsterdam

© DESIGN STUDIO OLYKAN, PAUL LAARHOVEN 1994